www.wadsworth.com

wadsworth.com is the World Wide Web site for Thomson Wadsworth and is your direct source to dozens of online resources.

At *wadsworth.com* you can find out about supplements, demonstration software, and student resources. You can also send e-mail to many of our authors and preview new publications and exciting new technologies.

wadsworth.com
Changing the way the world learns®

FROM THE WADSWORTH SERIES IN MASS COMMUNICATION AND JOURNALISM

General Mass Communication

Anokwa/Lin/Salwen	*International Communication: Issues and Controversies*
Biagi	*Media/Impact: An Introduction to Mass Media,* Seventh Edition
Bucy	*Living in the Information Age: A New Media Reader,* Second Edition
Craft/Leigh/Godfrey	*Electronic Media*
Day	*Ethics in Media Communications: Cases and Controversies,* Fifth Edition
Dennis/Merrill	*Media Debates: Great Issues for the Digital Age,* Fourth Edition
Fellow	*American Media History*
Gillmor/Barron/Simon	*Mass Communication Law: Cases and Comment,* Sixth Edition
Gillmor/Barron/Simon/Terry	*Fundamentals of Mass Communication Law*
Hilmes	*Connections: A Broadcast History Reader*
Hilmes	*Only Connect: A Cultural History of Broadcasting in the United States*
Jamieson/Campbell	*The Interplay of Influence: News, Advertising, Politics, and the Mass Media,* Sixth Edition
Kamalipour	*Global Communication*
Lester	*Visual Communication: Images with Messages,* Fourth Edition
Overbeck	*Major Principles of Media Law,* 2006 Edition
Straubhaar/LaRose	*Media Now: Understanding Media, Culture, and Technology,* Fifth Edition
Zelezny	*Communications Law: Liberties, Restraints, and the Modern Media,* Fourth Edition
Zelezny	*Cases in Communications Law,* Fourth Edition

Journalism

Bowles/Borden	*Creative Editing,* Fourth Edition
Chance/McKeen	*Literary Journalism: A Reader*
Craig	*Online Journalism*
Hilliard	*Writing for Television, Radio, and New Media,* Eighth Edition
Kessler/McDonald	*When Words Collide: A Media Writer's Guide to Grammar and Style,* Sixth Edition
Poulter/Tidwell	*News Scene: Interactive Writing Exercises*
Rich	*Writing and Reporting News: A Coaching Method,* Media Enhanced Fourth Edition
Rich	*Writing and Reporting News: A Coaching Method, Student Exercise Workbook,* Media Enhanced Fourth Edition
Stephens	*Broadcast News,* Fourth Edition
Wilber/Miller	*Modern Media Writing*

Photojournalism and Photography

Parrish	*Photojournalism: An Introduction*

Public Relations and Advertising

Diggs-Brown/Glou	*The PR Styleguide: Formats for Public Relations Practice*
Hendrix	*Public Relations Cases,* Sixth Edition
Jewler/Drewniany	*Creative Strategy in Advertising,* Eighth Edition
Newsom/Haynes	*Public Relations Writing: Form and Style,* Seventh Edition
Newsom/Turk/Kruckeberg	*This Is PR: The Realities of Public Relations,* Eighth Edition

Research and Theory

Baxter/Babbie	*The Basics of Communication Research*
Baran/Davis	*Mass Communication Theory: Foundations, Ferment, and Future,* Fourth Edition
Littlejohn	*Theories of Human Communication,* Seventh Edition
Merrigan/Huston	*Communication Research Methods*
Rubin/Rubin/Piele	*Communication Research: Strategies and Sources,* Sixth Edition
Sparks	*Media Effects Research: A Basic Overview,* Second Edition
Wimmer/Dominick	*Mass Media Research: An Introduction,* Eighth Edition

ETHICS IN MEDIA COMMUNICATIONS

5TH EDITION

ETHICS IN MEDIA COMMUNICATIONS
CASES AND CONTROVERSIES

Louis Alvin Day
Louisiana State University

THOMSON
™
WADSWORTH

Australia • Canada • Mexico • Singapore • Spain
United Kingdom • United States

THOMSON
WADSWORTH

Publisher: *Holly J. Allen*
Assistant Editor: *Darlene Amidon-Brent*
Editorial Assistant: *Sarah Allen*
Senior Technology Project Manager: *Jeanette Wiseman*
Marketing Manager: *Mark Orr*
Marketing Assistant: *Andrew Keay*
Advertising Project Manager: *Shemika Britt*
Project Manager, Editorial Production: *Jennifer Klos*

Print Buyer: *Lisa Claudeanos*
Permissions Editor: *Stephanie Lee*
Production Service: *Mary E. Deeg, Buuji, Inc.*
Copy Editor: *Linda Ireland, Buuji, Inc.*
Cover Designer: *Bartay*
Cover Image: Epoxy/Getty Images
Printer: *Malloy Incorporated*
Compositor: *International Typesetting and Composition*

Printed in the United States of America
1   2   3   4   5   6   7   09   08   07   06   05

For more information about our products, contact us at:
Thomson Learning Academic Resource Center
1-800-423-0563

For permission to use material from this text or product, submit a request online at **http://www.thomsonrights.com**. Any additional questions about permissions can be submitted by email to **thomsonrights@thomson.com**.

Library of Congress Control Number: 2004113700

ISBN 0-534-63714-0

Thomson Higher Education
10 Davis Drive
Belmont, CA 94002-3098
USA

Asia (including India)
Thomson Learning
5 Shenton Way
#01-01 UIC Building
Singapore 068808

Australia/New Zealand
Thomson Learning Australia
102 Dodds Street
Southbank, Victoria 3006
Australia

Canada
Thomson Nelson
1120 Birchmount Road
Toronto, Ontario M1K 5G4
Canada

UK/Europe/Middle East/Africa
Thomson Learning
High Holborn House
50–51 Bedford Road
London WC1R 4LR
United Kingdom

Latin America
Thomson Learning
Seneca, 53
Colonia Polanco
11560 Mexico
D.F. Mexico

Spain (including Portugal)
Thomson Paraninfo
Calle Magallanes, 25
28015 Madrid, Spain

BRIEF CONTENTS

CONTENTS

PART TWO: CASES IN MEDIA COMMUNICATIONS   77

Whenever the term "media ethics" is introduced into polite conversation, someone is sure to ridicule the reference as an oxymoron. Teachers of media ethics are painfully familiar with the looks of amusement or even disbelief when they acknowledge their complicity in what appears to be a frivolous academic pursuit. A sense of purpose can easily be replaced with a feeling of futility, as reflected in this cynical remark from Howard Good, the coordinator of the journalism program at the State University of New York: "You ought to feel sorry for me. I teach an undergraduate course in journalism ethics at a time when ethics seems to matter less and less in the conduct of professional journalists."[1]

At first glance, it does appear that we are engaged in a hopeless enterprise. Public opinion polls continue to show that media professionals are held in low esteem. For example, in 1985, 56 percent of the public believed news organizations usually got their facts straight, according to the Pew Research Center. By 2002, that figure had declined to 35 percent. In 1985, the public viewed the media as "moral" by a better than four to one margin; by 2003 public opinion was almost evenly divided on this issue.[2] Advertising executives are criticized for manipulating a vulnerable public. Public relations practitioners are depicted as representing special interests and disseminating disinformation to the detriment of the public interests. The entertainment industry stands accused in the court of public opinion of marketing gratuitous sex and violence to the nation's emotionally susceptible youth.

However, I must respectfully dissent from this cynical view of the value of ethics instruction within the public academy. Skepticism about moral education produces skepticism about moral responsibility, and this in turn produces leaders who lack a moral vision. In fact, the need for a renewed emphasis on ethics education has never been greater. Evidence of a general decline in ethical standards is all around us: political candidates who abandon any pretense of civility and launch "attack ads" to destroy their opponents, athletes whose record-setting performances are tainted by allegations that they used steroids or other performance-enhancing drugs, students expelled from school for cheating, and journalists for respectable news organizations fired for plagiarism and the fabrication of facts.

After thirty years of teaching, I am convinced that most students leave school without a meaningful understanding of the ethics of their profession or ethics in general for that matter. This depressing state of affairs calls for a more aggressive posture in the teaching of ethics, not cynical sighs of resignation by those who spend their time chronicling the media's frequent ethical lapses. My sense of optimism is fueled by the fact that, within the academy, professional schools—law, business, and journalism, for example—have reinvigorated their curricula with a renewed commitment to the teaching of ethics. And ethics, which was once the concern primarily of scholars, philosophers, and theologians, has even taken on a populist quality as the ethical dimensions of virtually any issue of substance are publicly debated. Or to state it in the vernacular, ethics has become a "hot button" issue.

Ethics in Media Communications is one small contribution to this pursuit of ethical knowledge. It offers a systematic approach to moral reasoning by combining ethical theory with the practice of ethics by media professionals. A moral-reasoning method is taught in the first three chapters, and in the rest of the book students are presented with hypothetical situations and asked to reach an ethical decision based on the principles they have learned. Some cases, though hypothetical in structure, are based upon real events while others are constructed from whole cloth.

The cases in this text represent the wide variety of moral dilemmas confronted by media practitioners. For example, an editor agonizes over whether to publish an embarrassing secret about a local military hero from the Iraqi War and a university's public relations department must decide whether to disclose a cheating scandal involving several basketball players just prior to the team's appearance in the NCAA's "Final Four" tournament. A marketing director for a drug company must confront some ethical questions surrounding the advertising of a new impotency drug. A Hollywood producer considers the ethical dimensions of "exploiting"

animals as actors in the film industry. A search engine operator explores the ethics of deceptive advertising on the unregulated World Wide Web. An editor for a college newspaper must decide whether to continue to run a graphic sex column that has generated a lot of campus controversy. A television news department must decide whether to report the truth about the infant daughter of a married lesbian couple. A public relations practitioner must decide whether political activism constitutes a conflict of interest, and the staff of an African American institute debates the ethics of commercializing the images of slain civil rights leaders in ads designed to counteract the marketing efforts of the tobacco industry within the black community.

Some cynics may question the value of using classroom simulations to teach real-world ethics, especially given the fact that media practitioners operate under time deadlines in pressure situations. However, even football teams must endure hours of skull sessions before they do combat on the gridiron, and experience in moral reasoning—even hypothetical experience—will help students prepare for the day when they must make ethical judgments on the job.

A final note: I do have some evidence, anecdotal though it may be, that this approach to teaching ethics is effective. After having used the moral-reasoning model in my classes, I have been told by students that it made them more ethically aware of the consequences of their behavior. If this book accomplishes nothing more than that, it will not have been in vain.

Notes

1. Howard Good, "We Need Ethics Examples," *Quill*, April 2001, p. 40.
2. See Robert J. Samuelson, "Picking Sides for the News," *Newsweek*, June 28, 2004, p. 37.

The study of ethics may be new and unfamiliar to you. Although most of us are obedient disciples of the values we learned in childhood, we spend few of our waking hours pondering the importance of these moral rules and how they might lead to a more virtuous life. Prohibitions against lying, stealing, and cheating, for example, are platitudes to which we pay homage, but we don't always comply with them. Our ethical conduct is often "situational" because we have no comprehensive moral framework to guide us in making judgments. In short, we lack experience in moral reasoning.

Public opinion polls continue to reflect a general wariness of the ethical deportment of media practitioners, the consequence of which has been an erosion of credibility. Mass communication educators have responded to this public impeachment by reinvigorating their curricula with required ethics courses or in some cases an infusion of ethics instruction across the curriculum. The primary goal is to initiate a moral discourse among faculty and students. This book is designed to engage you in this conversation through the process of moral reasoning. Of course, reading this book will not make you an ethically mature individual. But it will provide a blueprint for improving your ethical awareness. Nowhere is the need for moral reasoning more acute than in journalism and other areas of mass communications. The polls continue to show an erosion of credibility and confidence in the mass media, some of which is no doubt due to the public's perception that the media ship is sailing without a moral compass.

Because the frenzied environment of the newsroom or the advertising agency is no place to start philosophizing about moral reasoning, the classroom must serve as our point of departure. The exercises in this book represent a cross section of moral dilemmas confronted by media practitioners; you may encounter some of these on your first job or later in your career. If so, you will be called upon to make ethical judgments. The practice in problem solving and critical thinking afforded by these hypothetical cases will make you a more confident decision maker. Before confronting the dilemmas posed by these case studies, however, you must be familiar with the terrain of moral philosophy. Thus, *Ethics in Media Communications: Cases and Controversies* is divided into two parts.

Part 1, Foundations and Principles, is devoted primarily to a consideration of moral development and the formulation of moral rules and principles within a social context. The third chapter of Part 1 also draws on a fusion of important concepts from moral philosophy, media practice, and critical thinking to construct a moral-reasoning model that will be used as the blueprint for analyzing the hypothetical cases in Part 2.

The chapters in Part 2, Cases in Media Communications, present some of the major issues confronting media practitioners. The theme underlying this approach is that these issues affect all areas of mass communications. For example, moral principles involving truth telling and deception apply to journalists, advertisers, and public relations executives alike (as well as to society at large). Likewise, conflicts of interest are certainly not the exclusive preserve of journalists.

The hypothetical cases involve ethical dilemmas confronted by both lower-echelon employees and management personnel. In many cases you will be asked to assume the role of a management-level decision maker. Some may question the value of this kind of exercise because, as a *future* media practitioner, at least at the start you are likely to identify more closely with rank-and-file employees. However, role-playing can be an effective means of stepping into another person's shoes. By so doing, you should at least come to appreciate the management perspective on ethical issues, even if you do not agree with it. This ability might prove valuable once you enter the job market. Also, keep in mind that the real purpose of this text is to expose you to the process of moral reasoning and not just to discuss ethical issues. To this end, it makes little difference what your role as

ethical decision maker is as long as your judgment is based on sound moral principles.

In the book's Epilogue, I provide a final comment on the current state of the practice of media ethics. There is also some crystal-ball gazing and a look at the future of the teaching of media ethics. Ethical studies have a long and honorable tradition in programs of journalism and mass communications. *Ethics in Media Communications* is designed to help you become part of that tradition.

One final caveat before you confront the material in this text: Some ethicists and futurists have noted, correctly, the ethical challenges posed by the unregulated World Wide Web, and this text deals with these concerns. However, there is a tendency toward some hysteria each time that a new technology becomes available, leaving in its wake the mistaken impression that the ethical issues posed by that technology are unique. The digital manipulation of a news photo, for example, does not alter the fact that deception is involved, and deception is an enduring issue in the practice of journalism. Likewise, there is no doubt that concerns such as invasion of privacy, piracy of intellectual property, and the dissemination of false information are exacerbated on the Internet. But the technology has not altered the basic ethical issues. For example, the theft of intellectual property is wrong, regardless of whether it occurs in cyberspace or through more conventional low-tech means. Thus, the values discussed in this text are timeless and do not change with the introduction of new technologies.

ETHICS IN MEDIA COMMUNICATIONS

FOUNDATIONS
AND PRINCIPLES

The first part of *Ethics in Media Communications* lays a foundation for the study of moral philosophy (ethics) and moral reasoning. To accomplish this ambitious objective, I have divided Part 1 into three chapters.

Chapter 1, entitled "Ethics and Moral Development," begins with an overview of ethics as a subject worthy of exploration. It then documents the value of ethics instruction from the standpoint of both intellectual enrichment and professional practice. This first chapter also discusses how ethical values and attitudes are formed and how moral values sometimes collide, producing a crisis of ethical uncertainty. The theory underlying Chapter 1 is that an understanding of one's own ethical development—a development that should continue throughout one's lifetime—is a prerequisite for approaching the process of moral reasoning with any degree of confidence.

Chapter 2 focuses on the relationship between ethics and society. The need for a system of ethics is first established, followed by an examination of the requirements for a cohesive system of societal ethical standards. Because our ethical behavior is based, in part, on the rules and norms of society at large, the concept of moral duty and its relationship to virtuous behavior are examined. Chapter 2 also delves into the sometimes confusing relationship between law (what we are allowed to do or prohibited from doing) and ethics (what we should do). The chapter concludes with a discussion of the notion of social responsibility and how individual standards of moral conduct are reflected in media institutions' corporate attitudes toward the public interest. Chapter 2 also considers the impact of new technologies and the information superhighway on media ethics as we begin the twenty-first century.

Chapter 3 provides the connection between ethics and moral reasoning. It examines, among other things, the philosophical foundations of moral theory and the approaches to ethical decision making that have had the most profound impact on moral philosophy in Western civilization. These theories are then combined with the principles of critical thinking to develop a "model" for moral reasoning (the SAD Formula) that will be employed for analyzing the ethical dilemmas posed by the hypothetical cases at the end of Chapters 4 through 13.

1

Ethics and
Moral Development

THE STUDY OF ETHICS:
AN OVERVIEW

On May 11, 2003, readers of the *New York Times* were stunned by this front-page confession of journalistic transgression: *Times Reporter Who Resigned Leaves Long Trail of Deception.* In an unprecedented 13,900-word article, the paper then proceeded to document in painful and intricate detail how 27-year-old Jayson Blair had committed what it described as "journalistic fraud" in at least half the articles he produced as a national affairs reporter. "The widespread fabrication and plagiarism," lamented the *Times,* "represent a profound betrayal of trust and a low point in the 152-year history of the newspaper." [1]

The Jayson Blair affair—which will be examined in greater detail in Chapter 4—undoubtedly represented, as the *Times* itself acknowledged, the nadir of the paper's long and proud history, but its dramatic and highly publicized exposition obscures the less sensational ethical challenges confronted by media practitioners on a daily basis. This event, as embarrassing as it was to the nation's newspaper of record, did not represent a true ethical *dilemma* because dilemmas involve moral struggles and reflection in an effort to do the right thing. Ethical dilemmas engage the conscience, which must frequently respond to two or more competing and morally

defensible courses of action. However, Jayson Blair's behavior was indefensible under any standard of responsible journalism.

Ethical dilemmas are all around us. They are woven into the fabric of everyday life, persistently challenging our ethical sensibilities. Consider, for example, the following questions: Should I accept a music CD from a classmate illegally downloaded from the Internet, when to do so implicitly validates my classmate's behavior? Do I have a duty to report a crime I witness? Is physician-assisted suicide a moral affront to the sanctity of life? Is it ethically permissible for a TV reporter to use a hidden camera to document unlawful activity or scandalous behavior? Does Hollywood have a moral obligation to refrain from depictions of gratuitous sex and violence? Most of us could probably provide an answer to such questions based on our feelings about an issue. But could we defend our decision based upon some established ethical principle?

This is what the study of ethics is all about—learning to justify publicly our ethical choices based upon sound ethical precepts. A course in ethics can provide the tools for making difficult moral choices, in both our personal lives and our professional lives. Through the teaching of ethical principles and moral reasoning, educational institutions can fulfill one of their historically important responsibilities, the "cultivation of morality."[2]

But what exactly is *ethics,* and how does it differ from *morals? Moral* is derived from the Latin *mos, moris,* meaning (among other things) "way of life" or "conduct." It is often associated with religious beliefs and personal behavior. *Ethics,* on the other hand, is derived from the Greek *ethos,* meaning "custom," "usage," or "character." It is often thought of as a rational process applying established principles when two moral obligations collide. The most difficult ethical dilemmas occur when conflicts arise between two "right" moral obligations. Thus, ethics often involves the balancing of competing rights when there is no "correct" answer. A case in point is a student who promises to remain silent when a classmate confides that he has cheated. If a teacher attempts to solicit testimony from that student regarding her friend's nefarious behavior, the student must then weigh the value of loyalty to the friend (a moral virtue) against commitment to the truth (another moral virtue).

Despite this historical distinction between morals and ethics, in recent years many commentators have merged the two concepts to such an extent that they have become virtually indistinguishable. *Ethics,* in fact, is the branch of philosophy that deals with the moral component of human life and is usually referred to as *moral philosophy.* This semantical alliance between ethics and morals is not altogether an unwelcome development and reflects the approach used in this text. Thus, the terms *ethics* and *morals* will often be used interchangeably. This strategy is particularly useful in the study of media ethics (or any other profession, for that matter) because it reflects the growing realization that professional ethical behavior cannot be divorced entirely from the moral standards of society at large. A public relations practitioner, for example, who deliberately distorts the truth is violating a fundamental principle that has its genesis both in the moral systems of various religions and ancient ethical canons.

Ethics reflects a society's notions about the rightness or wrongness of an act and the distinctions between virtue and vice. To accuse someone of laziness or incompetence is not to accuse that person of immoral conduct. On the other hand, such actions as lying, stealing, and cheating do imply the violation of ethical norms. Thus, ethics is often described as a set of principles or a code of moral conduct.

Ethics involves the evaluation and application of those moral values that a society or culture has accepted as its norms. To suggest that individuals should set their own standards of conduct is to advocate ethical anarchy. One may derive a certain amount of satisfaction from adhering to a personal code of conduct, but the violation of this code does not necessarily raise serious ethical questions.

The study of ethics in the Western world began nearly 2,500 years ago when Socrates, according to his faithful student Plato, roamed Greece probing and challenging his brethren's ideas about such abstract concepts as justice and goodness. This Socratic method of inquiry, consisting of relentless questions and answers about the nature of moral conduct, has proved to be a durable commodity, continuing to touch off heated discussions about morality in barrooms and classrooms alike. Thus, the primary ingredient of ethical debate is conflict, because even within a given society or culture opinions can differ on standards of proper moral conduct.[3] This moral diversity can be intellectually stimulating and personally enriching, as depicted colorfully in this editorial comment from the *Quill,* the official publication of the Society of Professional Journalists:

> Ethical judgments are like that. No matter who makes them, they are seldom easy, and they are almost certain to strike some of us as perfectly proper while others regard them as wrongheaded, stupid, unfair, and—possibly—as evidence of intellectual and/or moral decay.
>
> All of which is a wonderful thing. Differing definitions of ethical behavior help keep our minds

awake and our spirits inflamed. If everyone agreed on all ethical principles, life might be more orderly, but it surely would be more boring.[4]

Discussions of the ethical behavior of media practitioners are usually anything but boring. The study of ethics in mass communications is a noble heir to the Socratic tradition, because the activities of journalists, advertisers, and public relations executives are being subjected to critical inquiry as never before, even among their fellows. We are in a constant state of agitation about the moral dimension of our lives. Our consciences tell us, often with brutal candor, that there is a real and important difference between actions that are right and those that are wrong. The knowledge of ethical principles and how they are derived can make a difference in our behavior. However, the goal is not to make ethical decisions with which everyone agrees or, for that matter, to make decisions that are necessarily in keeping with societal expectations. The most challenging ethical dilemmas involve the balancing of competing interests when there is no "right" answer. Nevertheless, such moral reflection should result in at least morally defensible decisions even if those decisions prove to be unpopular. Ethics instruction refines our ability to make critical judgments and to defend those decisions on some rational basis.

For example, journalists, when delving into others' private lives, often justify their decision to publish embarrassing revelations on the ground of "the people's right to know." The problem with this kind of rejoinder is that it doesn't answer the questions of what the people have a right to know and why the public has a right to this kind of information in the first place.

The Three Branches of Ethics

Ethics, as a formal field of inquiry, attempts to put such questions into perspective and, in so doing, includes three different but conceptually related enterprises: metaethics, normative ethics, and applied ethics.[5] *Metaethics* is concerned

with the study of the characteristics, or nature, of ethics. It also examines the meaning of such abstract terms as *good, right, justice,* and *fairness* and attempts to identify those values that are the best *moral* values. Metaethics is not concerned with making moral judgments but instead attempts to distinguish ethical values from those that involve merely matters of taste or attitude. For example, ethicists have identified a commitment to truth as a moral good, and this value underlies many of our societal norms. It is also the foundation of many media codes and standards of behavior, but it remains for media practitioners to adapt this rather abstract concept to specific moral dilemmas. Metaethics provides the broad foundation for ethical decision making, but it does not provide guideposts for how to get from point A to point B. When viewers or readers describe a news report as unfair, are they referring to an ethical concern or merely a matter of taste? Likewise, a media critic's description of a TV series as "good drama" does not necessarily denote any observations concerning the program's moral stature. It is the function of metaethics to define such vague concepts in ethical terms, providing precision of meaning so that all members of society can start with a level playing field in reaching moral judgments.

Normative ethics, on the other hand, is concerned with developing general theories, rules, and principles of moral conduct. The recent preoccupation with the ethical malaise within our society and the demise of traditional values centers on some of the fundamental societal principles of moral behavior—that is, normative ethics. These theoretical rules and principles are the ethical markers of any civilized society, guideposts designed to bring moral order out of chaos. They provide the foundation for ethical decision making in the real world. Some of society's prohibitions against lying, cheating, and stealing flow from our concern with normative ethics. For example, a media institution's proscription against reporters' employing deception to get a news story derives from the general societal norm concerning lying. Nevertheless, under deadline and competitive pressures, journalists are sometimes tempted to abandon such broad principles because they want an exclusive article or perhaps because they truly believe that the public interest will be served by ferreting out the story, even at the expense of violating a fundamental rule of ethical behavior. When moral norms undergo their baptism of fire in the real world, the media practitioner enters the practical realm of applied ethics.

Applied ethics is really the problem-solving branch of moral philosophy. The task here is to use the insights derived from metaethics and the general principles and rules of normative ethics in addressing specific ethical issues and concrete cases. Suppose that a reporter is asked by an attorney representing a man accused of murder to reveal the names of the sources of information for an article that the reporter has written about the case. The reporter has promised the sources to keep their identities secret. However, the attorney believes that such information could lead to his client's acquittal. One rule, or societal norm, in this case suggests that we should always keep our promises, because to do otherwise would violate the trust on which individual relationships are established. On the other hand, justice requires that we ensure a defendant a fair trial. In this case these two rather abstract principles would be on a collision course, but applied ethics is designed to guide us through this moral thicket by confronting issues within a real-world environment. There are not always right or wrong answers, but there should always be "well-reasoned" ones.

One reason, perhaps, that so many people are troubled and preoccupied with their moral existence is that they are unable to apply their beliefs to life's relentless barrage of ethical dilemmas.[6] Applied ethics is the vital link between theory and practice, the real litmus test of ethical decision making. Professional and occupational ethics reside here, and it is with this branch of ethics that the cases in Part 2 are concerned.

Ethical Communication

The study of ethics would be futile if it did not promote understanding, and understanding can best be achieved by examining any ethical situation from the perspective of the following communications process:[7] A *moral agent* (communicator) with a particular *motive* commits an *act* (either verbal or nonverbal) within a specific *context* directed at a particular *individual* or *audience* usually with some *consequence*.

Moral agents are the ones who make ethical judgments, regardless of whether they are acting on their own volition or as institutional representatives. All communicators become moral agents when they confront the ethical dilemmas of their professions and must bear full responsibility for their actions. An understanding of the role of the moral agent is essential because ethical standards often vary according to social roles. For example, most reporters and editors, because of their roles as agents for the public, could not in good conscience become politically active because to do so would compromise their independence. Those who fail to observe this journalistic axiom may quickly fall from grace in the eyes of their employers. Such was the fate of Sandra Nelson, a reporter for Tacoma, Washington's *News Tribune* who picketed for abortion rights outside a local hospital and campaigned on behalf of civil rights for gays and lesbians. Despite warnings from her superiors, Nelson continued her off-duty political activities and was reassigned from her position as education reporter to swing shift editor.[8] However, depending on their specific professional duties and the organizations for which they work, journalists have different obligations in this respect. A case in point is the editor of a politically conservative opinion magazine who is active in Republican party politics. The contract between such organs and their readers is different from the one between a general circulation newspaper and its audience.[9]

Ethical decisions are always made within a specific *context,* which includes the political, social, and cultural climate. Although the context does not necessarily determine the outcome of an ethical judgment, it exerts an influence that cannot be ignored. In fact, contextual factors often create the internal conflict that brings our conscience's admonition of what we ought to do into moral combat with what is the popular thing to do.

We must also examine the *motives* of the moral agent, because good motives can sometimes be used to justify what appears to be an unethical act. For example, a reporter may use deception to uncover governmental corruption, a journalistic technique most of us would be willing to tolerate (or perhaps even applaud) in the name of the public good. However, motives must not be examined based strictly on their popularity or public acceptability; they should be viewed in conjunction with the consequences of the action. National leaders would not be justified in carrying out a policy of genocide, even if it were ratified by their constituents.

The *act* is the behavioral component of the communications process. It is what draws our attention to the actions of others and may lead us to describe their actions as either ethical or unethical. These acts may be verbal, as when a reporter lies to a news source, or nonverbal, as when an advertiser omits product information vital to informed consumer choice.

An ethical situation should also be evaluated in terms of the moral agent's relationship to the *individual(s)* or *audience* most directly affected by the ethical judgment. For example, a magazine that appeals to a sophisticated audience might feel comfortable with including a quote containing offensive language, whereas a local community newspaper might sanitize such a quote. Or an advertiser that markets its products to children might employ less aggressive sales techniques than one that appeals to an adult audience. Likewise, the movie ratings

system and the TV networks' program advisories, whatever their shortcomings may be, are a tacit recognition that these industries have a duty to alert the audience to morally offensive content.

Finally, ethical judgments produce *consequences*—either positive or negative—for both the moral agent and others who may be touched by the agent's actions. These consequences may range from a stimulation of conscience to public approbation or disapproval of the moral agent's behavior. Sometimes these consequences are instantaneous and unambiguous, as when a newspaper's readers complain about a graphic photo of charred bodies on the paper's front page. But consequences may also be more subtle and long-term and usually form the foundations of individual and institutional reputations.

In an ideal world, moral agents could know the consequences in advance and act accordingly. But too often the consequences are either unanticipated or diverge from the expectations of the moral agent. Media practitioners should exercise extreme caution when their actions are likely to result in harmful consequences, particularly to innocent third parties. Julio Granados would be the first to agree with this moral admonition.

Julio Granados was a Mexican immigrant working at the El Mandado market in Raleigh, North Carolina. Gigi Anders, a reporter for the *Raleigh News & Observer,* produced a profile of Granados's life that she felt would be a tribute to all of the hardworking Hispanics who had migrated into the Raleigh community. Anders produced a two-page article that appeared in the paper's Sunday edition, a touching account of Granados's lonely life in America and the financial support that he provided for his family in Mexico. The article also mentioned his undocumented status. Agents of the Immigration and Naturalization Service (INS) in Charlotte read the article and decided to arrest Granados.[10]

Anders claimed she warned Granados that he might be deported if INS agents read the article. Granados disagreed and later told the paper that he had given the reporter permission to use his name but not the fact that he was here without the proper papers. Regardless, the Hispanic community was incensed and blamed the *News & Observer* for Granados's arrest, accusing the paper of "irresponsible journalism" that "destroyed this young man's life." After a rather spirited discussion among newsroom executives and staffers, executive editor Anders Gyllenhaal later acknowledged that they had not fully thought through the potential consequences of such a detailed article.[11] State government editor Linda Williams was less charitable. "We're telling the public we're neutral, we can't take sides," she said. "I think we erred by including all that information. We actually look like an arm of the INS."[12]

THE VALUE OF ETHICS EDUCATION

Can ethics be taught? This is a difficult and controversial question but must be confronted directly. There are two schools of thought on this matter. Cynics contend that ethics is not a proper subject for study at all, because it raises questions without providing clear answers. Besides, the skeptics argue, knowledge of ethical principles and norms does not necessarily produce a more moral person. On the contrary, in this view, when confronted with real ethical dilemmas, people will ignore whatever wisdom was dispensed in an ethics course and act in their own self-interest. And, in all candor, there is some credible evidence, spanning the last fifty years, that character education classes and conventional religious instruction programs apparently have no significant influence on moral conduct.[13] Skeptics also argue that children's moral development is completed before they reach school and thus that such character education classes can have little effect. This view assumes, of course, that moral maturity, unlike psychological and physical maturity, ends at a very early age, a dubious proposition

at best. Indeed, we are truly a work in progress, ethically speaking; age is no barrier to the cultivation of moral virtue or the accumulation of moral wisdom.

The cynical view is represented by the anecdote about the college student at a major university who was found guilty of plagiarism. Because this was his first offense, the student was sentenced to enroll in an ethics course taught by the Philosophy Department. He was finally expelled three months later, however, when he was caught cheating on an ethics exam.

Media practitioners, who are often skeptical of anything that smacks of ivory-tower elitism, have another complaint about ethics courses. Classroom discussions and simulations, they argue, cannot duplicate the frenzied pace and pressures of the real world. They have a point. But even military units must drill before they engage in actual combat, and the fact that battlefield conditions are not identical to maneuvers does not diminish the value of those simulations. Some media institutions have altered their thinking in this matter and are sending employees to seminars to increase their ethical awareness. Considering that the media often make pronouncements on the ethics of others, such as politicians and business executives, it follows that their own moral conduct must be sound.

Obviously, ethics cannot be injected with a hypodermic needle, and there are no guarantees that formal instruction in moral philosophy will turn sinners into saints. But neither are there any guarantees that the lessons learned in history and political science courses will produce better citizens or serve the cause of democracy.

The other school of thought, represented by the optimistic proponents of formal ethics training, holds that ethics is a subject like math, physics, or history, with its own set of problems and distinctive methods of solving them.[14] In this view there is a body of *moral knowledge* that awaits the ethically inquisitive mind. Thus, the study of ethics is the key to understanding moral conduct and to improving the human spiritual condition. Surely, the optimists contend, this objective is worthy of attention in academic curricula. Socrates reflects this view when he remarks rather bluntly in Plato's *Apology* that "the unexamined life is not worth living." However, even Socrates apparently doubted at one time that morality was teachable.[15] The persistent public criticism of the ethical standards of the professions in general, and the media in particular, compels us to accept the optimistic view of ethics instruction. We have little choice but to ponder, in a systematic and rational way, the ethical judgments being made in the nation's newsrooms, advertising agencies, public relations firms, Hollywood production studios, and by website operators. The media, it is safe to say, are operating in a hostile environment, although the polls differ on exactly how deeply public confidence has eroded.

Media practitioners are better educated and better trained than ever before. But many emerge from their college experience ill prepared to cope with the ethical exigencies of the real world. It is advantageous to the college student to first confront the tough ethical calls in the classroom, where they can be rationally discussed, rather than under deadline pressure later. Good professional ethics is a cherished commodity and builds respect among one's colleagues. Thus, the value of at least some formal ethics instruction would appear to be clear.

Contents of a Course in Media Ethics

What should one expect from a course in media ethics? An instructor probably cannot teach moral conduct in the sense that learning (or memorizing) ethical principles will produce a more virtuous person. But ethics instruction can *promote* moral conduct by providing the means to make ethical judgments, defend them, and then criticize the results of one's choices.[16] This process is known as *moral reasoning*, which is the primary focus of Chapter 3.

Our expectations should remain fairly modest, but a course in media ethics can have several realistic and practical goals. The following five educational objectives are drawn from a study published by the Hastings Center, a pioneer in the ethics of medicine, biology, and the behavioral sciences.[17]

Stimulating the Moral Imagination.   A course in media ethics should promote the notion that moral choices constitute an important part of human existence and that the consequences of ethical decisions can lead to either suffering or happiness. Stimulating the moral imagination develops an emotional empathy with others that is not elicited by discussing ethical issues in abstract terms. Sometimes our moral imagination needs gentle prodding; at other times it needs shock therapy.

Recognizing Ethical Issues.   Although most of us would like to believe that we know right from wrong, we do not always recognize the moral dimensions of a situation. Or at other times we simply allow our prejudices or self-interests to betray our moral compass. For example, in the fall of 1999 *El Nuevo Herald*, the *Miami Herald*'s Spanish-language newspaper, apparently saw no ethical problem in sacrificing its journalistic independence to the anti-Castro feeling in Miami. According to the *Columbia Journalism Review*, during a press conference to highlight atrocities against American prisoners of war in Vietnam by Cuban agents who now hold important positions in Castro's government, retired Air Force Colonel Ed Hubbard, survivor of torture at the hands of those agents, recommended that the United States establish relations with Fidel Castro. The atmosphere in the room was tense, and the press conference ended abruptly. The *Herald* covered the story by ignoring Colonel Hubbard's "heretical" remarks.[18]

Anticipation of possible dilemmas is an important objective of ethics education and the moral reasoning process. Of course, some ethical strictures are subject to change. The standards of professional behavior, like the sands of time, are constantly shifting as media practitioners realign their moral compasses to account for changing circumstances. For example, there was a time when reporters, underpaid and overworked, routinely accepted gifts and gratuities from news sources. Today, this practice is generally frowned on, although there is still some disagreement over where to draw the line.[19]

Media professionals, like alcoholics, must first learn to acknowledge the problem before they can do something about it. Training in moral reasoning can assist all of us in recognizing the ethical implications of the decisions we are about to make. As Professor Louis Hodges of Washington and Lee University observed in noting the long-term benefits of formal ethics training:

> A careful and systematic classroom experience with ethics can, I am convinced, be helpful. It does so by calling the mind's attention to important ethical issues, to the virtues, and, through cases, specifically to the needs of the audience. And that can help redeem the moral force of the profession.[20]

Developing Analytical Skills.   The ability to think critically about ethical issues is at the heart of the decision-making process. This goal involves examining fundamental abstract concepts such as *justice, moral duty,* and *respect for others* to see how they can be applied consistently and coherently to real-life situations. Critical examination of the arguments and justifications used to support one's moral decisions is also an important consideration.[21] The ability to reason is essential to problem solving in mathematics and the behavioral sciences; the same can be said of moral philosophy. Case studies and classroom simulations, in which students role-play moral agents in a hypothetical or real ethical situation, can be effective tools in developing analytical skills.

Eliciting a Sense of Moral Obligation and Personal Responsibility.   President Harry Truman had a sign on his desk that said, "The buck stops here." The language was simple, the meaning profound. With these four words Truman was telling anyone who cared to listen

that he accepted, without reservation, responsibility for all actions of the executive branch. He was also recognizing a simple moral truth: Responsibility cannot be delegated. As moral agents we are all accountable for our actions and should not blame others for our ethical lapses. Media practitioners often emphasize freedom at the expense of responsibility. A course in ethics can redress that imbalance.

Tolerating Disagreement.   Before moral agents can make informed ethical judgments, they must take into account and respect other points of view. A rational decision is based on a defensible moral foundation, ample deliberation, and consideration of the available options. As James Jaska and Michael Pritchard observed in an illuminating discussion on ethics in communications: "Tolerating differences in choice and refraining from automatically labeling opposite choices as immoral are essential. At the same time, seeking exact points of difference can help solve disagreements by eliminating false distinctions and evasions."[22] We live in an open and diverse society, and wisdom and reason suggest that we consult the moral views of others before rendering our personal judgments.[23]

Developing Ethical Fitness

Assume that you have read this entire text, comprehended all of the ethical principles, and agonized over the dilemmas posed by the various case studies. Assume further that you have excelled on all of the class assignments and examinations and for your diligence and hard work you have received an "A" in your course on media ethics. You might be forgiven a certain amount of vanity for your superior academic achievement, but does this certify you as a more virtuous person than when you enrolled in the course?

Absolutely not! This text and any formal instruction in ethics are merely a point of departure. Through the formal experience of agonizing over the ethical dilemmas posed in hypothetical cases you can begin to cultivate your ethical awareness and to understand the moral reasoning process, as described more fully in Chapter 3. But just as watching videotapes will not make you physically fit or reading a book on the fundamentals of football will not make you a gridiron great, reading a text on media ethics will not make you a more virtuous individual. Athletes excel because of years of continuous practice. And so it is with character training and the learning of moral virtues. The only way to *be* a more ethical person is to *do* (that is, practice) ethics. Rushworth Kidder, a journalist and the founder of the Institute for Global Ethics, refers to this as "ethical fitness."[24]

Virtuosity doesn't emerge from the endless philosophical debates about ethical issues or from analyzing a dilemma to death. Ethical fitness derives from confronting the tough moral issues of everyday existence and becoming an active participant in their resolution. To be ethically fit, according to Kidder's sage advice, you've "got to be mentally engaged" and "committed through the feelings as well as through the intellect."[25]

Kidder's point is worth pausing over for a moment. Although the intellect is essential to rendering sound moral judgments (and the focus of this text *is* on moral reasoning), it is insufficient for the truly ethically fit individual. Moral decision making also requires compassion—or in Kidder's words, "feelings." Without compassion, ethical decisions might be reduced to sterile exercises in logic. But ethical fitness requires a holistic approach to character building in which both our intellectual and emotional aspects are fully engaged. Of course, our reason and emotions often disagree. An editor, for example, considering whether to publish gruesome photos of American war dead is torn between the journalistic value of newsworthiness and compassion for the families of the victims, as well as the sensibilities of the readers.

Training for ethical fitness doesn't begin when you accept your first job. Although professions do impose certain unique duties on their members, what is often overlooked is that professional responsibilities cannot be completely divorced from society's fundamental values. The ethical decision-making process does not differ according to context or environment. In other words, there is not one ethical system for media practitioners and another for everyone else. The cultivation of moral virtue—that is, the ability to distinguish good from evil and to make ethically defensible decisions—must be a lifelong commitment that at once engages our intellectual, intuitive, and emotional faculties. Ethics cannot be turned on and off according to the situation. The principles and case studies in this text are only catalysts. However, they will acquire real meaning through *practicing* and *thinking about* what you have learned in the tranquility of the academic setting. That's how you become ethically fit!

THE FIRST PRINCIPLES OF MORAL VIRTUE

Moral knowledge, which is indispensable for ethical fitness, does not consist of memorizing a set of ethical principles. It entails, as suggested in the preceding section, having the capacity to distinguish good and bad behavior and the moral will to apply this knowledge to real ethical dilemmas. There is no greater joy than the conviction that we have done the right thing, even if it flies in the face of popular sentiment. Ethical fitness can never result in human perfectibility, which of course is always elusive. Therefore, we must settle for a more modest assessment of moral virtue. Any discussion of the "ethical markers" of a morally virtuous individual could engage us intellectually for quite some time, but there are three that are perhaps fundamental to all others: *credibility, integrity, and civility.*

Credibility

Credibility is discussed first because without it the other virtues have no meaning. To be credible is to be believable and worthy of trust. From an ethical perspective, credibility is the point of departure in our dealings with others and our full membership in the moral community. Credibility is a fragile commodity, and in today's highly competitive, materialistic, and permissive environment its preservation is sometimes tedious. Nevertheless, our faith in credibility as an energizing force must remain undiminished because the fact remains that a lack of trust can be deleterious to both individuals and corporate enterprises.

Such was the case when two reporters resigned from the *Salt Lake City Tribune* after admitting they sold unpublished scandalous rumors about the Elizabeth Smart kidnapping case to the *National Enquirer* for $20,000. The editor, who also resigned after twelve years at the helm of the *Tribune*, commented on this betrayal of trust in an article published in *Quill*, the official magazine of the The Society of Professional Journalists. "I feel saddened and angry that these two reporters damaged themselves, their colleagues and the reputation of *The Tribune* with their conduct," he said. "My trust in reporters was betrayed. I relied too much on that instinct."[26]

In still another ethical breach, two TV stations in San Antonio, Texas, interrupted regular programming to report that shots had been fired and children injured at a local elementary school. As it turned out there was no shooting at the school; the stations had reacted precipitously to police and emergency services scanner traffic concerning an investigation into a shooting involving a school custodian that occurred far from the school. Despite some efforts to verify the story, these stations continued to broadcast erroneous information, "hyped the story with breaking news live coverage, and scared the daylights out of many parents and other citizens."[27] In still another ethically dubious decision, Boston TV station WCVB may have lost some credibility points in early 2001 when it began running a promotional campaign featuring well-known political figures. Having politicians praise the station for its local programming

raised some ethical concerns, according to *Broadcasting & Cable* magazine, about the station's ability "to be independent of the influence of prominent newsmakers who endorse the station."[28]

At least since the 1960s the term *credibility gap* has become synonymous with a lack of confidence in statements made by government officials, corporations, and cultural institutions. But the media are certainly not immune from the ravages of this credibility gap, a fact sometimes reflected in public opinion polls. Fortunately, such instances as those recorded earlier are rare, but just one well-publicized ethical indiscretion can undermine respect from an already skeptical public.

Integrity

Integrity is also crucial to moral maturation. True ethical fitness demands integrity. In his recently published book on the subject, Stephen Carter defines integrity as "(1) *discerning* what is right and what is wrong; (2) *acting* on what you have discerned, even at personal cost; and (3) *saying openly* that you are acting on your understanding of right from wrong."[29] The willingness to take *responsibility* for the consequences of one's actions must also be added to this list. In other words, people of integrity must be proactive in determining the proper course of action, must be willing to act on the results of that intellectual and critical investigation, and must then be willing to live with the results of their behavior. These ideas are the heart of the moral reasoning process that will be discussed in Chapter 3.

Those with integrity not only are committed to discovering what is good; they spend much of their time attempting to improve the moral ecology. An opponent of physician-assisted suicide, for example, who honestly believes, after much soul-searching, that any form of euthanasia is immoral should actively oppose legislative attempts to legalize such activities. Similarly, a Madison Avenue advertising executive who is concerned about the persistent problem of un-fair gender stereotyping in TV commercials should work within the industry to eliminate such stereotypes. In other words, moral agents that possess integrity *practice* what they preach. They try to make a difference.

Of course, people of good will can disagree passionately about the correct course of action and still maintain their integrity. News executives, for example, might aggressively defend their institutions' policies against political activism among their reporters, even of those not involved in the coverage of such events, on the grounds that such partisanship compromises the news division's independence and integrity. Reporters, on the other hand, might argue that political activism does not involve a conflict of interest unless a journalist is actively campaigning on behalf of a cause that she is covering. Both sides maintain their integrity as long as they think critically about their position, are truly convinced of the ethical strength of their views (that is, they are based on sound moral principles), and are willing to publicly defend their position.

Civility

To the morally untutored, civility might appear to be out of place in a discussion of ethics. The term often conjures up images of Victorian-era manners and etiquette, long since abandoned by an increasingly permissive society. But though it is true that manners certainly matter, civility as used here has a much broader connotation. Civility might be described as the "first principle" of morality because it encompasses an attitude of self-sacrifice and respect for others. These ideas are reflected in all of the major religions of the world.

Whereas the value of civility can be traced to ancient Greece, its contemporary formulation dates from the sixteenth century when scholar Desiderus Erasmus wrote the first important work on the subject. Civility, in Erasmus's view, is what enables us to live together as a society.[30]

It embraces a set of rules, often based on convention, that provides the tools for interacting with others.[31] When projected against the tapestry of the various media enterprises, we can see the necessity for some consensus on rules of conduct that enhance the media's public credibility and esteem. If one examines closely the industry codes, for example, fundamental to all of them is respect for the reader, listener, or viewer.

Respect and self-sacrifice, then, are the energizing forces of the moral virtue we refer to as *civility.* Morality involves taking into account the interests of others; an entirely selfish person cannot, by definition, make ethical judgments.[32] This is not to suggest that we should never be guided by self-interest. A request for a pay raise is obviously motivated by self-concern. Even striving to become a more virtuous individual involves a degree of self-interest. But one can achieve this goal only by factoring a concern for others into the decision-making equation.

Of course, not everyone agrees with this view. There are those who feel that self-interest should always be the *primary* determinant in choosing which course of action to follow. Supporters of this belief are known as egoists. Egoists do not suggest that we totally ignore the impact of our behavior on others. After all, we often benefit when positive things happen to others. For example, when a business profits economically because of its record of public service to the community, the employees are likely to benefit through fatter paychecks. But egoists are always motivated by long-term self-interests, even if they have to resort occasionally to altruism to reach their goal.

Media practitioners are often viewed by the public as egoists, and this view has precipitated a crisis of confidence.[33] Attitudes concerning the media are increasingly negative, prompted no doubt by the perception that journalists will leave no stone unturned, even if it is an unethical stone, to uncover a story and that advertising and public relations executives are more interested in manipulating public opinion and consumer tastes than serving the public interest.

When referring to the news business, for example, phrases such as *ratings war, sleaze TV,* and *tabloid journalism* are now a familiar part of the audience's lexicon. In the competition of the market, sensational, shocking, and scandalous revelations have increasingly replaced serious and significant intelligence on the media's journalistic agenda. This trend is reflected in such media circuses as the coverage of the O. J. Simpson trial, coverage of the allegations of President Clinton's sexual relationship with a White House intern, and the media spectacle surrounding Elian Gonzalez, the 6-year-old Cuban child who was rescued off the coast of Florida and became the center of an international child custody battle between his father and relatives living in Miami. Critics often indict the media for pandering to the lowest common denominator in their relentless quest for greater profits.

When reporters are accused of showing a lack of respect for their subjects, in reality they are being charged with a lack of civility. While journalists must sometimes be aggressive in confronting newsworthy figures, crossing the imaginary line between acceptable professional behavior and incivility can precipitate a public backlash. Such was the case when NBC's Emmy Award–winning reporter Jim Gray confronted former baseball great Pete Rose just prior to game two of the 1999 World Series. Rose was on hand to be honored as a member of the All-Century baseball team, but unlike most of the other honorees, Rose was not in the Baseball Hall of Fame, having been banished from baseball for life for gambling on the game as manager of the Cincinnati Reds. Following the on-field ceremony, Gray asked Rose for an interview but instead of lauding or congratulating the legend, the reporter grilled Rose about his repeated refusal to acknowledge any guilt concerning the gambling allegations. Asserting that the evidence against him was overwhelming, Gray challenged Rose to show contrition and to acknowledge his guilt, which Rose again vehemently declined to do.[34]

Reaction from the nationwide television audience was swift and critical. A majority of the callers believed Rose had paid the price for his indiscretions and should have been allowed to savor his brief return to public acclaim. NBC was forced to replace Gray for the remainder of the series, but Gray defended his tactics as a "proper line of questioning" because Rose had "put himself in a position to be pressed like that."[35] Nevertheless, while Gray's questions had been asked many times, the rather festive forum for this intemperate exchange undoubtedly contributed to the public's perception of journalistic impertinence, disrespect, and incivility. We shall return to the importance of civility again within another context in Chapter 9.

THE FORMATION OF ETHICAL VALUES AND ATTITUDES

In the preceding section we noted the importance of developing a sense of self-sacrifice— that is, taking into account the interests of others. But what factors influence our moral development? The answer to this question lies in an understanding of how ethical values and attitudes are formed.

Defining Values and Attitudes

We must begin by defining what we mean by values and attitudes, the building blocks of ethical behavior. Although there are many kinds of values and attitudes, this book will be concerned primarily with those that relate to ethical judgments. Thus, a *moral value* is something that is "esteemed, prized, or regarded highly, or as a good."[36] Autonomy, justice, and the dignity of human life are examples of values that are important to large segments of society. Objectivity and fairness are often cited as values underlying the practice of journalism. Similarly, trust, integrity, and honesty are cherished values for any ethical public relations practitioner.

Values are the building blocks of attitudes— that is, the "learned emotional, intellectual, and behavioral responses to persons, things, and events."[37] For example, the attitudes of opponents of physician-assisted suicide may be predicated on such fundamental moral values as the sanctity of life. Contrarily, the attitudes of those who believe in a "right to die with dignity" are based on such underlying values as individual autonomy and the right to a quality of life. Thus, it is easy to see why ethical disagreements and debates generate such emotional rhetoric.

The ancient Greeks recognized the importance of *attitudes,* and since that time many writers have described three components: the affective, the cognitive, and the behavioral.[38] The *affective* component of an attitude is the emotional side of our beliefs about a situation. It consists of our positive or negative feelings toward people or events, pleasure or displeasure, or perhaps even uncertainty. For example, some TV personalities may elicit positive emotional responses because of their charisma, charm, or interesting commentary. Others may evoke negative emotions because of their insensitivity and ill-concealed ego. Of course, one of the wonders of human nature is that the same individual is often capable of producing a variety of responses in different members of the audience. This emotional incongruity is reflected in the phenomenon of controversial talk show host Rush Limbaugh, who is either loved or reviled by radio and TV audiences. The affective component is important to the moral agent in making ethical judgments because it provides an emotional dimension to those decisions. It would have been a callous reporter, indeed, who did not sympathize with the plight of the families of the 9/11 victims and thus approach those families for interviews with great sensitivity.

The *cognitive* component is the intellectual side of an attitude. It consists of what the moral agent believes, knows, or reasons about a person, thing, or event. For example, one person may believe that the rap group 2Live Crew poses a threat to cultural civility and sanity, whereas another may see the group as merely a harmless reflection of an uninhibited lifestyle.

The *behavioral* component of an attitude relates to the individual's predisposition to respond. When we speak of ethical conduct, or behavior, we are referring to moral action reflecting the affective (emotional) and cognitive (rational) components of a moral agent's attitudes about a situation. Either of these may dominate at a given moment, but true moral reasoning takes into account both feelings and beliefs.

As a case in point, a newspaper editor's decision to publish a rape victim's name is never an easy one. Many papers have policies against doing so; others will publish the names under some circumstances. The emotional side of the attitude about this dilemma would probably evoke feelings of compassion and sympathy for the victim. The rational, or cognitive, component might lead to the conclusion that the victim's name was not essential to the story and that nothing would be gained by publishing it. In addition, a policy against releasing the names of victims of sex crimes might encourage other victims to report their experiences to the authorities.

On the other hand, some editors, despite feelings of compassion for the victim and even some misgivings about publishing her name, might reason that the victims of crime have always been news and that their names should be published unless there is some unusual reason for not doing so. The media, they feel, should not be in the business of suppressing news; otherwise, their credibility will suffer. What is lost in this debate is the notion that the audience might support withholding the name of a rape victim without automatically assuming that news suppression was standard practice for the media. And as we have previously seen, the audience is an important consideration in making ethical judgments. In any event, both the rational and the emotional sides of our being are instrumental in moral reasoning.

Attitudes about morality, then, can be viewed as packages of values that combine feelings, thoughts, and actions.[39] But where do our attitudes and values come from? What forces shape our moral development? The answers to these questions are important, because individual moral behavior forms the foundation of institutional and professional standards of conduct. *Institutions don't behave unethically; people do.*[40]

Sources of Values and Attitudes

Four influential sources directly affect our formation of values and attitudes: the family, peer groups, role models, and societal institutions. The extent to which each of these is responsible for our moral behavior depends on the unique circumstances of each individual.

Not surprisingly, *parents* provide the first and perhaps most important behavioral models for children. Parents are the primary influence in instilling a conscience, a sense of right and wrong. Some values and attitudes are learned by a child through instruction and discipline, but others are acquired through imitating, or modeling, parental behavior. For example, parents who consistently blame others for their shortcomings and difficulties implant in their children the misguided belief that we are not responsible for our own actions. Likewise, a mother who writes an excuse to a teacher saying that "Johnny was sick yesterday," when in fact such was not the case, sends a cue to Johnny that lying is permissible. Ironically, such a parent would never instill deception in her child as a positive value, but her behavior sends a message that deception is socially acceptable in certain situations.

One measure of conscience is the ability to resist temptation.[41] This goal is achieved in the early stages of the child's moral development through a series of rewards and punishments,[42] but children increasingly internalize these lessons. At this stage children generally accept certain ideas advanced by their parents but are incapable of true moral reasoning. But in subsequent stages the beginnings of logical reasoning appear, and children's ever-developing moral blueprints become both reference points by which future ethical dilemmas can be resolved and defense mechanisms by which children can resist the challenges to their value systems.[43]

Peer groups are another important influence in moral development, especially among adolescents. The most significant peer groups are those encountered in our neighborhoods, schools, churches, social clubs, and, as we reach adulthood, working environment. Peer groups can exert enormous, sometimes irresistible, pressure to conform. It is here that the individual's moral values may undergo their most rigorous challenge and that ethical compromises may occur because of the social role required of group members. Of course, some peer group memberships, such as participation in a religious organization, can reinforce an individual's value system.

Role models are those individuals whom we admire, respect, and wish to emulate. They can teach us the ways of righteousness or wickedness (for example, drug dealers whose lavish lifestyles are sometimes attractive to impressionable youths), but they have a profound impact on the imitative behavior of others. Children and adolescents become psychologically involved with their role models and assume their ideas, attitudes, and conduct.

Sometimes, role models are ordinary people, such as teachers or ministers, who exert a subtle influence on those with whom they come in contact. Frequently, they are public figures who can set examples, either good or bad, for millions of followers. Tiger Woods, Ricky Martin, and Britney Spears appear to have very little in common except that they are all role models. Impressionable youths often take their ethical cues from such highly visible personalities. Beer commercials featuring well-known athletes, for example, convey a message that drinking is somehow a social virtue, a true test of masculinity. Likewise, the decrease in civility and the rather casual use of pejorative language among the nation's youth might be attributed, in part, to the examples set by their idols in the entertainment business and the sports world.

Role models and peers can exert as much influence, especially in later life, as family ties. The importance of selecting as models those individuals who exemplify positive ethical values was noted by the ethicist Michael Josephson in a conversation with the TV commentator Bill Moyers:

> We certainly get an inculcation from our parents, and that's a very important thing. But all that does is give us an orientation toward ethics. Now some people rebel against that orientation, and some people adopt it and follow it. We're also influenced by our peer groups. Ethics is taught from all sides, by a coach, for example, or a teacher, or a particular person who inspires someone to his highest self. . . . It is very important for leaders and role models, whether they be sports figures or politicians, to make positive statements of ethics, if they're not hypocritical.[44]

Do role models have any moral obligation toward their followers? Those who set bad examples are generally motivated by self-interest and thus are not worthy of emulation. But true moral leaders, those who are in a position to move the ethical development of others in a positive direction, have an obligation to set high standards of conduct for those who might be inclined to model their behavior.

Suppose that a college newspaper adviser, who is highly respected by the student staff and is thus somewhat of a role model, encourages his young reporters to do anything to get a story. Such advice can sometimes have the effect of instilling in journalistic neophytes the notion that reporters operate on an ethical plane separate from the rest of society. Likewise, a public relations instructor who counsels uncompromising company loyalty over public responsibility is providing her students with a distorted view of the ethical conduct expected of public relations practitioners.

Families, peer groups, and role models all exert powerful and demonstrable influences on our sense of ethics. But *societal institutions* should not be overlooked as important influences in the moral life of the individual. Do such institutions alter our ethical standards, or do they merely reflect them? This is a complex question,

but suffice it to say that society's institutions reflect the prevailing norms and at the same time are instrumental in bringing about changes in attitudes concerning standards of conduct. For example, the "sexual revolution" was well under way by the time TV jumped on the bandwagon, but it is likely that TV programming had a role in expediting public acceptance of greater sexual freedom, even if we cannot prove it scientifically.

I said earlier that institutions don't behave unethically—people do. However, the decision making within the institutional structure is sometimes so diffuse that individual responsibility is difficult to ascribe. A case in point is the TV drama, which necessitates a cadre of creative talent, each member with a stake in the content's moral tone. The path of responsibility begins in Hollywood and flows to the network corporate offices in New York. This division of creative labor within institutions often leads us to refer to the "ethical standards" of CBS, HBO, or Fox. Nevertheless, individuals make the moral judgments that emerge in the form of corporate policy or practice.

Institutions have a profound impact on their own members and set the ethical tone for their conduct. Within each organization there is a moral culture, reflected both in written policies and the examples set by top management, that inspires the ethical behavior of its members. The socialization of journalists and the development of professional values do not end at the schoolhouse gate. The moral education of media practitioners begins early in life but is a never-ending process.

Institutions also have a profound influence on the ethical values and attitudes of societal members because of the pivotal role they play in the dynamics of any culture. Thus, we often speak of those institutions that respect the needs and sensibilities of the publics they serve—which sometimes include media organizations—as acting with a sense of social responsibility.

The process by which all of these influences—families, peer groups, role models, and institutions—introduce the individual to the conventions and norms of a given society or sub-group is known as *socialization*.[45] For example, when an academic institution punishes students for cheating it is reinforcing the value of honesty that is a first principle of our culture's moral code. Likewise, advertising and public relations students, through their enrollment in university-level mass communication programs, are quickly "socialized" into the conventions of their profession. Socialization is a lifelong activity and serves as an agent of social control by providing for a certain homogenization of moral values.

All of these influences contribute to the moral development of the individual in a combination that social psychologists do not yet fully comprehend. We do know, however, that our attitudes about a situation do not always determine our moral judgments, thus suggesting that peer pressure and institutional influences sometimes take precedence over the values we consider important.

A legislator who is an outspoken advocate of gun control may, for example, vote against a ban on handguns to gain some concessions from his legislative colleagues on another matter pending before them. A magazine editor who has campaigned aggressively for more federal resources to fight the "war on drugs" may, nevertheless, look the other way when the ad manager accepts ads for alcoholic beverages, the nation's number one drug. There are many reasons for this inconsistency between belief and behavior,[46] but at the very least it reflects a conflict of ethical values.

Personal Values and Professional Ethics

Professions by their very nature often demand that practitioners subordinate their personal values or ethics to the standards of the profession. Criminal defense lawyers, for example, undoubtedly experience personal discomfort in defending unsavory clients they know to be guilty and whose community would be better off without their membership. As citizens, journalists might

enter the profession with a deep appreciation of the value of privacy, but their professional obligations frequently require painful intrusions upon the personal solitude of others, sometimes resulting in harm to innocent third parties. The dilemma for any media practitioner is stated rather succinctly in Thomas Bivens's recently published book on media ethics: "By letting our personal principles take first priority, we could be compromising our professional principles. The question then becomes, which do we want most to be, a private citizen or a media professional? Although the two roles are not mutually exclusive, there is an awareness that one assumes the mantle of professionalism willingly, accepting that a muting of personal values is part of the payment for doing so."[47]

Personal and professional ethics are not necessarily mutually exclusive. But when they do clash, as Bivens has remarked, "deference is usually, and possibly rightly, given to professional principles."[48] However, this observation should not be interpreted as an uncompromising preference for professional values by which personal ethics must be marginalized. In reality, personal and professional ethics share some common ground, and this makes the perceived clash between the two easier to digest. For example, human interaction often requires a course of action that may result in harm, either physical or mental, to others. But the harm principle admonishes us to "minimize" such harm, particularly as it relates to innocent third parties. This should be a guiding principle in our personal ethics, as well as our professional deportment. When we assume the responsibilities of a media practitioner, we willingly accept the standards of the profession, which may require the balancing of competing loyalties. But isn't this also true of our personal relationships in which competing values, such as justice versus mercy or truth versus compassion, painfully engage our moral sensibilities?

Professional standards are based upon experience and (hopefully) the best practices of the industry but frequently reflect community values. When viewed from the perspective of such values as credibility, trust, and respect for persons, among others, the nexus between professional and personal ethics becomes more readily apparent. The use of deception in investigative reporting, for example, can only be justified by some more compelling moral mandate, an ethical stance with which the average journalist would probably be personally as well as professionally comfortable. Inevitably, the tension between one's professional life and personal code can be untidy at times. Thus, in the final analysis "[t]he ultimate test of any principle, personal or professional, must be the efficacy of the resulting actions based on those principles—not just for the person acting (the moral agent) but for all those involved in or affected by the action."[49]

THE ETHICAL DILEMMA: CONFLICT OF VALUES

A man named Heintz has a wife who is terminally ill with cancer. He has tried, without success, to raise money to buy a drug that might save her life. A druggist is charging $2,000 for such a potion. Heintz has been able to raise only $1,000, and the druggist refuses to extend him credit. Should Heintz steal the drug to save his wife's life?[50] This famous hypothetical ethical dilemma was used by the social psychologist Lawrence Kohlberg and his associates to illustrate the conflicting values inherent in the notion of justice. On the one hand, Heintz loves his wife, and in the interest of the sanctity of life he may feel justified in stealing the drug. On the other hand, to do so would violate one of the fundamental moral tenets of the Western world, the proscription against stealing another's property.

Heintz dilemmas are all around us. They constitute the very essence of emotional debates about such diverse social issues as abortion, gun control, the death penalty, sex education, and pornography. Of course, not all moral judgments reflect the kind of life-or-death situation confronted by Heintz, but difficult ethical choices do involve conflicts in values. These conflicts can arise on several levels. Sometimes, there is an inner conflict involving the application of general societal values. For example, in times of military hostilities a Pentagon public affairs officer may have to choose between the value of revealing the *truth* to the press concerning battlefield casualties and the value of maintaining *public support* for American involvement in the conflict.

Sometimes, there is a conflict between general societal values (for instance, minimizing harm to others) and professional values. Consider, for example, the public uproar in Columbia, South Carolina, when a local TV station honored a police request to withhold information as a matter of safety and the newspaper did not. In Columbia, a policeman was wounded in a stolen car chase. The case was not connected with his regular assignment as an undercover narcotics investigator, and the police chief asked the news media not to reveal the officer's name lest they endanger him or his son or pregnant wife. As a result of the newspaper's decision not to comply, many subscribers were angry and some canceled their subscriptions.[51] In letters to defecting subscribers, editor Gil Thelen defended his decision: "We weighed the public's legitimate interest in the information with concerns about the officer's and his family's safety. No person in authority was able to provide specific information about any security threats to either."[52]

Another instance of conflicting values concerned Nike, which ran a billboard campaign in Chicago's South Side ghetto featuring famous African American athletes wearing Nike athletic shoes. Nike was careful to select athletes with "squeaky clean" images as role models for the African American youths who were the target audience of this campaign. But when several black inner-city youths were assaulted or murdered allegedly because their peers wished to look more like the celebrity role models,

Nike was criticized in the media for selecting black athletes as spokespersons. Such advertisements created a desire for material goods that were beyond the economic means of the average juvenile on Chicago's South Side. A Nike representative defended the practice as good marketing to use such credible personalities in appealing to black youths. Thus, what appeared to be a sound advertising and marketing strategy, based on noble principles, unintentionally ran afoul of social values and the stark realities of life in the inner city.[53]

When neither conflicting value appears to be satisfactory, we may examine third options. Suppose the dean asks a mass communication professor to reconsider a failing grade he awarded to a graduating senior in his media ethics course. *Loyalty* to the dean may propel him to honor her request. On the other hand, *honesty* suggests that the professor should not do so, especially if he is convinced of the correctness of the grade. However, he may appeal to a third value, *fairness:* Would it be unfair to the other students to reconsider the grade of one student and not the entire class?

Ethical judgments involving the clash of competing principles generally arise in rather untidy situations.[54] Such was the case when Minneapolis police asked the news media to assist in the disappearance of a 15-year-old boy who had allegedly been sexually assaulted. The primary suspect was a 30-year-old neighbor who had been charged with sexually assaulting the boy on a hunting trip two weeks earlier. The 30-year-old was free on bond and under a court order not to contact the boy. The Minneapolis *Star Tribune*'s story, which disclosed the victim's name and a description of the assault, also included the fact that the neighbor had called the boy's parents, had admitted the assault on their son, and said he felt like killing himself. The paper reported that the parents called police when they saw the older man point a gun at his head.[55]

The boy's father complained to the paper's ombudsman, Lou Gelfand, that the information

could "cause complications to getting them home" and could have adverse psychological consequences for the boy. Some readers complained that the details of the sexual assault were egregious. Reporter Mark Brunswick defended the coverage on the grounds that "it was essential to report the relationship between the two." "I think to simply say the boy was sexually assaulted, without elaboration," observed Brunswick, "might leave the reader to imagine many things that did not happen."[56]

The ethical concerns surrounding the coverage were exacerbated when a day after the story the newspaper published a report from a gay and lesbian organization from which the boy had sought counseling because he was concerned about his sexuality and could not get help from other channels. The paper was inundated with calls from outraged readers protesting the "outing" of the 15-year-old youth. They accused the *Star Tribune* of inexcusably publishing confidential information; some were concerned that troubled teenagers would be reluctant to seek counseling on sexual identity problems for fear their names might be made public.[57]

Editor Tim McGuire defended the paper's decision to print the confidential information about the boy's struggle with his sexual identity because it provided readers with a more complete understanding of the crime and the circumstances surrounding it. In addition, despite the delicate and sensitive nature of the story, the editor vindicated his paper's decision based on the greater good that might accrue to other troubled teens. "If we agreed not to publish we would have been buying into the premise that teen struggles with sexuality are something to be hidden and are, in fact, shameful," noted McGuire. "I could not get comfortable with that." Three days after the first story, the bodies of the boy and the man were discovered five miles from their homes, the victims of an apparent murder-suicide.[58]

This scenario exemplifies a conflict of competing values: the public's need to know versus the individual's right to privacy and confidentiality. It also illustrates how a news organization and its readers approached the issue from different ethical perspectives, both of which could be defended on rational grounds.

In ethical issues, no less than in legal ones, the key to dealing with Heintz dilemmas is to demystify the process by gathering as much evidence and formulating as many rational arguments as possible in defense of the ultimate decision. This is not to understate the difficulty of resolving conflicts between moral alternatives. Even after a decision is rendered, there will be some lingering uncertainty about whether the choice was proper or wise. The goal of moral reasoning is not to reach agreement on the ethical issues of our time. Instead, moral reasoning is a tool designed to assist us, as moral agents, in working our way out of the ethical morasses encountered in our personal and professional lives.

SUMMARY

Ethics is the branch of philosophy that deals with questions of moral behavior. The study of ethics can provide the tools for making difficult moral choices, both personal and professional. The goal is not to make ethical decisions with which everyone agrees but to increase our ability to defend our critical judgments on some rational basis.

Ethics, as a formal field of inquiry, includes three related subcategories. *Metaethics* attempts to assign meanings to the abstract language of moral philosophy. *Normative ethics* provides the foundation for decision making through the development of general rules and principles of moral conduct. *Applied ethics* is concerned with using these theoretical norms to solve ethical problems in the real world.

Ethical situations are usually complex affairs, in which a *moral agent* (the one making the ethical decision) commits an *act* (either verbal or nonverbal) within a specific *context* with a

particular *motive* directed at an *individual* or *audience* usually with some *consequence,* either positive or negative. Each of these factors must be taken into account before passing judgment on the outcome of any moral scenario.

There are two schools of thought on whether ethics is a proper subject for academic consideration. Cynics disparage the study of ethics, because it is a discipline that raises many questions without providing concrete answers. They also argue that such character education classes will do little to influence those whose moral education is virtually complete before they enter the academy. Media practitioners sometimes see little value in such courses, because classes cannot duplicate the frenzied pace and pressure of the real world.

Proponents of ethics instruction believe that although moral conduct itself probably cannot be taught, such courses can promote virtuous behavior through the teaching of moral reasoning. However, the ability to make sound ethical decisions comes only through practice and a lifetime commitment to the principles of virtuosity. This is known as *ethical fitness.*

Although media ethics courses cannot simulate the realities of the competitive marketplace, they can offer an intellectual moral foundation for future generations of practitioners. There appear to be at least five realistic and practical educational objectives for a course in media ethics: (1) stimulating the moral imagination, (2) recognizing ethical issues, (3) developing analytical skills, (4) eliciting a sense of moral obligation and personal responsibility, and (5) tolerating disagreement. Thus, the teaching of moral literacy is just as vital to the curriculum as the skills courses that will train students for their first jobs.

Moral development begins at an early age and is a lifelong process. Only through reflection and the *practice* of virtuous behavior can we become ethically fit. The cornerstones of ethical fitness are *credibility,* the moral virtue on which trust is built; *integrity,* which is essential to our own moral development; and *civility,* a device for interacting with others.

The study of ethics must include an understanding of how moral direction is acquired. Our ethical values form the foundation on which we make ethical decisions. These values underlie our attitudes about moral issues, and our attitudes are believed to consist of an emotional component, an intellectual (or rational) component, and a behavioral component. Thus, true moral reasoning takes into account both feelings and beliefs about an issue.

The acquisition of values and the formation of attitudes is a complex process and does not easily lend itself to scientific verification. However, for most of us the important forces that shape our moral development are family, peer groups, role models, and societal institutions. Parents are our first encounter with discipline, but as we evolve into autonomous individuals, peer groups, role models, and institutional forces play an increasingly significant role in shaping our moral destiny.

With so many diverse forces bombarding us with ethical cues, it is inevitable that conflicts between competing values will emerge. For example, personal and professional values sometimes collide. But in the final analysis the ultimate test of any principle, personal or professional, must be the efficacy of the resulting actions based on that principle—not just for the person acting (the moral agent) but for all those involved in or affected by the action. The study of ethics and moral reasoning cannot necessarily resolve such conflicts for us, but it can provide the tools to make it easier to live with our difficult ethical choices.

Notes

1. "Times Reporter Who Resigned Leaves Long Trail of Deception," *New York Times,* May 11, 2003, p. 1.
2. Lindley J. Stiles and Bruce D. Johnson (eds.), *Morality Examined: Guidelines for Teachers* (Princeton, NJ: Princeton Book Company, 1977), p. xi.
3. Ibid.
4. "Sports, Ethics and Ideas," *Quill,* January 1987, p. 2.
5. See Joan C. Callahan (ed.), *Ethical Issues in Professional Life* (New York: Oxford University Press, 1988), pp. 7–9; John C. Merrill and S. Jack Odell, *Philosophy and Journalism* (White Plains, NY: Longman, 1983), p. 79.
6. For a good discussion of applied ethics, see Baruch Brody, *Ethics and Its Applications* (New York: Harcourt Brace Jovanovich, 1983), p. 4.
7. This model is based on one described by Richard L. Johannesen in *Ethics in Human Communication,* 3d ed. (Prospect Heights, IL: Waveland, 1990), p. 16.
8. In response, the reporter also sued her newspaper employer, alleging a violation of the state's Fair Campaign Practices Act and the state and federal constitutions. The State Supreme Court eventually ruled in favor of the *News Tribune. Nelson v. McClatchy Newspapers, Inc.,* 25 Med. L. Rptr. 1513 (Wash. Sup. Ct. 1997), *cert. denied,* 118 S. Ct. 175 (1997).
9. For an elaboration of this point, see Jeffrey Olen, *Ethics in Journalism* (Upper Saddle River, NJ: Prentice-Hall, 1988), p. 25.
10. Sharyn Wizda, "Too Much Information?," *American Journalism Review,* June 1998, pp. 58–62.
11. Ibid., pp. 60–61.
12. Ibid., p. 61.
13. Stiles and Johnson, *Morality Examined,* pp. 11–12.
14. James Rachels, "Can Ethics Provide Answers?," in David M. Rosenthal and Fadlou She-haili (eds.), *Applied Ethics and Ethical Theory* (Salt Lake City: University of Utah Press, 1988), pp. 3–4.
15. This view was expressed, according to Plato, in the *Meno,* where Socrates stated that virtue is "an instinct given by god to the virtuous." See Stiles and Johnson, *Morality Examined,* p. 10, quoting Benjamin Jowett, Jr., *The Dialogues of Plato,* vol. 1 (New York: Random House, 1920), p. 380.
16. Reginald D. Archambault, "Criteria for Success in Moral Instruction," in Barry L. Chazan and Jonas F. Soltis (eds.), *Moral Education* (New York: Teachers College Press, 1973), p. 165.
17. Hastings Center, *The Teaching of Ethics in Higher Education* (Hastings-on-Hudson, NY: Hastings Center, 1980), pp. 48–52. These goals are also discussed in James A. Jaksa and Michael S. Pritchard, *Communication Ethics: Methods of Analysis,* 2d ed. (Belmont, CA: Wadsworth, 1994), pp. 12–18.
18. "Unliberated News," *Columbia Journalism Review,* January/February 2000, p. 19.
19. For a discussion of this issue, see Ron F. Smith, *Groping for Ethics in Journalism,* 5th ed. (Ames: Iowa State University Press, 2003), pp. 385–400.
20. Louis W. Hodges, "The Journalist and Professionalism," *Journal of Mass Media Ethics* 1, no. 2 (Spring/Summer 1986): 35.

21. See Jaksa and Pritchard, *Communication Ethics,* pp. 15–16.

22. Ibid., p. 9.

23. Hastings Center, *Teaching of Ethics,* p. 52.

24. See Rushworth M. Kidder, *How Good People Make Tough Choices* (New York: Morrow, 1995), pp. 57–76.

25. Ibid., p. 59.

26. Bonnie Bressers, "Rebuilding Trust: Newsrooms React as Ethical Breaches Erode Confidence," *Quill,* July 2003, p. 8.

27. Bob Steele, "Dull Tools and Bad Decisions," *Quill,* April 2000, p. 22.

28. "Credibility crisis?," *Broadcasting & Cable,* January 15, 2001, p. 103.

29. Stephen L. Carter, *Integrity* (New York: Basic Books, 1996), p. 7.

30. Ibid., pp. 14–15.

31. Ibid., p. xii.

32. For a discussion of this point, see Norman E. Bowie, *Making Ethical Decisions* (New York: McGraw-Hill, 1985), pp. 11–16.

33. Ted J. Smith III, "Journalism and the Socrates Syndrome," *Quill,* April 1988, p. 15.

34. Ben Scott, "Playing Hardball: The Pete Rose–Jim Gray Controversy," in Lee Wilkins and Philip Patterson, *Media Ethics: Issues & Cases,* 4th ed. (Boston: McGraw-Hill, 2002), p. 275.

35. Ibid., 275–276.

36. Peter A. Angeles, *Dictionary of Philosophy* (New York: Barnes & Noble, 1981), p. 310.

37. Albert A. Harrison, *Individuals and Groups: Understanding Social Behavior* (Pacific Grove, CA: Brooks/Cole, 1976), p. 192.

38. Ibid., pp. 192–195.

39. Ibid., p. 193.

40. This notion is challenged by Thomas Nagel in "Ruthlessness in Public Life," in Callahan, *Ethical Issues,* pp. 76–83.

41. Edwin P. Hollander, *Principles and Methods of Social Psychology,* 4th ed. (New York: Oxford University Press, 1981), p. 258.

42. See A. Bandura, *A Social Learning Theory* (Upper Saddle River, NJ: Prentice-Hall, 1977); J. P. Flanders, "A Review of Research on Imitative Behavior," *Psychology Bulletin* 69 (1968): 316–337.

43. The psychologist Lawrence Kohlberg, in challenging theories advanced earlier by Sigmund Freud, maintains that a child's moral development occurs in six stages.

44. Bill Moyers, *A World of Ideas* (New York: Doubleday, 1989), p. 16.

45. See Hollander, *Principles and Methods of Social Psychology,* p. 174.

46. For a discussion of the various theories in social psychology relating to this topic, see Harrison, *Individuals and Groups,* pp. 195–218.

47. Thomas H. Bivens, *Mixed Media: Moral Distinctions in Advertising, Public Relations, and Journalism* (Mahwah, NJ: Lawrence Erlbaum, 2004), p. 11.

48. Ibid.

49. Ibid.

50. Reported in Jaksa and Pritchard, *Communication Ethics,* p. 99.

51. Richard P. Cunningham, "Public Cries Foul on Both Coasts When Papers Lift Secrecy," *Quill,* April 1995, p. 12.

52. Quoted in Cunningham.

53. For a more thorough discussion of this case, see Gail Baker, "The Gym Shoe Phenomenon: Social Values vs. Marketability," in Philip Patterson and Lee Wilkins, *Media Ethics: Issues and Cases,* 4th ed. (Boston: McGraw-Hill, 2002), pp. 116–118.

54. For a more thorough discussion on this point, see Tom L. Beauchamp, *Philosophical Ethics: An Introduction to Moral Philosophy* (New York: McGraw-Hill, 1982), pp. 43–45.

55. Richard P. Cunningham, "Reporting Sexual Assault Crimes Can Be a Touchy Subject," *Quill,* March 1994, p. 10.

56. Ibid.

57. Ibid., pp. 10–11.

58. Ibid.

2

Ethics and Society

THE NEED FOR A SYSTEM OF ETHICS

When ABC's *PrimeTime Live* aired the results of an undercover investigation into charges that Food Lion, the nation's fastest-growing grocery chain, routinely sold rotting and infested food to an unsuspecting public, the network soon found itself confronted with a multimillion-dollar lawsuit and accusations of ethical misconduct. *PrimeTime Live* producers cited false references as a means to gain employment with Food Lion and then used cameras and other equipment concealed in their hair and bras to validate the charges. The broadcast was devastating to the grocery chain, resulting in the closing of eighty-four stores over the next two years and the termination of thousands of employees.[1] Food Lion did not contest the underlying truth of the report, but the jury, apparently reflecting the public's growing disaffection with such news-gathering conventions, found the network guilty of fraud and trespass and awarded Food Lion $5.5 million in punitive damages, an amount that was significantly reduced first by the trial judge and again by an appellate court.[2]

Despite the popularity of such undercover investigative techniques, especially among television magazine shows, the precariousness of the network's ethical position is reflected in the mixed reviews within the journalistic community. Whereas some feared that the Food Lion case would dampen the investigative ardor of future journalists,[3] others questioned whether the ends always justify the means. *Washington Post* columnist Colman McCarthy, for example, condemned the practice of lying to get a story as "lazy journalism, not aggressive reporting."[4] Dorothy Rabinowitz, a member of the *Wall Street Journal's* editorial board, was similarly unimpressed with the imperious attitude of some investigative reporters: "Many journalists continue to believe that they are involved in a calling so high as to entitle them to rights not given ordinary citizens."[5]

Society and Moral Anchors

As the Food Lion case illustrates, society is not always a gentle taskmaster when it comes to passing judgment on its moral agents. The standards against which society scrutinizes individual and institutional behavior are embedded in its code of moral conduct, its system of ethics. Thus, Rabinowitz's penetrating observation raises a profound question for the student of media ethics: Are media professionals bound by the same standards of moral conduct as the citizens they serve? If so, that is sufficient justification to explore the following question: Why does society really need a system of ethics? At least five reasons merit attention.

The Need for Social Stability. First, a system of ethics is necessary for social intercourse. Ethics is the foundation of our advanced civilization, a cornerstone that provides some stability to society's moral expectations. If we are to enter into agreements with others, a necessity in a complex, interdependent society, we must be able to trust one another to keep those agreements, even if it is not in our self-interest to do so.[6] Professional athletes who demand to renegotiate their contracts before they have expired may breed contempt and mistrust in the front office and the belief among the fans that they are placing self-interest over the interests of the team. While the public is accustomed to some puffery in advertising, they expect an uncorrupted flow of accurate information. When advertising executives fail in this expectation, public confidence is eroded. Likewise, the reading and viewing publics expect journalists to report the truth, even when there is no formal agreement to do so. When reporters fail in this expectation, their credibility is eroded. Suffice it to say that indiscretions by a few ethical miscreants can undermine the moral standing of an entire industry.

The Need for a Moral Hierarchy. Second, a system of ethics serves as a *moral gatekeeper* in apprising society of the relative importance of certain customs. It does this by alerting the public to (1) those norms that are important enough to be described as moral and (2) the "hierarchy of ethical norms" and their relative standing in the moral pecking order.

All cultures have many customs, but most do not concern ethical mores.[7] For example, eating with utensils is customary in Western countries, but the failure to do so is not immoral. Standing for the national anthem before a sporting event is a common practice, but those who remain seated are not behaving unethically. There is a tendency to describe actions of which we disapprove as immoral, although most of our social indiscretions are merely transgressions of etiquette. A system of ethics identifies those customs and practices of which there is enough social disapproval to render them immoral.

However, even those values and principles that have the distinction of qualifying as moral norms are not all on an equal footing. From time to time in this book I will refer to certain ideas, such as the commitment to truth and proscriptions against stealing, as *fundamental* societal values. This distinction suggests that some are more important than others. Trespassing, for example, although not socially approved, is generally viewed less seriously than lying. This may explain why the journalistic practice of invading private property to get a story, though not applauded in all quarters, does not usually meet with the same degree of condemnation as the use of outright deception.

The Need to Promote a Dynamic Moral Ecology. Three, an ethical framework serves as a social conscience, challenging members of a community to examine the ethical dimensions of both public issues and private concerns and to aspire to elevate the quality of the moral ecology. However, the goal should not be the *ideal* society (which is impossible) but a *decent* society. What should be avoided are claims of infallibility. Ethics is not a science, and trial and error are inevitable. In a not-so-perfect society some compromise and balancing are required because not every claim deserves equal attention.[8] A system of ethics provides an arena where ethical experimentation can occur, a process that is limited only by the admonition that moral progress should be the result, not moral retrenchment. Society must constantly seek moral progress, which involves a constant reevaluation of prevailing norms while not abandoning the civic community's most cherished moral precepts (such as justice and respect for others). This can sometimes be a painful process. The debate over stem cell research, for example, has publicly engaged the moral imaginations of ethicists, scientists, religious institutions, and the general public as they attempt to forge some ethical accommodation on this field of scientific inquiry. In the admittedly untidy process of establishing ethical norms, *exactly what the benchmarks should be is subject to some negotiation; whether to have such ethical benchmarks is not!*

The Need to Resolve Conflicts.   Four, a system of ethics is an important social institution for resolving cases involving conflicting claims based on individual self-interest.[9] For example, it might be in a student's own interest to copy from a classmate's term paper. It is in the classmate's best interest to keep her from doing so. Societal rules against plagiarism are brought to bear in evaluating the moral conduct inherent in this situation.

The Need to Clarify Values.   Finally, a system of ethics also functions to clarify for society the competing values and principles inherent in emerging and novel moral dilemmas. Some of the issues confronting civilization today would challenge the imagination of even the most ardent philosopher. A case in point is the controversy over the cloning of humans, a scientific breakthrough with unimaginable ethical consequences. Ethicists have already begun passionately debating this issue in the hopes of clarifying competing moral values and affording some time for reasoned reflection before such scientific experimentation becomes commonplace.

An ethical system encourages the debate and airing of differences over competing moral principles. In so doing, it crystallizes society's attitudes about ethical dilemmas and often leads to adjudication (if not a satisfactory resolution) of disputes. This point is illustrated by readers' complaints surrounding a California newspaper's coverage of a controversial ballot issue several years ago. The proposition, designed to cut off government services to illegal aliens, was supported by a group known as Save Our State (SOS), whose supporters were subjected to charges of racism and threats by militant opponents. Because of those threats, SOS sought to keep its address secret. But the Orange County *Register* learned the address and used it as the lead sentence in a story about the organization.[10] Furious readers, fearing that

bombers might be tempted to blow up the building, called the paper irresponsible. They believed the potential for harm, including possible loss of lives, outweighed any news value in revealing the organization's address. The *Register*'s topic editor defended the lead because of SOS's penchant for secrecy: "The decision to use the address as the lead was done to quickly focus on what has become a center of controversy about this group—its secrecy." But the paper's ombudsman was not impressed. "Leading the story with the address while knowing the group wanted secrecy for safety reasons," he wrote, "was a sorry example of in-your-face, gotcha journalism, precisely the type that has pushed journalism to a low rung on the public opinion ladder."[11] Although there may have been no meeting of the minds between the *Register*'s editors and their disgruntled readers, the ombudsman served as a forum through which to clarify the competing values and to foster a rational deliberation of the ethical concerns.[12]

In another case, the *Times-Union* in Jacksonville, Florida, published a page one article containing racist remarks by Chief Circuit Judge John E. Santora, Jr. Many readers were outraged, not at the remarks but at what they considered to be the newspaper's ill-considered judgment in printing them. Most callers said the *Times-Union* should not have published what the judge called "offhand remarks," and some accused the paper of fanning the flames of racial intolerance. The paper responded that the judge was interviewed twice and knew that he was being taped when he made the intemperate comments.[13]

Although the newspaper did apparently gain some public acceptance of the notion that it had done its job, the coverage precipitated a healthy debate about journalistic values and the role of the media as community activist. For example, the paper's ombudsman, Mike Clark, criticized the *Times-Union* for not doing more to combat racial injustice in Jacksonville. "We had an obligation to show our involvement in the community, not just to report the news," he said. Clark believed that more space should have been devoted to solutions.[14] But John Seigenthaler, publisher emeritus of the Nashville *Tennessean,* in an interview for *Quill,* appeared to take issue with Clark when he said that exposing racism in the community is the duty of the paper—"I'm not sure you have to go beyond that."[15]

The Functions of the Media within the Ethical System

If a system of ethics provides moral cohesion for society's individual members and institutions, media practitioners are in particular need of one. Why? The mass media are among the most influential enterprises in a democratic society, standing at the crossroads between the citizens and their political, economic, and social institutions. In addition, they are instrumental in the transmission of cultural values. They set the agenda for which values are important and offer symbolic cues for standards of conduct, including ethical behavior. This process is conveyed through the three key functions that media practitioners play in American society: dissemination and interpretation of *information,* transmission of *persuasive* messages and production, and marketing of mass *entertainment.* Each of these functions brings with it an array of ethical expectations that are not necessarily the same. For example, should the standards for truth and accuracy be the same for advertising as for news? What values—entertainment or news—should govern the production of a docudrama? Under what conditions may public relations practitioners withhold information from the media and the public and still maintain their own credibility and the credibility of their clients or companies?

First, the media are the primary source of *information* in a democracy. Accurate and reliable information is the lifeblood of the democratic process. Perhaps the most obvious players in this information flow are journalists,

who gain access to the day's intelligence and attempt to provide accurate information for citizens to make informed and intelligent political decisions. But in a capitalistic society news media must also respect the demands of the marketplace, thereby satisfying the public's craving for the more sensational and tantalizing aspects of the human condition. This is exhibited in tabloid journalism's insatiable appetite for violent and sexually explicit content and its unremitting fascination with the private lives of social luminaries. The so-called mainstream media, however, are also the captive of marketplace forces and spend an increasing amount of time producing news content that has little to do with the democratic process.

Journalists are not the only media practitioners who perform the essential function of providing information in a capitalistic society. The economic messages of advertisers and the corporate image building of public relations practitioners also provide relevant and beneficial information to consumers and other constituencies. The role of economic information in a democratic society was captured in a Supreme Court opinion recognizing the constitutional status of advertising. Justice Blackmun wrote, "As to the particular consumer's interest in the free flow of commercial information, that interest may be as keen, if not keener by far, than his interest in the day's most urgent political debate."[16] He continued with his defense of advertising as a worthy contributor to the capitalistic system:

> Advertising, however tasteless and excessive it sometimes may seem, is nonetheless dissemination of information as to who is producing and selling what product, for what reason, and at what price. So long as we preserve a predominantly free enterprise economy, the allocation of our resources in large measure will be made through numerous private economic decisions. It is a matter of public interest that those decisions . . . be intelligent and well informed. To this end, the free flow of commercial information is indispensable.[17]

Regardless of the source of information, society has a right to expect a certain level of ethical behavior from its media institutions, and when this conduct is not forthcoming, a crisis of confidence occurs between these institutions and the public. At a minimum media audiences demand information unencumbered by deliberate falsehoods, regardless of whether the source is a journalist or an advertising agency. But beyond that threshold expectation, ethical practices can vary, depending on the media practitioner's role. We expect reporters, for example, to include all relevant facts in their stories, unless they have a compelling reason for omitting some salient piece of information. We also expect their accounts of newsworthy events to be balanced—that is, not to favor one set of values over another. But society does not expect advertisers, public relations practitioners, and entertainment producers and executives to approach their tasks with a commitment to symmetry. They are mass marketers of products, ideas, and images, and their clients and audiences are fully aware that communications from these sources are motivated as much by self-interest as the public interest.

The second major function of media practitioners is the transmission of *persuasive* communications. Actually, persuasion enjoys a noble legacy, tracing its lineage to the ancient Greeks. Like the use of rhetorical persuasion in ancient Greece, contemporary persuasion techniques are considered an art form, particularly when they are adroitly used to alter public perceptions, attitudes, and even buying habits. However, unlike our Greek forbears, today's practitioners often use more subtle and sometimes indiscernible techniques to manipulate audiences and public opinion. Perhaps the most visible examples are TV commercials, which often include visual cues that shrewdly and skillfully promote the values (some would say "superficial" values) of sex appeal, perpetual youth, and social conformity as essential to our psychological tranquility and self-esteem.

Editorials and news commentaries, advertising, and public relations are the most prevalent sources for such content, although entertainment fare sometimes wraps persuasive messages in a sugar-coated genre. American society has embraced both advertising and public relations as legitimate functions—after all, advertising is the economic mainstay of mass media in a capitalistic system—but they have increasingly become ethically controversial. Defenders of advertising and public relations derive their support from classical liberal marketplace theory that emphasizes the competition of competing voices and the supremacy of the autonomous and rational consumer. The most extreme form of this philosophy is "let the buyer beware," which in effect absolves purveyors of persuasive messages of any moral responsibility for the consequences of their actions. Critics respond that advertisers and public relations practitioners are the true potentates in the communications process and take advantage of the inability or unwillingness of passive consumers to identify and discriminate among this relentless barrage of manipulative communications.[18] Thus, the public must be represented and protected by outside agencies, ranging all the way from government agencies such as the Federal Trade Commission to various consumer watchdog groups. Because practitioners and their critics hold such dissimilar perspectives, ethical conflict is inevitable. In a free society a reconciliation of these positions is unlikely. Perhaps the most that can be expected is to establish minimum standards of acceptable behavior (for example, prohibitions against the intentional transmission of false or deceptive information) and to apportion moral responsibility among the various players in the chain of communication, from the disseminators of persuasive messages to the ultimate gatekeepers in the process, the recipients.

The third function of media practitioners—the production and dissemination of mass *entertainment*—poses an ethical challenge perhaps because there is little agreement on what its role in society should be. Unlike journalism, which is designed to scrutinize the political system and contribute to the democratic process, entertainment has no clear-cut rationale. Thus, the ethical question is whether the media have an obligation to elevate tastes and promote virtuous behavior or whether "giving the audience what it wants," even at the risk of reinforcing dysfunctional attitudes and behavior, is sufficient.

In a democracy media practitioners produce material that they believe meets a perceived need of the heterogeneous audience. And the finicky public expresses its approval or disapproval in the marketplace.[19] In a pluralistic society with a diversity of artistic tastes, only an incurable optimist would argue that economic concerns and commercial motives do not matter. After all, one advantage of the mass production of entertainment is that a wide variety of content can be made available at little cost, thus providing enjoyment for consumers of all socioeconomic classes. On the other hand, critics complain that the inevitable consequence of such mass production is an appeal to the lowest common denominator of artistic tastes. They argue that commercialism should not be the only driving force in the production of popular entertainment and information and that producers of such material have a responsibility to contribute to an enrichment of cultural values. Thus, underlying any attempts at reconciling these two notions are two questions that must be confronted: Must all material produced for a mass audience have at least some modicum of social worth? Is it possible—or even morally desirable—to devise strategies that will meet the demands of a mass audience without resorting exclusively to fare that does nothing more than trivialize the human condition and then provide an escape from it?

Media practitioners, regardless of their societal function, are influential in that they touch the lives of all of us. Audience members, particularly those who are young and impressionable,

often take their ethical cues from media personalities. Thus, they should serve as role models and should reinforce society's ethical expectations. When they fail in this responsibility, each ethical indiscretion further erodes society's confidence in the media.

REQUIREMENTS OF A SYSTEM OF ETHICS

If society's norms are to serve as moral guideposts, what criteria should be used in constructing a workable system of ethics? There may be some disagreement on this issue, but the following five criteria should form the foundation for any ethical system. These requirements pertain both to general societal principles and to codes of conduct reflecting the standards of professional organizations.[20]

Shared Values

An ethical system must be constructed, first and foremost, on shared values. Although individuals and groups within society may apply these standards differently to specific situations, they should at least agree on common ethical norms. For example, the fact that some members of society choose to lie under some circumstances does not diminish society's fundamental commitment to the value of truth. In other words, deviations from the norm may be excused for substantial reasons, but exceptions to the rule do not automatically alter its value.

This commitment to shared, or common, values is often reflected in the codification of those norms. The Ten Commandments, for example, are part of the code of moral conduct underlying the Judeo-Christian heritage. Many media institutions have codified their ethical principles, and such codes can at least provide the journalistic novice with some idea of the dividing line between acceptable and unacceptable behavior.

Wisdom

Ethical standards should be based on reason and experience. They should seek to strike a balance between the rights and interests of autonomous individuals and their obligations to society. In short, ethical norms should be reasonable. It would be unreasonable, for example, to expect reporters to remove themselves entirely from involvement in community affairs because of potential conflicts of interest. In fact, wisdom suggests that community involvement can enrich journalists' understanding of the stories they cover.

Wisdom also demands breathing room for advertisers who use "puffery" in their commercial messages, as long as the ads are not deceptive. Hyperbole is the handmaiden of salesmanship, and the marketplace suffers little from the introduction of exaggerated commercial claims of enhanced sex appeal and social acceptance. A code based on wisdom promotes ethical behavior while avoiding excessive and unreasonable moral propriety. Application of this criterion to a system of ethics results in flexibility, which shuns the extremes of an intransigent code at the one end and moral anarchy at the other. In journalism, for example, the proper balance is considered to be somewhere between the sensational and the bland.

Of course, wisdom based on experience suggests that the solutions derived from a moral code should be appropriate to the problem. Ethical quandaries sometimes call for drastic remedies. An affirmative action program, which in some cases might appear to be extreme, is sometimes justified to correct past discrimination. A university that suddenly discovers pervasive cheating on its campus might, in a moment of moral indignation, impose harsh new penalties for academic violations of the student code of conduct.

The idea of moderation could also be applied to the controversy surrounding the responsibility of the advertising industry for the harmful consequences of alcohol consumption. Some conservatives favor an outright ban on such ads, particularly on radio and TV. Libertarians counter that any legal product or service should be allowed to promote its wares in the mass media. A temperate position—that is, between the extremes of banning the ads and accepting the ads while apprising consumers of the dangers of alcohol abuse—is to require health warning disclaimers in all alcohol advertising.[21]

Justice

Justice has to do with people's relations with one another and is often important to the resolution of ethical disputes. Central to the idea of justice is the notion of fairness, in which all individuals are treated alike in terms of what they deserve. In other words, there should be *no double standards,* unless there are compelling and rational reasons for discrimination.

This principle has important implications for the media. Media practitioners may employ it to decide what guidelines should be applied to using deception, establishing and maintaining confidential relationships, and intruding on the privacy of others. For example, justice requires that journalists report the embarrassing behavior of others, both public and private figures, based on what they really deserve rather than for the purpose of titillating the morbid curiosity of the audience. Hollywood could also benefit from this idea of justice by using it to eliminate its dramatic renditions of racial and sexual stereotypes. And in all fairness, there has been substantial progress in this area.

Freedom

A system of ethics must be based on some freedom of choice. A society that does not allow such freedom is morally impoverished. Moral agents must have several alternatives available and must be able to exercise their powers of reason without coercion. In the biblical account, the first moral choice was made by Adam and

Eve when they ate the forbidden fruit and were expelled from paradise. Of course, most ethical judgments do not result in such dire consequences. But without freedom there can be no moral reasoning, because moral reasoning, as we will see in Chapter 3, involves choosing from among several alternatives and defending one's decision based on some rational principle. In short, freedom provides the opportunity to raise one's ethical awareness, a goal that any system of ethics should encourage.

Accountability

As autonomous individuals, we are all responsible for our moral deeds and misdeeds, and the legitimacy of any ethical system depends on its facility in holding its participants to some standard of accountability. Accountability may range all the way from informal sanctions, as when an offending moral agent is tried in the court of public opinion, to more formal punitive measures, such as disbarment proceedings against attorneys who violate their codes of ethics or reprimands or dismissals of reporters who violate their companies' policies. An ethics system that does not include accountability encourages freedom without responsibility and thus lacks the moral authority to encourage virtuous behavior.

THE SOCIAL COMPACT AND MORAL DUTIES

When individuals emerge from their primitive stages of moral development and enter society, they assume certain obligations. There is a cost, in other words, of membership in a civilized society that values moral virtue. The ethics system is not a smorgasbord from which one can pick and choose moral delicacies. Society imposes certain responsibilities on its constituents as a condition of membership. These responsibilities are known as *moral duties*. The idea of duty to others is important to moral reasoning

because it is a way of paying homage to the triumph of virtue over self-interests.

The Two Levels of Moral Duty

Although there are many kinds of moral duties, for the sake of simplicity they can be divided into two categories: *general* and *particularistic*. *General ethical obligations* are those that apply to all members of society. Some are primary (or fundamental) in that they take precedence over other principles and should be violated only when there is an overriding reason for doing so.[22] Prohibitions against stealing, cheating, lying, and breaking promises are examples of fundamental duties. Others bind all of us, even though they do not occupy such a prominent position on the hierarchy of values as our primary general obligations. These secondary obligations, such as prohibitions against gambling and trespassing, have a weaker claim to moral permanence than our fundamental duties and are more likely to be violated or perhaps subordinated to competing interests. Charity bingo games and legalized state lotteries are two classic examples.

Of course, philosophers disagree greatly over the extent of our general obligations. Some believe, for example, that we have a moral duty to assist others in distress, to be a Good Samaritan. Others continue to ask, "Am I my brother's keeper?," and question whether such good deeds are really a general moral obligation. However, one could probably get agreement among philosophers and nonphilosophers alike that two general obligations underlie all others: to treat others with the respect and moral dignity to which they are entitled and to avoid intentionally causing harm to others.[23] You will notice that the latter duty is based on *intentional* harm, not *foreseeable* harm. For example, reporters know that scandalous revelations will harm others, but their *intent* is not to harm but to inform the public about matters of public interest. Even if their revelations are unwarranted, few journalists would embark on a story with the underlying motive of causing personal injury.

Particularistic obligations are determined by membership within a specific group, profession, or occupation. Practicing Roman Catholics, for example, have a moral duty to refrain from using artificial birth control. Doctors have a duty to maintain a confidential relationship with their patients, and attorneys have a responsibility to mount a vigorous defense for their clients, even if they believe them to be guilty. These are moral obligations that do not bind the rest of us.

A duty is often imposed on media practitioners to avoid certain conflicts of interest because of their unusual role within society. The National Newspapers Publishers Association (NNPA), which represents some two hundred African American–owned newspapers with a readership of eleven million in the United States, apparently ignored this obligation in 1996 when several of its officers and members accepted an all-expense-paid tour of Nigeria at the invitation of that country's military dictatorship. The trip was underwritten by Nigeria's leadership as part of an aggressive media campaign to counter reports of political repression, human rights abuses, and the censorship of journalists. That campaign, according to an article in *The Nation* magazine, was furthered by a series of editorials in NNPA papers and by lucrative ads and advertorial inserts placed by lobbyists for Nigeria in those same papers.[24]

Particularistic obligations for media practitioners, like those in other professions, are sometimes based on the more general societal obligations. Journalism's commitment to truth and fairness is a case in point. But occasionally the general and particularistic obligations collide, causing heated debate about which should prevail. Nowhere is this more apparent than in the love-hate relationship that sometimes exists between journalists and law enforcement agencies, which frequently pits journalists' commitment to independence against the obligations

of citizenship that are incumbent upon the rest of us.

This appeared to be the case in January 2001 when a young reporter in Phoenix, Arizona, found himself at the center of an ethical firestorm. A weekly alternative paper, the *Phoenix New Times,* published his interview with a man who claimed to be one of the arsonists who had destroyed mansions under construction on the outskirts of Phoenix. The interviewee described how and why they targeted the luxury homes. The article prompted a heated debate on media responsibility, with some critics denouncing the paper for conducting the interview without first alerting police.[25] *New Times* editor Jeremy Voas replied that his reporter arranged to meet the arsonist "because he and his editors believed the guy might say something of value" and that the story "would provide a glimpse inside the arsonist's psyche." Voas even speculated that the article might assist authorities in apprehending those responsible for the fires.[26] Fred Brown, capital bureau chief and political editor for the *Denver Post,* acknowledged the conflicting loyalties within the local journalistic community: "[I]t would have been totally unacceptable for the reporter to agree to an interview and then tell the police about it so they could lay a trap. Some local journalists, though, felt that would have been a good idea to get this maniac put away. But they were wrong. Betraying a source might be the worst thing a journalist can do."[27]

Deciding among Moral Duties

The duties just explored orchestrate our relations with one another and with society. Our moral calculations affect other humans, regardless of whether we know these individuals or they are members of that amorphous mass known as the public. Thus, our ethical judgments must take into account all parties, including ourselves, to which we owe allegiance.

Ralph Potter, of the Harvard Divinity School, has referred to these duties as "loyalties" in constructing his own model for moral reasoning.[28] Lawyers, for example, have obligations to their clients, their professional colleagues, the judicial system, and society at large, as well as to their own sense of ethical conduct. Teachers have loyalties to students, parents, academic colleagues, school officials, and the community at large. Sometimes these loyalties conflict, increasing the tension in the moral reasoning process. Clifford Christians and his coauthors in *Media Ethics: Cases and Moral Reasoning* make this observation:

> Many times, in the consideration of ethics, direct conflicts arise between the rights of one person or group and those of others. Policies and actions inevitably must favor some to the exclusion of others. Often our most agonizing dilemmas revolve around our primary obligation to a person or social group. Or, we ask ourselves, is my first loyalty to my company or to a particular client?[29]

The moral agent's responsibility consists of giving each set of loyalties its share of attention before rendering an ethical determination. Thus, as media practitioners we must identify those parties that will be most affected by our actions, sometimes referred to as *stakeholders*. For the purposes of the cases in this book, six *stakeholders* to whom we are obligated must be examined:[30]

1. Individual conscience
2. Objects of moral judgment
3. Financial supporters
4. The institution
5. Professional colleagues
6. Society

First, we should follow the adage "Let your conscience be your guide." Our *conscience* often tells us, if we are willing to listen, the difference between right and wrong. In other words, we should feel personally comfortable with our decision or at least be able to defend it with some moral principle. Being able to look ourselves in the mirror without wincing from moral embarrassment is a sign of our virtue.

The *objects of moral judgment* are those individuals or groups most likely to be harmed or affected directly by our ethical decisions. For example, racial and ethnic minorities are the objects of moral judgment when films depicting them are based on stereotypes. Certain specialized audiences should also be taken into account, as when a sexually explicit program is aired during the time of the day when children are most likely to be watching or listening. A public official whose womanizing catches the fancy of the media would also be in harm's way, much to the delight of his political opponents. It may seem strange to suggest that a loyalty is owed to such unsavory topics of news coverage. But there is a duty to take into account the interests of others, even if we believe that the target of our action deserves punishment or public scorn.

Media practitioners also must be loyal to their *financial supporters,* who pay the bills and make it possible to compete in the marketplace. These include, among others, advertisers, clients, individual subscribers, and other benefactors. Of course, loyalty to financial supporters may clash with obligations to other interests. For example, in the news business there will always be tension between the lure of profits and the ethical mandate to operate in the public interest, but the industry must sometimes strive to find an accommodation between them. This is not to suggest, of course, that the media must compromise their contract with society to present objective news coverage because of objections and pressure from advertisers or stockholders. It is an article of faith in many news organizations that advertisers should exercise no influence over editorial or news content. Thus, these loyalties to financial supporters must be carefully weighed, and in some cases the moral duty to society must override other considerations.

Allegiance to one's own *institution* is a noble gesture under most circumstances, because company loyalty is usually valued in corporate circles. Reporters often take pride in the news organizations for which they work and are concerned as much about their institutions' credibility as about their own. However, blind loyalty can work to the detriment of the company. For example, a public relations executive who recommends to management that the company "stonewall" the press concerning the effects of an environmental disaster disserves the company as well as the public. It should be noted that loyalty to one's organization may also take into account the stockholders (if any), because they are interested in improving the financial well-being of the company as well as in protecting their investments. Of course, media executives tend to be more concerned about the duties owed to investors than those owed to lower-level employees.

A practitioner's allegiance to *professional colleagues* is often powerful and unfaltering. When rendering a moral judgment, two questions are relevant: How will my actions reflect on my professional peers? Are my actions in keeping with the expectations of my colleagues? Suppose that a television news producer decides to air graphic death scenes from a satanic ritual. Public protests would suggest that this ill-advised decision might reflect poorly on all broadcast journalists. On the other hand, reporters often look to the expectations and practices of their colleagues for moral support to legitimize their actions. Protection of news sources is a case in point, and some reporters have gone to jail rather than breach these confidential relationships and risk the ostracism of their peers.

For media practitioners, obligation or loyalty to *society* translates into a sense of social responsibility. It goes without saying that ethical decisions cannot be made without factoring the public interest into the equation. Because our own sense of moral propriety—that is, our conscience—is based on societal norms, our obligations to ourselves and society are often in concert. This is not always the case, however,

as when reporters publish the contents of a stolen classified government document revealing American duplicity in foreign relations. In this case their consciences might override the concern for social prohibitions against stealing. However, if their motivations for releasing this information are related to self-interest (personal recognition, increased ratings, and the like), they have acted unethically.

Considerations of societal duties are more complex than they appear. In the real world society is not some monolithic entity but consists of many different groups, among which choices sometimes have to be made: news sources, public figures, minorities, senior citizens, children, people with disabilities. It is the balancing of these interests that presents a real challenge to media practitioners in the rough-and-tumble world of a diverse civilization.

THE NEXUS OF LAW AND ETHICS

Attorneys and judges tell us that laws are the cornerstone of our democratic civilization. *They are wrong.* It is the *moral respect* for the law that provides the foundation for our culture. Motorists do not refuse to run a red light just because there does not happen to be an officer of the law close at hand. They do so out of respect for legal authority (or perhaps fear of detection and punishment) and deference to the notion that limitations on individual liberty are sometimes necessary to bring order out of chaos in a complex society. Thus, there is what we might call a nexus, or connection, between the fields of law and ethics. But what is the scope of this relationship, and why should a media practitioner be concerned about this distinction?

We can begin by stating the obvious: Not all moral issues can be, or should be, legally codified. The law permits many immoralities that transgress against friends and enemies alike, such as the breaking of promises, uttering of unkind words, and certain forms of deception. In the course of our lives we often offend the feelings of others, an act for which the law provides no restitution to the offended party. A high school student, for example, might break his date for the senior prom at the last minute, but the lady kept in waiting cannot resort to the courts for redress of her tearful ordeal. Even in a litigious society it would be undesirable to open the floodgates to such deep interference into individual relationships.

Nevertheless, legal obligations are based on moral ones. The criminal and civil statutes codify some of our most important moral obligations, for example, proscriptions against killing, stealing, raping, or maliciously defaming another's reputation. Most of these statutes involve punishing direct harm to others, but some laws are based on moral principles that are not concerned with the well-being of others. Laws regulating sexual behavior between consenting adults and prostitution fall into this category. The moral justification for such laws is not as widely shared within society, and thus compliance is less certain.[31] Nevertheless, a fundamental distinction between our legal code and moral obligations is that legal violations involve prescribed penalties and ethical indiscretions do not.

But if the laws themselves are based on moral respect, are there circumstances when we are warranted in breaking a law? Does our ethical system provide for such waivers of our moral obligations?

Civil disobedience, in which citizens intentionally ignore laws that they feel are unjust, has received some moral respectability in recent years, particularly since the nonviolent civil rights demonstrations led by the Reverend Dr. Martin Luther King, Jr., in the 1960s. Most ethicists agree, however, that the legitimacy of civil disobedience depends on (1) the moral agent's true belief that the law is unjust, (2) nonviolence, and (3) the willingness of the protesters to face the consequences of their actions.[32] In addition, some people justify civil disobedience only if the legal avenues of redress have been explored. For example, an environmental group, having exhausted all legal avenues

to prevent the disposal of nuclear wastes at a site within their community, might resort to acts of civil disobedience to bring its concerns to the public's attention. In such cases, even when the legal questions have been settled, the moral issues persist.

What if the legal remedies have not been exhausted? Are moral agents then justified in violating the law? Perhaps, but it would appear that their actions are on shakier ground. A just law might be violated in emergency situations or when a higher moral principle is involved. For example, we would not think a husband immoral for running red lights to get his pregnant wife to the hospital in time for the delivery of their baby. On a more serious level, media practitioners may occasionally feel obligated to violate a just law if they believe that they must do so because of a more significant moral obligation. Journalists, for example, might be justified in ignoring a State Department ban on travel to a particular country if they felt compelled to document human rights abuses. Of course, the reporters would have to face the legal consequences of their transgressions, but their actions would still have some moral force behind them.

The point is this: Journalists serve a unique function as representatives of the public and may feel that their obligations to the audience outweigh their legal duties. And there is some merit to this argument. However, if a law has any moral force behind it—if it is a "just" law—it can be overridden only by a more compelling moral obligation.

This dilemma is exemplified by a case involving the Cable News Network (CNN) and the prosecution of former Panamanian dictator Manuel Noriega. General Noriega, of course, had been taken into custody after a massive deployment of U.S. troops in Panama and was awaiting trial in Miami. During his incarceration someone obtained tape recordings of jail cell conversations between Noriega and his attorney and provided them to CNN. After CNN announced that it had the tapes, U.S. District Judge William Hoeveler granted the defense's request for an injunction against the broadcast of the tapes,[33] an order upheld by the Eleventh Circuit Court of Appeals.[34] Although CNN did not broadcast conversations between Noriega and his attorney, they did use excerpts of calls to others. Judge Hoeveler, believing that the broadcast of the tapes was a violation of the attorney-client privilege and might be detrimental to Noriega's defense, eventually held CNN in contempt. In his opinion, which contained an exhaustive analysis of the competing claims of a free press and the general duty to respect judicial decrees, Judge Hoeveler appeared to be invoking the necessity for moral respect for the law when he observed: "The thin but bright line between anarchy and order . . . is the respect which litigants and the public have for the law and the orders issued by the courts. Defiance of court orders and, even more so, public display of such defiance cannot be justified or permitted."[35]

Journalists who complain bitterly that they have the right to ignore laws and court orders they believe to be unconstitutional miss the point. Statutes and court orders are legal until overturned by a higher authority. And in the CNN case, even the appellate court upheld the order because of the violation of a confidential relationship recognized by law and the possible threat to Noriega's right to a fair trial as a result of the broadcast of the jailhouse conversations. Thus, most legal issues confronting reporters also have an ethical dimension, a fact that is sometimes overlooked by media practitioners.

This inescapable alliance between law and ethics is often manifest when journalists view legal restraints, such as trespass laws, as impediments to their ethical mandate to serve the public interest. This notion is typified by a case that arose out of a protest in 2000 at Camp Garcia, Puerto Rico, against U.S. Navy training and bombing exercises conducted at the camp. Ten reporters covering the protest were arrested for criminal trespass. In a federal district hearing the journalists argued that the arrests violated their constitutional rights because they had entered the restricted area to cover the protest. However, the court rejected this argument on the grounds that journalists had no special right of access to the facility not available to the general public and that the First Amendment does not sanction the violation of law.

Thus, it is clear that most legal issues have moral dimensions as well, and we cannot necessarily settle ethical questions merely by resolving the legal ones. For example, the Supreme Court has held that journalists may report the names of rape victims obtained from public records or that were released through other governmental venues.[36] But these cases have not settled the ethical question of whether the names of rape victims *should* be published, even if they are a matter of public record. There are those who feel that the harm to the victims far outweighs the limited public good derived from release of this kind of information.

With some unusual exceptions, there is little that cannot be published under the First Amendment. However, the First Amendment says nothing about media responsibility. It is left to the consciences of practicing journalists to decide what is newsworthy. But constitutional freedoms are not just the point of departure for making ethical judgments. If irresponsible media come to be regarded as social parasites, these legal rights could be slowly eroded.

I conclude this section on the relationship between law and ethics as I began it, with the idea that it is the moral force of the law that provides the legitimacy for our legal codes. All parties have the same moral obligations to comply with the law. Thus, media practitioners are warranted in violating the law only if they can stand on some more important moral principle and are willing to endure the consequences of their disobedience.

INSTITUTIONAL AUTONOMY AND SOCIAL RESPONSIBILITY

"Institutions don't behave unethically; people do."[37] This statement from Chapter 1 would seem to suggest that any discussion of corporate morality is out of place here. However, despite the fact that ethical judgments are rendered by individuals within the corporate hierarchy, the public often associates images of moral or immoral conduct with the institutions themselves. Some media celebrities attract attention because of their conduct, but the institutional decision makers (the moral agents) are usually invisible to society. Nevertheless, the public has come to expect corporate sensitivity to their moral obligations, that is, a corporate culture built upon social responsibility—a commitment to the public welfare that outweighs short-term self-interests.[38]

In a case that still resonates within the industry as an example of social responsibility, Johnson & Johnson, a manufacturer of over-the-counter medications, confronted a public relations challenge when several people died from taking cyanide-laced Tylenol. The company took quick and decisive action by recalling and later repackaging the product.[39] Compare that with Exxon's public relations debacle when the company was accused of reacting too slowly to an environmental crisis precipitated by a massive oil spill from an Exxon oil tanker off the coast of Alaska. Despite Exxon's offer to pay for the cost of the cleanup, the company's image suffered.

The Libertarian View

The notion of corporate social responsibility is not without its controversial aspects. Although the "Let the buyer beware" philosophy that dominated until the early part of the twentieth century has been diminished by the efforts of consumer activists such as Ralph Nader, some still hold the libertarian view that "business is the business of business."[40] According to this view, a company is socially responsible if it provides employment and a stable financial base for the community. Within the libertarian framework, both individuals and corporations pursuing their own self-interests in a competitive marketplace will, in fact, contribute to the public welfare.[41] The only moral relationship is between management and stockholders; society should interfere in this arrangement only to prevent deception or fraud. In other words, the concept of the public interest is merely a by-product of corporate autonomy.

This libertarian philosophy is based on the notion of self-reliance and individual autonomy, free from governmental or societal restraints. Libertarianism is characterized by the notion of freedom without enforced responsibility, and it was within this kind of environment that the American press matured in the nineteenth century. Thus, the system nurtured a press that was free but that also resisted the development of strong ethical codes. This attitude is reflected in a comment years ago attributed to William Peter Hamilton of the *Wall Street Journal:* "A newspaper is a private enterprise owing nothing whatever to the public, which grants it no franchise. It is therefore affected with no public interest. It is emphatically the property of the owner, who is selling a manufactured product at his own risk. . . ."[42] Libertarians have also resisted government regulation of advertising, believing that in a free market economy autonomous consumers should cultivate their own sense of wariness and skepticism concerning commercial appeals.

Nevertheless, the libertarian press did subscribe to some fundamental values, many of which are still featured prominently in contemporary industry codes. As newspapers slowly acquired a reverence for facts and a preference for "hard news" over opinion, such notions as objectivity, fairness, and balance became a part of the journalist's ethical lexicon. Perhaps of primary importance was *objectivity,* a term that journalists began using in the twentieth century to "express their commitment not only to impartiality but to reflecting the world as it is, without bias or distortion of any sort."[43]

For most journalists objectivity is an article of faith, but there is also a recognition that absolute objectivity is an illusion. Thus, they have settled for a philosophically less demanding definition that allows them to practice their profession without feeling as though they have sinned. According to this more realistic view of objectivity, reporters strive to keep their personal preferences and opinions out of news stories, to achieve balance in coverage, and to rely on credible and responsible news sources. According to this traditional view, the ethics of newswriting is concerned with facts and impartiality in the presentation of those facts.[44]

Nevertheless, libertarians are opposed to enforced responsibility, even when there is a danger that some unscrupulous media executives might infect the public arena with falsehoods and half-truths. According to the libertarian view, it is better to leave the remedy for such moral indiscretions to the marketplace and the consciences of individual media practitioners.

Social Responsibility

The idea of social responsibility has developed as a counterpoint to libertarianism. Although this theory continues to emphasize freedom, it holds that responsibility is necessarily a partner to freedom in institutional behavior. Codes of ethics are encouraged as a self-regulatory device to promote social responsibility. Some have taken issue with Friedman's traditional views and believe that conducting business is not a right but a privilege granted by society.[45] Because the pursuit of profits has not automatically contributed to the public good, society has placed increasing demands on corporations to contribute to the correction of social ills. Affirmative action programs and increased availability of affordable legal services for the poor are two examples.

There is little doubt that corporate responsibility in contemporary society includes emphasizing ethical behavior for both management and employees. Some companies have instituted ethics programs, both for legal and public relations reasons. Some have even devised codes of ethics for their personnel. But the formality of written codes and policies does not ensure ethical conduct, as evidenced by the avalanche of scandals that has plagued corporate America at the dawn of the twenty-first century.

Social Responsibility in the Media. It is unclear when the notion of social responsibility first entered the consciousness of media practitioners, but five historical trends contributed to its emergence. First, the Industrial Revolution forever altered the American social landscape, fostering concentrations of capital and business ownership in fewer hands. Newspapers did not escape this reorganization of the free enterprise system, a trend that continues unabated.[46] Thus, with media control in fewer hands, some critics have questioned whether the libertarian intellectual ideal of a true competition of ideas continues to be a realistic expectation.

Second, despite this trend toward newspaper monopolies, an increasing number of media alternatives began to flood the marketplace in the form of magazines and radio. They placed pressure on newspapers to broaden their audience appeal. Thus, an economic imperative began to coexist with the media's journalistic mandate, and the idea of social responsibility became intertwined with commercial success.

Third, by the middle of the nineteenth century journalism had begun to attract people with strong educational backgrounds who established ethical standards for their industry and tried to live up to them.[47] In addition, a few publishers began to recognize that the freedom to publish carried with it a corresponding responsibility. Some, such as the legendary Joseph Pulitzer, even viewed a sense of social responsibility as the salvation of their profession from the ravages of the economic marketplace: "Nothing less than the highest ideals, the most scrupulous anxiety to do right, the most accurate knowledge of the problems it has to meet, and a sincere sense of moral responsibility will save journalism from a subservience to business interests, seeking selfish ends, antagonistic to public welfare."[48]

This early recognition of media responsibility has been manifested in more recent years in the establishment of various institutes, sometimes funded by the media themselves, committed to enhancing the professionalism of practitioners. The Poynter Institute in St. Petersburg, Florida, which sponsors workshops on topics ranging from newswriting to ethics, is a prime example of this kind of continuing education for journalists and journalism educators.

Fourth, schools of journalism began to appear in the early part of the twentieth century, an idea also supported by Pulitzer, and they contributed to the sense of professionalism within the industry. The teaching of practical skills was supplemented with instruction in social responsibility, and a cadre of practitioners educated specifically in the discipline of journalism entered the marketplace. This rising sense of professionalism led to the development of a social conscience among media practitioners, a belief that responsibility should be a welcome companion to press freedom. This belief was formalized in 1923, when the American Society of Newspaper Editors (ASNE) at its first meeting adopted the "Canons of Journalism" as its journalistic standards. Although some state press associations had already adopted codes, this was the first national code of ethics advanced by any organization of journalists.[49] It also flunked its first test as an enforceable code.

One year after the formation of the ASNE code, F. G. Bonfils, publisher of the *Denver Post,* was accused of having accepted $1 million in bribes for suppressing information from his reporters about wrongdoing in the Teapot Dome scandal. This scandal involved allegations that government oil reserves in the Teapot Dome field in Wyoming were being sold to private oil companies. Several members of the ASNE accused Bonfils of having violated the codified principles of the organization, including truthfulness, fair play, accuracy, and impartiality, and demanded that he be punished for these violations. The debate over code enforcement lasted for five years, but in 1929, under the threat of a

lawsuit from Bonfils, the newspaper editors voted for voluntary obedience rather than disciplinary action.[50]

The ASNE code was soon followed in 1928 by the first written principles for the electronic media, when the fledgling National Association of Broadcasters (NAB) adopted the industry's first radio code dealing with programming, advertising, and news. Since these early efforts at codification of professional ideas, such diverse groups as the Radio-Television News Directors Association, the American Advertising Association, the Public Relations Society of America, and the Society of Professional Journalists have adopted similar statements of ethical standards.

Social responsibility was also an outgrowth of the laissez-faire attitude of government, according to which the excesses of big business were allowed to run rampant. After the turn of the twentieth century, however, and particularly during the 1930s, wide government intervention in the marketplace brought applause from a public weary of economic and social turmoil and a business environment hostile to the interests of consumers. Advertising, the primary financial support for the media, was brought under governmental scrutiny in 1938 when Congress provided the Federal Trade Commission with new powers to oversee deceptive and unfair advertising practices. There was a fear by some that the government might next turn its regulatory arsenal on the media themselves and force social accountability on institutions that were perceived as having abused their constitutionally granted freedom under the First Amendment. The fact that the newly emerging radio medium had been brought under government regulation in 1927 did little to dispel this fear.

Finally, the idea of media social responsibility was given credence after World War II through the work of the so-called Hutchins Commission on Freedom of the Press. In 1942 Robert W. Hutchins, chancellor of the University of Chicago, was commissioned to study the future prospects of press freedom. Funding was initially provided by Henry R. Luce, of Time, Inc., and later by the Encyclopaedia Britannica. Hutchins appointed a panel of thirteen, including several distinguished educators, to carry out this ambitious assignment, and in 1947 the panel issued a report, "A Free and Responsible Press," which contained a well-reasoned and comprehensive analysis of the need for a socially responsible press.

Although the expression "social responsibility" was never mentioned in its report, the commission identified five obligations of the media in contemporary society.[51] Some of them are applicable primarily to journalism, but others are just as relevant to advertising and entertainment.

The first requirement, according to the commission, is to provide a "truthful, comprehensive, and intelligent account of the day's events in a context that gives them meaning." The press must not only be accurate; it must also clearly distinguish between fact and opinion. But facts by themselves are insufficient. The news media must also report the "truth about the facts" by putting stories into perspective and evaluating for the reader the credibility of conflicting sources. Interpretative reporting must extend beyond the pure facts and provide the relevant background surrounding the facts.

This was the issue when a reporter for a local newspaper covered a press conference in which the mayor accused a city councilman of distorting facts about the effects of certain pesticides on birds indigenous to the area and of being on the payroll of a local pesticide manufacturer. When contacted about the accusations, the councilman refused to comment except to say the mayor's accusations were "utter nonsense" and "politically motivated." The reporter's story included both the charges and the councilman's denial.[52] The paper's editor thought the story was fair and balanced, but the councilman was outraged. In a letter to the editor he denied lying about the effects of pesticides or being on the payroll of any pesticide company. "The story may have been fair,

balanced, and accurate," he wrote, "but it was not truthful."[53] The reporter should have held the story, in the councilman's view, until she had independently investigated the charges.

The commission's second recommendation is that the press serve as "a forum for the exchange of comment and criticism." This is an essential function in a system increasingly dominated by media giants. The press is urged to provide a platform for views that are contrary to its own while not abdicating its traditional right of advocacy.

A third requirement is that the press project "a representative picture of the constituent groups in society." In other words, racial, social, and cultural groups should be depicted accurately, without resorting to stereotypes. Social responsibility demands an affirmative role for the media in building positive images, both in their informational and entertainment content. Although some progress has been made in this area, stereotyping is still a common charge against the media.

The media should also, according to the commission, be responsible for "the presentation and clarification of the goals and values of society." They should transmit the cultural heritage, thereby reinforcing traditional values and virtues.

Journalism professor Ted Smith has rendered a strong indictment accusing the press of failing to live up to this obligation. Smith begins his critique by observing that the media, having ravaged most of the nation's established institutions, began a period of self-examination in the early 1980s. Several news organizations, he recalls, produced stories acknowledging the public's lack of confidence in the media. But after an initial flurry of stories on the subject of media credibility and ethics, he laments, the sense of urgency passed, and the self-scrutiny appeared to have no discernible impact on reporting practices. Although he attributes this renewal of self-assurance by the media to their perceptions that there is no "real crisis of credibility," he challenges this assertion and attempts to document the steady erosion of media believability since the early 1970s. This development represents a popular reaction against the mass media, which have come to view all traditional cultural values with some skepticism and have presented the public with a constant barrage of negative news coverage.

In comparing the media's skepticism with the critical dialogues of Socrates, Smith issues the following warning:

> Some journalists may be flattered by the thought that they are perpetuating the illustrious tradition of Socrates. They would do better to remember his fate: He was tried, convicted and executed for subverting religion and for corrupting the youth of his city.[54]

He accuses elite journalists of orchestrating "a relentless critique of all cultural affirmations as embodied in American policies, leaders and institutions."[55] Like Socrates, journalists have often reported from a vantage point outside the culture, rather than as a part of it. This stance has led, he says, to a collapse of confidence in the media by the society of which they are supposedly a part. Although we must await historical confirmation of Smith's dire prediction that the press may suffer the same fate as Socrates, recent polls showing a continuing decline of media credibility suggest that there may be a cause for concern.

The final requirement of the Hutchins Commission is that the press should provide "full access to the day's intelligence." This notion is reflected in the media's championing of the public's right to know, although this so-called right has yet to find expression in the Supreme Court's interpretation of the Constitution. From a philosophical standpoint the right to know is predicated on the notion that the media are the representatives of the public, a fourth branch of government (along with the executive, legislative, and judicial) with responsibility for informing the citizenry about governmental activities. The increase in the number and scope of laws regarding public

records and open meetings, at both the state and federal levels, is the manifestation of this right of access to government information. In recent years, however, the media have used the right to know to justify journalistic forays that extend beyond governmental activities into the private lives of individuals. This intrusion is sometimes viewed by an already skeptical public as social responsibility run amok, a sacrifice of personal autonomy for the sake of public curiosity.

Political Pressure and Social Responsibility. Politicians are often accused of being captives of special interests, but media enterprises are similarly vulnerable to pressures exerted by media watchdog groups or other citizen organizations. Some groups castigate the media for their crass commercialism and intellectual impoverishment of the nation's culture. Others accuse the media of moral insensitivity because of their preoccupation with sex and violence. Still others have a more overt political agenda, attempting to coerce the media through public pressure or even government regulation to conform to a more conservative or political agenda, depending upon the particular orientation of the pressure group. Is a decision to alter or even abandon objectionable content in response to such pressure merely a business decision or are there also ethical dimensions to such conduct?

This was the question provoked by the CBS network's controversial decision in the fall of 2003 to cancel the miniseries *The Reagans,* which had been scheduled to air during ratings sweeps. Based upon some leaked fragments of the script in advance of the planned broadcast, conservatives, including the former president's son, accused the network of distorting the legacy of Ronald Reagan. Brent Bozell, founder of the conservative Media Research Center, described the film as "a left-wing smear of one of the nation's most beloved presidents." CBS executives themselves expressed misgivings about the accuracy of some of the character portrayals.

Author Neal Gabler, in considering the broader implications of the brouhaha, denounced CBS's decision as unhealthy for democracy. "CBS, in pulling this film, did incredible harm, much more harm than they could ever have done in making the film," Grabler lamented. "What they've told us now is that a very small group of people have censorship power over the broadcast networks." For its part, the network denied bowing to political pressure, noting that its decision to cancel the movie was "based solely on our reaction to seeing the final film, not the controversy that erupted around a draft of the script."[56] CBS subsequently sold the program to the cable network Showtime, where the audiences are smaller and advertiser support less critical.

Media practitioners, of course, serve a broad spectrum of societal interests and cannot be impervious to their concerns and criticisms. They are particularly susceptible when the threats assume economic dimensions, as in the case of advertiser boycotts. But this raises a troubling question: Why should we be concerned with government censorship if private interests can exercise such formidable veto power over media content? In a democratic, market-driven society citizen organizations and more narrowly focused pressure groups certainly have a right to register their objections to or approval of media fare. But to the extent that these activities seriously diminish the diversity of content and compromise the independence of media enterprises, ethical concerns are implicated. While media practitioners cannot or should not ignore these critics, they must ultimately ask themselves to what extent their responsibility to society at large transcends the interests of individual groups, who may not represent a significant cross section of their constituents.

Promoting Social Responsibility from Within. In addition to organized efforts by public interest groups to promote their own views of social responsibility, there are also individual voices within the media that serve as society's "in-house" critics. For example, PBS film critic Michael Medved, Howard Kurtz, the respected media reporter for the *Washington Post*,[57] and the *Chicago Tribune*'s Larry Wolters are among the most visible and perhaps influential media reviewers. As Professor Peter Orlik has noted, in commenting on the role of electronic media critics, such authorities

> usually are in a much better position to propose change than are members of the public. That is because consumers seldom have the contacts and never have the time to acquire in-depth comprehension of radio/television workings for themselves. Consequently, it is the critic who must provide this knowledge for listeners and viewers.[58]

Although the real impact of critics, both individuals and public interest groups, is sometimes difficult to assess, they do serve as one more pressure point to remind media managers of their moral responsibility to the society that has given them sustenance. In addition, various segments of the public, which may be individually impotent in influencing media decision makers and gatekeepers, can at least feel they have an advocate in the information and entertainment marketplace. And although readers and viewers may not always agree with the critics, they at least share a mutual interest in not allowing the performance of media institutions to go unchallenged.

A Threat and an Obligation.   It is clear, from the preceding discussion, that the idea of social responsibility has become a part of the U.S. corporate landscape. But can media institutions maintain their autonomous status, which is essential in a democratic society, while at the same time fulfilling their mandate of social responsibility? Some traditionalists argue that such concepts as *duty, accountability,* and *obligation* are incompatible with the independence and freedom necessary for dynamic and vibrant media institutions. They believe that social responsibility is a euphemism for "lowest common denominator," which will result in bland, noncontroversial content. According to this view, the media are captives of public opinion and have thus abdicated their role as social and political gadflies.

This argument is rather dubious. As noted earlier in this section, the media have been criticized precisely because they are such gadflies, constantly casting aspersions on society's cultural values. They have continued to function as autonomous institutions, despite some loss of public confidence. Nevertheless, fundamental changes within the American economic system have forced consideration of a more expansive vision of social responsibility for all institutions to the top of the public's agenda. As corporations grow larger, more visible, and more powerful, consumers are increasingly aware of these companies' impact on their daily lives. Society is interested as much in whether General Motors makes safe and fuel-efficient automobiles as in the financial contributions it makes to the economic system.

As we inaugurate the twenty-first century, moreover, the media have witnessed some profound changes in their economic structures. The bottom line has become the ultimate barometer of success, and such terms as *merger, acquisition,* and *leveraged buyout* have become a part of the corporate lexicon. As *Newsweek* observed several years ago: "For the American news media, accustomed to thinking of themselves as a Fourth Estate, it has been something of a shock to be treated as Wall Street darlings instead."[59]

The media are among our most visible institutions, entering daily into the homes of millions of people. And because the bigness virus has also infected the media, it is only natural that consumers place increasing demands on an institution that plays such a pivotal role in the formation of public opinion. In other words, there is an expectation—a moral obligation, if you will—that the media will operate in the public interest. Thus, the concept of social responsibility has ethical implications when viewed in terms of moral duty.

THE CHALLENGES OF THE INFORMATION AGE

Convergence: New Media and Old Media

Although a thorough discussion of new technology and the information superhighway is beyond the scope of this text, a consideration of some of the ethical issues surrounding the application of this technology will be included in subsequent chapters. At this point suffice it to say that the convergence of communications media and sophisticated technology has revolutionized the world in which we live. Society's lexicon is now fraught with such fashionable terms as *Internet, cyberspace, digitalization, e-mail,* and *information superhighway.* The implications of this astonishing cultural reformation are both magnificent and terrifying, posing challenges to policy makers, sociologists, and philosophers alike.

Convergence is the latest conversation piece in the lexicon of techno-speak. Its meaning is multifaceted but needless to say it is revolutionizing the way we communicate. For example, cell phones can now double as Internet terminals, your computer can become your TV, wireless technology will soon become the delivery system of choice for your phone service, and Internet access is now available through your local cable company. And the list goes on.

The high-tech revolution is proceeding at incredible speed, but we should not approach this technological reformation with a sense of panic, fearful that the unregulated domain of the World Wide Web will stimulate cultural chaos or completely reconfigure the media industries. The cyberspace phenomenon is at once futuristic and tradition-bound. For example, online journalism is different from the coverage provided in conventional media and yet embraces them all:

It offers the depth of a newspaper (or, with hypertext links and electronic archives, even more depth). It offers the attitude and focus of a smart-mouthed magazine. It offers the immediacy and interaction of talk radio (with the added interaction of chat rooms, forums, and e-mail). It offers the visual impact of television. This seemingly chaotic medium is exploding with messages.[60]

The transition from traditional modes of communication, such as print and broadcast, to machine-to-machine distribution of information has spawned a growth industry in gathering and disseminating information. This has precipitated an explosion in the number of information consumers, as evidenced in the proliferation of online services, some of which are supplied by the news media themselves, in which consumers can select useful information from an endless array of menus and data banks. This in turn has increased the number of links (that is, potential moral agents) in the communication chain of data creation and distribution.

The Ethics of Cyberspace: Old Wine in New Bottles

At the outset, we should tone down the rhetoric emanating from some ethicists and futurists concerning the ethical challenges of cyberspace and other new media. There is no doubt that the new technologies will introduce novel approaches to unethical behavior, but the issues themselves are of ancient vintage. One of the most glaring concerns, of course, is the ease with which private information can be collected and shared via the Internet. But the underlying "value" here is still privacy. The use of the Web to pirate copyrighted music or movies, instead of using traditional dubbing techniques, does not alter the fact that the unethical conduct involves theft of intellectual property. And the use of digital technology to alter a news photo still involves questions of honesty and truth. An apt metaphor for this reality is "old wine in new bottles," although the unregulated venue of cyberspace does in fact make it more difficult to combat moral corruption.

Thus, the ethical concerns evolving out of this technological revolution confronting media practitioners of the twenty-first century are significant, and some of these are explored in subsequent chapters. In fact, we are already witnessing the tip of the iceberg, as media professionals and data collectors and distributors confront the moral intricacies of the information age. For example, as just noted, privacy has always raised troublesome ethical issues for media practitioners, but privacy assumes a renewed sense of urgency in the age of interactive media. Two-way media, e-mail, computer database access, and home shopping networks are all mechanisms that facilitate the information-gathering process about individuals. Because information is considered an asset with economic value, it is often processed and sold to mass marketers. In addition, computer-generated information might provide valuable information or tips for news stories, particularly as they relate to public figures or other high-profile newsworthy persons. For example, during the 1993 winter Olympics, several reporters were accused of unethical conduct for reading American figure skater Tonya Harding's e-mail. Harding attracted intense media scrutiny while she was under investigation for allegedly participating in a plot to disable her U.S. rival, Nancy Kerrigan. Reporters obtained her e-mail password using a camera and then gained access to her electronic communications. The journalists claimed they didn't read her messages; they just wanted to see whether it was possible to get into her e-mail.[61] If that's true, then one wonders what public interest was served by this unwelcome intrusion into Harding's private messages.

Individual access to computer bulletin boards and the Internet has also created a concern, both legally and ethically, about the use of cyberspace for the unregulated spread of pornography, electronic shouting matches (known as "flaming"), and the uncontrollable theft of intellectual property. Unlike traditional modes of communication, the global Internet is a loosely organized information system (or "web") of thousands of voluntarily interconnected computer networks, reaching more than 100 countries and serving over 25 million individual users. Cyberspace differs from conventional media distribution systems in that there is no central control or "ownership." Consumers now have access directly to the channels of distribution and thus have become major players in not only the mass consumption of information but also the creation and distribution of information.

However, this could be a mixed blessing. On the one hand, the communication system is now one of pure democracy. We can all become direct participants in the energizing force for the democratic process—the cultivation and dissemination of knowledge. On the other hand, ethicists must now ponder whether such an "infomocracy" is antithetical to the creation of a virtuous society. For example, news organizations have traditionally been the primary gatekeepers in the information flow process in our democracy. Under such a system, the public can usually be confident of a fairly high level of reliability and "quality" of information because of the elaborate system of rigorous scrutiny by professional journalists and editors. But with unrestricted access to the Internet and other computer-generated data sources, both for individual communicators and recipients, there is a danger that the overall quality of the information generated will diminish and along with it the quality of democratic discourse. The concerns range from just inaccurate information to the use of the Internet by extremist groups, such as terrorists, for propaganda purposes and to mobilize public opinion. One commentator, writing in the *American Journalism Review*, has posed this troublesome question: "Now that we can be our own editors and choose to read only the issues that engage us, who will participate in public debate?"[62]

Some of the most troublesome ethical dilemmas have resulted from the integration of computers and digital technology. *Digitalization* is a process by which pictures, sound, and text are converted electronically and stored as digits, which can later be decoded and reconstructed as the original product or an altered form of the original product. And because a "reconstructed" production is a perfect copy of the original, any transformation of the original content is impossible to detect. Simple alterations, such as the *St. Louis Post-Dispatch*'s decision several years ago to remove a Diet Coke can from a Pulitzer Prize winner, can be accomplished with only a few keystrokes using technology widely available in today's newsrooms. A new technology called "subtraction," for example, can be used to alter photos seamlessly. The cliché, "the camera never lies," has always been somewhat of a fallacy, but digital technology can be a seductive device in the hands of either overzealous or unethical media practitioners. One should not underestimate the potential for ethical mischief that the computer revolution has made possible. Consider this scenario described in a recent issue of *American Journalism Review:* A foreign power with which the United States is engaged militarily creates totally phony footage of American soldiers being tortured or shot in order to undermine the nation's will to fight.[63] An extreme example, perhaps, but one that should not be casually dismissed. Some of the ethical dimensions of digitalization and content alteration will be explored in Chapter 4.

The democratizing effect of cyberspace has piqued the interest of all Internet surfers in the ethical concerns of going online. The subject of "media ethics" is no longer the exclusive preserve of those who make their living collecting, editing, and distributing information to a mass audience. As Tim Atseff, chair of the Ethics Committee of the Associated Press Managing Editors, has noted: "What used to be discussed in newsrooms and at annual meetings is now daily discourse on the Internet and related discussion groups and forums. Something happens and instantaneously someone, for better or for worse, has an opinion about its ethical application."[64]

Ethicists are only now beginning to examine, in a systematic way, the ethical dimensions of our newly created technological universe. The danger is that the technology itself will become the scapegoat for an increase in unsavory behavior of both media practitioners and others in the communications chain, when in fact it can only facilitate unethical conduct or perhaps offer a tempting excuse for such deportment. We might be impressed by the potential of the new media but should not be awed by their technological charisma. Such blind loyalty could lead to technological slavery. If indeed the "high-tech" revolution does lead to an increase in moral mayhem, it will be the result of unvirtuous moral agents and not the ethically passive tools of their trade. Thus, it is important to remember that traditional ethical values and principles (for example, respect for persons, fairness, justice, honesty, and so forth) transcend the innovations of the information age and any strategies to harness the new technologies from an ethical perspective must place the individual at the center of the moral universe.

Unfortunately, with the accelerating tempo of technology and information transfer, quiet reflection is a luxury we cannot afford. Under such pressures it may be tempting to abdicate all responsibility to lawyers and policy makers. Of course, some legal regulation is inevitable and undoubtedly necessary. But a free and democratic society functions best when it leaves the resolution of its ethical quandaries to the reasoned judgment of its citizens rather than the regulatory authority of the government.

THE MEDIA AS SOCIALLY RESPONSIBLE INSTITUTIONS

Institutions, like individuals, must learn to be socially responsible. But there is no reason to believe that, in so doing, they must sacrifice their corporate autonomy. Institutional autonomy, like individual autonomy, consists of freedom of choice, but there is a price to be paid for making decisions that do not at least take into account the interests of others. Of course, this realization sometimes necessitates changing corporate attitudes.

For the media, attitudes of social responsibility can be acquired through a two-step process. The first step is to promote a positive corporate image and to improve the chances of gaining public respect. This can be done through an aggressive campaign of external communications and consideration of the impact on society of any ethical decisions made by media managers and employees. Although this step is based in part on self-interest—the idea that social responsibility is good for business—it creates a set of corporate values on which a more altruistic notion of responsibility can be built.

The second step is community involvement. This is accomplished by encouraging employees to participate in civic affairs and providing corporate financial support for community projects. It can also involve a high-level commitment to the resolution of social problems, even though it may not be economically advantageous to do so. Major newspapers, for example, might consider greater coverage of low-income and minority neighborhoods. Cable systems might increase their penetration in poor neighborhoods, thus enriching the program diversity for the lower rungs of society. Corporations (or their foundations) might endow libraries in the inner city to provide Internet access to those who are currently disenfranchised from the information society. Of course, these actions would necessitate restructuring the management philosophy of the communications industry. They are egalitarian ideas that may be hard for some corporate executives to swallow, especially when they have to confront the critical inquiries of stockholders, advertisers, or clients.

In addition to the involvement of some institutions in the communities of which they are a part, there are other visible signs that the media have at least recognized that freedom and responsibility can easily coexist on the same moral ground. The media have acknowledged that some self-regulation is essential because failure to regulate will result in further erosion of confidence and perhaps even public demands for governmental intervention. This recognition of social responsibility as a moral duty has been reflected in three self-regulatory mechanisms: codes of conduct, media ombudsmen (sometimes referred to as "readers' representatives"), and news councils.

Codes of Conduct

Although most media practitioners agree that ethical norms are important in their fields, formal codes of conduct are still controversial. Proponents of such codes argue that a written statement of principles is the only way to avoid leaving moral judgments to individual interpretations and that if ethical values are important enough to espouse publicly, they should be codified. Besides, codes provide employees with a written notice of what is expected of them.[65]

Opponents of such codes view them as a form of self-censorship, a retreat from the independence and autonomy necessary for a free and robust mass communication enterprise. In addition, the critics argue, such codes must, of necessity, be general and vague and thus are incapable of confronting the fine nuances of the ethical skirmishes that occur under specific circumstances.[66] In the field of journalism philosophy, such luminaries as John Merrill and S. Jack Odell have dismissed codes as meaningful tools for ensuring accountability:

> The problem with such codes and creeds, however, is that they are not even sufficient in what they do—develop a consensus in thought and action; reason: the rhetorical devices of the codes of ethics and the creeds are so nebulous, fuzzy, ambiguous, contradictory, or heavy-handed that the few journalists who do read them are perplexed, confused, bewildered, angered, and scared off. Journalists, of all people, should use the language skillfully, directly, and effectively, and in many instances they do. But when it

comes to codes and creeds they seem to retreat into a kind of bureaucratese, or sociological jargon that benumbs the mind and frustrates any attempt to extract substantial meaning from the writing.[67]

There is also a fear, sometimes justified, that formal codes of conduct will be used against the media in legal battles as evidence that employees have behaved negligently in violating their own standards of ethical deportment. Finally, opponents contend that codes are nothing more than statements of ideals and are conveniently ignored in the competitive environment of the marketplace.

Nevertheless, codes are viewed as a serious attempt to at least recognize the fundamental values and principles for which media organizations stand. They serve the dual purposes of establishing the common ground on which members of a profession stand and serving a public relations function of letting the public know the organization is serious about ethics.[68] These codes are of two kinds: professional and institutional.

Professional Codes.   All of the major professional media organizations, representing a broad constituency, have developed formal codes. For example, the Society of Professional Journalists (SPJ) has adopted standards for such things as truth, accuracy, conflicts of interests, and fairness.

There has been a recurring debate over whether the SPJ code should be enforced within the journalistic community, thereby ensuring adherence to the code's ideals. However, even the SPJ has resisted this idea, in part because they are afraid that attempts at making journalism a profession might encourage legislatures to license them, thus setting up a First Amendment confrontation. In 1985 its directors voted against enforcing the code on individual members because of a concern that such a stance would interfere with First Amendment freedoms. There was also a fear of litigation resulting from punitive action taken against some recalcitrant SPJ member for having violated the code.[69]

The American Society of Newspaper Editors, the Associated Press Managing Editors, and the Radio-Television News Directors Association have also adopted codes. The Advertising Code of American Business (developed by the American Advertising Federation and the Association of Better Business Bureaus International) sets forth the advertising industry's views on such things as truth in advertising, good taste and public decency, disparagement of competitors' products, price claims, and the use of testimonials. Likewise, the Public Relations Society of America (PRSA) has adopted a Code of Professional Standards to guide its members through the moral thicket of corporate responsibility. Hollywood has also mobilized its collective conscience in the form of the Motion Picture Association of America's rating system.

Codes of conduct, of course, are a prominent feature of the moral landscape for other professions. Lawyers, doctors, nurses, and psychologists all belong to professions with enforceable codes of ethics. The lack of enforceability, however, distinguishes media codes from those adhered to by other professional practitioners. Although the PRSA *can* expel a member for violation of its code under some circumstances,[70] it has no legal authority to prohibit an expelled member from continuing to practice public relations. In fact, the lack of an enforceable ethical code is cited by some as evidence of the media's lack of professional standing.

Institutional Codes.   In addition to these professional codes, many media institutions have their own policies regarding the conduct of employees. These codes are often comprehensive and deal with such diverse matters as the acceptance of gifts and other gratuities from outside sources, conflicts of interests, the use of offensive or indecent material, the publication of rape victims' names, the staging of news events, the use of deceptive news-gathering techniques, and the identification of news sources.

There are usually similar policies regarding advertising content, particularly in matters of decency and taste. Many of the issues covered by these codes will be dealt with in the hypothetical cases in Part 2.

Although these codes often reflect an organization's commitment to certain standards of conduct, they are sometimes criticized for failing to provide guidance for the myriad ethical dilemmas that confront media practitioners under the pressure of time deadlines. Nevertheless, such codes are helpful in socializing new employees to the ethical values of the organization and can also be used as a neutral standard to which both sides can appeal in an ethical dispute.[71] In addition, unlike professional codes, which are just voluntary statements of principles, industry codes are usually enforceable, sometimes resulting in either warnings or dismissal of ethically recalcitrant employees.[72]

Unfortunately, in the heat of battle and under deadline pressures some organizations ignore their own standards. Such was apparently the case when Jane Pauley, coanchor of *Dateline NBC,* opened a segment on the murder of James Jordan, father of basketball superstar Michael Jordan. In the segment she referred to criminal records of the two suspects charged in the murder and then introduced correspondent Brian Ross, who also dealt with the records and did so in the framework of "young criminals" moving through the justice system. This violated the NBC standards book, which cautioned against using criminal records on the air.[73]

Of course, institutional policies are not self-effectuating and depend on the diligence and good faith of management personnel to oversee their adherence. Each violation, particularly if ignored by media executives, erodes the integrity of the published ethical guidelines.

The Ombudsman System

Perhaps the most visible example of a commitment to self-criticism is the presence, in some media organizations, of an ombudsman, hired to investigate questionable journalistic conduct and to recommend action. Proponents of the ombudsman system argue that ombudsmen can most effectively "funnel" reader complaints, reduce the likelihood of libel complaints, help cement a paper's relationship with its readers, serve as a liaison with the public, and elevate the ethical awareness of the staff. Opponents insist that ombudsmen are expensive luxuries and that the money could be better spent on reporters and editors, that they are little more than window dressing and a public relations ploy, and that they create a bureaucratic layer between the audience and those who should be addressing the public's concerns, namely editors and reporters.[74]

The ombudsman idea originated in Sweden, where a government official with that title represents the public in its dealings with the bureaucracy, and ombudsmen have become a feature of the self-regulatory apparatus in other countries. Sometimes, they respond to complaints from irate citizens or the subjects of news coverage; at other times, they act on their own initiative.

A case in point is the controversy that engulfed the *Philadelphia Inquirer* when it published a photo of an African American man killed by police following a shooting incident at a high school championship basketball game on the University of Pennsylvania campus. The picture, which was prominently displayed on page one, prompted accusations from angry readers, many of them African American, who said the paper would not have run a similar picture of a white victim. Others vilified the paper for being insensitive and resorting to sensationalism. The *Inquirer* defended its decision on the grounds the picture conveyed a shocking but important story. But despite the paper's confidence in its ethical posture, the editors were not insensitive to their readers' concerns, and the *Inquirer*'s two ombudsmen reached out to readers, publicly acknowledging the debate over the gruesome photo and letting them vent their anger.[75]

The first newspapers to use an ombudsman in this country were Kentucky's *Louisville Times* and the Louisville *Courier-Journal* in 1967. However, the number of daily newspapers utilizing ombudsmen has never been impressive. Just a handful of the more than 1,400 dailies (only 40 were listed as members of the Organization of News Ombudsmen in 2003) employ ombudsmen, but ombudsmen occupy influential positions at some of the nation's largest metropolitan papers, including the *Washington Post, Minneapolis Star-Tribune, Chicago Tribune,* and *Boston Globe*.[76] At some newspapers the ombudsman's role has been expanded to include enhancing the papers' connection with their readers and improving the quality of news coverage before it happens rather than as an "after-the-fact critic in a public column."[77]

Ombudsmen do not base their advice on fixed codes; they are more interested in improving the social conscience of the institution than in adhering to a general and sometimes vague formal policy. Effective ombudsmen must be viewed both by management and the public as representatives of the community and should have access to space in the newspaper or airtime on the station to disagree with decisions by institutional personnel. Ombudsmen should also have seniority or some stature within the industry.[78]

Although ombudsmen are considered representatives of the public, they should also be even-handed in their handling of complaints. They must be fair to both readers and their newspapers and editors. One problem has been the public's perception of ombudsmen, who are sometimes viewed as a cosmetic response to reader criticism. Thus, an Organization of News Ombudsmen has been established to promote the positive role of these readers' representatives. Ombudsmen can provide an avenue for constructive criticism and a platform for a reasonable dialogue with the faceless institutional gatekeepers. The presence of ombudsmen can be an effective tool of corporate management to demonstrate to a skeptical public that they are serious about the idea of social responsibility. Unfortunately, staff members often resent ombudsmen and perceive them as in-house "snitches," not unlike the way in which members of some police departments view their internal affairs units with disdain. *HR?*

As to the future of ombudsmen as a self-regulatory device, there is both good news and bad news. The bad news is that several papers, apparently believing that too much self-criticism is destructive of corporate self-esteem, have fired or reassigned their ombudsmen for their brutal candor in assessing the ethical indiscretions of their employers.[79] The good news is that the electronic media, increasingly liberated from decades of government regulation that made self-policing largely redundant, have renewed their efforts at self-criticism and accountability in the form of audience feedback programs, on-air critics, and even ombudsmen.[80]

News Councils

News councils, arguably the most democratic of regulatory devices, are another breed of "watchdog" designed to foster a dialogue between the media and their various publics. These councils, which are usually composed of a cross section of the community and the media, are designed to investigate complaints against the media, investigate the charges, and then publish their findings. However, although such bodies are common in Europe, news councils have become virtually an ethical anachronism in this country.

In the 1950s and 1960s local councils sprang up in the United States, in large and small communities alike. The largest of these—the Minnesota Press Council—was statewide and remains the only visible force of its kind in investigating cases of alleged ethical wrongdoing. This grassroots movement provided the impetus for a national review panel, and in 1973 the National News Council came into existence. It was initially funded by the prestigious Twentieth

Century Fund and the Markle Foundation. Logically, the financial supporters should have been news organizations themselves, but the council was met with a predictable outpouring of disdain and even anger from print and broadcast journalists alike. Some felt that press freedom itself was being jeopardized, which in hindsight was a rather dramatic overreaction.

In 1984 the council died from neglect, a victim of media antagonism and dereliction. Richard S. Salant, a former head of CBS News and the council's president when it folded, noted that opposition to it was a reflection of the deep-seated hostility of the American media to any outside body looking over its shoulder and the belief that each news organization was capable of solving its own problems.[81] An editorial comment from the *New York Daily News* was typical: "We don't care how much the Fund prates its virtuous intentions. This is a sneak attempt at press regulation, a bid for a role as unofficial news censor."[82] The publisher of the *New York Times*, Arthur Ochs Sulzberger, called the idea "simply regulation in another form."[83] However, not all members of the media were as pessimistic. For example, the *Washington Post*'s publisher, Katherine Graham, observed, "If properly handled, it won't do any harm and might do some good."[84]

The council's detractors may have felt that a little social responsibility is good for the soul but that an overdose of anything can be terminal. Considering the hostile environment in which they are now operating, the media may have lost a valuable ally in their fight to be perceived as institutions of social responsibility. However, as the news media's credibility continues to tumble, some journalistic stalwarts are publicly resurrecting the idea of a news council. *60 Minutes'* senior correspondent Mike Wallace, for example, writing in the *Quill*, the magazine of the Society of Professional Journalists, lamented the fact that "there's a good deal less admiration in the public perception of us and our profession" and urged the industry again to consider a national news council.[85]

"What I'm suggesting is . . . [r]easonable, qualified people sitting down and considering whether or not they perceive a given piece of reporting warrants holding it up to public scrutiny as flawed, as dishonest," observes Wallace. "And if it is, then let the public know about it."[86]

SUMMARY

A system of ethics is a cornerstone of any civilization. It is essential for (1) building trust and cooperation among individuals in society, (2) serving as a *moral gatekeeper* in apprising society of the relative importance of certain moral values, (3) acting as a moral arbitrator in resolving conflicting claims based on individual self-interests, (4) improving society's moral ecology, and (5) clarifying for society the competing values and principles inherent in emerging and novel moral dilemmas.

Five criteria are the basis of any system of ethics. First, an ethical system must have *shared values.* Before ethical judgments can be made, society must reach agreement on its standards of moral conduct. Second, these standards should be based on reason and experience, that is to say, *wisdom.* Third, a system of ethics should seek *justice.* There should be no double standard of treatment, unless there is an overriding and morally defensible reason to discriminate. Fourth, an ethical system should be based on *freedom of choice.* Moral agents must be free to render ethical judgments without coercion. Only in this way will the individual's ethical level of consciousness be raised. Finally, there must be some means of *accountability,* either formal or informal. An ethics system that does not include accountability encourages freedom without responsibility and thus lacks the moral authority to encourage virtuous behavior.

Society imposes moral duties on individuals as a condition of membership in that society. These duties are of two kinds. *General* obligations are those that apply to all members of society. *Particularistic* obligations are determined by membership within a specific group, profession, or occupation. A real moral dilemma can occur when a conflict arises between our general and particularistic duties, as when a reporter refuses to divulge the name of a confidential source to a court of law.

In fulfilling these moral duties, we must take into account all parties, including ourselves, who may be touched by our ethical decisions. For media practitioners these include the individual's conscience, the objects of moral judgment, financial supporters, the institution, professional colleagues, and society at large.

There is obviously a connection between law and ethics, inasmuch as many of our felony statutes—for example, those involving murder and theft—are based on the moral precepts of civilization. However, not all moral issues are legally codified. But because compliance with the law in a democratic society depends on moral respect for its legal institutions, violation of the law can be justified only by some higher moral principle. Even then lawbreakers must be willing to accept the consequences of their actions.

Individuals are the primary moral agents within society. They are the ones who make ethical judgments within the institutional hierarchy. Nevertheless, the public often associates ethical or unethical behavior with the institutions themselves, especially when corporate executives are invisible to a skeptical populace. Thus, we often speak of social responsibility when referring to a company's image.

Some political and economic conservatives believe that the concept of the public interest is merely a by-product of corporate autonomy. According to this view, social responsibility consists primarily of serving the stockholders or other investors. Others have taken issue with this view and believe that conducting business is not a right but a privilege granted by society.

Because the media are now a big business feasting at the trough of Wall Street, the public has demanded accountability, just as it has from the rest of corporate America. This pressure for social responsibility, which has manifested itself through both mechanisms of self-regulation and external criticism, began around the turn of the twentieth century and has continued unabated.

The arrival of the information age has precipitated a new round of ethical soul-searching and may challenge traditional concepts of social responsibility. Such unethical conduct as invasion of privacy, theft of intellectual property, and deception using digitalization are among the concerns of ethicists as the convergence of communications media and sophisticated technology continues unabated.

There is no reason to believe that institutional autonomy and social responsibility cannot coexist in the media, but this goal necessitates the restructuring of corporate attitudes. This attitude realignment should begin, first, by convincing corporate executives that social responsibility is good for business and that little autonomy has to be surrendered in the process. Second, media institutions should be—and many already are—actively involved in the communities of which they are a part. Other promising signs indicate that the media have recognized that freedom and responsibility are not mutually exclusive. This recognition of social responsibility is reflected in two self-regulatory mechanisms: codes of conduct, both professional and institutional, and ombudsmen. News councils, perhaps the most democratic of self-regulatory devices, have all but disappeared from this country's ethical arsenal.

Predictably, all of these measures have met with some resistance from those who view social responsibility as a euphemism for censorship. But each, in its own way, has served to awaken the media to their obligations to the society from which they draw economic sustenance.

Notes

1. Dorothy Rabinowitz, "ABC's Food Lion Mission," *Wall Street Journal*, February 11, 1997, p. A-22.
2. On appeal, the Fourth Circuit Court of Appeals overturned some of the claims against ABC but allowed the trespass charge to stand. See *Food Lion Inc. v. Capital Cities/ABC, Inc.,* 27 Med. L. Rptr. 2409 (4th Cir. 1999).
3. For example, see Kyle Niederpruem, "Food Lion Case May Punish Future Journalists," *Quill,* May 1997, p. 47; Russ W. Baker, "Truth, Lies, and Videotape," *Columbia Journalism Review,* July/August 1993, pp. 25–28.
4. Philip Seib and Kathy Fitzpatrick, *Journalism Ethics* (Fort Worth, TX: Harcourt Brace, 1997), p. 93, citing Colman McCarthy, "Getting the Truth Untruthfully," *Washington Post,* December 22, 1992, p. D21.
5. Rabinowitz, "ABC's Food Lion Mission."
6. Jeffrey Olen, *Ethics in Journalism* (Upper Saddle River, NJ: Prentice-Hall, 1988), p. 3.
7. See John Hartland-Swann, "The Moral and the Non-Moral," in Tom L. Beauchamp, *Philosophical Ethics: An Introduction to Moral Philosophy* (New York: McGraw-Hill, 1982), pp. 7–10.
8. This point is discussed in greater detail in Edward Tivnan, *The Moral Imagination: Confronting the Ethical Issues of the Day* (New York: Simon & Schuster, 1995), pp. 263–265.
9. Olen, *Ethics in Journalism,* p. 3.
10. Richard P. Cunningham, "Public Cries Foul on Both Coasts When Papers Lift Secrecy," *Quill,* April 1995, p. 12.
11. Ibid.
12. Ibid.
13. Richard P. Cunningham, "Judge's Racist Comments Rip Scab Off City, Readers," *Quill,* June 1992, p. 10.
14. Ibid.
15. Quoted in ibid., p. 11.
16. *Virginia Pharmacy Board v. Virginia Consumer Council,* 1 Med. L. Rptr. 1930, 1935 (1976).
17. Ibid., p. 1936.
18. For a more thorough examination of this controversy, see Clifford G. Christians, Mark Fackler, Kim B. Rotzoll, and Kathy Brittain McKee, *Media Ethics: Cases and Moral Reasoning,* 6th ed. (New York: Addison Wesley Longman, 2001), pp. 127–132.
19. For a discussion of the relationship between "popular" culture and "high" culture, see Lee Thayer (ed.), *Ethics, Morality and the Media* (New York: Hastings House, 1980), pp. 19–22.
20. These criteria are based, in part, on the writings of ancient Greek and contemporary philosophers as well as some recommended by the ethics scholar John Merrill.
21. Such an approach is not unusual in cases involving harmful products, such as the warning labels now required on cigarette packages and tobacco advertising.
22. See Olen, *Ethics in Journalism,* pp. 2–3. One author refers to these as prima facie duties in Beauchamp, *Philosophical Ethics,* pp. 188–190.

23. See Norman E. Bowie, *Making Ethical Decisions* (New York: McGraw-Hill, 1985), p. 100.

24. "Darts & Laurels," *Columbia Journalism Review,* September/October 1996, p. 23.

25. "Paper Sparks Debate by Interviewing 'Arsonist,'" *Quill,* April 2001, p. 41.

26. Fred Brown, "Crossing the Police Line," *Quill,* March 2001, p. 30.

27. Ibid.

28. See Ralph Potter, "The Logic of Moral Argument," in Paul Deats (ed.), *Toward a Discipline of Social Ethics* (Boston: Boston University Press, 1972), pp. 93–114.

29. Christians, Fackler, Rotzoll, and McKee, *Media Ethics,* pp. 21–22.

30. Some of these categories are derived from those developed by Christians, Fackler, Rotzoll, and McKee in *Media Ethics,* pp. 22–23.

31. See Olen, *Ethics in Journalism,* p. 33.

32. Ibid., p. 34.

33. 18 Med. L. Rptr. 1348 (S.D. Fla. 1990).

34. 18 Med. L. Rptr. 1352 (11th Cir. 1990).

35. *United States v. Cable News Network,* 23 Med. L. Rptr. 1033, 1045–1046 (S.D. Fla. 1994).

36. For example, see *Cox Broadcasting Corp. v. Cohn,* 420 U.S. 469 (1975); *The Florida Star v. B.J.F.,* 109 S. Ct. 2603 (1989).

37. Not all ethicists agree with this view. Some believe that corporate morality exists apart from the ethical behavior of individual members. See Peter A. French, "Corporate Moral Agency," in Joan C. Callahan (ed.), *Ethical Issues in Professional Life* (New York: Oxford University Press, 1988), pp. 265–269.

38. For an insightful discussion and comparison of these two cases, see Philip Seib and Kathy Fitzpatrick, *Public Relations Ethics* (Fort Worth, TX: Harcourt Brace, 1995), pp. 101–111.

39. This case is discussed in James A. Laska and Michael S. Pritchard, *Communication Ethics: Methods of Analysis,* 2d ed. (Belmont, CA: Wadsworth, 1994), p. 48.

40. For a discussion of corporate social responsibility, see Conrad C. Fink, *Media Ethics* (Needham Heights, MA: Allyn & Bacon, 1995), pp. 111–160.

41. See Milton Friedman, "Social Responsibility and Compensatory Justice," in Callahan, *Ethical Issues,* pp. 349–350.

42. Fred S. Siebert, Theodore Peterson, and Wilbur Schramm, *Four Theories of the Press* (Urbana: University of Illinois Press, 1956), p. 73.

43. Mitchell Stephens, *A History of News: From the Drum to the Satellite* (New York: Viking Penguin, 1988), p. 264.

44. Ibid., pp. 263–268.

45. See Melvin Anshen, "Changing the Social Contract: A Role for Business," in Callahan, *Ethical Issues,* pp. 351–354.

46. See "Big Media, Big Money," *Newsweek,* April 1, 1985, pp. 52–59.

47. Fred S. Siebert, Theodore Peterson, and Wilbur Schramm, *Four Theories of the Press* (Urbana: University of Illinois Press, 1956), p. 83.

48. Ibid., quoting Joseph Pulitzer, "The College of Journalism," *North American Review* 178 (May 1904): 658.

49. Ron F. Smith, *Groping for Ethics in Journalism,* 5th ed. (Ames: Iowa State University Press, 2003), pp. 22–23.

50. Clifford Christians, "Enforcing Media Codes," *Journal of Mass Media Ethics* 1, no. 1 (Fall/Winter 1985–1986): 14.

51. Siebert, Peterson, and Schramm, *Four Theories of the Press,* pp. 87–92.

52. Theodore L. Glasser, "When Is Objective Reporting Irresponsible Reporting?," in Philip Patterson and Lee Wilkins (eds.), *Media Ethics: Issues and Cases,* 4th ed. (Boston: McGraw-Hill, 2002), pp. 39–40.

53. Quoted in Glasser.

54. Ted J. Smith III, "Journalism and the Socrates Syndrome," *Quill,* April 1988, p. 20.

55. Ibid.

56. David Bauder, "CBS Cancels Reagan Miniseries, Gives It to Showtime," AP dispatch published in *The Advocate* (Baton Rouge), November 5, 2003, p. 12A.

57. For an excellent book by Howard Kurtz that provides a penetrating and critical look at the newspaper industry, see *Media Circus: The Trouble with America's Newspapers* (New York: Times Books), 1993.

58. Peter B. Orlik, *Electronic Media Criticism* (Boston: Focal Press, 1994), p. 19.

59. "Big Media, Big Money," p. 52.

60. Jack Lule, "The Power and Pitfalls of Journalism in the Hypertext Era," *Chronicle of Higher Education,* August 7, 1998, p. B7.

61. Catherine Mejia, "E-mail Access v. Privacy," *Quill,* April 1994, p. 4.

62. Ed Fouhy, "Which Way Will It Go?," *American Journalism Review,* May 2000, p. 18. There is also a concern that journalists themselves may fall prey to inaccurate information on the Net and in computer data banks. However, a recent study reveals that stories using computer-assisted reporting are as credible as stories based on anecdotal evidence or authoritative sources. Justin Mayo and Glenn Leshner, "Assessing the Credibility of Computer-Assisted Reporting," *Newspaper Research Journal,* Fall 2000, pp. 68–82.

63. Ibid.

64. Quoted from "Ethics and the Rush of Cyberspace," *APME News,* July/August, 1995, p. 14.

65. See Christians, "Enforcing Media Codes."

66. For a consideration of arguments against formal codes of ethics, see Jay Black and Ralph D. Barney, "The Case against Mass Media Codes of Ethics,"

Journal of Mass Media Ethics 1, no. 1 (Fall/Winter 1985–1986): 27–36.

67. John C. Merrill and S. Jack Odell, *Philosophy and Journalism* (White Plains, NY: Longman, 1983), p. 137.

68. Jay Black, "Minimum Standards vs. Ideal Expectations," *Quill,* November/December 1995, p. 26.

69. Smith, *Groping for Ethics,* p. 23.

70. Under the 2000 revision of the code, the PRSA Board of Directors "retains the right to bar from membership or expel from the Society any individual who has been or is sanctioned by a government agency or convicted in a court of law of an action that is in violation of this Code."

71. For a more thorough discussion of the pros and cons regarding media codes, see Richard L. Johannesen, "What Should We Teach about Formal Codes of Communication Ethics?" *Journal of Mass Media Ethics* 3 (1988): 59–64.

72. See Jay Black, "Taking the Pulse of the Nation's News Media," *Quill,* November 1992, p. 32.

73. See Emerson Stone, "Going, Going, Gone . . . ?," *Communicator,* December 1993, p. 16.

74. Christopher Meyers, "Creating an Effective Newspaper Ombudsman Position," *Journal of Mass Media Ethics* 15, no. 4 (2000): 248.

75. Josh Getlin, "Monitoring Yourself," *Columbia Journalism Review,* March/April 2000, p. 51.

76. Organization of News Ombudsmen website, located at http://www.newsombudsmen.org/ (downloaded November 13, 2003).

77. Neil Nemeth, *News Ombudsmen in North America* (Westport, CT: Praeger, 2003), p. 142.

78. See William L. Rivers and Cleve Mathews, *Ethics for the Media* (Upper Saddle River, NJ: Prentice-Hall, 1988), p. 231.

79. For example, see Terry Dalton, "Another One Bites the Dust," *Quill,* November/December 1994, pp. 39–40; Richard P. Cunningham, "Third Canadian Paper Eliminates Ombudsman Post," *Quill,* September 1993, pp. 16–17; Richard P. Cunningham, "L.A. Riot Coverage Criticism Costs Ombudsman His Job," *Quill,* July/August 1992, pp. 12–13.

80. Sue O'Brien, "Electronic Ombudsmen," *Communicator,* March 1995, pp. 15–18.

81. "News Council Closes, Gives Files to Minnesota," *Quill,* May 1984, p. 44.

82. Rivers and Mathews, *Ethics for the Media,* p. 219.

83. "Judges for Journalism," *Newsweek,* December 11, 1972, p. 82.

84. Ibid.

85. See Mike Wallace, "The Press under Fire," *Quill,* November/December 1995, pp. 21–23.

86. Ibid., p. 23.

◀ C H A P T E R ▶

3

Ethics and
Moral Reasoning

MORAL REASONING AND
ETHICAL DECISION MAKING

Discussions about religion and politics are sure to liven up any party. Ethics deserves a place on that list. Everyone has opinions about unethical and immoral conduct, and arguments about morality usually produce more heat than light. When ethical issues are confronted in the classroom or in professional media seminars, the discussion often degenerates into passionate appeals for press rights or sympathy for the victims. Judgments are not well reasoned. In other words, they lack moral foundation.

Moral reasoning is a *systematic* approach to making ethical decisions. Like other forms of intellectual activity, it takes the form of logical argument and persuasion. Because ethical judgments, as we have seen in Chapters 1 and 2, involve the rights and interests of others, these decisions must be made with care and must be defensible through a reasoned analysis of the situation. An individual unschooled in the process of moral reasoning might assume that questions of ethical conduct, like those of personal taste, are nothing more than matters of opinion. Imagine trying to convince someone through rational argument that he should prefer colorful sports coats to more traditional blue business suits. Such an undertaking would

be an exercise in futility, because we cannot argue reasonably about matters of pure taste or opinion. We can, however, deliberate reasonably and persuasively about moral judgments.[1]

But moral reasoning consists of more than just offering reasons for our beliefs, opinions, and actions. After all, not all reasons are valid ones. Moral reasoning is a structured process, an intellectual means of defending our ethical judgments against the criticisms of others. This does not mean that reasonable people cannot disagree about the correct solution to an ethical dilemma. Two different moral agents may, through proper reasoning, arrive at opposing but equally compelling conclusions about the most virtuous course. The beauty of moral reasoning lies in the journey, not the destination.

Knowledge of ethical principles is important, but the application and defense of these rules of conduct in the drama of human interaction are at the core of moral reasoning. In other words, an attempt at moral justification is successful if it can be vindicated on rational grounds.

But if moral reasoning is such a deliberate process—after all, thinking and analyzing are time-consuming—how can media practitioners (or harried managers and employees in other lines of work, for that matter) who perform under deadline pressures expect to apply it? That, of course, is the purpose of teaching moral

54

reasoning techniques to aspiring practitioners within the relative tranquility of the classroom. The consciousness-raising and training that occur there should help the student confront moral dilemmas in the real world with more confidence. In addition, knowledge of moral reasoning principles provides a framework within which moral agents, once they have made ethical judgments, can review them with an eye to improving their performance in the future. Some consistency in decision-making will result, thus replacing the case-by-case approach that so often characterizes classroom discussions of ethical issues. However, one word of caution is in order: No approach to moral reasoning, no matter how structured or thorough, is a guarantee of success in ethical decision making under all circumstances.

Despite the rather untidy circumstances of some ethical dilemmas, the process of moral reasoning can be carried out if moral actors have knowledge and skills in three areas: (1) the moral context, (2) the philosophical foundations of moral theory, and (3) critical thinking. Each of these areas is important in its own way and plays an indispensable role in the moral reasoning model outlined later in this chapter.

THE CONTEXT OF MORAL REASONING

The making of ethical decisions does not take place in a vacuum. Moral agents must understand the *context* within which the dilemma has arisen. Before their powers of reason can operate at optimum efficiency, they must understand the issue itself, the facts of the situation, and the values, principles, and moral duties inherent in the case. In other words, the context consists of all of the factors that might influence an individual's resolution of a moral dilemma.

For example, White House press secretaries who knowingly disseminate "disinformation" to reporters to protect the security of delicate foreign policy negotiations not only must be thoroughly familiar with the facts that might justify such deception, but also should keep in mind the societal proscriptions against lying and be prepared to justify their actions on some higher moral ground. But the general societal norms aside, they should also be aware of the standards of ethical conduct expected of government officials in these circumstances and the particularistic moral duties that govern their behavior. After all, these expectations do change over time, as evidenced by the recent heightened sense of moral indignation in Washington over conflicts of interest.

The context of an ethical dilemma might involve making decisions about either our personal behavior or our professional conduct. Lying to a friend, for example, involves different considerations than using deception in gathering a news story. Even an ethical purist might be forced to admit that lying is permissible in extreme circumstances, such as to prevent harm to another. But the justifications for this deviation from societal norms would be different for a media practitioner than for others operating within a dissimilar environment.

Contextual factors are often culturally determined, whether through association with a close circle of friends or through the "culture" of the newsroom. Company value systems and behavioral codes cannot be ignored in rendering moral judgments. Before promising confidentiality to a news source, for example, a reporter must be guided by company policy on the matter as well as the views and advice of professional colleagues. Likewise, decision makers must consider certain competitive and economic pressures that are common to media institutions. All of the considerations that are unique to a particular dilemma constitute the context of the ethical case.

Thus, before moral agents can argue rationally about media ethics, they must know something about the environment—that is, the social and cultural context—within which the media operate. They must bring to the decision-making process at least a minimum body of knowledge about the media. Otherwise, it will be difficult to evaluate the strength and legitimacy of the arguments put forth in defense of moral judgments made by media practitioners.

THE PHILOSOPHICAL FOUNDATIONS OF MORAL THEORY

Many philosophers, both ancient and contemporary, as well as the ethical traditions they represent, have had a profound impact on the moral evolution of Western civilization. In the next few pages, we shall briefly encounter a few of the most significant. And while they may vary in substance, the reality is that each has contributed in some way to what might be referred to as the individual's *moral sense.*

The Greek Connection

Most would agree that the study of ethics had its genesis in the glory of ancient Greece. The Greeks, beginning with Socrates, believed that there are moral absolutes and moral knowledge and that they can be discovered by intellectually and persistently curious citizens. Or, to put it more indelicately, virtue is not imprinted on our genetic code at the moment of conception. It requires individual initiative, emotional stamina, critical reflection, and a great deal of determination. The Greeks would have been uncomfortable in a society without moral anchors. Those who share this vision are Greek, at least philosophically, if not through ethnic lineage.

Socrates (ca. 470–399 B.C.) believed that virtue could be identified and practiced. He was dissatisfied with his contemporaries' opinions about moral conduct and wanted to discover those rules that could be reasonably supported. He believed that anyone, through careful reflection, could arrive at some insights into these rules.[2] Although he did not pass on a philosophical system of his own, his "Socratic dialogues" were a significant contribution to what

we now refer to as moral reasoning. Of course, he would have been unnerved by the contemporary media environment, in which diatribes are as common as dialogues and reason often falls prey to intemperance.

Socrates's disciple, Plato (ca. 428–348 B.C.), argued in *The Republic* that justice is achieved through the harmony of wisdom, temperance, and courage. Translating into practice this philosophical observation from the ancient sage, we might say that moral conduct should be based on *experience and knowledge of the world, moderate behavior* as the means of achieving sound ethical judgments, and the *courage* to live up to those judgments. Plato believed that "good" was a value independent of the standards of behavior prevalent at any moment in society. An individual would be justified in defying conventional wisdom in the name of some higher moral good, even if that meant social ostracism. Thus, we might note these ancient seeds for the justifications that media practitioners (and other moral agents) sometimes use for behavior that runs counter to societal norms.

Aristotle (384–322 B.C.) was for many years a student of Plato, but he was more pragmatic in dealing with the world as he found it. He believed that moral virtue was obtainable but that tough choices had to be made in the process. The exercise of virtue, according to him, is concerned with means. Thus, the ends do not necessarily justify the means.

Aristotle's moral philosophy, sometimes referred to as *virtue ethics,* is based on the theory of the golden mean. He believed that virtue lay between the extremes of excess and deficiency, or overdoing and "underdoing." For example, courage is the middle ground between cowardice and foolhardiness. Pride is the mean between vanity and humility.[3] In contemporary journalism such concepts as balance and fairness represent the golden mean. Likewise, the banning of tobacco ads from radio and TV and the placement of warning labels on cigarette packages are a mean between the extreme of outlawing tobacco altogether and the other extreme of doing nothing to counteract the harmful effects of the product.

But Aristotle admitted that not every action could be viewed in terms of the golden mean: "The very names of some things imply evil—for example, the emotions of spite, shamelessness, and envy and such actions as adultery, theft, and murder."[4] In other words, some actions are always wrong, and there is no mean to be sought. Thus, Aristotle's theory of the golden mean is helpful in resolving many of life's difficult ethical dilemmas, but not the ones in which certain actions are clearly wrong.

Aristotle's virtue ethics emphasizes character. The development of a virtuous individual is the goal, not moral conduct in a particular situation or according to a specific rule. Aristotle believed that virtue was achieved through habit, which is perhaps an ancient expression of "practice makes perfect." Through repetitive moral behavior, the notion of "good" is inculcated into the individual's value system. Thus, moral virtue becomes a way of thinking as well as a way of acting. Without perhaps being aware of it, Aristotle made a major contribution to moral reasoning, because the practice of moral reasoning, if it becomes habit-forming, can realign one's way of thinking about ethics. This, at least, is one of the goals of this book.

ETHICAL PERSPECTIVES AND TRADITIONS

In addition to the Aristotelian focus on character, other ethical perspectives and traditions have evolved under the tutelage of both ancient and contemporary philosophers. Some of these are fully formulated guidelines for ethical decision making; others have simply added specific ideas and perspectives on what it means to be an ethical person or how ethical standards are determined. Space does not allow for a complete listing of the full array of ethical traditions or a complete delineation of those described in the following text. Nevertheless, those discussed here are representative of the most influential ethical traditions and perspectives.

Care-Based Ethics

Care-based ethics is the foundation of the world's major religions, including Judaism, Christianity, and Islam. Each has its own unique expression of this ideal, but the most familiar manifestation of care-based ethics is the Golden Rule: *Do unto others as you would have them do to you.* Care-based ethics is characterized by a feature philosophers refer to as *reversibility*. This is a classic case of role-reversal in which we are asked to put ourselves into the shoes of others and ask how we would like to be treated if we were the recipient rather than the perpetrator of our actions.[5]

Putting love for others first is the guiding principle of this form of ethical behavior. The fundamental creed of the Judeo-Christian tradition, for example, is the admonition to "love thy neighbor as thyself." The Judeo-Christian ethic is characterized by a love for God and all humankind. According to this notion, all moral decisions should be based on a respect for the dignity of persons as an end in itself rather than merely as a means to an end. All individuals—rich and poor, black and white, famous and ordinary—should be accorded respect as human beings regardless of their status in life.

Although the Judeo-Christian ethic sounds rather utopian, it offers some practical advice for moral behavior: Regardless of the approach we use to render ethical judgments, we should treat those affected by our decisions with dignity. In other words, the philosophy of respect for persons should underlie all ethical decision-making. This advice certainly has relevance for journalists who scrutinize others' affairs and subject them to the glare of public examination.

Kant and Moral Duty

The eighteenth-century German philosopher Immanuel Kant ushered in the modern era of ethical thought. Kant's theories were based on the notion of duty and what he referred to as the *categorical imperative.* In *Foundations of the Metaphysics of Morals,* he wrote, "I should never act in such a way that I could not also will that my maxim should be a universal one."[6] In other words, moral agents should check the principles underlying their actions and decide whether they want them applied universally. If so, these principles become a system of public morality to which all members of society are bound.

Kant believed that moral behavior was measured by living up to standards of conduct because they are good, not because of the consequences that might result. He argued that although individuals should be free to act (a fundamental requirement for a system of ethics, as noted in Chapter 2), they have a responsibility to live up to moral principles. Because Kant's theories emphasize duty, his ideas are sometimes referred to as duty-based moral philosophy. In other words, one has a duty to tell the truth, even if it might result in harm to others.

Kant argued that we should respect the autonomy of others and should never treat them as means to our ends. But how can one respect the dignity of another while at the same time obeying the rule to tell the truth if it might injure the other party? Kant knew quite well that obeying universal rules of conduct could result in harm to others. However, a reasonable interpretation of his writings is that he believed that we should never treat such persons exclusively as means and should accord them the respect and moral dignity to which everyone is entitled at all times.[7]

Kant believed that one's motives for acting must be based on acceptance of the duty to act rather than just on *performing* the correct act. The intent of the act is as important as the act itself. A public relations director who releases to the media truthful but damaging information just to injure a competitor would not, in Kant's view, be acting from sound motives. Likewise, an advertiser that avoids deceptive commercial messages just to escape detection by the Federal

Trade Commission cannot be said to be acting from any sense of moral duty.

Some wonder how Kant's absolutist view of the ethical landscape can be applied in today's complex society. A more liberal interpretation of Kant, one that still pays homage to his sense of moral duty, is that universal ethical principles— for example, truth telling, fairness, and honesty— should be obeyed unless there is a compelling reason for deviating from the norm. In addition, some contemporary duty-based philosophers have come to accept consequences as an important consideration in ethical decision-making, as long as such consequences are not the primary determinant of one's moral behavior.[8]

The Appeal of Utilitarianism

Another approach to morality, one that is popular in contemporary American society, is the idea of utilitarianism. Two nineteenth-century British philosophers, Jeremy Bentham and John Stuart Mill, are credited with introducing utilitarianism into the mainstream of modern Western ethical thought. Mill's version of this philosophy is often referred to as creating the greatest happiness for the greatest number of people. Later utilitarians have argued that happiness is not the only desirable value and that others should be considered as well.[9]

However, all versions of utilitarianism have one thing in common: They are concerned with the *consequences* of an ethical judgment. Rather than looking at the intention behind the act, as Kant suggested, one must explore the best outcome for the greatest number of people.

A case in point is a rather unusual situation that arose in Juneau, Alaska, in which two reporters searching a courthouse trash can discovered copies of a court clerk's notes on grand jury proceedings that were still under way. Of the four newspapers to which they offered the information, three refused to publish it, because they did not want to violate the integrity of the grand jury's secret proceedings. The editor of the fourth paper, however, had no such qualms and published the story. His job was to learn what was happening, according to the editor, and tell his readers,[10] thus suggesting that he had breached grand jury secrecy because of the utility of the information to the public.

Likewise, reporters who use deception to uncover social ills often appeal to the principle of utility on the ground that, in the long run, they are accomplishing some moral good for the public they serve. In other words, the positive consequences for society justify the devious means used in gathering the information.

Ethics as a Social Contract

While the notion of a social contract traces its lineage to the ancient Greeks, it is most famously related to the Enlightenment and the writings of such luminaries as Thomas Hobbes, John Locke, and Jean Jacques Rousseau. The social contract originated in political theory, but it has moral dimensions as well. It begins with a very simple premise: The purpose of morality is to enable us to live together. Unbridled individualism is antithetical to communal living. Thus, society's inhabitants must reach agreement on a set of principles that is conducive to peaceful coexistence or, even more idealistically, cultural harmony. We are free to do as we please as long as we do not harm others or cause serious social disruption. However, a perpetual problem is how to balance individual freedom against society's expectations. The issue of euthanasia is a case in point.[11]

Unlike some ethical theories that are inspired by outside forces such as God or nature or theories that hold certain values (such as truth or honesty) to be inherently good and universal, the social contract is strictly conventional. The ethical norms are respected as long as society agrees on their value or utility. (Imagine, if you will, a society in which all members agreed that lying is preferable to telling the truth.) Thus, some ethicists argue that the social contract is morally deficient because it is

incapable of envisioning or producing timeless ethical principles.

Nevertheless, the appeal of the social contract lies in the fact that it is quite egalitarian because the voice of each member of the moral community, at least in theory, is represented (if not always influential) in the formation of this contract. Under the contract, all individuals should be treated equally in terms of rights and opportunities. One contemporary version of the egalitarian idea is outlined by the philosopher John Rawls in his book *A Theory of Justice.* Rawls recommends that self-interested individuals enter into a social contract that minimizes harm to the weakest parties. They should step into what he calls an "original position" behind a hypothetical "veil of ignorance." They are temporarily deprived of knowledge about themselves that is likely to influence judgments in their favor, such as sex, age, race, and social standing.[12] In general, the public realm is characterized by reason, impartiality, and justice, the private realm by emotion, particularity, and caring. Minority views are to be accorded the same standing as those of the majority. Behind this veil individuals who have some stake in the outcome of an ethical dilemma propose their own principles of justice for evaluating the basic social and political institutions of their society. When the veil is lifted, they are asked to visualize what it would be like to be in each of these sociopolitical positions.[13] The goal is to protect the weaker party in the relationship and to minimize harm. This process forces self-interested moral agents to think impartially and to consider the views of others without regard to their own cultural biases. Thus, ethical decisions can be made independently of social, political, economic, and other distinctions.

A case in point is the TV executive (the powerful party) who decides to air commercial-free programming for children (the weaker party) out of respect for the psychologically vulnerable youthful segment of the audience. In such cases, the moral agent accomplishes a noble objective while justifying his decision economically by having the commercial lucrative fare subsidize the sustaining programs directed at children.

This veil of ignorance, though perhaps a romanticized parable, encourages the development of a system of ethics based on equality according to what individuals deserve rather than special privilege. This is an egalitarian idea, an admonition that king and knave alike must submit to the throne of moral judgment and that justice should not be meted out arbitrarily. In other words, there should be no double standard of ethical treatment *unless there is an important and morally defensible reason to discriminate.* This principle is particularly relevant to journalists, who must make decisions about news coverage of individuals of diverse backgrounds, from the famous to the ordinary.

Feminist Ethics

Historically speaking, feminist ethics is a relatively new field of inquiry and at first glance may evoke images of moral behavior based primarily upon our biological predispositions as males or females. Or as one ethicist who has explored this issue thoroughly inquired: *Is there something distinctively male about ethics, or about the way in which we currently understand ethics? Is ethics really something that can properly take forms that differ according to gender?*[14] While some feminist ethicists have explored these enticing questions,[15] feminist ethics is primarily a critique of traditional theories of ethics and morality.[16] It is an attempt "to revise, reformulate, or rethink those aspects of traditional western ethics that depreciate or devalue women's moral experience."[17]

Feminists complain that traditional accounts of ethics are deficient because they focus primarily on the public realm, our political and social interactions in the marketplace, rather than the private domain of interpersonal relationships. This occurs, in the feminist view, because conventional theories of ethics (formulated, incidentally, by males) omit some important concerns.

Take, for example, the following dichotomies: *reason versus emotion, impartiality versus attachment,* and *pure justice versus caring.* In general, the public realm is characterized by reason, impartiality, and justice, the private realm by emotion, particularity, and caring. Feminist ethicists assert that traditional theories are concerned only with the first in each pair of these dichotomies but that both are essential to a fully developed moral life.[18]

The feminist critique has made a valuable contribution to the study of ethics because it reminds us of the complexities of our moral development and the connectedness of our public and private lives. In this respect, feminist ethics has expanded our ethical horizons and can provide some valuable insights for media professionals. The moral environment of practicing journalists, for example, is usually typified by reason and impartiality, but there are times when emotion and attachment must surface as moderating influences. In fact, the readers of this book are admonished that, despite the preoccupation with moral reasoning in resolving the ethics cases at the end of Chapters 4–13, in the real world emotion and intuition are vital sources of the moral sense that animates our ethical behavior.

The Rise of Relativism

Partially in response to the absolutist ideas of Kant, a school of philosophers has arisen espousing the virtues of relative values. These thinkers have rejected the approach of basing moral choice on immutable values.

Bertrand Russell (1872–1970) and John Dewey (1859–1952) are the most notable proponents of this philosophy, sometimes referred to as "progressivism." Dewey, in particular, is credited with (or blamed for, depending on your point of view) convincing the public schools in the United States that they should not be preoccupied with inculcating moral values in their students. Of course, there are those who believe that this progressivist movement has worked to the detriment of the moral stability of youth. This movement may also explain why, until recently, the teaching of ethics in public schools was looked on with suspicion.

Relativists believe that what is right or good for one is not necessarily right or good for another, even under similar circumstances. In other words, moral agents determine what is right and wrong from their own point of view but will not judge the adequacy of others' ethical judgments.[19] Relativists have the attitude that "I'll determine what's right for me, and you can decide what's right for you."

Carried to its outer limits, relativism can lead to moral anarchy by which individuals lay claim to no ethical standards at all. A less extreme view, however, is held by those who believe in certain moral principles, such as telling the truth, but are willing to deviate from them if certain circumstances warrant. Thus, the term *situation ethics* has entered our moral lexicon.[20] Situationists decide on a case-by-case basis whether it is expedient to deviate from the rule. This is ad hoc decision making at its worst and can hardly be used as a model of ethical decorum. Professor Bert Bradley offers this negative assessment of situation ethics: "It appears that situation ethics has an unsettling ability to justify a number of diverse situations. It is not difficult to see how situation ethics can be used to rationalize, either consciously or unconsciously, decisions and actions that stem from selfish and evasive origins."[21]

John Merrill, one of the nation's leading scholars on the philosophy of journalism, agrees with Bradley. Writing in *The Imperative of Freedom,* he refers to this approach as "nonethics":

> When the matter of ethics is watered down to subjectivism, to situations or contexts, it loses all meaning as ethics. If every case is different, if every situation demands a different standard, if there are no absolutes in ethics, then we should scrap the whole subject of moral philosophy and simply be satisfied that each person run his life by his whims or "considerations" which may change from situation to situation.[22]

ETHICAL THEORIES IN MORAL REASONING

From the foregoing discussion one could construct many different approaches to evaluating ethical behavior. But the perspective to which I am committed in this text is derived from three kinds of ethical theories, based primarily on the teachings of Aristotle, Mill, and Kant. Thus, the guidelines that will be used in the moral reasoning model presented later in this chapter fall into three categories: *deontological* (duty-based) theories, *teleological* (consequence-based) *theories,*[23] and *virtue theories,* represented by Aristotle's golden mean.

Deontological (Duty-Based) Theories

Deontologists (derived from the Greek word *deon,* or "duty") are sometimes referred to as "nonconsequentialists" because of their emphasis on acting on principle or according to certain universal moral duties without regard to the good or bad consequences of their actions. The most famous deontologist is Kant. As noted earlier, his fundamental moral principle is his categorical imperative, which is based on moral rules that should be universally applied and that respect the dignity of people.

According to this duty-based theory, prohibitions against certain kinds of behavior apply, even if beneficial consequences would result. Rather than focusing on the consequences (after all, foul deeds might produce good results), deontologists emphasize the commitment to principles that the moral agent would like to see applied universally, as well as the motive of the agent. Thus, in this view Robin Hood would have been a villain and not a hero for his rather permissive approach to the redistribution of the wealth. Duty-based theories do not approve of using foul means to achieve positive ends. The moral agent's motives are important. According to Kant, people should always be treated with respect and as ends unto themselves, never as means to an end. Simply stated, *the ends do not justify the means!*

Because of their emphasis on rules and commitment to duty, deontological theories are sometimes referred to as "absolutist," admitting of no exceptions. Under a duty-based approach to ethical decision making, for example, reporters would not be justified in using deception in ferreting out a story, and Hollywood producers could not defend their use of gratuitous sex or violence just to achieve higher ratings or audience appeal. It is little wonder that many media practitioners dismiss this absolutist approach as unrealistic and even as a threat to their First Amendment rights.

Nevertheless, duty-based theories do have some advantages. First, concrete rules that provide for few exceptions take some of the pressure off moral agents to predict the consequences of their actions. There is a duty to act according to the rules, regardless of the outcome. Second, there is more predictability in the deontological theories, and one who follows these ideas consistently is likely to be regarded as a truthful person.

In addition, rules can be devised for special circumstances to take some of the ambiguity out of ethical decision-making.[24] For example, in cases in which reporters refuse to divulge the names of their sources to a court, even when these sources may have information relating to the innocence of a criminal defendant, a special rule might be devised to compel disclosure on the ground of justice to the defendant. Such rules would then have to be applied in all such circumstances, without regard to consequences in particular situations. The problem is that such rules often collide with other fundamental principles, such as the obligation to keep one's promises.

This situation illustrates one of the shortcomings of duty-based theories. In cases in which a conflict exists between two equally plausible rules, deontologists have a difficult time resolving the moral standoff. The "Heintz dilemma" described in Chapter 1, in which Heintz was trying to decide whether to steal an expensive life-saving drug for his terminally ill wife, is an example of such a rule conflict. Deontologists do not provide very satisfactory solutions to this problem.

In addition, even when there is no rule conflict, it is sometimes difficult to apply general principles to specific unusual circumstances. For example, should a TV reporter knowingly broadcast false information at the request of the police to save the life of a hostage being held at gunpoint? Most of us would probably vote in favor of doing anything to save the life of the hostage, but strictly interpreted duty-based theories might suggest otherwise.

It can also be argued that moral duties cannot be separated from the consequences of fulfilling those obligations. For example, the reason that the duty to tell the truth is such a fundamental principle is that truth telling produces good consequences for society. And even Kant, despite his condemnations of consequential reasoning, sometimes acknowledges the link between universal moral duties and the positive consequences of carrying out those ethical responsibilities.[25]

Nevertheless, from this description it would appear that the Kantian approach to ethical decision making is too uncompromising for the complex world in which we live and would thus not provide a sound theoretical foundation for moral reasoning. However, the contemporary interpretation of deontological morality reflects a more liberal attitude and suggests that we have a duty to obey specified rules unless there is a *compelling* reason not to do so. In any event the burden of proof is on the moral agent to prove that an exception is justified in extreme or rare circumstances, such as telling a lie to prevent a murder.

Teleological (Consequence-Based) Theories

Teleological, or consequentialist, theories are popular in modern society. They are predicated on the notion that the ethically correct decision is the one that produces the best consequences. Consequentialists, unlike deontologists, do not ask whether a particular practice or policy is always right or wrong but whether it will lead to positive results.

There are, of course, variations on the teleological theme. At one extreme are the *egoists,* who argue that moral agents should seek to maximize good consequences for themselves. They should, in other words, *look out for number one.*[26] But as suggested in Chapter 1, egoism should be rejected as a viable avenue for moral behavior because it is based essentially on self-interest.

At the other extreme are the utilitarians, represented primarily by the writings of philosophers such as Mill. As noted previously, utilitarians believe that we should attempt to promote the greatest good (the most favorable consequences) for the greatest number of people. Utilitarianism is appealing because it provides a definite blueprint for making moral choices. When confronting an ethical dilemma, moral agents should analyze the benefits and harms to everyone (including themselves) affected by the decision and then choose the course of action that results in the most favorable outcome for the greatest number.

Appeals to the public interest to justify certain unpopular decisions by media practitioners is a contemporary manifestation of utilitarianism at work. Thus, a socially beneficial consequence is sometimes used to justify an immoral means. Reporters who accept illegally recorded conversations from news sources on the ground of the "public's right to know" are attempting to justify what they believe to be good consequences, even though the means of accomplishing the ends are rather questionable.

Another aspect of teleological theories, particularly utilitarianism—and one that is often overlooked—is the focus on minimizing harm. Consequentialists recognize that difficult moral choices sometimes cause injury to others. When news stories are published that reveal embarrassing facts about private individuals, the potential for harm is great. On balance, the consequences for the public might be greater than the harm to the subject of the story, but the reporter has a moral obligation to inflict only the harm required to put the story into perspective. To do more would be merely an appeal to the morbid curiosity of the public. For example, a story concerning a malpractice suit should not include allegations concerning the doctor's personal life unless these facts relate directly to questions of the physician's negligence or professional competence.

The consequentialist approach to resolving ethical questions does have a certain appeal. It is more flexible than the duty-based theories and allows greater latitude in prescribing solutions in difficult situations. Teleological theories also provide a clear-cut procedure for confronting moral choices through listing the alternatives, evaluating their possible consequences, and then analyzing each option in light of its impact on others.

However, some people object to these theories on the ground that they rely too much on unknown results and the predictive powers of moral agents. How can we know, for example, that the government's withholding of vital information relating to national security will be in the best interest of the American people?

Another objection to consequentialism is that it does not always take into account the special obligations to individuals or small groups that may conflict with our moral duties to society at large. Media practitioners who are intent on producing the greatest good for the greatest number of people often overlook the needs of special audiences. This neglect results in a form of artistic majoritarianism, in which minority needs are slighted in the media marketplace.

Despite these objections, consequentialist ethics is a valuable tool in moral reasoning, because it does force us to weigh the impact of our behavior on others. It provides a rational means for extricating ourselves from the confusion of rule conflict and thus helps to demystify the process of ethical decision making.

Virtue Theories: Aristotle's Golden Mean

Although duty-based and consequence-based theories differ in many respects, they have one thing in common: They are concerned with standards and principles for evaluating moral behavior. They focus on what we should do, not on the kind of person we ought to be. The ancient Greeks, on the other hand, were more concerned with character building than with what we think of as moral behavior. Plato and Aristotle viewed the acquisition of virtuous traits as central to morality. They believed that acts performed out of a sense of duty did not necessarily reflect a virtuous character. Theories that emphasize character are often referred to as virtue theories.

However, if virtue theories are directed at the building of moral character—a long-term proposition, at best—what relevance can they have for moral reasoning, which is a systematic means of arriving at ethical judgments in specific situations? How can virtue ethics assist us in confronting the moral dilemmas posed by the cases in this book?

Many writers in philosophy have rejected the idea that virtue ethics has an independent and primary status—that it can be useful in the process of moral reasoning.[27] However, one helpful theory can be extracted from virtue ethics: Aristotle's theory of the golden mean, discussed earlier. The golden mean provides a moderate solution in those cases in which there are identifiable extreme positions, neither of which is likely to produce satisfactory results.

Aristotle's golden mean, however, is not analogous to the kind of weak compromise or middle-of-the-road "waffling" that one finds in political circles. The mean is not necessarily midway between the two extremes, because a moral agent must sometimes lean toward one extreme or the other to correct an injustice. Thus, an employer might be justified in giving larger pay increases to some workers than others in order to remedy the effects of past salary inequities. As Clifford Christians and his colleagues have observed in their casebook, *Media Ethics*: "The mean is not only the right quantity, but it occurs at the right time, toward the right people, for the right reason, and in the right manner. The distance depends on the nature of the agent as determined by the weight of the moral case before them."[28]

Aristotle's approach to achieving a virtuous resolution of a dilemma is exemplified by the Federal Communications Commission's approach to regulating broadcast indecency. Although federal law prohibits the transmission of indecent material over radio and TV,[29] the commission has decided to prohibit such content only during times of the day when children are likely to be in the audience—an approach endorsed by the Supreme Court in 1978.[30] This time period, which has actually shifted over the years, is referred to as the "safe harbor."

At one extreme is the "vice" of doing nothing and allowing the airwaves, which carry programs into the privacy of the home, to become a 24-hour repository of scatological language indiscriminately broadcast to children and adults alike. At the other extreme is a total ban on such program fare that could result in censorship of some speech with literary and artistic value, as well as speech lacking in any discernible social worth. Thus, the safe harbor is an attempt, in a libertarian society, to achieve a balance between the extremes of moral anarchy on the airwaves and moral prudery that manifests itself through overzealous government regulation. Although the remedies are legal ones, it is clear that the golden mean has widespread application in the unpredictable drama of human affairs. Aristotle, it seems, continues to speak to us through more than two thousand years of history, thus affecting our destiny and our views on moral virtue.

CRITICAL THINKING IN MORAL REASONING

Understanding the context of an ethical situation and the philosophical foundations of moral theory are necessary but insufficient for sound moral reasoning. There must also be critical thinking about the dilemma. Critical thinking is the engine that drives the moral reasoning machinery and thus leads us away from knee-jerk reactions and toward a more rational approach to decision making. There is nothing more frustrating than classroom discussions in which students express their opinions about ethical issues without having thought critically about them. This is not to suggest that such discussions should end with a consensus on the correct course of action. It does mean, however, that most of the time should be devoted to analyzing and evaluating the reasons for the ethical judgments rendered.

Critical thinking is not a mysterious phenomenon, available only to philosophers and others of superior intellect. We do not all possess the talent to become athletes, musicians, or great literary figures, but we do all possess critical-thinking abilities.[31] And because critical thinking is a skill, it can be learned. The moral reasoning model outlined in the next section is designed to encourage the learning of this skill.

Critical thinking, like the moral theories described earlier, has a long and honorable tradition in Western history, tracing its origins to the ideas of Socrates, Plato, and Aristotle. Like his teacher Plato, Aristotle believed that moral principles separating right from wrong could be derived through the power of reason. To these ancient Greeks skepticism was a healthy occurrence, because it led to relentless questions about the meaning of moral virtue. Thus, critical thinking involves, to some extent, learning to know when to question something and what sorts of questions to ask. Some of the recent political scandals in Washington (the most egregious of which are often accompanied with the suffix "-gate," a candid reference to President

Nixon's Watergate scandal) might have been avoided if the deviant public officials had critically questioned the propriety of their conduct.

Critical thinking begins with something to think critically about. In other words, there must be knowledge of the subject to be evaluated. For media practitioners engaged in moral reasoning, this knowledge would include an understanding of the facts and context surrounding a particular case, and some comprehension of the principles and practices of their own profession, as well as the moral theories that might be brought to bear on ethical decision making. For example, students of critical thinking about media ethics (and this includes you, as you attempt to resolve the hypothetical cases in this book) cannot critically examine the use of deception in news gathering unless they understand the role of the media within society and the ethical norms that the industry itself has established for sanctioning or condemning such behavior. It would be expedient to offer an opinion that reporters should be held to the same standards as the rest of us, but this statement neither answers the question of "why" nor allows for any reasonable defense of an exception to the general rule.

Second, critical thinkers must be able to identify problems (or in the case of this text, to recognize ethical issues) and to gather, analyze, and synthesize all relevant information relating to those problems. They must also be able to identify all stated or unstated assumptions concerning the problems.

Finally, critical thinking also requires that alternatives be evaluated and that decisions be made. In so doing, the critical thinker must examine the consequences and implications of the alternatives, each of which may have at least some validity. In some respects, this is the most intimidating aspect of critical thinking, because it requires that we make choices—choices that may be subjected to severe criticism from others. However, successful salespeople have learned that the best techniques in the world fail without the ability to close the sale. The same is true of critical thinking. One can analyze (or study) an issue to death, but at some point a decision must be made. The hope is that it will be a well-reasoned decision, based on the most rational analysis of the situation.

In summary, the critical thinking component of moral reasoning involves a three-step process: (1) acquisition of knowledge and an understanding of the context of the ethical dilemma, (2) critical analysis of that knowledge and a consideration of ethical alternatives, and (3) a decision based on the available alternatives.

The moral reasoning model outlined in the next section reflects the notions about critical thinking described earlier and should be used in exploring Part 2. Thus, the integration of this model for ethical decision making with the case study method is a functional vehicle for retreating from an ivory-tower approach to teaching media ethics and for developing critical-thinking abilities that should awaken the powers of reason within even the most reluctant individual.

A MODEL OF MORAL REASONING

As noted earlier, moral reasoning is a systematic process. It involves numerous considerations, all of which can be grouped into three categories: (1) the situation definition; (2) the analysis of the situation, including the application of moral theories; and (3) the decision, or ethical judgment. For the sake of simplicity I will refer to this as the *SAD formula*.[32] There are, of course, other models available, but the SAD formula seems particularly adaptable to the needs of the moral reasoning neophyte.

However, this model can also be a valuable tool in creating a discourse among media professionals. Some news organizations, for example, regularly conduct sessions or hold discussions on ethical problems. The SAD formula could be used to respond to either hypothetical or real ethical issues, with individual reporters and editors working through these problems. A dialogue with professional colleagues and a critique

from management personnel or an ombudsman could follow.

The following explanation of this model is designed with written case studies in mind, although it can be used for oral discussions as well. But written analyses, at least until one becomes comfortable with the moral reasoning process, help attune the mind to logical thinking and sharpen intellectual faculties. Following the discussion of the SAD formula, a sample case study is presented (in abbreviated form) to illustrate this approach to moral reasoning.

The Situation Definition

The situation definition is designed to identify the ethical issue and to list or examine those facts, principles, and values that will be important to the decision-making process. The first step is to describe the facts and to identify the relevant conflicting values and principles implicated in this ethical dilemma. Sometimes the conflicting values and principles will be obvious; at other times their discovery may require some thought on your part. They will obviously vary from case to case, but such things as truth telling, the right to privacy, conflict of interest, the right of the public to receive information, fairness, justice, loyalty, media credibility, harm to others, confidentiality, and economic concerns are representative of the values and principles lurking in the hypothetical cases in this book.

Students of media ethics should also have an appreciation for the role that competition and economic factors play in decision-making in a deadline-oriented environment. These "values" are at the heart of the media enterprise and will be a consideration in most ethical judgments. In the real world such factors often dominate. But experience in moral reasoning, even within the more sanitized classroom situation, can create an appreciation for other values that should be considered in rendering moral judgments. In any event, the facts and competing values and principles should be described in the *situation definition* section so that they can be easily applied to the analysis portion of your written case study.

Second, there should be a clear statement of the ethical question or issue involved. It provides a logical lead-in to the analysis section and can be done only after some understanding of the facts. The question should be specific, not general. For example, an issue statement regarding whether a reporter should go undercover in a Veterans' Administration (VA) hospital to investigate rumors of unsanitary conditions might be written as follows: "Is it ethical for reporters to conceal (or lie about) their identity to gain employment at a VA hospital for the purpose of investigating rumors of unsanitary conditions at the facility?" When dealing with individual cases, this form is preferable to a more general question—for example, "Is it ever permissible for reporters to use deceptive news-gathering techniques?"—because it relates to the specific circumstances and thus provides a more solid foundation for debate. Of course, more general questions are acceptable when debating broader issues of ethical significance, such as "Is society justified in passing laws that limit the distribution of sexually explicit material?"

A statement of the ethical issue would appear to be a simple task. But if you do not fully understand the dilemma, clarity of moral vision will be replaced by confusion and uncertainty, and the reasoning process will become defective. It is imperative that you spend a great deal of time fleshing out all of the relevant considerations for inclusion in the situation definition. The time spent in brainstorming here will diminish the likelihood of faulty reasoning during the analysis phase.

Analysis of the Situation

Analysis is the real heart of the decision-making process under the SAD formula. In this step you will use all of the available information, as well as your imagination, to examine the situation and to evaluate the ethical alternatives.

There is surely no limit to the things that might be included here, but any analysis of a media ethical dilemma should include at least four considerations. First, there should be a *discussion,* pro and con, of the relative weights to be accorded to the various conflicting values and principles. This is a fertile field for imagination, and you should not be afraid to engage in a certain amount of intellectual experimentation, as long as your arguments are reasonable and defensible.

Next comes an examination of *factors external to the case situation itself* that might influence the direction of moral judgment. Or, as another way of putting it, an external factor is one that was there prior to the particular case at hand and is likely to be there after the specifics of this case are resolved. Illustrative of such factors are company policy, legal constraints, and the demographic composition of the local community, which may determine how the citizens will react to decisions made by media practitioners. For example, reporters who electronically eavesdrop on unsuspecting public officials in violation of company policy (and possibly the law) may undermine their claim of moral virtue unless there is an equally persuasive countervailing reason for doing so. Demographic considerations, for example, might lead a TV station manager in a predominantly conservative Catholic community, for fear of protests, to preempt a controversial network movie that probes too deeply into sexual misconduct by members of the Catholic clergy.

One external factor that is sometimes valuable in rendering moral judgments is an appeal to precedent: "What do we normally do under similar circumstances?" For example, if a newspaper usually reports all misdemeanor violations, even those of public figures, on an inside page, it must justify deviating from that practice in a particular circumstance. Otherwise, it will be suspected of ulterior motives or perhaps even malicious intent.

Third, you should examine the various individuals and groups likely to be affected by your ethical judgments. In Chapter 2 we explored the moral duties and the loyalties owed to several parties: individual conscience, objects of moral judgment, financial supporters, the institution, professional colleagues, and the various segments of society. These parties should be weighed, or evaluated, in terms of their relative importance and impact on the ethical issue under consideration. Of course, some may not figure in the moral equation at all in some situations. Financial supporters (advertisers, stockholders, subscribers), for example, are usually concerned with issues that affect their own well-being, the financial viability of the institution, or, in some cases, issues in which they have a vested interest.

In Chapter 1 we noted the role that emotions play in attitudes about ethical behavior. With all of this talk about reason in moral decision making, does that mean that our emotional side has no role to play? Not at all. In fact, emotions often do, and should, influence the evaluation of our duties or loyalties to others. A reporter's sympathy (or perhaps empathy) for a victim of tragedy, even when the reporter feels obliged to intrude into the victim's privacy, is an emotional response but is also certainly a rational one. It should be factored into the decision-making equation, because actions taken with the interests of others in mind (rather than self-interests) are a product of both our intellectual and our emotional components.

Finally, the ethical theories discussed earlier should be applied to the moral dilemma. Examine the issue from the perspective of consequences (teleology), duty-based ethics (deontology), and Aristotle's golden mean. In those cases in which a particular approach might not be applicable—for example, where there does not appear to be a middle ground—you should also note this in the analysis. Each of these theories should be evaluated with the idea of rendering what, in your opinion, is the most satisfactory ethical judgment.

Decision

In the final section you must make your decision and *defend* your recommendation. Your discussion should include an appeal to one or more of the moral theories outlined earlier. Keep in mind that a deontologist and teleologist might arrive at the same decision, but they do so for different reasons. For example, if you apply deontological ethics to a case involving the use of undercover reporting, you would categorically oppose deception as an acceptable news-gathering device. Applying teleological ethics, you would weigh the harms and benefits and might still conclude that the use of deception in the case under consideration is more harmful than beneficial. But in this case you are focusing on the consequences rather than on the universal rule that says lying (that is, deception) is always wrong. In your decision-making section of some cases, you might also wish to point out that a particular course of action could never be justified under any of the ethical theories described in this text.

Although your defense may be somewhat redundant of some of the points outlined previously, it will serve to reinforce your arguments and allow you to justify them with greater moral certainty. In summary, the SAD formula for moral reasoning can be diagrammed as shown in Figure 3.1.

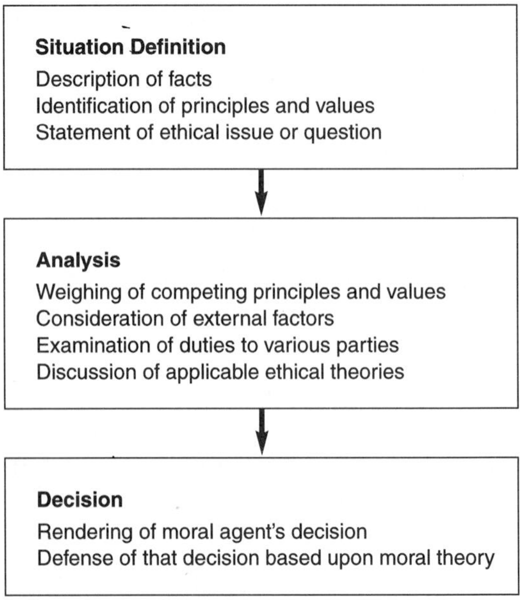

Situation Definition
Description of facts
Identification of principles and values
Statement of ethical issue or question

Analysis
Weighing of competing principles and values
Consideration of external factors
Examination of duties to various parties
Discussion of applicable ethical theories

Decision
Rendering of moral agent's decision
Defense of that decision based upon moral theory

Figure 3.1   The Moral Reasoning Process

A SAMPLE CASE STUDY

The following sample case is based on actual circumstances.[33] It concerns a decision by editors at two newspapers to break promises of confidentiality made to a news source by their reporters. The discussion that follows is not intended to exhaust all possibilities for resolving the issue; you are encouraged to add your own perspectives. For example, one issue that could be considered in this case is whether the reporters should have made the promises in the first place. However, because our discussion focuses on the conduct of the editors as the moral agents, any consideration of whether the promises should have been made is omitted. Of course, in this case we are playing the role of neutral observer (and critic), whereas in the hypothetical cases in Part 2 you are asked to assume the role of the moral agent.

Situation Definition

Six days before the Minnesota gubernatorial election Dan Cohen, an employee of an advertising agency working for Republican candidate Wheelock Whitney, approached reporters from four news organizations, including the *Minneapolis Star Tribune* and the *St. Paul Pioneer Press,* and offered to provide documents relating to an opposition candidate for lieutenant governor in the upcoming election. Cohen had been encouraged by a group of Republican supporters to release this information. In exchange for a promise that he not be identified as the source of the documents, Cohen revealed to the reporters that Marlene Johnson, the Democratic-Farmer-Labor candidate for lieutenant governor, had been convicted of shoplifting twelve years earlier, a conviction that was later vacated.

After discussion and debate, the editorial staffs of the two papers independently decided to publish Cohen's name as part of their stories concerning Johnson. The Minneapolis paper made this decision after its reporter had contacted Cohen to ask whether he would release the paper from its promise of confidentiality.

Cohen refused. In their stories, both papers identified Cohen as the source of the court records, reported his connection to the Whitney campaign, and included denials by Whitney campaign officials of any role in the matter. The same day the stories were published Cohen was fired. The editors justified their decision on the grounds that (1) Cohen's actions amounted to nothing more than a political dirty trick, and thus his motives were suspect; (2) Cohen's name was essential to the credibility of the story; and (3) reporters should not make promises of confidentiality without authorization from their superiors.[34]

Cohen sued the papers for breach of contract and won a jury award of damages. The U.S. Supreme Court eventually ruled 5–4 that such promises of confidentiality are legally enforceable. Although Cohen won his lawsuit, the ethical issues surrounding the newspapers' decision to break the promise of confidentiality and publish his name remain.

The moral agents in this case are the editors of the two papers, because they are the ones who breached the promise of confidentiality. (There is also an ethical question on whether the reporters should have promised confidentiality in the first place, but that isn't an issue here because this case focuses on the editors' conduct.) In this case the conflicting values and principles are not too difficult to identify. On the one hand, there is the right of a source to expect a news organization to honor a promise of confidentiality. And closely connected to this expectation is the value of reporter autonomy—that is, a news organization's obligation to honor promises made by its reporters. The value of loyalty is also implicated, because a newspaper's refusal to honor commitments made by its reporters could create morale problems and discord within the newsroom. Because arguably the public has a "need to know" anything about political candidates that might affect their fitness for office, the use of anonymous sources can sometimes be justified to obtain such information. On the other hand, the use of anonymous sources can erode the credibility of a news organization. Thus, the "need to know" principle might also be used to justify publication of Cohen's name so that readers can consider the source's motivation in releasing this information.

Moreover, the editors felt that Cohen's motivation was newsworthy; they thus believed that it provided journalistic *balance* (or symmetry) to the potentially damaging information concerning the Democratic candidate.

The harm principle is also implicated in this case. At a minimum the parties who might be harmed through a breach of confidentiality are Cohen, Cohen's employers, and the credibility of the reporters themselves and perhaps their paper. On the other hand, if the promise is kept, Johnson could be injured in her electoral bid, although it isn't clear what effect such a specious charge might have on her campaign.

Thus, the ethical issues are as follows: (1) Were the editors ethically justified in breaching the promises of confidentiality made by their reporters? (2) Are such promises made by reporters, without authorization from management, morally binding on their news organizations?

Analysis

Evaluation of Values and Principles.   One could argue that the reporters should never have made the promise in the first place, but the fact is that they have done so and now the editors (the moral agents) must decide whether to honor that promise. Because breaking promises should never be taken lightly, any breach of a promise must be based on some other overriding principle. Can the editors absolve themselves of responsibility simply by refusing to honor the promises made by other staff members? Probably not, because the average news source is unlikely to distinguish reporters from the organizations for whom they work. If they enter into an agreement with a reporter from the *New York Times,* for example, they assume that the newspaper will honor that agreement.

Even if a paper's policy requires an editor's approval before any such agreement is made—and the reporter violates that policy—that is a management problem for the paper and should not have to be a concern for the source.

Thus, if the editors in this case are justified in breaching confidentiality, their decision must be based on some more compelling principle. Was the information provided by the source of such overriding public interest that a promise of confidentiality was warranted? In this case, the public's "need to know" that Johnson was convicted of shoplifting twelve years ago, a charge that was later vacated, is questionable. In fact, the editors could have refused to publish the story, thus avoiding the ethically controversial decision to breach the promise of confidentiality. But in so doing they might also be accused of suppressing information.

Nevertheless, the editors apparently felt the story was newsworthy because of Cohen's motivation in damaging the Democratic ticket just prior to the election. Cohen is obviously a key figure in this campaign, and his involvement in "dirty tricks" (in the editors' view) is newsworthy, which in turn justifies publishing the information concerning Johnson's past. And because of Cohen's tactics and out of fairness to Johnson, the editors have concluded that the source's name must be included. They are appealing, in other words, to the fundamental journalistic principle of balanced coverage of newsworthy events. Although the paper might risk some loss of credibility in not standing behind their reporters and perhaps even an erosion of loyalty among their staff, the editors might argue that the story itself lacks credibility without the source's name. In addition, the editors might include some explanation to the readers concerning the promise of confidentiality and the reasons that they decided not to honor this pledge.

Regardless of the editors' decision, harm will accrue to some of the parties involved. If Cohen's name is included in the story, he will probably be fired. In addition, the credibility of the reporters and the paper might suffer. Johnson could be harmed, perhaps needlessly, by the release of this information, although it isn't clear whether the electorate will hold her past against her, especially because her record for shoplifting was expunged. But the editors might argue that including Cohen's name and letting the readers evaluate his motivation for themselves might work to Johnson's advantage, thus negating any potential harm to her from the story.

External Factors.   One important factor external to the facts of this case might be the absence of any clear-cut policy on source confidentiality. (This is considered an external factor because it is a situation that apparently existed prior to this case and that will remain after this issue is resolved, unless the newspaper moves to implement a written policy on the matter.) The reporters apparently did not feel that they needed to seek management approval, and this factor could be cited in favor of reporter autonomy. One might also point to society's attitude toward political dirty tricks as an external factor in favor of including Cohen's name in the story.

Moral Duties (Loyalties) Owed.   As noted in Chapter 2, media practitioners must take into account the interests of six *stakeholders*—parties to whom they owe an ethical duty—before rendering an ethical judgment: the individual conscience, the objects of moral judgment, financial supporters, their institution, their professional colleagues, and society at large. Thus, the editors in this case owed a duty, first, to their *consciences* to do what is morally right. Unfortunately, professional obligations and pressures sometimes lead us away from what we would consider to be the ethically virtuous course of action under other circumstances. In this case the editors' consciences should have spoken to them clearly on the matter of breaking promises. However, they might also have rationalized their decision on the grounds that Cohen was acting from impure motives. But again, if this were a concern, they could have chosen to suppress the story. At this point, however, competitive pressures could become a factor. If the story is suppressed, other news organizations might run the story, thus causing some journalistic embarrassment to the Minneapolis and St. Paul papers.

The moral agents in this case (the editors) also owe a duty to those who are most likely to be directly affected by this decision. These parties are identified in the SAD formula as the *objects* of the ethical judgment. In this case Cohen, Johnson, and the reporters are the major objects. The reporters promised Cohen anonymity, and he acted on that promise in good faith. Regardless of Cohen's motives, which were known at the time the promises were made, the editors owed a duty to the source to keep this promise and to minimize harm. On the other hand, a duty is also owed to Democratic candidate Johnson, the target of the information provided by Cohen. Although this information had the potential for harming Johnson, the editors apparently believed that out of fairness Cohen's name should be included. In this way readers could decide for themselves, based on the source's questionable motives, what relevance to accord this information in terms of the campaign. In this way the harm to Johnson might be minimized. The reporters are also *objects* in this case because their editors' failure to support them could harm their professional credibility. It has certainly eroded their relationship with the management staffs of their respective newspapers. One could argue that, in the absence of any policy requiring management approval of promises of confidentiality, the editors were duty-bound to support their reporters.

Media practitioners must also be loyal to their *financial supporters*—those who pay the bills. In the case of a newspaper the supporters are primarily advertisers, although some revenues are also derived from subscribers. Advertisers rely on the media to help sell their products. Newspapers have only their credibility to sell, and a loss of credibility could result in an erosion of circulation and reader support. It is unlikely that, regardless of the editors' decision in this case, merchants would withdraw their advertising, unless perhaps they were staunch supporters of one candidate or the other. But over time an erosion of credibility could hurt the newspaper's bottom line.

The editors also owed a duty to their *institution*. Whatever their decision, they must take into account how it will reflect on their respective newspapers. Because promises of confidentiality have become a mainstay of investigative reporting, any breach of such a promise will reflect unfavorably on the institution, unless this decision is based on some overriding and more important principle.

In most ethical dilemmas involving professionals, there is always the nagging question of whether moral agents have complied with the standards of their profession. Thus, they must be loyal to their *colleagues*. In this case the editors clearly violated acceptable practice, although the breaking of promises to sources is not unheard of. Each such ethical lapse tends to erode the credibility of the profession. Of course, editors must have the flexibility to render judgments contrary to acceptable practice for compelling reasons. How would most editors have responded in this situation? The question is whether the reasons given for breaking the promise were compelling enough to satisfy most journalists who have always considered anonymous news sources to be an essential ingredient in the news-gathering process.

Finally, a duty is owed to *society*. Some journalists apparently believe that their unique roles in society entitle them to special moral exemptions. But all media practitioners are bound by the same fundamental principles as the rest of us, and any deviation must be justified (as in the case of any other societal member) by some overriding principle. In this case, the reporters made a promise, and any breach of that promise, without some compelling reason, is a violation of cultural norms. On the other hand, the editors could argue that the reporters had no right to make such a promise and that their obligation lies in the direction of journalistic fairness and balance, which necessitated the inclusion of Cohen's name.

Moral Theories.   A person rendering a moral judgment has no benefit of hindsight. A Kantian (deontologist) evaluating this case would follow a rule that can be universally applied. The very fabric of society is predicated, in part, on faith in the promises of others. Thus, "never break a promise" becomes a maxim that should be applied universally and that includes promises of confidentiality made by reporters to news sources. And in this case, the editors could not absolve themselves of responsibility simply by refusing to honor promises made by their reporters. The fact is that Cohen believed that he was dealing in good faith with reporters who came to the bargaining table with their employers' full authority. A deontologist would argue strenuously that the editors had a moral obligation to honor the promise and that perhaps they should use this case as a catalyst for devising a company policy requiring reporters to obtain management approval before entering into a moral contract (and perhaps a legal one as well) with a news source.

This case can also be viewed from the perspective of anticipated consequences (teleology)—that is, the relative benefits and harms for the individuals or groups affected by this decision. If the source's name is included in the story, the greatest harm, of course, will accrue to Dan Cohen. He will probably lose his job. On the other hand, his motives are suspect. His willingness to release such questionably relevant information so close to the election is nothing more than a dirty campaign trick. Therefore, perhaps he deserves the consequences of his ethically dubious behavior.

The Democratic candidate, Marlene Johnson, could be hurt by the revelations, although the electorate may attach little importance to a twelve-year-old conviction on a minor charge that was overturned anyway. And whether Cohen's name is included in the story probably won't alter this equation substantially.

Morale in the newsroom—and hence employee loyalty to the paper—could suffer as a result of the failure of the editors to support their reporters. Perhaps the reporters used poor judgment in making the promises in the first place. But considering the questionable newsworthiness of the information, perhaps the story should have been killed. One could argue that the breaking of a promise—which is a serious matter—could not, in this case, be justified just for the sake of journalistic balance when the story itself is of questionable validity in the overall scheme of the campaign.

Is any real benefit to be derived from this breach of confidentiality that would outweigh the harms described here? One could argue that the inclusion of Cohen's name might serve to inform the public about the character of those who are running the Republican campaign. And it still isn't clear whether this character flaw is confined to Cohen or reflects on the ethical stature of his employer. Therefore, the various harms that will occur from this breach of confidentiality appear to outweigh any modest benefit that might result.

Decision

The foregoing analysis strongly opposes the editors' breach of confidentiality. Breaking a promise is a serious matter. Credibility is a mainstay of the journalistic enterprise, and the failure of the editors to support their reporters, even if the promises were ill advised, erodes the credibility of both the reporters and the newspapers. Promise keeping is a fundamental societal value. And in this case a great deal of harm can occur without any comparable benefit. In addition, an evaluation of the duties owed to the various parties in this ethical dilemma point, on balance, in the direction of keeping the promise. The sanctity of promises and credibility seem to permeate the discussion of the loyalties to the six parties identified here; and these were more important, in this case, than the editors' concern for journalistic balance. Thus, the editors' decision to break their reporters' promises cannot be supported under either a deontological or teleological perspective.

SUMMARY

Moral reasoning is a systematic approach to making ethical decisions, relying primarily on logical argument and persuasion. Moral judgments should be based on sound ethical theories and should be defensible through a reasoned analysis of the situation. The process of moral reasoning requires knowledge and skills in three areas: (1) the moral context, (2) the philosophical foundations of moral theory, and (3) critical thinking.

First, the moral agent must understand the context within which the dilemma has arisen. This understanding includes some comprehension of the issue, the facts of the situation, the values and principles inherent in the case, and the social and cultural environment within which the media operate.

Second, moral theory must be brought to bear on the problem. The writings of the ancient Greeks—Socrates, Plato, and Aristotle—and those of John Stuart Mill and Immanuel Kant provide the philosophical foundations for the moral theories described in this chapter. These theories are of three types: *teleological*, based on the consequences of the moral agent's actions; *deontological*, in which moral duties and the actors' motives are more important than the consequences of their actions; and *virtue*, focusing on character rather than moral behavior in specific situations. For the purpose of the moral reasoning model outlined in this book, Aristotle's golden mean, which seeks a solution between the extremes in a given situation, has been selected as a practical example of a virtue theory.

Third, critical thinking is essential to moral reasoning. Success in critical thinking requires some knowledge of the subject, practice in analyzing and reasoning, and the willingness to make decisions.

Although there are many approaches to moral reasoning, the model employed in this book is the *SAD formula*, consisting of the situation definition, the analysis, and the decision. The situation definition is a description of the facts, identification of the principles and values inherent in the case, and a clear statement of the ethical issue under review. The analysis section is really the heart of the moral reasoning process. In this tier of the SAD model, the moral agent weighs the competing principles and values, considers the impact of factors external to the case facts themselves, examines the moral duties owed to various parties, and discusses the application of various ethical theories. The final step consists of rendering the moral decision. Here the moral agent makes a judgment and defends it.

Notes

1. For a discussion on the differences between morality and other forms of human activity, see Joan C. Callahan (ed.), *Ethical Issues in Professional Life* (New York: Oxford University Press, 1988), pp. 10–14.

2. Anders Wedberg, *A History of Philosophy, vol. 1: Antiquity and the Middle Ages* (Oxford: Clarendon, 1982), p. 139.

3. For other examples of virtuous behavior, see W. T. Jones, *The Classical Mind* (New York: Harcourt, Brace, 1969), p. 268.

4. "Moral Virtue," in Tom L. Beauchamp, *Philosophical Ethics: An Introduction to Moral Philosophy* (New York: McGraw-Hill, 1982), p. 161. This writing is an excerpt from Aristotle's *Nichomachean Ethics,* Book 2, Chapters 1, 2, 4, 6, 7, and 9.

5. See Rushworth M. Kidder, *How Good People Make Tough Choices* (New York: William Morrow, 1995), p. 25.

6. Immanuel Kant, "The Good Will and the Categorical Imperative," in Beauchamp, *Philosophical Ethics,* p. 120. This is an excerpt from Kant's *Foundations of the Metaphysics of Morals,* trans. Lewis White Beck (Indianapolis, IN: Bobbs-Merrill, 1959), pp. 9–10, 16–19, 24–25, 28.

7. Beauchamp, *Philosophical Ethics,* pp. 123–124.

8. Callahan, *Ethical Issues,* p. 20.

9. Clifford G. Christians, Kim B. Rotzoll, Mark Fackler, and Kathy Brittain McKee, *Media Ethics: Cases and Moral Reasoning,* 6th ed. (New York: Longman, 2001), p. 16.

10. Conrad C. Fink, *Media Ethics: In the Newsroom and Beyond* (New York: McGraw-Hill, 1988), pp. 53–54.

11. See Robert C. Solomon and Clancy W. Martin, *Morality and the Good Life: An Introduction to Ethics Through Classical Studies,* 4th ed. (Boston: McGraw-Hill, 2004), pp. 20–21.

12. See John Rawls, *A Theory of Justice,* rev. ed. (Cambridge, MA: The Belknap Press of Harvard University Press, 1999), pp. 118–123.

13. For a discussion of Rawls's theory, see James A. Jaska and Michael S. Pritchard, *Communication Ethics: Methods of Analysis,* 2d ed. (Belmont, CA: Wadsworth, 1994), pp. 111–112; Norman E. Bowie, *Making Ethical Decisions* (New York: McGraw-Hill, 1985), pp. 268–269.

14. Peter Singer (ed.), *A Companion to Ethics* (Malden, MA: Blackwell, 1991), p. xvi.

15. E.g., see Jean Grimshaw, "The Idea of a Female Ethic," in ibid., pp. 491–499.

16. Solomon and Martin, *Morality and the Good Life,* p. 23.

17. "Feminist Ethics," *Stanford Encyclopedia of Ethics,* online at http://plato.stanford.edu/entries/feminism-ethics.

18. Solomon and Martin, *Morality and the Good Life,* pp. 23–25.

19. Deni Elliott, "All Is Not Relative: Essential Shared Values and the Press," *Journal of Mass Media Ethics* 3, no. 1 (1988): 28. See also William Frankena, *Ethics* (Upper Saddle River, NJ: Prentice-Hall, 1973), p. 109.

20. See Joseph Fletcher, *Situation Ethics: The New Morality* (Philadelphia: Westminster, 1966). For a discussion of various views of situation ethics, see Richard L. Johannesen, *Ethics in Human Communication,* 3d ed. (Prospect Heights, IL: Waveland, 1990), pp. 79–88.

21. Quoted in Johannesen, *Ethics in Human Communication,* p. 79. See Bert E. Bradley, *Fundamentals of Speech Communication: The Credibility of Ideas,* 3d ed. (Dubuque, IA: Brown, 1981), pp. 27–29.

22. John C. Merrill, *The Imperative of Freedom: A Philosophy of Journalistic Autonomy,* 2d ed. (New York: Freedom House, 1990), p. 169.

23. Ibid., pp. 167–170; Baruch Brody, *Ethics and Its Applications* (New York: Harcourt, Brace, 1983), pp. 9–35.

24. See Brody, *Ethics and Its Applications,* p. 31.

25. Although Kant often condemned consequential reasoning, most scholars seem to agree that even he did not believe that an action could be universalized without universalizing its consequences. Thus, the consequences of an action sometimes cannot be separated from the action itself. For example, the reason that the duty to tell the truth is a fundamental societal value is that truth telling has general positive consequences for society. See Beauchamp, *Philosophical Ethics,* p. 139.

26. Jaksa and Pritchard, *Communication Ethics.*

27. For a discussion of this idea, see Beauchamp, *Philosophical Ethics,* pp. 163–166.

28. Christians, Rotzoll, Fackler, and McKee, *Media Ethics,* p. 13.

29. 18 U.S.C.A. § 1464.

30. *FCC v. Pacifica Foundation,* 438 U.S. 726 (1978).

31. For more discussion of critical thinking, see Robert E. Young (ed.), *New Directions for Teaching and Learning: Fostering Critical Thinking* (San Francisco: Jossey-Bass, 1980).

32. This model is based, in part, on ideas advanced by Ralph B. Potter in "The Logic of Moral Argument," in Paul Deats (ed.), *Toward a Discipline of Social Ethics* (Boston: Boston University Press, 1972), pp. 93–114.

33. For example, see *Cohen v. Cowles Media,* 18 Med. L. Rptr. 2273, 2274 (1991). For different ethical perspectives on this case, see "Confidentiality and Promise Keeping," *Journal of Mass Media Ethics* 6, no. 4 (1991): 245–256; Theodore L. Glasser, "When Is a Promise Not a Promise?" in Philip Patterson and Lee Wilkins, *Media Ethics: Issues and Cases,* 2d ed. (Dubuque, IA: WCB Brown & Benchmark, 1994), pp. 104–106; Jay Black, Bob Steele, and Ralph Barney, *Doing Ethics in Journalism: A Handbook with Case Studies* (Greencastle, IN: Society of Professional Journalists, 1993), pp. 190–191.

34. On appeal, the Minnesota Supreme Court changed the legal basis for the lawsuit from breach of contract to promissory estoppel (breach of promise), which was more suited to the facts of the case.

CASES IN MEDIA COMMUNICATIONS

The chapters in Part 2 examine some of the most important ethical issues confronting media practitioners. Each chapter begins with some background and an overview of the issue. Where appropriate, examples are provided to illustrate a point, but I make no attempt to discuss fully every possible ethical dilemma that might arise in connection with the issue. The goal of this book is to help you become a critical thinker, regardless of the specific moral dilemma that might confront you.

Each chapter also includes several hypothetical cases designed to challenge your moral imagination and allow you to apply the moral reasoning model outlined in Chapter 3. The cases are followed by some suggestions on how to deal with the issues, but you are expected to make a serious effort to reason out the solutions and to defend your decisions based on the ethical approaches suggested in Chapter 3.

4

Truth and Honesty
in Media Communications

A WORLD OF LIMITED TRUTH

Lying, deception, and dishonesty are so pervasive in contemporary society, it seems, that some ethicists must feel like moral dinosaurs in their continued defense of truth as a fundamental value. Take, for example, this recent disturbing headline: *E-mail urges lying for blood drive.* In April 2004 the press reported that "members of the Gamma Phi Beta sorority at Missouri were urged to lie about their health to qualify as donors in a competitive blood drive" at the university. In her e-mail to sorority members, the chapter's blood donation coordinator threatened punishment for those members refusing to donate blood. They were instructed to lie about recent tattoos and piercings and colds—anything that might disqualify them as donors.[1] Far from being a harmless sorority prank, this kind of dishonesty could have posed a threat to the blood supply.

Despite such continuing anecdotal evidence of a rather cavalier attitude toward the truth, we are placing ourselves at great risk if we abandon truth as a fundamental cultural norm. Truth breeds trust—a precious and essential commodity within a democratic system—and trust is an energizing force of social intercourse and civil society. Unfortunately, the media themselves sometimes operate within a world of limited

truth and thus must bear some responsibility for the loss of reverence for truth and honesty. Consider the widely publicized case of Stephen Glass. By the time he was 25, Glass was a rising star in Washington journalism and an associate editor of the *New Republic.* His colorful details about such fascinating topics as the small religious sect that worshipped George Bush and the Las Vegas casino that took bets on whether the next space shuttle would explode captivated his readers and earned him a reputation for journalistic enterprise and creativity. Unfortunately, his stories did not originate with real life but from Glass's vivid imagination. After a month-long investigation, the *New Republic* editors confirmed that 27 of the 41 pieces Glass had written for the magazine were full of fabrications,[2] thereby "destroying a portion of the always-fragile bond of trust journalists try to form with their readers."[3]

Glass's fall from journalistic grace was soon followed by the tragedy of Jayson Blair, described briefly in the opening to Chapter 1, in which the 27-year-old *New York Times* prodigy was accused of fabricating or plagiarizing material in over half his stories, thereby precipitating an ethics scandal of staggering proportions and a crisis of confidence in American journalism.[4]

Unfortunately, these recent blows to the credibility of journalism may be symptomatic of an escalating assault on the values of truth and honesty in both the media professions and society at large. For example, when *Primary Colors,* a best-selling novel that was eventually made into a movie by the same name, was published in early 1996, it set off a wave of speculation within the journalistic community. The book, a thinly disguised portrait of the Clinton campaign and the national press corps, carried only the pseudonym "Anonymous," a fascinating attempt at literary camouflage that was rivaled only by the plot's political intrigue. After months of denials to his professional colleagues, including those at CBS News, the *Washington Post,* and the *New York Times, Newsweek* columnist Joe Klein confessed his authorship of *Primary Colors* but offered no apologies for lying to friends and colleagues. The plot thickened when a *Newsweek* editor, Maynard Parker, acknowledged that he was aware of Klein's involvement in the project but declined to inform the magazine's staff despite the fact that *Newsweek* had been among those that had joined in the speculation.[5]

In 1996, in conjunction with the baseball All-Star Game in Philadelphia, the tabloid *Philadelphia Weekly* published a 4,000-word cover story on the "recently discovered love letters between Jimmie Foxx, one of Philadelphia's all-time great ballplayers, and starlet Judy Holliday." Writer Tom McGrath's highly detailed exposé included a personal account of the relationship that began in April 1945 and ended in late September when the movie star dumped Foxx. The *Weekly* later admitted that the story was a hoax, a rather clinical way of semantically reducing this piece of journalistic deception to nothing worse than a practical joke. Editor Tim Whitaker offered no apologies for this shocking admission, although he promised in his column not to do it again.[6]

The reactions to such desecrations of the truth have often been swift and unforgiving from both journalists and media critics. For example, following the Jimmie Foxx hoax, a columnist for the *Philadelphia Daily News* wrote:

"The most shocking part of this mess is that Whitaker offers no apologies. Since he says he's done nothing wrong, he's free to fake another story."[7] Similarly, CBS News, which featured Joe Klein as a news consultant and commentator on its weekend news program, castigated the columnist for not being more forthcoming with them.[8] Suzanne Braun Levine, editor of the *Columbia Journalism Review,* was unforgiving in her assessment: "Journalists think of themselves as a fraternity," she said, "and that journalists are straight with each other even if nobody is straight with them. They are extremely sensitive to being criticized or being duped. And what could be worse than being duped by one of your own?"[9]

Reactions such as these from within and outside the media are refreshing in that they serve as evidence that such deceptions are not necessarily the industry standard. And a continuation of this moral guardianship may serve to prevent such ethical lapses from becoming pathological. This is the optimistic view. A more bleak appraisal is that episodes such as these represent an increasingly casual attitude toward truth as an ethical imperative. Truth, in this view, has not fared well in the moral pecking order. This attitude is captured in a rather startling assessment several years ago by a public relations practitioner for one of the ten largest U.S. corporations: "Does the word 'lie' actually mean anything anymore? In one sense, everyone lies, but in another sense, no one does, because no one knows what's true—it's whatever makes you look good."[10] The reality probably lies somewhere between the optimistic and pessimistic views.

Some authors of nonfiction works attempt to justify their deceptions or outright fabrication of facts by an appeal to a "higher truth." In this view, it matters little whether the specific facts underlying the story are true. Instead, they are merely surrogates for the author's view of political reality. This form of ethical relativism is exemplified by the controversy that arose in 1999 over the book *I, Rogoberta Menchu,* a captivating chronicle of the political violence that engulfed Guatemala from 1979 to 1983. Written by Nobel Peace Prize winner Rogoberta Menchu, the book purported to be based upon the author's personal experience with the alleged oppression of Mayan Indian peasants by Guatemalan landowners and the struggles between the author's family and the landowners. However, part of Menchu's story began to unravel when anthropologist David Stoll published a book, based upon exhaustive research and interviews, in which he claimed that Menchu described experiences she never had and consistently altered facts and stories.[11]

Unfortunately, *I, Rogoberta Menchu* is not the only award-winning author recently to stand accused of fabrication. Benjamin Wilomirski won the National Jewish Book Award for *Fragments,* his celebrated memoir of the Holocaust. However, as it turned out, the author's real name was Bruno Doesseker, and he was the son of a Protestant mother who never witnessed the Holocaust.[12]

The evidence increasingly suggests that, as a society, we view the world from a perspective of greater moral relativism. Even those of us who do not consciously condone lying are often unwilling to acknowledge publicly a bright line between truth and falsehood. In addition, we are less inclined to be judgmental of those who lie. "It's not my problem" is a common refrain. Consider, for example, the results of a student role-playing exercise in a class on "The Presidency and the Press" at the University of Southern California. The topic involved the sexual relationship between President Bill Clinton and former White House intern Monica Lewinsky. The instructor, columnist Richard Reeves, divided the class into two groups, half designated as advisers to President Clinton and half as Washington reporters. The students each wrote memos to their superiors about how to handle the Lewinsky affair. Although there were differences between the two groups, both agreed that it did not matter whether the information they were giving out or writing down was true. The

Clinton advisers said it did not matter whether their boss was telling the truth. *It wasn't their problem!* The student reporters said it did not matter whether "sources" were telling the truth. Nor did it matter that reports in other media were accurate. *It wasn't their problem!* Neither group assumed any responsibility for helping to spread disinformation, even if it turned out later that their information was false. They could distance themselves from their involvement in this episode with clear consciences. Their instructor, in a follow-up column, described the lesson of the class as "[l]iving in a world of limited truth."[13]

TRUTH AS A FUNDAMENTAL VALUE

Are lying and deception ever justified? If you put this question to your friends, you would probably receive several different responses. Some would answer with an unqualified "Never!" Others would say that it depends on the circumstances. Still others would try to evade the question directly by cautiously noting that the answer depends on the definition of the word *lie*. These responses, as simplistic as they are, represent the wide range of answers provided by moral philosophers in their tireless efforts to answer this question.

At the outset it should be acknowledged that lying and deception are related but are not necessarily the same thing. For the purposes of this chapter, *deception* means "the communication of messages intended to mislead others, to make them believe what we ourselves do not believe."[14] Deception may result not only from words but also from behavior, gestures, or even silence. Thus, under some circumstances the withholding of information from the public might be considered a deceptive act.

Lying is really a subcategory of deception and involves the communication of false information that the communicator knows or believes to be false. Although media practitioners have been known to deliberately transmit false information, many of the contemporary ethical problems involving the ethics of truth telling fall under the broad category of deception.

The commitment to truth is perhaps the most ancient and revered ethical principle of human civilization. Despite our constant temptation to lie and use deception in our self-interest, the idea of truth as a positive value is well entrenched in moral and legal philosophy. Some of the earliest condemnations of lying were contained in judicial laws against false witnesses and perjury, such as the ancient Code of Hammurabi, which stated unequivocally, "If a citizen appears as a false witness in court . . . , he shall be put to death."[15] We find the Judeo-Christian expression of this ideal in the Ninth Commandment's dictum "Thou shalt not bear false witness against thy neighbor."

On a more secular level both ancient and modern philosophers have been preoccupied with the role of truth in human affairs. Of course, Socrates was eventually sentenced to death for his critical inquiry, thus becoming possibly the first martyr to free speech.[16] Kant, as noted in Chapter 3, felt that the truth was a universal value that should be brought to bear in all circumstances, regardless of the consequences. John Milton, in his *Areopagitica*, published in 1644, made a compelling argument for freedom of thought when he depicted truth and falsehood as combatants in the marketplace of ideas. The truth, Milton felt, would always win in a fair fight. More than two hundred years later John Stuart Mill was still promoting this idea in arguing for people's right to express opinions free from government censorship: "If the opinion is right, they are deprived of the opportunity of exchanging error for truth; if wrong, they lose, what is almost as great a benefit, the clearer perception and livelier impression of truth, produced by its collision with error."[17] Of course, Milton and Mill were perhaps more interested in the *intellectual* meaning of truth than its application to moral philosophy.

But if the truth is so sacred, why is honesty so often the first thing to be compromised when it is in our self-interest to do so? The answer may lie, in part, in that the tendency toward dishonesty is as much a part of human nature and our societal norms as telling the truth. In fact, the art of deception enjoys a history at least as ancient (if not as honorable) as the commitment to truth. Deception was linked irrevocably with the idea of original sin when the serpent deceived Eve, who in turn persuaded Adam to eat the forbidden fruit of the Tree of Knowledge. This propensity for lying was passed on to Adam and Eve's offspring, as evidenced by Cain's response when the Lord questioned him on his slain brother's whereabouts: "I know not. . . . Am I my brother's keeper?" And still later in the Old Testament, Jacob's children, in a fit of jealousy directed against their brother Joseph, deceived their father by telling him that Joseph had been ravaged by a wild beast, when in fact they had sold him into bondage.[18]

As we saw earlier, the ancient philosophers may have been committed to the ideals of truth, but even Plato questioned whether the truth was always beneficial. When confronted with the proposition of whether one should lie to save someone from a murderer, Plato said yes. And when the truth is unknown, we can even make falsehood appear to be truth and thus turn it to our advantage.[19] This advice, of course, blurs the distinction between fact and fiction and raises contemporary ethical questions concerning such issues as the use of composite characters in news stories and the use of the docudrama—the dramatic blending of fact and fiction—as a credible TV format for communicating historical events.

Our mythology, folklore, and literature are replete with dramatic examples of deception and lying as legitimate means of fulfilling one's self-interest. As consumers of fictional drama we are generally impressed with the cunning and cleverness of acts of deceit of some of our favorite characters. In fact, it is safe to say that deceit, rather than truth, is featured more prominently in literature to reflect the human condition.

Thus, those who are prone to deception have an impressive array of witnesses in their corner. Moreover, many contemporary philosophers, unlike their ancient predecessors, have virtually ignored the importance of truth in human intercourse. We are living, it seems, in an age of relativism, when accusations of moral misconduct are met with the rather cavalier retort "Everything's relative." The problem is not that the relativists are entirely wrong; sometimes deception may be justified. But if we are to remain moral beings, both in our personal and professional lives, we should be prepared to defend our deviations from the path of truth based on some firm moral foundation. *Telling the truth never needs any moral justification; lying and deception do.*[20]

THE IMPORTANCE OF TRUTH

Some ethicists are uncompromising in their defense of truth as a fundamental value and adhere to the Kantian view that lying is inherently wrong. Others are more forgiving but still insist on a heavy burden of proof to justify any lie. Ethicist Sissela Bok, for example, adheres to what she refers to as the *principle of veracity,* which does not condemn every lie but requires that moral agents prove their lies are necessary as a last resort. And even then, alternatives to lying must be explored and chosen if available.[21] Nevertheless, because so many of the contemporary writings on moral philosophy have failed to establish the continuing importance of truth as an essential ingredient in our value systems, it would be instructive to do so here. There are several reasons that civilized society should embrace the commitment to truth as a fundamental principle.

First, a lack of integrity in human communications *undermines the autonomy of the individual.* As rational beings we depend on truthful and accurate information to make informed

judgments about a whole host of activities, including the election of public officials, what products to buy, what TV programs to watch, and even the selection of friends and professional colleagues. Consider, for example, the potential consequences of a phony film critic scam perpetrated by two Sony Pictures executives in 2001. They had fabricated a film critic named David Manning, who gave rave reviews to Sony-distributed films *Hollow Man, Vertical Limit, A Knight's Tale,* and *The Animal.* When the scam was discovered, the executives were suspended without pay for 30 days,[22] but this may have been little comfort to those who depended upon these reviews and assumed they were the product of an independent film critic.

Because many of our waking hours are spent consuming the visual and auditory stimuli provided by the mass media, we have a right, as autonomous individuals, to expect media practitioners to behave with the same degree of integrity as the rest of society. When inaccuracies, rumor, and unsubstantiated allegations replace truth based upon personal knowledge, evidence, or corroboration, then informed decision making, and thus individual autonomy, is prejudiced.

The damage that can result from an assault on the truth is clearly illustrated by the contentious senatorial debate surrounding the confirmation of Supreme Court Justice Clarence Thomas in 1991. Confronted with allegations of sexual harassment from former law school professor Anita Hill, Thomas vehemently denied the allegations and called the proceedings a "high-tech lynching." While the truth may never be known, ten years after the hearings, David Brock, a former *American Spectator* writer, acknowledged in a book that in the wake of the hearings he had been designated by Thomas's right-wing supporters to destroy Hill's reputation and scrub Thomas's. According to Brock, he had printed "virtually every derogatory and often contradictory allegation" about Hill to make her appear "a little nutty and a little bit slutty."[23] In the meantime, in the collective mind of the public a cloud still hangs over a Supreme Court justice and his accuser.

The notion of individual autonomy is based, in part, on freedom of choice. Deception may undermine the confidence we have in our choices, which may make us reluctant to exercise our autonomy in the future.[24] For example, a lack of veracity among advertising and public relations practitioners would understandably create a climate of public distrust of the business community. Thus, the term *social responsibility* has entered the lexicon of media practitioners alongside the word *freedom,* a concept that is also reflected in the codes of the various media professions.

The second reason for a commitment to truth is that it demonstrates a *respect* for persons as ends rather than as tools to be manipulated. Deception usually places self-interest over the interests of others. There are exceptions, of course, such as in *some cases* when a doctor refuses to tell a patient the truth about a terminal illness. But by and large a lack of veracity in the communication process places the recipient of the deceptive information at a competitive disadvantage. Where media practitioners are involved, the problems are magnified, because consumers are either more unlikely to discover the deception than they would be in person or have no way to register their disapproval immediately with any real hope of having an impact.

Of course, the fallacy in this "respect for persons" rationale for truth telling is that it can also be used to *justify* deception, as when someone avoids unbridled candor to salvage the feelings of others. At a higher level, journalists sometimes defend their deceptive practices in the name of the public interest. Some investigative reporters use misrepresentations to uncover official corruption or other unsavory activities inimical to society's well-being. From an ethical standpoint this practice is defended on the ground that it will benefit the public at large while harming (deceiving) a small number of unsuspecting persons. Those who question

the practice believe that reporters are too inclined to become undercover sleuths before exhausting other means of getting the story. From a duty-based perspective two wrongs don't make a right (even in the name of the public interest), and deception as a *routine news-gathering technique* should be rejected.

The belief in the truthfulness of communications also builds *trust* between individuals and between individuals and society's institutions. Deception constitutes a breach of faith and makes it less likely that relationships based on trust and credibility will succeed in the future.[25] One writer has even described the practice of lying as "parasitic on the social process."[26] For example, a public relations practitioner for a chemical company who is not completely honest with the press concerning a toxic spill may have something to gain in the short term but will soon discover that the company's (as well as her own) credibility has suffered a serious blow. Likewise, misleading or deceptive advertising practices constitute a breach of faith with the consumer, because it is usually more difficult for the consumer to discover the truth about commercial speech than about political speech, which receives such intense scrutiny from the press. Because trust is built on truthful communication, lying and deception undermine the very foundations of society.

Finally, truth is *essential to the democratic process.* Democracy depends on an informed citizenry, one that approaches the political and economic marketplace armed with the knowledge that inspires studious deliberation. In a complex democratic society, the media are the primary conduits of information flow, and to the extent that they do not provide truthful, accurate, and meaningful information, they deprive their audiences of the intellectual nourishment necessary for rational decision making. The recent trends toward "sound-bite" journalism and the displacement of thoughtful reporting and analysis with the sensationalism and triviality of the tabloid media are troubling manifestations of how truth is often vulnerable to the lure of commercial values. Certainly nothing is ethically amiss in the media's appealing to the popular tastes of their audiences. And to the extent that the public abandons serious content for banality, they must share the moral responsibility for the depreciation of democratic values. But when the media are not faithful to the democratic mandate to service the political and economic system that has provided them sustenance in the first place, they become culturally dysfunctional and deprive the system of its vitality.

MEDIA PRACTITIONERS AND THE TRUTH–FALSEHOOD DICHOTOMY

In theory, it would appear that absolute truth is an ideal for which all media practitioners should strive. In practice, however, the application of this principle often depends on the circumstances and the role of the moral agent. Although outright falsehoods can seldom be justified, exactly how much truth is good for the public soul depends on our expectations. For example, we expect journalists to be unbiased and to report the truth (that is, as many of the known facts as possible that are important to a story). On the other hand, consumers realize that public relations practitioners and advertisers are advocates and do not expect them to do anything that would be contrary to their self-interest or the interests of their clients. This is not surprising considering the fact that advertisers and public relations professionals come from a different tradition than journalists. Thus, the question becomes one of how much of the truth should be revealed and under what circumstances public relations professionals and advertisers may withhold information that might be important to consumers.

In assessing the role of truth as it pertains to the various forms of media practice, Professor Frank Deaver of the University of Alabama

suggests that we construct a continuum, a form of ethical "gray scale," from one extreme to the other.[27] In so doing, absolute truth will reside at one end and deception and blatant lies at the other. Those whose purpose it is to provide facts and information (for instance, ethical journalists) will lie near the "truth" end of the scale. Those who intend to deceive, even if for justifiable purposes, will occupy the other end of the continuum. Unethical journalists and advertisers and public relations practitioners who knowingly dispense falsehoods are the most prominent inhabitants of this position on the scale. Somewhere between these two extremes, according to Deaver, are two other points: those who intend to persuade by using selective information (that is, not the whole truth), such as advertisers and public relations professionals, and those who engage in nontruths without intent to deceive. Fiction (such as media entertainment that does not purport to be a truthful account of events), parables, allegories, and honest error fall into this latter category. *New journalism,* which achieved popularity in the 1960s, resides here because it often uses parables, allegories, and fictional characters to achieve a "greater truth." It is often justified on the grounds that a fictional approach to real events and ideas appeals to a larger and more diverse audience than the more conventional structured approach to journalism.[28]

Truth in Journalism

The Standard of Journalistic Truth.   From a journalistic perspective, expert opinion abounds on what constitutes a truthful news account. At the minimum, three concepts appear to underlie the notion of truth in reporting.[29]

First, and most obviously, the reporting of a story must be *accurate.* The facts should be verified; that is, they should be based on solid evidence. If there is some doubt or dispute about the facts, it should be revealed to the audience. This is a threshold requirement, because inaccurate, unsubstantiated, or uncorroborated information can undermine the credibility of any journalistic enterprise. The failure of CBS News to observe this basic canon of responsible journalism created an ethical firestorm in the fall of 2004 during that network's coverage of the bitter and hotly contested presidential race between President George W. Bush and Senator John Kerry. Pursuing what had already become a contentious campaign issue, CBS News broadcast reports on both its evening news program and *60 Minutes* raising new questions about President Bush's Vietnam-era National Guard service. Despite a mounting body of evidence that the documents were forgeries, CBS News and Dan Rather continued to express confidence in their authenticity, but after nearly two weeks at the center of a public brouhaha finally acknowledged that they could not authenticate the documents. The disclosures that the source who gave the network the documents had lied about where he got them and that a *60 Minutes* producer acted as a conduit between the network's source and Senator John Kerry's presidential campaign led some media pundits to speculate on the future of CBS News, its top executives, and the 72-year-old Rather himself.[30] CBS and Rather issued a public apology,[31] but the harm to the network's journalistic stature was incalculable.

From the standpoint of accuracy, quotes should be used with precision. As an ethical practice, the altering of direct quotes to avoid embarrassment to the speaker is questionable. If there is a problem in this respect, indirect quotes or paraphrases should be used. Nevertheless, some reporters believe that "cleaning up" an interviewee's faulty grammar is justified out of fairness to the person.

What if the quotes are accurate but contain assertions that the reporter believes may be untrue? Is there an obligation to investigate the truthfulness of every statement (often an impossibility during the frenzy of a political campaign, for example), or does the reporter's obligation end with quoting the speaker accurately? Surely the failure to investigate may deny the audience some access to the truth, but there is some question whether this duty amounts to a moral imperative. Nevertheless, when reporters do not personally witness an occurrence or when the information is not general knowledge, they should be sure to attribute the source of their information. This is a fundamental requirement of accurate reporting.

Unfortunately, inaccurate quotes and stories often assume a life of their own when reporters fail to conduct their own independent investigations and simply accept the accounts of their colleagues as gospel. For an unsuspecting public, such stories may be uncritically embraced as journalistic truth. One of the most highly publicized examples occurred when Democratic presidential candidate Al Gore was quoted directly as claiming that he "invented" the Internet. In reality, what he told CNN's Wolf Blitzer in an interview was, "During my service in Congress I took the initiative in creating the Internet." When Gore was derided by both Republicans and the news media for this comment, several Internet experts noted that Gore did indeed play an important role while in Congress in developing the Internet.[32]

With the advent of the Web and the inevitable attractiveness of online journalism, the problem of incestuous news coverage, in which journalists borrow liberally from each other, is likely to increase. While inaccuracies can be corrected immediately by the original publisher, they are likely to endure as the number of derivative stories proliferates. Admittedly, the solution might elude even the most passionate and reflective ethicist, but the gauntlet has been thrown down. "If integrity isn't a compelling enough reason to think about these things," writes Barb Palser in the *American Journalism Review*, "consider the fact that content sharing is making errors harder to erase. With more sites grabbing one another's content outright or referencing it in research, slipups are more likely to be immortalized. Now imagine getting caught trying to swallow your own words."[33]

A particularly troublesome weakness in journalistic accuracy (and hence the overall truth of the story) is in the reporting of research. This is significant because the marketplace is increasingly dominated by studies and surveys for public consumption. Many journalists, never having had a statistics or experimental design course in their liberal arts education, are awed by scientific studies. Without the necessary intellectual tools to evaluate the methodology or conclusions, they often accept them uncritically. This is not the place to embark on a crash course in the scientific method. However, journalists do not have to be scientists to at least question the source of the study and to attribute this in their stories. This within itself may say something about the credibility of the study.

For the sake of accuracy, should reporters ever allow sources to review their stories prior to publication? At one time prepublication review was a taboo, and the notion is still not popular with many journalists because of what they perceive as a threat to their independence. However, Fred Brown, the Ethics Committee cochair of the Society of Professional Journalists, notes that in the past couple of decades "[w]e've put accuracy above independence, and we've decided it's more important to serve our readers than to be overly protective of what we're writing."[34] Steve Weinberg, former head of Investigative Reporters and Editors, routinely allows prepublication review because "the offer of review makes sources more willing to talk on the record" and "it doesn't compromise the writers' control over their stories."[35] Sources who wish to alter the interpretation or tone of an article should be reminded that their review is limited only to confirming the accuracy of the information. Supporters of at least limited prepublication review also point out that the ultimate goal of ethical journalism is the truth, which can be compromised by inaccurate information. According to this view, if sources can insure the accuracy of information, which is frequently the case in complex stories involving

tax policy or scientific discoveries, reporters should not hesitate to consult with them prior to publication.

While most reporters embrace accurate reporting as a first principle of ethical journalism, time and competitive pressures sometimes compromise the accuracy of news coverage. The biggest blunder in recent memory occurred when the four major broadcast networks, CNN, the Associated Press, and many of the nation's leading newspapers incorrectly named Democrat Al Gore as the winner in the 2000 presidential contest.[36] The critics could not agree on the cause of this debacle. Some blamed faulty data from the service that provides exit polling and raw vote counts to the networks and the Associated Press. Others blamed Florida for producing flawed election results.[37] However, there was virtual unanimity on one point: The news media, particularly the television networks, had suffered an incredible loss of credibility. Representative Billy Tauzin, chair of the House Telecommunications Subcommittee, even accused the networks of "disenfranchising Americans from their right to vote" and promised to hold hearings on the networks' election night faux pas.[38]

Battlefield coverage is particularly vulnerable to accusations of inaccurate reporting, a result in part of heavy dependence upon military sources of information, the inherent complexities of modern military operations, and the rapid pace of battlefield engagements that is antithetical to journalistic reflection and perspective. During the invasion of Iraq in the spring of 2003, for example, the term *embedded* quickly attached itself to the public consciousness as the Pentagon permitted reporters to accompany military units as they marched on Baghdad and engaged the Iraqi military in an effort to unseat Saddam Hussein. Journalists were thus provided with a ringside seat for the engagements of individual units. Nevertheless, from the outset the war coverage was plagued by numerous inaccuracies precipitated by the reporting of rumors and information frequently based upon faulty intelligence. An article in *USA Today*, for example, attributed some of the inaccuracies to the "fog of war, a place where fact, fiction and battlefield exaggeration merge into a muddle." Among the incidences cited were reports that Saddam Hussein may have died in an air strike when in fact his fate remained unclear; that a captured chemical plant produced banned weapons, which was false; that thousands of Shiites had revolted against Saddam in Basra, also false; and that bodies found in a warehouse in southern Iraq were victims of Saddam's brutal regime when in fact the remains were from the war in the 1980s against Iran.[39]

A second requirement for journalistic truth is that, in addition to being accurate, a truthful story should *promote understanding.* Time and space limitations preclude providing a comprehensive understanding of any situation. The goal should be to provide an account that is *essentially complete.* A story should contain as much relevant information as is available and essential to afford the average reader or viewer at least an understanding of the facts and the context of the facts. This places the working journalist somewhere between the extremes of full disclosure and no disclosure.[40]

The fact is that the whole truth can probably never be known about any situation, but ethical issues arise when moral agents *intentionally* withhold all or some facts relevant to the public interest. This practice is antithetical to the journalistic imperative of reporting all of the known relevant facts, but *sometimes* threats to the lives of individuals or the public's welfare lead to withholding or delaying certain kinds of information. Fast-breaking stories relating to terrorism and hostage takings are two prime examples.

There are other occasions when the journalistic imperative to report the truth is held hostage by more powerful forces that are just as determined, for their own ends, to control the flow of information to the public. As noted earlier, media coverage of military conflicts is a

challenging undertaking, particularly when, in the heat of battle, journalists attempt to provide perspective and understanding for what is admittedly a complex story. Chastened by what they believed to have been unrestrained negative coverage of the Vietnam War, the Pentagon, many of whose senior brass were veterans of that unpopular conflict, was determined not to repeat their earlier mistakes during Operation Desert Storm, which successfully thwarted Iraq's aggressive intentions in Kuwait in 1991. In this relatively short hundred-day campaign, the military severely limited media access to the combat zone. And reporters, many of whom were covering their first war, seemed so mesmerized by the Pentagon's relentless flow of sanitized information that *Newsweek* described them as "callow children of the video arcades, stupefied by the high-tech at press briefings." "At times," *Newsweek* observed, "news organizations seemed so busy courting generals they forgot to ask questions. Competing correspondents, papers and networks played right into the Pentagon's hands."[41] The more restrained commentators chided them for being uncritical. Their less charitable critics accused them of being government collaborators.[42]

Twelve years later, when the United States and its coalition partners invaded Iraq, the press was accused of jumping to unwarranted conclusions that seemed to change by the day— conclusions that did little to enhance the public's understanding of the military or public policy implications of that engagement. Media critics accused journalists of mood swings, morphing rapidly from a sort of prewar optimism to predictions of a quagmire (invoking memories of Vietnam) shortly after the commencement of hostilities. These mood swings, according to this view, "magnified both expectations of an instantaneous victory and grumbles about military stumbles, resulting in schizophrenic coverage that distorted public perceptions of the military campaign."[43] "Bounding between spurts of overly optimistic expectations and overly pessimistic fits of defeatism may fill newspaper columns and TV air time," declared an editorial in the *Houston Chronicle*. "But it doesn't necessarily reflect reality."[44]

However, some reporters and editors countered that journalists simply recorded the progress of the war, both successes and setbacks. In their view, the media justifiably reported the Pentagon's predictions of an early victory, but when current and retired military officers expressed consternation about the war strategy and the stiffer-than-expected guerilla resistance in southern Iraq, the media also reported these concerns.[45] Regardless of one's perspective on the media's performance in this particular conflict, professional journalists should strive for clarity and promote understanding and thus should avoid the temptation to render judgments unless they are reasonably supported by factual assertions and accompanied by source attribution.

The third criterion for a truthful article is that it be *fair and balanced*. These twin concepts involve, first, the avoidance of any discernible reporter bias. While reporters, like the rest of us, bring a certain amount of cultural baggage to their jobs, is it asking too much to expect them to leave their prejudices at the newsroom door? No accusation is more frequently heard against the news media or has the potential to be more damaging to credibility than that of biased coverage. Consider, for example, the results of a study conducted by the Pew Research Center and the Project for Excellence in Journalism concerning the coverage of the 2000 presidential campaign. Based upon a survey of 2,400 newspaper, TV, and Internet stories during five different weeks, researchers found that a staggering 76 percent of the coverage included one of two themes: that Al Gore lied and exaggerated or was marred by scandal and that George W. Bush was a "different kind of Republican."[46] The Pew study also included this damning indictment of the press, a conclusion also supported by an anecdotal survey reported in the *Columbia Journalism Review*: "Journalists' assertions about Bush's character were more than

twice as likely than Gore's to be unsupported by any evidence. In other words, they were pure opinion, rather than journalistic analysis."[47]

In addition to avoiding bias, fairness and balance require that journalists accord recognition to those views that enhance the understanding of the issue. Every effort should be made to represent them fairly and in proportion to their significance to the issue.

The greatest threat to journalistic truth is likely to occur during periods of crisis. Reporters covering the horrific events of September 11, 2001, for example, confronted unprecedented ethical challenges in attempting to convey accurate information to a nation gripped by fear. On that date, Americans watched in horror as two passenger jets crashed into the World Trade Center in New York City and another left a gaping hole in the Pentagon in Washington, DC, the symbol of our nation's military might. These aircraft had been converted into weapons of mass destruction by Arab terrorists motivated by their passionate hatred for the United States. A fourth plane crashed into a field in Pennsylvania when several passengers successfully confronted their hijackers, thus heroically thwarting their captors' plans for further destruction of American institutions. While the nation was attempting to cope with the fear generated by these attacks on American soil and the loss of thousands of innocent civilian lives, a bioterrorist attack in the form of anthrax was launched through the U.S. mail, placing political leaders, journalists, and postal workers at risk. Several deaths resulted from this assault from an unknown source.

Coverage of any national tragedy is risky, from an ethical perspective, but the enormity of 9/11 and its aftermath confronted journalists with a daunting challenge—how to provide an accurate account of events within a context that promotes understanding while not fueling the flames of fear and panic. In the weeks following the terrorist attacks, reporters were confronted with a deluge of information, much of it contradictory and inaccurate, emanating from the

White House, various public officials, and other sources. In the process, factual information sometimes became a casualty. In the anthrax story, for example, editors struggled to provide useful information to the public to help them guard against anthrax infection, while trying to avoid creating hysteria. As one commentator frankly acknowledged in the *American Journalism Review,* "The media were being held hostage by an unfolding drama over which they had no control."[48] And the fact that some journalists were targeted by the perpetrator(s) of the anthrax scare made it difficult for those affected to retain the emotional detachment usually expected of professional journalists. NBC anchor Tom Brokaw, himself a target, may have expressed the feelings of some of his colleagues when he closed his evening news broadcast of October 15th displaying a vial of pills and proclaiming, "In Cipro we trust."[49] Cipro, a popular treatment for the anthrax virus, soon became a household name.

In the immediate aftermath of 9/11, the public accorded the news media high marks for their coverage. For example, in a survey conducted by the Pew Center following the attacks, an impressive 89 percent of respondents rated the coverage as "excellent" or "good" in mid-September. A month later this figure still stood at 85 percent.[50] Perhaps one reason the public was favorably disposed toward the media's treatment of the events surrounding 9/11 was because of the patriotic fervor that seemed to embrace news organizations themselves. American flags appeared on news sets and lapels of news anchors, and reporters uncritically accepted information provided by government leaders and other officials. Some of the coverage assumed a decidedly patriotic tone, an understandable response to a horrific act perpetrated against innocent civilians. "One problem," noted Jane Kirtley, Silha Professor of Media Ethics and Law at the University of Minnesota, "is that it's difficult to be critical when the audience is swept up in patriotism."[51] However, public approbation may also have resulted from the fact

that the predictable flood of rumors and unsubstantiated facts was carefully evaluated by credible journalists,[52] not an easy task in an environment in which reporters had no precedents to guide them.

Nevertheless, there were dissenting voices. Some critics faulted journalists for abandoning their traditional role of independent government watchdog and of reporting on the foreign policy implications of the "war on terrorism" with an uncritical eye.[53] In a democratic society committed to the free flow of information, factual accuracy is clearly an ethical imperative, even when it reflects unfavorably on government policies. For example, once the shock of the terrorist attacks had subsided and journalists attempted to regain some measure of perspective, they increasingly turned their attention to stories concerning America's policies in the Middle East and the societies that were the breeding grounds for terrorists such as Osama bin Laden.

Efforts to enhance the American public's understanding of the context surrounding the 9/11 story, of course, necessitated interviews with Arab subjects who could provide unique insights into the culture in which bin Laden grew up. Such journalistic overtures run the risk that the subjects will attempt to control the interview agenda. Such was the case when ABC and CBS sought an interview with Carmen bin Laden, Osama bin Laden's estranged sister-in-law. To get the interview, Carmen bin Laden's attorney insisted on a number of conditions, including his right to prescreen the interview and to make changes, a violation of the standards of both news organizations. To their credit, the networks refused these demands. ABC was eventually granted the interview.[54]

CNN raised some ethical eyebrows when it apparently gained the inside track on being the first Western media outlet to question Osama bin Laden following the September 11th attacks. According to *Broadcasting & Cable* magazine,[55] CNN said it had been contacted by Al Jazeera, the Arab-language network, regarding the submission of questions for an interview with Osama bin Laden and had pursued the arrangement. CNN defended its actions by admitting that such preinterview submissions were not consistent with its policy but that the unusual circumstances warranted an exception. The network tried to counter expected criticism by declaring that it had not agreed to any preconditions regarding questions nor had it committed itself to airing bin Laden's responses. Bob Steele, a journalism practice expert with the Poynter Institute, also defended CNN's decision on the grounds that "[t]here is value in hearing what's inside bin Laden's head, even if it is propaganda."[56] Steele also noted that CNN promised appropriate editorial oversight and that there was no guarantee they would use the material. "It's a chip out of journalistic independence, but it's not a shattering of that independence," he concluded.[57]

Withholding Information.   Journalists are in the business of revelation, not concealment. In the minds of some it is antithetical to the practice of journalism to sit on a story. The stakes are high—the erosion of the public trust if readers and viewers believe vital information is being concealed from them. Nevertheless, there are frequently competing claims on the loyalties of journalists. They may "kill" a story to avoid harm to others or perhaps pull their journalistic punches in anticipation of gaining an advantage at some future date.

But regardless of the reasons, whether noble or self-serving, public trust is frequently the first casualty when news organizations suppress the truth. This was the concern in the spring of 2003 when Eason Jordan, CNN's chief news executive, acknowledged in the *New York Times* that for twelve years his network refused to report stories of Iraqi brutality and atrocities out of concern for the safety of its employees and sources.[58] Eason stated he made numerous trips to Baghdad to lobby the government to keep the CNN bureau open and to arrange interviews with Iraqi officials. During these visits

he became painfully aware that some of CNN's sources had been tortured and that the regime had threatened to kill CNN employees.

Critics accused Jordan of trading "truth for access" and betraying the public trust.[59] Several journalism professors and commentators said the CNN news executive had compromised his network's journalistic mission so that it could continue to report from Iraq. Jordan responded that the issue was not about access but life and death. "It's very simple," he replied. "Do you report things that get people killed? The answer is no." Jordan also stated that his network's reporting on the Iraqi regime was "fair and tough-minded."[60] However, CNN never reported these death threats, prompting one commentator to remark unsympathetically, "If it couldn't tell viewers how its newsgathering was shaped by implicit death threats, it was time to get out of Baghdad."[61]

But Jordan also had his share of supporters, who believed he was being unfairly singled out. "If we thought that we were endangering somebody we had hired to help us to report, that would be something that we would weigh very heavily," proclaimed Michele Grant, director of development for the British Broadcasting Corporation in the United States. Alex S. Jones, director of Harvard's Sorenstein Center on the Press, Politics and Public Policy, agreed: "I think every news organization has to make those kinds of calls from time to time."[62]

The "Feeding Frenzy."   One disturbing tendency that compromises all three standards discussed here is the media's rush to judgment in covering a sensational story, sometimes referred to as a "feeding frenzy" or the "herd mentality." If such journalistic stampedes are also accompanied by inaccuracies in the original account, then the harm is exacerbated and media credibility again stands indicted in the court of public opinion. Consider, for example, the media feeding frenzy set off by an article in the *New York Times*. In its March 6, 1999, edition the *Times* reported that China had used secrets stolen from the Los Alamos National Laboratory to advance its nuclear weapons program. The story did not identify the suspect but noted that he was a scientist at the lab. It also quoted a CIA operative as comparing the case with that of Julius and Ethel Rosenberg, a couple executed in 1953 for allegedly supplying secrets to the Soviet Union.[63] The *Times'* story quickly moved onto the national agenda, with unsettling consequences. "While a few journalists and news organizations took a skeptical view of the mounting near-hysteria," observed an article in the *American Journalism Review,* "many others did little original reporting, settling for wildly simplified versions of the *Times* coverage."[64] Two days following the initial report, Wen Ho Lee, a 60-year-old Taiwanese American working at the lab, was fired. Despite his denials that he had supplied China with official secrets, Lee spent 278 days in solitary confinement but was never charged with espionage. The government eventually dropped all but one of the 59 counts against him.[65]

In a postmortem of its Wen Ho Lee coverage, the *Times* acknowledged "flaws" in its original coverage and an uncritical reliance upon government sources. But as *U.S. News* noted in its own assessment of the situation: "Normally, a newspaper's blunders wouldn't attract so much attention. But lapses by the *Times* take on added significance because the newspaper is the national agenda setter."[66]

However, feeding frenzies do not always begin with such prominent news organizations. Consider the biggest story of 1998 concerning what transpired in the Oval Office between President Clinton and White House intern Monica Lewinsky. The story broke first on the Internet site of Matt Drudge, whose stock in trade was rumor and gossip, not accurate and reliable news. Because this relationship, among other things, was the subject of an investigation by a federal special prosecutor, no one can seriously deny the news value of this event. However, the quality of reporting, particularly in the early days, was distressing. In a cover story two

months after the first reported accounts of the affair, *Quill* magazine,[67] the publication of the Society of Professional Journalists (SPJ), questioned whether there had been a rush to judgment. Steve Geimann, former SPJ president and the chair of its Ethics Committee, provided this assessment:

> Instead of seeking the truth—the foundation of the SPJ Code of Ethics—newspaper and broadcast journalists were more interested in copying and chasing each other. Instead of identifying anonymous sources, otherwise respected journalists abdicated their responsibilities to other reporters and editors who often seemed to follow a looser set of ethical guidelines.[68]

This appraisal is supported by a study commissioned by the Committee of Concerned Journalists that evaluated the performance of major TV programs and newspapers during the first six days of the story. The conclusion? Forty-one percent of the coverage was analysis, opinion, speculation, or judgment instead of factual reporting.[69] Attribution was noticeably lacking from much of the early reporting. And this distressing conclusion did not go unnoticed by readers and viewers. In an opinion poll conducted just one month after the story broke, the top two adjectives Americans agreed they would use to describe news media coverage of the story were *excessive* (80 percent) and *embarrassing* (71 percent). When provided with two options as to why the media were focusing heavily on the story, 81 percent said that the media were more interested in attracting a large audience, whereas only 14 percent believed they were mostly interested in getting to the bottom of the story.[70] Space limitations preclude any meaningful reprise of the many ethical lapses that occurred in this case, but the reader is referred to the March/April 1998 edition of the *Columbia Journalism Review* for an interesting appraisal on the media coverage of the Clinton–Lewinsky affair.[71]

Such feeding frenzies, of course, are the result of instant news and the herd mentality, exacerbated by instantaneous electronic communication, and follow a predictable pattern. In the early stages the media are caught off guard and scramble to catch up, usually reporting as much opinion and innuendo as they do fact. Depending on the nature of the story and its duration, the mainstream media may settle into a more responsible form of reporting. Then there will be a period of self-flagellation in which some journalists lament their rush to judgment. And just as predictably, the next time that such a story breaks, the lessons of the past will be conveniently ignored in the passion of competition.

Deception in Journalism.   Any ethical debate about the use of deception in news gathering and reporting must take into account its various nuances and forms. Some moral purists argue that because truth is an animating principle of the journalistic profession, any form of deception is taboo. According to this Kantian view, such behavior erodes the bond of trust between reporters and their audiences. Others are not so austere in their ethical approach, acknowledging that sometimes deception must be used to uncover stories of overriding public importance.

As the media continue to be plagued by a public crisis of confidence, certain journalistic devices have increasingly been put under an ethical microscope. One such practice is the use of surreptitious investigative techniques, such as undercover reporting and the use of hidden cameras and microphones. Journalists defend such tactics on the grounds that as fiduciaries of the public, they are sometimes required to employ deception to uncover a greater truth. In other words, the end justifies the means. Such was the case when freelance reporter Jonathan Franklin posed as a mortician and entered Dover Air Force Base, where casualties of the Persian Gulf War were processed. In so doing, he confirmed that the military had underestimated the number of casualties. Franklin's article was eventually published in the *Bay Guardian*,

a weekly paper in San Francisco. The managing editor, acknowledging that he usually turned down stories based on undercover work, justified this exception on the grounds that the deception was directed against government misconduct, not an individual.[72]

Some undercover activities, however, are based on less noble motives. Take, for example, the sweeps-week exposé of security in the public schools undertaken by a TV station in Portland, Maine. A member of the station's investigative team, posing as a family friend of a particular second grader, arrived at an elementary school and said he had been asked by the family to take the child to the dentist. In reality, the student's mother was a station employee and was waiting in the car outside. Because the man was without a note, the child's mother could not be reached, and the dentist's name provided by the undercover reporter did not match the name of the dentist in the student's file, the principal correctly refused to release the child into the visitor's custody. The school superintendent accused the station of an "abuse of trust" and charged that the station "had engaged in a deliberate, cynical deception of the school staff in order to manufacture a news story."[73]

Although the use of deception is probably as old as journalism itself, many news managers are uncomfortable with the practice and have instituted policies that, while not banning undercover reporting altogether, are designed to prevent its abuse. However, one could hardly fault a news organization if it chose to ban the use of deceptive undercover reporting practices altogether. After all, adherence to the truth hardly needs any justification. Those who find such moral conservatism too restrictive in a highly competitive media environment must still defend their use of deception based on some overriding principle and some fairly demanding criteria. Investigative techniques, such as undercover reporting and the use of hidden cameras, should be employed only after a full and deliberate discussion in which the principles of sound moral reasoning are employed. Bill Kovach and Tom Rosenstiel, in their illuminating book on the enduring principles of journalism, have apparently rejected the Kantian view of deception as too austere for practicing journalists but suggest that reporters should use a test similar to the concepts justifying civil disobedience in deciding whether to engage in the technique. According to Kovach and Rosenstiel, a three-step test should be applied for employing deceptive news-gathering techniques.

1. The information must be sufficiently vital to the public interest to justify deception.

2. Journalists should not engage in masquerade unless there is no other way to get the story.

3. Journalists should reveal to their audience whenever they mislead sources to get information, and explain their reasons for doing so, including why the story justifies the deception and why this was the only way to get the facts.[74]

News staging is another deceptive practice that raises serious ethical questions, and, unfortunately, it is not that rare in either print or electronic journalism. Take, for example, the photo that accompanied a story in the *Indianapolis Star* in the summer of 2002—a photo the newspaper later acknowledged was staged. The photo and caption depicted a nurse giving a boy a vaccination when in fact he was at the Health Department for a different procedure. The boy was asked to pose for the photo as though he were getting a shot. The *Star* subsequently apologized for the misrepresentation. "Such distortion of the truth is a violation of our policy on ethics and our commitment to readers to always be honest in our delivery of the news," the newspaper wrote.[75]

In still another ethical blunder, the consequences were more dire for the perpetrators. When a reporter at WCCO-TV in Minneapolis couldn't find appropriate visuals to illustrate a story about underage drinking, he purchased two cases of beer for six teenagers and then filmed them drinking the beer. When this journalistic duplicity was discovered, the reporter and photographer were not only fired; they were arrested and charged with violating state liquor laws.[76]

Closely related to staging is the practice of news reenactments or re-creations. Not surprisingly, such techniques are controversial among professional journalists. The most severe criticism has been leveled against the use of reenactments in catastrophes or tragedies. For example, in 1996 listeners of WGST-AM/FM in Atlanta were treated to an almost two-minute cockpit voice recorder reenactment of the last minutes of ValuJet Flight 592 as the plane plunged into the Florida Everglades. For the sake of realism, the station added sound effects, such as wind rushing and people screaming. WGST news director Al Gardner defended the broadcast as an attempt "to put a face and a human behind the story." ValuJet officials called the report "outrageous" and "irresponsible."[77]

Not all electronic journalists are willing to rule out the use of reenactments entirely, but caution their use must be limited. For example, Nancy Sanders, assistant news director of WKBW-TV in Buffalo, New York, notes: "I do think there are times when you have to cross the line and do re-enactments, and I do think it possibly is helpful in crime situations. But in catastrophes, I don't know that I would endorse doing that. It smells of docudrama." On the other hand, Paul Perillo, news bureau chief of Metro Networks' Philadelphia office, believes that any re-creation "flies in the face of all the basics of good journalism." He fears that competition for ratings may oblige more and more stations to embellish their news reports for shock value.[78]

As noted in Chapter 2, the introduction of computer-assisted digital technology poses still another challenge to the moral imagination of media practitioners. Digital-imaging technology itself is ethically neutral, but its deceptive capabilities are worrisome. Alteration of still pictures, of course, predates the arrival of digitalization, but the new technology makes such manipulation of both still and moving pictures easier and virtually undetectable. Because of these factors, will media professionals now be more tempted than ever to alter visuals?

The jury is still out on that question, but there are already some disturbing trends. Consider a photo that ran in several newspapers, including the *Hartford Courant, Chicago Tribune,* and *Los Angeles Times,* during the invasion of Iraq by the American military and its coalition partners. A *Times* photographer took two photos of a British soldier in front of a crowd of Iraqi civilians and, using his laptop, composed an image using the left side of one photo and the right side of the other. He transmitted his composite photo to the *Times,* along with twelve other images, but the altered photo was unwittingly selected for publication by the *Times* and other papers. The digital manipulation was discovered when an employee of the *Hartford Courant* noticed that several civilians crouching in the background of the photo appeared twice.[79]

And then there was the controversial decision by CBS news executives in which they apparently sacrificed journalistic principles to a clever market strategy. During the New Year's Eve newscast from Times Square leading into the new millennium, CBS technicians digitally removed a giant NBC logo, as well as a Budweiser ad, from the video image of Times Square behind Dan Rather and replaced them with their own CBS corporate logo. "It's a classic case of technological expertise," lamented media ethicist Bob Steele, "at the expense of ethical principles."[80]

In November 1999 *Stars and Stripes,* the daily newspaper for U.S. armed forces overseas, featured on its front page a color photo of an Apache helicopter maneuvering high above a mountain range. The accompanying headline read: "To better prepare for mountainous terrain, Apache pilots are getting their training." However, the photo was a phony, a creation of the paper's central office in Washington, DC, which

had employed modern technology to produce "a picture of an Apache with a shot of an awesome mountain view."[81]

Even institutions of higher education, supposedly the bastions of intellectual honesty, are not immune from the allure of digital manipulation. In September 2000 an attempt by the University of Wisconsin to display its commitment to racial diversity turned into a public relations fiasco. The original cover photograph for its new admissions brochure showed happy Wisconsin students attending a football game. When university officials noticed that the picture contained no black faces, they used photo-design software to add the face of an African American. "Our intentions were good, but our methods were bad," declared the public relations director once the deception was exposed. Similarly, two weeks after the Wisconsin incident the University of Idaho digitally pasted two faces—one black and one Asian—onto white bodies in a photo at the top of the university's website. An official from the university blamed the episode on an overzealous computer technician but acknowledged that "other administrators had urged the technician to find a picture showing minority students."[82]

Certainly the alteration of the "content" of visuals in such a way as to distort the reality of the event raises serious ethical questions and erodes the confidence that readers and viewers have in the editorial process. But what if the alterations are made primarily for considerations of design or taste, as when the editors of *American Photo* digitally removed for matters of "taste" the nipples of model Kate Moss who appeared on the magazine's cover in a tight-fitting gauzy top?[83] Under such circumstances, the ethical slope becomes more slippery as media practitioners balance competing concerns.

Many news organizations have policies against alteration of the content of photographs, and the need for new ethical constructs to deal with the deceptive capabilities of digital imaging is not yet manifest. After all, if certain forms of manipulation are unacceptable under current policies, the arrival of a new technology should not alter the unethical nature of that practice. The ultimate test is still, purely and simply, one of honesty.

Fabrication: The Unpardonable Sin. To the loyal readers of the *New York Times*, it was inconceivable that an employee of the nation's journalistic icon would fabricate information and steal material from other news organizations. And yet, as described briefly in the opening narrative of Chapter 1, in the late spring of 2003 the *Times* declared in a lengthy front-page story that Jayson Blair, a prolific young reporter who had recently been promoted to the national desk, had resigned amidst allegations of journalistic fraud. As described in the *Times*'s own account, an investigation revealed that at least half the stories produced by Blair while covering national assignments were tainted by fabrications or other forms of deception, and a spot-check of more than 600 of Blair's stories written prior to that time also contained apparent fabrications. "His tools of deceit were a cellphone and a laptop computer," wrote the *Times*, "which allowed him to blur his true whereabouts—as well as round-the-clock access to databases of news articles from which he stole."[84]

The public remains blissfully unaware of most incidences of journalistic malpractice, but the Jayson Blair affair riveted both the mainstream and tabloid press, fascinated the eager listeners and viewers of the radio and TV talk shows, and was featured prominently as the cover story in the major news magazines. Several accounts chronicled Blair's troubled personal life and his disrespect for professional standards and deportment that dated to his days as a high school journalist.[85] This publicity was accompanied by some anguished soul-searching within the *Times* that focused on the controversial executive editor, Harold Raines, who prided himself on nurturing new talent and ignored complaints from other editors concerning Blair's job performance. Three weeks after the *Times*

published its exhaustive account of the Blair debacle, Raines, along with Managing Editor Gerald Boyd, resigned after deciding that "the backwash from the Blair affair was keeping them from providing the effective leadership" the paper needed.[86]

Most journalists are hardworking and honorable and are a credit to their profession. But as *Newsweek* candidly acknowledged in the wake of the Blair revelations: "Jayson Blair isn't the first journalist to deceive readers—and he probably won't be the last. It's no wonder, then, that the profession is struggling with a credibility problem."[87] In what the magazine referred to as the *Hall of Shame*, it briefly described a legacy of deception originating with the infamous era of Yellow Journalism in the 1890s during which New York publishers Joseph Pulitzer and William Randolph Hearst sensationalized and manufactured events to boost paper sales.[88]

Newsweek was certainly prescient in its prediction that Jayson Blair "probably won't be the last" to commit journalistic malpractice. Less than a year after Blair and the *Times* parted company, *USA Today* veteran reporter Jack Kelley was fired for fabricating stories and plagiarizing other material. Some staff members speculated that the paper's managers were lax in their editorial supervision because of Kelley's potential for enhancing the publication's prestige (Kelley had been nominated for a Pulitzer Prize, only the second such nomination in the paper's 22-year history.).[89]

The profession of journalism is built on trust. The loss of credibility can be ethically fatal to a news organization. Journalists who approach a story with an ax to grind or who intentionally slant their reporting to favor one ideology over another are kindred souls with propagandists. Of course, journalists are not perfect. Under time deadlines they frequently make mistakes, and some are unnecessarily careless in gathering the facts. And the public is frequently willing to forgive the trespasses of those who make mistakes and acknowledge them.

What is unpardonable in the practice of journalism, however, is the fabrication of stories or quotes. This has not become common fare within the industry, but several highly publicized cases in recent years have raised some profoundly disturbing questions concerning the ethical direction of the profession. The highly respected *Washington Post* is credited with running what one author has described as "the most famous hoax of the modern era."[90] The *Post* was forced to return a Pulitzer Prize for feature writing after the paper's editors discovered that one of their young reporters, Janet Cooke, had fabricated a dramatic account of an 8-year-old heroin addict. Although the case was dismissed as an isolated incident, other cases have arisen in some of the nation's leading publications. In August 2000, for example, ABC News' John Stossel apologized to millions of TV viewers for his role in an incredibly distorted report on the news magazine show *20/20*. Seven months earlier Stossel had reported that "organic" foods were not safe or more nutritious than food grown with chemicals. His report was based upon tests commissioned by ABC that found no pesticide residues on either organic or regular produce. In fact, the network later admitted that no tests had been done on produce, and environmentalists concluded that some of the other research findings included in the story were also misleading. Stossel was reprimanded and a producer was suspended, but the loss of credibility resulting from such ethical indiscretions is incalculable.[91]

Two years earlier, the *Boston Globe* had asked a prize-winning Boston columnist, Patricia Smith, to resign because of fabricated people and quotes in four of her columns.[92] This case is worth pausing over for a moment because of the reporter's attempt to rationalize her unethical behavior. In her apology to the paper's readers, Smith said she wanted her writing to come across as exciting and wished "to leave the reader indelibly impressed," acknowledging that she

sometimes quoted nonexistent people to "create the desired impact or slam home a salient point."[93] But the *Globe*'s ombudsman, Jack Thomas, was unimpressed with this morally ambiguous defense, accusing Smith of continuing to compromise the truth. "Making up an entire column of fictitious people and fictitious quotations is not, as she would have us believe, slamming home a point," wrote Thomas. "It's lying."[94]

It would be difficult to improve on Thomas's description of the situation. In some ethical dilemmas confronting journalists, there is room for legitimate disagreement on the most morally permissible (or justifiable) solution. *The fabrication of information is not one of them!*

Where Truth and Fiction Collide: The Docudrama

The docudrama is probably the most popular version of fact-based entertainment, sometimes referred to as "infotainment." Docudramas have appeal because they are based on actual incidents, and, in the case of current events, the audience can usually identify with the featured characters. The blending of historical fact and fiction has a lineage that can be traced at least to Greek drama, but the docudrama genre, at least in its current incarnation, is a little over three decades old. Prior to the 1970s TV documentaries were substantially fact-based, but the tragic political misdeeds and fall of Richard Nixon afforded an irresistible temptation to blend historical facts with fictional episodes allegedly to serve a "higher truth." Thus was born the docudrama, and by the 1990s Nixon was "being depicted in film as an epithet-swearing drunk who suffered from hallucinations."[95]

In assessing the historical relevance and value of docudramas we must remember the producers of these films are not journalists. Their goal is to create an interesting story. In some cases modifications are made or inaccuracies tolerated primarily for dramatic effect; sometimes producers approach their work with a political agenda. The question then arises whether the writers and producers of docudramas should have the same degree of ethical commitment to the truth as practicing journalists. Some producers have been careful to note the fictionalized nature of their creations. But when a producer markets a revisionist version of history and cleverly disguises theories and rumors as fact, then serious ethical concerns must be addressed. The docudrama genre is not new, but it has become increasingly controversial.

The most severe indictment of docudramatists is that they frequently alter or distort historical facts to support a preconceived bias. A classic example was Oliver Stone's film *JFK,* which was savagely characterized by critics as entertainment masquerading as history and as little more than propaganda for a huge conspiracy theory of the Kennedy assassination.[96] Stone himself acknowledged that his version of events was not a "true story" but said his film spoke to "an inner truth." And *JFK* star Kevin Costner admitted that the film's whole case might be dismantled and discredited but that the "movie as a whole has an emotional truth."[97] Such linguistic spins led columnist John Leo, writing in *U.S. News & World Report,* to offer the following rebuttal:

> But inner truths and emotional truths are the stuff of fiction, or used to be. What I think Stone and his actor are saying here is that it doesn't much matter whether this is literally true or not, so long as it steers the culture where we want to go. This has become an increasingly modish opinion as the line between fact and fiction grows ever more blurry in the culture.[98]

Following the release of his historically based film *Amistad*—the story of fifty-three captive Africans who revolted aboard the slave ship *Amistad* in 1839 and then were recaptured and finally freed by the Supreme Court after a two-year battle—producer Steven Spielberg came under fire for his excessive use of dramatic

license in depicting the historical truth of the event. Spielberg's coproducer, Debbie Allen, described the movie as an allegedly "suppressed" story of black rebellion and victory. However, historian Warren Goldstein was unforgiving in his denunciation of the film as "frequently incomprehensible, and misleading when it isn't just plain wrong." In castigating the producers for compromising historical accuracy for dramatic license, Goldstein referred to *Amistad* as "downright slanderous."[99] Other academics defended the film's overarching political perspective of African American empowerment, even at the risk of historical inaccuracy.[100]

Even if we accept the notion that docudramatists should not be held to the same standards of truth as journalists—after all, some artistic license is inevitable in transforming historical events into a dramatic structure—they nevertheless owe a duty to their audiences to present a faithful re-creation of at least the substantive aspects of those phenomena. They should not offer as fact what is clearly fiction or mere theories or unsubstantiated rumors. "It can be argued coherently that the public has a legitimate interest in knowing the amount of truth in historical films, docudramas, and similar productions."[101]

Of course, time is an ally of producers who wish to tap the rich annals of history for arresting topics that lend themselves to dramatic re-creation. Reflection and perspective are essential to the search for truth. Unfortunately, the recent plethora of TV docudramas, ripped from today's headlines, is lacking in both.[102] Consider, for example, the made-for-TV movie *Saving Jessica Lynch,* a dramatic account of the capture and rescue of an American soldier during the early days of the U.S.-led invasion of Iraq that aired on CBS in November 2003. As the *New York Times* observed in a review of this made-for-TV film: "The facts surrounding Private Lynch's capture and rescue were [hazy], with so many conflicting reports that despite countless news articles, magazine show segments and television biographies, there is still no complete picture of what really happened during those fateful days in Iraq last spring." Nevertheless, the article concluded, "its makers did the best they could without access to primary sources to fill in the blanks."[103]

The docudrama feeding frenzy has become so frenetic that some scripts go into production even before the stories have run their course, which compromises any sense of historical perspective. A case in point is the emotionally charged and fatal confrontation between federal agents and the Branch Davidians in Waco, Texas, the first docudrama about a real-life tragedy that was filmed *while the tragedy was still unfolding*. Similarly, a USA Network movie about the highly publicized case of Scott Peterson, accused of murdering his wife and unborn baby, was produced even before Peterson had gone to trial. The filmmakers claimed to be unfazed about the potential impact of the docudrama on jury selection, but Court TV anchor Nancy wasn't so sure. "You'll have to ensure which jurors have seen it and what impact it had on them," she remarked in an interview for *TV Guide*. "Sometimes, frankly, even the most honest juror doesn't know the impact."[104]

Critics complain that docudramas pulled from today's headlines are driven more by ratings than any allegiance to balance and proportion and that these made-for-TV movies simply repackage real-life tragedies as home entertainment.[105] In the process, as *Newsweek* observed in its rather terse assessment of what it referred to as "headline TV," truth often falls prey to fantasy.[106] Defenders of docudramas based on current events respond that such programs often address important social issues. Indeed, contemporary docudramas can illuminate social issues and even provide psychological insights into the dimensions of human tragedy. In a highly competitive marketplace, using today's headlines as the artistic cue for a TV movie is not inherently unethical, as long as producers adhere

to a "truth-in-labeling" standard. They should not promote as reality a product that is nothing more than a fictionalized account of events. But ethical concerns do arise when fantasy subtly and skillfully replaces truth and the audience remains an unenlightened hostage to the producer's deception.

Truth in Advertising and Public Relations

Clearly, the standards outlined for journalists cannot be entirely applicable to the other forms of media practice with which we are concerned in this book. Advertisers and public relations practitioners, for example, are in the business of persuading. They come to the marketplace with a bias, and there is nothing wrong with that. Public relations practitioners have a right to defend their clients' interests in the court of public opinion, and in such circumstances the audience expects that the dissemination of information will be more selective.

Although the ethical expectations of mass persuaders may vary from those of journalists, we still expect advertisers and public relations personnel to adhere to the threshold requirement of truth—that is, that they not knowingly disseminate inaccurate information. The various professional codes of the public relations and advertising industries commit their practitioners to standards of truth and accuracy. Unfortunately, such standards are ignored when company executives allow their allegiance to the bottom line and unharnessed competitive instincts eclipse their responsibility to the society that has given them their corporate privilege. Such was the case when Columbia Pictures executives had an advertising department employee pose as a movie critic to lavish praise on such movies as *The Animal* and *A Knight's Tale*. The studio also confessed to using actors and its own employees in testimonial ads for such movies as *The Patriot*.[107] Apparently the practice is widespread in Hollywood, which is puzzling since such lies apparently have little impact among consumers. "No one believes these people anyway," proclaims Tom Sherak, a partner in Revolution Studios. "Even well-known critics have trouble getting people to believe them."[108]

Although mass persuaders are just as morally culpable as journalists for deliberately telling a lie, they are under no ethical obligation to provide balance in their public proclamations. A cereal company, for example, while extolling the health benefits of its oat bran flakes in a TV campaign, is unlikely to acknowledge the presence of sugar in its product.[109] Nor would a spokesperson for a "low-fat" product, which appeals to the health-conscious consumer, voluntarily admit to its high caloric content resulting from sugar. Likewise, a public relations spokesperson for a corporation will attempt to put the best foot forward and not dwell on the company's shortcomings.

In other words, mass persuaders—public relations practitioners and advertisers—employ selective truth to construct their messages, and there is nothing inherently unethical about this. As noted in Chapter 2, persuasion is one of the legitimate functions of mass communication, and society does not expect the same level of truth here as they do from practitioners of the information function (that is, journalists). We expect accurate information, but we do not expect balance or objectivity. Public relations professionals, for example, to retain credibility should provide accurate information, but, as Professor Deaver cautions us, "we should know that it is not necessarily objective and unbiased, that it is certainly not the whole story."[110]

Advertising is a little more problematic[111] because of two related and controversial techniques: linguistic ambiguity, in which no specific product claims are made (for example, Allstate's "You're in good hands"), and puffery, which is the use of superlatives, exaggerations, and subjective opinions that do not implicate specific facts (such as "the best deal in town" and "number one in sex appeal"). Most people would probably agree that intentional ambiguity is unethical in situations "where accurate instruction or efficient transmission of precise information is the acknowledged purpose."[112] But in a competitive media environment often driven by entertainment values, advertising's purpose transcends the provision of accurate information. Its purpose is to create a favorable image about the product or company and thus to increase sales or to hold onto market share. In most advertising messages, therefore, ambiguity is usually recognized as such and accepted by consumers.[113]

Puffery is also a ubiquitous technique in contemporary advertising, but it isn't without its critics. Ivan Preston, for example, in his book *The Great American Blow-up,* argues that all puffery is false by implication and should be illegal. Philip Patterson and Lee Wilkins, in their illuminating discussion of the ethics of persuasion, assert that "[t]he absence of a verifiable claim, for example ads employing ridicule or commercials promoting 'image,' should alert the consumer to a potentially unethical approach to persuasion."[114] Opponents might counter, however, that this is ethical prudishness and that such a narrow posture is neither realistic nor desirable. And indeed, it isn't at all clear as to why an advertising message designed to create an image or a "feel good" mood among consumers is unethical, even if it is devoid of information (unless, of course, the advertiser promises accurate information and fails to deliver). If consumers expect information from ads, they will demand it. In a marketplace economy, the audience should assume some degree of responsibility and must be discriminating and ponder commercial messages with a healthy degree of skepticism.

However, when advertisers omit important information that could mislead consumers and that actually affects a consumer's purchasing decision, such ads are deceptive and raise more serious ethical concerns. For example, the Federal Trade Commission ruled that an advertisement by Beneficial Corporation, a finance company, stating that it would provide customers with an "instant tax refund" if individuals' tax returns entitled them to a refund was misleading. What was unstated, according to the Commission, was that the customer had to first qualify for a loan, and "there was nothing instant about the loan procedures."[115]

Public Relations and Journalism: A Love–Hate Relationship

Public relations practitioners and journalists often view each other with suspicion. Some journalists consider the practice of public relations as parasitic, populated by "flacks" who derive their livelihood by using the media to their own advantage. Public relations practitioners, on the other hand, often look at newsrooms as repositories of cynicism, where journalists eagerly survey the landscape for governmental or corporate malfeasance or irresponsibility. "Good news," according to this view, is an oxymoron.

The fact is, however, that neither profession can claim moral superiority over the other because they derive their principles from different intellectual moorings. The mission of journalists is to uncover facts, report on society's institutions, and present a fair and balanced account (some would describe this as "objectivity") of the day's intelligence. Ethical journalists, according to the traditional view, should have no causes to promote, no axes to grind. Public relations practitioners, on the other hand, are by definition advocates and are committed to achieving their organizations' goals. They, too, provide information for public consumption, but they usually do so in a manner that will achieve the most favorable results for their company or client.

The journalist's stock-in-trade is revelation, the public dissemination of as much relevant and significant information as possible. On the other hand, confidentiality of information and relationships plays an important role in the life of the public relations practitioner. Proprietary information that might work to the advantage of a competitor is one example. As advocates, public relations practitioners usually view a certain degree of confidentiality as essential to advancing a positive image for their companies and clients. Thus, they are more likely to be selective in the information they provide the public and the media. However, when the public interest requires full disclosure (as noted earlier), even when to do so might be initially detrimental to the public image and corporate profits, the long-term public relations benefits can be tremendous. Sincerity and self-criticism can be ethically invigorating in the arena of public opinion.

Despite this apparent mistrust between reporters and public relations practitioners, the relationship is really more symbiotic than adversarial. News organizations depend on public relations information (in some cases quite heavily) for both economic and journalistic reasons. The cost of gathering information from every possible organization within a community would be prohibitively expensive without the assistance of representatives from those organizations. In addition, company officials and their public relations representatives are good sources of information that might not be available elsewhere, and they provide a constant flow of free information to the news media. In this respect, public relations practitioners serve as extensions of the news staff: "They play a specific, functional, cooperative role in society's information-gathering network, even though they owe no loyalty to specific news outlets, are not paid by them, and may never set foot in the building in which the news is produced."[116]

In return, the media serve as a willing and sometimes uncritical forum for the dissemination of governmental and corporate messages and information. Public relations releases provide an opportunity for companies to tell their side of the story, especially in an environment where public relations practitioners distrust the media's objectivity in their own accounts of events. The most visible and controversial evidence of this symbiotic relationship is the widespread dissemination and use of video news releases (VNRs). VNRs resemble typical TV news stories in their packaging but are produced on behalf of a client in attempt to get free airtime to promote a cause, product, or service.[117] They are distributed free to stations and often come with scripts for local anchors or reporters to read as "voice-overs." In other cases, they are downlinked from satellites. VNRs are an efficient and effective way for public relations firms to represent their clients to a mass audience. And in economic hard times VNRs are a cost-effective means for a station to produce more material for local broadcast without adding more employees.[118]

Charitable and nonprofit organizations are just as aggressive as commercial enterprises in competing for the public's attention. In the fall of 1998, for example, when an autopsy revealed that the three-time Olympic gold medalist Florence Griffith Joyner ("Flo-Jo") had died of a "seizure," the Epilepsy Foundation swung into action, blanketing the country with publicity releases, including a VNR designed for transmission to every TV station in the country. The tragic death of Flo-Jo provided the catalyst for the normally low-profile Epilepsy Foundation to raise public awareness of an often-ignored disease.[119]

The production and use of VNRs impose ethical obligations on both public relations practitioners and the stations to which they disseminate this material. Some practitioners believe, for example, that as long as the information contained in a VNR is accurate and true and the production standards are high, they have conducted themselves in an ethical manner. The rest is up to the journalists.[120] News organizations then have an ethical obligation to identify the source of the VNR, regardless of whether it is substantially edited or aired in its entirety. And yet, in a Nielsen survey of news directors several years ago, only 60 percent of the respondents said VNR sponsors should be identified when a VNR is aired.[121] And unfortunately,

unattributed VNRs are not that rare among news departments.

INTELLECTUAL DISHONESTY

The unauthorized or unacknowledged use of someone else's literary or artistic creation is dishonest. Society does not abide theft of the fruits of one's physical labors. There is no reason that it should be any more tolerant of the piracy of intellectual property. For the sake of simplicity, we can divide intellectual dishonesty into two categories: plagiarism and misappropriation. Although misappropriation also has a specific legal meaning, within the ethical context we shall take it to mean "the *unauthorized use* of someone else's literary or artistic expression." Plagiarism, on the other hand, refers to "the taking of another's ideas or expression and passing it off as your own." Plagiarism often revolves around the question of attribution, whereas misappropriation occurs when a use of intellectual property is not authorized by the owner. It reflects the moral right of creators to control the use and dissemination of their intellectual property. Such misappropriation not only raises ethical concerns but can also run afoul of copyright law. A classic example, and one that has precipitated an angry and aggressive response from the recording industry, is the illegal downloading of music (and movies) from the Internet. Companies such as Napster have facilitated the practice of file-sharing, the process by which computer users all over the world can share music stored on their hard drives. Napster was eventually forced to the sidelines through litigation, but others have stepped in to fill the vacuum. File-sharing is particularly rampant among the young, a generation nurtured within an Internet culture where everything appears to be free for the taking. In the meantime, the music and film industries claim they are losing millions of dollars because of illegal downloading.

Plagiarism has been described as "the unoriginal sin."[122] Take, for example, the following unfortunate events: During the 1991 David Duke campaign for the Louisiana governorship, the Fort Worth *Star-Telegram* published a story under the byline of political writer James Walker, a thirteen-year veteran at the paper. Quotes in the story were attributed to various speakers but not to the Louisiana television report and the New Orleans *Times-Picayune* from which they were lifted. Walker resigned, attributing his indiscretion to an "error in judgment."[123] A reporter for the *St. Petersburg Times* resigned after she claimed as her own about a third of an article on credit cards from *Changing Times* magazine. On the day of her resignation she apologized to her colleagues, describing her indiscretion as a "stupid mistake."[124] In November 2000 the *Sacramento Bee* fired a political writer for plagiarizing and fabricating material in his stories on the presidential campaign.[125] Shortly thereafter, a reporting intern was suspended and later fired from the *Mercury News* for plagiarizing material from other newspapers.[126] "Plagiarism is unacceptable in our newspaper and in our business," declared managing editor Susan Goldberg in a memo to the paper's staff. "It is an inherent violation of the trust we have with our readers and with our professional colleagues."[127]

Each fell from journalistic grace for allegedly committing the mortal sin in media communications, plagiarism—using someone else's intellectual property without attribution. Because a media professional's stock-in-trade is artistic originality and creativity, the unattributed use of someone else's work violates the virtue of honesty. When it is necessary to borrow from another source, that source should be attributed.

Although attribution is the cornerstone of media credibility, the practice of nonattribution is quite common, as reflected in this lament from columnist Garry Wills:

> [P]rofessional writers, who take on subjects of their own volition, regularly commit plagiarism. Very intelligent people do this, some of them repeatedly. What are they doing in their line of work? Why do they talk on subjects about which they have nothing of their own to say?
>
> The excuse regularly used is that the writers have made the words of somebody else, encountered some time ago, part of their own "mental furniture," so that they can no longer distinguish what others said from what they think.
>
> Writers should have some pride in their own style. If they cannot identify their own words, why should others value them?[128]

A classic illustration of Wills's concern is the *Boston Globe*'s decision in the summer of 1998 to fire and then reinstate star columnist Mike Barnicle after he published a column that used, without attribution, jokes that resembled those in George Carlin's book *Brain Droppings*. When confronted by his editors, Barnicle said he had not read the book and had received the material from a friend without checking its origins.[129] The *Globe*'s editor apparently did not consider Barnicle's indiscretion serious enough for termination. But Barnicle's reinstatement brought an angry response from the newsroom staff, with at least fifty employees signing a petition of protest. One complained that the reprieve "not only cripples the paper's integrity but undermines the efforts of staff members who work daily to produce a newspaper that is beyond reproach."[130] When questions later arose concerning another column, Barnicle abruptly resigned.

While it is tempting to dismiss high-profile cases, such as the Jayson Blair affair, as aberrations, the incidence of plagiarism cases among journalists does appear to be on the rise. For example, in its March 2001 issue, the *American Journalism Review* chronicled twenty-three episodes that had been acknowledged during the past two years.[131]

This rash of cases involving intellectual dishonesty is particularly disturbing to journalism educators who spend much of their time attempting to instill high standards of professional deportment in their young charges. When the highly publicized cases of fabrication and plagiarism in the professional ranks are combined with the proliferation of cheating on college campuses, it should not be surprising that such pathologies should infect the college newsrooms. In early 2004, for example, the editor-in-chief of Clemson University's *Tiger News* resigned after acknowledging he had borrowed outside sources. Shortly thereafter, a columnist for the *Iowa State Daily* newspaper was fired for plagiarism for lifting material from other sources.[132]

It is ironic that in the news business in particular, which depends so heavily on attribution for its credibility, journalists are so careless in identifying the real origins of their information. Some reporters, for example, often incorporate information from stories in their newspapers' morgues for historical background and perspective without sufficient verification or attribution. Wire stories sometimes appear under the bylines of local reporters. Broadcast and print reporters often steal from each other to preserve the myth of exclusivity.[133]

But ethicist Deni Elliott, commenting on plagiarism in the news business, says there is a greater need for attribution today and in the future, "not because of declining morality, but because our notion of news is changing."[134] In the days when news was "out there" waiting to be discovered, observes Elliott, everyone was chasing the same story, and not much counted for plagiarism. Competitive reports often resembled each other. But in today's journalistic culture reporters' accounts are more likely to be individualized, the result of painstakingly synthesizing, analyzing, and interpreting.[135]

There is a lively debate within journalistic circles as to what actually constitutes plagiarism. The excuses range all the way from "a lack of clear industry standards" to "the line between ethical behavior and plagiarism depends upon context." However, such relativistic arguments are nothing more than an attempt to

rationalize the predatory practices of both charlatans and those who surrender to deadline pressure or moments of weakness. It is ironic that journalists, who have always embraced attribution as one of the "first principles" of ethical reporting, should equivocate on the issue of plagiarism. According to Elliott, such ethical indiscretions violate the moral duty owed to at least three parties:

> A reporter who passes off some other reporter's reporting as her own cheats her boss by violating a rule of research that she knows she is expected to follow. She cheats the original author by not recognizing her claim of ownership. Most importantly, she cheats her reader because she doesn't have the background that she implicitly promises with her byline or on-air appearance.[136]

Like most ethical thickets concerning media practitioners, there is undoubtedly some room for ambiguity in what constitutes plagiarism. But in searching for guidelines, you might ask yourself two questions: (1) Have I clearly attributed all information derived from other sources? (2) Will the average reader, viewer, or listener be able to clearly distinguish my work from others in terms of style, structure, and expression? These two questions should not exhaust your inquiry into what constitutes plagiarism, but they can serve as a barometer in measuring the intellectual honesty of your own work.

TRUTH TELLING AND APPROACHES TO MORAL REASONING

In working your way through this ethical thicket involving truth telling, you should return to the various approaches to moral reasoning discussed in Chapter 3. You may recall that deontologists, represented by the views of such philosophers as Kant, hold that something other than consequences should determine the rightness or wrongness of an act. The important thing is the "rule" against lying, despite the fact that telling the truth might result in bad consequences, as when a journalist reports the facts about a public figure that might injure that person's reputation.

Because of its absolute prohibition against lying and deception, the Kantian (nonconsequentialist) model has been rejected by some as unrealistic and even undesirable. However, some contemporary authors have suggested that we should not construe Kant's categorical imperative so narrowly.[137] All lies or acts of deception are not, after all, on the same moral footing. Under this more moderate Kantian view, the touchstone test would be whether there was a compelling reason to deviate from the truth, and even then the burden of proof would be on the one who was engaging in the deception. This *compelling-reason* test would require the following: (1) the reason(s) for the deception must be extremely important, (2) the deception must be done for humanitarian purposes devoid of self-interest, (3) the arguments in favor of deception must far outweigh the arguments against the compromising of the principles of truth telling, and (4) the moral agent must act with good motives based on the respect for persons as ends unto themselves rather than means to an end.

A different perspective on the question of truth and deception is provided by the teleologist. As noted in Chapter 3, teleologists (represented by the utilitarians) are sometimes referred to as consequentialists, because they gauge the consequences of an act before making an ethical judgment. Because utilitarians believe in promoting the greatest good for the greatest number, a media practitioner following this approach would weigh the relative harm or good done to various individuals or groups that results from deceptive behavior. However, utilitarians do not assume that lies and deception are harmless. In fact, "liars are presumed guilty until proven innocent, rather than innocent until proven guilty."[138] In other words, the burden of proof is still on the moral agent to prove

that a lie or deceptive act will promote the greatest good for the greatest number of people and that the benefits outweigh the harmful consequences.

Aristotle's golden mean, the example of *virtue ethics* described in Chapter 3, is also a valuable approach in providing a sense of balance and proportion in cases involving how much truth to reveal about a situation or the kind and scope of coverage to provide for a news story. In news stories in which there is a tendency toward excessive and sometimes sensational coverage—for example, in the case of a terrorist hijacking—the golden mean can be a helpful guideline in exercising more restraint in reporting. There are also occasions when this approach can be applied by advertisers and public relations executives in an attempt to maintain that delicate balance between social responsibility and corporate self-interest. A case in point are beer commercials that contain a subtle admonition to the audience not to drink and drive.

TRUTH AND DECEPTION: HYPOTHETICAL CASE STUDIES

The following cases give you an opportunity to examine a variety of issues dealing with the principle of truth. The scenarios cover a wide range of deceptive practices, from communicating outright falsehoods to withholding information and using the literal truth to deceive an audience. Several kinds of moral agents are represented in these cases: reporters, advertisers, public relations practitioners, and those who make decisions regarding television entertainment.

Each case begins with a set of facts and an outline of the ethical dilemma. Next, I briefly discuss the case study and the role that you are asked to play. You are asked, in some situations, to assume the role of a moral agent. In every case you should apply the material and the moral reasoning model outlined in the first three chapters of this book.

CASE STUDIES

> ## CASE 4-1
> ### Undercover Advertising in the Public Square

"Is this the future of advertising?," Lydia Mitchell wondered reflectively as she completed perusing the proposal submitted to her by Warren Douglas, her company's Director of Marketing and Sales. Mitchell was Vice President for Corporate Communication and Strategic Planning for SolarLink Technologies, a financially thriving electronics firm that catered to the American consumers' addictive appetite for the latest high-tech communications hardware. Mitchell had cultivated her managerial skills and competitive instincts in a variety of corporate venues before joining SolarLink Technologies, but the competition in the consumer electronics industry was unrivaled in her prior experience. Marketing and advertising her company's vast menu of innovative products was a risky enterprise and demanded creative strategies to counter the equally aggressive campaigns of SolarLink's commercial adversaries. She was buoyed by the talents of her staff, who micromanaged and integrated the company's multifaceted corporate affairs, including sales, marketing, advertising, and public relations.

Mitchell was painfully aware of the clutter of the commercial marketplace and the constant challenge to market and advertise SolarLink's products amid this cacophony of competing voices. She credited Warren Douglas and Susan Rabinowitz, her director of advertising and public affairs, with SolarLink's ascendancy from commercial obscurity to an industry leader. Douglas, in particular, shared his supervisor's understandable apprehension over what he believed was an increasingly difficult challenge in promoting SolarLink's futuristic and complex products in a world of competing electronic innovations. In his view, more aggressive and unorthodox strategies were called for.

Douglas decided that the Astrolight, a palm-size electronic information center, should serve as the test case for SolarLink's maiden foray into undercover advertising, sometimes referred to as viral marketing. Viral marketing had already proven its effectiveness in the marketplace, according to preliminary reports from companies that had pioneered this rather audacious marketing strategy. The concept is simple: A company contracts with actors who pose as tourists or ordinary consumers and then engage unsuspecting potential customers (referred to in Douglas's proposal as *consumer targets*) in conversation. Once they have the attention of their subjects, they then produce the company's product and in a casual, conversational manner begin promoting the product features. While there is no attempt to consummate a sale at that point, the objective is to spread the news about the product by word of mouth, like a virus, hence the name "viral marketing."

As was customary in developing marketing strategies for new products, Douglas prepared a proposal for Lydia Mitchell's review, highlighting the natural "fit" between Astrolight and the viral marketing technique. The Astrolight was a palm-size communications center that integrated cell phone, digital photography, and computer technology and was supplemented with a satellite link to greatly expand Astrolight's multifaceted horizons. According to the proposal, the company would hire two actors to masquerade as tourists on Madison Avenue in downtown New York. They would accost unsuspecting pedestrians and ask them to take a picture of the couple. The actors would first instruct the subjects on how to operate the Astrolight and then very casually begin plugging the other product features. If asked if they worked for the company, they would acknowledge their affiliation but otherwise would not disclose their real purpose in promoting the Astrolight's impressive features to willing pedestrians on Madison Avenue.

Mitchell was aware that a delay in marketing a new product could be a fatal flaw and immediately summoned Douglas and Rabinowitz to discuss the merits of Douglas's viral marketing proposal for the Astrolight. The meeting quickly turned into a discourse between Douglas and Rabinowitz on the ethics of undercover advertising. Mitchell listened intently because in the final analysis she would be the moral agent in deciding whether to implement Douglas's controversial plan.

"Viral marketing is the latest in marketing techniques," Douglas declared in his opening salvo in defense of what he believed was an imaginative strategy. "And those who have tried it say it works. The media advertising marketplace is so cluttered that individual sponsors are being drowned out. It's difficult to get your message across. Viral marketing, on the other hand, allows us to go one-on-one with the consumer."

"I have ethical concerns about this proposal," responded Rabinowitz. "Undercover advertising—or viral marketing as its called—is deceptive. It takes advantage of strangers who aren't aware they are talking to actors promoting a product."

"So who is being harmed?," asked Douglas. "As you will note in my proposal, the actors would be instructed to never lie about who they are. The consumer targets can assume anything they wish, and if they inquire about whether the salespeople actually work for the company, our representatives must be honest."

"But promoting the benefits of a new electronic gadget without revealing the motivation for the endorsement is taking advantage of total strangers," contended Rabinowitz. "Besides, in addition to being deceptive, this practice is intrusive. It's worse than telemarketing because there is no do-not-call list. It's an 'in-your-face' kind of marketing strategy that makes it difficult for consumers to say no."

"But we're not attempting to sell these people the Astrolight on the spot," replied Douglas. "All our actors are doing is providing information. And then, hopefully news of our product will spread by word of mouth. That's why it's called viral marketing. We're just providing information about our new product, and then the consumer targets can take it from there. Based upon industry research, this strategy is very effective. Many companies are already using it. If we don't do likewise, we'll be at competitive disadvantage."

The appeal to marketplace realities usually resonated with Susan Rabinowitz who, after all, was the corporate superintendent for SolarLink's aggressive and highly successful advertising agenda. Nevertheless, she persisted in her reluctance to associate herself with Douglas's marketing proposal.

"I don't believe that what our competitors do or are likely to do should be the pivotal factor in this case," said Rabinowitz. "Admittedly, the traditional advertising marketplace is cluttered, but if we're creative enough we can still compete. We don't need to stoop this low to peddle our products."

"If you believe undercover advertising is unethical," responded Douglas, "then we're already operating on an ethically slippery slope. Two years ago we contracted with a product placement firm to have some of our products featured prominently in a couple of TV series, as well as one movie for theatre release. Although our name was mentioned in the closing credits, most viewers were probably unaware that we paid for these product inserts."

"But product placements are different," replied Rabinowitz without hesitation. "Even if viewers are unaware of the commercial nature of these inserts—an assumption that may not be true considering the increasing sophistication of consumers—at least our corporate name is prominently displayed. And since the entertainment content is wrapped around the product inserts, which receive only a brief mention, the viewer is unlikely to feel abused in the process. But in viral marketing the consumer must deal directly with the commercial agents—the actors—and thus they are a captive audience. And it's not clear at the outset that they are representing SolarLink Technologies."

"But the Astrolight has so many attractive features—how do you explain this in a magazine ad or 30-second television commercial?," asked Douglas. "Even if there is some deception involved in undercover advertising, it may be the only effective means for truly marketing such a complicated product. Traditional media don't lend themselves to such a broad spectrum of rational appeals and the practical utility of such a product. And as I stated earlier, no one is really getting hurt. We're not asking the target consumer to actually purchase the product from our reps."

After five minutes of this frank exchange between her two subordinates, Mitchell felt reasonably attuned to the ethical dimensions of utilizing undercover advertising as a marketing strategy. As she stared out the window of her twelfth-story office to the busy thoroughfare below filled with potential customers for the Astrolight, she agonized over whether her company should embrace this new-fangled advertising pitch known as viral marketing.

THE CASE STUDY

Although undercover advertising—viral marketing— is viewed as an innovative strategy for positioning a company's products in a highly competitive marketplace, it has the trappings of an old idea. Prior to the advent of mass media, products were often peddled by door-to-door salespeople who promoted the virtues of their wares in a one-on-one encounter with the consumer. Mass media, of course, are much more efficient in reaching a large audience, and door-to-door advertising has become prohibitively expensive for most nationally sold products. When advertising is mediated rather than interpersonal, commercial messages cannot be tailored to the individual consumer.[139] But in the previous scenario, the sales reps can respond instantly to comments or even objections from target consumers.

Viral marketing does remedy the deficiency inherent in mediated communication, but it differs from the traditional door-to-door sales pitch in that consumers may be unaware they are being manipulated. Practitioners of undercover advertising must plead guilty to accusations of deception. Nevertheless, they are not without some interesting rebuttals in defending the practice. First, while viral marketing may be deceptive, it causes no harm, particularly since the sales reps do not attempt to sell directly to their targets. They rely upon word of mouth to promote their products. Second, while some may view viral marketing as a form of manipulation, all advertising involves manipulation at some level. Third, in response to the complaint that viral marketing is intrusive, proponents point out that advertising today is ubiquitous and is inherently intrusive, particularly TV ads that penetrate the sanctity of the home. Why, they ask, is a brief encounter with total strangers on a busy pedestrian thoroughfare any more intrusive, even if they are unaware of the real purpose of the encounter? Those who venture forth into the public

square run the risk that they will be accosted by strangers with hidden agendas.

For the purpose of confronting the ethical dimensions of undercover advertising, also known as viral marketing, assume the role of Lydia Mitchell, the Vice President for Corporate Communication and Strategic Planning for SolarLink Technologies. And then, applying the SAD model for moral reasoning outlined in Chapter 3, make a decision on whether you will approve Warren Douglas's proposal to market your company's new product.

 CASE 4-2

Crisis Management on the Web and the Framing of Truth

It was an airline's worst nightmare! A brief Mayday distress signal, followed by an abrupt disappearance from the air controller's radar screen, and then an eerie silence. Transnational Airlines Flight 680 had crashed in a heavy thunderstorm just 300 yards from the runway at Atlanta's Hartsfield International Airport. As an emergency response team and airport officials rushed to the scene of devastation, members of the National Transportation Safety Board (NTSB) were packing their bags for what they knew would be another lengthy investigation of an airline disaster involving a substantial loss of life.

Transnational had been in the air for only ten years, the latest major entry into the increasingly competitive airline industry, and it had been blessed with a perfect safety record. Its low-cost fares and convenient schedules had endeared it to both corporate and pleasure passengers, and its profitability seemed secure, at least for the short term. CEO Wallace Brewster, who had assumed the helm of Transnational after eight years as a vice president of an industry competitor, felt acutely any loss of life resulting from an airline catastrophe, but he was also aware of the public relations implications of such tragedies. One of his first moves as Transnational's corporate head was to hire David Lane as his director of marketing and communications. Brewster also assembled a crisis management team, which would be responsible for handling all aspects of the airline's public response to any unforeseen misfortune. Like a military unit that trains constantly but hopes that their preparation will never be tested in combat, the crisis management team's preparedness was assured through a constant series of well-orchestrated but unannounced drills. When the team's alert was sounded just minutes after the crash of Flight 680, accompanied by a "this is not a drill" advisory, Transnational's crisis management operatives knew their baptism of fire was about to begin.

As Subteam A—a group of fifty airline employees especially trained in grief counseling and family assistance—embarked immediately from the airline's headquarters in St. Louis and flew directly to the crash site in Atlanta, Subteam B busied themselves with notifying family members and arranging transportation for those who needed it to Hartsfield International. David Lane, who just prior to the crash was known simply as the director of marketing and communications, now became the head of Subteam C, which would handle all media relations and information flow about the crash to the bereaved family members of the crash victims. Lane, who by temperament always prepared for the worst-case scenario, did not underestimate the complexity of his mission. Initial reports indicated there were no survivors.

When Lane joined Transnational Airlines at its inception, he had devised a public relations crisis management plan, which he reviewed and updated every six months. The emergence of Web-based communications had afforded the energetic corporate executive opportunities that were unavailable during his maiden voyage with the company. With the crash of Flight 680, Lane and his small staff of public relations artisans responded with alacrity to the accident's inevitable emotional aftermath.

Within a couple of hours of the crash, Lane met with the news media to provide them with any available information on the crash, which of course amounted to very little. He then announced, much to the annoyance of the assembled journalists, that his company's primary concern was the care and comfort of the family members who had suffered the loss of loved ones and that this would be

Transnational's last press conference for the foreseeable future. Instead, the airline was establishing a website on which all information originating from Transnational would be posted. Transnational had promised the families they would provide information directly to them through the website rather than disseminating it secondhand through the media, while continuing its personal contacts with the families. The online site would ensure that the media, the public, and family members would have simultaneous access to the unfiltered latest developments on the airline's handling of the tragedy's aftermath. Details of the investigation into the causes of the crash, of course, would come from the NTSB. This was a risky strategy in terms of media relations, but Lane believed the Web had reduced the need to rely on journalists for mass dissemination of their corporate messages.

In addition, Lane told the assembled reporters that part of the website would be secure and access granted only to family members through a password provided by the airline. This link would allow airline officials to keep family members updated instantaneously without having to contact each family individually to inform them of new developments. However, Subteam A would continue its program of assistance and counseling as long as it was needed.

In the weeks following Transnational's untimely catastrophe, Lane continued to receive inquiries from the press, but his staff unfailingly referred them to the company's online crisis communications center. When reporters complained about a lack of access to corporate officials, Lane reminded them that the airline was holding back nothing and that all relevant information was available to both the media and the public on the company's website. Meanwhile, the NTSB investigation had initially focused on the poor weather conditions at Hartsfield International as Flight 680 made its final approach. But that was about to change.

Six weeks after the crash and the 132 funerals and memorial services that were held to commemorate those who lost their lives at the nation's busiest airport, Lane was watching glumly as CNN's live telecast of the NTSB's latest news conference unfolded on the 25-inch monitor in his corporate office. "We believe that poor weather conditions may have been a contributing factor in the crash of Flight 680," NTSB Chair Simon Yates announced, "but we are now looking at the possibility of pilot error."

Pilot error! The two most feared words in the lexicon of airline public relations officials. But Lane was not immobilized by the agency's announcement. "We must be proactive in dealing with this new blip on our radar screen," he declared confidently as he invoked his favorite airline metaphor in referring to this new public relations challenge. His two staff members, Allison Peachtree, Transnational's associate director for media relations, and Rondell O'Neil, the associate director for corporation communications, had joined their superior for the NTSB's latest pronouncement. O'Neil handled the internal information flow within corporate headquarters and between the headquarters and the airline's field operations, but he frequently participated in decisions involving media and public relations.

"We have anticipated this kind of situation," noted Peachtree. "It's part of our crisis management plan. At this point we should say as little as possible except to note that the pilot of Flight 680, Thomas Kinko, was a veteran with twenty-two years in the cockpit, including ten with Transnational, and that we shall await the results of the NTSB investigation before commenting further."

"It's not that simple," responded Lane. "An hour ago I had a meeting with Brewster. He had some warning of what the NTSB Chair was going to say, and they may be on to something."

"How does Brewster know that?" O'Neil demanded. "Kinko was one our best. Has he been provided some inside information on this investigation?"

"So far he's cooperated fully," replied Lane. "But some of the questions of the field investigators have raised the issue of pilot fatigue. The NTSB has our personnel files on the flight crew and our own flight and maintenance logs. Some of the logs show that Kinko frequently spent too many hours in the air, in violation of FAA regulations."

"That's obviously a problem," affirmed Peachtree, "but this is common among almost all airlines, according to the FAA's own records. Pilots routinely fly too many hours without a break. And it certainly doesn't prove that Kinko's fatigue contributed to

this accident. Most veteran pilots are used to putting in overtime."

But then Lane dropped his bombshell. "Well, this case may be different. Brewster shared with me two letters that Kinko had sent to our local representative of the Airline Pilot's Association. He met with Brewster on Kinko's behalf to discuss the matter. The letters are essentially complaints about the number of consecutive hours that Kinko had been required to fly during a two-month period. He also complained about fatigue, admitted he had actually dozed off in the cockpit on several occasions when the aircraft was on autopilot, and expressed a concern about the safety of his passengers. Brewster acknowledged Kinko's concerns and directed that the work schedules of all pilots be reviewed by their supervisors, but apparently little changed in the way of the pilot's working conditions. It's Brewster's understanding that the union head will testify about Captain Kinko's complaints and might even provide the letters."

Although Lane's inclinations had always been to be proactive, he advised his two staff members that they should await the NTSB's findings before issuing a public response. "After all, we don't know what their conclusions will be," he noted.

Two months later the government agency completed its investigation and released its findings. It noted the testimony and evidence about pilot fatigue and observed rather cautiously that that *could* have been a factor, but there was no direct evidence of fatigue. However, they identified the culprits as inclement weather accompanied by a critical error in the pilot's flap adjustment during the final approach. The report noted that inbound pilots had warned others on final approach about the severe turbulence in the area.

The airline had been provided with an advance copy of the agency's findings, and Lane quickly convened a meeting with Peachtree and O'Neil. "I have to recommend to Brewster what our course of action should be. There are two key issues here: first, what will be our response to the Board's findings and, second, will we abandon our website-only communications policy and deal directly with the media?"

"I think we have to hold a news conference," responded Peachtree. "The press is already unhappy with what they perceive as a lack of cooperation on our part. In this way, if they have questions we can respond on the spot. In addition, I think that a live, televised news conference is more effective than the austerity of narratives on the Web. We could transmit a statement by real-time video on the Internet, but that won't generate the broad-based audience that network television does. Besides, David is a very credible and persuasive speaker."

"I'm still uneasy about abandoning our pledge to communicate only through our website," replied O'Neil. "This is what the victims' families expect. On the secure link we can also target them with special messages in an attempt to restore some measure of credibility if the NTSB's announcement raises questions in their mind about our corporate responsibility. Our family assistance efforts have paid handsome dividends since the crash. We don't want to suffer a reversal on that front."

"I'm more concerned about our corporate line than how we disseminate this information," declared Peachtree. "The NTSB has found pilot error but hasn't clearly linked it to fatigue. It may well be that he was fatigued, but we don't know that. Of course, the public might think the worst, and link pilot error with fatigue in their collective minds. Nevertheless, our strategy should be to emphasize the fact that we have no reason to believe that Kinko was not fully alert during his final approach. He was one of our most experienced pilots."

"We could leave it at that," replied O'Neil, "but there *was* pilot error, and the issue is whether it was his mistake alone or whether we share corporate responsibility. We'll never know the answer to that question, but we can't just leave it to the mercy of public speculation. Perhaps we should attempt to deflect attention away from Captain Kinko and release a statement acknowledging that pilot fatigue is an industry-wide problem caused not by corporate malfeasance but unavoidable flight delays and the complex logistics of responding to such delays through the reassignment of flight crews. Under such circumstances, some overtime is unavoidable. We could then reemphasize the fact that we have no reason to believe that Captain Kinko was not fully alert on his final approach to Hartsfield. That's true because I don't believe there's any evidence to the contrary.

It's my understanding that the communication with the control tower prior to impact was normal. He certainly had enough presence of mind to issue a Mayday call a short time before impact."

"But the most damaging part of the NTSB's report is Kinko's complaints," observed Peachtree correctly. "Do we just ignore this fact? The media will certainly press us on this issue. If we acknowledge the complaints and our company's subsequent review of our pilot's work schedules, we could note that Captain Kinko was the only one who protested to corporate management and that we attempted to address his concerns. Of course, journalists are by nature suspicious and they aren't likely to buy the 'Captain Kinko as lone protestor' explanation. They will suggest that other pilots were probably afraid to come forward for fear of losing their jobs in an industry that is at the mercy of unpredictable market forces."

David Lane listened to this civil exchange between his two staff members and told them he would reflect upon their comments before preparing a draft recommendation for Wallace Brewster's perusal. He promised them an opportunity to review his proposal before presenting it to Transnational's beleaguered CEO.

THE CASE STUDY

Public relations professionals are frequently confronted with moral dilemmas concerning how much of the truth should be released to the public. But exactly what is the truth as developed in this narrative? There are clearly some unanswered questions, as there are in any ethical dilemma. Thus, the problem becomes one of how to "frame" the story to protect the company's own interest and yet keep faith with the flying public.

How to balance corporate self-interest against the public's interest is a perennial question for public relations practitioners. This case is particularly complex because full disclosure can have devastating effects on Transnational Airline's image in the court of public opinion. The airline is in an awkward position because they are not fully in command of the information flow to the public. When they established their website to control the flow of information, they did not anticipate that the finger of responsibility would point directly at Trans-national's corporate headquarters. There appeared to be an underlying assumption that the accident was entirely weather related. However, the NTSB investigation took an unexpected turn.

Since the "truth" behind this accident is at issue here, perhaps a good way to begin is to review the facts. First, Flight 680 crashed in extremely poor weather conditions. Other pilots attempting to land reported a great deal of turbulence just prior to the plane's impact. Second, there is no evidence that Captain Kinko was not alert in the cockpit; he managed to blurt out a distress call a minute before the crash. Third, Captain Kinko had ex-pressed a concern to his union representative about his work schedule, a complaint that was for-warded to Transnational's CEO. Four, CEO Brewster ordered a review of all pilot work schedules but apparently nothing changed. Five, pilot fatigue is an industry-wide problem, and many airlines systematically violate FAA guidelines concerning work hours.

There are several stakeholders in this ethical narrative: the victims' families, the public, the media, the pilots, and the company itself. Pilot fa-tigue is an industry-wide problem, but if Transna-tional shifts the focus away from Captain Kinko and his complaints, then this might be construed as an affront to the bereaved families of the vic-tims. Transnational's emergency response team has worked diligently to cultivate their faith in the com-pany's sense of compassion, and the shifting of blame to a higher plane could undermine the air-line's humanistic efforts. On the other hand, the company can truthfully point to the fact that there is no evidence that pilot fatigue contributed to this particular accident. And CEO Brewster was not un-responsive to Kinko's complaints, although for whatever reason no major changes resulted from his directive that pilot work schedules be reviewed. Perhaps this tragedy should serve as a clarion call for corporate management to address more effec-tively the problem of pilot fatigue.

The other issue, of course, is whether to deal with this embarrassing revelation through a stan-dard news conference or to continue to rely solely on the website. This decision is not unrelated to the slippery slope of truth since the website allows the company to control its response to the NTSB report, both to the media and a national (as well as international) audience, whereas a news con-ference will subject Transnational to the vagaries of hostile questioning. Journalists will argue that corporate officials should subject themselves to cross-examination. Do public relations practition-ers owe a special duty to journalists as fiduciaries of the public, or are corporate websites making journalists increasingly anachronistic (or at least less important) in the dissemination of corporate communications? Which is likely, in the long run, to better serve the public's interest in uncorrupted and truthful information?

With these ideas in mind, assume the role of David Lane, Transnational's director of marketing and communications, and describe the recommen-dation you will present to CEO Wallace Brewster. In analyzing this case, you should apply the SAD for-mula for moral reasoning outlined in Chapter 3.

 CASE 4-3

Hidden Cameras and the Journalist as Social Conscience

Proposition 120, a rather innocent-sounding label for a very controversial ballot initiative, had been the brainchild of state senator Hugh Wilson. Wilson, a conservative lawmaker and perennial opponent of big government, was determined to stem the flow of illegal immigrants into his state from Mexico. And the most effective means of accomplishing this goal, in Wilson's view, was to deny them access to the state's bountiful cafeteria of social services. His supporters championed Wilson as a fiscal knight in shining armor. His detractors disparaged his pro-posal as an assault of draconian proportions on innocent human beings.

Nevertheless, Wilson's proposal struck a re-sponsive chord among a large segment of the electorate and was soon featured prominently as Proposition 120 on the November ballot, along with the plethora of state and local elections and the hotly contested races for the U.S. House of Representatives. Specifically, Proposition 120 would cut off most social services to illegal immigrants, including educational opportunities for their children. Although the rather formal-sounding language of the proposition obscured the emotional and human dimensions of the debate, the message to the nation's lawmakers in Washington was unmistakable: *Stop the flood of illegal immigrants into our state, or we'll do it for you!*

Manny Fernandez watched with concern on election night as the returns were tabulated by his newsroom computers. Within a couple of hours after the last polls closed, it was clear that Proposition 120 would pass overwhelmingly. As news director of Channel 5 in San Jacinto, one of three network affiliates located in a metropolitan center of 650,000 near the Mexican border, Fernandez knew that Proposition 120 would just exacerbate the growing ethnic strife in his city. With its proximity to the Mexican border, San Jacinto was the entry point for many of the immigrants. On election night the Hispanic population stood at 40 percent; the city had become a true melting pot. And the pot was beginning to boil.

San Jacinto voters had defied the trend statewide and narrowly defeated the proposal. But an influential and very vocal minority had campaigned aggressively for Proposition 120. The best-case scenario, in Fernandez's view, would be a court injunction that would halt the implementation of the measure until its constitutionality could be decided. This would allow time for the cooling of passions. But what Fernandez feared most was a violent uprising by the Hispanic community and perhaps even a defiance of the measure by local school officials, who considered the denial of educational opportunities to the immigrants' children as tantamount to child abuse.

Channel 5's news staff had reported on the "immigrant problem," as it was referred to in the newsroom, almost from its inception. The alarming drain on the state's dwindling financial resources precipitated by the staggering costs of social services to the immigrants had been the centerpiece of the station's coverage. And although the hiring of these immigrants was illegal, the station had documented repeatedly the rather casual violation of the law by local merchants. Of course, neither employers nor employees were willing participants in these stories, and Channel 5 had often relied on confidential sources and concealed identities to document this illegal behavior. One of the station's reporters had even spent a few days in jail rather than reveal a source to a grand jury investigating the situation.

Fernandez viewed these reports with mixed emotions. As a journalist, he felt an undeniable commitment to the first principles of journalism, fairness and balance. This was a complex and contentious issue, and he was determined that all credible voices should be heard. On the other hand, as the son of Mexican immigrants himself, he felt an emotional bond with those who had crossed the border, either legally or illegally, in search of a better life. Fernandez had harbored expectations that the newly ratified trade agreement between the United States and Mexico would improve economic conditions south of the border, but the continuing pilgrimage of immigrants into his state had dampened his cautious optimism.

As expected, within a week after the passage of Proposition 120, a federal court blocked implementation of the measure until its constitutionality could be tested. And with the endless hearings that were likely to ensue, Fernandez felt relieved that other stories could at last compete for top billing in his station's newscasts. Ron Mackey had other ideas.

Mackey was the producer of Channel 5's top-rated early evening newscast. Mackey had joined the staff three years ago and had quickly molded a rather lethargic news operation into an aggressive and creative journalistic enterprise. But Mackey was not one to be complacent, and his antennae were constantly scanning the horizon for visually appealing, dramatic, and controversial story ideas. His enthusiasm sometimes tested the limits of ethical propriety, but his arguments in favor of the public's right to know were usually convincing to his superiors, particularly in San Jacinto's competitive marketplace.

Two weeks after the election, Fernandez turned first to Mackey during his morning staff meeting. "I'll discuss tonight's lineup in a minute. But we have something new on the immigrant problem. Ortego has confirmed the rumors." Fernandez recognized Ortego as a confidential source the station often relied on in covering the hiring of illegal immigrants. And the rumors referred to unsubstantiated accounts of manufacturers that had set up sweatshops in San Jacinto.

"We have confirmation from a second source," Mackey continued. "There may be more than one shop in the area, but the one that's been identified is Alton Enterprises on Third Avenue." Alton was a locally owned company that produced a line of cheap ready-to-wear garments with its own label. But it also did contract work for several major retailers and discount stores, and it was in this manufacturing arena that illegal immigrants were forced to work fifteen to eighteen hours a day for less than the minimum wage. Some workers, according to the information provided by the sources, were under 18 years of age. And there was also evidence that some plant supervisors physically abused the workers when they fell behind the company-imposed production quota.

Fernandez realized that, if the charges were true, the issue of employment of illegal immigrants would reach a new plateau. It was one thing for small merchants, who often worked on small profit margins and experienced a large employee turnover, to ignore the sometimes complex requirements in documenting the legal status of immigrants. But it was quite another for a large company to exploit their workers under such inhumane conditions.

"So how should we handle this?" Fernandez directed the question to Mackey, but he welcomed suggestions from assistant news director Andrea Cobb and assignment editor Marci Gonzalez.

"We can't just rely on sources in this case," stated Gonzalez. "We have to name the company, and we need authentic visual evidence. This is different from the other stories, where some small merchants are too busy eking out a living to document the legal status of their employees. In this case, Alton is running a sweatshop; they're exploiting and abusing their workers. We have to go in undercover with concealed cameras. Jose can be our mole."

Jose was a young photographer who had been with the station for two years. With his youthful appearance and fluent Spanish, he should have little trouble, in Mackey's judgment, in passing himself off as an undocumented immigrant and gaining employment at Alton. His concealed camera could record the daily activities of the plant, including the alleged abusive behavior of the plant's supervisors. Eventually Jose could also gain the confidence of his coworkers to capture, on tape, their own personal testimonials of economic woes. "Don't we have other options?" Fernandez asked. "Jose will obviously have to lie on his job application to get hired. And besides, I've always been uncomfortable with the use of hidden cameras. Let's face it. Most of our network's magazine shows have used concealed cameras and microphones, and now they're being accused of practicing tabloid journalism. This isn't good for our credibility." In staking out the moral high ground, perhaps Fernandez was remembering a tongue-lashing he had suffered on this issue at the hands of a student during a visit to a journalism ethics class at a local college.

"I agree," Cobb said. "Surely there must be other ways to approach this story. Perhaps our sources can arrange for us to talk to some of the employees; we could even interview them on tape and mask their identities. And keep in mind, some of these people may not be illegals. We have to be careful to document each worker who appears on tape. If we go into this plant and surreptitiously record these employees on tape, even if we don't identify them, we may never again get cooperation from the Hispanic community. Even if there is some exploitation, at least the company does provide employment. Many of our Hispanic citizens may not appreciate this kind of public exposé and breach of trust with these immigrant workers. In their view, after all, these sweatshops may be no worse than the conditions they left in Mexico. I would feel more comfortable if there were other companies involved—if the practice were widespread. Alton is a large company, but it *is* only one manufacturer among many in this region."

"Interviewing them really isn't an option," Gonzalez responded in apparent agreement with Mackey. "They aren't likely to talk; they need the job, and they're afraid of retribution. Besides, TV is a visual medium. We need to use the tools of our trade. The hidden camera is our way of documenting this story. We can mask the faces of the workers. So who will get hurt? The public needs to know that this kind of exploitation is occurring here in San Jacinto, even if only one company is involved. Isn't it our job to call attention to a problem before it spreads? And I don't really have a problem with Jose's using deception to get this job or using a hidden camera, for that matter. There are times when reporters must take extraordinary measures to help cure society's ills. *And this is one of those times.*"

Fernandez wasn't so sure. But he promised to keep an open mind on the subject. After all, his station had acquitted itself well, in his judgment, in its coverage of the immigrant problem over the past several years. The Hispanic community had given Channel 5 high marks, overall, for its balanced treatment of the issues. Would this story be greeted with similar acclaim? Fernandez ended the staff meeting and pondered the ethical concerns raised by Mackey's proposal.

THE CASE STUDY

Are journalists ever justified in using deception to collect information in the name of the public interest? Investigative reporting demands documentation, and as a visual medium, TV is at its best when it provides photographic evidence of its discoveries. And as technological advances have produced small cameras that can shoot in poor lighting conditions, the temptation to use concealed cameras has, in many cases, been irresistible. But despite the widespread use of hidden cameras and other forms of deception in news gathering, these techniques remain controversial.[140] Misrepresentation and deception, of course, are a violation of society's norms. Thus, such practices must be justified based on some overriding moral principle.

Two salient values in this case appear to be the "public's need to know" and the "minimization of harm." Some would argue that the information in this story is of profound public importance. It certainly represents a new chapter in the ongoing saga of the illegal immigrants. But at this point the evidence points to only one company that is engaged in worker exploitation. Many others hire legal immigrants and appear to be law-abiding. Is the station justified in going undercover to expose one company? Mackey might argue that such aggressive journalism would prevent others from setting up sweatshops in San Jacinto to take advantage of the abundant labor supply.

Anticipating the consequences in ethical dilemmas of this kind is fraught with uncertainty, and the question of harm is certainly problematic in this case. Channel 5's news staff may truly believe that they are coming to the aid of these workers by exposing their life of misery and abuse. Under most circumstances, the station would be applauded for such journalistic enterprise. But if the illegal workers are identified by immigration officials and returned to Mexico, some Hispanic viewers may be less than enthusiastic about the station's role in unmasking the sweatshop. After all, are the conditions here much worse than the poverty experienced in their homeland? But should Fernandez be concerned about such consequences? After all, Alton's actions are morally and legally indefensible. If the station doesn't confront publicly such affronts to human decency, then it might be accused of abandoning its mandate as the guardian of the public's interest.

Fernandez should be convinced that the harm prevented by the misrepresentation and use of hidden cameras outweighs the harm that may occur from the act of deception. As news director, Fernandez is concerned with the station's credibility. On the one hand, the failure to investigate this story for fear of alienating the viewers with the use of deception could damage the station's reputation as an aggressive journalistic enterprise and a defender of the public's interest. On the other hand, the use of hidden cameras and undercover reporters could result in a loss of credibility for the station, especially if the station's viewers consider such tactics unnecessary or unreasonable.

Using the SAD formula for moral reasoning described in Chapter 3, assume the role of Channel 5's news director, Manny Fernandez, and ponder whether you will approve the use of misrepresentation and hidden cameras to document the existence of sweatshops and the exploitation of illegal immigrants in San Jacinto.

▶ **CASE 4-4**

Political Communication on the Net: Is Voter Targeting Responsible Behavior?

Thirty-six-year-old Anthony Satterfield and 34-year-old Benjamin Marsh had launched their political consulting firm, Satterfield and Marsh (S & M), in 1982 just as the Reagan administration's agenda had captured the imagination of an increasingly conservative American electorate. In their maiden voyage, they had represented several Democratic hopefuls and worried incumbents, and in a political climate not conducive to Democratic victories had scored a series of impressive victories. With its reputation as an aggressive and effective advocate for Democratic candidates thus assured, Satterfield and Marsh quickly evolved from a fledgling political consulting firm to one of the most influential and successful firms in the Democratic camp. While the Democratic leadership remained tentative in its attempt to rescue the party from a crisis of confidence and political disarray in the wake of Republican victories in key congressional districts and senatorial races, S & M had exerted a steadying influence on party loyalists. Through aggressive and creative campaign strategies, the firm had turned the tide in favor of the Democratic Party in several key races, frequently against formidable opposition.

S & M's founders would concede no political venue to their Republican rivals, but from the outset Satterfield and Marsh had set ethical boundaries for their assertive and relentless campaigns on behalf of their clients. They accepted some negative campaigning as inevitable and perhaps even desirable in the highly contentious enterprise of party politics, but as attack ads became increasingly the norm during the decade of the nineties, Satterfield and Marsh refused to dignify these political assaults with retaliatory responses. In light of polling data showing that attack ads were frequently effective, S & M's strategy was risky, but the firm's success rate on behalf of its Democratic clientele continued unabated. The firm considered responding in kind to the political brutality of attack ads but had

rejected the notion and had emerged with its integrity intact.

Even as they approached middle age, Satterfield and Marsh were not inclined toward complacency or traditionalism and readily embraced the Internet as the new frontier of political campaigning. Their initial attempts at fund-raising using a designated website had produced impressive results, and as the political consultants perfected their use of the Net, the number of "hits" on their clients' Web pages increased dramatically.

Of course, campaign strategizing was fraught with ethical pitfalls, and as his firm's senior partner and moral gatekeeper, Anthony Satterfield insisted upon a reasonable amount of reflection and deliberation by S & M's talented and loyal staff on any proposal with ethical implications. Lewis Barnes's recommendation was such a proposal.

Barnes was S & M's Senior Campaign Strategist and saw his firm's representation of Democratic presidential contender John Cardwell as an opportunity to experiment with using the candidate's website to "target" specific individuals with interest in certain political issues utilizing information about these individuals mined from various sources on the Net. The process would work as follows: Through site tracking, the firm's computers would monitor user engagement with various websites and infer from these movements which issues a potential voter might be interested in. A related technique would involve reading the information biscuits in a user's "cookie jar"—the device that stores information about sites users have previously visited, thereby revealing their interests and concerns. For example, a cookie jar full of visits to websites of various antiabortion groups would be helpful in targeting a candidate's message to those who share similar views. Similarly, environmental messages could be framed to coincide with the views of those voters whose cookie jars reveal an interest in environmental concerns. All of this data gathering, of course, would transpire without the users' knowledge.[141]

The firm's long-standing policy required Satterfield's benediction for such a controversial campaign tactic, and he quickly summoned Barnes and Media Director Marsha Moore to his office for what he anticipated would be a spirited exchange.

"As you know," said Barnes, as he began the defense of his proposal, "we're in a dead heat with our Republican opponent. We need every vote we can get. We must pull out all the stops and maximize the use of the Internet as a vehicle for political communication. We'll continue to use the traditional media to get our messages across, but the strategy I've devised also calls for using the Net to match our various agendas with receptive target audiences. Cardwell is pro-choice on the abortion issue; when someone from this target audience hits our website, a pop-up message will outline his views on abortion. Those opposed to our candidate's position will not be exposed to his pro-choice message. Similarly, a voter who is a strong environmentalist will be treated to our candidate's strong beliefs about protecting the environment. Senior citizens will be reassured of Cardwell's determination to protect Social Security from the conservative tax cutters in Congress. And so on."

"But this is manipulative and dishonest," replied Moore without hesitation. "We're setting different agendas for different demographic groups—groups whose profiles we have gathered from the various Internet cookies and catalogued according to their political views. Voters who are likely to disagree with Cardwell on abortion will be treated to a different set of issues. This is a divide-and-conquer strategy that could boomerang if voters feel they are being manipulated."

"Agenda setting is nothing new," responded Barnes. "We've known for years that the media help set the agenda for debate about public issues. Political campaign strategists are also pivotal to the agenda-setting process. What I am proposing is simply a highly refined form of agenda setting. We are giving various groups a view of our candidate that coincides with their own interests. Why waste time and money communicating with audiences whose views are firmly entrenched in opposition to Cardwell's positions?"

"But Cardwell is running for president," complained Moore. "If elected, he will deal with an entire range of issues. Your proposed strategy would divert the attention of voters from Cardwell's much broader agenda. While I believe in an aggressive campaign strategy, targeting of this kind is antithetical to the democratic process. It balkanizes the voters in such a way that they can't make a truly informed choice. And it deprives voters of knowing the full truth about Cardwell's views on matters of public concern."

"I think you're overreacting," declared Barnes. "Most voters aren't interested in the entire panoply of issues that Cardwell has to deal with during this campaign. Most make their decisions based upon one or two issues. My strategy is designed to reassure voters who are already predisposed toward Cardwell on the issues in which they have an interest. Why is this any different from other forms of target marketing?"

"We're not selling toothpaste or automobiles," countered Moore. "For better or worse, we're part of the political process. When potential voters hit our website they expect to receive credible information on what our candidate stands for—not just pop-up links that discuss single issues. They're not aware that we have essentially prescreened most of them using cookies to construct personal dossiers that will then be matched to their political preferences. Most are probably not even aware that these technologies exist."

"I'd like you to consider this question," replied Barnes. "Is what I'm proposing really new? Targeting has always been the hallmark of effective marketing. We're simply using technology to make data collection more efficient. They're not interested in our candidate's stand on a wide variety of issues. Why not just give them what they're interested in?"

"I'm not convinced that this isn't manipulative," declared Moore. "Directing potential voters to some issues and diverting them away from others, without their knowledge, is deceptive and dishonest. It shaves the truth about Cardwell's beliefs as a political candidate."

"I disagree," responded Barnes, who had never agreed entirely with the firm's ethical squeamishness about attack ads. "All persuasive communication is to some degree manipulative. That's certainly true of targeted messages in advertising. Data gathering without the knowledge of consumers as a technique for target marketing has been a standard practice for years. Consider, for example, telemarketing and direct mail advertising. My proposal is certainly ethically acceptable within the highly competitive framework of political communication.

Since voters are interested in only selected issues anyway, I don't believe my proposal for targeting significantly conceals the truth about our political agenda."

Manipulative! Dishonest! Deceptive! Marsha Moore's unflattering portrayals of her colleague's high-tech proposal troubled Satterfield as he listened to this spirited exchange between his firm's two staff members. Were her concerns overblown or did targeting of the kind recommended by Barnes pose a true ethical dilemma? On the one hand, Satterfield agreed that there was something manipulative and even deceptive in the process. On the other hand, he recognized that target marketing was so ingrained in the American cultural experience that perhaps it did not pose a serious ethical concern. Satterfield's candidate was in a close and highly contentious race; his firm's goal was to help ensure a victory. But as he pondered whether to approve the proposal tendered by his Senior Campaign Strategist, Satterfield was still concerned about the consequences of such targeting on the political process.

THE CASE STUDY

Political consultants acting as communication strategists for political candidates owe their first loyalty to their clients. Their primary objective is to help ensure a campaign victory. Some operate in an ethically ambiguous universe with seemingly few scruples to animate their campaign strategy. The firm described in the previous scenario has, thus far, rejected attack ads as being counterproductive, but that appears to be the only clear-cut ethical limitation. Considering the role of political communication as an indispensable ingredient of any campaign, is targeting without the knowledge of potential voters, utilizing the technology of the Internet, an unethical practice? Or is this just a high-tech version of a practice that has become so ingrained and accepted by consumers that its ethical dimensions have become inconsequential?

Communications scholar Gary W. Selnow, in an essay on Internet ethics, disparages Web-based targeting as "manipulative." The problem, according to Selnow, is that when candidates "direct voters' attention to one or two issues and divert their attention

from the rest . . . the candidate will have been successful in reaching isolated groups with congruent images, while concealing the total picture from all groups. Voters thus can be manipulated by the agenda-setting process. Each group has a vision of the candidate. Few have the full view."[142]

Is Selnow attempting to convert unjustifiably an accepted campaign practice into an ethical issue? One could argue, first, that Barnes's proposal is nothing more than a Web-based version of a marketing technique that has been around for years and, second, that the fact that voters may be unaware that their personal Web browsings are being used to a candidate's political advantage does not truly undermine their autonomy, since in the final analysis they will vote for whom they believe to be the most qualified candidate anyway. In addition, the reality is that most voters are interested in particular issues, not a candidate's entire political platform. If voters truly desire a "full view" of a candidate, they should not rely strictly upon the candidate's website; they should seek alternative sources of information.

Nevertheless, the spirited discourse between Lewis Barnes and Marsha Moore has engaged the moral imagination of senior partner Anthony Satterfield, and he must decide whether to approve Barnes's proposal. Is the practice of targeting described in this case manipulative and dishonest or deceptive? Does this technique of political communication seriously compromise the truth about a candidate? For the purpose of responding to these troubling questions and evaluating the ethical issues posed in the previous scenario, assume the role of Anthony Satterfield and, applying the SAD model for moral reasoning described in Chapter 3, render your own decision on this matter.

 ## CASE 4-5

The Careless Chaperons and the Unbridled Teens

"Please don't publish this story. We're not asking on behalf of ourselves. It's our daughter we're concerned about. She's just a teenager who made a mistake!"

This plaintive plea sounded uncommonly familiar to Frank Littenfield as he politely listened to the distraught voice on the phone. As the managing editor of the *Columbia Gazette,* Littenfield was accustomed to requests from unwilling subjects of news coverage to "kill" or modify a story. In most cases, these frantic entreaties were pathetically frivolous or unreasonable, and Littenfield rejected the callers' complaints courteously but firmly. However, in those cases in which innocent victims or juveniles were involved, Littenfield's forbearance usually trumped his natural inclination to deny straightaway the validity of the complainant's request. As his newspaper's primary gatekeeper, he labored under the dual loyalties of keeping faith with the canons and expectations of his profession and maintaining a genuine feeling of moral compassion for those who were the focus of the *Gazette*'s journalistic enterprise.

On this occasion, the caller identified herself as Virginia Martin. Her husband and she were plaintiffs in a rather unusual lawsuit, based on circumstances that, in Littenfield's view, should never have resulted in litigation. According to the complaint filed in the state district court in Columbia, the Martins' 15-year-old daughter had attended a Christmas party at the home of Michael and Virginia Pike, who served as chaperons for the party and whose son attended the same school as the Martins' daughter. During the evening, the girl retreated to an upstairs bedroom, unnoticed by the Pikes, and had sex with a 16-year-old classmate. The girl got pregnant and later gave birth.

The girl's parents were suing the Pikes for negligence, claiming that they were careless in not properly supervising their teenage charges. "A complete lack of supervision, guidance, and discipline provided the opportunity for this sexual encounter," according to the court records.

Virginia Martin had learned of the *Gazette*'s interest in the story when Leslie McDougald, the paper's government affairs reporter, had contacted the Martins' attorney seeking additional information. McDougald had also approached the Pikes' attorney for a response to their antagonists' legal expression of indignation. The plaintiffs' counsel, predictably, accused the defendants of being delinquent in their stewardship of the teenagers entrusted to their care. The Pikes' attorney responded that "the expectations reflected in this lawsuit are unreasonable in that parents cannot be expected to oversee the unbridled passions of sexually active teenagers. There is simply no legal duty of the kind alleged in the plaintiffs' complaint."

The story was slated for tomorrow morning's edition of the *Gazette,* according to the rundown provided at the staff meeting earlier that afternoon by city editor Thomas Sizemore. As he extricated himself from the anxious caller, Littenfield made no promises to Virginia Martin but said he would consider her request for journalistic charity.

"I received a call from Virginia Martin," stated Littenfield as Sizemore and McDougald settled comfortably into their chairs for what the managing editor assumed would be a brief meeting. "She wants us to kill the story on the negligent chaperons. She claims that her concern is primarily with her daughter."

"I assume that the Martins are distressed because of what the publicity might do to their daughter," noted Sizemore. "She isn't named in the court papers or our story, but let's face it—she will be identified by association with her parents. Her sexual rendezvous and pregnancy will no longer be a personal matter if this story is published."

"That's true," replied McDougald. "But this lawsuit is a matter of public record. Once the Pikes decided to litigate this issue rather than settle it away from the glare of publicity, it became a matter of public interest."

"It may indeed be newsworthy," said Sizemore, responding more as a devil's advocate rather than from conviction, "but the fact that it's now a matter of public record doesn't automatically answer the ethical question of whether it should be published. After all, the publicity surrounding this case will result not from the court record itself but from our reporting of what's in the court record."

"True enough," admitted McDougald, "but this case clearly meets the test of newsworthiness. It involves the court system and the circumstances themselves are highly unusual. There are a lot of teenage parties in our community, most chaperoned by parents. This suit could serve as a warning to them. Besides, we're in the *truth* business. We should not get in the habit of suppressing news just because someone whose name will appear in our paper is unhappy."

"I agree, as a matter of principle," replied Sizemore. "But in a sense, the Martins' daughter has been victimized once in that she had an unwanted pregnancy. A story on this lawsuit will just victimize her again. We make editorial judgments all the time about what is or is not newsworthy. And we've been known to delete information or occasionally to preempt a story altogether if the potential harm is much greater than the news value. Is this one of those cases?"

With Sizemore's closing query, Littenfield decided to adjourn the meeting. As the moral agent in this case, he would make the final call. As a journalist, he knew that the burden of proof is on those who counsel restraint in publishing a story that a paper deems to be newsworthy. To assume otherwise is to compromise the independent status of reporters and editors. But as he pondered the situation, the managing editor acknowledged that Sizemore had raised some intriguing points that could not be dismissed out of hand.

THE CASE STUDY

At first glance, this case appears to be uncomplicated. The Martins have filed a lawsuit against another couple claiming that they were negligent in chaperoning a party, an act of carelessness that led to the pregnancy of their daughter. And despite the fact that the suit is a matter of public record, they are asking the *Gazette* to withhold the story because it will further embarrass their daughter. Such requests are not uncommon in newsrooms, and most are summarily dismissed. After all, the news media are in the business of revelation, not concealment.

But there are some countervailing arguments in this case. First, this story is not of great moment. It does not involve politics, crime or corruption, or some large-scale human tragedy. The civil complaint here is a matter of public record—a fact that offers legal refuge for the media in case of a lawsuit—but, as the city editor suggests, this doesn't automatically provide an ethical justification for publishing the story. Second, although the Martins'

daughter will not be named in the story, she will be identified through association with her parents. Thus, her own behavior will be subjected to the glare of publicity because of her parents' actions and through no fault of her own.

Managing editor Frank Littenfield is the moral agent in this case. For the purpose of examining the issues raised by the facts of this case, step into the editorial shoes of Littenfield and then, using the SAD formula for moral reasoning, render a judgment in this case.

▶ **CASE 4-6**

Digital Photography and the Manipulation of Reality

It was a classic confrontation in the abortion wars. The Reverend Joshua Saint Clare, the national leader of the Lifeline Coalition, had rallied his anti-abortion legions for another skirmish in front of the Maplewood Women's Pavilion, one of only two abortion clinics in Lewiston. Carla Alvarez was just as determined to defend the women of Lewiston against the moral onslaught of the Reverend Saint Clare. As a prominent attorney committed to rekindling the feminist liberation movement of the 1970s, Alvarez was uncompromising in her view that the right for a woman to control her own body was precedent to all other rights.

The drama that was unfolding at the Maplewood Women's Pavilion was a reenactment of similar confrontations between Saint Clare and Alvarez in five other cities, three of which had sparked sporadic violence but no serious injuries. And each time, local and national media descended on the scene with an unquenchable thirst for conflict, emotional impact, and undeniable visual appeal. The fanaticism displayed on both sides had resulted in a cult of personalities that virtually silenced the more moderate voices on the abortion issue. The high-decibel verbal sparring between the charismatic Saint Clare and the combative Alvarez was irresistible in the competitive journalistic marketplace. The characters had overshadowed the plot on the nation's front pages and the evening newscasts.

As usual, correspondents from the TV networks, several large newspapers, and the news magazines were on hand in Lewiston to chronicle the next chapter in this morality play. The *Lewiston Gazette* was on hand too. This story was made to order for chief photographer Brian Fogle.

Fogle had joined the *Gazette* ten years ago after serving a three-year apprenticeship on a small-town weekly just seventy-five miles from Lewiston. He had thrived at a paper that was becoming increasingly more visual in its coverage and where color was often featured conspicuously on both the front page and the metro page. The *Gazette*'s impressive list of awards for photojournalism since Fogle's arrival at the paper bore testament to the photographer's talent as both journalist and artisan. Fogle prided himself on his journalistic instincts in ferreting out the "real" story and then packaging it in the most vivid and dramatic way possible.

The abortion story was no exception. Fogle, along with reporter Mickey Chambers, had arrived early at the Pavilion, and with the police standing by in case of violence, the two groups of demonstrators soon began to exchange insults. And once again, the Reverend St. Clare and Carla Alvarez squared off in their all too familiar public exhibition of mutual disdain. Fogle moved quickly through the mob, capturing the growing hostility in color and preserving this dramatic confrontation for posterity. Most of his pictures, Fogle knew, would simply wind up in the newspaper's morgue. But not the profile shot of St. Clare and Alvarez standing toe-to-toe engaged in their verbal duel in front of the abortion clinic, while their supporters, armed with placards bearing a variety of messages, cheered them on. Fogle was confident that this photo had captured the very essence of the story that was unfolding at the Maplewood Women's Pavilion and that it would be featured prominently in color on the *Gazette*'s front page.

Editor Samuel Gates wasn't so confident. In reviewing the front-page layout for the next day's edition, Gates was immediately impressed by the hostility that radiated from the photo. This was certain to convey the electric atmosphere surrounding the confrontation to the reader. But it was not the profile shot of the two combatants that concerned Gates. Although it was clear from the photo that St. Clare and Alvarez were surrounded by demonstrators, one was featured more prominently than others. In the center of the photo, in the background but clearly visible, was a placard with an aborted fetus in a jar.

With the deadline approaching, Gates quickly summoned Fogle and photo editor Bill McBride to his office and expressed his concern. "This is a fantastic shot, Brian," Gates declared sincerely, "but there is a problem. Quite frankly, I feel uneasy with running this photo on the front page with the aborted fetus. This could offend some of our readers, especially if we run it in color. Do you have another shot without any signs?"

"Not really," Fogle responded somewhat defensively. "I had to move in a hurry, and the crowd was making it difficult to get near enough for any kind of close-ups. I was lucky to get this. Besides, Saint Clare and Alvarez were surrounded by demonstrators carrying signs. This is part of the story."

"If there's a problem with the sign, we can take it out or smear the message on the sign," McBride volunteered. Gates knew that McBride was referring to the paper's multimillion-dollar investment in digital technology that allowed technicians, among other things, to reconstruct or alter photographs without the faintest hint of hand retouching.

"But that's deceptive to the readers," Fogle responded indignantly. "The photo should run as it is, or it shouldn't be used at all. But I'm opposed to just killing it because it's essential to give our readers a feel for the hostility that I felt at the clinic." At this point Gates wasn't sure whether his chief photographer was taking the ethical high road or just reacting from a sense of artistic pride.

"We have other pictures," Gates said. "Of course, they are mostly crowd scenes, and they aren't as personal or dramatic. But there are some where the messages on the signs are not as visible."

But Fogle persisted. "This story is no longer just about abortion. It's about the personal animosity between Saint Clare and Alvarez. And this photo captures this hostility. This picture *is* the story."

"Then if that's the case," Gates responded, "why not remove or smear the sign? It detracts from the focus of the story. This sign might be offensive to our readers without adding anything to the photo. Why take a chance?"

The photo editor had to concede the validity of this argument. "If you're concerned about offending the readers," McBride said, "then what's the difference between altering this photo and deleting foul language from quotes in news copy? That is common practice at this paper."

As the deadline approached, Gates began to feel the tug of competing ethical loyalties. As a journalist and editor, he was usually opposed to deleting substantive content that contributed to an understanding of the story. The sign may not have been essential to the photo, but it did provide context. And he did not believe that this background sign necessarily detracted from the dramatic face-to-face encounter of the two antagonists. And even if it did, the paper might still be accused of altering reality just for the sake of dramatic effect. Would removing or smearing the sign through digital manipulation be deceptive to the readers? Would they really care?

But editors often edit stories for length, tastes, and even superfluous content. Was this offensive visual message really important to the story? If the story was no longer abortion itself but the repeated and increasingly vociferous confrontations between Saint Clare and Alvarez, then perhaps the background sign in the photo *was* superfluous. Besides, the *Gazette* was a family newspaper and owed a duty to its readers to treat them with civility, while providing them with an accurate account of the day's events. This could be accomplished in the narrative part of the coverage without such a morally challenging photograph. On a couple of occasions, the paper had "cleaned up" the background and composition of feature photos. Was this any different?

As Gates pondered his decision, he realized that the temptation to take advantage of his technology's capabilities was almost irresistible. But he had to remember that his computers and software were only tools and that machines were incapable of making ethical judgments. Digital technology, he knew, should be the servant, not the master, of practicing journalists.

THE CASE STUDY

This case does not involve digital manipulation just to delete extraneous material or to adjust a photo for space considerations. The editor is concerned about the potential reaction of readers to this offensive sign between the profile shots of the two abortion combatants. On the one hand, the alteration of any photo might be considered deceptive unless the readers are informed as to how and why the photo was altered. On the other hand, if one accepts McBride's argument, then deleting material from photos is really no different from editing news stories for content for overriding ethical reasons (for example, deleting offensive language or cleaning up the grammar in a quote).

Under time pressures, such ethical dilemmas are often subjected to ad hoc decision making, without concern for long-range consequences. But as editor, Gates must protect the integrity of his enterprise. If the *Gazette* acquires a reputation, for example, of doctoring photos, even if the readers are informed of such manipulation, then the paper has sacrificed its only stock-in-trade: the truth. Nevertheless, there are those rare exceptions when journalists must deviate from standard ethical practice for other overriding considerations. Is this such a situation? If so, what are the overriding considerations?

Gates has four choices. First, he could publish the photo in color on the front page. He would then run the risk of offending some readers.

Gates's second option is to alter the photo, either removing or smearing the sign. In this case, the paper will avoid offending its readers. But, on the other hand, if the *Gazette* readers learn of this manipulation the paper's credibility could suffer.

Third, Gates could decide to omit the photo from the paper's coverage entirely. This would avoid his ethical quandary. But would this decision be journalistically sound, especially because the photo is important to the overall story? In addition, the omission of this dramatic photo would certainly undermine the *Gazette*'s goal of improving its visual coverage to enhance the paper's marketing potential.

Finally, the paper could publish the photo in black and white or perhaps move it to an inside page to lessen its impact. Would this lessen the chance that it might offend some readers?

As the deadline approaches, assume the position of editor Samuel Gates and, using the SAD formula for moral reasoning, decide how you would handle this ethical dilemma.

CASE 4-7
Tainted Research and the Right to Know

Dr. Franz Heimlich was the jewel in the crown of the Hudson Institute of Science and Technology. Like many German intellectuals, following the defeat of Nazi Germany he had fled his homeland in advance of the Allied assault and eventually had immigrated to the United States, evading the exacting governmental scrutiny to which the more prominent officials in the Hitler regime were subjected. Heimlich's impressive academic credentials in biology, physiology, and medicine, as well as his fluency in English, eventually earned him a position at the prestigious Hudson Institute, a private college in New York state devoted to research and the training of scientists to accommodate the nation's unquenchable thirst for medical knowledge. For several years he toiled in anonymity, quietly conducting experiments, attempting to unravel the mysteries of the brain that might eventually lead to treatments or cures for a variety of neurologically based diseases and afflictions. His impressive results brought both admiration and envy from his scientific colleagues and a healthy and continuous infusion of grant money to fund his ambitious research enterprises. In the twilight of his career, Heimlich's experiments in genetics earned him the scientific community's most coveted honor, the Nobel Prize, the rewards for which accrued not only to Heimlich, the college's most distinguished scholar, but also to the institute in the form of international approbation and additional research grants.

The scientific community was not unanimous in its public applause for Heimlich's accomplishments, however. A small group of Jewish scientists, some of whom had come of age in Nazi

Germany, were deeply suspicious of their colleague's credentials and identity, and following further investigation their suspicions appeared to be confirmed: Franz Heimlich's real name was Hans Stein, who at the time of the Jewish Holocaust had served as a young associate to Dr. Josef Mengele, who was responsible for possibly as many as 400,000 Jewish deaths during the Holocaust and was quite deservedly referred to as "The Angel of Death" and "The Butcher." Stein (a.k.a. Heimlich) had also assisted Mengele in conducting medical experiments on thousands of unwitting Jews, leaving many of those who survived with permanent physical and emotional scars.

The group turned their findings over to the Simon Wiesenthal Foundation, which is committed to apprehending and bringing to justice as war criminals those who committed the atrocities during Hitler's reign. Investigators for the Wiesenthal Foundation confirmed the circumstantial evidence tendered by the concerned scientists and contacted the State Department about deporting Heimlich to Germany to stand trial as a war criminal. The Hudson Institute, fearing a loss of funding and recriminations from within the scientific community for their failure to investigate more fully Heimlich's mysterious past, quickly severed its relationship with their Nobel Prize winner and issued a press release denying (truthfully) any knowledge of Heimlich's sordid past and condemning the application of science to such evil and unethical purposes. While the dishonored scholar was awaiting his deportation hearing, his body was discovered in his small off-campus apartment, an apparent victim of a self-inflicted gunshot wound. Franz Heimlich had eternally escaped his rendezvous with justice.

While the Hudson administration and staff slowly recovered from their institutional chagrin and regained the public relations initiative as a credible center of scientific wisdom, Heimlich's young associate and protégé, Dr. Myron Summerfield, quietly determined that he would continue his mentor's promising investigation into the mysteries of neurology and gene therapy. However, Summerfield's endeavors concealed a ghastly truth that Heimlich had confided to him following the award of the Nobel Prize: Many of Heimlich's successful projects were based on knowledge gleaned from the experiments on the unwilling Jewish subjects conducted under the diabolic auspices of Josef Mengele. Heimlich told his associate that he had lived with the horrors of his role in Hitler's regime and that he viewed his present research, which he hoped would eventually abate the suffering for those afflicted with various neurological maladies, as a form of ethical redemption.

Summerfield, whose memories of World War II and Nazi Germany were mostly uninformed beyond those gleaned from courses in world history and an occasional article on the Holocaust, had accepted Heimlich's moral resurrection at face value and now silently pledged that he would continue his mentor's significant endowments to medical science.

Several years following Heimlich's untimely demise, Summerfield published an article in the *Journal of the American Medical Association* describing his research that held out the promise of a cure for Alzheimer's, a disease that afflicts thousands as they approach old age. The publication of the article was accompanied by a press release from the Hudson Institute's Office of Public Relations applauding Summerfield for his success based on experiments with white mice and promising controlled experiments on humans within a short period of time pending approval by the Institute's Human Subjects Committee and the appropriate government agencies. This medical breakthrough attracted the attention of the scientific community. It also attracted the attention of Joanne Raab, a science writer for the *Albany Tribune,* a daily newspaper in the state's capital just thirty miles from the Hudson Institute.

With an undergraduate degree in microbiology and a master's degree in journalism, Raab was no scientific neophyte and skillfully blended her empirical education with her professional journalistic skills. To keep herself abreast of the latest scientific research, Raab read the leading scientific journals, including the *Journal of the American Medical Association.*

Keisha Cantrell's call from Joanne Raab was not unexpected. As director of public relations for the Hudson Institute, Cantrell frequently received inquiries from Raab following public relations releases announcing various scientific breakthroughs.

On this occasion—one day before the next press release officially announcing the proposed experiments on human subjects—Raab called with some questions about Summerfield's studies, his plans to begin trials on human subjects, and the prospects of an imminent cure for Alzheimer's. She was particularly interested in how the Institute had made such great strides in finding what could perhaps be a cure for Alzheimer's, whereas other researchers had had only modest success in arresting the progression of this debilitating disease. Raab requested an interview with Summerfield, the approval for which was the prerogative of the public relations office.

However, Summerfield was uncharacteristically reticent in acceding to Raab's request as forwarded to him through Cantrell, a reluctance that did not go unchallenged by the Institute's public relations director. Cantrell's aggressive interrogation, induced as much by curiosity as frustration, led to Summerfield's confession of the ethically shaky foundations of the Institute's research project on Alzheimer's, as well as other neurologically based afflictions. Cantrell immediately notified the Institute's president, who instructed her to forward a recommendation within twenty-four hours on how to handle the public relations aspect of this startling revelation. In the meantime, Joanna Raab would have to wait.

"And that's where we are on this issue," Cantrell said with an air of resignation as she closed her briefing with public relations News Division chief Charlotte Horner and assistant public relations director James Roider. "Very shortly we'll issue a press release concerning our human subjects experiments on the Alzheimer's project. The issue is whether we acknowledge what we've learned from Summerfield or just leave well enough alone. But of more immediate concern, of course, is the request from Joanne Raab. I don't know whether she really knows anything—perhaps a rumor she's picked up—or whether this is just natural journalistic curiosity."

"The potential consequences for the Institute could be staggering," acknowledged Horner. "If we admit that the Alzheimer's project—as well as some of our other research enterprises—is based, in part, on scientific data generated by Mengele's 'mad scientist' experiments, we'll be savaged by some segments of the scientific community. And of course, this could cost us some funding."

"That may be true," replied Roider. "But I think we should take the initiative and be out front on this. After all, this doesn't involve an institutional cover-up—at least, not at this point. We just discovered the truth ourselves. It was concealed from us by Heimlich's associate. Surely the public, as well as the scientific community, will be somewhat forgiving under the circumstances. We can schedule a press conference, state categorically that we do not condone Summerfield's lack of candor, but point out the medical benefits that may soon derive from this research."

"I have reservations about this approach," responded Horner. "Heimlich is dead. His research and Summerfield's follow-up studies have contributed significantly to medical science. Perhaps some of the data on which the Alzheimer's project is based is tainted, morally speaking, but at least it's being used for a noble purpose. If we release this information, the ethical purists within and outside the scientific community may demand that we scrap the studies based on this data—or at least postpone indefinitely the human subjects trials. This could delay a much-needed medical breakthrough while the ethical debate rages."

"I still think the public has a right to know how this research originated," said Roider, although he silently acknowledged the appeal of the News Division chief's arguments. "After all, the benefits will accrue to them. Besides, much of the funding for this research came from the public till."

"Does the public really care?" inquired Horner. "It seems to me that the public mood on such matters is rather permissive—as long as there is some benefit to society."

"I'm not so sure," replied Roider, not willing to concede the public's apathy on issues of scientific or medical ethics. "There's more and more coverage of scientific discoveries, especially when they involve some kind of medical breakthrough. And medical and scientific ethics is also increasingly grist for the journalistic mill. I don't doubt that there will be public interest in this issue. The question is whether the public in general, and the scientific community in particular, has a right to know.

And there's one segment of the public that may have a lot to say—the Jewish community, particularly the remaining Holocaust survivors."

At this point Cantrell's two staff members fell silent, tacitly signifying the end of their spirited debate. The public relations director had listened attentively as she began mentally to frame the issues that must be addressed. "The first thing we must do is buy time," she told her two colleagues. "I'll phone Raab and tell her that Summerfield can't meet with her today because of a heavy lab schedule, which is true. But I'll also tell her that a press release on the human subjects trials will be issued tomorrow and that if she still has questions we'll consider an interview with Summerfield. Beyond that, I'll work up a public relations strategy to present to the president for approval, and we'll meet first thing in the morning to go over it."

THE CASE STUDY

What should the public relations strategy be in this case? One could argue that the public acknowledgment of the tainted data on which much of this research is based is unnecessary because it doesn't involve crisis management in which the public's health or safety is in immediate peril. On the other hand, many of the experiments have been conducted with public funding. But more important, from an ethical perspective, Heimlich's and Summerfield's impressive medical breakthroughs were made possible through data gleaned from diabolical experiments performed on victims of the Holocaust and their relatives. Does the public have a need to know this information?

The scientific method is based, among other things, on disclosure, a value that usually parallels those of the public relations practitioner. But Cantrell's problem is that she must also safeguard the long-term interest of the Hudson Institute, its reputation, and its financial viability. Does this reality favor disclosure or nondisclosure?

The issues here are complex, but from a public relations perspective Cantrell has several options:

Option 1: She could issue the press release concerning the anticipated human subjects experiments without mentioning Summerfield's confession. As a corollary, she could then stonewall Raab, hoping that the reporter would not persist in her desire to interview Summerfield.

Option 2: She could issue the press release without mentioning Summerfield's confession but could then submit to Raab's request for an interview, with instructions to Summerfield to say nothing about the tainted data.

Option 3: She could issue a press release (or perhaps hold a press conference) in which the Institute acknowledges what it has learned from Summerfield, recognizes the profound ethical implications of this turn of events, and expresses regret for its lack of diligence in not ferreting out this morally distasteful practice.

Option 4: Cantrell could follow the approach in Option 3, except that she could move the institutional *mea culpa* to the background and instead attempt to put a positive spin on the situation by concentrating on the medical advances that have derived from this research and which will have profound positive consequences for the public welfare.

For the purpose of discussing this case, assume the role of public relations director Keisha Cantrell. And then, using the SAD formula for moral reasoning, construct a public relations strategy that, in your judgment, is based on sound ethical principles. In so doing, you should consider the pros and cons of each of the options.

▶ **CASE 4-8**

Vow of Silence

This was the year of Brandon Layfield's discontent. As CEO of Actron Pictures, he had endured a strike by Hollywood actors, barely staved off a hostile takeover bid by a formidable competitor, and suffered through harsh questioning from a congressional committee accusing Hollywood of being Satan's disciple in emasculating the nation's family values. And now he watched with growing annoyance at the parade of devout Catholics in the street below with their picket signs that indicted his cinematic empire for being in league with the Devil. Layfield could sum up the source of their anger in two words: *Aaron Moeller.*

Moeller was one of Actron's most imaginative producers but he was also a cultural gadfly, always eager to challenge social conventions and to "push the envelope" on matters of artistic propriety. His graphic films on child prostitution, the drug culture, and the realities of the gay lifestyle, including violence within the gay community, had been box office hits but had also earned him the enmity of his conservative detractors. While his films generally won critical acclaim, Moeller was also accused of fueling a "culture of cynicism" toward society's various pathologies. His latest film, *Vow of Silence,* was proving to be the most controversial of his professional career.

Vow of Silence took an unvarnished and dramatic look at an unpleasant fact that challenged the very foundations of Catholic Church doctrine—the fact that Catholic priests are dying of AIDS at four times the rate of the general U.S. population. Moeller's project was prompted by a well-researched article published in the *Kansas City Star,*[143] but he believed that a dramatic rendition of this issue on the big screen would place the matter on the national agenda and provide a sense of urgency to its resolution. His sense of realism propelled him toward an actual case history, but this was no mean task considering the resistance of the Catholic Church to any discussion of the issue. Undaunted by such obstacles, Moeller had put out "feelers" in various venues in the hopes that his contacts might provide an entrée to someone with knowledge of such a case history. His break came when a Hollywood agent and friend phoned Moeller and told him that she knew a woman whose brother, a priest, had died of the AIDS virus. "She might be willing to cooperate because she is still upset that her brother's superiors misled her as to his affliction," she said. "They told her that her brother had contracted hepatitis. She is his only surviving family member and feels she should have been told the truth."

Moeller lost no time in contacting the woman, informed her of his proposed project, and over time gained her confidence. The woman told Moeller that her brother confided to her just before his death that he had AIDS and confessed that he had probably contracted the disease from a brief relationship he had with a church employee.

The bishop had compelled his silence during this tragic ordeal, but the young priest was inspired by guilt to divulge his secret to his sister.

Moeller took voluminous notes, turned them over to a scriptwriter, and assembled a cast and staff to produce a fictionalized rendition of this heart-rending story. While he planned to take the appropriate poetic license with some of the details, Moeller's film would remain faithful to the "greater truth"—that priests are dying of AIDS, a tragedy that has not been publicly acknowledged by the Catholic Church. For the sake of realism, the film's director decided to employ the documentary technique, similar to Steven Soderberg's award-winning film, *Traffic,* and Steven Spielberg's *Saving Private Ryan.*

In Moeller's fictional account, the film opens with Father Michael, a much-beloved young parish priest at St. Thomas, in a hospital bed dying of AIDS. At his bedside is his sister, Rebecca, to whom he begins a confession of how he contracted the disease and how his superiors dealt with it. Many of the plot transitions are executed through interviews with Rebecca that are inserted at strategic points throughout the film, thus adding to the documentary demeanor of the project. The director also introduces a series of flashbacks that begins with a brief scene of Father Michael as a priest fresh out of seminary. He quickly befriends a troubled parishioner, a young advertising copy-writer, and an affectionate relationship emerges. In one poignant scene Father Michael confides to his friend that he is having a difficult time dealing with his sexuality, a topic that was not adequately explored in seminary. The audience is led, through a sequence of creative and subtle interactions between the two, to believe that the priest is gay, although this is never fully explored in a dramatic fashion. Nevertheless, as the flashbacks continue, Father Michael is diagnosed with the HIV virus, a fact that he initially conceals from his bishop and the other parish priests. But over time he becomes ill with AIDS, and his bishop, fearing a scandal because of the imputations of homosexuality that usually accompany this frequently fatal disease, puts in place an elaborate cover-up. He commands Father Michael to remain silent about his condition, even to his parents and siblings, and

arranges for medical treatment outside the parish. He also forbids the young priest to wear his clerical garb when undergoing periodic blood tests and filling prescriptions intended to prolong the life of the young priest. The underlying theme of *Vow of Silence* is unmistakable: There is a serious AIDS problem among the Catholic clergy, and the Church is attempting to cover it up.

At the conclusion of the flashbacks Father Michael soon dies, but when his sister examines the death certificate she notices the cause of death is listed as "unknown" and that his occupation is listed as "clerk." Her faith in the Church shaken, Rebecca is determined to force the parish clergy to confront the realities of her brother's death and begins a lengthy search for the truth. In the end, she fails, unable to penetrate the veil of secrecy that appears to stymie her inquiries, and she even experiences some self-doubt as other family members attempt to convince Rebecca that her brother would not have approved of her relentless crusade.

The advance publicity on *Vow of Silence* had galvanized the Catholic faithful into action, and weeks before the premiere of Moeller's latest film demonstrators arrived at Actron Pictures and theatres in the major markets that had booked the controversial movie. The Catholic hierarchy condemned Moeller's project and publicly denied the major premise of the movie—that AIDS is a serious problem within the Catholic Church. Noting that priests take a vow of celibacy, Catholic clergy publicly savaged the film and condemned it as an insult to the priesthood and as an assault on the fundamental values of Catholic doctrine. They also objected to the film's apparent conclusion—that Catholic clergy are involved in some kind of cover-up. They demanded that Actron Pictures cancel the scheduled release of *Vow of Silence.* The news media ensured that the protests would receive national exposure, while Actron Pictures executives fretted about how to respond to this assault on their artistic freedom.

Layfield and his minions had weathered public censure and critical condemnation before, but the Catholic Church was a formidable foe. As he surveyed the cacophony of critical voices piercing the tranquility in the street below his twelfth-floor office,

Layfield decided to consult with Bess Cooper, his studio's director of publicity, and Renita Marcos, Actron's vice president for domestic distribution. Aaron Moeller was also summoned to the meeting.

"We're under a lot of pressure," declared Layfield in an understatement, as Cooper, Marcos, and Moeller settled comfortably into their chairs. "We've received calls from several worried theatre managers, the Catholic clergy have incited their parishioners to write letters and join in protests, and we're getting a lot of bad press. It hasn't all been negative, of course. Some groups have urged us to release the film, but we need to make a decision soon. *Vow of Silence* is scheduled to open in three weeks."

"I'll go first, since it's my film that's causing the ruckus," volunteered Moeller. "If this were a news story about the prevalence of AIDS cases among Catholic priests, we might get some complaints but we wouldn't be here talking about self-censorship. This is an important topic, and the premise of the film is based upon facts. We can't cave in to pressure."

"But this *isn't* a news story," responded Cooper who, as Actron Picture's publicity director, was acutely aware of the fragility of public tastes. "It has alienated a large segment of our audience. The film is morally offensive to many Catholics because they believe this is a problem for the Church to handle, assuming there is a problem in the first place. They particularly object to the insinuation that Father Michael is a homosexual. Some are even accusing us of being anti-Catholic."

"I sympathize with this view," replied Marcos, herself a practicing Catholic. "We have to ask ourselves whether this film is really designed to bring an important issue to light or is it just a form of exploitation. News accounts are different. The story runs and if the Church chooses to ignore it and if they're lucky, it might just die a natural death. Besides, reporters always provide an opportunity for a response from the targets of their investigation. If the Church chooses to remain silent, that's their choice. At least there is some fairness in the process. In the case of *Vow of Silence* the controversy itself will undoubtedly increase the box office receipts, and this will ensure a longer life span for the film. Catholics can take to the streets, but this will only serve to enhance people's curiosity about the movie."

"I object to the characterization of my film as sensational," responded Moeller testily. "The fact is that the Church does have a problem with priests dying of AIDS. There has been some news coverage of this, but it hasn't received national exposure. Sure, *Vow of Silence* was inspired by an actual case history, but it's a fictionalized account. Nevertheless, there is some fundamental truth in the film, and this dramatic portrayal may even have more of an impact than a news account. I regret that some Catholics are offended, but this shouldn't be our concern."

But Marcos was unwilling to concede Moeller's point. "The disclaimer that *Vow of Silence* was inspired by an actual event and the use of the documentary technique will lead many moviegoers to conclude that your portrayal is typical of the way the Catholic Church handles AIDS cases. This is unfair because the conflict between the requirement for celibacy and a priest's sexuality is complex; it can't be encapsulated in one feature-length film. In addition, this film depicts the Church as involved in a cover-up. It's possible that such things might happen, but the truth is more complex than this. While some in the Church hierarchy might refuse to discuss the issue of AIDS among priests, the notion of a cover-up of the type described here reflects upon the entire Church."

"I'm not attempting to deal with every facet and nuance of this issue," replied Moeller. "My film represents a greater truth—that the Catholic Church does have a problem, namely that the violation of their vows of chastity are costing many priests their lives. In addition, this kind of reaction from the Church is not unusual when there's an embarrassing revelation. My film is inspired by an actual case, but the story line is not accurate in many of the details. My depictions are fictionalized accounts—but the underlying message is that the Church is in denial. At the least I can make the public aware of this problem. And perhaps this controversy may precipitate a more open dialogue within the Church."

"This is a hot topic," responded Cooper. "We might justify this film based upon an appeal to some higher truth, but in this case I wonder whether the dramatic format can do justice to this issue. Once we acknowledge that *Vow of Silence* is inspired by a true event, many moviegoers will assume that the story itself is truth and that in fact the Church is involved in a cover-up. I realize we have a lot of money invested in this project, but we're also getting a lot of bad publicity out of this. Perhaps now is not the time to push the envelope."

"Well, the buck stops here," said Layfield with an air of resignation. "I could let someone else make this decision, but it's really my call. I don't like self-censorship, but I also must take into account the interest of our company and the audiences we serve." With that Layfield adjourned the meeting and once again peered out the window at the protestors below as he prepared to render his verdict.

THE CASE STUDY

Vow of Silence falls somewhere between a true docudrama and a work of fiction. It is inspired by an actual case history, and the filmmaker uses the documentary technique to add authenticity to his project. Moeller has taken one event and represented it as the way the Church deals with a problem that challenges fundamental doctrine, such as clerical celibacy. His use of the cover-up may or may not be accurate as a general proposition, but in this film it becomes a metaphor for what Moeller believes is a state of denial among Church officials. This is what he means when he refers to a "greater truth," which is constructed using fictional characters and a fictionalized story line.

Moeller obviously believes that the dramatic format is a legitimate means of alerting the public to a serious problem that, in his view, hasn't been accorded sufficient attention through the traditional news media. Should filmmakers have more latitude in interpreting reality? Or is there a greater risk of distorting the truth when a social issue is distilled through a work of cinematic fiction that attempts to enhance its credibility utilizing some of the tools of the documentarian?

Fictionalized accounts always run the risk of complicating or obscuring the truth. Moeller may be on solid ground with his claim that there is a problem with AIDS within the priesthood. However, there is clearly more than one interpretation of the

facts concerning the Church's response to this problem, and Moeller has chosen to present one of them—that the clergy are involved in a cover-up. Is this a true ethical dilemma or just an agonizing public relations problem for Actron Pictures?

For the purpose of considering this issue, assume the role of Brandon Layfield, the CEO of Actron Pictures. And then, utilizing the SAD formula of moral reasoning described in Chapter 3, make a decision on whether you will put Aaron Moeller's film, *Vow of Silence,* into distribution.

Notes

1. "E-mail Urges Lying for Blood Drive," *The Advocate* (Baton Rouge, LA), April 13, 2004, p. 2A.
2. David Goldman, "Storyteller: Stephen Glass Makes Fact from Fiction," *Biography Magazine,* October 1999, p. 22.
3. Seth Mnookin, "Total Fiction," *Newsweek,* May 19, 2003, p. 70.
4. See Joellen Perry, "Sign of the Times," *U.S. News & World Report,* May 26, 2003, p. 46.
5. Doreen Carvajal, "Columnist's Mea Culpa: I'm Anonymous," *New York Times,* July 18, 1996, p. A11; "Not Very Neatly, 'Anonymous' Comes Clean," *U.S. News & World Report,* July 19, 1996. The deception began to unravel when the *Washington Post* published the results of a comparative handwriting analysis between Klein's handwriting and notes on an early manuscript of *Primary Colors.*
6. "Darts & Laurels," *Columbia Journalism Review,* January/February 1997, p. 22.
7. Ibid.
8. Carvajal, "Columnist's Mea Culpa."
9. Quoted in Carvajal, "Columnist's Mea Culpa."
10. Marvin N. Olasky, "Ministers or Panderers: Issues Raised by the Public Relations Society Code of Standards," *Journal of Mass Media Ethics* 1 (Fall/Winter 1985–1986): 44.
11. John Leo, "Academia's Lust for Lies and Disregard for Truth," *Seattle Times,* January 19, 1999, online article at http://216.247.220.66 /archives/academia/leo1–20-99.htm
12. Charles Krauthammer, "The Case of the Suspect Bios," *Time,* October 4, 1999, p. 122.
13. Richard Reeves, "Living in a World of Limited Truth," syndicated column published in *The Advocate* (Baton Rouge, LA), February 6, 1998, p. 8B.
14. See Sissela Bok, *Lying: Moral Choice in Public and Private Life,* 2d ed. (New York: Vintage Books, 1999), p. 13; Richard L. Johannesen, *Ethics in Human*

Communication, 3d ed. (Prospect Heights, IL: Waveland, 1990), p. 110.

15. Quoted in Warren Shibles, *Lying: A Critical Analysis* (Whitewater, WI: Language Press, 1985), pp. 19–20.

16. For a good scholarly analysis of the trial of Socrates, see I. F. Stone, *The Trial of Socrates* (Boston: Little, Brown, 1988).

17. John Stuart Mill, *On Liberty* (New York: Bobbs-Merrill, 1956), p. 21.

18. *Genesis* 4:37, cited in Arnold M. Ludwig, *The Importance of Lying* (Springfield, IL: Thomas, 1965), p. 7.

19. See William L. Rivers and Cleve Mathews, *Ethics for the Media* (Upper Saddle River, NJ: Prentice-Hall, 1988), p. 15.

20. Clifford Christians, Mark Fackler, Kim B. Rotzoll, and Kathy Brittain McKee, *Media Ethics: Cases and Moral Reasoning,* 6th ed. (New York: Addison Wesley Longman, Inc., 2001), p. 85.

21. Bok, *Lying,* pp. 30–31.

22. "Studio Pair Return to Work after Critic Scam" (online dispatch from *Variety,* July 10, 2001, accessed July 10, 2001), available from http://news.findlaw.com/entertainment/s/20010710/filmphonydc.html

23. Quoted in Margaret Carlson, "Pleading Guilty," *Time,* July 9, 2001, p. 28. The allegations against Hill are contained in David Brock, *The Real Anita Hill: The Untold Story* (New York: Free Press, 1993).

24. Johannesen, *Ethics in Human Communication,* p. 110.

25. James A. Jaska and Michael S. Pritchard, *Communication Ethics: Methods of Analysis,* 2d ed. (Belmont, CA: Wadsworth, 1994), p. 132.

26. Shibles, *Lying,* p. 19.

27. See Frank Deaver, "On Defining Truth," *Journal of Mass Media Ethics* 5, no. 3 (1990): 168–177.

28. Ibid., p. 174.

29. Some of these are discussed by Stephen Klaidman and Tom L. Beauchamp in *The Virtuous Journalist* (New York: Oxford University Press, 1987), pp. 34–55.

30. Dan Gilgoff, "A Fine Mess at CBS," *U.S. News & World Report,* October 4, 2004, p. 29.

31. E.g., see Jim Rutenberg and Kate Zernike, "CBS Apologizes for Report on Bush Guard Service," *New York Times,* September 21, 2004, Section A, p. 1.

32. Jane Hall, "Gore Media Coverage—Playing Hardball," *Columbia Journalism Review,* September/October 2000, p. 31.

33. Barb Palser, "Virtual Wite-Out," *American Journalism Review,* May 2001, p. 70. Ms. Palser conducts technical and editorial training for online news editors at television stations in the U.S. and Canada.

34. Fred Brown, "Balancing accuracy with independence," *Quill,* May 2004, p. 30.

35. Ibid.

36. See "It's Gore! It's Bush! It's a Mess!," *Broadcasting & Cable,* November 13, 2000, pp. 6–7.

37. For example, see Meredith O'Brien, "How Did We Get It So Wrong?," *Quill,* January/Feburary 2001, pp. 14–18; Gary Hill, "Election Coverage: A Major Media Mistake," *Quill,* January/February 2001, p. 19.

38. Paige Albiniak, "Coverage on the Carpet," *Broadcasting & Cable,* November 13, 2000, p. 12.

39. Steve Marshall, "Accuracy of Battlefield News Often Hazy," *USA Today,* April 8, 2003, p. 7A.

40. For further discussion of this point, see Klaidman, *The Virtuous Journalist,* pp. 40–41.

41. "Not Their Finest Hour," *Newsweek,* June 8, 1992, p. 66.

42. For a critical analysis of the role of the media in Operation Desert Storm, see John R. MacArthur, *Second Front: Censorship and Propaganda in the Gulf War* (New York: Hill & Wang, 1992).

43. Rachel Smokin, "Media Mood Swings," *American Journalism Review,* June/July 2003, p. 17.

44. Quoted in ibid.

45. Ibid.

46. Jane Hall, "Gore Media Coverage—Playing Hardball," *Columbia Journalism Review,* September/October 2000, p. 30.

47. Ibid.

48. Sherry Ricchiardi, "The Anthrax Enigma," *American Journalism Review,* December 2001, p. 18.

49. Ibid, p. 21.

50. The Pew Research Center for the People & the Press (online report, November 28, 2001, accessed January 7, 2002), available from http://www.people-press.org/112801s1.htm

51. Quoted in Maria Trombly, "Ethics and War," *Quill,* December 2001, p. 15.

52. For example, see Fred Brown, "Journalists Rise to Challenge of Tragedy," *Quill,* October 2001, p. 31.

53. For example, see Trombly, "Ethics and War," 14–17.

54. Elizabeth Jensen, "Interview Subjects Try Bending Rules of Journalism," AP dispatch published in *The Advocate* (Baton Rouge, LA), October 31, 2001, p. 11A.

55. Dan Trigoboff, "CNN's bin Laden Dilemma," *Broadcasting & Cable,* October 22, 2001, p. 14.

56. Ibid.

57. Ibid.

58. Eason Jordan, "The News We Kept to Ourselves," *New York Times,* April 11, 2003, Section A, p. 25.

59. James Poniewozik, "The Trouble with Sitting on the Story," *Time,* April 28, 2003, p. 92.

60. Jim Rutenberg, "A Nation at War: The News Media; CNN's Silence about Torture Is Criticized," *New York Times,* April 15, 2003, Section B, p. 2.

61. Poniewozik.

62. Rutenberg.

63. James Risen and Jeff Gerth, "Breach at Los Alamos: A Special Report; China Stole Nuclear Secrets for Bombs, U.S. Aides Say," *New York Times,* March 6, 1999, p. A1.

64. Lucinda Fleeson, "Rush to Judgment," *American Journalism Review,* November 2000, p. 22.

65. Angie Cannon and Jay Tolson, "The Old Gray Lady Is in the Spotlight," *U.S. News & World Report,* October 9, 2000, p. 56.

66. Ibid.

67. For another assessment of the quality of news coverage of the Clinton–Lewinsky story, see Jules Witcover, "Where We Went Wrong," *Columbia Journalism Review,* March/April 1998, pp. 19–28.

68. Steve Geimann, "Not Our Finest Hour," *Quill,* March 1998, p. 24.

69. "Bill Kirtz, "Was Truth the Standard?" *Quill,* March 1998, p. 34.

70. "Concerns about Accuracy, Reliability: Television Top Information Source," *Quill,* March 1998, p. 27.

71. Wiscover, "Where We Went Wrong."

72. Jay Black, Bob Steele, and Ralph Barney, *Doing Ethics in Journalism: A Handbook with Case Studies,* 2d ed. (Boston: Allyn & Bacon, 1995), p. 121.

73. "Darts & Laurels," *Columbia Journalism Review,* March/April 1996, pp. 17–18.

74. Bill Kovach and Tom Rosenstiel, *The Elements of Journalism* (New York: Crown, 2001), p. 83. For further insights on the use of hidden cameras, see Bob Steele, "Hidden Cameras: High-Powered and High Risk," *Communicator,* September 1999, pp. 73, 75.

75. "Paper Apologizes for Staging Photo," *Quill,* September 2002, p. 53.

76. Ron F. Smith, *Groping for Ethics in Journalism,* 4th ed. (Ames, IA: Iowa State University Press, 1999), p. 99, citing "2 Plead Guilty to Buying Beer for Teens for TV Story," *Orlando Sentinel,* February 24, 1993, p. A6; "TV News Pair Get Jail Time for Buying Beer for Teens," *Orlando Sentinel,* March 24, 1993, p. A19.

77. Carol Anne Strippel, "Not Necessarily the News," *Communicator,* April 1997, p. 24. Gardner also acknowledges that the station briefly considered using actors for the voices.

78. Ibid.

79. Cheryl Johnston, "Digital Deception," *American Journalism Review,* May 2003, p. 10.

80. See Bob Steele, "Dull Tools and Bad Decisions," *Quill,* April 2000, p. 21.

81. "Darts & Laurels," *Columbia Journalism Review,* March/April 2000, p. 14.

82. Roger Clegg, "Photographs and Fraud Over Race," *Chronicle of Higher Education,* November 24, 2000, p. B17.

83. Several such examples of digitally altered photos based on design or taste considerations were contained in a paper delivered to the 1994 annual convention of the Association for Education in Journalism and Mass Communication in Atlanta, Georgia: Tom Wheeler and Tim Gleason, "Digital Photography and the Ethics of Photofiction: Four Tests for Assessing the Reader's Qualified Expectation of Reality," pp. 5–6.

84. "Times Reporter Who Resigned Leaves Long Trail of Deception," *New York Times,* May 11, 2003, p. 1.

85. E.g., see Seth Mnookin, "The *Times* Bomb," *Newsweek,* May 26, 2003, pp. 41–46.

86. "Leadership at *The Times,*" *New York Times,* June 6, 2003, Section A, p. 32.

87. Karen Yourish, "The News NOT Fit to Print," *Newsweek,* May 26, 2003, p. 44.

88. Ibid, pp. 44–45.

89. Matthew Cooper, "Too Good to Check," *Time,* March 29, 2004, p. 20. For a more thorough analysis of this case, see Jill Rosen, "Who Knows Jack?," *American Journalism Review,* pp. 29–38.

90. Smith, *Groping for Ethics in Journalism,* p. 94.

91. "Distorted 'News,'" *USA Today,* August 11, 2000, p. 15A.

92. Robin Pogrebin, "Prize-Winning Boston Columnist Losing Job over Faked Articles," *New York Times,* June 19, 1998, pp. A1, A21.

93. Quoted in John Leo, "Nothing but the Truth?," *U.S. News & World Report,* July 6, 1998, p. 20.

94. Ibid.

95. William A. Rusher, "Fiction Problems with Docudramas," syndicated column published in *The Advocate* (Baton Rouge, LA), November 13, 2003, p. 8B.

96. "Twisted History," *Newsweek,* December 23, 1991, pp. 46–49, citing comments made to the New Orleans *Times-Picayune* and *Vanity Fair.*

97. Ibid.

98. Warren Goldstein, "Bad History Is Bad for a Culture," *Chronicle of Higher Education,* April 10, 1998, p. A64.

99. "Movie Makers and the Historical Record: When Accuracy and Drama Intersect," *Chronicle of Higher Education,* May 22, 1998, pp. B3, B9.

100. Michael Nelson, "'Thirteen Days' Doesn't Add Up," *Chronicle of Higher Education,* February 2, 2001, p. B16.

101. See "Racing the News Crews," *Newsweek,* May 24, 1993, p. 58.

102. For example, see "Ripping Off the Headlines," *Newsweek,* September 11, 1989, pp. 62–65.

103. Allessandra Stanley, "Battle of the Network Docudrama," *New York Times,* November 7, 2003, Section E, Part 1, p. 1.

104. Bruce Fretts, "Pretrial Motion Picture," *TV Guide,* January 3, 2004, p. 45.

105. "Ripping Off the Headlines," p. 63.

106. "Ripping Off the Headlines," p. 65.

107. Betsy Streisand, "An Underpowered Hollywood Summer," *U.S. News & World Report,* July 2, 2001, p. 35.

108. Ibid.

109. For those who care to read them, however, the ingredients will be listed on the product package itself.

110. Deaver, "On Defining Truth," p. 172.

111. For a thorough discussion of the ethics of advertising, see Michael J. Phillips, *Ethics and Manipulation in Advertising* (Westport, CT: Quorum Books, 1997).

112. Johannesen, *Ethics in Human Communication,* p. 113.

113. Ibid., p. 115.

114. Philip Patterson and Lee Wilkins, *Media Ethics: Issues and Cases,* 3d ed. (Boston: McGraw-Hill, 1998), p. 64.

115. Don R. Pember, *Mass Media Law,* 2003/2004 (Boston: McGraw-Hill, 2003), p. 531.

116. Otis Baskin and Craig Aronoff, *Public Relations: The Profession and the Practice,* 3d ed. (Dubuque, IA: William C Brown, 1992), pp. 207–208.

117. For a good discussion on the ethical concerns involved in the use of VNRs, see K. Tim Wulfemeyer and Lowell Frazier, "The Ethics of Video News Releases: A Qualitative Analysis," *Journal of Mass Media Ethics* 7, no. 3 (1992): 151–168.

118. See Joan Drummond, "Ethics vs. the Economy," *Quill,* May 1993, pp. 35–38.

119. Judith Havemann, "A Healthy Dose of Buzz: Madison Ave. Tactics Aid Medical Charities," *Chicago Sun-Times,* December 6, 1998, Section LI, p. 43.

120. Wulfemeyer and Frazier, "The Ethics of Video News Releases," p. 156, citing "VNR's—A New Tool Needing the Same Care," *PR Week,* September 5, 1988, p. 4.

121. Doug Newsome, Alan Scott, and Judy VanSlyke Turk, *This Is PR* (Belmont, CA: Wadsworth, 1989), p. 353.

122. See Roy Peter Clark, "The Unoriginal Sin," *Washington Journalism Review* 5 (March 1983): 43–48.

123. Black, Steele, and Barney, *Doing Ethics in Journalism,* p. 172.

124. Clark, "The Unoriginal Sin," p. 47.

125. Lori Robertson, "Ethically Challenged," *American Journalism Review,* March 2001, p. 21.

126. "Second Merc News Intern Fired for Plagiarism," *Quill,* March 2001, p. 31.

127. Quoted in ibid. For further examination of this issue, see Meredith O'Brien, "When the Words Aren't Our Own," *Quill,* October/November 2000, pp. 24–25.

128. Garry Wills, syndicated column published in *The Advocate* (Baton Rouge, LA), January 4, 1998, p. 12B.

129. Howell Raines, "The High Price of Reprieving Mike Barnicle," *New York Times,* August 13, 1998, p. A22.

130. Felicity Barringer, "50 Globe Employees Protest Columnist's Reprieve," *New York Times,* September 13, 1998, p. A14.

131. Robertson, "Ethically Challenged," pp. 24–25.

132. "Students Caught Lifting Material, *Quill,* May 2004, p. 31.

133. Clark, "The Unoriginal Sin," p. 45.

134. See Deni Elliott, "Plagiarism: It's Not a Black and White Issue," *Quill,* November/December 1991, p. 16.

135. Ibid.

136. Ibid.

137. Ray Eldon Hiebert, Donald F. Ungurait, and Thomas W. Bohn, *Mass Media IV: An Introduction to Modern Communication* (White Plains, NY: Longman, 1985), p. 549.

138. Jaska and Pritchard, *Communication Ethics,* p. 128.

139. See Kathleen Hall Jamieson and Karlyn Kohrs Campbell, *Interplay of Influence: News, Advertising, Politics, and the Mass Media,* 3d ed. (Belmont, CA: Wadsworth, 1992), pp. 161–162.

140. For example, see Russ W. Baker, "Truth, Lies, and Videotape: *Prime Time Live* and the Hidden Camera," *Columbia Journalism Review,* July/August 1993, pp. 25–28; Black, Steele, and Barney, *Doing Ethics in Journalism,* pp. 123–125.

141. This information is taken from Gary W. Selnow, "Internet Ethics," in Robert W. Denton, Jr. (ed.), *Political Communication Ethics: An Oxymoron* (Westport, CT: Praeger, 2000), pp. 205–206.

142. Ibid., p. 219.

143. See Judy L. Thomas, "A Church's Challenge; Catholic Priests Are Dying of AIDS, Often in Silence," *Kansas City Star,* January 30, 2000, p. A1. Also see "Religion and Reality," *Columbia Journalism Review,* July/August 2000, p. 15.

5

The Media and Privacy: A Delicate Balance

ETHICS AND PRIVACY: THE SEARCH FOR MEANING

In early 2000 NBC *Today* show host Katie Couric, an advocate of preventative cancer screening, provided viewers with a ringside seat during her own colonoscopy. In the same year ABC's *Good Morning America* featured a live broadcast of a woman giving birth.[1] The Internet treats us to graphic portrayals of teens having sex. Ordinary, uninhibited individuals disgorge themselves of their pathologies on TV talk shows. And otherwise serious newspapers offer descriptions of the presidential penis and "also the testimony of anonymous sources who were said to have watched that organ in action."[2]

In a media-dominated culture, our private and public selves have become indistinguishable. We remain emotionally tentative when it comes to how much we value privacy. We grumble about unwelcome spam on the Internet, for example, and yet eagerly provide Internet marketers with a wide variety of private information. We complain about unwelcome dinnertime intrusions from telemarketers while we carry on cell phone conversations in public places, often to the amusement (or annoyance) of others.

Such apparent contradictions are due in part to the fact that privacy is an ambiguous concept that does not easily lend itself to definition.[3] One common view is that the right to privacy means the right to be left alone or to control unwanted publicity about one's personal affairs. Of course, the media are in the business of *not* leaving people alone. Their tendencies are in the direction of revelation, not concealment. Thus, the balancing of the individual's interest in privacy against the interest of the public in access to information about others is one of the most agonizing ethical quandaries of our time.

Invasions of privacy by the media encompass a broad spectrum, ranging from incursions on another's physical solitude, or "space," to the publication of embarrassing personal information. Some invasion of privacy is essential to the news-gathering process and a well-informed public. But the ethical dilemma arises in deciding where to draw the line between reasonable and unreasonable media conduct.

Reporters are not the only media practitioners who invade our private domain. Most disseminators of mass media content, including advertisers and those who produce entertainment, are inherently intrusive. They seek us out in an effort to dominate our aesthetic tastes and economic choices. In a highly competitive media environment, this process is probably inevitable, but its very pervasiveness adds an ethical dimension to the relationship between media professionals and the audiences they serve.

Most of us value privacy, and yet we are ambivalent about how much we should retain and how much we should relinquish. We object to government spying and intelligence gathering on private citizens but are willing to tolerate TV cameras and two-way mirrors to discourage shoplifting. Some workers object to polygraph exams as a condition of employment but accept drug testing as a necessary evil, although society is certainly divided on this issue. The media are frequently accused of unwarranted invasions of privacy, but the fact is that incursions into our private domain are rampant. We seem to relinquish more privacy with each passing year, turning over to governmental and private agencies volumes of data about our personal affairs.

Society's concern about invasions of privacy by the media lies just beneath the surface of public discourse and, like an active volcano, occasionally erupts into a raging debate whenever the standards of proper decorum appear to have been transgressed. Such was the case when the media asked a medical examiner for autopsy photos of NASCAR champion Dale Earnhart, who died in a crash during the 2001 Daytona 500.

Of course, the line between public and private matters is particularly fragile where public persons are involved. The opening salvo in the contemporary media's fascination with the lives of public officials may have been fired in May 1987 when the *Miami Herald* staked out the apartment of Democratic presidential contender Gary Hart to document his allegedly adulterous affair. In the aftermath of the *Herald*'s report, Hart's popularity plummeted, and he soon withdrew from the Democratic race. Five years later it was then presidential candidate Bill Clinton who provided tantalizing coverage as reporters relentlessly pursued allegations of his twelve-year affair with Gennifer Flowers. While the networks basked in the glow of sizable ratings, news executives had to defend themselves against charges that they had lost sight of other campaign issues.[4]

Such cases generate a lot of heat but are not always illuminating in our search for the delicate balance between public and private interests. Privacy is usually a prominent feature of media ethics texts and professional seminars in which hypothetical and real-life ethical issues are explored. Yet precise rules remain elusive, although some broad guidelines have emerged. "Few ethical issues will cause you more difficulty," observes Professor Conrad Fink in *Media Ethics,* "than the godlike attempt to balance the individual's right to privacy, the right to be left alone, against your responsibility to inform readers and viewers about matters in which they have justifiable news interest."[5]

This is an awesome responsibility for media practitioners who must make difficult judgments under deadline pressures. In all likelihood the search for the meaning of privacy will proceed unabated, and the distinction between reasonable and unreasonable violations of privacy will continue to elude us. Nevertheless, sensitivity to the privacy interests of others is an essential ingredient of moral reasoning.

THE VALUE OF PRIVACY

Why do we value privacy? Why is it so important to us?[6] First, the ability to maintain the confidentiality of personal information is the hallmark of an autonomous individual. It can be taken as an article of faith that others are not entitled to know everything about us. To the extent that this principle is breached, we lose control, and our sense of autonomy is undermined. Consider, for example, the media coverage surrounding the crash of TWA Flight 800 in 1996 soon after its departure from JKF Airport in New York. While Donald Nibert and his wife, whose daughter was a passenger on the flight, anxiously awaited details of the crash, they became magnets for media attention. In the aftermath of this tragedy, Nibert had nothing but harsh words for the media, which he accused of aggressive and intrusive deportment. "We had a guy crawling under a bus with a TV camera trying to get a picture of [my wife] because she was crying," he complained. "We were going through a grief period, which should be private, and the media interfered in that process." Nibert said the lowest point came when a New York newspaper ran a picture of the Niberts, taken without their knowledge, as they selected a burial plot for their daughter.[7]

The principle of autonomy is also at the core of the prohibitions against false and deceptive advertising. When TV commercials, for example, enter the privacy of our home, we have the right to expect messages that will assist us in making informed product choices. Deceptive ads undermine our autonomy in making those decisions in the marketplace.

Second, privacy can protect us from scorn and ridicule by others. In a society in which there is still intolerance of some human tragedies, lifestyles, and unorthodox behaviors, no one wants to be shamed. Alcoholics, homosexuals, and AIDS victims, for example, know only too well the risk of exposing their private lives to public scrutiny.

Third, privacy produces a mechanism by which we can control our reputations. "Who cares what others think?" is a common refrain, but the fact is, we do care. The more others really know about us, the less powerful we become in controlling our destiny. Congressman Gary Condit found this out the hard way when his political future was jeopardized by a reported admission to police of an affair with 24-year-old Washington intern Chandra Levy, whose disappearance prompted an intensive police investigation and national news coverage.[8] While Condit's attorney assailed the media for focusing on his client's personal life,[9] *New York Times* reporter Maureen Dowd offered this blunt assessment: "Given the last few years in Washington, any politician who wants a zone of privacy shouldn't lie publicly."[10]

Fourth, privacy, in the sense of being left alone, is valuable in keeping others at a distance and regulating the degree of social interaction

we have. Our laws against trespassing and intrusion reflect this concern. Electronic eavesdropping and telephoto lenses have rendered personal solitude more difficult, but our interest in maintaining some semblance of privacy remains undiminished.

Finally, privacy serves as a shield against the power of government. Knowledge is power! As individuals relinquish their privacy interests to the government, the dangers of manipulation and subservience to the state increase, as in a totalitarian society. Thus, privacy is a value that lies at the heart of a liberal democracy and is an essential ingredient in protecting the political interests of the individual.[11]

There is, then, a moral right to privacy that has value for those who wish to maintain a sense of individuality. However, as a *fundamental value* it is of recent vintage. As such it must compete aggressively with other values (such as truth and justice), particularly in our information society. We are curious about the activities of others, and revelations of facts by the media and other agencies have eroded our expectations of privacy. In other words, we are at once *private* beings and *social* beings, and these two roles collide, sometimes to our detriment.

The Emergence of Privacy as a Moral Value[12]

The concept of privacy, unlike that of truth, does not find its root in ancient history. In discussing such fundamental cultural values as privacy, it is always tempting to search Genesis for confirmation, as when Adam and Eve covered themselves with fig leaves. However, Adam and Eve's sense of modesty was in no way comparable to the contemporary meaning of privacy. Anthropologists tell us that our modern ideas about privacy were absent from ancient and primitive societies.[13] The origins of the word *private* in classical antiquity suggest that it was not a term of endearment. Because citizens were expected to be involved in public affairs, to refer to someone as a "very private person" (as we sometimes hear today) was to disparage that individual's sense of citizenship.[14] The average American voter would have failed miserably this rigid test of public responsibility.

It took centuries for the idea of privacy to gain respectability, but we find some appreciation of the advantages of physical solitude in the seventeenth century, as landholders retreated to their estates and gardens to escape the concerns and pressures of public life.[15] The birth of the United States was founded, in part, on the lack of religious privacy in England, and demands for religious tolerance—the privacy of one's conscience—were later codified in the First Amendment's guarantee of religious freedom. The colonists were also concerned with protecting their homes from unreasonable searches by government agents and preventing forced quartering of troops in their private residences, both of which are also dealt with in the Constitution. Nevertheless, protection against unwanted invasions of privacy by their fellow citizens was not an overwhelming concern to the colonists, because their agrarian society was characterized by considerable physical distance between villages and farms. On the other hand, within homes and public accommodations there was little real privacy, no sense of one's own space.

The press of the late eighteenth and early nineteenth centuries was also vastly different from the contemporary mass media. Newspapers contained more commentary and opinion than news, and the lives of average citizens attracted little attention. With education still the preserve of the elite,[16] the press was unavailable to the illiterate mass audience. The emergence of mass public education in the 1830s greatly expanded the potential newspaper audience and paved the way for the "penny press," thus democratizing the media's content for the masses. Following the Civil War, rapid urbanization revolutionized the economic, social, and cultural underpinnings of American society. The rugged individualism and frontier mentality of Jefferson's day retreated as city dwellers became dependent on their neighbors for survival.

In addition, the overcrowded cities virtually precluded any sense of real privacy, and fascination with the intimate lives of one's neighbors became a spectator sport.

These population centers created a lucrative marketplace for the development of the urban mass media. Advertisers eagerly sought space in the thriving press to tap the buying power of the newly affluent consumers. For millions of readers newspapers became a welcome daily diversion from the humdrum existence of the workplace, and editors and publishers adjusted their content accordingly. They retreated from the intellectually appealing articles of colonial America and replaced them with stories selected more for their excitement, entertainment, and human interest than their news value.[17] Of course, not all papers succumbed to these temptations, but there is no doubt that those that did profoundly influenced the course of American journalism.

This new brand of sensational reporting was characterized, in part, by frequent exposure of the affairs of both public and private figures, as the collective audience became increasingly fascinated with the foibles and misfortunes of both the famous and not-so-famous members of society. This form of journalistic enterprise was no laughing matter to the victims of such publications, especially the "blue bloods," who rapidly grew tired of the press's nosy inquisitions. Media critics were quick to accuse the press of engaging in sensationalism and boorish behavior to satisfy the morbid curiosity of some segments of society.

Thus, as the United States entered the twentieth century, the value of privacy as a moral right increased dramatically because there was less of it. The right to privacy became an ethical concern in a complex urban society that still prized individual autonomy. The Industrial Revolution had resulted in crowded cities with little space and privacy, and newspapers had subjected human foibles to the glare of publicity as never before. This situation posed a moral dilemma for a culture that valued both privacy and press freedom: Whereas the press defended its intrusions on the ground of newsworthiness, its critics sought to impose public accountability on what they perceived to be unethical breaches of journalistic decorum. It was within this environment that the right to privacy became a legal concept, as well as a moral one.

Privacy as a Legal Concept

Until the turn of the twentieth century, there was no legal right to privacy in the United States. By common agreement the contemporary notion of privacy as a legal concept began in 1890 with the publication of an article in the *Harvard Law Review*. In this scholarly treatise two young lawyers, Samuel D. Warren and Louis D. Brandeis, proposed a legal recognition for the right to be left alone. Offended by newspaper gossip and what they saw as violations of the standards of decency and propriety, the authors proposed monetary damages for citizens who had suffered from the prying and insatiable curiosity of an unrestrained and unrepentant press.

The Warren and Brandeis proposal initially fell on deaf ears. Nevertheless, if they were alive today, they would surely be humbled by contemporary privacy law, which has greatly exceeded their modest proposal. In the hundred years since the publication of the *Harvard Law Review* article, the courts or the legislatures in most states have recognized some legal protection for the right to privacy. In American jurisprudence, however, the right to privacy has actually developed into four separate and distinct torts.

Intrusion is what many people think of when the subject of privacy invasion arises. The media can be held liable for an unwarranted violation of one's physical solitude. A journalist who enters a private home uninvited, even at the invitation of law enforcement authorities, may be sued for intrusion. The use of telephoto lenses to capture the private moments of an unsuspecting subject and electronic eavesdropping can also pose legal problems.

The second area of privacy law is *publicity of embarrassing private facts.* This is the kind of privacy protection that Warren and Brandeis had in mind when they published their treatise on the subject. The media can be held liable for publicizing embarrassing revelations about someone if the information (1) would be highly offensive to a reasonable person and (2) is not of legitimate concern to the public.[18] Legal victories for disgruntled plaintiffs are rare, however, because most courts are reluctant to impose liability against the media for the reporting of truthful information.[19] But this attitude has angered some members of the public, who believe that the media use this freedom to rummage, often irresponsibly and unnecessarily, through the private domains of both the famous and the obscure. Although most journalists may not do this, those who do create feelings of animosity and distrust.

The media can also be held liable for publishing information that places someone in a *false light.* Legal problems can arise when a newspaper, magazine, or broadcast station reports falsehoods or distortions that leave an erroneous impression about someone. False-light cases often arise within the context of the mismatching of stories and pictures. A newspaper should use extreme caution, for example, in using a file photo to illustrate a current story, unless its purpose is clearly identified. TV stations are sometimes confronted with a legal problem when the audio and video are not properly matched and an erroneous impression is left concerning an individual who happens to be included in the news coverage.

Appropriation is the oldest of the four types of invasion of privacy. Appropriation consists of the use of a person's name, picture, or likeness without that person's permission, usually for commercial exploitation. This is the least ambiguous area of privacy law and is designed to protect the right of individuals, both public and private figures, to exploit their personal identities for commercial and trade purposes. However, news coverage is not considered a trade purpose, and those who are featured in news stories cannot collect damages for appropriation.

This framework of civil privacy law, designed to shield us from the excesses of the press and one another, has been supplemented by some constitutional protection from the excesses of government. In the past forty years the Supreme Court has discovered, among other things, a constitutional guarantee of access to contraceptives without government interference and a right to enjoy pornography within the privacy of our homes.[20]

Privacy is also a concern of our criminal laws, and although these statutes serve as legal restraints on all of us, they are particularly relevant to the news-gathering process. Our laws against criminal trespass are of ancient vintage and should serve as a strong deterrent to any reporter considering a transgression against private property, especially over the objection of the property owner. Electronic eavesdropping and recording have become commonplace within the journalistic community. Although the law is fairly tolerant of the use of such techniques in public places, some states prohibit the recording of a conversation without the consent of both parties. The ethical problems associated with surreptitious recording will be dealt with in a subsequent section.

Such legal proscriptions are a reflection of society's public policy on the matter of privacy. Thus, media practitioners have a moral obligation to respect the solitude of others unless they have relinquished their privacy (either voluntarily or involuntarily) through participation in some newsworthy event or unless there is some overriding public interest in violating this right in a specific instance.

It is clear, therefore, that our preoccupation with privacy and the legal protection against violations of our right to privacy have increased dramatically as we seek solitude and attempt to maintain some modicum of autonomy over our personal affairs. It is equally clear, however, that privacy law has not achieved the balance between public and private interests envisioned

by media critics at the turn of the twentieth century. Thus, there is a need for an "ethics" of privacy that goes beyond the legal principles and provides a moral compass for media practitioners in fulfilling their obligations to society.

THE NEED FOR AN ETHICS OF PRIVACY

Basic Principles

Legal principles are not a worthy foundation for making ethical judgments concerning the lives of others. They cannot be fitted neatly to individual cases, and, where the media are concerned, the courts have gone out of their way to ensure a minimum of interference with reporting and news gathering. It is a rare invasion-of-privacy case that does not go the way of the media defendant. In view of the law's strong presumption in favor of the media, there are several convincing arguments for a system of ethics that transcends legal considerations.[21]

The law of privacy, first, has virtually stripped away protection from public officials and public figures. Little about the lives of public people is sacred in the eyes of the law. The fact that they have chosen to inject themselves into the public arena suggests a willingness to undergo rigorous scrutiny and to suffer the consequences of embarrassing revelations.

From a legal standpoint this argument has some merit; from an ethical perspective it is suspect. Undoubtedly, public figures must expect some fallout from the glare of publicity, and it is true that their "zone of privacy" is more narrow than that of the average citizen. But this is not to say that they must sacrifice all privacy and relinquish all autonomy over their personal affairs. Unfortunately, the media, believing that they are satisfying their audiences' insatiable appetite for probing accounts of the sinful ways of public persons, have often justified their behavior by refusing to recognize any zone of privacy for such individuals, a view that may not be shared by their readers and viewers.[22]

The threshold question should be to what extent the information relates to the public person's performance, image, or involvement in some specific newsworthy event. But even here there is no bright-line rule that can serve as a moral beacon in every situation. For example, in the wake of the tragic death of Dale Earnhardt, who was killed in a crash during the Daytona 500, the *Orlando Sentinel* attempted to view Earnhardt's autopsy photos as part of its investigation to determine if his life could have been saved by further safety measures now used by other racing leagues. Although the family eventually allowed a medical examiner to review the photographs for the *Sentinel*, Earnhardt's widow also successfully lobbied for legislation limiting the media and public's access to such photos.[23]

Privacy concerns can be particularly thorny in news coverage of the families, friends, or associates of public figures. The media have a credible record on this score, usually crossing the line only when news judgments require further scrutiny. For example, reporters generally respected President Clinton's desire to shield daughter Chelsea from the glare of publicity. Conversely, when President George W. Bush's daughter, Jenna, pleaded "no contest" to a charge of underage drinking, reporters played it down. But when she got into a second alcohol-related scrape just a few weeks later, the media could no longer let it pass.[24] It would be difficult to argue with the story's news value, since it involved a violation of law. "Like all presidential kids they're entitled to a zone of privacy, and the press is not out there stalking them," observed Tom DeFrank, the *New York Daily News*'s Washington bureau chief. "But as long as these girls keep doing things that give their father headaches, they're making news and we've got to cover it."[25]

Of course, ethical concerns about media coverage of public figures extends beyond embarrassing private information. The relentless pursuit of the rich and famous as they emerge from seclusion is a familiar trait of the tabloid media (and increasingly the mainstream media

as well). Should such subjects of public curiosity have any expectation of privacy in public places?

Journalists argue that public figures "use" the media for their own publicity purposes and are being hypocritical in complaining about the press's relentless pursuit of a story. This is a fair point, but the dividing line between legitimate news coverage and harassment can be a slippery slope. In recent years, photographic stalkers, known as *paparazzi,* have epitomized the darker side of celebrity journalism and have severely strained the public's tolerance for such distasteful news-gathering tactics, as evidenced by the outcry over the alleged role of paparazzi in the death of Princess Diana in 1997. Princess Di's untimely death was also the catalyst for congressional consideration of an antipaparazzi bill that, although of dubious constitutional validity, reflected Hollywood's frustration with the paparazzi's uncivil behavior toward its film stars.[26]

The second reason that an ethics of privacy is needed revolves around one of the primary legal defenses for the publishing of embarrassing private information: newsworthiness. The courts have taken a very liberal approach in allowing the media to define what they consider to be news or matters of public interest. Taken to the extreme, anything that is disseminated by a news organization might be considered news. But from an ethical standpoint more precise criteria are needed. More attention should be paid to what the public needs to know rather than to merely what it has a curiosity about.

One problematic situation arises when a private person is not inherently newsworthy but is included in a story by way of illustration. Illustrative of this concern is a TV documentary about child abuse that included a therapy session with a 9-year-old abuse victim. During the session, the child was shown talking with her mother and demonstrating with anatomically correct dolls how her father allegedly abused her.[27] The child's father sued on behalf of his daughter, and the Lifetime Cable Network and the British Broadcasting Corporation eventually settled out of court without admitting liability.[28]

This case illustrates the legal pitfalls of invading the privacy of innocent parties who do not intentionally seek publicity. But legal issues aside, an ethics of privacy should be concerned with the real public interest value in information rather than how much appeal to mere curiosity can be tolerated under the law. As Clifford Christians and his colleagues have observed in their casebook on media ethics: "Clearly, additional determinants are needed to distinguish gossip and voyeurism from information necessary to the democratic decision-making process."[29]

Finally, the law of privacy has accorded substantial latitude for news gathering in public places. The general rule is that anything that takes place in public view can be reported on. The idea is that activities that transpire in public are, by definition, not private. But even in public we sometimes covet some degree of solitude. Take, for example, lovers seated on a park bench. From a legal standpoint photographers might be within their rights to capture this moment on film and publish it as an item of human interest. A sense of ethics would suggest, however, that they obtain permission from the couple for two reasons: (1) common decency requires permission before intruding into this private moment, and (2) minor inconvenience may turn to acute embarrassment if these two lovers are married, but not to each other.

Beyond the human interest realm, even "hot" news stories may require some restraint. There are times when good taste and simple compassion for the victims of unfortunate circumstances require a heightened degree of moral sensitivity on the part of media practitioners. This is particularly true in situations involving victims of accidents or other tragedies. The public, of course, has an interest in learning about accidents and tragedies. But such an interest does not, in every circumstance, demand a public airing of a tape of an accident victim or

an interview with a grief-stricken parent who is probably still in a state of shock. From an ethical perspective, Jeffrey Olen, in *Ethics in Journalism*, makes the following salient observation regarding the ethical conduct of reporters covering accidents: "If we take seriously the claim that journalists are our representatives, then their moral rights at the scene are no greater than our own."[30]

An offshoot of this public property defense is the use of material obtained from public records or government sources. Such information is generally privileged under the First Amendment,[31] and the media have enjoyed some immunity from liability for the fair, accurate, and nonmalicious publication of this material. The theory underlying this principle is simple: a state is not *required* to place such embarrassing information in the public record, but once it does so, the matter is no longer private. Any citizen could conceivably examine this record. Thus, the press is merely providing publicity for what individual citizens could see for themselves if they wished.

This is a convincing argument from a legal standpoint. From an ethical perspective, it is less so. The reality is that most private facts committed to public records remain unknown to society unless publicized by the media. Lawyers may rest easier if their clients rely on public records for their stories, but moral agents should still balance the public benefits against the possible harm that will accrue under such circumstances.

Data Mining and Privacy in Cyberspace

Technology's challenge to our right to privacy did not begin with the invention of the Internet. Tape recorders and photographic surveillance have for decades posed a threat to our desire to be left alone. One cannot venture very far into the public arena without being recorded. Automatic cameras at intersections that visually document automobiles driving through red lights and surveillance cameras in stores, banks, garages, and airport terminals are now a well-entrenched feature of modern life.

We have accepted some of these intrusions as the cost of living in a secure society. Although there are many dimensions to our concerns about the impact of the unregulated World Wide Web on our privacy, the most immediate fear appears to be the ease with which others can collect data about our individual lives, preferences, and tastes. In a sense, this is not a revolutionary development. Both the profit and nonprofit sectors have for years collected these kinds of data through conventional means. Perhaps it is the facility with which the Web allows such data mining and the lack of technological sophistication of many consumers that have generated such disquiet concerning the protection of our privacy interests in cyberspace. In any event, it is apparent that advertisers, public relations firms, and any other entities that wish to direct their messages to particular target audiences can use computers and networks "to pull together those little bits of data into a picture that may be much more revealing than we realize or appreciate."[32] Our interaction with the Internet leaves an electronic trail of our activities that can be appropriated by those who wish to communicate with us in the privacy of our homes or in the workplace. By utilizing devices known as "cookies," commercial websites can track an individual's buying habits and purchases and can thus develop "consumer profiles" that can be used to fashion messages for particular target audiences.

While some electronic defenses have emerged to safeguard our privacy, they are still primitive. At this juncture there is a healthy degree of on-line mistrust of the unregulated venue of cyberspace, the consequence of at least three factors. First, much of the activity on a computer is invisible from the data subject. Second, there is a lack of accountability in much of the data transfer. When information travels from one computer to another, it frequently carries no identification tag as to its source or limitations on its use. Third, while traditional modes of

communication are limited by geography, the sheer scale of the Net is staggering, linking people and organizations on a global scale.[33]

As is the case with most "frontiers," there are countless rogues and pirates operating in the unregulated cyberspace. Nevertheless, there is nothing about this technological revolution that should change the ethical environment for traditional or unconventional media practitioners. Such values as *respect for persons and their privacy, trust, fairness, honesty,* and *minimization of harm* have not become anachronisms just because these new technologies have provided unprecedented opportunities to interact directly with individual consumers. None of the ethical guidelines discussed in Chapter 3 would sanction the abdication of traditional values simply because the Net is an unregulated universe. The ethical principles that should guide media professionals are of ancient vintage and are still worthy guideposts. If anything, the lack of legal regulation in cyberspace demands a greater degree of moral vigilance and deportment. Thus, advertisers, journalists, public relations executives, and other media practitioners must carry their moral compasses with them as they enter the increasingly competitive environment of cyberspace.

PRIVACY AND THE JOURNALIST: SOME SPECIAL PROBLEM AREAS

Any story, even one that appears to be innocuous, has the potential for raising complaints from those who are featured in it. Some people might object to a funeral notice, for instance, for fear that a burglar might use that information to invade their home while they were at the service. Sensitive elderly citizens might even object to the publication of their age. Because some members of the public view such innocent intrusions as matters of privacy, the media should be sensitive to their concerns. But some areas of news coverage dealing with private and sensitive information and certain techniques of news gathering raise special problems for journalists. The discussion that follows is not intended to be exhaustive but simply to identify several areas that are ethically troublesome.

Contagious Diseases and Disabilities

When Dorothy Barber entered a Kansas City hospital in 1939 for treatment for an unusual eating disorder, she did not anticipate that her medical condition would attract the attention of the press. When *Time* magazine published a story and a picture that had been taken without her permission by a wire service reporter, she sued the magazine for invasion of privacy and won damages of $3,000.[34]

More than sixty years have elapsed since Dorothy Barber's public humiliation at the hands of *Time* magazine, but an individual's medical history continues to enjoy a zone of privacy that the media transgress at their peril. Particularly where private persons are concerned, journalists must be convinced of the newsworthiness of any potentially embarrassing medical condition. And newsworthiness should *not* be defined simply in terms of the public's morbid curiosity.

At one point in history leprosy was considered one of the most loathsome diseases. And today, of course, AIDS presents a real challenge for the media.[35] Despite a widespread public education program about AIDS and a more enlightened public, for some a stigma is still attached to the disease that could result in loss of a job, alienation from friends and relatives, and even expulsion from school. There is usually no public interest rationale for publishing the names of AIDS victims unless their disease is directly related to some newsworthy event. A case in point is estranged lovers who sue their sex partners for the failure to have warned them that they were suffering from AIDS.

Where public figures are concerned, of course, society's interest in their private lives is more acute. One could not argue with any degree of confidence, for example, that the public should be kept ignorant of a medical condition that threatened the life or well-being of the nation's president. But even public figures are entitled to a certain zone of privacy, and the journalistic treatment of their medical conditions should be approached with caution.

Former tennis great Arthur Ashe died of AIDS-related complications in February 1993 but not before bitterly denouncing *USA Today* for invading his privacy. As an African American, Ashe had overcome racial barriers to win the U.S. Open and Wimbledon tennis championships. He retired from tennis because of heart problems and later tested positive for the HIV virus as a result of a blood transfusion during one of his open-heart bypass operations. In April 1992 Ashe was contacted by a *USA Today* reporter about a rumor that he had AIDS. During the interview Ashe asked to speak with the managing editor of sports, Gene Policinski. In response to a question from Policinski concerning whether Ashe had AIDS, the former tennis star answered "could be" but said he would neither confirm nor deny the information. He then asked whether he could have some time to call friends and other journalists and to prepare a public statement. Believing that he had no choice but to confront the issue directly, he met again with a *USA Today* reporter and confirmed he had AIDS. The story was quickly provided to *USA Today*'s international edition and circulated to other news organizations.[36]

Like most difficult ethical decisions, the Arthur Ashe case divided the journalistic community. Jack Shafer, editor of the Washington, DC, *City Paper,* was sympathetic to Ashe but nevertheless found no fault with *USA Today*'s decision: "My heart goes out to Ashe for whatever anguish the news stories caused him, but news stories cause anguish all the time." But *USA Today* columnist DeWayne Wickham was less enthusiastic about his paper's controversial decision: "Journalism teeters on the edge of a very slippery slope when, by confronting Ashe with rumors of his infection, and thus forcing him to go public or lie, it attempts to pass off voyeurism for news judgment."[37] The paper's readers were unforgiving in their assessment of the revelation. About 95 percent of the 700 readers who contacted *USA Today* about the Ashe story protested its appearance.[38]

Columnist Murray Kempton has decried what he regards as reporters' willingness to apply their own standards of newsworthiness, often to the detriment of simple respect for others. "Journalists sometimes forget they are reporting on human beings," he said.[39] This respect-for-persons notion is always at the heart of the privacy debate and can be pivotal in the search for the delicate balance between news values and the value of individual autonomy.

Homosexuality

With gay characters appearing with increasing frequency in television dramas and sitcoms and with more homosexuals being willing to acknowledge publicly their sexual orientation, it is reasonable to conclude that society's views have moderated somewhat on this issue. Nevertheless, one's sexual orientation is still viewed as a private matter, unless it involves a matter of clear public interest. The media's comfort level in discussing homosexuality has noticeably improved only within the past several years. A news event from the late 1970s exemplifies how the media have historically dealt with gays and lesbians.

In 1979 the editors of the *Washington Post* and the now defunct *Washington Star* were confronted with an ethical dilemma: How far should they go in identifying the victims of a fire at a homosexual club?[40] The dead and injured had been watching all-male, X-rated films on the second floor of the Cinema Follies and had been unable to escape the flames, which were blocking the only unlocked exit. Eight men died in the fire, and six others required hospitalization. Most of the men were married, but none was well known in the city.

The *Star* decided to fully identify the eight men who had died because of the tragic circumstances surrounding their deaths. The *Post* published some of the names but buried them in the middle of the story about the fire.[41] Both papers reported the nature of the club, but neither published the names of the injured. Both papers also later carried feature articles on the previously identified victims, delving into their backgrounds, their families, and what their friends had to say. The *Star* used the full names of the deceased, whereas its competitor published only the first names. The *Post's* managing editor, Howard Simons, said that the paper's primary motivation in not using the names was compassion for the wives and children of the men. The *Star's* editor, James Bellows, said he felt that the names were news and should be published.[42]

About a week after the tragedy, the *Post's* ombudsman, Charles Seib, in an editorial, criticized the paper's decision to omit the names from the feature article. "In effect, *Post* editors said that homosexuality is so shameful," wrote Seib, "that extraordinary steps had to be taken to protect the families of the victims."[43] Seib also contended that the names of the victims should have been reported because they were news, according to the paper's conventional yardsticks for measuring newsworthiness.[44]

Until the 1980s, references to homosexuality in the media were virtually taboo. Although public attitudes toward homosexuality have softened considerably in the past twenty years, the frank discussion of homosexuality within the media can still challenge moral conservatives' comfort level, as evidenced by the controversy surrounding the TV character Ellen's "coming out" on the TV sitcom by the same name. At times, the labeling of someone as gay or lesbian can still be harmful. However, the national controversy over same-sex marriages has in a sense "mainstreamed" news coverage of the gay lifestyle. Nevertheless, in terms of news coverage, the key test for the moral agent is still whether a person's sexual orientation is *relevant* to the story, such as when a police officer is fired or a service member is discharged from the military because of sexual orientation.

This test of *relevance,* a key ingredient of newsworthiness, was at the heart of the debate over whether to reveal the sexual orientation of Pentagon spokesperson Pete Williams. While the rumors had circulated for months, the first revelation came in a column from Jack Anderson and Dale Van Atta in which they reported that Williams was considering resigning in the face of efforts by a "radical homosexual group" to out him as a closet gay.[45] Many of the 800 papers that subscribed to the column published the story, while others "spiked" it. In Williams's home state, six dailies in 1991 subscribed to the column and all six ran it. The Wyoming editors unanimously agreed that Williams's sexual preference was irrelevant to his ability to perform as assistant secretary of defense. But they also saw some irony in the fact that gays were being ousted from the military while being allowed to serve as civilian employees of the Pentagon.[46] This apparent contradiction, in the minds of the editors, met the requirement of *relevance*—in other words, it was newsworthy.

The ethical concerns surrounding sexual orientation and privacy simmer because of attacks on sexual privacy from an unexpected source: gays themselves. In a controversial tactic known as "outing," several years ago gay activists began publicizing the names of alleged homosexuals who have chosen to conceal their sexual preferences. The activists claim that by forcing reluctant gays into the open (that is, forcing them out of the "closet"), their numbers will swell, thus helping to eradicate the stigma attached to being gay.

The comfort level of the news media in reporting upon the activities of gays and lesbians has undoubtedly increased, but one's sexual orientation still has significant privacy implications. Just as most reporters have abandoned the use of race in their stories unless race is journalistically significant, the same consideration should be applied to the sexual orientation of a subject of news coverage.

Sex Crimes

In August 2002 two teenage girls from Lancaster, California, were abducted at gunpoint from a "lovers' lane" near Lancaster, California, while their boyfriends stood helplessly by. The girls' pictures and the story of their abduction were the television story of the day. They were identified in both conventional news media and on Internet websites. The girls were soon freed following a shootout with their kidnapper, who was killed. Reporters covering the case had heard the girls were raped, a tragic twist to the story that was confirmed by a local sheriff on CNN's *Larry King Live.* As the story quickly shifted from the kidnapping to the rape, newsrooms struggled to define their options in framing the coverage. There was no clear consensus. The *Los Angeles Times,* the *Dallas Morning News,* and the *Washington Post* withdrew the victims' identities. The *Boston Globe* and *Newsday* named the girls and reported the rapes.[47]

Despite much discussion within newsrooms and professional soul-searching, the coverage of sex crimes is still one of the most troublesome for journalists.[48] News gatekeepers have struggled with this dilemma for more than a century. Its resolution, if there is one, has been complicated by such diverse factors as definitions of sex, gender roles, the dignity of women, and race (e.g., some critics complain that an African American accused of raping a white woman still generates more coverage than other rapes).[49] In a male-dominated society, there has also been, until recently, a tendency to "blame the victim." For this reason, journalists have been reluctant to name rape victims because of the "stigma" attached to such an experience. "It took the rise of the women's movement in the early 1970s," wrote Helen Benedict in her 1992 book on rape, "to bring society to an awareness of rape as a crime that mattered not as a violation of male property or of white dominance, but as a violent act that causes human beings harm."[50]

Occasionally, the lives of public figures and the coverage of sex crimes intersect, but usually "the dilemma of privacy invasion and sex crime victims revolves around intrusion by the media into public lives of *private* individuals who quite unwittingly have been thrust into public notice. Being involved in a sex crime is a guaranteed way to receive such notice."[51] Crime, of course, is by virtually any definition of news a matter of public interest, and the identities of crime victims are usually included in the accounts of these events. But the tradition among journalists in the United States is to omit the names of rape victims unless the victims have been murdered or are well known.

The rationales for withholding the names of rape victims are familiar ones: Rape is different from other crimes because of the stigma attached, because victims are less likely to report the crimes if they know their names will be in the news, and because rape victims deserve a level of privacy not afforded other crime victims due to the public's insensitivity toward them. However, critics of these arguments respond that rape has lost some of its social stigma, and thus the traditional rationale that women must be protected is no longer valid.[52] In addition, because the names of the accused are usually reported, withholding the names of rape victims violates the principles of fairness and balance.[53] Some note that once the charges are filed and as long as the issue is an open one before the courts, the media should be even-handed in their coverage. This policy necessitates the publication of the names of both the victim and the accused, because the question of guilt or innocence has yet to be determined. Reporters and editors who subscribe to this view are appealing to our sense of justice.

Needless to say, there is some moral ambivalence among those who have reflected upon this ethical dilemma. For example, one recent study found that the inclusion of victims' names had little effect on how readers viewed either the rape story or the crime. That being the case and considering the possible harm to the victim, this author concluded that withholding the name would appear to be the best policy.[54]

Of course, the increasing presence of TV cameras has done little to reassure rape victims in their search for both privacy and justice. This is particularly true of high-profile cases, which are the only ones likely to merit the attention of electronic media coverage. A classic example is the highly publicized 1991 rape trial in West Palm Beach of William Kennedy Smith. Under Florida law, identifying rape victims through the media was illegal,[55] and the televised coverage featured a blue dot to mask the features of Smith's accuser.[56] The fact that this sensational trial, featuring the nephew of Senator Edward Kennedy, was televised nationally provided the catalyst for still another debate on whether rape victims should be identified. Nevertheless, when a supermarket tabloid, the *Globe,* published the victim's name, NBC, the *New York Times,* and several other newspapers followed suit. But overshadowing the controversy about naming the alleged victim was the decision by the mainstream media to take its ethical cues from the tabloid press. Both NBC and the *Times* were accused of using the *Globe*'s revelation as an excuse for their own journalistic deportment. For example, in his on-air introduction to the story Tom Brokaw explained, "While Smith has become a household word, the identity of the woman has been withheld by the news media until now, and this has renewed a journalistic debate over naming names."[57] The next day the *New York Times* not only named the victim and members of her family but also profiled her sex life.[58] But even within the *Times* organization feelings ran high, and more than 100 staffers signed a petition expressing "outrage" over the naming of the woman.[59]

To the extent that a news organization predicates its own judgments on others' decisions, it is on rather shaky ethical terrain. Such behavior deprives the moral agent of the requisite degree of independence to formulate ethically reasonable and defensible judgments. And in this case, there was undoubtedly some of the copycat journalism mentality involved in the decision-making process. But in fairness to NBC and the *Times,* it should be noted that the decisions within both news organizations were arrived at after exhaustive discussions and a great deal of soul-searching. For example, NBC News president Michael Gartner, in spite of some powerful arguments against doing so from his senior staff, decided after a 36-hour debate that his network should report the name.[60] Gartner, who has always been a strong advocate of naming rape victims, defended his decision in a column in the *Communicator,* the publication of the Radio Television News Directors Association. Because these reasons constitute the most compelling arguments in favor of naming rape victims, they are worth noting.

First, according to Gartner, names and facts are news and they add credibility to the story. They round out the story and give readers or viewers all the information they need to understand the issues. Second, producers, editors, and news directors should make editorial decisions, including what information to include in a news account. The subjects of news should have no veto power over editorial judgments. In no other category of news do news managers and journalists give the news-maker the option of being named. Third, by withholding the names of rape victims, journalists become a part of a conspiracy of silence, reinforcing the idea that being raped is shameful. "One role of the press is to inform, and one way of informing is to destroy incorrect impressions and stereotypes." Finally, because news organizations always name the suspects in a rape case, fairness demands that the accusers should also be identified.[61]

As news organizations continue to approach this ethical thicket with a healthy degree of caution, most are aware of the sensitive nature of stories involving the victims of sex crimes. Identifying the victims of sex crimes should be justified by some overriding public interest

in the news value of the name. The fact that so many news organizations continue to struggle with this issue at least demonstrates a willingness to continue a healthy ethical dialogue and to calibrate carefully the relative harms and benefits to the naming of victims of sexual assaults.

Juvenile Offenders

Youthful lawbreakers have also traditionally been protected from the glare of publicity. Since the nineteenth century such offenders in the United States have been dealt with through a separate juvenile justice system committed to rehabilitation rather than punishment. To this end most states have historically closed juvenile proceedings to the press and the public, although this practice has begun to change. And until recently, the media have honored this code of silence by withholding the names of juvenile offenders. But with the increase in the commission of serious crimes by juveniles, a trend that has led some states to try youthful perpetrators of violent crimes as adults, journalists have begun to challenge these ethical norms and even the state laws that threaten the press with punitive measures for publishing the names of juvenile offenders. The Supreme Court provided the media with an important victory in 1979 by ruling that a state cannot punish the press for identifying a juvenile accused of a crime when the information is lawfully obtained.[62]

Despite this reinforcement by the nation's highest court, some reporters and editors are still reluctant to publish the names of juvenile offenders. Traditionalists argue that the release of this information will impede rehabilitation by subjecting such youths to the embarrassing glare of publicity. In addition, children and adolescents, whose moral guideposts may not yet be firmly anchored, are entitled to a mistake without being stigmatized in their later social relationships and employment opportunities.

Nevertheless, the increase in juvenile crime has piqued the public's interest, and there seems to be a growing feeling that many juvenile offenders, particularly teenagers, know the difference between right and wrong and that there is no compelling ethical justification to shield them from the consequences of their deeds, including the media spotlight. And the increase in violent crime among juveniles, including the rash of senseless school killings in 1997 and 1998 that shocked the conscience of the nation, has resulted in their early introduction to the adult criminal system. The majesty of childhood innocence, it seems, has vanished.

Such heinous crimes among the young has prompted some journalists to reevaluate their policies against identifying children. For example, Joe Kollin, a reporter for the *Sun-Sentinel* in Ft. Lauderdale, Florida, believes the media should take a more proactive role in confronting the realities of juvenile crime. Conventional recommendations, such as tossing parents into jail or assessing them for damage caused by their children, are ineffective in Kollin's view. "[T]he only way to get the attention of parents is to put the fear of God into them," Kollin declared in a recent issue of *Quill Magazine*. "We can do what juvenile justice systems can't; we can embarrass the hell out of parents. The threat of embarrassment and humiliation can have more impact on how parents raise their children than anything a judge can do. . . . Their fear, of course, is that neighbors will wonder what kind of parents they are. They fear the whispers, gossip and stares in the supermarket, on the golf course, at work, at the beauty shop. What parent wants that?"[63]

The threat of publicity may deter some forms of juvenile misconduct, but it may be wishful thinking to believe that the incidences of violent juvenile crime will decline with more intense media scrutiny. There are still those within the industry who believe the media should not retreat entirely from their sensitivity in dealing with juvenile offenders. In this view, rehabilitation of juvenile offenders is still a worthy goal, a goal that could be rendered more difficult by exposing them to the glare of news coverage. Whether to include the identity of a youth accused of breaking the law will depend, among other things, on the nature of the crime, the age of the juvenile, and perhaps the circumstances surrounding the incident. Nevertheless, in view of recent court decisions stripping away the cloak of anonymity from youthful criminals and the trend in some states toward a presumption of public openness in their legal dealings with juveniles, media practitioners can no longer use the law as a crutch in their ethical decision making. They are now confronted directly with the dilemma of balancing the privacy interests of youthful offenders against the public's need to be apprised of one of the nation's most serious social ills.

Using Children as Sources

When three middle school boys in Jonesboro, Arkansas, opened fire on their classmates, a TV reporter asked two students not only what they knew about the boys' earlier behavior but why they had not reported it to the principal. That question prompted this strong rebuke from Richard Lieberman of the National Organization of Victims Assistance, who counseled the traumatized Jonesboro students: "These kids were consumed with guilt and shame, more so than the others. They had been given the idea that they should've done something."[64]

Interviewing children has always been risky business, but the recent wave of school shootings and violence has elevated the intensity of newsroom discourse on how to use children as sources of information. Because of their lack of maturity and proclivity for fantasizing, particularly with younger children, reliability has always been an issue in using juveniles as eyewitnesses or new sources. But this is overwhelmingly a privacy issue, considering their inability to make informed judgments and difficulties in handling the glare of publicity. Since there are no legal prohibitions on using children as news sources, the ethical concerns are even more pronounced. Elizabeth Stone, writing in the *Columbia Journalism Review*, has framed the ethical issue using a series of questions:

> Should journalists interview children after they've been involved in a tragic or traumatic event? What about when kids are witnesses to a crime or to violence or trauma? Or even charged with a crime? And how reliable are they as sources, anyhow? Adults suddenly thrust into the limelight are often unprepared for what may follow, so don't children need even more protection in order not to jeopardize their rights to privacy, or harm themselves or others, emotionally or legally?[65]

Like most ethical issues in journalism, the use of juvenile news sources involves the balancing of the child's interest against the public interest in accurate and truthful information. "In the end, I have the obligation to tell the truth, and that supersedes what may be the wish to protect," declared CBS producer Abra Potkin in a recent interview. Al Tompkins of the Poynter Institute agrees: "We do not start with minimizing harm. We must first consider our journalistic mission." On the other hand, Anne Gudenkauf, a senior editor at National Public Radio, believes that a journalist's "obligation to protect the children is a higher obligation than our obligation to report stories."[66]

After reviewing comments from several news executives and journalists, Elizabeth Stone offers this conclusion: "Overly elaborate instructions as to how to proceed in interviewing children are probably as much a mistake as no guidelines at all. The best approach is for journalists to familiarize themselves with the factors they ought to be looking at well before the next crisis comes, as it surely will."[67]

But what if the juvenile is not just an information source but is instead the focus of the news coverage? In such cases, the journalistic equation may change in terms of the news value of the interview but certainly not in the delicacy of dealing with the interviewee. The most vivid example in recent memory concerns the tragic plight of the 6-year-old Cuban refugee Elian Gonzalez, who was the subject of intense media scrutiny. Elian's mother had drowned during their perilous voyage from Cuba, and he had been taken in by relatives in Miami. In the ensuing weeks, an international custody battle followed with Elian's father, who still resided in Cuba. Following an interview with ABC's Diane Sawyer, Dr. Alvin F. Poussaint, a Harvard professor of psychiatry, took Sawyer to task for probing Elian with "highly charged questions" that posed a "considerable emotional risk for this little boy" in reliving the memories of his mother's death. Dr. Poussaint challenged ABC to "rethink its ethical guidelines for interviewing children, especially where there is a possibility of doing more harm than good."[68]

Boston Herald columnist Howie Carr, in responding to Dr. Poussaint, acknowledged that Elian had been exploited but defended his relatives' willingness to use any means at their disposal to prevent his return to Cuba, including interviews with journalists in which the child professed his desire to remain in the United States. "[Y]ou can rage all you want about Diane Sawyer and all the TV coverage, but that's how the game is played now," declared Carr.[69]

While overarching guidelines may be difficult to formulate in dealing with children, the following are worthy of consideration. The reporter should take into account: (1) the age and emotional maturity of the child, (2) the nature of the news event about which the child is being questioned, and (3) the extent to which the child's information and knowledge are vital to the story. In addition, reporters should avoid a confrontational, investigative type of interrogation and, where appropriate, should make every effort to obtain the permission of a parent or guardian before using the intelligence provided by a youthful news source.

Suicides

The coverage of suicides is such a sensitive issue that many editors contacted for an article on the subject in *American Journalism Review* declined to comment on their policies, even in hypothetical terms.[70] Many news organizations have no standing guidelines and deal with the issue on a case-by-case basis.

The right to die with dignity is almost an article of faith in our society. For this reason most news stories concerning deaths and obituaries reflect an acute sensitivity to the circumstances surrounding the death. Except in the case of a public figure, the cause of death is often unreported, and the media will generally defer to the wishes of the family in deciding what to include in the published account.

Suicides present a ticklish problem for reporters and editors. There is the omnipresent possibility of copycat suicides, but from a privacy perspective the focus is upon victims and their families and friends. When the suicide is that of a public figure or when it occurs in public view, it should probably be reported. But even here journalists should approach such stories with a sense of compassion and an appreciation for the privacy of the family and friends of the victim.

Consider the case of former Enron Vice Chair Cliff Baxter who shot himself with a pistol in his car in January 2002 and left a suicide note in his wife's car in the couple's garage. Baxter took his own life in the wake of a huge financial scandal that eventually led to the company's demise. Baxter allegedly had complained to Enron's president concerning the appropriateness of Enron's financial transactions. News organizations clamored for the contents of the note, claiming that in light of the pervasive coverage surrounding the Enron debacle, Baxter was a public figure and thus the suicide note was a matter of public interest. Baxter's family argued that the correspondence was private and had no public interest. The Texas attorney general eventually ruled that the note was a public record and ordered release of the note, excerpts of which were published or broadcast by several media outlets. Some journalists defended the publication and broadcast of the Baxter note on the grounds of its news value, but others chided the media for a lack of sensitivity to the family's concerns.

While the development of formal policies for suicide coverage may not be feasible, considering the wide variety of circumstances under which such tragedies occur, *promotion of public understanding* is certainly worthy of consideration as a guiding principle. Deni Elliott, director of the Practical Ethics Center at the University of Montana–Missoula, concurs. "It's important to report that deaths are suicide in order to help alert people to the high number of suicides in this country," she says. "But publishing suicide notes and gratuitous gory details is voyeurism. Those details are important for families and professionals trying to figure out what happened."

Television coverage of suicides is particularly susceptible to an accusation of sensationalism because of its visual impact. Where suicides or suicide attempts are captured on videotape, a distinct possibility in today's electronic age, TV stations should use such footage with caution. Competitive pressures and the excitement of such dramatic footage can lead to a moral lapse on the part of some producers and news directors. Not only is the respect for persons an important value in the ethical decision-making process under such circumstances, but matters of taste, especially where the suicide is graphic or gruesome, require that the moral agent be sensitive to the viewing audience as well.

In addition, journalists should report on suicides in a straightforward manner, without romanticizing or sensationalizing the act or presenting it as an attractive alternative to depression or pain.[71] Some commentators urge a more aggressive journalistic stance in combating suicides by going beyond the threshold mandate of serious, fact-based reporting and balancing the tragic aspects with information for their audiences on where to go for help in resolving their problems. In 1992, for example, the Nashville *Tennessean* reported the contents of a suicide note left by deputy police chief John Ross. In the note Ross defended suicide as "a rational act (Japanese style) when one brings disgrace to those whom he loves."[72] Frank Ritter, the *Tennessean*'s reader advocate (ombudsman), justified the publication of the suicide note but criticized the paper for not doing more:

> It was news, and the newspaper is obligated to report the news, no matter how painful that might be for us, or for the suicide victim's family. But I would have felt more comfortable if the story had been accompanied by information on where people can seek help for problems that bring them to the brink of self-destruction. . . . [W]e needed to give expression to a voice of sanity: Suicide is not "a rational act."[73]

Of course, as morally noble as this tactic is, it is likely to be controversial because it requires news organizations to abandon their traditional posture of neutrality and in a sense become activists within their news coverage.

When a suicide occurs within the privacy of one's home, the public's need to know such details may be less compelling than when the victim is a public figure or commits the act in public view. One might inquire, for example, why a cause of death by suicide is any more essential to a news story or obituary involving a private person than the revelation that the deceased died of cancer or a heart attack. Nevertheless, some newspapers do report routine suicides, at least in news accounts if not in the obituaries. It would appear that suicides are no longer sacred cows for the press, but this does not lessen the moral responsibility of media practitioners to weigh the news value of such sensitive facts against the possible loss of dignity for the victim and the intrusion into the privacy of family and friends.

Secret Cameras and Recorders

The ethics of privacy is just as concerned with *how* reporters acquire their information as with the distribution of the embarrassing facts themselves. Journalists are quite inventive, or even ingenious, in their detective work. The electronic age, plus a continuing interest in and demand for investigative reporting, has made video and audio recording devices an important part of the journalist's arsenal for documenting discoveries.

Reporters sometimes lie in wait in unmarked vans or in other inconspicuous positions, waiting for their prey to engage in some illegal or other form of nefarious conduct. When a hidden camera merely records a transaction in a public place, such news-gathering techniques can usually be justified from an ethical standpoint, although reporters must be careful not to implicate innocent persons in their surveillance. Of course, the use of hidden cameras should be the exception and not the rule, lest reporters be accused of becoming electronic "snoops" rather than protectors of the public's interest.

The surreptitious recording of a conversation between a reporter and a source also poses an ethical dilemma, as well as a legal one. Under federal law, and in some states as well, a conversation may be recorded with the consent of only one party to the exchange. In other states both parties must consent. But even when the conversation is recorded illegally, the Supreme Court has shielded individuals and the media from civil liability for disclosing its contents when they have been obtained lawfully from third parties.[74] However, legal considerations aside, journalists disagree on the seriousness of the ethical dilemma involved in secret recordings or even whether an ethical problem exists at all. Some view secret recordings of conversations and interviews as more of a practical aid in the news-gathering process than as an attempt to subvert the privacy rights of the individual being interviewed. Tape recordings assist in documenting the accuracy of the facts and quotations to be included in the story and are used by both print and broadcast journalists. As long as the interviewees know that they are talking to a reporter, a recording device is no more intrusive than the reporter's questions. Of course, assuming the validity of this view, the question then arises as to whether the reporter, having secretly recorded the conversation, should obtain the subject's permission before airing the recorded interview. One could counter this argument by raising the following question: If a secret recording device is just an aid in the news-gathering process, why not ask the interviewee for permission to record the conversation? Needless to say, this would be foolish when a reporter is attempting to procure evidence of wrongdoing, and under such circumstances surreptitious taping of a conversation might be justified.

An article in the *Journal of Mass Media Ethics* offers a reasonable approach to the ethical dilemma posed by surreptitious recordings. The author suggests that the proper focus for determining the morality of secret tapings should be based on the rules governing privacy, confidentiality, and source attribution:

> Rules about privacy require that both the reporter and the source are in their public roles as journalist and source, not in their private roles as human beings. Rules about confidentiality establish what information is intended for public consumption and what is not. And rules about attribution establish the extent to which the source will be publicly known.[75]

Thus, according to this view, journalists who employ surreptitious recording "do not engage in deception and they do not violate a source's privacy."[76] The ethical issues are settled by the rules established for the interview. If the source strongly objects to a recorded interview, journalists who do so anyway are on shaky ethical terrain without some compelling justification. Such practices may also violate company policy. This was the case several years ago when *60 Minutes* correspondent Mike Wallace and producer Bob Anderson were reprimanded by CBS News president Eric Ober for secretly taping a story source, who made it clear that she didn't want to do an on-camera interview. Ober said this was a clear-cut violation of CBS News rules. Wallace said the tape would not have been used without the source's permission.[77]

Accidents and Personal Tragedies

Accidents and personal tragedies are often newsworthy, but victims may be unsophisticated in dealing with the media. Thus, reporters should

be careful not to take advantage of the situation and to respect the privacy of those who find themselves in such unfortunate circumstances. There are times, of course, when it is necessary to acquire certain information and to interview the victims of accidents or personal tragedies. But such requests should be handled with diligence and sensitivity. A TV reporter, for example, should not stick a microphone in the face of an unsuspecting grieving relative of an accident victim just to capture this dramatic and emotional moment on tape.

The media are particularly vulnerable to charges ranging from insensitivity to prurience when they publish "broken-heart" photos that capture an individual's private grief. Although we shall return to this subject in Chapter 10, we pause briefly here because of the privacy dimensions of such visuals. A case in point is the publication in the *Minneapolis Star Tribune* of a photo of Esteban Marques kneeling in grief over the slaying of his 8-year-old daughter. Readers complained that the picture shredded the man's right to privacy. Shortly thereafter, the paper published the picture of Curt Hanson weeping when he learned that his former girlfriend had been found dead in her wrecked car. Readers again objected to the publication of the photos.[78]

It should be noted, however, that the protests did not come from the people whose pictures were published. And executive editor Joel Kramer defended the use of the photos as essential elements of the stories. *Star Tribune* ombudsman Lou Gelfand, while advocating a moratorium on broken-heart photos, also noted that neither picture had been taken surreptitiously. Marques fell to his knees as he was talking with the photographer, and Hanson was aware of the presence of the photographer in the restaurant where he and his friends and other news people awaited word from the search for his former girlfriend.[79] Thus, although it might be emotionally tempting to discard such visual portrayals of life's most tragic moments, contextual factors such as those described here are always essential ingredients in the moral reasoning process. In this way prurient interest becomes more readily distinguishable from the public interest.

Sometimes media gatekeepers defend their use of disturbing visuals, not on the grounds of contextual relevance per se, but on the basis of some greater public good. Such was the case when a photographer for the *Bakersfield Californian* snapped a picture of a 5-year-old drowning victim moments after his body was retrieved by divers. The picture depicted the grieving family surrounding the boy's lifeless body. The publication of this picture prompted 500 letters of complaint. The *Californian*'s managing editor, who chose to use the picture, defended his decision on the ground that he thought the photo might remind people to be more careful when their kids are swimming.[80]

Similarly, the editors of the *Riverside Press-Enterprise* appealed to a greater public good that extended beyond the specific journalistic context when they ran a photo of the prayerful mother of a 22-month-old boy who had been hit by a car in front of his home. As paramedics attempted to save him, the child's mother, covered by the blood of her son, knelt beside him; all of this was captured vividly in the paper's photo. Photo editor Fred Bauman, who shot the picture, said that after a lengthy discussion in the newsroom, the paper decided to publish the graphic photo on the grounds that the realism of the picture might prevent future accidents by encouraging safer drivers or more vigilant parents.[81]

Such arguments, however, are not entirely persuasive. In most cases the personal tragedy and privacy concerns overshadow the alleged public benefit, which is marginal at best. The public does not need such graphic visuals to remind them of the dangers of children left unattended while swimming or playing in streets or driveways.

At times, some invasion of privacy may be justified, especially when a firsthand account is essential to the audience's understanding of the story. But competitive pressures can also lead to unwarranted invasions of privacy and harassment. The public sometimes sees such journalistic vigils as rather ghoulish. And such glaring displays of moral insensitivity, even if they are unusual or relatively rare, can further erode media respectability.

Computers and Database Journalism

Several years ago the *Seattle Times* used computer data on everything from parking tickets to a detective's expense vouchers to prove how a police investigation into the deaths of forty-six women was botched. At about the same time reporters at Knight-Ridder's Washington bureau uncovered unusually high death rates at several hospitals around the country by analyzing computerized Medicare records of open-heart surgeries. And when three Rhode Island children were hit and killed in three separate school bus accidents, the *Providence Journal* cross-checked its list of bus driver licenses with its reports of traffic accidents. The paper discovered that some bus drivers had been ticketed as many as twenty times over a three-year period. That information, coupled with the tape of criminal convictions, showed that several drivers were convicted felons. As a result, licensing procedures were improved and buses were made safer.[82] These are all examples of investigative journalism in the finest tradition of the craft. But these stories would have been difficult, if not impossible, without the use of computers. Computer networks with their virtually endless storage and retrieval capacity have revolutionized investigative reporting. But when government accumulates so much data on so many people—information that is easily accessible by third parties (for example, reporters)—the potential for mischief is intensified. Under such circumstances, public knowledge must sometimes give ground to other competing values. And chief among these moral claimants is the individual's interest in privacy.

Government public records have traditionally provided a bountiful repository of information for investigative reporters, but the use of computers and government databases has expanded their horizons exponentially. The sheer drudgery of physically perusing "hard copies" of documents has been replaced by the facility of accessing data banks directly from the newsroom or even from the comfort of a reporter's home.

Like any technology, computers provide a seductive tool for improving the quantity and quality of communication. But no innovation has so crystallized the conflicting values inherent in the individual's right to privacy, media access to information, and the public's "right to know." Journalists have long relied on the wealth of information available in public records, but members of the public are discovering, much to their consternation, that a lot of identifying information about themselves can be accessed from government files. In addition, some news organizations are now posting public records on their websites, allowing readers to mine the raw data for themselves and in effect become their own editors. While this process may be more "democratic," it also challenges the traditional role of the media as filters, synthesizers, and purveyors of "value-added" information.[83] It remains to be seen whether this use of technology will be healthy for the democratic soul.

Recognizing the threats that lurk in public data banks to their privacy, some citizens are beginning to fight back. In response to pressure from their constituents, legislators across the country have begun to seal some databases, such as voter registration lists, vital statistics, and land transfer records. Perhaps the most visible example of this frenzied legislative activity was the congressional passage, in 1994, of the Driver's Privacy Protection Act, a federal mandate requiring the states to limit access to drivers' license and car registration records, which contain personal information.[84]

But these legislative initiatives, the result more of political pressure than intelligent deliberation of policy issues, have left the ethical questions unresolved. As noted earlier in this text, technology is ethically neutral. It enters society in neither a virtuous nor a corrupt state. Thus, computers are the obedient servants of the moral agents who use them. The most visible example of this is the Internet, which is a repository of useful consumer information while also serving as a platform for the dissemination of hate speech and pornography.

On the positive side, computer databases can assist journalists in fulfilling their role as government watchdogs. The media's exposure of government wrongdoing instills confidence in the media as fiduciaries of the average citizen and assures them of some degree of governmental accountability.[85] The use of computers can also bring reporters to "a new level of activism" in their reporting,[86] providing quick access to a wealth of information, reducing the time for data collection and thus freeing them up to analyze the data, to develop relationships and correlations among diverse information, and to reflect on its significance.

On the other hand, indiscriminate access to government data banks does raise privacy concerns, particularly when the information is used for a purpose other than that for which it is retrieved. For example, as private economic enterprises media might be tempted to use news-gathering computer tapes for marketing purposes, such as developing a potential subscriber list from the wealth of demographic information yielded by the tapes.[87] In addition, the inaccuracy of some of the database information is well documented, as evidenced by the trials and tribulations of those who have attempted to get a false credit record expunged. Thus, the fact that information is retrieved, through an elaborate computer network, from government data banks does not relieve news organizations of the responsibility of corroborating the accuracy of that information. The use of computer data banks is no substitute for fact checking, as the *Boston Globe* discovered in preparing a series on money laundering across the United States. In analyzing the data, the paper discovered large and unexplainable swings in cash transactions reported in certain cities. Ultimately the discrepancies were traced to a clerk in Detroit, who occasionally added five zeroes to the actual figures—just to ease boredom.[88]

THE SEARCH FOR JOURNALISTIC GUIDELINES

The infinite variety of situations in which concerns about privacy can arise precludes the identification of specific criteria that will accommodate every contingency. But at least four moral values should provide the foundation for an ethics of privacy for media practitioners.

The first guideline is based on the notion of *respect for persons* as an end in itself. This idea is based, in part, on the Judeo-Christian creed described in Chapter 3. As autonomous individuals we are all entitled to a certain amount of dignity, which should not be arbitrarily compromised for the sake of some slogan such as "the people's right to know." Particularly when covering those who involuntarily become the subject of newsworthy events, reporters and editors should apply this value with exacting scrutiny.

The second value is that of *social utility*. The moral agent must decide what information is essential or at least useful to the audience in understanding the message being communicated. This principle eliminates appeals to sensationalism, morbid curiosity, ridicule, and voyeurism as a justification for invasion of privacy.

The third principle is based on the notion of *justice*. In Chapter 2, you may recall, I defined justice in terms of what one deserves. Moral agents are obliged to render judgments based on how much privacy their subjects really deserve under the circumstances. Public officials who are accused of violating their oath of office would, under most circumstances, deserve less privacy than victims of human tragedy. Certainly, the degree of "voluntariness," or purposeful behavior, is a consideration in deciding what kind of treatment an actor really deserves.

Finally, in making decisions that may offend or intrude into the private lives of others, moral agents should strive for a *minimization of harm*. This value is closely related to that of *respect for persons*. When invasions of privacy are inevitable, as they sometimes are when journalists report on matters of public interest, the goal should be confined to the coverage of those details that are essential to the newsworthiness of the event. The failure to heed this admonition, for example, is at the heart of many of the complaints about the news media's treatment of the victims of crime and other tragedies. Such was the case when several Ohio newspapers published a graphic account of the rape and murder of two women near Akron. A friend of one of the victims, a student at Ohio University, criticized the papers for including the sordid details of the sexual assault, the physical abuse, and her slow and painful death in their account of this vicious crime. He accused the papers of violating the privacy of the victims and their family and friends.[89]

James Fallows, writing in *U.S. News & World Report,* places journalists in the company of a select group who are "authorized," because of the nature of their responsibilities, to do harm: doctors (who must sometimes administer harmful treatments to save lives), soldiers, police, judges who deprive people of their liberty, and business competitors "who deprive rivals of markets and their employees of jobs." All are limited, in some respect, by legal proscriptions and codes of conduct that are unique to their particular professions and occupations. "Yet for all these groups," observes Fallows, "the internal constraints are more important: the daily judgments, by individuals whose daily decisions may harm others, about how many normal 'human sympathies' they can maintain and still do their job." Of course, journalists can never fully escape the occasional public flogging for their alleged moral indifference in pursuit of a good story. However, the "inner awareness of the struggle to remain human"— that is, to balance news values against humanistic considerations—might serve to revitalize the public's respect for the journalistic enterprise.[90]

ADVERTISING AND PRIVACY

Advertising is ubiquitous. It not only intrudes into the privacy of our homes, but it also competes for our attention on billboards at athletic events, in the skies overhead on the sides of blimps, at movie theatres, in public transportation, on the Internet, and even on gas pumps. Advertising relentlessly seeks us out, marketing everything from fast foods to feminine hygiene products. The average American sees an estimated 3,000 advertisements per day.[91] The sheer volume of ads that consumers must endure has led to complaints.

Because we willingly relinquish a certain amount of privacy by venturing into public places, advertising prominently displayed in such arenas does not generally give rise to privacy concerns. But advertising that enters our home— even by tacit approval through the purchase of a radio or TV set or a computer—does implicate privacy interests. Under such circumstances, advertising might be viewed as a guest. It is welcome to stay (or at least tolerated) as long as certain minimum standards of decorum are maintained. Ads that are too loud or offensive in their delivery offend these standards. Likewise, exaggerated claims that exploit consumer ignorance or insult their intelligence are problematic.[92] But what about ads that are simply in poor taste? Some commentators believe that matters of taste are not serious enough to raise ethical concerns.[93] In their view, concerns about taste belong to the more genteel domain of etiquette rather than the more probing realm of morality. Certainly this argument holds some appeal. But when advertisers seek us out in our private spheres and offend our sensibilities with tasteless messages, then the line between etiquette and ethics is at the least ambiguous. If advertisers have any responsibility for their content—and they certainly do—then part of that responsibility must be moral in character.

Protecting one's privacy has always been a challenge for the individual consumer, but the allure of the Web for advertisers has increased the stakes considerably. For example, an ad-server company can insert banner ads and other promotional material on websites targeted toward the most desirable consumers. The device used to track consumers and to develop profiles of their purchasing habits is known as a "cookie," as described earlier. While some ad-server companies have provided only anonymous data about Web surfers to marketers, others have offered online profiles that help identity the surfers. Most consumers are unaware of this practice, although there does appear to be a heightened sense of awareness concerning the threats to privacy in cyberspace.

Regardless of where the ad messages occur, the industry has been accused of promoting superficial values such as sex appeal, the connection between materialism and happiness/self-esteem, and stereotypes. To the extent that this accusation is true, advertising competes with the primary societal unit (the family) for control of the socialization process. For advertising critics, this is particularly troublesome when children are exposed to such unfiltered commercial messages.

In the not-too-distant past there were certain advertising "guests" that were never welcome, particularly in the electronic media. At one time, for example, feminine hygiene and condom ads were considered taboo. Today, it seems, there are few legal products that have not found their advertising niche. Defenders of unfettered access argue that any lawful product should have the right (both legally and ethically) to advertise. Opponents contend that, at least where the electronic media are concerned, advertisements for some personal products (such as condoms) should be rejected because they are *inherently offensive*, even if the ads themselves are in good taste. In other words, because radio-, TV-, and computer-transmitted ads do seek us out in the privacy of our homes, privacy concerns should be greater than in other situations.

PRIVACY: HYPOTHETICAL CASE STUDIES

The cases that follow represent a wide range of privacy issues, although they are by no means exhaustive. In applying the moral reasoning model outlined in Chapter 3, you should keep in mind the three primary philosophical approaches. Because privacy is a fundamental value, duty-based moral agents (deontologists) believe that the consequences of one's actions are always subordinate to the ethical principle itself. Thus, invasions of privacy cannot always be justified on the ground that society will somehow benefit. The value of privacy can be overridden only in the face of some more compelling principle. For example, a reporter might feel obliged to report a case of apparent child abuse even if it meant intruding into the privacy of a family relationship. Thus, a journalist's commitment to truth, which also embraces a moral duty, can justify invasions of privacy when individuals become newsworthy and can then be said to have relinquished their privacy. As always, duty-based theorists confront difficult choices when two equally compelling principles compete for their allegiance.

A consequentialist (teleologist), as noted earlier, examines the potential consequences of the decision. The public good is always a consideration here. Teleologists, although certainly not oblivious to the harm to individuals, look at the impact of the moral choice. In some cases, such as the utilitarian variety of teleology, the moral agent will consider the consequence to the greatest number of people. At other times the consequence to individuals or small groups will be of primary concern. In applying the guidelines outlined here for an ethics of privacy, however, even consequentialists must justify invasions of privacy based on some competing principle(s) and, in so doing, should not cause more harm than is justified by their decision.

A virtue ethicist, in applying Aristotle's golden mean, searches for some mean position between two extremes. Of course, in invasion-of-privacy cases this approach is not always possible, but some situations do provide an opportunity to limit the intrusion or to make its impact more palatable. Television advertising, for example, is by its nature intrusive and invades the privacy of our home. Of course, commercials are here to stay, but the advertisers have an obligation not to offend the sensibilities of the audience. In other words, making TV a welcome guest in the home is a reasonable accommodation between banning intrusive advertising altogether and not having any standards at all.

CASE STUDIES

▷ **CASE 5-1**

News Values versus Privacy: The Case of "Designer Baby" Anna Marie

Laura Chaplin and Sarah Betts were lesbian partners residing in a middle-class and demographically diverse suburb of New Portsmouth, a scenic community of 300,000 located just 50 miles inland from the middle Atlantic coastline. Besides their sexual orientation, they shared one other common bond: Both were deaf, Laura because of an ear infection suffered in early childhood and Sarah as a result of a genetically inherited trait. After they had lived together for five years, they decided to become parents. Sarah was impregnated through artificial insemination with sperm provided by a donor through a sperm bank in New York, and daughter Anna Marie quickly became the focus of the couple's affection.

Although Chaplin and Betts had participated in a couple of gay rights demonstrations prior to the commencement of their relationship, they did not consider themselves political activists and lived rather unobtrusive lives as they focused most of their energies upon their careers and the nurturing of their infant daughter. Since their state did not permit same-sex marriages and they did not expect the conservative legislature to initiate any change in the marriage laws that would sanction such unions, Chaplin and Betts were exultant when the Massachusetts Supreme Judicial Court opened the doors to same-sex marriages in that state. Six weeks after the Massachusetts court's controversial decision, Chaplin and Betts traveled to Boston and were married in a civil ceremony, a legal bond they hoped would open the door to a variety of benefits enjoyed by heterosexual married couples. However, their optimism was short-lived. When Chaplin and Betts attempted to submit a joint state income tax return as a married couple, they were summarily rebuffed, prompting the couple to file suit against the state in federal district court on the grounds that the U.S. Constitution requires states to give "full faith and credit" to the laws of other states. The state, according to the couple's petition, was constitutionally obligated to recognize the marriage performed in Massachusetts, thereby extending to them the same rights enjoyed by heterosexual couples.

Chaplin and Betts had both declined interviews from the local media following their marriage ceremony, citing a right to privacy, but the lawsuit and its potential legal ramifications if they should prevail propelled their case to the top of the national and local news agenda. Channel 8, New Portsmouth's ABC affiliate, assigned Harrison Waters, a veteran reporter and award-winning journalist, to chronicle the legal proceedings and to illuminate them for an audience untutored in the intricacies of the legal system. He first sought an interview from the previously publicity inhibited couple, and this time they were less reticent in taking their case to the court of public opinion. Harrison's lead story, which focused primarily on the legal proceedings, included a brief reference to their hearing impairments and 2-year-old Anna Marie, but the couple was loathe to discuss their daughter in an effort to shield her as much as possible from the glare of publicity.

Harrison attached no special significance to the fact that both Chaplin and Betts were deaf until he received a rather startling call from Linda Carr, the head of the local Association for the Hearing Impaired, who had consulted with the deaf couple. She had witnessed their rapid evolution from relative obscurity to objects of public curiosity and provided the following remarkable account: When the couple began seeking a donor through a sperm bank in New York by the name of Certotron Enteprises, they had one unusual request: The sperm donor had to be deaf as a result of a genetic defect. A local doctor had told Betts that if she were impregnated with the sperm of a male who had a genetic defect similar to hers, the odds were significant that she would produce a deaf baby. When Anna Marie was born, an audiology test confirmed she was indeed deaf.

Carr also told Waters that she had moral reservations about such "designer babies" and had strongly urged Chaplin and Betts not to pursue this option. She also asked Waters not to attribute this information to her, a request that Waters readily agreed to. Not content with this singular source of the startling revelation concerning Anna Marie's conception, Waters contacted Certotron Enteprises in an effort to confirm the information. Unsurprisingly, the reporter's overtures were not productive, but working through a journalistic colleague in New York, who was also intrigued by Waters's story, Channel 8's reporter soon received confirmation from a source inside Certotron of the accuracy of Linda Carr's report.

For Waters, the news value of the circumstances surrounding Anna Marie's conception and birth was indisputable, not only because they were unique but also because they implicated profound questions of human morality concerning genetic engineering. On the other hand, he was sensitive to the infant's privacy interests and the potential harm to both the parents and Anna Marie if he should divulge what he had learned. Waters knew that on such a sensitive issue Channel 8's news director, Samantha Edwards, would serve as the moral gatekeeper, and he quickly summarized for his superior what he had learned about Anna Marie's birth. Edwards decided that before she made a decision, she wanted input from the station's early evening news producer, Latrelle Brown. As Edwards convened a hastily called meeting in her office, it was clear that Waters and Brown harbored different opinions on the news value of the unusual mode of Anna Marie's creation.

"As you know," said Waters, "Anna Marie, Laura Chaplin and Sara Betts's daughter, has remained in the background of our coverage. I've mentioned her in passing, but it's obvious the couple prefers to protect her from the glare of publicity. But in my judgment, this new information changes things. Anna Marie is a designer baby, produced essentially through the union of a sperm and egg from two genetically deaf people. This sort of genetic manipulation is controversial and is therefore newsworthy."

"The procedure itself is a matter of public interest," agreed Brown, "but Anna Marie is only 2 years old. If we divulge the unique circumstances of her conception and birth, this unwelcome intrusion upon her privacy could haunt her for the rest of her life. Admittedly, the circumstances of her birth are unique, but this has nothing to do with the story that has made her parents the focus of news coverage."

"I agree that Anna Marie's handicap has nothing to do with our coverage of the couple's marriage and legal proceedings against the state," replied Waters. "Chaplin and Betts are clearly newsworthy, and under *normal* circumstances Anna Marie would not be a matter of public interest. However, this is a couple that deliberately set out to produce a deaf baby, a child with a handicap like theirs. They apparently believed they would be better prepared to care for a deaf child and that their daughter, in her later years, would more easily identify with her deaf parents. One could argue that their motivations in creating a deaf baby are selfish and in fact deliberately producing a handicapped child is an act of cruelty. This entire procedure is controversial and that, in my judgment, makes Anna Marie newsworthy, as unfair as it might be to the couple's unfortunate daughter."

"We're in no position to judge the motivations of the parents," responded Brown bluntly. "They obviously love this child, and there's no reason to doubt their parenting skills. Anna Marie may in fact be what we refer to as a designer baby but that by itself doesn't make her a matter of public interest.

Anna Marie can't speak for herself; she is still entitled to a zone of privacy."

"Normally I would agree," declared Waters. "But her lesbian parents are matters of public interest because of their marriage in Boston and their efforts to seek marital recognition in this state. The notion of homosexual couples having children is increasingly common but is still controversial. The circumstances surrounding the marriage of Laura Chaplin and Sarah Butts are certainly a matter of public interest. Anna Marie came to be a part of this family under rather unusual and perhaps even disturbing circumstances. This, in my judgment, makes her a matter of public interest."

"But your claim is still based upon the newsworthiness of the parents," replied Brown. "Assume that Anna Marie's parents were not gay and that there was no controversy surrounding their marriage. Would Anna Marie still be newsworthy? Before we trample upon her privacy we need to be convinced that she is somehow independently newsworthy. And I don't believe a sufficiently compelling case can be made that would justify invading her privacy."

"I agree that under normal circumstances Anna Marie's handicap would not be a matter of public interest," said Waters. "But the fact is that her parents are newsworthy, and the circumstances of her birth are highly unusual. Children frequently become newsworthy because of the behavior of their parents. The zone of privacy has to be expanded because this couple's decision to seek legal redress has thrown the spotlight on their family situation, and that includes Anna Marie."

News Director Samantha Edwards listened attentively to this lively exchange between Harrison Waters and Channel 8's news producer. As a parent herself, she empathized with the plight of 2-year-old Anna Marie who could not enter into this conversation concerning the proposed publicity surrounding the circumstances of her birth. Despite the characterization of Anna Marie as a "designer baby," Edwards conceded the strength of the privacy claims under normal circumstances. However, as Waters had noted, the newsworthiness of her parents had changed the equation somewhat. The question was whether the publicity swirling around the marriage of Laura Chaplin and Sarah Betts justified the incursion upon the privacy interests of their 2-year-old daughter.

THE CASE STUDY

One of the most difficult ethical judgment calls for journalists is in deciding whether the public interest surrounding newsworthy individuals extends to those who are closely affiliated with them, such as friends and family members. In some cases, the answer may be obvious. But in others it would appear that the burden of proof is on the moral agent to demonstrate that those who are connected in some way with the newsworthy subjects are themselves independently newsworthy. When an individual is newsworthy, there may be legitimate public interest in reporting private information, although in doing so the goal should be to at least minimize the harm.

In this scenario, the lesbian partners, Laura Chaplin and Sarah Betts, are clearly newsworthy because of their lawsuit to compel the state to recognize their marriage consummated in Massachusetts. While the initial reports mentioned their 2-year-old daughter Anna Marie—a degree of publicity to which even her parents would not object—at first glance she has no independent news value. In any event, the infant Anna Marie cannot represent herself in making her wishes known.

The circumstances surrounding Anna Marie's creation are certainly intriguing, but are they newsworthy? They are unrelated to the newsworthiness of her parents, but this case broaches the issue of motivation on the part of Chaplin and Betts in intentionally seeking to produce a deaf child. There is no evidence that their actions were not inspired out of love, but one could argue that deliberately "designing" a child with a handicap is cruel, even if the parents suffer from the same affliction. And beyond the specific case of Anna Marie, this form of genetic manipulation is controversial. Nevertheless, the moral agent must still struggle with the question of whether the newsworthiness of Anna Marie's parents coupled with the unusual circumstances of her conception are sufficient to strip the zone of privacy from the 2-year-old infant.

For the purpose of weighing the public interest in Anna Marie's creation against potential harm to

all parties involved, assume the role of Channel 8 news director Samantha Edwards and, applying the moral reasoning model outlined in Chapter 3, render your judgment in this matter.

 ## CASE 5-2

The Supreme Court Candidate's Untimely Withdrawal[94]

Chief Justice Byron Fitzhugh's retirement had come as a surprise to the nation's legal watchdogs, but the still robust 70-year-old jurist had decided to leave the bench to pursue other interests, confident that his successor would continue his legacy of constitutional restraint. The White House lost no time in organizing a search for Justice Fitzhugh's replacement amidst presidential assurances that he would appoint a judge whose "record reflects an unwavering faithfulness to the constitutional text." In the weeks following Fitzhugh's announcement, media pundits and the White House press corps pursued leaks and rumors on the "vetting" process by which potential nominees for the federal bench are subjected to a vigorous FBI background check and their fitness is appraised by the American Bar Association. But while reporters kept up a relentless barrage of news dispatches from inside the beltway, fueling public speculation, the White House press secretary remained customarily evasive in her frequent briefings of White House reporters. Nevertheless, as the president's staff worked tirelessly to develop a "short list" of potential nominees, confidentiality yielded to the inevitable leaks that fuel journalists' insatiable appetite for inside information. According to "sources close to the president," three candidates remained on the list, with Judge Harlan Askew as the odds-on favorite to receive the president's benediction.

Judge Askew had served both as a New York state prosecutor and a federal district court judge and had been appointed by the president's predecessor six years earlier to the Second Circuit Court of Appeals. While his legal inclinations were those of a constitutional strict constructionist, he was not considered to be an ideologue, thus earning him accolades from both legal scholars and fellow jurists. His opinions were lucid and well-reasoned and described as "intellectually rigorous" even by his critics. Even in his relatively short tenure at the appellate level, Judge Askew had exhibited impressive leadership qualities among his fellow judges, a trait that further commended him for the center seat on an increasingly fractured court.

The press corps dutifully reported what they had gleaned from their White House sources, including Judge Askew's apparent preeminent standing as a finalist for the Supreme Court vacancy. Based upon their triweekly dispatches, syndicated columnist Maxwell Knight and his partner Louis Raymond, 12-year veterans of the capital's political milieu, had penetrated the veil of official secrecy surrounding the nomination and had successfully extracted newsworthy details that had escaped the grasp of their competitors. The columnists were the first to report Judge Askew's emergence as the front-runner, precipitating a mad scramble among their journalistic brethren to regain the initiative in the intensely competitive news environment of the nation's capital. As reporters waited expectantly for an announcement from the White House, Knight learned from his usually reliable source inside the Oval Office, presidential aide Michael Palmer, that Askew had withdrawn his name from contention, citing "family" reasons. Knight pressed Palmer for more details, but the presidential aide was evasive. The columnist shared this information with his coauthor, and they quickly conveyed this shocking revelation to their geographically diverse readers, who had remained attentive to the president's progress in filling the Supreme Court vacancy, according to the daily e-mail correspondence. They allowed the story to resonate for a couple of days before Knight again approached Palmer for more information on the real reason for Askew's untimely retreat. He was determined not to be outmaneuvered by his highly competitive peers. Palmer was reticent in his second meeting with Knight on the subject of Askew's withdrawal but eventually succumbed to the columnist's irresistible and persistent entreaty.

Even for the veteran journalist, Palmer's disclosure was a surprise and confronted the columnist with an unexpected ethical dilemma. He quickly returned to his cramped quarters in the White House press room and summoned his partner Louis Raymond and their editorial assistant, Janice Meehan, both of whom were opinioned and could be counted on to provide counsel, usually accompanied by a rather energetic debate.

"I've discovered why Askew withdrew from the nomination process," Knight began as his two colleagues listened attentively. "This information comes from Michael Palmer, the presidential aide. He's asked not to be quoted by name, but I've found him to be a credible source in the past. He tells me that Askew's 8-year-old son, Chad, is adopted, but the boy has never been told."

"And so Askew is afraid this might crop up amidst the pervasive public scrutiny he and his family will undergo if he should be nominated?," Meehan asked rhetorically.

"Precisely," replied Knight. "And he's deeply concerned about the psychological impact this kind of sudden revelation might have on Chad. Askew just doesn't want to take a chance that his son's adoptive status will be made public."

"I'm perplexed as to why the Askews decided to keep the fact of his adoption from their son," Raymond said. "Most parents today believe that adoptive children should be told as soon as they are old enough to understand."

"I posed this question to Palmer," responded Knight, "and he said Harlan Askew is old-fashioned. He's 56, and his wife is sixteen years his junior. The judge's personal beliefs are apparently as conservative as his judicial ideology. During an interview with the White House staff, Askew said he and his wife had agreed to break the news to Chad when he became a teenager and would be mature enough to handle such an unanticipated confession."

Knight paused briefly and then posed the question that would precipitate a vigorous ethical discourse between his two professional colleagues: "Do we disclose this information in tomorrow's column—do we tell the nation that Harlan Askew withdrew as the front-runner because of concerns his 8-year-old son, Chad, would find out through press coverage he's adopted?"

"As painful as it is, I think we have to," Raymond declared unhesitatingly as he rose to the challenge. "By all accounts, Askew was the front-runner for the nation's highest judicial post. The president was only days away from the nomination and suddenly Askew withdrew his name. We know the reason, and I think our readers have a right to know."

"I couldn't disagree more," noted Meehan emphatically. "The publication of this information would be an invasion of privacy. It's a private matter for the Askews to deal with. They've decided to conceal from Chad his adoptive status for several more years. This may appear to us to be unwise and even an outmoded way of thinking, but that's not a decision for us to make."

"Normally I might agree with you, Janice," Raymond replied, "but Askew is a public figure. He's currently serving on the appellate bench, has written some controversial and highly publicized opinions, and until a couple of days ago was the leading candidate for Chief Justice. The public was expecting this nomination, and for some inexplicable reason Askew withdrew. We have the answer to this puzzle, and I believe we have a responsibility to share it with our readers."

"Although there was never an official announcement of Askew's withdrawal since the president was still considering the matter," declared Meehan, determined to defend the Askews' right to privacy and the sensibilities of their young son, "the fact is that Palmer confided to Max that Askew was withdrawing for family reasons. That's what we initially reported. Why can't we just leave it at that? Do our readers really need to know the specifics?"

"In this case I believe they do," replied Raymond. "I can appreciate Palmer's attempt to shield Askew from unwelcome publicity by just citing family reasons for his withdrawal. But this vague account raises more questions than it answers. Askew knew when he started this process that the press coverage would be intense and relentless and that his family might even become a subject of media scrutiny. If he had apprehensions about the public disclosure of his family secret, he should never have become a candidate for Chief Justice."

But the young researcher was unconvinced. "If Askew had been officially nominated, then perhaps this would be a different matter," she answered. "But he withdrew before any announcement was made. Besides, I have a child of my own. He's not adopted, but I can sympathize with the Askews'

dilemma. I don't agree that they must relinquish all right to privacy simply because Harlan Askew is on the federal bench and was considered for a Supreme Court appointment. His son's adoptive status is not a matter of public interest, and keep in mind that Chad Askew is a stakeholder in this ethical dilemma concerning whether to reveal the real reason for his father's withdrawal. The emotional impact could be tremendous."

"You may have a point," Raymond conceded. "But I still say that Harlan Askew invited public scrutiny when he accepted the president's invitation to become a candidate. Surely he must have known the risk, particularly once the senatorial hearings began on his nomination. It's possible that the press would never have learned about his adoptive son, but on the other hand in today's celebrity-obsessed media environment that is improbable. As a potential nominee for the nation's highest court, I don't see how Askew can claim a right to privacy for himself or his family when a member of his family is the reason why he is withdrawing from consideration."

"But this private information—his son's adoptive status—has nothing to do with Askew's fitness for the position of Chief Justice," Meehan replied. "And besides, now that he's withdrawn from contention, your rationale for publishing what we know is even less convincing."

Maxwell Knight listened attentively as his two staff members engaged in their spirited verbal dual, summoning to their defense the countervailing values of newsworthiness and the right to privacy. Since the inception of their journalistic alliance, Knight, as senior partner, had assumed the mantle of senior editor when ethical dilemmas arose. Thus, as moral agent, he would make the final decision on whether to reveal publicly the real reason for Harlan Askew's sudden withdrawal, but the dialectic between Raymond and Meehan helped to crystallize the competing claims on his moral sense. On the one hand, the privacy argument registered high on his ethical barometer because of the rather dubious news value of Chad Askew's adoptive status. On the other hand, despite the official White House silence on the matter, Harlan Askew had become a candidate for nomination to the Supreme Court's center seat, knowing that his life would soon become an open book. And then he suddenly withdrew with an abrupt announcement that was curiously vague.

The *Knight/Raymond Report* had an exclusive, but the ethical dimensions of this story mitigated the usually passionate temperament of the two prominent Washington columnists.

THE CASE STUDY

Awkward situations involving children can be ethically troublesome for practicing journalists. In this case, the potential harm to young Brad Askew is real if he discovers his adoptive status through news accounts. Depending upon his emotional maturity, he might survive this shock with few aftereffects or he might suffer severe trauma. Thus, the moral agent in this case must ask whether the journalistic imperatives of this story outweigh the potential harm to Judge Harlan Askews's adoptive son and the privacy interests at stake here.

But *whose* privacy interests are implicated? Do the Askews have a privacy interest in maintaining their family secret? Since Harlan Askew was never officially named as the president's nominee and withdrew before the expected announcement, should he have a greater expectation of privacy? Does 8-year-old Chad Askew have a privacy interest in being shielded from the glare of publicity? If so, how does his father's sudden withdrawal as a candidate for Chief Justice—a withdrawal based specifically upon his desire to protect his son—affect the newsworthiness argument surrounding the disclosure of this information?

These are vexing questions, but professional journalists must sometimes step back from the emotional precipice and render a rational judgment based upon what they believe to be sound and defensible ethical principles. The zone of privacy, particularly where the vulnerabilities of young children are at stake, should be penetrated with reluctance and only where the public interest is clearly manifest. Of course, the cognitive components of moral reasoning cannot always be easily segregated from the affective dimensions of our humanity, which is why ethical dilemmas sometimes challenge the limits of our moral endurance.

For the purpose of analyzing the ethical dilemma posed in this scenario, assume the role of syndicated columnist Maxwell Knight and, applying the model for moral reasoning outlined in Chapter 3, decide whether you will report the real reason for Judge Harlan Askew's sudden withdrawal as a candidate for Chief Justice of the United States.

 CASE 5-3

The Pregnant Place Kicker

Football was a secular religion to the citizens of South Platte, and the Jefferson High Panthers were their sacred altar. Each Friday night in the fall, when the local gridiron powerhouse was playing on its home field, the team's supporters gathered to cheer their high school heroes to victory over their hapless opponents. Fanaticism reigned supreme in South Platte on Friday evenings. The faithful not only expected the Panthers to win; they demanded it. Memories faltered when attempting to recall the team's last losing season. They were perennial contenders for state playoff honors and on several occasions had made it to the final round, claiming the much-coveted prize of state champions three times in the past ten years.

The coaching staff was always blessed with a boundless pool of football talent at their disposal. Virtually every athletically inclined young male aspired to don the Panthers uniform and perform before the hometown crowd. Judith Watkins also aspired to join the Panthers.

Fifteen-year-old Judith had played on a recreational football team before entering high school, where she had displayed an incredible aptitude for the game. She had played some defense, but her specialty was place kicking. The kicking game had been the Panthers' Achilles heel for several years, and Judith assumed her talents would be a blessing to head coach Mackie Jones and his staff. However, when she appeared for spring tryouts, the coach informed her brusquely that football was a male sport and that she could not participate. Under the threat of a court order, Mackie relented but warned Judith that he was according her a right to compete for the position of place kicker and nothing more. By the end of spring training, it was clear to the coaching staff that they could not deny Judith Watkins a place on the football squad. She had range and accuracy, both desirable traits in a field goal kicker.

Judith's admission to the previously all-male bastion of gridiron prowess was not applauded by the team's loyal fans, whose conservative community still celebrated traditional gender roles as the natural order of things. The publicly stated reasons for their disenchantment varied, but they were united in their condemnation of coach Jones's controversial decision. Some supporters opposed the move on principle. Others, noting Judith's physical attractiveness, worried that her presence on the team would be a distraction for the other players. Still others were concerned for her safety, anxious that an opposing player might risk a "roughing the kicker" penalty just to prove that women were not cut out to be football players. The sight of Judith Watkins being taken from the field on a stretcher, they feared, would place a pall over the entire season.

Judith's first appearance in the inaugural game of the season precipitated the predictable boos and jeers from the stands, but they quickly subsided as the young woman kicked a 38-yard field goal in the face of a stiff breeze. By the end of the season, some unreconstructed critics were loathe to acknowledge Judith's contributions to the team's winning season, but much of the public censure had subsided. She not only had the best kicking percentage of any high school player in the state, her "golden toe" was directly responsible for two of the team's victories, when the offense faltered on fourth down.

In her second season, the young place kicker continued her impressive performance, and by midpoint in the season she was being touted for all-state honors. In addition, the Panthers appeared to be on their way to an undefeated season and the postseason playoffs. However, with only two games remaining, Coach Jones's unexpected announcement quickly changed the dynamics of the Panthers' prospects. During a press conference just four days prior to his team's matchup against their archrival, the Avondale Wildcats, Jones announced

that Judith Watkins was leaving the team for medical reasons. Because of privacy concerns, he said, no further details would be provided. "She's under the care of a doctor, and we wish her well," noted Jones in a prepared statement read to the assembled reporters.

Victor Simms was curious about Judith Watkins's sudden departure from the team, but he respected Coach Jones's plea for privacy during the press conference. Simms was perhaps best known for his colorful commentary on the local cable system's weekly telecast of the Panthers' games, which was fed to cable outlets in surrounding communities. But Simms was also a journalist and anchored the sports segment of a locally produced cable newscast. He was well respected by the entire Jefferson High coaching staff, and his entrée for weekly interviews and insights into the school's athletic program was always assured.

Three days following Coach Jones's startling announcement, Simms was interviewing the team's part-time trainer, Nathan Brown, about the players' overall physical condition as the season neared its climax. At the close of the interview, when the camera was no longer rolling Brown volunteered some astonishing information: Judith Watkins had left the team because she was pregnant. The reporter was unsure why Brown felt compelled to reveal this piece of intelligence that Coach Jones had described as a matter of "privacy," but Simms was aware that Brown had never reconciled himself to Judith's membership on the Panthers football squad. At this point Simms was unsure of the news value of what he had learned, but in a subsequent meeting with assistant coach Paul Samuelson he raised the issue. Samuelson confirmed what the trainer had told him and added that they had known about her pregnancy for three weeks but were undecided what to do about it. The team doctor recommended she quit the team.

Simms returned to his office at the cable system building and hastily arranged a meeting with his producer, Katheryn Cross, and Oliver Holmes, the system's director of program origination. The sports journalist then briefed his two colleagues on the unexpected details of Judith Watkins's departure from the team.

"This is very interesting," volunteered Holmes when Simms had completed his summation. "The question is what we should do with this information, if anything. This will be my call, but I would like your views." South Platte Cable's rather modest staff had no news director, but Holmes was nominally in charge of all locally produced programming, which included the daily newscast. He would be the moral agent in deciding the news value of the reason behind Judith Watkins's untimely departure from the Panthers football squad.

"During his news conference Coach Jones referred to Judith's 'medical condition' as a private matter, and normally I would agree," responded Simms. "A teenager's pregnancy is hardly newsworthy, and the publication of such information would be an invasion of privacy. But this case is different. Despite her youth, Judith Watkins is newsworthy. She broke the gender barrier for the first time in our state's history of high school athletics. She is the number one place kicker in the state. And she was in line for all-state honors before leaving the team. The public has a right to know why their team's first female player has left at the end of only her second year."

"I agree that all of these things make her a matter of public interest," admitted Cross. "But why is her pregnancy newsworthy? This is a private matter and is particularly sensitive for a teenager. She's only 16."

"The question I've asked myself," replied Simms, "is whether Judith's pregnancy is sufficiently related to her public persona to make this matter newsworthy. I believe that it is. Her sudden absence from the team could diminish the team's chances in the playoffs, particularly in close games. In addition, Coach Jones announced that Judith was leaving the team for medical reasons. I suppose that's technically true, but it's also misleading. Just in the past couple of days I've heard a lot of speculation around town concerning Judith's departure, ranging from academic problems to fraternization with another team member. No one really believes the medical excuse. Perhaps we should set the record straight."

"If Judith were a professional athlete, I might agree with you," asserted Cross, who was determined to defend the honor of Jefferson High's first female football player. "But she's a student first—an adolescent student—who just happens to be playing football for the local high school team."

"I'm not sure that any of these players are really amateurs," noted Simms. "They are given almost as much press coverage as college and pro athletes. They are treated like heroes by the loyal citizens of South Platte. And everyone knows that the academic program can't compete with these adolescent superstars. When was the last time a football player flunked a course?"

"Your argument is unpersuasive, Victor," replied Cross. "We can't do anything about the rumor mill concerning Judith's departure, but in this case I don't think it's our job to set the record straight. Coach Jones was acting in good faith when he ascribed Judith's untimely exit to medical reasons. I don't think that news values should trump her right to privacy in this case."

"This is a small town, and her pregnancy won't remain a secret for long," noted Simms realistically. "Reporting what we know will at least satisfy the public's curiosity and stop the rumor mill. And since Judith's pregnancy is directly related to her inability to continue on the team, I think it's newsworthy."

"I have no doubt that her pregnancy won't remain a secret for long. But should we be a party to divulging this kind of personal information? Shouldn't that decision remain with Judith and her family?"

With those final queries, Holmes told Victor Simms and Katheryn Cross that he would consider their arguments and render a decision within 24 hours. He was not unaware of the possible legal consequences if South Platte Cable were to publicize Judith Watkins's pregnancy. His company could face an invasion-of-privacy lawsuit, but for the moment he was preoccupied with the ethical dimensions of the issue. Besides, Holmes believed that the burden of proof was on those counseling publicity of embarrassing private information, and if he were convinced by his reporter's newsworthiness argument in favor of disclosure, a similar rationale might serve as a legal defense.

THE CASE STUDY

Concerns over personal privacy are enduring in our society, and the unregulated domain of the World Wide Web has simply exacerbated those fears. But as ethicists and media critics struggle to cope with these new challenges, the traditional media must continue to cope with ethical concerns of their own.

Hovering over many privacy cases is the possibility of a lawsuit concerning the revelation of embarrassing personal information. That's particularly true in the case of those who are not of the age of majority. However, the legal defenses underlying the privacy lawsuits are not entirely distinct from the ethical rationales advanced in support of publicizing such embarrassing information. Newsworthiness is foremost among these rationales, but journalists are frequently too casual in using the "public's right to know" as a justification. Such platitudes are empty vessels without some ethically defensible explanation as to *why* the public has a right to know certain information.

This concern must animate Oliver Holmes's moral reasoning process. However, in any privacy case involving a private individual the first question that must be resolved is whether the subject herself is newsworthy. Is Judith Watkins newsworthy? If so, why? Assuming that she is newsworthy, is the fact of her pregnancy newsworthy? Is there some public benefit to be derived from this knowledge, that is, do the benefits outweigh the harms in this case? Should the fact that she is a high school athlete rather than, say, a professional athlete be a significant factor in your decision-making process?

For the purpose of addressing these challenging questions, assume the role of Oliver Holmes, the local cable system's director of program origination, and applying the model for moral reasoning described in Chapter 3, render a judgment on whether to include the fact of Judith Watkins's pregnancy in your next sports report.

▶ **CASE 5-4**

The Massacre at Langdale High and Laura's Secret Diary

High school senior Laura Devlin was looking forward to graduation day, the ritualistic validation of an academic milestone. May 16, just three weeks before she was to receive her diploma, was indistinguishable from any other school day as Laura

moved almost absentmindedly through the cafeteria line following her fourth-period social studies class. As she turned from the cashier in search of her 15-year-old brother Jeffrey, who had preceded her through the line, she spotted him standing alone at a far table—and then watched with horror as he pulled a .38-caliber pistol from beneath his windbreaker and methodically began pulling the trigger. Within a matter of seconds four classmates lay seriously wounded, and three students and a teacher lay dead.

From that moment on the events resembled those that had transpired at too many high schools across the nation: A frantic call went out to 911, police and paramedics rushed to the scene to confront the tragic consequences of a disturbed teenager's violent deportment, counselors were brought to the school to assist its inhabitants in coping with the unexplainable, and a community mourned and asked "How could this happen here?"

It did not take long for the police to take Jeffrey Devlin into custody. Moments after the shooting the police found him sitting calmly behind the gym, still holding the weapon that had turned the Langdale High cafeteria into a monument to death. Jeffrey was charged as an adult with first-degree murder and was held without bail in the city jail. In the meantime, the police used a search warrant to retrieve three weapons and five boxes of ammunition from Jeffrey's room, along with other material evidence that might be useful in his prosecution. On the advice of Jeffrey's court-appointed attorney, Laura and her divorced mother rejected all overtures from the local and national media.

Like other members of the community, Sharyn Lassiter was shocked by the shootings. Lassiter was the police and court reporter for the *Andersonville Tribune,* a four-year veteran of the local paper. During her relatively brief tenure at the *Tribune,* Lassiter had compiled an impressive portfolio of articles documenting her community's law enforcement and juristic activities. Most of her coverage dealt with the more sinister side of human nature and the community's disaffected rogues whose social obscurity was transformed only through their arrest for some felony or misdemeanor. Lassiter's diverse journalistic menu ran the gamut from murder, rape, and simple burglary on the criminal side to the civil docket's less sensational array of lawsuits alleging a variety of physical and emotional injuries.

While Lassiter was sometimes repelled by what she heard in court or by the evidence provided by her police sources, she had fostered an emotional detachment in reporting on the legal foibles of society's miscreants. But the Devlin story was different. *Kids killing kids!* did not follow the script of the typical criminal case. Nevertheless, the young reporter covered the initial phases of the case with her usual commitment to journalistic objectivity and neutrality, the animating principles of her university education and the *Tribune*'s newsroom culture. But like most good journalists, Lassiter was not satisfied to report just the facts surrounding the tragic events at Langdale High. The citizens of Andersonville deserved answers, and the *Tribune* was the proper forum in which to satisfy her readers' justifiable curiosity.

Because Laura Devlin and her mother, perhaps as much out of shame as the legal advice provided by Jeffrey's attorney, had refused any public comment and had consistently rejected the media's requests for interviews, Lassiter began her investigation by talking to the principal and several teachers at Langdale High, neighbors of the Devlin family, and, with their parents' permission, several of the Devlin children's classmates. To probe beyond the information contained in the official crime report, she also interviewed detective lieutenant Andy Cherry, a source with whom the reporter had had a cooperative relationship since her arrival at the *Tribune* four years ago. Cherry was in charge of the Devlin investigation.

From these disparate sources, a rather grim assessment of the Devlins' family life emerged. Neighbors remembered Laura and Jeffrey as quiet but friendly children in their formative years. But shortly after Laura's tenth birthday, according to their recollections, she suddenly had become sullen and withdrawn. Her high school classmates rendered a similar verdict. She counted few friends among her classmates, with the exception of three girls who frequently came to her house to study.

Jeffrey was described as very bright, a good student, and socially well adjusted—that is, until his father abandoned the family when Jeffrey was 13.

From this point on, the teenager's good-natured disposition changed. Several classmates recounted his growing fascination with guns and even a threat to bring one to school to "liven up the place." However, they had not taken him seriously. His mother, who had never been a strict disciplinarian, was unable to compensate for her husband's faithful influence in Jeffrey's life, and his obedience to her maternal commands became increasingly erratic. Perhaps Jeffrey's unanticipated rampage was triggered by his unforgiving resentment against his father.

Some of these details were confirmed by Lieutenant Cherry in recounting some of the conversations that several witnesses had had with the investigating officers. But it was not Cherry's confirmations that piqued Lassiter's journalistic curiosity; it was Laura Devlin's diary. The diary—which actually consisted of three separate books covering eight years—had been seized by the police to be used as possible evidence in the case against Jeffrey Devlin. Perhaps the diary would provide some clue as to her brother's motivations in carrying out his armed assault.

Lassiter, who felt uncomfortable at the idea of penetrating the unspoken code of privacy that surrounds a diary, nevertheless buried herself in Laura's personal musings. The diary was a virtual tour de force through Laura's childhood and adolescent fantasies and dreams, but it also revealed a worldview of an increasingly troubled young woman. Laura's chronicle began when she was about 8 and reflected a fairly happy, well-adjusted child. It provided some keen insights into her personal world, a father who was domineering but suitably attentive, and a mother who was loving but clearly unassertive in her relationship to the children's father.

But shortly after Laura's tenth birthday there was a noticeable change in the tone of her youthful literary recollections. Her father figured even more prominently in her accounts, which revealed a pattern of sexual abuse that continued until his departure when Laura was 15. Her increasingly desperate entries, a cathartic attempt to cope with her victimhood, described an emotional evolution from confusion and fear to loathing for her oppressive father. Some of her notations were suicidal, although there was no evidence that Laura had ever attempted to take her own life. She had tried drugs but apparently decided that her personal diary was more therapeutic than the unpredictable consequences of marijuana and speed.

The diary's references to her brother were somewhat circumspect and not entirely illuminating of the case at hand. However, it did contain regret at Jeffrey's apparently blissful ignorance of his father's sexual perversion and some evidence of her brother's growing disaffection with their father's authoritarian impulses, which seemed to contradict Lassiter's accounts from other sources of Mr. Devlin's departure as the immediate cause of Jeffrey's psychological demise. Despite the apparent estrangement between father and son, several entries also recorded, paradoxically, Jeffrey's depressed state following his father's untimely desertion and his subsequent experimentation with drugs. There were other incidents of his youthful rebellion recorded in the diary. It was clear that Jeffrey had lived a life of quiet desperation.

Lieutenant Cherry allowed Lassiter to take notes and even to photocopy pages of the diary; the original would be retained in the event that the district attorney decided to use it as evidence. Laura's diary helped to explain the pathologies that had engulfed the Devlin family. As a first-person account of wasted youth, it would also make an interesting story—but not before it underwent the ethical scrutiny of managing editor Douglas Hawthorne.

Lassiter had not yet written her proposed story when she met with Hawthorne and city editor Marcia MacKenzie. She understood Hawthorne's ethical concerns but was prepared to argue in favor of a human interest story based on Laura Devlin's diary.

"The information in that diary is indeed interesting," began Hawthorne in convening the meeting in his rather spacious office on the third floor of the *Tribune*'s new headquarters. "But I am concerned that we may be crossing the line here in terms of Laura's right to privacy."

"I've thought of that," replied Lassiter somewhat reflectively. "But much of the information is a matter of public interest because of its connection to the school shootings. It helps to explain the circumstances that may have turned Jeffrey Devlin from an apparently normal teenager into a killer."

"In a sense that's true," responded MacKenzie. "But much of this material is very personal and private information, particularly the part about sexual abuse. If we publish this, its impact on Laura could be devastating. Diaries are by definition private; there's nothing to be gained by publishing the contents of this diary."

"But the confidential nature of the diary has already been breached," asserted Lassiter. "The police department has examined it; it could even become evidence in Jeffrey's trial, although the DA hasn't made up her mind about that. And, of course, Lieutenant Cherry let me peruse it at will."

The city editor was obviously not persuaded by this line of argument. "It may be true that a handful of people have examined this diary," said MacKenzie, "but the contents are still not public knowledge. The real embarrassment will come if we publish a story based on this diary in our newspaper."

"I realize that Laura is truly a victim and did nothing to invite this kind of public scrutiny of her family," Lassiter replied, attempting to alter the line of argument somewhat. "And even though she won't talk to the press, her life and that of her mother have been put under a microscope—all because of what Jeffrey did. They're hounded by the media every time they visit him in jail or accompany him to a court appearance. The fact is that they're newsworthy by association with the suspect."

"I'm not so sure," responded MacKenzie, who silently acknowledged the superficial appeal of her reporter's claim but was not quite willing to concede its moral merit. "Where matters of privacy are concerned, we should be clear about where to draw the line between the real public interest and what the public is interested in. I question using any of the diary's contents as the basis for a story, particularly the personal details of her father's sexual abuse. How is that relevant to this case?"

"It's relevant because it places this whole episode into context," Lassiter asserted. "It places part of the blame right at the father's doorstep—a fact that can be most forcefully documented through the pages of this diary. Besides, the diary contradicts the rumors that are floating around that Jeffrey went into a tailspin entirely because of his father's desertion. This may be partially true, but the diary suggests a problem of longer duration. It may be a little more complicated than people realize, and this story could help to set the record straight."

"In addition," Lassiter continued, "stories such as this could serve as an early warning to the community about the dire consequences of not intervening sooner in the lives of troubled kids. I don't know whether anything could have been done in this case, but the signs were there. And that alone justifies using this diary as a source for my story."

At this point Hawthorne decided that all relevant arguments had been vented and dispatched his two staffers with the promise of a quick decision. As his newspaper's managing editor, Hawthorne was the moral agent because, assuming that he approved this project, the story would be published in both the paper and the *Tribune*'s online edition.

THE CASE STUDY

Are the contents of Laura's diary newsworthy? Does the public interest in this information override the privacy interests of Laura and her mother? Does the teenager's relationship to the accused diminish her expectation of privacy, particularly in matters that are tangential to the crime under investigation?

The privacy concerns arise at two different levels. First, there is the status of the diary itself as a viable source of news. Second, the *nature of the information* must be the focus of the moral reasoning process.

An ethical purist might argue that diaries by definition are sacrosanct; except in highly unusual circumstances, a diary's contents should not be violated. The writer has an expectation of privacy that even parents must respect unless a child's safety or well-being is at stake. In this view, the police might be entitled to review the diary to collect evidence in the case against Jeffrey Devlin. But this gives them no right to reveal its contents to third parties. Of course, if some of the contents are introduced into evidence during the trial, then the privacy rights are clearly diminished as far as press coverage is concerned. But this isn't a factor in this case study. On the other hand, one could argue that once the diary is removed through official action from the custody of its owner, it is no longer strictly a private document.

The other issue in this case focuses on the content itself. Sharyn Lassiter apparently believes that there can be no line-drawing here in terms of the news value of the contents. Admittedly, some of the diary's commentary is directly relevant to Jeffrey's state of mind and motivations; some, such as the father's sexual abuse of Laura, appears at best to be tangential to the case. But Lassiter contends that the totality of the diary's contents helps to explain the family circumstances that may have led to Jeffrey's psychological demise.

The counterpoint to this is that, *assuming that the use of any material from the diary is justified,* the reporter should use a fine scalpel and include in her story only the material that directly relates to Jeffrey Devlin's personal behavior and his relationship with his family.

For the purpose of exploring these issues, assume the role of managing editor Douglas Hawthorne, and using the SAD formula, decide whether you will authorize a story based on Laura's diary and, if so, what limits (if any) you would place on the use of its contents.

▶ **CASE 5-5**

Electronic Billboards on the Freeway and Motorist Privacy

For Timothy McNabb, the president and CEO of the McNabb Outdoor Advertising Agency, the steady stream of commuters on San Fernando's north-south freeway was a much-coveted target audience. Where motorists saw gridlock and road rage, McNabb saw a mobile consumer market ready to be cultivated. Billboards, of course, were an important venue in his agency's advertising arsenal, and McNabb did not underestimate the importance of commuters to a successful outdoor advertising campaign.

Under his aggressive and innovative stewardship, the McNabb agency had emerged as a powerful presence in the outdoor advertising industry, and McNabb's devoted and talented workforce remained vigilant for opportunities to expand the agency's horizons and hence its clients' commercial exposures. McNabb had taken a rather modest

inheritance from his father and invested in a financially floundering and creatively stagnant outdoor advertising enterprise headquartered in San
Fernando's vibrant commercial district and within
five years had triggered a creative renaissance and
profitable resurrection within the agency. From the
outset, McNabb's entrepreneurial mind-set was
analogous to that of a defense attorney; he accepted any client (within reason) who had money
to spend. His client list was not determined by
whether he personally approved of their products.
McNabb believed that any client had a right to promote its wares in the economic marketplace, and
his agency would be a willing partner in forging a
psychological bond between corporate America
and the nation's acquisitive consumers.

Among his advertising contemporaries, McNabb
was known as an innovator, but he was also willing
and even eager to embrace successful techniques
employed by agencies in other markets. Imitation
was the sincerest form of flattery, in McNabb's view,
and besides, his clients did not scrutinize closely
the genesis of his creative ideas. They were interested in results.

McNabb believed that electronic billboards
would produce such results. He had read an article in the trade press describing the installation of
electronic billboards along a California freeway
equipped with sensors that scan the traffic and
register the radio station frequencies (and hence
the musical tastes) from passing motorists. This information is fed into a central computer, which
correlates it with certain products favored by such
consumers. The computer then selects an ad for an
appropriate product from among a data bank of pre-
programmed ads and displays that product ad on
the billboard. The products can continually change
depending upon the musical tastes of a majority of
automobiles scanned at any particular time.

McNabb had presented this idea to his staff,
who enthusiastically developed a proposal to erect
an electronic billboard along the San Fernando
north-south freeway on a three-month trial basis.
A successful experiment here would then be followed by a proliferation of electronic billboards on
other San Fernando thoroughfares, as well as in
other communities with agency branch offices. Sara
Lockett, McNabb's director of sales and marketing,

had been commissioned to begin lining up potential clients. Lockett issued a brief press release
indicating that the agency expected the experimental sign to be operational within 30–45 days.
However, the brief announcement in the *San
Fernando Chronicle* did not go unnoticed by
Marsha Britt, president of Citizens for Responsibility in Advertising, a consumer watchdog group that
kept a wary eye on each new advertising initiative.
She asked for and was granted an audience with
Timothy McNabb. The agency's CEO was reluctant
at first but knew from experience that Britt could
be a formidable adversary. At least a meeting with
her would allow for a frank exchange of views.
McNabb was determined to listen attentively and
summoned Sara Lockett to represent the agency's
position on the proposed electronic billboard.

After a brief exchange of pleasantries, Britt
got to the point. "We're asking you to scrap your
plans to install electronic billboards along the San
Fernando freeway," she declared bluntly. "It's one
thing to place billboards along a highway with a
message that motorists can choose to view or ignore. But you're using personal information to target drivers with a variety of advertising messages."

"We don't see it that way," responded Lockett.
"Advertisers are constantly gathering demographic
information and facts about consumers' product
choices. What's the difference?"

"I'll concede the fact that there's a lot of personal information already available to marketers
and advertisers," acknowledged Britt. "But in this
case you're electronically eavesdropping on motorists while they're driving. With the sensing devices on the electronic billboards, you can tell what
stations these people are listening to. That's how
you select the particular product ad at any given
moment. This is an invasion of privacy."

"I disagree," replied Lockett. "Our device merely
scans the automobile pool within its range at any
given moment and provides information on the
most popular stations. Our computer then matches
this with a profile of consumer product preferences
and selects an appropriate ad from our data bank.
How can this be an invasion of privacy?"

"It's a privacy issue," responded Britt emphatically, "because the motorists are unaware they're
being electronically monitored. The stations they

listen to on their way to work are their own business. This process is not like a ratings survey where listeners agree to participate in the data gathering."

"I would like to return to a point I made earlier," said Lockett. "Advertisers and marketers constantly gather data on consumers from a variety of sources. This personal information is all over the place, including the Internet. In today's consumer-driven market economy, I'm not sure that a claim of privacy is any longer valid."

"That may be the view from the vantage point of advertisers," declared Britt, confident that she spoke for a majority of citizens, "but loss of privacy is a big issue among consumers. That is why there has been such a backlash against telemarketers and junk mail. These electronic billboards are just one more device to intrude into individuals' private domain without their consent. An automobile is private space, and motorists have a right to know when they're being monitored, even if they can't be individually identified in the computer data bank."

"Motorists are on a public freeway," responded Lockett. "We're using the information on listening habits simply to target an advertiser's product to consumers with particular product preferences. They can choose to ignore the ads. I disagree that this is really an issue of privacy."

"It's true that drivers can ignore the ads," conceded Britt. "In that respect the electronic boards are like other forms of outdoor advertising. But it's the electronic eavesdropping to collect data on personal listening habits without the knowledge of motorists that we object to. This is a violation of personal autonomy. In our judgment, this is clearly a privacy concern."

During this spirited exchange between Marsha Britt and his director of sales and marketing, Timothy McNabb had listened attentively. He thanked Britt for her candor and concern for consumers' well-being and promised to give her remarks serious consideration. Sara Lockett had also defended her agency's interests quite well and competently deflected their visitor's privacy arguments. As president and CEO of the McNabb Outdoor Advertising Agency, Timothy McNabb would be the moral agent in deciding to pursue the firm's plans to install an electronic billboard along the San Fernando north-south freeway. His entrepreneurial instincts

naturally propelled him in the direction of utilizing this innovative technique of targeting mobile consumers. But he was also acutely sensitive of the privacy concerns raised by Marsha Britt. Aroused consumer activists had succeeded in procuring government intervention against telemarketers. Public opinion was a formidable foe when aroused, and McNabb wondered if the kind of data gathering envisioned by his plans for electronic billboards would cross the line. Of course, his "test" clients—those who had signed up for the agency's freeway experiment—would have little sympathy for Marsha Britt's privacy arguments, particularly in light of the massive personal data gathering that was endemic to advertising and marketing strategies. With little time remaining before the proposed launch date for the electronic billboard, Timothy McNabb reflected upon the competing interests that had emerged in the dialogue between Sara Lockett and consumer activist Marsha Britt.

THE CASE STUDY

Advertising is ubiquitous, and data gathering by the advertising industry is commonplace. Personal facts and statistics on consumers are catalogued in corporate and governmental computer data banks, and the Internet offers a virtual bonanza of information for demographic profiles. Advertisers and marketers make liberal use of this information in targeting consumers and discovering their product preferences and purchasing habits. Advertising itself can pose privacy concerns when it intrudes unreasonably and perhaps objectionably into our personal domain. However, this case is not about the intrusiveness of ads themselves but rather about the techniques employed to target potential consumers.

In the view of consumer activist Marsha Britt, the NcNabb agency's proposal to install an electronic billboard that would scan the morning rush-hour traffic to ascertain listening preferences which would then be correlated with ads for particular products constitutes an invasion of privacy. Her premise appears to be that the electronic scanning collects personal information without the knowledge or consent of unwitting motorists. In another words, the information-gathering process is intrusive.

Sales and Marketing Director Sara Lockett, responding on behalf of the NcNabb agency, rejects this complaint. Such data gathering is already so pervasive, she argues, that this is no longer a privacy issue.

However, considering the litany of complaints that continue to emanate from disaffected consumers, particularly as they relate to the intrusiveness of marketing strategies and advertising messages, one cannot dismiss the privacy issue so casually. Although the ethical dimensions of privacy are often associated with the practice of journalism, I noted earlier in this chapter that advertising can also raise privacy issues. And because advertising seeks us out, it is by definition intrusive. In this case, the intrusiveness occurs at the data collection stage used to present advertising messages to particular target audiences. Personal autonomy includes the right to be aware of and have the opportunity to reject electronic data-gathering techniques that invade one's private domain. At the same time, in a highly competitive market economy, advertisers have the right to employ reasonable means to confront consumers and to use innovative devices to gain their attention.

For the purpose of considering these competing interests and the ethical implications of this case, assume the role of Timothy McNabb and, using the SAD formula for moral reasoning outlined in Chapter 3, decide whether you will follow through with your agency's proposal to place an electronic billboard on the freeway. In so doing, construct arguments to explain your decision to those who are most likely to be unhappy with it.

CASE 5-6
The Right to Die with Dignity

To his supporters, Dr. Michael Dvorak was an angel of mercy. To his detractors, he was possessed of a God complex that manifested itself in his arrogant defense of euthanasia as a morally acceptable solution for terminally ill patients. Dvorak, a rather controversial internist, had acquired a reputation as a medical gadfly and had lobbied relentlessly with the legislature for a "right-to-die" law that would institutionalize physician-assisted suicide for terminally ill people who freely choose to end their lives with dignity. He was viewed with some annoyance by the medical establishment, who still believed that euthanasia was an assault on the Hippocratic oath's prescription to *do no harm.* But opinion polls reflected increasing public support for Dvorak's legislative agenda and a law that would legalize physician-assisted suicide.

Nevertheless, the legislature, under pressure from the medical establishment, repeatedly rebuffed the right-to-die initiative while various special interest groups debated the ethics of euthanasia. But Dvorak grew impatient with the tediousness of the political process and decided to take matters into his own hands. When one of his patients, a 54-year-old woman who was in the terminal stages of multiple sclerosis, asked for his assistance in ending her life, he readily agreed. Dvorak's participation in the carbon monoxide death of his patient brought a quick response from Riverside County District Attorney Robert Nix. As a conservative Christian, Nix was a foe of euthanasia and relished the opportunity of bringing the unrepentant physician to justice. The DA obtained a murder indictment against Dvorak, but following a six-day trial, with both national and local media in attendance, the jury acquitted him of the charge.

Emboldened by this legal triumph, Dvorak pledged to continue his assistance to any terminally ill patient who expressed a desire to die with dignity. Nix was equally determined to resist what he considered to be the doctor's insane disregard for the sanctity of life and the laws of the state.

Three months after his acquittal, Dvorak was again front-page copy with reports that he had assisted a terminally ill cancer patient, 62-year-old widow Helen Tate, commit suicide, and again he was indicted for murder. The opening salvo was fired in this high-profile trial when the district attorney released statements by two of the woman's children disputing the doctor's claims that their mother wanted to die. "At times she did express a desire to end her life," according to one of the statements, "but in the couple of weeks prior to her death she told me she had had second thoughts because of what this might do to her family." Nix knew that the children's testimony would be crucial during the trial.

Dvorak's attorney, Melvin Sanderson, also a veteran litigator in the court of public opinion, retaliated by releasing to the media, a week before the commencement of Dvorak's trial, a videotape of his patient's "last wish" that was allegedly made about an hour prior to the time of death listed on the coroner's report. The tape showed an emaciated, pathetic woman, whose body and spirit had been ravaged by the months of chemotherapy treatments. On the tape Tate is heard, in a barely audible whisper, apologizing to her children for causing them so much grief and begging their forgiveness. But the sound track also contained an unmistakable desire to end her life and a request for Dvorak's assistance in doing so. "This tape should remove any doubt as to Ms. Tate's desires to end her suffering," the defense lawyer announced confidently in his public statement accompanying the much-publicized release of the visual documentation of Tate's last moments. "And my client is not guilty of murder," continued Sanderson. "He did not kill Helen Tate. He just provided a means for her to end her own suffering."

This was quickly followed by a statement from Tate's children denouncing Sanderson's disgraceful behavior and calling on the news media to repudiate this "blatant and sensationalistic attempt to manipulate public opinion." "This tape was made as a personal farewell to her children," the statement said. "We believe that the expression of her wish to die was coerced by Dr. Dvorak when our mother was no longer in full control of her faculties. To broadcast this tape or to publish pictures of our mother in this condition would constitute a gross violation of her privacy, as well as that of her family."

For Sanderson, this videotape was defense Exhibit A in the case of *People v. Dr. Michael Dvorak.* To Sandra Feinstein it represented a challenging ethical dilemma. Feinstein was the news director of Channel 8, a CBS affiliate in the competitive three-station market of Harrisburg, the Riverside County seat. Two hours before Channel 8's *News at 6,* Feinstein was huddled with producer Bruce Baxter and Stephanie Hunter, the reporter who was covering the criminal proceedings against Dvorak.

The tape they were watching was a solemn testament to the ravages of disease and the pathos of human suffering.

"We have to decide whether to put this tape on the air," Feinstein broke the silence with her usual air of authority. "Both Channel 3 and Channel 12 have this tape; I don't know what their plans are, but we must assume that at least one of them will run this tape—especially Channel 12. They run a lot of graphic video and tabloid-type stories."

"This *is* news," responded Hunter. "This tape represents one of the key issues in this case. Was Ms. Tate's desire to die unequivocal or did she, as her children claim, have second thoughts about her decision?"

"But what about the privacy issue?" responded Baxter. "Her children have asked the media not to use the tape. Despite the fact that Dvorak's attorney released this tape, I certainly don't think Ms. Tate expected her dying moments to become a public spectacle. This tape was clearly intended as a personal farewell message to her children."

"Ms. Tate is dead," said Hunter. "I don't see this as a privacy issue in her case. As far as her children are concerned, they are key witnesses in this trial. Whether they like it or not, they have become matters of public interest. Besides, once this tape is entered into evidence at the trial it will become a public record—and anyone can attend this trial and see the tape. Hasn't the privacy surrounding this case really been lost because of the criminal proceedings against Dr. Dvorak?"

"I'm not so sure," replied Baxter with increasing defiance. He enjoyed challenging Hunter, with whom he often disagreed, and probing for the weaknesses in her arguments. "It's true that this tape will become a matter of public record and that those in the courtroom can view the tape. But the fact is that most of our viewers will not be in the courtroom. They'll be watching this tape at home. Obviously, we should report the proceedings of the trial itself. But if Channel 8 airs this graphic videotape that was not originally intended for public dissemination, then we're the primary culprits here. Ms. Tate might be dead, but she has a right to die with dignity. And as far as her children are concerned, they didn't ask to become a part of this spectacle."

"I question Sanderson's motives in releasing this tape," said Feinstein. "But I'm also concerned about our viewers' reactions. They might see this as nothing more than journalistic exploitation and a ratings ploy. The tape is a good visual. But is it *essential* to the content of the story?"

But Hunter was persistent. "Perhaps Sanderson's motives are less than pure in releasing this tape at this time. But we just have to bite the bullet and run it anyway. This is a key piece of evidence in a murder trial; our viewers should understand this. The tape is essential to the story and provides context. We are a visual medium. Pictures can't be divorced from the other content of the story. In this case the news value of this tape outweighs any privacy interests of Ms. Tate or her children."

As Hunter made her final plea for what she viewed as the integrity of the station's news judgment, Feinstein began pondering this ethical dilemma. It was now only an hour until airtime. The notion of delaying a decision on the matter and perhaps airing the tape on another night occurred to Feinstein, but she knew that at least one of her competitors, and perhaps both, was likely to include the tape in that night's newscast. She regretted that her reporter and producer had brought different perspectives to the table. A consensus would have made Feinstein feel more comfortable if not fully confident in her role as moral agent.

THE CASE STUDY

Helen Tate made this tape as a private farewell message to her children. She apparently never anticipated the public scrutiny to which this visual account of her last moments of suffering might be subjected. She is not alive to express her own wishes, but one might argue that the airing of the tape could serve to remove any doubt in the public's mind as to her desire to die with dignity. On the other hand, the graphic image of this frail, pathetic woman might raise some questions about whether she made this declaration with a clear mind. Would the airing of this tape undermine the respect that is due Tate, even in death?

Reporter Stephanie Hunter argues that the privacy question as it pertains to Tate is moot, because she is deceased. From a legal standpoint,

Hunter is essentially correct. Is this also a compelling ethical argument?

The privacy of Tate's children is also at stake here. They argue that the tape contains a personal communication to them from their mother and that their own privacy should be respected. Have they relinquished this privacy through their public statements concerning the tape or through their willingness to serve as prosecution witnesses against Dvorak?

For the purpose of analyzing this case, assume the role of news director Sandra Feinstein and, applying the SAD formula, render an ethical judgment as to whether you will include this videotape in tonight's rendition of *News at 6*. From an ethical perspective, you must decide whether the news value of this tape and its importance to the trial coverage outweigh the family's request for privacy. As the moral agent, you must decide whether the tape is essential or useful to the audience in understanding the context of the story. It is a key piece of evidence in this case. The tape could be instrumental in the jury's deliberations, and Tate's children have challenged the defense's explanation of the tape. The tape clearly does have news value.

But because the case hasn't yet gone to trial, it isn't entirely clear as to how this evidence will be used or explained to the jury. Sanderson's claim that this tape shows an autonomous woman expressing, with a clear mind, her desire to die will certainly be challenged by the prosecution. Thus, is it even possible to really place this tape into the overall context of the story? On the other hand, the station is faced with competitive pressures. Channel 8 could air the tape and let the audience render their own judgment concerning its meaning.

 CASE 5-7

Cyberspace Data Mining as a Public Relations Tool

To Nicholas Wentworth, the Internet was not an unmixed blessing. As the director of public relations for Samacme Pharmaceuticals, one of the nation's largest manufacturers of prescription drugs, Wentworth fully appreciated the public relations potential of cyberspace and his company's attractive and informative website. On the other hand, Samacme was plagued by attack sites, some of which provided a safe haven for those who desired anonymity as they cast stones at the pharmaceutical industry. However, Wentworth had reconciled himself to such unregulated assaults and was determined to respond in kind on the *Samacme.com* website. His discomfort was ameliorated in part by the Internet's potential as a marketing and public relations venue. While his public relations strategies still encompassed traditional media and other conventional public relations activities, Wentworth was attracted by the new technology's low-cost means of communicating directly with Samacme's target audiences in the privacy of their homes. The Web was a virtual gold mine of data about the preferences, tastes, and purchasing habits of individual consumers, but Wentworth moved cautiously in the unchartered waters of cyberspace in an effort to strike an ethical balance between the marketing and public relations objectives of his company and the privacy interests of individual consumers.

Government regulation of the advertising of prescription drugs had been relaxed several years ago, and Samacme had moved aggressively into television and magazine advertising. These campaigns were accompanied by an assertive public relations blitz, under the capable management of Nicholas Wentworth and his talented staff. Although patients still needed prescriptions to purchase these drugs, advertising and marketing directly to consumers was effective, in Wentworth's view, because they provided much-needed product information that might prompt patients to request a Samacme product from their physicians.

Wentworth was concerned that some of his competitors might be developing public relations and marketing strategies that included data mining of the Web, but his own moral compass advised caution. Before unleashing his creative energies on devising a full-fledged Web-based public relations plan, Wentworth sought the counsel of two Samacme executives whose departments were instrumental to the success of any public relations initiative: Latoya Hampton, the director of consumer relations, and Louis Salbo, the company's director of marketing.

"As you know, the Web is full of data about our potential customers," began Wentworth as he convened a meeting of his two colleagues. "Every time they hit a website they leave a trail. Some of these may be secure sites, but the unsecure ones are particularly valuable. There are many sites where customers provide medical information or ask questions concerning various medical conditions and the drugs that are most effective in treating these problems. Most of the HMOs have their own sites where consumers can look for information, and they frequently provide personal data. There are tools for gathering all of this data and then collating it according to certain demographic and other personal criteria. Using this data that we have mined from cyberspace, we could identify potential customers of our prescription drugs and communicate with them directly. We could pass this along to our ad agency, and they could handle the commercial end of this operation. Our public relations department would handle the informational aspects of this campaign, developing messages that would enhance our corporate visibility and cultivate a positive image of the company. I do have some reservations concerning privacy, however, and I would like your feedback."

"This sounds like a great marketing and public relations opportunity," responded Hampton. "But I also have some concerns about privacy. These consumers that we plan to target may not be aware that some of their hits on other sites may provide information for our database. While most people understand, I think, that the Web is not a secure form of communication, many do not fully understand that a simple click on a site may provide commercial enterprises with a plethora of personal information."

"I don't see the problem with privacy," replied Salbo, who was eager to tap the Web for its abundance of personal data that could figure prominently in his company's aggressive computer-based marketing and public relations strategies. "When consumers are linked to the Net, they know they are relinquishing some of their privacy rights, in the same manner as when they leave the seclusion of their homes and travel to a public location. And, as you know, the swapping of information among commercial enterprises has long been standard practice. When individuals order from catalogs, for example, their names are entered in data banks, and these lists are frequently sold to other companies. Consumers are accustomed to this practice. Why is the Web so different?"

"First of all," responded Hampton without hesitation, "consumers can have their names removed from these lists. But in addition, when individuals order through catalogs, they usually provide, along with their credit card number, only a limited amount of information. Of course, they reveal a lot about their preferences through these catalog purchases. On the Web, however, consumers often surf the Net looking for sites that will provide them with information without realizing they are leaving an electronic trail. They may not be aware that there are programs that can record every file they read and even how long they remain linked to a particular site. If we mine the Web for this data, I have no doubt that we'll be able to develop consumer profiles that will be of immense benefit to our company. But at what costs? If we expect to attract potential customers, this approach may result in some resentment among those who object to our unexpected access to their computers. If we truly personalize our messages for maximum effectiveness, consumers may wonder how we obtained so much personal data on them. They may consider this to be an unwelcome intrusion on their privacy."

Salbo was unmoved at what he considered to be a rather austere ethical concern for consumer privacy. "Our job is to promote our corporate image and to cultivate a favorable environment in which to promote our products," declared Salbo. "Computers are the latest venue for such marketing and public relations efforts. Consumers are so accustomed to receiving direct marketing mail— some refer to this as junk mail—that they probably won't even consider the privacy implications of how we obtained so much information on them."

"Let's assume you are correct," replied Hampton, willing for the moment to concede the point. "Even if our target audience doesn't object to this intrusion—perhaps they are so conditioned to direct marketing that computer-based strategies don't give them pause—does this really relieve us

of our own ethical responsibilities to avoid unreasonable invasions of privacy? As I noted before, many consumers aren't aware of how easy it is to mine this data from the Web. It's still a mystery. The question we have to ask ourselves is whether, if they were fully aware of this process, would they object to our using this personal information to promote our company and our products? After all, they are autonomous individuals. In traditional direct marketing, they can request that their names be removed from mailing lists. Their failure to do this, I suppose, carries with it a tacit consent. But the average consumer may feel that it's not that easy with electronic lists compiled from the Web."

This brief conversation with his two colleagues had been instructive but had provided no easy solutions to Wentworth's discomfort. As the director of public relations, he had seldom encountered privacy concerns. Much of his effort had been directed toward media relations, but the Internet provided new opportunities to incorporate individual consumers directly into his public relations strategies. He contemplated the ethical dimensions of his concerns, even as he wondered whether his counterparts at other drug companies were experiencing similar moral qualms.

THE CASE STUDY

Privacy is among our most vulnerable values in the unregulated recesses of cyberspace. Consider this commentary from a recent book on the social, legal, and technical challenges of the Internet:

> As we increase the amount of information and entertainment we receive through digital devices, it becomes more and more possible to collect detailed data about our reading and viewing habits. In principle, it would be quite easy to develop systems and programs that notice what we read or watch, when we read or watch it, and how long we spend doing so. A profile of our interests could be generated from such records, making it easy for advertisers to target us with junk mail, junk e-mail, or even personalized television advertisements. Net browsers already target our interests in this way.[95]

As noted previously, the device used to develop these profiles is known as a "cookie," which allows marketers to "target advertising to users who have previously visited related sites, and thus are presumed to have an interest in related merchandise."[96] In this narrative, the public relations director for a pharmaceutical company is considering the ethical implications of using this data-mining technique as part of his public relations strategy, whereby he can target specific corporate and product messages to individual consumers. His ethical concerns, of course, involve privacy. In addressing this question, he must acknowledge that direct marketing is well established in our consumer society and, except perhaps for an occasional offensive ad, privacy concerns have never been that apparent. Most unwanted solicitations are either discarded or the unconsenting recipients request that their names be deleted from the mailing list. Under new federal do-not-call laws, citizens can also request that telemarketing calls be blocked. But these options are not practical in cyberspace, at least at the moment.

Are there unique characteristics of the cyberspace culture that raise the ethical bar for privacy concerns? Exactly how does data mining on the Web to devise consumer profiles differ from traditional means of tabulating personal data in order to construct advertising or public relations messages for individual consumers? Historically, public relations communications have been directed to mass audiences. Will cyberspace significantly alter the practice of public relations in such a way that one-on-one communication assumes a role as prominent as communication through traditional media? If so, what effect will this have on the ethical concerns of public relations practitioners, such as the value of privacy? Do you agree with Latoya Hampton's concern that her company has a moral responsibility to avoid unreasonable invasions of privacy even if consumers aren't fully aware that their privacy is being invaded?

These are daunting questions and not susceptible to easy solutions. However, as a point of departure assume the role of Nicholas Wentworth, the director of public relations for Samacme Pharmaceuticals, and utilizing the SAD formula for moral reasoning described in Chapter 3, render a judgment on whether you will follow through with your proposal to target individual consumers using

personal data mined from the vast recesses of the World Wide Web.

Notes

1. Craig L. LaMay (ed.), *Journalism and the Debate Over Privacy* (Mahwah, NJ: Lawrence Erlbaum, 2003), p. vii.
2. Max Frankel, *Media Madness: The Revolution So Far*, Catto Report on Journalism and Society (1999), p. 1, quoted in ibid.
3. For a fairly wide-ranging discussion on various ethical concerns of privacy, see *Journal of Mass Media Ethics* 9, no. 3–4 (1994).
4. "Clinton Coverage: Media Get Mileage, Flak," *Broadcasting*, February 3, 1992, p. 13.
5. Conrad C. Fink, *Media Ethics* (Needham Heights, MA: Allyn & Bacon, 1995), p. 44.
6. For a good discussion on the value of privacy, see W. A. Parent, "Privacy, Morality, and the Law," in Joan C. Callahan (ed.), *Ethical Issues in Professional Life* (New York: Oxford University Press, 1988), pp. 218–219.
7. Deborah Potter, "How the Media Treated Me," *Communicator*, September 2000, p. 46.
8. For example, see Megan Garvey, "More Unease for Condit Colleagues," *Los Angeles Times*, July 14, 2001, p. 15; Marc Sandalow, "Scandal Changes Condit's Career Forever, Spotlight's Glare Will Outlive Mystery," *San Francisco Chronicle*, July 16, 2001, p. A3.
9. For example, see Richard A. Serrano, "Rep. Condit's Lawyer Chastises the Media," *Los Angeles Times*, July 9, 2001, p. A8.
10. Maureen Dowd (*New York Times*), "Next Disappearance Should Be Condit's Career," article published in the *Milwaukee Journal Sentinel*, July 12, 2001, p. 13A.
11. Louis Hodges, "The Journalist and Privacy," *Journal of Mass Media Ethics* 9, no. 4 (1994): 201.
12. For a discussion of the moral foundations of privacy, see Samuel P. Winch, "Moral Justifications for Privacy and Intimacy," *Journal of Mass Media Ethics* 11 (1996): 197–209.
13. For a discussion of this point, see Alan Westin, "The Origins of Modern Claims to Privacy," in Ferdinand David Schoeman (ed.), *Philosophical Dimensions of Privacy: An Anthology* (Cambridge: Cambridge University Press, 1984), pp. 59–67.
14. Richard A. Posner, *The Economics of Justice* (Cambridge, MA: Harvard University Press, 1983), pp. 268–269.
15. Ibid., p. 268.
16. Ibid.
17. Don R. Pember, *Privacy and the Press* (Seattle: University of Washington Press, 1972), pp. 12–13.
18. William L. Prosser, *Handbook of the Law of Torts*, 4th ed. (St. Paul, MN: West, 1971), pp. 810–811.

19. For example, see Don R. Pember, *Mass Media Law* (Madison, WI: Brown & Benchmark, 1997), p. 262.

20. See *Griswold v. Connecticut,* 381 U.S. 479 (1965); *Stanley v. Georgia,* 394 U.S. 557 (1969).

21. Clifford G. Christians, Kim B. Rotzoll, Mark Fackler, and Kathy Brittain McKee also discuss the need for a system of ethics in *Media Ethics: Cases and Moral Reasoning,* 6th ed. (New York: Longman, 2001), pp. 113–115.

22. E.g., see James Glen Stovall and Patrick R. Cotter, "The Public Plays Reporter: Attitudes toward Reporting on Public Officials," *Journal of Mass Media Ethics* 7, no. 2 (1992): 97–106.

23. "Access Battle for Earnhardt Autopsy Photos Puts SPJ in National Spotlight," *SPJ Report,* May 2001, p. 1.

24. Bill Keveney and Gary Levin, "How Can You Not Comment on Bush Twins?," *USA Today,* June 7, 2001, p. 6D.

25. Quoted in Howard Kurtz, "Jenna Bush Gets No Pass from Press This Time; Privacy Bubble Shrinks with Second Incident," *Washington Post,* June 1, 2001, p. C1.

26. See Tony Mauro, "Paparazzi and the Press," *Quill,* July/August 1998, pp. 26–28.

27. *Foretich v. Lifetime Cable,* 777 F. Supp. 47 (D.D.C. 1991).

28. Kent R. Middleton, William E. Lee, and Bill F. Chamberlin, *The Law of Public Communication* (Boston: Pearson Education, 2003 Edition), p. 168.

29. Christians, Rotzoll, Fackler, and McKee, *Media Ethics,* p. 114.

30. Jeffrey Olen, *Ethics in Journalism* (Upper Saddle River, NJ: Prentice-Hall, 1988), p. 71.

31. See *Florida Star v. B.J.F.,* 491 U.S. 524 (1989); *Cox Broadcasting Corp. v. Cohn,* 420 U.S. 469 (1975).

32. Mark Stefik, *The Internet Edge: Social, Legal, and Technological Challenges for a Networked World* (Cambridge, MA: The MIT Press, 1999), p. 211.

33. Ibid., p. 223.

34. *Barber v. Time, Inc.,* 159 S.W.2d 291 (Mo. 1942).

35. For a discussion of this issue, see Estelle Lander, "AIDS Coverage: Ethical and Legal Issues Facing the Media Today," *Journal of Media Ethics* 3, no. 2 (Fall 1988): 66–72.

36. "Sports Editor: It's a News Story," *USA Today,* April 9, 1992, p. 2A.

37. "Arthur Ashe AIDS Story Scrutinized by Editors, Columnists," *Quill,* June 1992, p. 17.

38. Anne Wells Branscomb, *Who Owns Information?* (New York: Basic Books, 1994), p. 65, citing Christine Spolar, "Privacy for Public Figures?," *Washington Journalism Review,* June 1992, p. 21.

39. "AIDS and the Right to Know," *Newsweek,* August 18, 1986, p. 46.

40. Ron F. Smith, *Groping for Ethics in Journalism,* 5th ed. (Ames: Iowa State University Press, 2003), pp. 158, 160.

41. Charles B. Seib, "How the Papers Covered the Cinema Follies Fire," *Washington Post,* October 30, 1977, p. C-7.

42. Ibid.

43. Ibid.

44. Ibid.

45. Sue O'Brien, "Privacy," *Quill,* November/December 1991, p. 10.

46. Ibid.

47. Kelly McBride, "Rethinking Rape Coverage," *Quill,* October/November 2002, p. 8.

48. For a thorough examination of news media treatment of sex crime victims, see Helen Benedict, *Virgin or Vamp: How the Press Covers Sex Crimes* (New York: Oxford University Press, 1992).

49. Ibid., p. 9.

50. Ibid., p. 39.

51. Jay Black, "Rethinking the Naming of Sex Crime Victims," *Newspaper Research Journal,* Summer 1995, p. 106.

52. E.g., see Smith, *Groping for Ethics in Journalism,* pp. 214–215.

53. McBride, p. 9.

54. Michelle Johnson, "How Identifying Rape Victims Affects Readers' Perception," *Newspaper Research Journal,* Spring 1999, pp. 64–80.

55. The Florida courts have now declared certain aspects of this law unconstitutional.

56. See David A. Kaplan, "Remove That Blue Dot," *Newsweek,* December 16, 1991, p. 26.

57. Judy Flander, "Should the Name Have Been Released?" *Communicator,* June 1991, p. 10.

58. Ibid.

59. "Naming," *Newsweek,* April 29, 1991, p. 29.

60. "NBC Creates Stir with Rape Report," *Broadcasting,* April 22, 1991, p. 25.

61. Michael Gartner, "Why We Did It," *Communicator,* June 1991, pp. 11–12.

62. *Smith v. Daily Mail,* 443 U.S. 97 (1979).

63. Joe Kollin, "Why Don't We Name Juveniles?," *Quill,* April 2003, p. 12.

64. Quoted in Elizabeth Stone, "Using Children as Sources," *Columbia Journalism Review,* September/October 1999, p. 33.

65. Ibid., p. 32.

66. Ibid.

67. Ibid., p. 34.

68. Dr. Alvin F. Poussaint, "The ABC's of Exploitation," *TV Guide,* April 29, 2000, pp. 18–19.

69. Howie Carr, "Manipulation, American-Style," in Poussaint, "The ABC's of Exploitation," p. 19.

70. See Mark J. Miller, "Tough Calls," *American Journalism Review* (December 2002): 43–47.

71. Frank Ritter, "Reporting on Suicide Is Not Easy, and Needs Sensitivity," *Tennessean,* January 12, 1992, p. 5-D.

72. Ibid.
73. Ibid.
74. *Bartnicki v. Vopper,* 29 Med. L. Rptr. 1737 (2001).
75. Louis W. Hodges, "Undercover, Masquerading, Surreptitious Taping," *Journal of Mass Media Ethics* 3, no. 2 (Fall 1988): 34, citing T. L. Glasser, "On the Morality of Secretly Taped Interviews," *Nieman Reports* 39 (Spring 1982): 17–20.
76. Ibid.
77. "In Brief," *Broadcasting & Cable,* November 21, 1994, pp. 80–81.
78. Richard P. Cunningham, "Seeking a Time-Out on Prurience," *Quill,* March 1992, p. 6.
79. Ibid.
80. Smith, *Groping for Ethics in Journalism,* p. 315, citing "Graphic Excess," *Washington Journalism Review,* January 1986, pp. 10–11; Nick Russell, *Morals and the Media: Ethics in Canadian Journalism* (Vancouver: UBC Press, 1994), p. 121.
81. This case is discussed in Philip Patterson, "Public Grief and the Right to Be Left Alone," in Philip Patterson and Lee Wilkins (eds.), *Media Ethics: Issues and Cases,* 4th ed. (Boston: McGraw-Hill, 2002), pp. 130–132.
82. Gregory Stricharchuk, "Computer Records Become Powerful Tool for Investigative Reports and Editors," *Wall Street Journal,* February 3, 1988, p. 25.
83. See Jeff South, "No Secrets," *American Journalism Review,* April 2000, p. 52.
84. "When Privacy Trumps Access, Democracy Is in Trouble," *News Media and the Law,* Spring 1995, p. 2. The Supreme Court later upheld the constitutionality of the law.
85. Karen Reinboth Speckman, "Using Data Bases to Serve Justice and Maintain the Public's Trust," *Journal of Mass Media Ethics* 9, no. 4 (1994): 236.
86. Ibid.
87. Ibid., p. 237. For an example, see Karen Reinboth Speckman, "Computers and the News: A Complicated Challenge," in Patterson and Lee, *Media Ethics,* pp. 139–146.
88. Stricharchuk, "Computer Records Become Powerful Tools," p. 25.
89. Michael J. Bugeja, *Living Ethics: Developing Values in Mass Communication* (Needham Heights, MA: Allyn & Bacon, 1996), pp. 256–257.
90. James Fallows, "Are Journalists People?" *U.S. News & World Report,* September 15, 1997, pp. 31–32, 34.
91. "It's an Ad, Ad, Ad, Ad World," *Time,* July 9, 2001, p. 17.
92. For a discussion of ethical standards in advertising, see Richard L. Johannesen, *Ethics in Human Communication,* 3d ed. (Prospect Heights, IL: Waveland, 1990), p. 93.
93. For example, see Richard T. DeGeorge, *Business Ethics,* 2d ed. (New York: Macmillan, 1986), p. 274.
94. The idea for this case was derived from a real event reported in John W. Dean, *The Rehnquist Choice* (New York: Free Press, 2001), pp. 119–121.
95. Mark Stefik, *The Internet Edge: Social, Legal, and Technological Changes for a Networked World* (Cambridge, MA: The MIT Press, 1999), p. 211.
96. Madeleine Schachter, *Law of Internet Speech* (Durham, NC: Carolina Academic Press, 2001), p. 319.

6

Confidentiality
and the Public Interest

THE PRINCIPLE
OF CONFIDENTIALITY

In the summer of 2003 columnist Robert Novak revealed that Valerie Plame, wife of Joseph Wilson, former ambassador to Gabon, was a CIA operative. Novak and perhaps as many as five other reporters had obtained this information from an official of the Bush administration. There was speculation the source was motivated by revenge. Wilson had previously undertaken a mission at the request of the administration to determine whether Saddam Hussein had purchased uranium from Niger. His report debunked the allegation that Iraq had tried to buy Niger uranium, and Wilson later wrote an op-ed piece for the *New York Times* questioning whether the Bush administration had suppressed his report and manipulated intelligence to justify the war in Iraq.[1] After some hesitation, the Justice Department eventually opened an investigation into the source of the leak. However, the manner in which Plame's CIA connection was made public received as much attention as the story itself, leading Fred Brown, cochair of the Ethics Committee of the Society of Professional Journalists (SPJ), to remark that the reporters "allowed themselves to become a major part of an important news story," which is "hardly in the

journalistic tradition of at least trying to be objective and detached."[2]

In the summer of 1996 three Republicans were locked in a close race for their party's nomination for a U.S. Senate seat in Maine: Susan Collins, Robert A. G. Monks, and W. John Hathaway. Just days before the primary election, the *Boston Globe* received a tip that Hathaway had abruptly moved back to Maine from Alabama because of a sex scandal involving a 12-year-old babysitter. The *Globe* quickly confirmed the story with sources in Alabama and published a front-page story outlining an 18-month affair between Hathaway and the young girl. State and local prosecutors were thwarted in their efforts to prosecute Hathaway for statutory rape because the girl's family had refused to allow the case to go forward. According to the paper's assistant managing editor, the girl's parents were friends and business associates of Hathaway and "did not want to put the girl through the ordeal of a trial and instead essentially drove the guy out of town." Hathaway later denied the charges and suggested that his accuser was mentally unstable. He then accused Monks of being the source of the accusations against him. Monks and his staff initially denied the charge but Monks later acknowledged that he had hired a political consultant to conduct opposition research on Hathaway. In the meantime, the *Globe* refused to identify the source of the damning information but shrewdly noted with such phrases as "widely held perception" that many believed Monks had tipped reporters to Hathaway's dubious past. While Hathaway and Monks slung mud and exchanged insults, Susan Collins won the primary and later the November general election.[3]

In 1995 reporter John Rezendes-Herrick used a confidential source in preparing a series of stories for the *Inland Valley Daily Bulletin* in Ontario, California, about an agricultural company that opposed a planned landfill project. When the project later became the focus of a grand jury investigation, he was summoned to appear but refused to answer questions about the source of his information. A trial judge sentenced Rezendes-Herrick to spend five days in jail.[4]

What do these three situations have in common? All are based on the value of confidential relationships or information, an important principle in the practice of media communications. The principle of confidentiality imposes a duty to withhold the names of sources of information or the information itself from third parties under certain circumstances. Although this obligation is not absolute, neither is it a mere rule of thumb. The consensus among philosophers is that confidentiality is a prima facie duty that can be overridden only by other, weightier considerations.[5] Thus, the burden of proof is generally on those who wish to override it.[6] This is familiar terrain for media practitioners, who must decide, in an endless variety of situations, whether confidentiality or candor is the more desirable servant of the public interest. Of course, these ideas are not mutually exclusive, because a promise of confidentiality to a news source can lead to candor in the uncovering of corruption or other illegal activities.

The notion of confidentiality, however, goes beyond the protection of news sources. Sometimes news organizations must decide whether to publish secret or confidential information provided to them by a source. Classified government documents and grand jury investigations are two prime examples. Under such circumstances the issue is not just one of *source* confidentiality but also of whether the media should release *information* they may not be entitled to in the first place.

Because media practitioners are in the information business, they often have an irresistible urge to prefer disclosure over secrecy. But the notion that revelation and openness are always in the public interest is presumptuous at best. There are times when the court of public opinion is not entitled to information the release of which could offend or perhaps even cause harm to other parties. Thus, the case for confidentiality as an important societal value worth salvaging is a compelling one.

The role of confidentiality in our social relationships is one that we learn early in life. Our parents instill in us the value of keeping secrets and admonish us never to break a promise. This is part of the socialization process by which we develop loyalty to our peers. In fact, secrets can provide a sense of power, because we are privy to information that is not widely shared by others. But promises of confidentiality also limit our freedom of action. An oath of secrecy places a burden on the moral agent to withhold information even in the face of conflicting (and sometimes more compelling) demands.

Confidential relationships usually arise in three circumstances. First, there are *express promises,* as when a reporter promises anonymity to a news source. These are often oral commitments, but they may also be written. The oaths of secrecy signed by CIA agents are a case in point.

A promise of confidentiality from a reporter, however, involves more than just a pledge not to reveal a source's identity. The conditions of this "contract" of secrecy should be clear to both reporter and source. To this end, the journalistic establishment has developed its own lexicon to describe the different kinds of confidential relationships.

"Off the record," for example, is supposed to mean that the information provided to the reporter is not for public release. But sources sometimes interpret this to mean that they do not want to be identified with the information, which in the journalist's mind is usually defined as "without attribution." Thus, when some sources say "off the record," they really mean that they don't want to be quoted.

"On background" generally refers to an arrangement whereby government officials or other sources call in reporters to brief them on some matter of public interest. The source is then usually identified in the story by such references as "White House aide," "senior Pentagon official," or "State Department spokesman."[7] It is not unusual for journalists to negotiate with their sources over which of these forms of confidentiality will be employed. Nevertheless, such ground rules are subject to interpretation, and it is important that reporter and source have a meeting of the minds on the conditions of their contract before any agreement on confidentiality.[8] For example, sometimes background sessions are held between reporters and government leaders for the purpose of a candid exchange of views on public issues. Participants agree in advance whether the information will be on or off the record.[9]

Confidential relationships may also be formulated out of a sense of *loyalty*. In such cases there may not be an express promise of secrecy in every situation, but a sense of loyalty to an individual or company propels the moral agent in that direction. A personal secretary to a recently deceased celebrity who refuses to write a kiss-and-tell book and thereby eschews personal enrichment is acting out of a sense of loyalty. Public relations practitioners are expected to serve the best interests of their companies and not to release information detrimental to the corporate welfare. They are expected, in other words, to be loyal. Indeed, the Code of Ethics of the Public Relations Society of America (PRSA) requires a member to "[a]ct in the best interests of the client or employer, even subordinating the member's personal interests" and to avoid "actions and circumstances that may appear to compromise good business judgment or create a conflict between personal and professional interests."

But how should ethical public relations practitioners respond when their company is engaged in behavior inimical to the public welfare? Such conduct, of course, can erode company loyalty, and if the public relations practitioner cannot effect change from within the corporate structure, her conscience may compel her resignation. Resignation is a drastic remedy, however, for conflicting loyalties, and as a staff member a greater good can probably be derived from staying on the job and arguing one's case directly to corporate management. Some practitioners elect to stay but become frustrated in their failure to change the system from within and become *whistle-blowers*. In other words, they secretly inform the media about their employer's irresponsible deportment to bring public pressure on the organization.[10] Whistle-blowing, however, is a controversial practice. Some argue that if practitioners cannot be loyal to their employers, they should resign as soon as they become disaffected with the company's questionable conduct. Practitioners themselves may also actually participate in the unethical or illegal activities before acting on their moral qualms, thus subjecting them to charges of "unclean hands" in leveling the charges against the company. In addition, although whistle-blowing might stop unethical corporate practices, it still usually costs the whistle-blowers their jobs in the long run. Such was the case when a public relations practitioner charged his company, a multinational fruit conglomerate, with the manipulation of media coverage, as well as with political and military action in a Latin American country where the company was operating.[11]

Loyalty in the marketplace is not always based on genuine affection but is more often a reflection of a feeling of obligation. Thus, such loyalties are transitory and may lose their moral force when the circumstances under which they are formed are altered. What if public relations representatives, for example, move from one agency to another? Are they acting unethically if they use the knowledge of their former employer to lure away clients? The PRSA code admonishes members to "safeguard the confidences and privacy rights of present, former, and prospective clients and employees." Nevertheless, loyalty, like patience, does have its limits, but the use of confidential information from a now-terminated relationship poses some intriguing moral dilemmas.

The third type of confidential relationship is one *recognized by law.* Society has determined that some relationships are so important that they deserve legal protection. The protection accorded to confidential communications between doctors and patients, lawyers and their clients, and priests and penitents are examples. It is unnecessary for an attorney to make an express promise of confidentiality to a client; this relationship is automatically protected by law. In addition, many states and courts now recognize a privilege for reporters to maintain the confidentiality of their sources, a tacit acknowledgment of the role of the media as representatives of the public.

Unlike other societal privileges, however, a reporter's privilege is not predicated on the danger of personal embarrassment or a threat to the privacy rights of the parties per se. Instead, the rationale is that compulsory disclosure would lead to serious consequences for both the reporter and the source. For example, sources who pass on information about government or other corruption may fear for their jobs or even their physical well-being. On the other hand, reporters may be subject to contempt charges if they refuse to divulge the source's identity.[12]

In those confidential relationships recognized by law, journalists share moral obligations similar to those imposed on the society they serve. For example, reporters who testify before grand juries are subject to the same oaths of secrecy as other witnesses. Thus, they should not divulge in the media the contents of their testimony, unless they are released from

their commitment to confidentiality through due process of law.

One reporter who chose to honor his commitment to confidentiality until it could be challenged through the legal system was Michael Smith of the *Charlotte-Herald News* in Florida. Smith was subpoenaed to testify before a special grand jury investigating activities in the Charlotte County state's attorney's office and the sheriff's department. The reporter was warned that disclosure of his testimony was prohibited by Florida law. On completion of the grand jury's investigation Smith wanted to publish a news story and possibly a book about the investigation, including his observations of the grand jury process and the matters about which he had testified. To the reporter's credit he did not simply ignore the statutory ban on publication but sued in federal court to have the law declared unconstitutional as a prior restraint on his First Amendment right of free speech. The U.S. Supreme Court eventually upheld Smith's constitutional claim.[13]

THE JUSTIFICATION FOR CONFIDENTIALITY

The principle of confidentiality has taken a beating in recent years. In our information-rich society, the public's demand for knowledge about all manner of things is insatiable. Thus, other duties are sometimes seen as more important than secrecy. This trend, which is disturbing to some, is described by the ethicist Sissela Bok:

> So much confidential information is now being gathered and recorded and requested by so many about so many that confidentiality, though as strenuously invoked as in the past, is turning out to be a weaker reed than ever. . . .
>
> Faced with growing demands for both revelation and secrecy, those who have to make decisions about whether or not to uphold confidentiality face numerous difficult moral quandaries.[14]

Despite this assessment, several justifications exist for a reaffirmation of the principle of confidentiality.[15] First, there is a concern for human autonomy in safeguarding personal information and knowledge. The ability to keep secrets—and to feed information to others selectively—provides a sense of power over the individual's sphere of influence. In fact, most disputes over secrecy boil down to conflicts over power, the power that comes through controlling the flow of information.[16]

This power is of particular relevance to journalists, who value openness over secrecy in a democratic society. The press is the most important counterbalance against the natural tendencies of government and other institutions to control the flow of negative or sensitive information. The media, therefore, have a much clearer *public* mandate to challenge such policies of concealment than some other members of society, such as social scientists and private detectives.[17]

News sources are exerting their sense of autonomy (or power) when they channel confidential information to reporters. This is an important concept for journalists to remember, because anonymous sources act with a variety of motives. Some have an ax to grind, and others may breach confidentiality with the public's interest in mind, as in the case of a whistle-blower. Of course, the idea of autonomy in maintaining confidentiality does have its limits. For example, an individual who knows that a crime is about to be committed (and this includes reporters) is obliged to relinquish this secret to the proper authorities.

The second justification for confidentiality is that it establishes a feeling of trust among individuals within society. The respect for the secrets of others is essential to maintaining relationships. Trust, the keeping of promises, and loyalty are the foundations of confidentiality, and it is against these cherished values that third parties who seek to breach the cloak of confidentiality must compete. Reporters who insist on complete candor from their public relations contacts in sensitive situations are asking them to place truth over institutional loyalty. Likewise, law enforcement authorities who insist on knowing reporters' confidential sources are asking that promises be broken in the name of an overriding principle, the fair administration of justice.

Confidentiality is also sometimes necessary to prevent harm to others. Committee personnel decisions, even at public institutions, are usually closed to the press and the public because of the potential harm flowing from the rather candid and sometimes brutal comments during the deliberations. Reporters' offers of confidentiality to news sources are usually grounded in the perceived harm that might accrue to those individuals if their identities should become known.

Finally, confidentiality serves the ends of social utility. Without assurances of confidentiality, the trust surrounding certain professional relationships would be eroded. Clients would be less than candid with their attorneys, which could undermine the cause of justice. Patients might lose confidence in their doctors, diminishing the quality of personal health care. And, of course, reporters argue that confidential sources are often essential to uncovering crime and bringing it to the public's attention. Thus, for a journalist secrecy can become a tool for ensuring the public's access to the day's intelligence.

SEEKING DISCLOSURE: THE MORAL POSITION OF THE ACTOR

Because of the value attached to the principle of confidentiality in our society, the moral positions of the party seeking disclosure and the one claiming confidentiality must be considered in deciding whose claim should be accorded greater significance. Motivation is helpful in evaluating whether there are overriding reasons for disclosure. For example, an individual whose neighbor pleads that she cannot afford to repay a loan might desire a peek at the neighbor's income tax returns, but his moral position is a weak one. Likewise, a reporter who seeks copies of a company president's personal financial statement is also in a weak position unless the executive is involved in a matter of public interest to which the statement might relate.

Public interest (as opposed to merely private curiosity or self-interest) is perhaps the most compelling justification for disclosure. Information is the lifeblood of democracy, and where certain knowledge is essential either to rational consumer choice or collective political decision making, the arguments favoring publicity over confidentiality assume critical dimensions. A case in point is Hill & Knowlton's representation of "Citizens for Free Kuwait," a lobbying group that sought to foster Kuwait's interests in the United States at a time when this country was contemplating military action against Iraq to free Kuwait. According to the public relations firm, they made prompt disclosure under the Foreign Agents Registration Act of its relationship with the Citizens and the fact that the bulk of its fees were being paid by the Kuwaiti government.[18] Among President Bush's justifications for initiating military action against Iraq were Saddam Hussein's atrocities against the Kuwaiti people. Perhaps the most sensational claim was that Iraqi soldiers removed hundreds of Kuwaiti babies from incubators and left them to die on the hospital floors.[19]

In October 1990 the Congressional Human Rights Caucus held a public hearing on conditions in Kuwait under Iraqi occupation and heard testimony from witnesses who had escaped from Kuwait after the Iraqi invasion. The most dramatic incubator story—and the one that attracted the most media coverage—was that of Nayirah al-Sabah, the 15-year-old daughter of the Kuwaiti ambassador to the United States. Hill & Knowlton had offered her testimony to the committee. At her father's request, the girl's last name and her relationship to the Kuwaiti ambassador were omitted from public testimony for fear of reprisals against her family in Kuwait. The claims of incubator atrocities were apparently influential in convincing some senators to support the resolution authorizing war.[20] Several news organizations later challenged her

testimony, suggesting that the girl had committed perjury and questioning whether she had even been in Kuwait and whether there had been any atrocities. Hill & Knowlton, citing evidence of atrocities after the liberation of Kuwait, stood by the maligned witness's testimony.[21]

Regardless of the truth of Nayirah al-Sabah's testimony, the more significant ethical question, from the public relations firm's perspective, was Hill & Knowlton's relationship with members of the congressional caucus conducting the hearings. In an op-ed piece in the *New York Times,* John R. MacArthur wondered why the caucus did not investigate Nayirah's story. As it turned out, the committee's chair, Tom Lantos, a California Democrat, and John Edward Porter, an Illinois Republican, had a close relationship with Hill & Knowlton. The company's vice president had helped to organize the Congressional Human Rights Caucus hearings in meetings between the two congressmen and the chair of Citizens for a Free Kuwait. In addition, Hill & Knowlton provided office space in Washington at a reduced rate and phone message service for the Congressional Human Rights Foundation, a group founded in 1985 by Congressmen Lantos and Porter. A year after Nayirah's appearance before Lantos's committee, the foundation also named Frank Mankiewicz, Hill & Knowlton's vice chair, to its board. Although the public relations firm came in for a great deal of public censure for representing a controversial client and a questionable cause, it was the testimony of the Kuwaiti ambassador's daughter in a congressional hearing without full disclosure that raises serious ethical concerns. As Susanne Roschwalb observes in her rather exhaustive examination of the public relations firm's involvement in the Kuwaiti hearings, "Hill & Knowlton becomes the focal point for the discussion of ethics because the basic concerns about public relations, media management and lobbying were magnified during a time when the country was debating war and Hill & Knowlton's client was a foreign country with a direct interest in the outcome of the debate."[22]

The moral position of mass media institutions is often at issue when the release of confidential information is sought. From the standpoint of motivation, the media are at least on respectable moral ground when they publish sensitive information because they believe it to have news value. Such decisions, of course, do involve subjective judgments, but they are at least news judgments born out of public interest considerations.

This is not to suggest that public interest concerns are the only noble ethical motivations. Obviously, the potential for harm to individuals, small groups within society, or even large institutions can provide a morally justifiable rationale for breaching confidentiality. But actors' moral position is an important consideration in evaluating their claims of access to confidential information.

CONFIDENTIALITY IN JOURNALISM: SOME SPECIAL CONCERNS

In early January 2002 aspiring author Vanessa Leggett was released from the Federal Detention Center in Houston after 168 days of incarceration. She thus achieved the rather dubious distinction of spending more time in jail than any other journalist in U.S. history for refusing to provide confidential tapes and notes to a federal grand jury seeking to charge millionaire bookmaker Robert Angleton with conspiring to kill his wife. The government claimed that Leggett, who was writing a book about the case but had no publisher and had never published a news story, was not a representative of the media and was thus not entitled to any form of reporter's privilege.[23]

The duration of Leggett's imprisonment may be an anomaly, but the issue of reporters' privilege—the right to maintain the confidentiality of news sources and documentary materials—remains controversial, both legally and ethically. For many journalists, the right of confidentiality

is fundamental to the news-gathering process, but the punishment of reporters through judicial contempt for refusing to cooperate with law enforcement agencies is rather common.

The issue of confidentiality confronts all media practitioners, but among journalists the ethical dilemmas posed by confidential relationships with their news sources are particularly acute. However, in staking out a claim to openness, as opposed to secrecy, journalists should beware of moral hypocrisy. Reporters serve a legitimate function as government watchdogs, and in this capacity they correctly view secrecy as antithetical to the democratic process. But from an ethical perspective this claim is undermined somewhat by the use of clandestine operations, surreptitious surveillance, and reliance on confidential sources whose veracity may never be subjected to public scrutiny. These practices may lead to credibility problems for the media, as Bok notes in her book on secrecy and confidentiality:

> The press and other news media rightly stand for openness in public discourse. But until they give equally firm support to openness in their own practices, their stance will be inconsistent and lend credence to charges of unfairness. It is now a stance that challenges every collective rationale for secrecy save the media's own. Yet the media serve commercial and partisan interests in addition to public ones; and media practices of secrecy, selective disclosure, and probing should not be exempt from scrutiny.[24]

The Case for and against Confidentiality

In 1972 the U.S. Supreme Court denied constitutional protection for the reporter–source relationship. In *Branzburg v. Hayes,* which was really a combination of cases involving three reporters, a 5–4 majority ruled that the reporters had no privilege under the First Amendment to refuse to testify before grand juries.[25] The *Branzburg* decision sent a shiver through the journalistic community. However, the impact of this decision has been offset in recent years by the recognition of a First Amendment privilege in the lower federal courts and many state courts. In addition, many states have extended protection to journalists through "shield laws," statutory privileges designed to protect reporters from having to reveal the identities of their confidential sources to judicial or investigatory bodies. In some jurisdictions the privilege is absolute; in others the shield laws provide only qualified protection.

Some reporters have welcomed the arrival of shield laws within their states (there is no federal shield law), because such legislation reflects public policy and recognizes the importance of the reporter–source relationship. Others oppose shield laws, preferring to base a reporter's privilege on the First Amendment, which is not subject to legislative whims. Even a liberal or absolute statute can be amended or repealed, depending on the political makeup of the lawmaking body.

In carving out a privilege for reporters, some states and courts have relied on the dissenting opinion by Justice Potter Stewart in the *Branzburg* case. Stewart noted that he would require the government to demonstrate three things before compelling grand jury testimony from a reporter regarding a confidential source: (1) that there is probable cause to believe that the reporter has information "clearly relevant to a specific probable violation of law"; (2) that the information sought cannot be obtained by alternative means less destructive of First Amendment values; and (3) that there is a "compelling and overriding need" for the information.[26] This three-part test, because it has been embraced in one form or another by lower courts and some states through their shield laws, represents an important summary of the circumstances under which journalists might be required to divulge their sources.

Nevertheless, even where the law works to the advantage of reporters, the ethical quandary regarding the protection of sources remains problematic. The threshold issue is whether to promise anonymity in the first place. This is a critical decision because it sets in motion a potential conflict with other competing interests, particularly when the information provided by the sources relates to criminal or civil investigations or litigation. Thus, a promise of confidentiality should be used with extreme caution in the news-gathering process.

News sources are the cornerstone of good investigative journalism. And reporters sometimes feel compelled to promise confidentiality to solicit candid testimony from those who bear witness to the unsavory conduct of others. Reporters point out, perhaps correctly, that without the assurance of anonymity, some sources would dry up. Thus, the audience would be deprived of valuable information about matters of public interest. In such cases reporters are laying claim to a fiduciary relationship with their readers and viewers, whereby they serve as representatives of the public in its quest for information.

There is also resentment in the journalistic community at being used as an arm of law enforcement, a pawn for lazy prosecutors and other officials who are unable or unwilling to develop their own sources. At times, however, no alternative sources are available, and thus this argument loses some of its appeal as a defense for reporters' privilege. But in general, confidentiality in a reporter–source relationship does serve a valid social purpose, and a promise to a source should be broken only when there are overriding reasons for doing so.

Nevertheless, some serious reservations have been advanced about the use of confidential sources. Because the credibility of sources is one of the barometers of truthful communications, confidentiality deprives members of the audience of the opportunity to decide for themselves how much faith to put in the information. In addition, news sources, as noted earlier, act from a variety of motives, some of which are not commendable. Some like to influence public opinion by leaking information to reporters in exchange for a promise of confidentiality. Such sources are described variously as "authoritative," "highly placed," "unimpeachable," or "well-informed." Others act from self-interest or with such objectionable motives as hatred or revenge. Still other sources are more altruistic and appear to be acting out of a legitimate concern for the public interest.

Another concern is that sources sometimes use their cloak of confidentiality to attack third parties who cannot defend themselves against an unidentified opponent. They venture opinions and observations that might remain unexpressed if the source were quoted by name.

There is also concern that such a privilege could serve as a license for irresponsible behavior by the media. Instead of searching for facts, they could spin webs of fantasy, maligning both public officials and private citizens in the process. There would be no means of redress, because the reporter could not be called as a witness to corroborate the allegations.[27]

Critics of reporters' privilege, especially as it relates to criminal cases, also contend that journalists should not be exempt from the moral and legal duties imposed on the citizenry at large. According to this view, people have a general obligation to assist the cause of justice by offering any evidence at their disposal, and there is no compelling reason to relieve reporters of this moral responsibility. And the critics may have a point: Journalists, who are quick to point out that politicians are not above the law, are often reluctant to apply the same egalitarian ideals to their own professional conduct.

This was the issue in late 1999 when a source confessed to *Philadelphia Inquirer* reporter Nancy Phillips that he had arranged the grisly murder five years earlier of Rabbi Fred Neulander's wife, Carol, at the request of her husband. However, before confessing, the source had insisted that the conversation be "off the record," and while police continued their investigation of the murder, Phillips harbored a secret that, if true, would have solved the case and could have earned the rabbi the death penalty.[28] While the source, with the reporter's assistance, eventually confessed to

the police, the ethical postmortems on Phillips's conduct were predictable. For county prosecutor Lee A. Solomon, Phillips's duty as a citizen should have served as her moral beacon. "Journalists have a moral and ethical obligation to come forward," he declared categorically. "To cloak themselves in privilege and allow someone to get away with murder is unconscionable to me. Maybe it is legally permissible, but it's morally unconscionable."[29]

Media ethicist and University of Minnesota law professor Jane Kirtley was just as resolute in support of the reporter's decision. "The definition of good citizenship for a journalist is different because of the constitutionally protected role we enjoy in our society," Kirtley said. "One of the ways you fulfill your duty to the public is by maintaining your independence from the government. Police have a role to fulfill, but it's not identical to journalists'. Keeping the line firmly drawn is tremendously important."[30] *Inquirer* Editor Robert J. Rosenthal, in a statement that undoubtedly reflected the ethical posture of the journalistic community, agreed. "It's crucial for our long-term credibility to not be seen as a branch of law enforcement."[31]

A promise of confidentiality might exempt a reporter from the normal editorial review processes, at least insofar as the credibility of sources is concerned. In the strictest sense the promise precludes disclosure even to the reporter's employer, but some debate persists within the journalistic community over whether promises of anonymity are really the reporter's or the institution's. For example, if reporters reveal their sources to an editor, has the promise of confidentiality been breached? Regardless of the views of individual journalists and editors on this issue, there is a moral obligation to clarify this point with the source before extending an offer of unqualified confidentiality. In addition, at the risk of offending the sense of journalistic independence and autonomy, news organizations should develop a written policy on this matter to serve as a moral beacon for employers and employees alike.[32]

Indeed, most news organizations now routinely require reporters to reveal their sources to their editors, a practice that was once opposed by both editors and independent-minded reporters. Some news organizations have specific policies stating that promises of confidentiality can flow only from the institution itself, not from individual reporters. Many news organizations discourage the use of confidential sources altogether. Only when all other "on-the-record" avenues of investigation have failed, according to these policies, should confidentiality be considered. It is also common practice to confirm the information provided by a confidential source with at least one other source. And when a story is based on a confidential source, the reason for the source's anonymity should be explained to the audience.

A Delicate Balance: Confidentiality and Competing Interests

The ethical dimensions of the reporter–source relationship are anchored in two important principles. First, the moral duty to keep a promise of confidentiality to a source is derived from the general obligations imposed on each member of society. Keeping promises, as pointed out earlier, is a value considered worthy of protection. A breach of secrecy should be the exception, not the rule. Second, the confidentiality of the reporter–source relationship is based on the reporter's *particularistic* obligations (see Chapter 2) to the field of journalism. Such obligations are set out in the professional codes.

Given this impressive array of moral support, some reporters have apparently concluded that their duty to protect their sources overrides all other obligations. And it is true that the special nature of the reporter–source relationship serves important societal functions, a reality that does not apply to most citizens in terms of their confidential relationships. Thus, the burden of proof is on those parties seeking the breach of confidentiality and the revelation of the sources' identities.

It does not follow, however, that journalists are *exempt* from competing obligations. A system of ethics cannot excuse any group from the rules of moral reasoning predicated simply on the *role* of that group within society. Reporters must engage in the same process of moral reasoning as the rest of us, in which competing values are weighed against the principle of confidentiality.[33] If confidentiality is then deemed to override other duties, reporters will have some justification for defending these decisions against the critics of their ethical behavior.[34]

In summary, ethical concerns affecting the reporter–source relationship arise at three points: (1) when the reporter decides whether to promise anonymity to a source; (2) when the reporter decides whether to divulge the source's identity to an editor or other supervisor, especially when there is no clear-cut company policy on this matter; and (3) when the journalist contemplates breaking a promise of confidentiality because of some conflicting moral principle or perhaps under penalty of law. The existence of a reporter's privilege is, for some members of the journalistic community, an essential tool of investigative reporting. But this does not exempt reporters from the obligation to follow the normal procedures of moral reasoning and to acknowledge that there are competing moral claims to their promises of confidentiality.

CHANGES IN THE REPORTER–SOURCE RELATIONSHIP

Journalists clearly face more pressure than ever before to reveal their sources of information. In the past some reporters have gone to jail rather than reveal their confidential sources, but the reporter–source relationship has changed perceptibly. Floyd Abrams, a prominent First Amendment attorney, once asserted that breaking promises to sources is more common than one might suspect and that there is a lot of "fibbing" about this practice because news organizations do not want to acknowledge it to the rest of the journalistic community.[35]

Needless to say, the breaking of a promise is not a casual enterprise and should be done only after much reflection and only when based upon some more overriding ethical consideration. The moral agent should always keep in mind that the consequences of naming a confidential source can be quite painful. Consider, for example, the TV news reporter in South Carolina whose husband was forced to reveal her news source to a grand jury. The source, an attorney who served as president of the state's trial lawyers association, was sentenced to four months in jail and was forced to resign his law practice. Similarly, a former corporate attorney in Ohio was sentenced to two years of unmonitored probation and forty hours of community service for his involvement in illegally accessing corporate employees' voice mail after a reporter named him as the source for a story critical of the corporation's business practices.[36]

Perhaps the greatest source of pressure comes from the legal fraternity, especially in libel suits. In such cases journalists and their employers are confronted with the prospects of huge damage assessments, particularly when a plaintiff argues that the truth or falsity of an allegation can be determined only if the identity of the source is revealed. If reporters refuse to comply with a court order to divulge the source's name, the judge may well enter a default judgment in favor of the plaintiff, a judgment that could run into the millions of dollars.[37]

A reporter might also justify the breaking of a promise based upon "altered circumstances," that is, facts that are not in evidence at the time the agreement with the source was consummated. This was the dilemma faced by Howard Weaver, editor of the *Anchorage* (Alaska) *Daily News,* when he was confronted with whether to break a promise to an AIDS victim and his family. A young man, a hemophiliac, was suing a blood supplier, alleging that he had contracted AIDS from tainted blood he bought. In response to a plea from the man and his family,

Weaver agreed not to use his name in their coverage of the story. The stigma of having AIDS, they argued, was equal to that of being raped. But the paper later discovered the victim was having unprotected sex after he found out he had AIDS. "We were faced with the question of violating our pledge of confidentiality," said Weaver, "stacked up against what could have been obvious life-and-death circumstances to his partners." The editor told the victim's mother he had a moral responsibility to warn his partners, and if he didn't the paper would take action. The victim later notified his partners, and the paper was taken off the horns of an ethical dilemma.[38]

Although confidential sources will probably continue to occupy an important niche in investigative reporting, the trend away from the traditional view that the reporter–source relationship is sacred is unmistakable. News organizations have tightened their policies and have reined in reporters who might, in their enthusiasm to get an exclusive, make unnecessary promises of confidentiality to their sources. Nevertheless, in those cases in which promises are made—wisely or unwisely—reporters who are asked to break their pledge of confidentiality must still wrestle with the moral dilemma of whether to do so.

THE PRINCIPLE OF CONFIDENTIALITY: HYPOTHETICAL CASES

The cases in this chapter provide the opportunity for you to examine several issues involving the principle of confidentiality. Although the scenarios deal primarily with the relationships between reporters and their sources and the ethical responsibilities of public relations practitioners, confidentiality is a value that affects all of us, regardless of our professional interest.

In analyzing these cases, keep in mind the three approaches to ethical decision making described in Chapter 3: deontological (duty-based) ethics, teleological (consequence-based)

ethics, and Aristotle's golden mean. Of course, any ethical dilemma involving confidentiality must begin with the general rule outlined at the outset of this chapter: The burden of proof for breaching confidentiality is on the party seeking disclosure.

A duty-based theorist would consider confidentiality a basic right grounded in the principle of autonomy. Thus, a breach of secrecy, especially when made pursuant to a promise, would be justified only when confidentiality must be overridden by some other basic right. An example would be the right to a fair trial, the outcome of which depends, in part, on a defendant's access to a reporter's sources of information. But even here there is a duty to keep promises, and the abrogation of a promise can seldom be justified, according to the deontological perspective.

Consequentialists, on the other hand, would examine the potential impact of disclosure before breaching confidentiality. This process involves, first, measuring the *short-term harm (or benefits)* of the decision. Second, the *long-term consequences* must be evaluated. For example, in deciding whether to break a promise of confidentiality, a reporter should weigh not only the relative harm to the source and other interested parties but also the long-term impact on the journalist's (and perhaps the institution's) credibility and future effectiveness as an investigative reporter.

Aristotle's golden mean requires a search for a "mean" between two extremes. In most cases, however, there may not be a middle ground for exploration, because any release of information effectively violates the principle of confidentiality.

CASE STUDIES

▶ CASE 6-1

Guarding a Secret about a Military Hero

In March 2003 the 3rd Infantry Division crossed the border between Kuwait and Iraq and headed for Baghdad. *Operation Iraqi Freedom had begun.* Bypassing most of the major centers of resistance, the 3rd Division moved with dispatch toward the Iraqi capital, capturing the international airport and entering Baghdad from the west virtually unopposed. Pursuant to President Bush's orders to topple Saddam Hussein's regime, the military buildup of coalition units had occurred so rapidly that planning was still underway as the lead elements of America's fighting forces began their incursion into the Iraqi homeland. CBS News correspondent Jim Axelrod, embedded with the 3rd Division, reported that they had made it from the Kuwait-Iraq border to the edge of the Euphrates River valley in less than six hours, an amazing feat considering the anticipated resistance from elements of Saddam's armed forces.

While most of the American public watched with stunned fascination the televised accounts of what appeared to be a quick and decisive victory, the families of the soldiers left behind at Fort Stewart, Georgia, the home base for the 3rd Infantry, were understandably apprehensive about the potential dangers, including the reported weapons of mass destruction, that awaited their loved ones. Laura Sinclair, a bride of only three months, was among those who attempted to remain stoic while coping with her husband's abrupt departure for Operation Iraqi Freedom.

Jason and Laura Sinclair had been high school sweethearts at Roosevelt High in Annistonville, where Jason's athletic prowess earned him letters in three high school sports and made him a local celebrity. Jason's decision to enlist in the army shortly after graduation came as no surprise to his family and friends, who admired the youth's patriotism and commitment to public service. Following his basic training at Fort Benning, Jason was assigned to the 3rd Infantry Division at Fort Stewart, where he was soon promoted to corporal. When the unit was alerted for its deployment to Kuwait and then Iraq, Jason and Laura decided to marry prior to Jason's departure for Operation Iraqi Freedom.

In her husband's absence, Laura returned to Annistonville to live with her parents. She monitored the nightly television accounts of the 3rd Infantry's operations and the optimistic reports from those journalists embedded with various units of the 3rd Infantry. Much to her relief her husband returned safely to Fort Stewart, where he was awarded the Silver Star for valor for liberating his squad from an ambush by Iraqi soldiers just 20 miles from Baghdad. Corporal Sinclair's bravado under fire was front-page news in the *Annistonville Courier,* and he was quickly anointed a hero.

Shortly after returning from Iraq, Jason's enlistment ended, and he took a job as a security guard at a plant in his hometown. Laura took a job as a teller in a bank, and life appeared to resume some degree of normalcy for the Sinclairs. Friends and neighbors detected a more somber mood from the usually gregarious Jason Sinclair but attributed this to the period of decompression required for any soldier reentering civilian life from combat duty. Three months after he left military service, Jason was found dead in his car in a wooded area not far from the Sinclairs' home, the victim of a self-inflicted gunshot wound.

Kurt Bannister, the senior reporter for the *Courier,* was assigned to write the front-page account of Jason Sinclair's tragic death. However, Bannister felt unfulfilled by his initial news report on Corporal Sinclair's death and decided a few days after the funeral to write a more in-depth feature that would serve as a sufficient commemoration of the life of the young man who had served his country and risked his life for his fellow soldiers. He quickly gathered background material on his community's military hero and interviewed friends, teachers, former classmates, and even those who had served with him in Iraq. The picture that emerged was of an optimistic, selfless individual who was always willing to make sacrifices for others. Some observed that Jason had been rather moody since his return from Iraq but ascribed this

to the difficulties of readjusting to civilian life after several months of intense combat and security operations. During a brief interview with Sinclair's father, the reporter asked the senior Sinclair if he knew why his son committed suicide, and he reluctantly replied that Jason and his wife were having financial and marital problems but requested that Bannister not include that in his story. Bannister readily agreed, reasoning that this was a personal matter that his readers did not need to know. Besides, such a revelation might tarnish the community's image of Jason as a well-adjusted family man, and the tarnishing of this image, in Bannister's mind, would serve no purpose.

However, Jason Sinclair's brother, David, also a resident of Annistonville, tendered a somewhat more disturbing account of his sibling's life following his return from Iraq. His interview with Bannister commenced with a rather mundane description of their childhood and adolescence but quickly turned to Jason's decision to join the army and his subsequent deployment to Iraq. "I was opposed to my brother's joining the army," David Sinclair revealed to Bannister, "and I was opposed to our going into Iraq. Fortunately, Jason returned alive and was even honored as hero. He received the Silver Star for valor. But there's another side to his combat experiences in Operation Iraqi Freedom. It's all here in a journal he kept while on active duty. I discovered it among his personal belongings a couple of days ago. Since you're doing a feature on my brother, including his military experience, I thought you might find this interesting."

Bannister reviewed the rather fascinating first-hand chronicle of one soldier's triumphs and tribulations as his division marched relentlessly toward Baghdad and eventually occupied the Iraqi capital. Jason's description of how he rescued his fellow soldiers from an ambush, for which he was awarded the Silver Star, was particularly tantalizing. The journal's tone was decidedly upbeat, reflecting the optimistic disposition for which Jason was renowned during his high school years. But as the 3rd Infantry neared Baghdad, the realities of war began to take their toll on Corporal Sinclair. According to Jason's account, on the outskirts of Baghdad his company encountered fierce resistance from an unknown number of Iraqis firing rifles and grenades from a series of reinforced bunkers and an old farmhouse. Jason's squad was assigned to assault the farmhouse with heavy weapons and to neutralize the enemy combatants inside. After 30 minutes of intense fighting, the squad accomplished its mission, but in surveying the consequences of their assault discovered the bodies of not only three Iraqi paramilitary soldiers but also seven civilians, including two women and three children.

Although Jason's unit was unaware of the civilian occupants of the farmhouse, his journal revealed a deepening despair at this sobering but inevitable facet of war. As Bannister turned the pages of the journal and scanned the entries posted after the young soldier's return from Iraq, Jason appeared to become increasingly despondent, and the recollections manifested a quiet desperation. It was clear that his role in an operation that had resulted in the deaths of innocent civilians had taken a psychological toll on the previously gregarious Jason Sinclair. Near the end, suicide was mentioned more than once as a permanent escape from the demons that continued to haunt Jason upon his return from Operation Iraqi Freedom.

Bannister thanked David Sinclair for sharing his brother's journal with him, although he was uncertain as to Sinclair's motivation or how he might incorporate the journal's contents into his feature on Annistonville's hometown hero. The journal had clearly revealed the reason for Jason Sinclair's despondency that was probably responsible for his suicide. As the *Courier's* senior reporter contemplated his human interest feature on Annistonville's military hero, he recognized the potential ethical quandary posed by his unexpected exposure to Corporal Sinclair's anguish over his possible contribution to the deaths of innocent civilians and the role that this played in his decision to commit suicide. And because the revelation of such confidential information might tarnish the image of a local citizen who was revered as a military hero and thus subject his paper to public censure, Bannister asked for a meeting with Managing Editor Murphy Truscott, who would be the moral agent in this case. Truscott usually erred on the side of caution and listened to all points of view before rendering a judgment. He asked City Editor Lauren Anderson, Bannister's immediate supervisor, to participate in

the ethical discourse on whether to reveal the real reason for Jason Sinclair's tragic death.

"The buck stops here," declared Truscott as he opened the dialogue with Bannister and his city editor. "I must give the green light on whether we run a follow-up story on Jason Sinclair and reveal our discovery on the probable motivation for his suicide. But first, I want your views."

"As you know," began Bannister, "during the interview Jason's father cited financial and family problems as the reasons for his son's drastic action. I promised that I would not report this information because it really wasn't a matter of public interest. But this changes things. Mr. Sinclair may have known more than he revealed. In any event, David Sinclair let me read his brother's journal, which provides some pretty graphic insight into his mood change upon his return from Iraq and his ultimate decision to take his own life; he was despondent over what he believed was his role in the killing of innocent civilians."

"I have a different view," responded Anderson. "You made a promise to Jason's father that you would not reveal his family problems as a possible cause of his suicide. When you interviewed him, he may very well have been aware of this journal. We should assume he was. But in my opinion that doesn't change the decision to omit any reference to the reasons for the suicide. Your information came from a journal that Corporal Sinclair clearly did not intend to be released to the public. The fact that his brother made it available to you doesn't alter this fact."

"I'm not so sure," replied Bannister. "I agreed to omit any reference to family and financial problems as a possible cause of suicide because these were personal matters, the discussion of which would serve no public purpose. And I don't believe that Mr. Sinclair was attempting to deflect me from the real reason for his son's tragedy. I'm inclined to believe that Jason's Iraq experience and subsequent depression contributed to his family problems. However, I do believe the circumstances surrounding Corporal Sinclair's suicide may justify the inclusion of this information in my story."

"I disagree," responded Anderson. "Sinclair is a local hero. He won the Silver Star. What's to be gained by reporting that he may have been responsible for civilian casualties, a mistake that apparently tormented him to the point that he was willing to take his own life? This could cause needless anguish for the family and friends of the victim. Combat casualties, civilian or military, are newsworthy, but this episode is not the focus of your story. If there had been an official investigation of this incident that focused on Sinclair—and so far we have no evidence of this—then I would have a different view."

"I'm aware of the potential reaction among our readers," declared Bannister. "But describing this event through Jason's eyes might help our readers to understand the unpredictable nature of war and its psychological impact on the individual soldier. Jason is a local hero—a soldier who committed suicide apparently because of an event that transpired during the same military campaign that turned him into a decorated hero."

"But doesn't using this private account to inform readers about the human tragedies of war turn this article into a political statement?," replied Anderson. "Besides, your information came from a personal journal—journals contain the private musings of their authors. They're not intended to be made public. Jason Sinclair's brother should never have showed it to you, but the fact that he did does not remove its cloak of confidentiality. Besides, David Sinclair admitted to you that he was opposed to Jason's enlistment and in fact was opposed to the war. His motives are somewhat questionable."

But Bannister persisted in his defense of including some of the material from Jason's journal, becoming increasingly confident of his rationale for doing do. "My original intention was to write a human interest story—a commemoration of the life of a local hero—but this new information casts this project in a different light. Civilian casualties are an unfortunate consequence of war, but Jason's journal provides a personal account of one soldier's psychological reaction to such tragedies. Perhaps family problems played a role in his death—they may even have been the result of his Iraqi experiences—but the journal leaves little doubt as to the underlying cause of his mood swings and the probable cause of his suicide. Since his suicide may have been the result of his

role, as unintended as it was, in the deaths of Iraqi civilians, this is a matter of public interest and should be reported."

Sensing that Bannister and Anderson had fully delineated their positions, Managing Editor Murphy Truscott instructed Bannister to continue work on his story, assuring him that he would consider the ethical dilemma posed by the just completed discourse and quickly render a judgment on whether to reveal the personal lamentations of a young soldier who could no longer speak for himself.

THE CASE STUDY

This case raises some troubling questions concerning the use of confidential information that could cause harm to innocent third parties, as well as to the memory of a suicide victim who cannot object to publicity surrounding his private thoughts. Journalistic reporting on suicides is never easy, and in this case the difficulty is more acute because of the status of the victim within the community. Nevertheless, the newspaper's reporter, Kurt Bannister, believes that the reasons underlying the young soldier's suicide, which at first he believed to be strictly personal, are now a matter of public interest because of their connection to the same military campaign that resulted in his being anointed a local hero in the first place. Bannister may believe, although this is left unstated in the case, that the fact Jason Sinclair's brother provided access to the victim's journal constitutes tacit consent to include this information in the feature story concerning Corporal Sinclair's combat experiences.

Jason Sinclair's involvement in an operation that killed innocent civilians and his subsequent despondency over this episode are chronicled in a private journal, the contents of which were certainly not intended for public consumption. Does the fact that the tragic results of this mission are a matter of public interest and are directly related to Jason Sinclair's suicide alter the equation in favor of publication? The reporting of the contents of Sinclair's journal will undoubtedly tarnish, at least in the minds of some, his status as a local hero. Should this be of paramount concern to Murphy Truscott as he decides whether to support Kurt Bannister's point of view?

Truth versus confidentiality! For the purpose of engaging these competing ethical values, assume the role of Managing Editor Murphy Truscott and, applying the SAD formula for moral reasoning outlined in Chapter 3, make a decision on whether the *Annistonville Chronicle* should divulge the real reason for Corporal Jason Sinclair's suicide.

▶ CASE 6-2

A Public Relations Challenge: Fraud in a University's Basketball Program

The Fighting Tigers, North Central University's Cinderella basketball team, were poised for their return to national prominence. After eight years of exile from the postseason tournaments, the Tigers had posted an incredible regular season record, which brought a well-deserved invitation to the NCAA tournament. They had vanquished their foes decisively in the first rounds and were now among the much-coveted final four. Only three teams stood between them and a national championship.

For almost two decades the Fighting Tigers had been a perennial contender for regional or national honors, and their demise had not been accepted graciously by fans and alumni. Their overtures to the university's administration to restore some measure of dignity to North Central's flagging basketball fortunes had produced a series of coaching changes, all to no avail. President Julius Dickins was not unmindful of the correlation between a successful athletic program and alumni donations to the North Central University Foundation. He frequently compared a public university, not entirely facetiously, with the stock market. "Good economic news produces a rise in the stock market," he declared realistically during a local Lions Club speech. "And a winning basketball team enriches our financial coffers." Nevertheless, Dickins had been unable to stop the bleeding—until the arrival of Latrelle Savage.

Savage had arrived with impressive credentials, with coaching experience at both the college and professional levels, but university alumni were skeptical that he could salvage the athletic debris

inherited from his two predecessors. Nevertheless, team supporters were patient as Savage aggressively recruited a group of talented young freshmen from a nationwide pool and then proceeded to mold them into a formidable basketball presence. His first two "rebuilding" years did not produce any postseason tournament bids, but in his third year the Tigers had defied the lackluster predictions of most prognosticators and after only five games were listed in the top ten, a position that the university's basketball upstarts never relinquished.

The North Central faculty were less enthusiastic about the arrival of the much-heralded coach because they had always harbored a suspicion that the administration favored athletic success over academic excellence. However, Savage had moved quickly to assuage their concerns with promises to require class attendance, to promote the benefits of a college degree, and to improve upon the team's dismal 21 percent graduation rate. How he planned to accomplish this latter objective he did not share with the alumni or the media.

As the Fighting Tigers were moving confidently toward postseason tournament play, an internal university investigation was underway that threatened to derail the team's bid for national glory. In early February a staff member employed by the athletic department's Athlete Counseling Center notified her superiors that two of the center's counselors were doing more than offering advice and tutoring to the basketball team. For those players who were in academic trouble, they were actually writing papers for their young charges, and on three occasions they arranged to have a "proxy" take exams for players. True to her expectations, no action was taken, and two weeks later the whistleblower reported these academic indiscretions to the university provost, Judith Whalen. The provost appointed a committee to investigate the allegations, which included the faculty senate president. Coach Savage was made aware of the charges but said he was confident that the counselors would be cleared of any wrongdoing. The provost cautioned the committee that the investigation was strictly confidential because any premature release of its findings would be embarrassing to the university and would be an untimely distraction for the team as it focused on basketball's Holy Grail. The university notified the NCAA of its investigation, but the chair of the organization's Committee on Infractions told President Dickins that they would await the results of the investigation before taking any action of their own.

As the buzzer sounded signaling the Fighting Tigers' final victory before beginning the final four competition, the committee delivered its report to President Dickins's office. The accusations of fraud were confirmed, according to the forty-page document. Two counselors, two team starters, and one sub were implicated. One of the starters was an All-American candidate; the other was the team's reliable three-point shooter. Dickins had traveled with the team to support them in their NCAA tournament play, but when he received news of the investigation's conclusions he returned promptly to the North Central campus. The president recognized this debacle for what it was: a public relations disaster in the making. Thus, the focus now must be on damage control. To assess the situation, he quickly assembled his "brain trust," whose composition always varied depending upon the issue at stake. In this case, Dickins's brain trust consisted of Director of University Relations Lewis Hale, Sports Information Director Joseph Sawyer, and Provost Whalen.

"Let me make one thing clear," Dickins declared as he nervously fingered the explosive report of athletic fraud. "In the future any communications concerning our investigation will be disseminated through University Relations, as always. However, this is going to be an unpleasant journey. My office must personally approve any contacts with the media, NCAA investigators, or any member of the public. Now, as far as I know this whole matter is still confidential, but it won't stay that way forever. At some point we must go public, but the question is when. Whenever we make an announcement, we'll just cite disciplinary reasons for our decision because if we pursue this matter under the Code of Student Conduct, the proceedings will be confidential anyway."

"I hate to rain on your parade so early in our proceedings," Hale stated, "but just before I left my office to come here I received a call from a local reporter who apparently has heard rumors of

our investigation. He wanted an update. I stalled him but I don't know for how long."

"If we suspend these players and release this report just as we're preparing for the final four," said Sawyer, reflecting the athletic department's view, "we may as well concede the national championship to one of the other teams. We could be forced to suspend three players, two of them crucial to our chances, until a hearing can be held."

"I'm well aware of the potential consequences of player suspensions which will then necessitate a public announcement on our findings," responded Hale. "We could hold this report until the finals are concluded. But if the press finds out that we knew about this fraud but kept the report confidential just to protect our position in the playoffs, we'll lose a lot of credibility, and we'll be denounced in the media. In addition, the faculty senate, which has always been deeply suspicious of the administration's motives, will undoubtedly turn this into a debating point at one of their meetings, which I might remind you is open to the media and the public."

"As you know," replied Whalen, "the provost is the chief academic officer of the university. It's my responsibility to protect the academic integrity of this institution. But the athletic department is an integral part of our university community, and I must also work with them. They are part of our team. My academic training tells me to move quickly to discipline the players and release this report to show good faith with the public and the state's taxpayers—and then let the chips fall where they may. On the other hand, these players have worked so hard to get where they are. The other members are not responsible for the bad judgment of two counselors and three of their teammates. What difference will it make if we keep this report under wraps for another week or two?"

"So what in the hell is your position, Judith?" demanded Hale. "Your waffling makes it sound as though you're running for public office. And incidentally, what you refer to as bad judgment some of us would consider cheating."

Before Whalen could reply to this assault on her integrity, the sports information director unloaded his trump card. "Let me remind each of you," he said, "that our alumni and boosters have waited a long time for this moment. It's true that even without a victory in the final four our faith in Coach Savage will have been vindicated. But that isn't likely to satisfy our rabid fans. They smell blood. And if we do anything to undermine our chances for a national championship, not only will we be viewed as pariahs, but the contributions to our endowment fund will inevitably decline as well. If we suspend these players and release this report now, we can congratulate ourselves on doing the 'honorable' thing from a public relations standpoint, while the university suffers economically from our moral intransigence."

"But if we sit on this report until after the final four and the media find out about it—as we must assume they will—then this will just confirm the faculty and our board's suspicion that we care more about athletics than we do about academics," responded Whalen, attempting to restore some measure of self-respect in the eyes of Lewis Hale. "In addition, we must remember that the public, the state's taxpayers, are stakeholders in our decision, and I'm afraid of losing credibility and trust in their eyes. I must acknowledge, however, that if we release this report we'll feel the heat financially."

"I think you're operating under a faulty premise," asserted Sawyer. "The faculty senate may condemn us for our actions, but many of these taxpayers are our boosters. They will not send accolades our way if we trash our chances for a national championship. Keep in mind that restoring prestige to a university that until fairly recently prided itself on its winning basketball program is high on the agenda of both alumni and fans. I'm still puzzled as to why we can't protect the confidentiality of this report for a few more days and allow our players to participate in the final four."

"But it's not just about making the report public," responded Hale. "It's what's in the report that really matters. We now know that fraud was committed by members of the athletic department. I have a reservoir of trust with the media. If we have this report and fail to release it, my credibility will be eroded. Swift action must be taken, even if it includes suspending three players just prior to the final four. That will necessitate a public announcement. If we fail to act expeditiously, at the best we'll be impeached for prostituting our academic integrity; at the worst we'll be accused of a cover-up."

"Time is short," concluded President Dickins. "The buck stops here, and I'll make the decision. But I still want a formal recommendation from the director of university relations. After all, you're our expert in public relations. I know how you feel now, Lewis, but I want you to take into account the views expressed here, including your own, and by tomorrow morning have a recommendation on my desk." With that, North Central University's beleaguered president adjourned the meeting as he contemplated the inauspicious climax to the Fighting Tigers' basketball season.

THE CASE STUDY

When the *St. Paul Pioneer Press* published a story in 1999 of academic fraud within the University of Minnesota men's basketball program the day before the Golden Gophers were to face Gonzaga University in the first round of the NCAA tournament, the reader backlash and vehemence of their condemnation was astonishing. Some questioned the timing of the story, accusing the paper of "sensationalism." Even Governor Jesse Ventura joined the cacophony of voices arrayed against the *Pioneer Press*.[39] Ralph D. Barney, editor of the *Journal of Mass Media Ethics,* responded (correctly) that "[t]he underlying principle is, without worrying about the timing . . . you publish when it is ready."[40]

Public relations professionals, however, operate in a somewhat different ethical orbit than journalists. While they should still subscribe to the fundamental values of truth and honesty, the self-interest of their clients must not be far from center stage. In this narrative, of course, Lewis Hale's "client" is also his employer. The decision on the timing of the disciplinary actions will be left ultimately to the university president, but this event cannot be divorced from the public relations considerations. If suspensions are handed down prior to the final four, they must be accompanied by an announcement, which might also entail the release of the report itself. The other extreme is to keep the university's findings confidential, await the tournament's conclusion, and then suspend the players (which may mean little if their eligibility has expired). Hale is concerned that if the university is aware of academic fraud but fails to release immediately the results of the investigation, his unit will lose credibility with the media. Is there a middle ground—an Aristotle's golden mean—that might accommodate both the athletic department's anxieties and Lewis Hale's determination to maintain his own integrity as director of university relations?

This is an intriguing case because the salvation of Hale's own credibility with the media could result in a public relations disaster among the team's boosters and alumni. There are several stakeholders here: university relations, the university administration, the faculty, the alumni and team supporters, the general public, the athletic department, and of course the team itself. For the purpose of weighing your options and then making a recommendation on whether to publicize the results of the university's investigation, assume the role of Lewis Hale. And then, utilizing the SAD formula for moral reasoning outlined in Chapter 3, outline your recommendation to university president Julius Dickins.

▶ **CASE 6-3**

Allegations of Sexual Harassment: Newsworthy or Political Dirty Tricks[41]

After three terms as mayor of Titusville, a community without term limits, Alton Fitzhenry was now fighting for his political life. His tenure as mayor had been preceded by four terms on the city council representing a precinct whose voters regularly tendered their patronage at the ballot box on behalf of his candidacy, and his first three mayoral races had similarly produced little effective opposition. But by the time that Fitzhenry announced he would seek a fourth term, Titusville's voters were becoming restless, and polls reflected a growing disaffection with what one community leader described as "political stagnation coupled with a lack of civic vision" on behalf of the city's leadership, a thinly veiled reference to Mayor Fitzhenry. Simon McCain, a highly successful and charismatic litigator with the law firm of Maxwell, Reynolds and Abercrombie, sensed Fitzhenry's vulnerability to the vicissitudes of political life and aggressively challenged the incumbent's bid for a fourth term.

McCain's decision to abandon, at least temporarily, his lucrative law practice was fueled by a nagging political ambition that he had harbored since his graduation from law school. He aspired to higher office, but the mayor's race would provide a fruitful learning experience for the political neophyte. With the support of a talented campaign staff and a progressive and ambitious political agenda, McCain's candidacy resonated with the Titusville electorate, and just two weeks prior to the election he led Fitzhenry in opinion polls by two percentage points. The incumbent's bid for a fourth term was clearly in jeopardy.

Tonya Vergara was professionally obligated to neutrality in the mayor's race, but she savored the spirited mudslinging that had emerged with a vengeance as the contest entered its final days. Vergara was the senior political reporter for the *Titusville Ledger*, covering the daily activities of local government and coordinating the paper's coverage of local and state races during the political season. Vergara had joined the *Ledger* just prior to the mayor's second campaign and was chagrined by the lack of serious competition for a political leader who once had been described by local pundits as unbeatable. Like most political journalists, Vergara relished the unpredictability and energy of competitive races and was stimulated by the vigorous contest between the seasoned politician and the young but politically savvy challenger.

As the campaign entered its final two weeks, Vergara received an unexpected call from Samuel Cousins, the incumbent mayor's campaign manager, who requested a secret rendezvous with the *Ledger*'s senior political reporter. Intrigued, Vergara agreed to meet Cousins at a park several blocks from the newspaper. Cousins told Vergara that he had done some research on McCain's background and had uncovered a civil complaint that had been filed against him by a female paralegal and a clerk at his law firm accusing him of sexual harassment. As far as he could tell, the case had never received any news coverage and had been settled out of court for an undisclosed amount. The settlement included an agreement that neither party could discuss the case or the terms of the settlement. Cousins said the material had been provided to him by a friend at the district court. "We are concerned that if McCain becomes mayor," Cousins nobly proclaimed, "he might subject the city of Titusville to civil liability if he repeated the kind of behavior toward city employees alleged in the sexual harassment complaint." Left unsaid, of course, was the less virtuous motive of obliterating McCain's slim lead among the voters. Cousins offered Vergara copies of the legal settlement on the condition that the source of the information concerning the civil complaint and its disposition remain confidential. Vergara agreed, with the caveat that her editors would have to be informed, but did not immediately pass judgment on its journalistic value.

Vergara returned to her office, where she studied the confidential documents in greater detail. According to the civil complaint the paralegal had accused McCain of attempting to grope her on more than one occasion; the legal secretary attributed "lewd and sexually suggestive remarks" to the attorney in the workplace. According to the settlement, the complainants had been awarded $175,000 and $135,000, respectively, but there had been no admission of culpability on McCain's part. The reporter then contacted the mayoral challenger and asked for his reaction to the sealed judicial settlement. McCain acknowledged that a civil complaint had been filed against him three years ago, but stated he was prohibited by the terms of the settlement from commenting on the case.

As a veteran journalist and one who prided herself on her professional deportment, Tonya Vergara recognized the ethical implications of publishing the details of the confidential civil settlement provided by the mayor's campaign manager. It could certainly influence the dynamics of McCain's well-orchestrated campaign. With the election rapidly approaching, Vergara briefed the *Ledger*'s managing editor, Wallace Holbrook, and city editor Sofia Lamb on what she had learned about the previously unpublicized sexual harassment suit against Simon McCain and her conversation with Mayor Fitzhenry's campaign manager. Because of the potential consequences of the injurious information for McCain's mayoral bid, Holbrook would be the moral agent in deciding whether his newspaper would inject this unexpected revelation into the campaign.

"I must confess to some ambivalence about publishing this information," Vergara acknowledged in her meeting with Holbrook and Lamb. "Cousins's overture to me and the provision of this information are clearly designed to sink McCain's candidacy. On the other hand, he has a point when he notes that there's a risk of electing someone mayor who has been accused of sexual harassment. If this kind of behavior should occur on his watch as mayor, the city could be exposed to civil liability. And then the taxpayers will be the losers."

"But we don't really know whether he was guilty of sexual harassment," replied Lamb. "He was sued for harassment, but there was never a jury verdict. An out-of-court settlement was reached without McCain admitting any liability."

"But the fact that a political candidate has been sued for sexual harassment in the past may have news value," responded Vergara, "especially if there's a good chance he'll be our next mayor. "For some reason this suit was not reported when it was first filed, and the plaintiffs' attorney apparently did not make a public issue of it. But this settlement involving a candidate for Titusville's highest office could be a matter of public interest."

"But this settlement is confidential by order of the district court. I'm not suggesting that we should refuse to publish all officially sealed information. It's our job to keep the public informed. But at the time of this suit McCain was not a public figure, and reporting it now rather than at the time the suit was filed may raise questions in the public's mind as to our motivation. We may be accused of 'dirty tricks,' especially since we can't name our source."

"At the time the suit was filed," noted Vergara, "McCain was not a political candidate. His guilt or innocence on the issue of sexual harassment was not a matter of profound public interest. But the fact that he is now running for mayor has changed the equation somewhat."

Despite Vergara's professed ambivalence about publishing the nature of the civil complaint and the settlement, she appeared to be building a case favoring publication, but the city editor was not persuaded. "McCain is prohibited by the terms of the settlement from discussing this matter," observed Lamb. "He can't even deny that he was guilty of sexual harassment. While most public figures can publicly respond to accusations against them, McCain has been deprived of this option. If we reveal what we have learned about this sexual harassment suit, this will be unfair to the candidate, and the voters may be the losers in the long run. And keep in mind that an out-of-court settlement is not proof of liability. Some attorneys advise settlements to avoid protracted and expensive litigation, even when the merits of the case favor the defendant. Sexual harassment law is still evolving. What constitutes sexual harassment is not always clear. From the materials that Cousins provided, we simply can't draw any conclusions about McCain's alleged nefarious behavior."

"His guilt or innocence is not the issue," replied Vergara emphatically. "The fact that a suit was filed and a settlement reached is what's newsworthy—more so now than when McCain was a private citizen. In this respect, a comment from him, which is prohibited by the settlement, is not really required for journalistic balance."

Wallace Holbrook listened intently to this ethical sparring between the paper's senior political reporter and the city editor. He was troubled by the prospect of publicly confronting the mayoral candidate with this previously confidential information just a few days before the election, especially since McCain was legally prohibited from commenting on the matter. On the other hand, within the journalistic framework, everything that related to a candidate's fitness for public office was fair game. In reflecting upon the facts of this case, Holbrook wondered whether this confidential legal settlement in a sexual harassment lawsuit three years ago met this standard.

THE CASE STUDY

Journalists frequently publish officially sanctioned confidential information under the claim of the public's right to know. And in most cases the press has a legitimate moral claim in publishing such information. But in this case, the confidential information concerns a civil lawsuit filed three years before Simon McCain entered the political arena. Under normal circumstances, this suit and its officially sealed settlement would be of marginal public interest. But if the allegations are true, then

serious questions about the candidate's character are implicated. However, unlike most allegations introduced during political campaigns, the candidate in this case is legally prohibited from responding to them.

The newspaper's senior political reporter, Tonya Vergara, argues that McCain's inability to respond publicly to the revelations concerning the lawsuit is, in the final analysis, not relevant to the news value of the material. The fact that a mayoral candidate was sued for sexual harassment and a settlement was reached with the plaintiffs is newsworthy. While there may be an element of unfairness in McCain's forced silence on the matter, this does not outweigh the public's need to know about the sexual harassment allegations.

Vergara's antagonist in the ethical debate, city editor Sofia Lamb, disagrees and believes the confidentiality of this information that includes a requirement that McCain refrain from public comment trumps any claims of newsworthiness. The harm to the candidate's political campaign will be too great, and this last-minute entry into what is already a contentious and hard-fought campaign will smack of "dirty tricks."

The paper's managing editor, Wallace Holbrook, is the moral agent in this case. For the purpose of tendering your own judgment in this matter, assume the position of Wallace Holbrook and, utilizing the SAD model for moral reasoning described in Chapter 3, decide whether the *Titusville Ledger* will publish the information provided to it by the mayor's campaign manager.

▶ **CASE 6-4**

Gender Norming and the Admiral's Public Relations Problem

Admiral Jason McAlister was no fan of the news media. As a young ensign during the Vietnam War, McAlister had witnessed America's first military defeat from offshore and, like many military officers who suffered in silence, blamed the Washington politicians for his nation's humiliation. If America's military arsenal had been unleashed against North Vietnam, in his view, the fortunes of war would have produced a swift victory. But McAlister had also embraced another facet of conventional military wisdom at the time—the liberal news media had turned the tide of public opinion against America's involvement in the conflict, thus ensuring a loss of political will to continue the engagement.

Thus, as a senior naval officer assigned to the Pentagon thirty years later, Admiral McAlister had applauded the military's tightly controlled flow of information during the Persian Gulf War. Like his military brethren, many of whom were veterans of the Vietnam debacle, he was now painfully aware of the perils of an unrestrained press in a military theater. McAlister's belief in the First Amendment's free press guarantees was tempered by his professional commitment to military security.

In the interval between Vietnam and McAlister's present assignment as chief of naval operations (CNO), the media, especially the national press corps, had done little to redeem themselves in Admiral McAlister's eyes. Vietnam had been followed by Watergate, which, McAlister believed, had reenergized the media's emerging cynicism concerning the conduct of all government officials. And the military had been a favorite target of their journalistic prowess, as evidenced by the periodic investigations on the network news magazine programs of various alleged nefarious or irresponsible activities and policies condoned by the Pentagon brass. McAlister candidly admitted the accuracy of much of the networks' information but faulted them for a lack of balance and perspective. He was particularly chagrined at the willingness of some retired military officers and those enlisted men who were apparently willing to risk censure by their superiors to serve as sources for myriad prime-time news magazine shows.

Diane Kole's overture to Admiral McAlister was not unexpected. Kole was a field producer for *Dateline America,* the latest addition to the prime-time news magazine genre, and was working with correspondent Jeffrey Hughes on the safety record of the navy's FA-18 fighter aircraft. As reported in the media during the past four years, the navy had experienced several crashes and other operational mishaps with the FA-18, four of which had resulted in fatalities. Although official reports released to the media blamed most of the incidents on mechanical

failure, Kole told McAlister that she had learned a disproportionate number of the ill-fated aircraft had been piloted by women; *Dateline America* wanted the admiral's perspective on this situation.

The decision to place females at the front lines of the nation's air defenses had not been made on Admiral McAlister's watch and was widely believed to have resulted from pressure from congressional liberals and women's groups. The navy's top brass had had reservations, but these paled in comparison to the outright antipathy by the "top guns" whose machismo and bravado were legendary and who considered the flight line to be an all-male preserve. Nevertheless, the navy had admitted women into its pilot training program accompanied by repeated public proclamations of its confidence in the ability of women to perform admirably in training missions and aerial combat.

In his current position as CNO, McAlister was an unapologetic disciple of gender equity in the navy. His subordinates considered him to be enigmatic. On the one hand, his temperament and experience inclined toward tradition. On the other hand, McAlister believed that the military should reflect the political realities of the society that sustains it. Thus, one of his priorities when he became CNO was to order an acceleration of the training of female pilots, a directive that some unit commanders apparently interpreted as moving women ahead of men in aviation assignments, if necessary.

However, the performance records of some female pilots to date had betrayed the navy's confidence in their program of gender equity. During the past four years, for example, there had been a number of crashes or other operational anomalies involving several FA-18 fighters, the navy's most sophisticated aircraft carrier–based jet, a disproportionate number of which were piloted by women. Three of the four FA-18 fatalities had involved female pilots, two of which were assigned to one aircraft carrier. In all but one of the mishaps investigators had attributed the causes to equipment malfunctions, but flight instructors were dubious.

Admiral McAlister was also dubious and ordered a more comprehensive investigation. His instincts and common sense, which had been reliable guides throughout his career, told him that human factors were somehow implicated in the disproportionate number of mishaps involving women pilots. The report of the investigation confirmed his suspicions.

According to many of the instructors interviewed, they were under pressure to train women pilots and move them to their duty assignments on aircraft carriers as soon as possible. To fulfill this mandate, some female trainees were given preferential treatment, a practice referred to as "gender norming." In a few cases, including one who died in one of the fighter mishaps, women pilots who had received lower evaluations than their male counterparts had nevertheless received earlier assignments to the carrier fleets. A couple of instructors, according to the report, complained that some women trainees with lower scores needed more flight time in the FA-18 before joining the carrier-based flight crews.

Admiral McAlister's investigators were unmerciful in their assignment of blame to "pilot error" in many of the FA-18 crashes and other operational abnormalities. They also documented incidents of gender norming by some overzealous commanders, which tracked closely the subsequent increase in FA-18 mishaps. The study that covered four years revealed a clear correlation, in McAlister's view, between the alleged policy of gender norming and the increase in FA-18 crashes but stopped short of proving a cause and effect in individual cases. Nevertheless, McAlister appreciated the report's candor but worried about its impact upon the many women pilots who had received exemplary evaluations and had moved to their duty assignments in the normal rotation.

And now, just two weeks after receiving this troubling account of preferential treatment in some naval training facilities, *Dateline America* was on Admiral McAlister's doorstep. As always, he sought the counsel of the navy's highest-ranking public affairs officer, Rear Admiral Nathaniel Washington, the chief of naval information. McAlister's query to Washington was simple: Should I meet with Kole, and should we release the most recent report of our internal investigation? He wanted a recommendation within 48 hours.

Admiral Washington, who prided himself on efficiency, promised a recommendation within twenty-four hours. He quickly summoned Public Affairs

Officer Michael Donovan and Geneva Roundtree, a GS-14 civilian who served as the assistant public affairs officer.

"As you know, the admiral is disturbed by the *Dateline America* inquiry on the FA-18 accidents," Washington stated matter-of-factly as he met behind closed doors with Donovan and Roundtree. "We're not sure how much they know. The field producer is focusing on the fact that a disproportionate number of women have been involved in these incidents. But there's no indication that she has any knowledge of the report's conclusion on gender norming. Admiral McAlister wants a recommendation on how we should deal with this issue."

"We've all seen the report," said Donovan. "It's pretty damning. It doesn't indict the entire system, but it's clear that some women pilots have been given preferential treatment. The one thing that isn't certain is to what extent this so-called gender norming is responsible for the disproportionate number of accidents involving women. There's a definite correlation, but the report doesn't clearly establish cause and effect."

"That's an argument that could cut both ways," responded Roundtree. "If we release this report with a statement that we're taking steps to correct the situation, it might work to our advantage in a public relations sense. On the other hand, the report is likely to be misinterpreted. There's a danger the media will focus on the gender-norming findings and ignore the fact that it doesn't clearly establish a cause and effect between this preferential treatment and the FA-18 mishaps."

"The only information that is public knowledge at the moment," observed Washington, "is the reports that were released to the media following each incident. Most of these, of course, attributed the crashes to mechanical failures. Admiral McAlister's investigation contradicts these findings. I could recommend that the admiral refuse to meet with the *Dateline America* crew on the ground that there is nothing to add—or that if he does meet with them, that he just refer to the reports that have already been released."

"I realize that the findings of Admiral McAlister's investigation are confidential," said Roundtree. "But if we don't release the report and it's leaked to the media, this will look like a cover-up."

"I question the wisdom of going public with this information," Donovan countered with growing concern about the document's embarrassing revelations. "Those commanders who practiced gender norming were not reflecting official navy policy. And because there is still some 'wiggle room' in this report to deny the cause and effect between the alleged preferential treatment of women and the placement of marginally qualified pilots into the cockpits of the FA-18, I see nothing to be gained by releasing it."

"But this isn't exactly a matter of military security," replied Roundtree. "It's a classic example of how a good-faith effort to diversify the navy's flight crews can go awry. I think the public needs to know. And when we release the report, we can also include a statement that applauds the overall success of the program, while noting that we're taking steps to correct the deficiencies."

"But if gender norming isn't official policy and most women pilots have performed admirably, then what's to be gained by releasing the report?" asked Donovan. "It will reflect unfairly on those who do measure up. Besides, does the public's right to know really outweigh the damage to the navy's credibility that might result? There are still plenty of critics out there—and not just a few within the navy itself—who would like to bring an end to gender equity within the services. This report, despite its highly qualified nature, could provide a lot of ammunition for our detractors. And in the process it might even hurt our recruiting efforts if women believe they are being stigmatized by suspicions of preferential treatment. Even if we publicly confess our sins and promise improvements in our flight-training procedures, there will always be a lingering suspicion that we are providing preferential treatment to female pilot trainees."

Admiral Washington had had such spirited discussions with his staff members before and was never disappointed in their candid assessments of the available options. He particularly appreciated their abstention from ideological imperatives and their pragmatism in balancing the public's interest in receiving information with the military's demand for confidentiality. As a navy public affairs officer, Washington had never viewed the media as enemy terrain and had counseled his superiors in the necessity of cooperating, when possible, with inquisitive reporters.

On the other hand, he accepted the control of the flow of information about military training and preparedness to be a legitimate role for a public affairs officer. It was his job to provide intelligence that met the standards of accuracy and fairness without unduly harming the navy's credibility. As he pondered the recommendation that he would offer to Admiral McAlister, Nathaniel Washington wondered whether releasing this confidential report would comport with this demanding standard.

THE CASE STUDY

Military public affairs operatives are like other public relations professionals in that they must balance the interests of their employers against the public's need to know. However, unlike public relations practitioners who work for the private sector, Admiral Washington is a public employee, although the needs of the military are admittedly different from those of other government agencies. When Admiral Washington synthesizes the views of his two subordinates, the concerns will come down to these: On the one hand, the CNO's confidential report reflects unfavorably on the navy because it does document incidents of gender norming to increase the number of female pilots in the cockpits of the FA-18. But the report is highly qualified in that it (1) contradicts earlier reports of mechanical failures and (2) shows a correlation but *not* a cause and effect in individual cases between gender norming and operational mishaps with the fighter aircraft. When put into context, the report reflects unfairly on those women pilots who have performed admirably. There is a danger that the media will focus on the most damaging aspect of the report, the documented cases of gender norming.

On the other hand, the fact that this report, based on more in-depth interviews with flight instructors, contradicts earlier published reports of mechanical failure is significant, and release of this information could actually enhance the navy's credibility by setting the record straight. By the same token, if the report is leaked the service's credibility could suffer.

What recommendation should Rear Admiral Washington make to his superior officer? For the purpose of responding to this question, assume the role of Admiral Washington and, using the model for moral reasoning outlined in Chapter 3, render a judgment in this matter.

CASE 6-5

Attorney–Client Privilege and the Public's Right to Know

The FBI was still basking in the publicity of its latest law enforcement triumph. Mohammed Ahmed, who had been indicted in absentia for masterminding the bombing of the Empire State Building just three years prior to 9/11, had finally returned to confront his accusers. Ahmed, a Palestinian by birth, had been a rather shadowy figure and a minor player on the international stage of terrorism until he had publicly claimed credit for the brutal bombing of a commercial jetliner over Greece in February 1995, which had resulted in the deaths of 325 passengers and crew. Ahmed was subsequently linked to a rather obscure Iranian-sponsored fundamentalist group committed to the destruction of Israel and its Western supporters.

But Ahmed apparently had not been content to confine his terrorist activities to the Middle East and Europe. According to the FBI, he had slipped undetected through U.S. customs using a fake passport and had quickly organized a group of followers who had preceded him. Their goal was to carry out attacks on symbols of American power and prestige and to humiliate their antagonists in their own backyard. The Empire State Building was the first of several landmarks targeted by Ahmed's group, but the mission had not been entirely successful. Although the first two floors of the structure were gutted in the explosion that killed three people, the edifice remained defiantly intact in response to this unprovoked assault.

An FBI informant fingered Ahmed as the mastermind behind this plot, and the agency moved quickly to take him into custody. However, even as his lieutenants were planting the bomb in a remote corner of the Empire State Building, the elusive Ahmed had crossed the border into Canada and returned to his base of operations in the Middle East. Within a few weeks the FBI had compiled enough evidence on Ahmed to link him to the crime, and a grand jury indicted the terrorist for his role in the bombing. The State Department was determined to bring Ahmed to justice and offered a $2 million reward for information that would lead to his arrest.

This rather lucrative financial incentive soon produced results, as an informant in Pakistan, motivated more by self-interest than principle, led police to a local hotel where Ahmed had registered under an assumed name. The Pakistanis were anxious to rid themselves of this controversial guest and quickly extradited the terrorist to the United States and into the custody of the FBI.

Ahmed was housed in a maximum security cell just a few blocks from where the bombing that had led to his arrest occurred. He was arraigned before a federal magistrate in New York, who appointed an Arab-speaking attorney, Yassir Assad, to represent the unrepentant defendant. During the next several weeks, Assad met repeatedly with Ahmed in an effort to forge a meaningful attorney–client relationship and to plan an aggressive defense against what Assad believed was a rather dubious chain of evidence against the accused.

As the trial date approached, the media prepared for the high drama that was sure to emerge as Mohammed Ahmed was given his constitutional right to due process. Network reporter Daniel Thorn was among those journalists who eagerly awaited the jury selection process, which would signal the official beginning of the trial. Thorn had paid his dues as a foreign correspondent for twelve years in the Middle East and was culturally attuned to, if not a master of, the rather mysterious workings of the Arab fundamentalist mind. He had never met Ahmed, but during his tenure in the Persian Gulf region, he had often visited the breeding grounds of such religious and political fanatics. Since his return to his homeland, his fascination with and revulsion of state-sponsored terrorism remained undiminished.

Thorn was looking forward to his journalistic role in this high-profile drama and had prepared thoroughly for his engagement. Three weeks before the commencement of the trial, the veteran correspondent was reviewing some notes in his New York office when he received a call from a government source, Jacob Marley, who had often supplied Thorn with inside information. Marley again asked for a meeting with Thorn.

"I have something you might be interested in," said Marley as he sipped a cup of black coffee in a diner just a few blocks from network headquarters. "You're covering the Ahmed case, aren't you?" Thorn responded affirmatively to what he considered a rhetorical question.

"The government has been monitoring the conversations between Ahmed and his attorney," continued Marley. "I'm sure they know nothing about this. I have dubs of two of the tapes here. I don't know if they contain anything interesting. Most of it's in Arabic. But you can have it translated."

As usual, Thorn did not inquire into how Marley had acquired the tapes. In the past Marley had been a valuable source of information, and he was confident that this instance would prove to be no exception. Thorn retreated to what he often described as the organized chaos of the network newsroom, where he found Joel Silverman, the executive producer of the evening news, huddled with several writers. He briefly described his journalistic coup to Silverman. The producer was impressed but immediately recognized the ethical and legal implications of the network's use of these surreptitious recordings. Silverman asked for a meeting with Malcolm Sikes, whose position as news division president compelled a divided loyalty between the journalistic imperative and corporate responsibility. Unfortunately, sometimes the two seemed incompatible.

Sikes, Silverman, and Thorn were joined in the meeting by a translator, who was also a network consultant on the Middle East. They listened intently as the recordings disclosed, often in barely audible tones, the confidential conversations in Arabic between Ahmed and his attorney in his maximum security residence. The two tapes, which ran for a total of ninety minutes, focused primarily

on the credibility of two government witnesses, both of whom had been former lieutenants of the accused terrorist. Apparently Assad had succeeded in forging a bond of trust with his reluctant client as Ahmed chattered incessantly and candidly about his relationship with those he termed "traitors." There was no admission of guilt on the tapes, but on two occasions he expressed sympathy for the holy war being waged against the "enemies of Palestine" and repeatedly accused his former associates of duplicity in attempting to undermine his leadership among his fundamentalist followers. To his attorney, Ahmed denied any involvement in the bombing of the Empire State Building.

Sikes finally broke the silence. "You're sure these tapes are authentic?" he asked Thorn.

"Yes. I got them from a source who has always proved to be reliable in the past. And I recognize the voices on the tape. In addition, since receiving these tapes I've heard through other contacts that the feds have been monitoring the conversations between Assad and Ahmed."

"The tapes are quite interesting," replied Sikes. "I don't know whether Ahmed is telling the truth, but these conversations really raise some interesting questions about the credibility of the government's two key witnesses. But if we air these tapes, we could be asking for trouble."

"But these recordings provide a rare glimpse into the defense strategy in this case," responded Thorn. "The FBI, at least publicly, has always maintained that a conviction is a virtual certainty. But the defense apparently plans to attack the credibility of the two key witnesses. If they succeed, this case could come apart. The FBI has other circumstantial evidence, but in my judgment these witnesses are crucial to their case. I think these tapes are newsworthy. They relate to a high-profile case—the public interest here is high."

"I'm not so sure," said Sikes, who held a law degree but had never joined the legal fraternity. "This could be a violation of the attorney–client privilege. This network did not actually monitor these conversations—that was the government's misconduct—but if we air these tapes, we'll certainly have to share part of the blame. And we could take a public beating on this, especially from the legal profession. And they won't have any trouble catching the attention of our competitors and our print brethren."

"But like you said, we didn't make these recordings," replied Silverman. "If Assad has a complaint, he should direct it against the government. These tapes provide a rare insight into this case even before it goes to trial. Our job should not be to worry about the attorney–client privilege. The breach of confidentiality occurred when the recordings were made. But this case—every aspect of it—is a matter of public interest. We shouldn't be in the business of suppressing relevant and newsworthy information relating to such an important story."

"Exactly where is the public interest?" asked Sikes rather testily. He didn't disagree with Silverman entirely, but he felt compelled to play devil's advocate out of allegiance to his managerial responsibilities. "Ahmed may be a despicable human being to the average American, but he is still entitled to a fair trial. And that's what the public interest really is. I don't see any compelling news value in violating attorney–client privilege and airing part of the defense strategy on national TV. There will be plenty of grist for the journalistic mill as the trial unfolds."

But Thorn was persistent. "But there's more to this story than just this confidential conversation. Doesn't the public have a right to know about possible government misconduct in prosecuting this case?"

Sikes conceded that both points of view had merit. The tapes did add a dimension to this story that would certainly be of interest to the network's viewers—an inside look at the defense strategy—as well as the government's role in monitoring the conversations between Ahmed and his attorney. On the other hand, if they aired the tapes, the news division would become a major player in this breach of confidentiality. The network could suffer a public relations debacle. In addition, Sikes wondered whether Ahmed's emotional and often fanatical recorded comments contributed much to the underlying search for truth that is the cornerstone of the American justice system. While the accused terrorist and his attorney continued their preparations for the trial unaware of this breach in their privileged relationship, the head of a premier news organization wondered whether the public's need to know was sufficient to justify this violation of the attorney–client privilege.

THE CASE STUDY

The attorney–client privilege represents one of the most strongly defended confidential relationships in American society. It is considered fundamental to our system of justice. However, in this case the news organization is not responsible for the initial violation of the attorney–client privilege. The government, apparently without the knowledge of Ahmed and his attorney, secretly monitored their conversations, and these tapes wound up in the hands of the network. Are the networks also guilty of exacerbating the problem by airing these tapes to a national TV audience? Malcolm Sikes, the news division president, questions whether the network should participate in this breach of confidentiality. After all, *both* the government's alleged misconduct and the broadcasting of these confidential conversations might adversely affect Ahmed's constitutional guarantee of a fair trial. He is also concerned about the public relations fallout from what some might perceive as journalistic arrogance in the handling of this matter.

But the network's correspondent, Daniel Thorn, is less concerned with the constitutional implications and the intricacies of the attorney–client privilege than with what he feels is the journalistic imperative to evaluate the newsworthiness of the recorded conversations themselves and to accommodate the public's need to know about alleged government misconduct in the case.

As noted earlier in this chapter, confidentiality is a prima facie duty that can be overridden only by other, weightier considerations; thus, the burden of proof is generally on those who wish to override it. Can the network justify its participation in this breach of the attorney–client privilege on some overriding moral principle? Respond to this question by assuming the role of news division president Malcolm Sikes and, applying the formula for moral reasoning outlined in Chapter 3, decide whether the network is ethically justified in breaching the attorney–client privilege between Yassir Assad and his controversial client.

> ▶ **CASE 6-6**

Client Confidentiality in Radio Sales

Brad Dillon was not a happy camper! As the general sales manager of North Hampton's only adult contemporary FM radio station, often promoted and identified simply as 106 FM, he had presided over a financial malaise as his staff struggled to extricate themselves from the recession that had ravaged his city's economy for almost two years. Local merchants had responded to this economic downturn by trimming advertising expenditures, a move that had contributed significantly to the budgetary austerity of the media. Dillon had watched solemnly as revenues fell, along with staff morale, and as sales quotas had to be adjusted downward to accommodate more realistic expectations.

But as the dog days of summer approached, the economic benchmarks began to show signs of a gradual recovery, and the station's clients reassessed their rather fragile disbursements for advertising. The most optimistic clients, in Dillon's view, were the automobile dealers who relished the prospect of an economic recovery as the new car models made their debut in the early fall. During the summer, the current stock had begun to move swiftly off the lots, and North Hampton's car merchants were looking forward to the arrival of the latest in automotive craftsmanship from Detroit, Japan, and Germany.

The significance of the automobile clients to the station's recovery was evident in Dillon's weekly staff meeting in early August, devoted almost exclusively to two of their most loyal clients. "Let's begin with the Brian-Miller and McKay accounts," Dillon said as he surveyed the meeting room expectantly. Brian-Miller Toyota and John McKay Chrysler-Plymouth had been two of the station's most lucrative accounts until two years ago, and Dillon appreciated their allegiance. He also knew that their expenditures for the first six months of the new model year would be an important ingredient in the station's own economic recovery. He quickly focused on Rashaneka Brown and Mark Todson as they opened their clients' sales portfolios. Todson handled the Brian-Miller account, and

Brown had adroitly courted John McKay in adding McKay's dealership to her impressive account list.

"I'm having a problem with my client," Todson said. "Jason Miller makes most of the budgetary decisions for the dealership. He decides how much they will spend on advertising. But as you know he cut back a couple of years ago. Miller is apparently concerned that his dealership will not share in the recovery. American models are now more popular than ever—foreign dealers are having to play catch-up. Miller says he wants to wait awhile before increasing his advertising budget."

"Then we need to change that," responded Dillon optimistically. "After all, McKay is a major competitor—and they're coming back into the market in a big way. Because the car dealers will be instrumental in the economic recovery here in North Hampton, we need to develop a comprehensive strategy that will help them—and, of course, convince them to devote a large chunk of their advertising budget to advertising on 106 FM."

"I'm not sure what you mean by a 'comprehensive strategy,'" replied Brown defensively. "I'm not keen about discussing my client's campaign in a meeting like this, even if it is among our own staff. I realize that knowledge of McKay's advertising plan might help Rashaneka sell Brian-Miller and develop a campaign for her client. It could certainly help Brian-Miller to become competitive again, and this would send some advertising dollars our way. But I have a problem with this from an ethical standpoint."

"But this is all in-house," said Todson. "It's not as though we're divulging privileged information to another station or agency. We're trying to do what's best for all of our clients. And if they win, we win! How can we plan strategy in helping to sell our clients' products—clients that are in the same business—without some coordination among ourselves and the sharing of information?"

"That *is* a problem," acknowledged Brown. "But much of the information provided to me by Brian McKay—much of what I know about his business—is confidential. There's a bond of trust between us. Of course, we're all working for a common purpose. But we should not use inside information from one client to gain a sales advantage with a competitor."

"But how is McKay Chrysler-Plymouth being hurt?" asked Todson. "Their campaign will stand on its own merits. And if we use what we know about their plan to help Brian-Miller, then another of our clients will benefit. After all, the real choice will be made in the marketplace; the consumer will decide. The effectiveness of these campaigns will reside in the creative aspect—that is, how good a job they do selling automobiles. If we can use some confidential information about one client to help another, then I don't see a real ethical dilemma here."

Dillon listened intently to this debate. Brown was one of his most productive account executives, and he respected her views. She obviously saw a clear ethical dilemma in revealing her client's plans in a sales meeting. On the other hand, Todson apparently viewed this as more of a simple business decision than an ethical dilemma. The objective, in Todson's view, was to develop a comprehensive plan to benefit all clients—and if this meant using some confidential information, then so be it. And because all the information remained in-house, then Todson did not see this as an ethical breach. The loyalty, therefore, should be between client and station—not between the client and the individual account executive.

With some time remaining before the arrival of the new car models, Dillon decided to put off further discussion of this issue until the next meeting. These assemblies were usually devoted to discussions about client problems, selling techniques, rates, and promotions. But now a moral dimension had intruded into these strategy sessions. Dillon's responsibility was to improve his station's financial posture, and the automobile clients would be important to his mission. As he prepared for his next staff meeting, he pondered his loyalties to the various parties directly implicated in this ethical decision: his clients, other advertisers, his station, and the sales staff.

THE CASE STUDY

Is it unethical to use knowledge about one advertiser's business and campaign to obtain an order from another client or to construct a campaign for that client? When an advertiser signs a contract with an account executive and provides information

to that salesperson, a special relationship develops in which the client has a right to expect that the station's representative will operate in the client's best interest. Does that include not divulging confidential information among members of the same sales staff?

In this case, Rashaneka Brown argues that it is a breach of confidentiality to reveal strategies and campaign plans during a sales meeting. To do so, she says, is a violation of the account executive–client relationship analogous to the attorney–client privilege or the doctor–patient relationship.

Mark Todson doesn't see it that way. He believes that the bond of confidentiality is between the advertiser and the station, not the individual account executive and the client. He also believes that some knowledge of the client's plans is essential both to the station's overall sales strategy and as a means for helping the client's competitors who advertise on the same station.

For the purpose of examining this dilemma, assume the role of the general sales manager of 106 FM and, using the SAD formula, render an ethical judgment on this issue.

 CASE 6-7

The Student Newspaper and Faculty Evaluations

As a senior at Southwestern State University, Jonathan Southall was feeling more impoverished than he had as an entering freshman. For four years he had subsisted on a series of low-interest student loans and the meager income from his part-time job as a waiter. But each year Southall watched helplessly as the relentless tuition increases exceeded the cost of inflation, further eroding his confidence in the administration's financial management capabilities. Southall did not dispute the chancellor's defense that competitive salaries, funded in part by the tuition hikes, were essential to attracting and keeping quality faculty. He was not convinced, however, that the tuition increases had been accompanied by a comparable increase in the quality of education.

But now, as the newly elected president of the Student Government Association (SGA), Southall demanded accountability. He had been elected overwhelmingly on a platform committed, among other things, to "opening up" the faculty evaluation process and publicizing the results of the student surveys required in all courses at the end of each semester. Within the first two weeks of his nine-month tenure as SGA president, Southall moved expeditiously to fulfill his passionate campaign promise. However, his overtures to the university's administration were rebuffed, as they invoked various claims of confidentiality, privacy rights, and academic freedom. "The faculty evaluation results are for the eyes of administrators and faculty only," said the vice chancellor for academic affairs in summarily dismissing Southall's initiative. "They are used in the university's tenure and promotion process and that ensures sufficient accountability to Southwestern's teaching mission." She also cited a court decision four years ago that, in effect, exempted faculty evaluations from the coverage of the state's public records law.

Undeterred by what he perceived as the administration's cloak of secrecy designed to protect the substandard performance records of some of the university's faculty, Southall continued to pressure the chancellor's office through statements made to the SGA that were dutifully reported in the student newspaper. His flirtation with liberalism, albeit on a rather modest scale, had challenged one of the university's sacred cows. He acknowledged to his political allies in the SGA that his campaign might not produce instant intellectual gratification, but he would not be denied his day in the court of public opinion.

If the Southwestern State administration did not share Southall's unbridled enthusiasm for complete faculty accountability, Felicia Cobb did. Cobb was the *Watchdog*'s SGA correspondent and was an unapologetic advocate for openness in government (and that included student government) and public accountability. She believed strongly that her classmates had a right to know how their peers assessed the faculty's pedagogical handiwork.

Andrew Jenner thought so, too. Jenner was a graduate assistant assigned to work in the Office of Data Processing and Retrieval, which was responsible for feeding the results of the faculty evaluations into the university's mainframe computer.

Cobb was intrigued when Jenner contacted her in her dorm and requested a clandestine rendezvous in a coffeehouse just off campus. "Shades of Watergate," she thought, recalling the historical accounts of the clandestine meetings and anonymous sources surrounding the downfall of the Nixon presidency.

Jenner was nervous but got right to the point. "I support Southall's campaign to release the results of the faculty evaluations," he began. "But that'll never happen, at least not in the near future. I feel strongly that we students have a right to know. This is all the data on the individual faculty evaluations," he told Cobb pointing to a package in his hand. "I have access to this information in my position as a graduate assistant. You can have this on the condition that you not reveal the source. If my department head finds out, I'll lose my assistantship and be kicked out of school." Cobb readily agreed. The young student reporter was only too eager to indulge Jenner's request for anonymity as she savored her journalistic triumph.

"I've finally recovered from my bout with information overload," Cobb told Lyle MacArthur, the student editor of the *Watchdog*. "There are more than 1,200 faculty included in this survey from last semester, and most of them taught two or three courses. We can publish the results in a tab insert, and then include a story highlighting the results in a front-page story." The paper's faculty adviser, Richard Hammock, wasn't sure the evaluations should be published at all.

"We'll take a lot of heat from the administration *and* the faculty if we publish these faculty evaluations," stated Hammock matter-of-factly three days before the scheduled publication date in a hastily arranged meeting with MacArthur, Cobb, and student managing editor Amanda Tedrick. "The results of these evaluations are supposed to be confidential."

"I have no doubt that we'll be under a lot of pressure," acknowledged Cobb. "But the students have a right to know about the quality of teaching at this university and how their classmates rate their teachers. This is one factor that students use in choosing their classes, particularly when they have a choice of more than one instructor."

"This may be true," said Tedrick. "But why is this news? Even if we assume that students have an interest in knowing how their teachers rate, I'm not sure that the results of the faculty evaluations are newsworthy. There's even some doubt as to their reliability. I'm a senior, and I've filled out these forms faithfully every semester. But quite frankly, I'm convinced that the way students evaluate their teachers is related to the difficulty of instruction. That may not be true in all cases, but there's certainly a tendency in that direction. The point is that faculty evaluations are inexact. I doubt that the results necessarily identify the good or the bad teachers. There too many other factors involved. Such surveys sometimes are nothing more than popularity contests that do not necessarily measure teaching effectiveness."

"That may be true," acknowledged MacArthur, who was impressed by his reporter's enterprise, "but it's not our job to be concerned about whether these surveys measure teaching effectiveness. The only issue is what students think of their teachers. And this university has made the results of these surveys a part of the tenure and promotion process. And because the quality of faculty affects all students, that makes these surveys newsworthy."

"I am concerned about how we acquired this information," said Hammock. "The university has determined that these evaluations should be confidential. We haven't done anything illegal, but the publication of these survey results will violate university policy. And it could cause a rift between the faculty and the administration concerning a lack of security for what the faculty assumed was confidential information."

"That's not our problem," countered Cobb. "If we believe the students have a right to know this information, then we should publish it. The professional media often publish confidential information if there is a legitimate public interest in doing so. What makes us so different?"

"We are different," responded Hammock, "because of the relationship of the *Watchdog*'s staff. You are all students, and the faculty still hold the keys to your academic future here. This could blow over, and perhaps there won't be any retribution. But most of our paper's staff are enrolled in journalism courses. A professor whose evaluations

are poor could find ways to retaliate. In that respect, our reporters do not stand in the same relationship as the professional media in terms of the newsworthy individuals they cover."

"That could be a problem," agreed Tedrick. "Of course, I don't believe our paper should avoid controversy just because it makes the administration unhappy. Otherwise, we lose credibility with our readers. On the other hand, if we break the rules, we're putting ourselves into an adversarial relationship with the administration *and* the faculty. They provide much of our information. The fact is that we breached the confidentiality of these evaluations. The faculty have always assumed that they would be seen only by the department chairs and deans."

"It's true that we gained access to confidential information and in so doing perhaps we broke the rules," said Cobb, who was a true believer in the people's right to know. "But these evaluations are paid for by public funds. In addition, we pay tuition and have a right to demand accountability. In covering the SGA, I have discovered that there is a great deal of concern about recent tuition hikes, but there's a perception that the quality of education hasn't improved. We're the voice of student expression. It's our responsibility to look into these questions. And the only measure of teaching effectiveness currently employed to evaluate professors is this student survey."

"It's your call," Hammock said to MacArthur. "You're the editor. As the faculty adviser, I have no control over what you publish. I can only advise. All I ask is that you weigh the benefits—that is, the news value of these evaluations—against the potential harm of releasing this confidential information."

Although the editor had sided with Felicia Cobb during this rather intriguing discussion, he now found his role as moral agent more challenging. Because the faculty evaluations were confidential under university policy and academic freedom and professional reputations were perhaps at stake, MacArthur knew that the burden of proof was on the student newspaper to justify any breach of confidentiality on the grounds of newsworthiness or public interest. In addition, he harbored no illusions concerning the consequences of publishing these evaluations: The access that the *Watchdog* had enjoyed to sources in the upper administration would evaporate. Of course, that was the risk that any newspaper confronted in offending their news sources.

It was true that the surveys were conducted at taxpayer expense and that his classmates had a vested interest in the quality of their educational experience at Southwestern State University. But student grades were also the product of a heavy investment of public funds and yet were confidential. What was the difference? he wondered. As a student, would he be happy if his grades were available for public inspection?

In confronting the ethical dimensions of publishing this confidential information, MacArthur was troubled by his conflicting loyalties. As a student, he had faithfully filled out these student questionnaires each semester, and he believed that he had the right to see the results. But he was a participant in the process, not an entirely disinterested observer. His role as a journalist-in-training also propelled him in the direction of disclosure, but unlike most professional journalists, MacArthur was a part of the institution whose policies favoring confidentiality were about to be breached. Nevertheless, the *Watchdog* was a student newspaper independent of administration control. It was supported by student fees and advertising, not state funds. The paper owed its primary allegiance to its student readers. And undoubtedly this information would be helpful to students in selecting their professors and courses. But he wondered whether even this justification was sufficient to overcome the officially imposed shroud of secrecy surrounding the faculty evaluation process at Southwestern State University.

THE CASE STUDY

Most colleges and universities do not release the results of student evaluations of individual faculty members, although student governments sometimes conduct their own surveys and publish the results. School administrators view confidentiality of such material as essentially a personnel matter predicated upon privacy and academic freedom concerns. But such a system can also conceal substandard performance records by public employees. Thus, students might argue that they have a

vested interest in the quality of their education and a right to know how their professors measure up in the classroom.

In this scenario, both university policy and the state's public records law (as interpreted by the courts) exempt faculty evaluations from disclosure. In addition, in most cases involving confidentiality, the party seeking disclosure must carry the burden of proof. Thus, the *Watchdog*'s moral claim in support of its decision to publish this information—particularly because it was obtained through an anonymous source—must be based on some overriding principle. Although the promise of confidentiality and the circumstances under which the paper received the material also raise ethical concerns, these issues are not central to this case study, since they are a fait accompli.

In contemplating his decision, the editor, Lyle MacArthur, might consider the following questions: (1) Are the results of the individual faculty evaluations a matter of public interest? (2) Are students entitled to this information because the surveys are publicly funded? (3) Are the students entitled to this information because they pay tuition and have a right to demand accountability? (4) Should the paper decline to publish the evaluation results because they are an inaccurate barometer of the quality of teaching, or is the fact that they are taken seriously by the administration in their tenure and promotion decisions sufficient justification for reporting students' collective opinions regarding the quality of their instruction?

For the purpose of resolving this ethical dilemma, assume the role of student editor Lyle MacArthur and then, using the moral reasoning model outlined in Chapter 3, render a judgment on whether you will publish the results of Southwestern State University's faculty evaluations.

Notes

1. See Maureen Dowd, "The Spy Who Loved Him," *New York Times*, October 2, 2003, Section A, p. 31.
2. Fred Brown, "Anonymity Hurts Reporters and Politicians," *Quill*, December 2003, p. 38.
3. Steven R. Knowlton, *Moral Reasoning for Journalists: Cases and Commentary* (Westport, CT: Praeger, 1997), pp. 74–75.

4. "California, North Carolina Reporters Held in Contempt," *News Media and the Law,* Winter 1999, p. 4. This order was stayed pending an appeal.

5. Nancy J. Moore, "Limits to Attorney–Client Confidentiality: A Philosophically Informed and Comparative Approach to Legal and Medical Ethics," *Case Western Law Review* 36 (1985–1986): 191.

6. Sissela Bok, "The Limits of Confidentiality," in Joan C. Callahan (ed.), *Ethical Issues in Professional Life* (New York: Oxford University Press, 1988), p. 232.

7. For a more thorough discussion of these categories of confidentiality, see Ron F. Smith, *Groping for Ethics in Journalism,* 5th ed. (Ames: Iowa State University Press, 2003), pp. 179–181.

8. For an interesting discussion of the reporter–source relationship, see John L. Hulteng, *The Messenger's Motives: Ethical Problems of the News Media,* 2d ed. (Upper Saddle River, NJ: Prentice-Hall, 1985), pp. 79–96.

9. Smith, *Groping for Ethics in Journalism,* p. 180.

10. Otis Baskin and Craig Aronoff, *Public Relations: The Profession and the Practice,* 3d ed. (Dubuque, IA: Brown, 1992), pp. 90–91.

11. Ibid., p. 91.

12. Maurice Van Gerpen, *Privileged Communications and the Press* (Westport, CT: Greenwood, 1979), p. 171. In recent years, some courts have held that agreements of confidentiality between reporter and source constitute an enforceable contract. See *Cohen v. Cowles Media Co.,* 16 Med. L. Rptr. 2209 (1989).

13. *Butterworth v. Smith,* 17 Med. L. Rptr. 1569 (1990).

14. Bok, "Limits of Confidentiality," p. 231.

15. Ibid., pp. 232–234.

16. Sissela Bok, *Secrets: On the Ethics of Concealment and Revelation* (New York: Pantheon, 1982), p. 19.

17. Ibid., p. 249.

18. Cornelius B. Pratt, "Hill & Knowlton's Two Ethical Dilemmas," *Public Relations Review* 20 (1994): 286.

19. Susanne A. Roschwalb, "The Hill & Knowlton Cases: A Brief on the Controversy," *Public Relations Review* 20 (1994): 271.

20. Ibid.

21. Pratt, "Hill & Knowlton's Two Ethical Dilemmas," p. 287.

22. Roschwalb, "The Hill & Knowlton Cases," pp. 271–272.

23. See Ross E. Milloy, "Writer Who Was Jailed in Notes Dispute Is Freed," *New York Times,* January 5, 2002, Section A, p. 8; David D. Kirkpatrick, "Book Contract for Writer Jailed for Contempt," *New York Times,* April 30, 2002, Section A, p. 26.

24. Bok, *Secrets,* p. 264.

25. *Branzburg v. Hayes,* 408 U.S. 665 (1972).

26. Ibid., p. 743 (Stewart, J., dissenting).

27. Van Gerpen, *Privileged Communications,* p. 172.

28. For a discussion of this case, see Alicia C. Shepard, "The Reporter and the Hit Man," *American Journalism Review,* April 2001, pp. 18–27.

29. Quoted in ibid., p. 23.

30. Quoted in ibid.

31. Quoted in ibid., p. 24.

32. For an examination of one newspaper's approach to this problem, see Richard P. Cunningham, "Should Reporters Reveal Sources to Editors?" *Quill,* October 1988, pp. 6–8.

33. See Jeffrey Olen, *Ethics in Journalism* (Upper Saddle River, NJ: Prentice-Hall, 1988), pp. 40–41.

34. For a discussion of the reciprocal nature of the reporter–source relationship, see Stephen Klaidman and Tom L. Beauchamp, *The Virtuous Journalist* (New York: Oxford University Press, 1987), pp. 163–177.

35. Monica Langley and Lee Levine, "Broken Promises," *Columbia Journalism Review,* July/August 1988, p. 21.

36. "Sources Disclosed by Reporter, Spouse Loses Job," *News Media and the Law,* Fall 1999, pp. 21–22.

37. Ibid., p. 22.

38. Howard Weaver, "Unnamed Problem," *Fineline,* November/December 1990, p. 7.

39. Lori Robertson, "Body Slam," *American Journalism Review,* May 1999, pp. 53–56.

40. Ibid., p. 55.

41. The idea for this case is derived from a case decided several years ago by the Minnesota News Council (*In the Matter of the Complaint of Roy Carlson,* who was mayoral candidate in Savage against the Savage Pacer). This case can be accessed at the Council's home page: http://www.mtn.org/~newscncl/

7

Conflicts of Interest

CONFLICTS OF INTEREST: REAL AND IMAGINED

As Fox News Channel reported election results on the night of November 7, 2000, John Ellis, director of the channel's decision desk, was on the phone with Republican candidate George W. Bush and Jeb Bush, the governor of Florida, a pivotal state in the presidential race. Ellis was the executive responsible for collating and analyzing the exit poll information used to determine the winners in each state. He is also a first cousin to the Bush brothers. In the aftermath of the election, Bob Steele, director of the ethics program at the Poynter Institute, a journalism training and research center, described Ellis's position as one of "irreconcilable competing loyalty." Marvin Kalb of Harvard's Shorenstein Center on the Press, Politics, and Public Policy said he was "surprised" and "dismayed" that Ellis remained in contact with the Bushes while working at Fox News.[1] Fox executives said they had been unaware of the contact but acknowledged that "Mr. Ellis had misused his role with the network, perhaps damaging its reputation."[2]

Several years before this election night ethical indiscretion, the usually conservative National Conference of Catholic Bishops, disturbed by the growing number of pro-choice church members, solicited the help of Hill & Knowlton, the nation's largest public relations firm, to help recruit antiabortion Catholics and non-Catholics. When it was discovered that Hill & Knowlton also represented organizations that support abortion rights, the firm's management was accused of violating Article 10 of the code of the Public Relations Society of America (PRSA), which prohibited a member from representing "conflicting or competing interests without the express consent of those concerned after a full disclosure of the facts."[3] Hill & Knowlton was also castigated by many of its female employees for accepting an assignment "whose ultimate goal is to limit our fundamental rights."[4]

Conflicting loyalties were also at issue in March 2002 when the *Wall Street Journal* reported that recently retired GE chief executive Jack Welch had had an affair with Suzy Wetlaufer, a divorcee who edited the *Harvard Business Review*. Several of the magazine's senior editors asked her to step down, and Wetlaufer resigned after conceding that "she had lost the confidence of her colleagues."[5]

These three seemingly unrelated events share one of the most troublesome ethical terrains for media practitioners: conflict of interest. Simply stated, a *conflict of interest* is a clash between professional loyalties and outside interests that undermines the credibility of the moral agent.

Conflicts generally arise from the roles we play within society and, for that reason, appear to involve *particularistic* duties (see Chapter 2) rather than our general societal obligations. Unlike the value of truth, there does not appear to be any all-encompassing moral rule urging our consciences to reject all conflicts of interest. A reporter, for example, should avoid endorsing political causes, but the rest of us are not so constrained.

It is tempting, therefore, to say that divided loyalties do not involve any fundamental moral values. Our parents tell us never to lie, cheat, or steal. They say nothing about conflicts of interest. The fact is, however, that a conflict of interest raises some basic questions concerning fairness and justice, two important and fundamental values. A judge who owns stock in a company accused of violating the antitrust laws, for example, could not be counted on to conduct a fair and impartial trial. Likewise, a reporter who is married to a city official might be tentative in uncovering governmental corruption at the local level.

Many news organizations have specific policies relating to conflicts of interest, such as banning the acceptance of perquisites and freebies from news sources or the participation in political and community organizations by members of the editorial staff. The professional codes also admonish media practitioners to avoid conflicts of interest. The code of the PRSA, for example, prohibits members from representing conflicting or competing interests without the express consent of those involved or from placing themselves in a position in which the member's interest might conflict with those of a client. The code of the Society of Professional Journalists (SPJ) reflects a concern with *potential* conflicts of interest, as well as actual conflicts, when it observes that journalists should avoid conflicts of interest, "real or perceived." The SPJ code also discourages secondary employment, political involvement, holding public office, or service in community organizations if it compromises journalistic integrity.

Some are troubled by the sweeping nature of these restrictions and believe that they are not required by our ethical system. Jeffrey Olen, for one, writing in *Ethics in Journalism,* has this to say about the code's pronouncement: "If media organizations wish to adopt that policy in order

to protect an enhanced image of trustworthiness to their audiences, that is one thing. But such a policy is not morally required. All that is morally required is that journalists, like anyone else, be trustworthy."[6] What Olen ignores is that even the appearance of impropriety can undermine the credibility of moral agents in the eyes of an ever-skeptical public. A music critic who accepts free tickets to an opera may be perfectly capable of writing a detached and objective account of a performance, but readers will have lingering doubts.

Olen is right about one thing, however. The appearance of conflict is often difficult to avoid. And there are reasonable or acceptable conflicts of interest that do not necessarily undermine the credibility of the moral agent. But at a minimum the public should be apprised of the situation. A case in point is the control that professional baseball teams often exercise over the selection of announcers to broadcast their games on local stations. This fact is made known to the audience through a "disclaimer" broadcast during the game. The audience has no aversion to this practice, because it usually expects local commentators to be supportive of the home team. In other words, these announcers, like advertisers and public relations practitioners, operate with an acknowledged vested interest, and they are not expected to abandon the goals of their employers in the name of objectivity.

One problem with confronting the ethical behavior of individual media practitioners is that potential conflicts of interest begin at the top. The mass media are big business and depend on advertisers for their support. The editorial side of the ledger is beholden to the commercial side for its daily bread. And many of these advertisers, particularly large corporations, could someday be the subject of news stories. Whereas large newspapers and broadcast entities are better able to insulate their journalistic integrity from commercial pressures, smaller news operations might be forced to pull their punches to avoid coverage that would reflect unfavorably on an advertiser.

Some news organizations are also owned by parent companies whose allegiance is more to the bottom line than to journalistic independence. ABC, for example, is owned by the Walt Disney Company. Could the network's news division be expected to aggressively cover a story adverse to the interests of the Disney corporation? Perhaps, but the evidence thus far is not encouraging.[7] In a world of conglomerates the possibilities for conflicts of interest are boundless, and it becomes even more incumbent on media managers at the corporate level to be sensitive to the ethical dilemmas posed by such conflicts.

RECOGNIZING CONFLICTS: THE MOST TROUBLESOME TERRAIN

If we are to avoid conflicts—or at least learn how to deal with them—we should acknowledge them for what they are. Some people become ensnared by competing loyalties without even recognizing the ethical dimensions of their actions. Life is full of such traps awaiting the uninformed and unwary. In other cases we are aware of the potential conflict but are helpless to do anything about it. All college journalists, for example, are at the mercy of the administration. Even if administrators have limited powers of censorship over the student press, there are more subtle ways of dealing with recalcitrant student reporters, both inside and outside the classroom. Thus, there is a potential conflict between the roles of student and journalist.

Although conflicts of interest can arise in many situations, those confronting media practitioners tend to fall into three broad areas: conflicting relationships, conflicting public participation, and vested interests and hidden agendas.

Conflicting Relationships

It is always difficult to serve two masters. Our independence of action is severely limited when we are involved in conflicting relationships. The code of the PRSA, for example, admonishes its

members to avoid "actions and circumstances that may appear to compromise good business judgment or create a conflict between personal and professional interests." Advertising agencies' and public relations practitioners' primary duties are to their clients, and when conflicting loyalties intrude, their independence of action on behalf of those clients is compromised. It would clearly be a conflict of interest, for example, for a public relations firm to represent both an oil company and an environmental group in their dispute over what to do about developing a wilderness preserve. The following are examples of some of the more common conflicts confronting practicing journalists.

Gifts and "Perks." Journalists' primary responsibility is to their readers and viewers, and when they accept favors, gifts, or other special considerations from vested interests or news sources, it raises serious questions about their objectivity. Although unspectacular freebies, such as meals provided by a news source, may not be problematic, over time the reporter's professional detachment could be undermined. In the eyes of the public, the appearance of a conflict can be as damaging as the conflict itself. The mere acceptance of the thing of value raises questions about the moral agent's credibility and future independence of action, even if no favor is promised in return.

There was a time when reporters, who tended to be underpaid, less educated than they are now, and less attuned to the ethics of the profession, routinely accepted gifts from news sources. The rules, to the extent that they existed, were lax, to say the least. However, contemporary reporters are more sensitized to ethical concerns. Many news organizations have specific prohibitions against accepting gifts or anything else of value. Although the specific language of these policies may vary, a basic text on news broadcasting has captured the practical flavor of their concerns: "Reporters shouldn't accept any gifts from the people they may have to write about—no bottles of Scotch, vacations, fountain pens or dinners. Reporters don't even want to be in a position of having to distinguish between a gift and a bribe. Return them all with a polite thank you."[8]

An ethical purist might reject the idea of accepting even a cup of coffee from a news source. Although most reporters might not go this far, many now refuse to accept meals from outside parties. One of the most troublesome kinds of freebies, from an ethical point of view, is the "junket," a free trip (and perhaps food and lodging) paid for by some vested interest or a news source. The expenses-paid trip is a valuable public relations tool for some organizations, and in the past reporters have not been loath to take advantage of such offers. The movie industry and the television networks participate in the junket game to promote their new films and shows, although more and more news organizations are now paying their reporters' own way to these extravaganzas.

The public relations profession, which is the source of many of the organized media visits, is not without its ethical scruples in the matter. For example, the PRSA code requires its members "to maintain the integrity of relationships with the media, government officials, and the public" and to preserve "the free flow of unprejudicial information when giving or receiving gifts by ensuring that gifts are nominal, legal, and infrequent." Arguably, payment or other forms of compensation to a member of the media in order to obtain preferential or guaranteed news or editorial coverage in the medium would violate the spirit of this provision. However, the code does not prohibit media tours when media representatives have a legitimate news interest in the event or product under review. Trips for no purpose other than pleasure (junkets) are ethically dubious.

Reporters who travel with those they cover have also fallen prey to conflicts. Sports reporters, for example, sometimes travel with the teams they are covering, although this practice has been viewed with increasing skepticism. Some news organizations now either pay the way for their employees or require that they travel separately from the team. However, those reporters who still ride free with the team seldom reveal this fact to the public, exacerbating an already serious conflict of interest.

At one time political reporters eagerly took advantage of free rides with the candidates they were covering, but this practice has virtually disappeared.[9] The acceptance of any such gift from a candidate or any governmental agency is one of the most flagrant examples of a conflict of interest. Under such circumstances, the objectivity of the reporter immediately becomes suspect. Of course, there is an exception to any rule, and reporters operating in a war zone are usually at the mercy of the military for transportation. Such was the case in the Persian Gulf War, when journalists had to depend on the military to provide access to the combat zone, and even then under tightly controlled reporter "pools." The debate over journalistic independence and objectivity during wartime was reignited during the Iraqi invasion in the spring of 2003 when reporters, for the first time, were "embedded" with specific military units. CBS news anchor Dan Rather undoubtedly expressed the concerns of many journalists when he warned, "There's a pretty fine line between being embedded and being entombed."[10] In any event, one postwar critique concluded that, while the embed program was effective in terms of providing a unique perspective on the military operations, the coverage lacked a more comprehensive view of the war.[11]

Like any other profession, journalism has its share of perks. Some special interests try to curry favor with reporters by offering them discounts, special memberships, or other privileges. Government officials, particularly, recognize the power and influence of the press and often provide such benefits as free parking or special seating for media personnel. The executive and legislative branches of both the federal and state governments have set up press galleries and special working accommodations for reporters. Although some news organizations, having undergone an ethical revelation in the light of the Watergate scandal in the 1970s, now pay for their space in the pressrooms, many still take advantage of this perk. Perhaps they feel that such access is a right rather than a privilege and that they should not have to pay for their proximity to the seat of government.

The ethical problems with journalists accepting freebies can be summarized rather succinctly. *First*, those who offer gratuities to reporters are not motivated by mere humanistic or altruistic instincts; they want to influence coverage. *Second*, even if journalists were not influenced by freebies—which is a distinct possibility—the public might suspect that they were. *Third*, there is a certain hypocrisy in journalists exposing politicians and other power brokers who are "on the take" and yet being the recipient of perks from outside sources. *Four*, while journalists deny they can be influenced by perks and freebies, sometimes the influence can be subtle, and they can never be absolutely confident that their objectivity has not been compromised. *Finally*, there may be direct pressure from gift givers, as when movie studios invite critics to special screenings to get favorable reviews.[12]

Checkbook Journalism. Robin Wyshak had lived in relative obscurity until it was discovered that she had been the next door neighbor to Monica Lewinsky, the former White House intern who alleged she had a sexual relationship with President Clinton. Wyshak decided to cash in on her recollections of the Lewinsky family and attempted to peddle her story to, among others, *Hard Copy, Inside Edition,* the *National Enquirer, Star,* and the *Globe.*[13] Some potential news sources have become increasingly mercenary in their relations with reporters. In February 1994, for example, Jacquee Petchel, head of the investigative unit of WCCO-TV in Minneapolis, was preparing a story on dangerous doctors. When Petchel sought an interview with a woman who had sued a Minnesota doctor for malpractice in connection with the death of her

husband, the woman told Petchel she would not discuss the lawsuit without getting paid. Similarly, after the second Rodney King trial, in which several Los Angeles police officers were accused of using excessive force to subdue a speeding motorist, *Los Angeles Times* reporters were effectively excluded from posttrial interviews with certain jurors because they weren't willing to pay for them.[14] These three circumstances exemplify a practice that ethical journalists derisively refer to as *checkbook journalism.* It raises serious conflict-of-interest questions because of the traditional journalistic commitment to truth and accuracy. Paying interviewees and sources, some say, may well taint the quality of the information because of the economic motives involved. Checkbook journalism also raises questions about journalistic independence because an economic investment in information may elevate it to a position of unjustified prominence relative to other sources of information.

However, despite its recent ethical censure by mainstream journalists, paying for news is not a long-standing taboo, and in the competition of the marketplace few news enterprises are completely immune from the lure of exclusive or inside information. In 1912, for example, the *New York Times* paid $1,000 for an exclusive interview with the wireless operator of the ill-fated *Titanic.* Two decades later the Hearst Newspaper chain covered the legal bills for the defendant in the Lindbergh baby kidnapping/murder case to guarantee scoops during the trial. In the 1960s *Life* magazine was criticized by their journalistic brethren when it compensated the original Mercury astronauts for their stories.[15] Similarly, critics accused CBS News of checkbook journalism when it paid H. R. Haldeman, the most powerful and least accessible of President Nixon's convicted staff members, $100,000 for his insights into the Nixon White House and the Watergate affair.[16]

Large payments for interviews with high-profile public figures attract a lot of attention and a predictable round of criticism, even from within the media establishment itself. Check-book journalism raises the ethical hackles of some reporters and editors because it encourages the marketing of information that may not be accurate. But this criticism overlooks the fact that much of the checkbook journalism occurs in less publicized ways and involves ordinary citizens. Some news organizations, for example, have been known to pay accident victims for exclusive interviews. The commercial link to newsworthy subjects is sometimes more subtle than direct cash payments. It is not uncommon for news organizations to pay for transportation, lodging, and meals when they fly newsworthy subjects to designated locations for interviews.

Although paying sources for news or exclusive interviews is common in other parts of the world, it is still publicly disparaged (though sometimes privately practiced) among most mainstream American news organizations. But the pervasiveness of the practice among TV talk shows and in the tabloid media has certainly increased the pressure on all news organizations to conform to the economic realities of the business. In fact, many news figures now expect to be paid for their "inside information." For example, in 1994 figure skater Tonya Harding, following allegations that she conspired to injure Olympic rival Nancy Kerrigan, was paid several hundred thousand dollars for a series of exclusive interviews with *Inside Edition*.[17] Checkbook journalism certainly flourished during the O. J. Simpson media frenzy, with tabloid newspapers and TV shows picking up the tab.[18] When federal authorities laid siege to the compound of a religious cult in Waco, Texas—a siege that ended in a bloody shootout—one of the tabloid TV programs paid the mother of cult leader David Koresh for interviews. In another case, a ratings war turned into a bidding war among several programs that sought to interview several teenage boys who had formed a club that awarded points for sexual conquests of girls at their school.[19]

Competitive pressures have made the temptation to resort to the herd mentality quite

alluring, and checkbook journalism is not that uncommon even among mainstream media, although some are reluctant to acknowledge their participation. Some reporters (usually off the record) challenge the orthodoxy that investigative journalism should somehow be immune from economic reality. News is simply a commodity, they argue, not unlike a tangible product that is bought and sold in the marketplace. *Newsweek* contributing editor Gregg Easterbrook imbued this argument with an air of respectability when he described the practice as an intellectual property issue: "I don't see why professional reporters should be the only ones to profit from producing news. We in the press seem to think [people] should surrender their privacy and submit to our embarrassing questions so that we can make money off it."[20]

Nevertheless, each incident of checkbook journalism among the mainstream media sets off a new round of ethical soul-searching. In January of 2004 *U.S. News & World Report* reported that CBS's *60 Minutes* had paid Michael Jackson $1 million for an interview, apparently as a prelude to airing a Jackson gala on the network. While CBS insisted that its premier news magazine show does not pay for interviews, *U.S. News*, citing sources quoted in the *New York Times*, noted that the entertainment division had footed the bill for the interview. "No question," lamented the magazine, "CBS gains viewers, but it risks losing their respect."[21]

In the spring of 1999, ABC was taken to task for its decision to pay a friend of one of the teenage gunmen in the Columbine High School shootings $16,000 for the exclusive broadcast rights to home videos and other materials containing details about the killers. The network then aired what it referred to as an "exclusive interview" with the 18-year-old, Nathan Dykeman, on *Good Morning America*. The network did not disclose on the air that it had paid the teenager, acknowledging only that it had recently obtained the rights to his home video and other materials.[22]

Ken Bode, at the time the dean of Northwestern University's Medill School of Journalism, called the decision "exploitative" and "improper." But Tom Goldstein, the dean of Columbia University's Graduate School of Journalism, was more reserved in his assessment: "I find the whole notion of checkbook journalism very complicated. Some of the greatest photographs ever taken were by passersby or participants. It makes us uneasy that somebody is profiting from the misfortune of others, but that's what a lot of journalism is about."[23]

Perhaps! But most traditional reporters still deride checkbook journalism as nothing more than a needless capitulation of journalistic values to commercial interests. If financial incentives for gathering information become a mainstay, they argue, then news organizations will become little more than conduits for those who have an interesting story to tell.

So how can reporters who don't pay compete with those who do? Some journalists believe that the issue should be made part of the story, thus bringing to public attention the question of payment to news sources.[24] If this becomes a common tactic among investigative reporters, it could at least make for an interesting intramural squabble and might even produce some serious ethical soul-searching.

Personal Relationships. Of course, conflicts of interest do not always revolve around financial considerations, gifts, or perks. Reporters are human and sometimes develop personal relationships with or are perhaps even related to their sources. Under such circumstances, it may be difficult to maintain a sense of detachment. During a sweeps-week ratings period, for example, WTVJ-TV in Miami aired an exposé of a local chain of funeral homes. However, the series failed to mention that the reporter was the daughter of a former supplier to the chain who had been involved in a bitter business dispute with its owner.[25] Similarly, the *Columbia Journalism Review* accused *Daily Oklahoman* theater critic Franci Hart of an "amateurish

performance" for her enthusiastic appraisal of thespian newcomer Wendy Hart in a local production for her failure to acknowledge the mother–daughter relationship.[26]

Journalists must be particularly cautious if they are romantically involved with or married to a potential news source. Such was the case when an NBC correspondent became romantically involved with a presidential candidate. NBC learned of the relationship from outside sources and transferred her immediately off the campaign. Although there was no detectable bias in her reporting, the mere perception of a personal stake in the story was sufficient to merit a reassignment.[27]

Employment of more than one family member by the same organization, particularly if they work in the same department, can be viewed as an ethical problem. A city editor whose wife is a staff reporter, for example, would be under pressure from other newsroom personnel to avoid even the appearance of favored treatment. Because of the potential for conflicts of interest that might develop from these kinds of familial relationships, some institutions have nepotism policies that forbid or limit such employment practices.

The Journalist as Citizen. Amidst the emotional fervor surrounding the invasion of Iraq by the American military and its coalition partners in the spring of 2003, Peter Arnett, legendary war correspondent under contract with NBC News and MSNBC, gave an interview to Iraqi TV in which he assertively praised the courtesy of Iraqi information ministers, declared that the original war plan had "failed" because of Iraqi resistance, and asserted that reporting of civilian casualties had aided the antiwar movement. A U.S. senator accused Arnett of treason. His network employers fired him, which occasioned a demurrer from *Time* magazine that "[a]mid questions of loyalty, TV news should recall that being on 'our side' doesn't mean pandering."[28] While Arnett was assaulted with accusations of anti-American bias, *Time* detected a degree of hypocrisy in this ethical brouhaha: "The network flies a flag in its lower left-hand corner and uses the military's name for the war, Operation Iraqi Freedom, to brand its coverage."[29]

But defending one's professional principles does not always engender public approbation. In the fall of 2001, for example, Stacey Woelfel, news director for KOMU-TV in Columbia, Missouri, was caught in the ethical crossfire between what he viewed as his professional duty and what his critics viewed as his paramount responsibility as a citizen. Several days after the terrorist attacks of 9/11 Woelfel, reiterating a long-standing policy, warned staff members by e-mail against on-air displays of patriotism. Woelfel was in a particularly precarious position because KOMU-TV is owned by the University of Missouri and employs student interns year-round. The public's e-mail response to Woelfel's ethical posture was excruciatingly intemperate, ranging from accusations of unpatriotic behavior to foul language to threats. At least two advertisers withdrew their spots from KOMU, and some Republican state representatives threatened to evaluate "more carefully" the state funding for the university's School of Journalism because some journalism faculty worked at the station.[30]

Patriotism is a formidable opponent for journalists attempting both to maintain a residue of healthy skepticism and to fulfill their responsibilities of citizenship (which, incidentally, are not necessarily mutually exclusive), as evidenced in the disturbing case of 23-year-old Tom Gutting, a reporter for the *Texas City Sun*. Following the tragic events of 9/11, Gutting published a column in which he criticized President Bush's leadership in responding to the first attack on America's homeland. Gutting was subsequently fired for his journalistic impertinence, which attracted international attention and criticism from the worldwide group Reporters Without Borders concerning the security of press freedom in the United States.[31]

Gutting criticized his professional colleagues for jumping on the Bush bandwagon and not asking the tough questions expected of journalists. In his view, the red, white, and blue ribbons that adorned the lapels of many TV news anchors and the use of star-spangled newspaper logos with slogans like "America fights back" were evidence of "some sort of patriotism gone bad."[32] Gutting was not the only journalist to lose his job, prompting concerns about their employers' commitment to the First Amendment.

There is no doubt that in the weeks following the attacks American journalists had to walk a thin ethical line between serving as an uncritical conduit for information provided by the White House, State Department, and Pentagon and giving aid and comfort to the enemy or serving as a propaganda forum for Osama bin Laden and his supporters. Some critics framed the issue in terms of competing loyalties between journalists' role as an independent watchdog and their obligations as citizen patriots.[33] But are these roles mutually exclusive? A concise and reasonable response to this question was captured in this headline published in *Quill Magazine* two months after the September attacks: "Search for truth is journalism's patriotic role."[34] In other words, in a democracy the pursuit of truth and a healthy dose of skepticism and detachment are themselves acts of patriotism. While reporters must be careful not to divulge secrets that will compromise military operations or allow themselves to become pawns of terrorists, neither should they abandon their critical assessment of government policy. "It is hard to think of a time, even in the toughest moments of these past forty years," declared Michael Hoyt, executive editor of the *Columbia Journalism Review*, "when the country was more in need of an independent press that is both measured and aggressive, wise and brave."[35]

Needless to say, the events of September 11, 2001, were unique in the lives of American journalists and posed conflicting loyalties that are not common in routine news coverage. Nevertheless, journalists are frequently confronted with apparent conflicts between their professional obligations and their humanitarian instincts as citizens. For example, in the summer of 1997, reporter Sonia Nazario and photographer Clarence Williams of the *Los Angeles Times* were spectators to the cruel reality of American poverty. For several months they observed the tortured existence of the neglected and abused children of drug-addicted parents, eventually documenting the tragic results of their investigation in a powerful two-part series titled "Orphans of Addiction." Subscribing to the journalistic tenet that reporters must remain completely detached from the stories they cover, Nazario and Williams did nothing to intervene on the children's behalf or to notify the proper authorities. Their responsibility, according to Nazario, Williams, and editor Joel Sappell, who supported the two journalists, was to *hold a mirror up to society* without tampering with the environment they were covering.[36]

However, their enterprise was not universally applauded. Many agreed with the notion of journalistic detachment as a guiding principle but "not when it comes to watching powerless children suffer, especially over a period of months." Harvard law professor Elizabeth Batholet, for example, who specializes in child welfare, abuse, and neglect, called the "reflective mirror" justification "outrageous." "The only moral defense possible for not calling social services," she said, "is that they felt they were accomplishing some greater social purpose with these articles. If they're just trying to hold up a mirror to society, then how do they escape their responsibility as members of the public to help helpless children?"[37]

But Jerry Ceppos, executive editor of the *San Jose Mercury News,* disagreed: "I believe I would have done what the *Times* did. I can see not calling authorities. I can see the thinking that writing about these children in a moving way would yield longer-lasting results."[38]

Was criticism of the *Times* justified? Did Nazario and Williams unreasonably allow their journalistic instincts to overshadow their duties

as citizens? On the one hand, the media have been criticized for ignoring the poor and the pathologies that are so prevalent among the economically and socially disenfranchised. The coverage that does exist is pathetically superficial. From this perspective, one must admire the journalists' dedication. Such stories often win Pulitzers. On the other hand, journalists are sometimes in a unique position to observe and to document such abuses. Do they have a responsibility to shed their observer status and to become a partner with government agencies in resolving society's ills?

Reporters are citizens too. They cannot completely divorce themselves from the culture that has nurtured them. Most journalists, for example, would undoubtedly intervene to save the life of someone or to prevent serious injury. And yet, the canons of journalistic deportment insist on a healthy degree of detachment and neutrality. There is clearly no bright line between these competing loyalties of citizenship and professional obligations. Under such circumstances, reporters must rely on moral reflection and common sense. Media codes usually don't address such contingencies, but we might begin with a threshold standard that appears to be the prevailing view in the industry: Unless journalists are on a specific assignment to cover an event where people's lives are in danger, they should render aid when no one else is present to do so.[39] But even when reporters are on assignment, they do not shed their obligations of citizenship. If someone is in need of assistance, they should render it (assuming they can do so without peril to their own safety) until emergency personnel have arrived. In this manner, journalists can fulfill their duties as citizens without significantly compromising their journalistic goal of impartiality.

Conflicting Public Participation

The Two Views in Journalism. At one end of the ethical spectrum, some news organizations discourage membership or participation in any

community organizations. Once reporters become "joiners," according to this view, they
become part of the system they are assigned
to cover. In addition, this traditional view of
journalism holds that news organizations must
remain civically detached, surveying their communities from afar in order to render an "objective" and impartial account of their fates and
fortunes. At the other end of the spectrum are
those who encourage civic participation and
activism as a means to stay attuned to the needs
of the community and, not coincidentally, to
develop news sources.

Perhaps the best approach to this dilemma
is to apply the "rule of common sense." Journalists cannot be social hermits and retreat
from all involvement in their communities. In
fact, some civic activity sensitizes reporters to
the problems they are assigned to cover. In this
view, reporters need to be "wired in" to the dynamics of their communities. Thus, in modern
society the avoidance of all conflicts of interest
may not be feasible, but journalists are still
under a moral obligation to disclose such conflicts to the public.

Nothing is more troubling to news executives than reporters who harbor political ambitions while working as journalists. This was
evident in the fall of 2000 when NBC suspended
Geraldo Rivera for even "exploring" a run for
the mayor of New York City. NBC News vice
president David Corvo informed Rivera that he
had run afoul of news division policies and
"created a conflict between [his] politics and
[his] journalism." Confronted with a choice between politics and journalism, Rivera bowed
out of the race.[40]

The lesson is clear: Journalists should be
wary of outright political activism, because that
is likely to be viewed as a partisan undertaking
(which it is!). If reporters might be perceived by
the audience as having a vested interest in the
story they are covering, they should be reassigned. Some consideration might even be given
to alerting the public to the staff's external activities. Can reporters expect public officials whom

they cover to disclose their conflicts of interests
and not do so themselves?

Some argue, however, that membership in
political organizations is not necessarily the
cause of reporter bias and that journalists with
strong political beliefs would be biased regardless of their official ties with such organizations. Thus, a resignation from such affiliations
would be primarily cosmetic and symbolic. The
question, of course, is whether the public will
be willing to overlook such political memberships, even if the reporter is capable of impartiality under the circumstances.

Even an appearance at a political event will
frequently seize the attention of media critics,
particularly if the journalist is nationally prominent. Dan Rather's invitation to be the star attraction at a Democratic fund-raiser was duly
noted by the *Washington Post,* which observed
that Rather's appearance "will undoubtedly provide ammunition to critics who have long accused Rather of leaning to the left." Rather's
ethical problems were compounded by the fact
that the event was also hosted by his daughter, a
Texas environmentalist and marketing executive
who was reportedly considering a run for mayor.
Rather later apologized for what he described as
a "regrettable error in judgment."[41]

Similarly, political contributions from journalists can also provoke accusations of conflict
of interests. In the summer of 2002, for example, the *Boston Globe* reported that a number of
journalists had contributed to political candidates' campaigns. "This is not a good idea," observed Fred Brown, cochair of the SPJ Ethics
Committee, "and it is unquestionably a bad idea
for anyone who's actually covering politics or
editing copy about government and elections."[42] Nevertheless, 18 months later, during
California's 2003 gubernatorial recall election,
an Oakland television station's business editor,
Brian Banmiller, contributed $1,000 to candi-
date Arnold Schwarzenegger. Banmiller allegedly
wanted to meet the movie star, and so he purchased a ticket to a private campaign fund-raiser
near his hometown. Although the contribution

violated no station policy, Banmiller asked the Schwarzenegger campaign to return the money following inquiries from the Associated Press, according to the station's news director.[43]

In recent years reporters have been admonished by their superiors for participating in public demonstrations on controversial issues, even on their own time. For example, when several female reporters for the *New York Times* and the *Washington Post* joined thousands of marchers in a Washington, DC, abortion rights demonstration, they apparently believed they were exercising their constitutional right to free speech. However, the *Post*'s managing editor Leonard Downie Jr. and executive editor Benjamin C. Bradlee viewed this reporter activism through a different ethical prism and issued a memoradum ordering anyone who had participated in the march to refrain from further coverage of the debate.[44]

Gay journalists who are active in gay rights organizations have also run into resistance from their editors. A case in point is Sandy Nelson, a reporter for the Tacoma, Washington, *Morning News Tribune,* who sued her employer for allegedly reassigning her to the copy desk because of her activism in a gay rights organization. "Journalists are like serfs," she said. "We have become the company's property twenty-four hours a day." But managing editor Jan Brandt responded that they were just protecting the paper's integrity: "This case is not about lifestyles, freedom of speech or an individual. . . . When a journalist takes a highly visible political role, it undermines the credibility of the paper."[45]

But contrast this view with that of media ethicist Valerie Alia, who was asked to contribute to a study by the Associated Press Managing Editors concerning the participation in 1995 of an African American newspaper editor in the "Million Man March" in Washington. The march was sponsored by the Nation of Islam, headed by its controversial leader Louis Farrakhan. Some reporters and editors thought the editor should not have marched because it suggested alignment with Farrakhan's "anti-Semitic and racist" views. The editor's response was that his participation was a personal, not a political, decision. Alia agreed, observing that journalists are not "blank slates or neutral absorbers and disseminators of information."[46] She also offered this counsel concerning the editor's moral duty:

> The editor had the right to attend the event, as a citizen acting from personal convictions and conscience. He was obligated to make certain that his participation did not affect the content, slant, or overall coverage of that or other events, by his news organization. He was obligated to disclose to his employer and the public his involvement in the march, and to remove himself from any professional task which might involve a conflict of interest.[47]

Civic activism by newspaper publishers and station owners presents a related conflict-of-interest dilemma. Media executives are generally well-known and influential members of the community. Most are not journalists and often feel more comfortable in the business world than the newsroom. Nevertheless, their loyalties must lie, first and foremost, with their journalistic enterprises, and civic activities that conflict with those loyalties must be avoided. For example, memberships in such social organizations as the Lions Club or Rotary International would probably pose no problem. But serving on the board of directors of a chemical plant that has been under constant government scrutiny for pollution violations would place the newsroom staff in an awkward position. Of course, the range of civic activities to which media executives might become a party is so great that once again the rule of common sense should be used as a moral guidepost. When conflicts of interests are apparent, they should be avoided. When they are unavoidable or unforeseen, the public should be apprised of the situation, and every effort should be made to insulate newsroom personnel from the pressures for favored treatment.

The Rise of Public (Civic) Journalism. When almost 90 percent of Baltimore's third graders received less-than-satisfactory ratings on their reading assessments, the *Baltimore Sun* not only reported on the disturbing results, they decided to do something about it. Defying the conventions of objectivity and journalistic neutrality, the paper enlisted employee volunteers to teach reading and marshaled its own news resources in an impressive campaign to improve test scores. In a clear example of activist journalism, the *Sun* embarked upon a five-year program to get all third graders to read by age 9.[48] This is an example of what is referred to as public, or civic, journalism, a controversial movement that is more than a decade old.

For most of our history, the news media in this country have adhered to the traditional view that they should serve as society's watchdogs and gadflies and that this role necessitates a respectable psychological distance from the affairs of their communities. But with media credibility continuing to erode (and with it, newspaper readership), proponents of the public journalism movement hope to reconnect journalists and the institutions they represent to their civic roots. Its broad goals, according to Al Cross, the president of the Society of Professional Journalists, include "fighting cynicism about politics, government and institutions, getting editors and reporters out of their ivory towers, and recognizing that a news outlet must be an active player in the community that it serves."[49] Supporters view this ideology as a mechanism to force news organizations to "think of themselves as part of a system"[50] and possibly as the salvation of American journalism. Opponents see it as a threat to the sacred cows of independence and objectivity.

Arthur Charity, in *Doing Public Journalism,* declares that public journalism "is a work in progress, and that is the most important thing anyone can say about it."[51] Each newspaper that uses it puts its own gloss on the practice, and the lack of a universal definition may have added to the confusion surrounding the ethical debate. However, the following commentary from political science professor Anthony J. Eksterowicz presents a concise perspective on the public journalism movement:

> Public journalism is concerned with developing productive relationships with the communities that journalists serve. Journalists are not mere observers but rather are participants and facilitators in such relationships. Such efforts engage journalists, within the confines of their communities, as champions of political and perhaps social reform. There is an end result or product to many public journalism projects. . . . This new movement strikes at the heart of more traditional tenets of journalism that emphasize the concepts of "objectivity" and "fairness," or so the critics charge. Public journalism offers a different route to community problem solving. Whereas traditional journalism may stress the complex nature of modern problems, public journalism stresses empowerment via increased information, resulting from civic action.[52]

Thus, the animating principle of the public journalism movement appears to be that news media should serve as agents of change by focusing not just on problems but also solutions.[53] This includes asking readers and viewers to decide what the media should cover and even how they should cover it and then becoming active partners with the community in confronting social problems. Consider these examples of regular journalism stories using a public journalism approach. The *Detroit Free Press* exposed children's charities wasting money in connection with a project that also featured public forums on children's issues and dispatched reporters to volunteer in schools. The *New Orleans Times-Picayune* overcame its own newsroom racial divisions to devote a year, 23 staff members, and 163 full pages to a series on race relations.[54] We The People, Wisconsin, Inc., a group of Madison-based media organizations, convened citizens as mock grand juries and legislatures to deliberate a property tax plan, the national budget, gambling, and health care reform.

Although public journalism poses a direct challenge to entrenched views about the media's presumed role, it has attracted a rather significant following. In two University of Kansas surveys of editors and publishers during the early days of the public journalism movement, nearly half of the publishers reported sponsoring town meetings to identify community expectations for newspaper leadership. Ninety-seven percent said they were personally involved with community organizations, and 74 percent said their editors were too. Only 3 percent of the editors responding to the surveys said newspapers should "never" become directly involved in community affairs.[55]

Since those early surveys, public journalism apparently has gained an increasing number of adherents. In 2002, for example, Lewis Freidland, a sociologist and journalism professor at the University of Wisconsin, noted that 560 projects had been self-identified as civic journalism by 322 newspapers since 1993.[56]

As civic-minded as advocates of public journalism appear to be, some have denounced what they perceive as a desertion of traditional values, such as detachment, objectivity, and impartiality. "I have an obligation not to be involved in a community I write about," declared one editor. "It's more important that the people I write about trust that I'm impartial than it is to be involved in that part of the community."[57] One respondent to the University of Kansas survey agreed: "We must stay out of the community power structure if the newspaper is to sustain its credibility," he said.[58] In addition, the critics complain that public journalism initiatives too often substitute the judgments of community leaders for those of editors. In responding to referenda, the media are merely feeding citizens what they want to know rather than what they need to know.[59]

Davis "Buzz" Merritt, one of public journalism's founding fathers, describes the conventional views of such concepts as objectivity and detachment as "false demons" that result in an abdication of responsibility:

Objectivity, or whatever has replaced that arguably invalid concept, provides a comforting—and confining—shelter for journalists. Limiting the journalistic task of telling the news without regard for outcomes avoids accepting any responsibility for whether any outcome occurs at all. In a modern, information-soaked, physically dispersed society, that is a recipe for social and political gridlock.

Moving beyond detachment does not, however, mean that journalists must be—or ought to be—or could be—responsible for which outcomes occur. Rather, moving beyond aloofness means vigorously pursuing, in our reporting role, all of the possibilities of resolution or problems. It does not mean trying to determine outcomes, but it does mean accepting the obligation to help the process of public life determine the outcomes. It is clear from recent history that simply "telling the news" does not sufficiently activate the process.[60]

Space limitations preclude any exhaustive examination of the implications of the public journalism movement. Needless to say, the ethical debate surrounding this phenomenon will continue. However, if the reformers succeed in subduing the traditionalists in this journalistic tug-of-war, the aftermath could forever alter the ethical landscape for the practice of journalism within American culture.

Vested Interests and Hidden Agendas

In the summer of 1999 the mayor of Pittsfield, Massachusetts, asked *Pittsfield Eagle* publisher Andrew Mick if the *Eagle* would consider donating a one-acre parking lot near the newspaper for the site of a new baseball stadium to prevent the town's minor team from leaving. Several months later the paper's parent company agreed to donate the parking lot plus $2 million for the new stadium in exchange for naming rights for the stadium. The *Eagle* campaigned aggressively for the new baseball facility to help revitalize downtown Pittsfield but never disclosed the naming rights agreement.

The voters rejected the plan, and "the *Eagle*'s community activism exposed its news reporting to a charge of hidden agendas." "It's difficult," admitted David Scribner, the *Eagle*'s editor, "because it seems to put the newspaper in a position of being an advocate rather than a trustworthy and credible objective observer, gathering facts and letting people make decisions."

Conflicts between media practitioners' professional duties and their personal interests and agendas pose some intriguing questions. Financial reporters, for example, should obviously not trade in stocks they cover, but does that mean that they should shun the market entirely? The ethical issue usually revolves around the degree to which outside relationships and vested interests are likely to influence one's professional judgment. When such conflicting loyalties remain undisclosed or when hidden agendas motivate the moral agent, then ethical concerns are implicated.

A prime example are the circumstances surrounding the publication of a *Newsweek* article in December 2003 titled "Fear of Litigation Is Paralyzing Our Professions." Stuart Taylor Jr.'s 3,400-word article, which *Columbia Journalism Review* described as an amicus brief for so-called tort reform, provided a litany of extreme cases as evidence that "frivolous, greed-driven lawsuits are jeopardizing medicine, education, and the ministry—and therefore society itself."[61] However, the article failed to mention that a specialty of *Newsweek*'s law firm, Covington & Burling, is defending employers against discrimination lawsuits and that during the past three years *Newsweek* and its sibling, Post-Newsweek Stations, had been the target of such discrimination lawsuits at least three times.[62]

Most conflicts involving vested interests would probably go undetected except for the vigilance of the news industry's moral sentinels. Consider, for example, the rather unusual editorial in the *New York Times* in the days leading up to the 2003 World Series. "With all due respect to our New York readership," the editorial declared, "we find it hard to resist the emotional tug" of a Cubs–Red Sox World Series. Why would the paper risk the ire of Yankee fans and possibly the alienation of some of its readers? It so happened that the *Times* had a minority stake in the company that owned the Red Sox, a fact that it neglected to disclose.[63]

Unfortunately, hidden agendas and vested interests are not that rare among news organizations and sometimes cloud their editorial (and ethical) judgments. Such was the case when the *Union-News* in Springfield, Massachusetts, refused to publish William Safire's column (a regular feature in the paper) on the evils of state-sponsored gambling. One possible explanation is that the paper supported the construction of such a casino in Springfield, preferably on land next door. The column was finally published when a mayoral candidate called attention to its absence in an ad in the *Union-News*.[64] Similarly, the readers of the *Times Union* in Albany, New York, were treated to a story on the front page of its business section, which carried an 8-by-11-inch box on its newly inaugurated service between Albany and Orlando. The story mentioned Delta's name twenty-two times, an explanation for which was contained on the jump page: "Integral to the airlines' decision to come to Albany was commitments from regional businesses, including the *Times Union* and other media companies, to offer marketing assistance to Delta Express. . . ."[65]

These representative examples beg the question: If the parties involved had publicly acknowledged their vested interests, would this have resolved the issue of a conflict of interest? One could maintain that revealing such vested interests, which carry the perception of hidden agendas, is the honest thing to do and fulfills the moral agent's duty to the audience. Armed with this information, readers and viewers are perfectly capable, so the argument goes, of determining for themselves how much credibility to place in the communicator's message.

On the other hand, audience members, particularly in a fast-paced culture that does not afford many opportunities for quiet reflection, may have neither the inclination nor the ability to evaluate the motivation and sincerity of the moral agent. For example, if Stuart Taylor Jr.'s *Newsweek* article on the fear of litigation had disclosed the magazine's posture as a target of discrimination lawsuits, would readers have considered the article more credible if they had known of *Newsweek*'s vested interest in the issue? Regardless of whether one prefers the more permissive (full disclosure ethically sufficient) or austere (no reporting or commentary where vested interests are involved) view, most would probably agree that the minimum requirement is for the moral agents to reveal any vested interest or hidden agenda that inspires their public pronouncements.

APPROACHES TO DEALING WITH CONFLICTS OF INTEREST

Obviously, no clear-cut solution can be provided for avoiding every conflict of interest. But the following three-step approach should serve as a guide through this moral thicket and should bring some degree of sanity to the moral reasoning process. First, of course, the goal should be to avoid personal conflicts that are likely to undermine the media practitioner's professional obligations. Duty-based theorists (deontologists) would avoid foreseeable conflicts as a matter of principle. Consequentialists (teleologists) would examine the potential harm to various parties caused by the conflict as a means of resolving the dilemma.

Second, if the conflict cannot be anticipated, every effort to resolve the dilemma, even after the fact, should be made. For example, newspaper publishers may not be able to anticipate that a company in which they hold stock will become the subject of an official investigation. But if their paper is covering the story, they should

consider ridding themselves of their financial investment to avoid the appearance of a conflict of interest. We can see this principle in action when public officials who do not choose to divest themselves entirely of their investments nevertheless place them in a blind trust until they have withdrawn from the political arena.

Third, if a conflict of interest cannot be avoided, it should be acknowledged to the public or clients. Those travel writers, for example, who must rely on the good offices and the financial support of the tourist industry to cover their stories should acknowledge their source of sponsorship. A public relations practitioner who discovers a conflict of interest in serving two clients with opposing agendas should acknowledge that conflict (as is required by the PRSA code) to both clients. Aristotle's golden mean is sometimes valuable in applying this third principle, because it provides a reasonable accommodation between unrealistic moral purity and the callous disregard of the public's right to know about the existence of the conflict.

CONFLICTS OF INTEREST: HYPOTHETICAL CASE STUDIES

The cases in this chapter provide some insight into the diversity of situations that can pose conflicts of interest for media practitioners. In confronting the dilemmas posed by these scenarios, pay particular attention to the conflicts between the *particularistic,* or role-based, obligations of the moral agents and the *universal* obligations, as described in Chapter 2. You may also wish to reread Chapter 3, outlining the three primary approaches to ethical decision making: duty-based ethics (deontology), consequence-based ethics (teleology), and Aristotle's golden mean. These will be the keys to stimulating your imagination as you apply the moral reasoning process to the issues raised in these hypothetical cases.

▶ **CASE 7-1**

The PR Practitioner as Political Activist

Lancaster was a picturesque and progressive urban center just 60 miles from the Canadian border. For several decades its economy had been fueled by a variety of highly successful service industries; and the city's proximity to thousands of acres of pristine wilderness, populated with nature's bountiful supply of wildlife and creeks brimming with rainbow trout, had made Lancaster and its environs a mecca for tourists seeking to escape the tedium of their daily routines. As long as the forests that separated Lancaster from its Canadian neighbors, known as the Blue Falcon Forest Preserve, served as a magnet for tourists and thus enriched the financial coffers of the merchants and city government, the preserve's unmolested natural beauty was secure from the impatient cravings of land developers. But a lingering economic recession and competition from other tourist areas that offered a greater diversity of family-oriented entertainment, including attractive theme parks, had taken their toll on Lancaster's economy as several significant tourist-related businesses were forced to abandon their host city.

Lancaster's political leadership and civic leaders lost little time in attempting to resurrect their community's economic vitality, but after a study by a marketing research company, they painfully concluded the tourist industry, at least as a mainstay of the local economy, was beyond redemption. The city council, under the mayor's leadership, proposed to establish the Lancaster Development Commission, whose mandate would be to plan for and spearhead the commercial cultivation of at least part of the Blue Falcon Wildlife Preserve. The public hearings prior to the council's vote on the proposal were raucous, as local merchants favoring the commercial development squared off against Citizens for the Preservation of Blue Falcon, an environmental group composed of a cross section of local activists, the most vocal of which

was the Citizens for Environmental Responsibility (CES). Despite the deep civic divisions, the city fathers approved the proposal. The Commission's first order of business was to lobby the state legislature to release the acreage necessary for private development in close proximity to Lancaster, but Commission members were acutely aware that strong public support was essential to their ultimate legislative success. According to the polls, local citizens were about evenly divided on the issue of land development, prompting the Commission to retain professional public relations counsel to argue its case in the court of public opinion and to lobby the legislature to release part of the wildlife preserve for commercial development. Because of its reputation as an aggressive advocate for its clients, including the local tourist industry, the Gould & LaFleur PR agency was selected as the Commission's representative in the public square.

The agency had started rather modestly in 1992 as a partnership between Wesley Gould and Darrell LaFleur with its headquarters in Lancaster and from its inception had played an instrumental role in the promotion of the tourist industry. The firm had benefited impressively from the economic boom of the late 1990s, resulting in a diversification of its clientele and expansion into neighboring states. However, the tourist industry retained a position of prominence among Gould and LaFleur's mix of clients. The sudden decline in the viability of tourism in the region around Lancaster, therefore, was of more than passing interest to Wesley Gould and Darrell LaFleur, and the partners quickly accepted the Development Commission as a client.

A few days after the firm had signed an agreement to represent the Commission, its Creative Director, Marilyn Durr, asked for a meeting with senior partner Wesley Gould and Laurie Dyer, the senior account manager, who had been instrumental in presenting the agency's plan to the Development Commission in competition with two other PR firms and finalizing the agreement with the Commission. The meeting took place in Gould's office.

"As you may recall from my resumé," Durr began, addressing her opening remarks to Wesley Gould, "I did some freelance publicity work for Citizens for Environmental Responsibility five years ago before joining this firm. I also personally support environmental causes and would like to participate in their public meetings and demonstrations. On my own time, of course. I wouldn't do any publicity work for them, but since our firm is representing the city on the Blue Falcon development project and CES is opposed to this project, you might consider this a conflict of interest. I don't believe it is, but I would like your permission to participate in the CES activities."

"What do you think, Laurie?," Gould asked, turning to his senior account executive.

"Since we would not ask Marilyn to work on this account—that would certainly be perceived as a conflict of interest—we could avoid the issue of conflicting loyalties as far as Marilyn is concerned. However, the public and certainly the Development Commission might have a problem with this. They might have questions about our commitment to this project."

"If I were a journalist, I would agree," countered Durr. "Journalists are expected to remain free from entangling alliances. Such relationships can undermine their credibility and that of their news organizations. But I don't see that such standards can apply in our industry. We are advocates by nature. If I were working on the Blue Falcon project, then this would be a different matter. But I feel I should be free on my own time to participate in political causes and to exercise my right of free expression."

"It's true that the standards of journalism don't work exactly for our profession as they relate to conflicts of interest," replied Dyer. "But the underlying rationales are the same—the avoidance of relationships that compromise your professional integrity or the credibility of your company. PR firms represent a variety of interests, institutions, and causes. You never know when your company will provide public relations counsel to some party with which you have had an adverse relationship in the past. I don't believe that PR professionals are required to be social monks, but I do believe they must be cautious about the political causes they become embroiled in. In your case, there's no issue

of personal integrity, especially since you won't be working on this project, but there is a potential that your activism could reflect poorly on the firm."

"I disagree," replied Durr. "If anyone—the Commission, for example—raises questions we can point out that I won't be working on this account and that Gould & LaFleur allows its employees to participate in community activities on their own time."

"But our firm's critics might question our commitment to the project," observed Dyer. "There's also the ethical issue of whether, assuming we allow your activism on behalf of the environmentalists, we should formally disclose your participation. If we do, of course, that will invite criticism. Silence might be a virtue in this case. On the other hand, your presence will probably be noted and if we don't disclose your involvement with the environmental cause, then our firm might suffer even greater censure."

"I'll leave the disclosure issue to Wesley," declared Durr. "I certainly don't intend to conceal my involvement. However, it seems to me that disclosure is required when a PR practitioner has a conflict of interest. But I don't believe that's true in this case."

Wesley Gould had listened attentively to the exchange between Dyer and Durr. He appreciated Durr's candor and her recognition of what might be construed by some to be a conflict of interest, even though she would not work on the Development Commission's account. As senior partner, Gould would be the moral agent in this case since Marilyn Durr was asking for the firm's benediction in pursuing her own political interests. There were two ethical questions that had to be addressed: (1) Is it a conflict of interest for a PR firm's employee to participate in a political activity that is adverse to the interest of one of the agency's clients, even if the employee is not working on the client's account? (2) Should the PR firm officially reveal the employee's involvement in that cause? Gould promised to discuss the matter with Darrell LaFleur, the agency's junior partner, before rendering a decision.

THE CASE STUDY

In assessing the ethical dimensions of this case, we might begin with the provisions of the Code of Ethics of the Public Relations Society of America

(PRSA). The "intent" of the provision on conflicts of interest, according to the code, is twofold: (1) to earn trust and mutual respect with clients or employers and (2) to build trust with the public by avoiding or ending situations that put one's personal or professional interests in conflict with society's interests.

The code then declares that to fulfill this intent a PRSA member shall (1) act in the best interests of the client or employer, even subordinating the member's personal interests, (2) avoid actions and circumstances that may appear to compromise good business judgment or create a conflict between personal and professional interests, (3) disclose promptly any existing or potential conflict of interest to affected clients or organizations, and (4) encourage clients and customers to determine if a conflict exists after notifying all affected parties.

Do any of these provisions address the issues raised in this scenario? An employee of the Gould & LaFleur PR agency, Marilyn Durr, has revealed that she would like to participate actively in a cause that is adverse to the interest of one of her agency's clients. She would do this on her own time and would not simultaneously work on the client's account. Durr argues that public relations operates on a somewhat different ethical plane than journalism and that her political activism will not undermine the credibility of her agency. In her view, as a citizen she has a right to freedom of expression. Her antagonist in the discussion, Laurie Dyer, responds that from an ethical perspective the fundamental concerns surrounding conflicts of interest are not that different between journalism and PR. Since public relations firms serve a variety of interests in the public arena, should PR practitioners be as cautious as journalists about becoming politically active? Assuming that Wesley Gould sees no reason to prohibit Durr's off-duty activities, is the agency under a moral obligation to reveal her political engagement with the environmental group?

These are intriguing questions, and for the purpose of responding to them, assume the role of senior partner Wesley Gould and, utilizing the SAD formula for moral reasoning outlined in Chapter 3, decide whether you will approve or object to Marilyn Durr's proposed political activism. You might

begin with the code provisions described here and interpret them in light of the facts of this case.

 CASE 7-2

DNA Testing: A Journalist's Call for Justice

For twelve years death row inmate Washington Brown had proclaimed his innocence to an unresponsive criminal justice system. Brown, an African American, was facing execution by lethal injection because of his conviction for the murder and rape of 18-year-old Adrienne Lattimore, a college freshman and daughter of a local prominent bank president in North Haven Ridge, an affluent and culturally diverse Midwestern community. According to police records, the young girl's partially nude body was discovered in the woods just before dawn about one hundred yards from her abandoned automobile. A photograph of the young woman was included in all local news accounts of the homocide, and within days a potential witness contacted North Haven Ridge police and provided a lead that eventually led to the arrest and indictment of Washington Brown for the rape and murder of Adrienne Lattimore. The witness, a 40-year-old plant manager named Louis Shadetree, claimed that late in the afternoon on the day of the murder he was driving along Mulberry Lane, a little-traveled road on the eastern perimeter of the city, when he noticed the victim talking to a black male. He provided a description of the suspect to police, who then distributed a composite sketch and a physical description to the news media. Within days, based on an anonymous tip, Brown was located and taken into custody.

During the interrogation Brown, an alcoholic indigent with an IQ of 82, never denied he had been with the victim on the night of the murder but claimed that he was walking along Mulberry Lane when he noticed a parked car with a flat tire and a female driver standing next to the vehicle. She had retrieved the jack and lug wrench from the trunk but had made no move to change the tire herself. Needing money for "booze," according to the suspect's account, he picked up the wrench and offered to change her tire for ten dollars. When she declined his less-than-altruistic overtures, Brown admitted that he cursed the young woman but denied striking her or any involvement in her rape and murder. He had left her to fend for herself or to await the arrival of a Good Samaritan, according to the indigent suspect's rather rambling account.

The police investigation did in fact reveal a flat tire in the trunk in the space normally reserved for the spare. The spare was on the left rear of the vehicle. A lug wrench was found near Lattimore's body with the victim's blood and Brown's fingerprints on it. The wrench had apparently been used as a weapon to incapacitate the unfortunate young woman, but the cause of death was listed as strangulation. No other prints were found at the crime scene. However, a sample of semen retrieved from the victim matched Brown's blood type, although this type of evidence is not conclusive. At the time of Brown's arrest DNA testing was not widely used in most states to provide positive identification of suspects.

During their investigation the North Haven Ridge police never considered the possibility of other suspects. Under pressure from a restless public demanding expedient justice, law enforcement officials were satisfied with their incarceration of one of society's disinherited. Since Brown could not afford an attorney, the judge provided him with a public defender, who later admitted that he was an inexperienced criminal trial lawyer. Brown was subsequently sentenced to die by lethal injection.

To death penalty proponents, Brown's case was unexceptional. For opponents of the death penalty, Brown's looming rendezvous with the state's executioner was one more manifestation of the moral depravity of the criminal justice system. On the other hand, Jerry Greenberg's interest in the Brown case was not driven by ideology or any overarching moral concerns, but his investigation of the inmate's case had created a reasonable doubt in his own mind even if not in the jury's.

Greenberg was Channel 8's investigative reporter who had spent two years in between other assignments exploring the case histories of several death row inmates in Leavenwood Penitentiary, the state's maximum security prison for convicted

felons. A few had admitted their guilt following a lengthy incarceration on death row while their appeals were exhausted, but most continued to deny their culpability, even when the evidence was irrefutable. However, as his investigation entered its final phase, Greenberg had bracketed Washington Brown's case for further exploration. Perhaps it was his journalistic intuition that provoked his skepticism about Brown's guilt. Or perhaps it was the inmate's conviction based upon the single blood test and the fingerprints on the lug wrench. In addition, the most serious offense on record against the 28-year-old Brown, until his conviction for murder and rape, were three citations for public drunkenness. Washington Brown might have been an alcoholic and uncouth in his personal deportment, but in the reporter's estimation he was no threat to society. Greenberg's doubts were intensified when another inmate serving a twenty-year sentence for armed robbery and aggravated assault confessed to the murder of Adrienne Lattimore. Appellate courts were unimpressed with this rather tardy admission of guilt and refused to overturn Brown's conviction.

Just three weeks before Brown's scheduled execution, Channel 8's news director, Jennifer Clausen, settled comfortably into her chair as she convened her weekly staff meeting for what she assumed would be a routine review of news assignments and other administrative matters concerning her domain of station operations. On hand were several producers, the assignment editor, and the assistant news director. Jerry Greenberg did not always attend—he was frequently on assignment—but the investigative reporter approached this meeting with a sense of purpose. After the completion of the day's official agenda, Clausen recognized each subordinate in turn.

"I've looked into the Brown case," Greenberg said in responding to his news director's acknowledgment, "and I have serious doubts about his guilt. The evidence against him during the trial was distressingly circumstantial. His prints were on the wrench that was used to assault the victim, but Brown admitted that he picked up the tool before Lattimore declined his offer for help in exchange for money. And the blood test proved only that the assailant could have been Brown but others should not have been ruled out. In addition, Brown has no record of violence."

"So what are you proposing?" inquired Clausen who had grown accustomed to Greenberg's sometimes unorthodox approach to journalism.

"As you know, many states now allow postconviction DNA testing for crimes like murder, but ours is not one of them," replied Greenberg. "At the time of his conviction DNA testing was not widely used. I've talked to Brown's court-appointed attorney. His client is so insistent on his innocence that he is willing to undergo DNA testing to prove his claim. Unfortunately, the state will not pay for it. In addition, in this jurisdiction new evidence must be introduced within six months of the trial. Nevertheless, it would be an abomination if the state executes an innocent man who might have been cleared by a DNA test. I would like for this station to pay for this test. Prosecutors have told me they will not object and that it might convince the judge to take a fresh look."

"I have an ethical problem with the station getting actively involved in this case," responded Sandy Cheng, producer for Channel 8's early evening news. "We're journalists, not defense attorneys. Brown was convicted after a fair trial. He's had several appeals, and if there are any further avenues of redress, his lawyer should pursue them. If we pay for this DNA test, it's a conflict of interest—a violation of our professional responsibility to be objective."

Greenberg was undeterred by his colleague's ethical austerity. "I don't believe that our code of ethics requires that we stand on the sidelines while an innocent man is put to death," he asserted. "After all, this will not affect our coverage of this case. If we pay for the test, I do believe we have an obligation to include this in our reports. But I don't see how this will affect our objectivity."

"Just for the sake of argument, let's assume you are correct," Cheng responded, confident in her stance but willing for the moment to concede Greenberg's point. "Our viewers—at least those who support the death penalty and are skeptical of claims of innocence from death row inmates—may not believe that we can remain unbiased. Even a *perception* of a conflict of interest can affect our credibility."

"I disagree," replied Greenberg. "If our efforts succeed in freeing an innocent man and we explain our motivations to our viewers, I doubt that our credibility will suffer."

"I think the issue of credibility may well fall along ideological lines," Cheng said. "Death penalty opponents will applaud us. But others will condemn us. Even if Brown's innocence can be irrefutably established, they will criticize us for our involvement in this case. Remaining entirely neutral, even if Brown is put to death, is a safe position to take; no one will condemn us for *not* getting involved in the DNA issue."

"I'm not interested in playing safe when the state may be making a mistake," declared Greenberg, in an attempt to persuade Cheng and his news director of the moral virtue of his plea. "Of course, the DNA test may establish Brown's guilt. But there is precedent for the media's offer to pay for such a test. A couple of years ago a TV network and several major newspapers offered to pay for DNA tests on evidence from a 1981 murder case in Georgia to examine whether the man executed was in fact innocent. They apparently were unconcerned about the ethical implications of their proposal."

"The fact that other news organizations have considered this doesn't allay my concerns," Cheng said. "I admit that paying for a DNA test that might exonerate an innocent man doesn't make us an advocate for or against the death penalty. But I still think it crosses the line from neutral observer to participant in the criminal justice process. I sympathize with Brown's plight, but in my view it's not our station's role to try to exonerate him."

"I agree that we must adhere to our professional responsibilities," admitted Greenberg. "But journalists are also citizens and citizens have civic obligations. If our investigation raises serious doubts about an inmate's guilt, I have no qualms about our station's paying for a test that might exonerate him."

"If we pay for a DNA test for Brown," Cheng countered, "then where will it stop? Will we assume this responsibility for every inmate whose guilt is in doubt? What about other defendants who are denied the benefits of DNA evidence because the state won't pay for it? Through our own involvement we will introduce an element of un-fairness into the system."

Greenberg was frustrated that he had made lit-tle progress in tempering the producer's ethical absolutism. "I don't find this line of reasoning con-vincing," he replied, referring to Cheng's concern about fairness. "I'm not arguing that we have a moral *obligation* to see that justice is done through subsidizing a DNA test for this inmate. And even if our effort results in Brown's exonera-tion, this doesn't mean that we have to intercede on behalf of other death row inmates."

As she listened to this vigorous exchange be-tween her investigative reporter and news pro-ducer, Jennifer Clausen was ambivalent in her own evaluation of this ethical dilemma. Did the conflict in this case really involve an inviolable "bright line," or were Cheng's concerns unjustified as a matter of ethical deportment? If Channel 8 agreed to pay for the DNA test, would the station's viewers regard this as a form of unwarranted intrusion into the criminal justice system, regardless of the outcome? She doubted the station's efforts would be per-ceived as a form of social activism, since they could not reasonably be construed as expressing a view on the morality of the death penalty itself, and yet some line crossing was inevitable. Granted, news organizations had traditionally recused themselves from this kind of initiative, but perhaps such con-ventions were unfashionable as a guide to ethical behavior. With only three weeks until the state's discharge of Washington Brown's death warrant, Jennifer Clausen promised her investigative re-porter a timely decision on his proposal.

THE CASE STUDY

This case confronts its participants with the quin-tessential question of the extent to which news organizations may depart from their traditional posture of neutrality and involve themselves di-rectly in the community's affairs. In this scenario, unlike one concerning political activism, for exam-ple, the stakes for death row inmate Washington Brown are quite high. At this juncture no one has volunteered to be proactive in procuring a DNA test for the condemned prisoner, assuming that a court will even consider the results. However,

tradition is on the side of producer Sandy Cheng in this debate. Justice is a cherished commodity within American society, but Cheng doesn't believe that her station should be a participant in determin-ing Brown's fate. She is also concerned about where such intervention will end. If Channel 8 funds a DNA test for Brown, will it then be morally obligated for the sake of fairness to do so for other prisoners whose guilt may be in doubt?

Reporter Jerry Greenberg is more concerned about *this* case rather than any future obligations. He also raises a pertinent question: If his station pays for a DNA test that might result in Brown's release, how does this compromise the news de-partment's objectivity? Is the station really likely to lose credibility over this issue?

With these conflicting ideas in mind, assume the position of news director Jennifer Clausen and, utiliz-ing the SAD formula for moral reasoning described in Chapter 3, render an ethical verdict on whether you will approve Jerry Greenberg's proposal.

▶ **CASE 7-3**

The NABJ and Divided Loyalties[66]

As the newly elected president of the National Association of Black Journalists (NABJ), Mathias Washington was rightfully pleased with his organiza-tion's accomplishments. Washington was a charter member when the NABJ was founded in 1975 to monitor racial discrimination and to help to open up employment opportunities for African American journalists. The initial meetings had been rather sparsely attended, but its founders had infused the organization with a noble mission and a social con-science that increasingly attracted African American writers, reporters, and editors to its agenda for racial justice. And now, two decades later, the associa-tion's annual conventions had become a significant rendezvous point for recruiters and eager job seek-ers, and its rather modest activities of the early days had given way to lavish concerns in which scholar-ships and awards were handed out.

But it was not scholarships or awards that were on the minds of the NABJ board members as the association prepared for its annual convention in

Atlanta. They were preoccupied with the case of Glendell Watts, the charismatic past president of the NABJ who was widely credited with invigorating the organization with its sense of purpose and journalistic brotherhood. But as NABJ members arrived in Atlanta, Watts was not practicing journalism; he was sitting on death row.

Watts had been convicted seven years ago in Pittsburgh of shooting a white police officer. From the moment of his arrest and indictment, Watts maintained that he was being beaten by the officer for no legitimate reason and that he had acted in self-defense. The prosecutor countered that Watts had been stopped for speeding and had shot the officer in cold blood without any provocation. Whatever the truth, an all-white jury had taken only two hours to convict Watts, and the former NABJ president was sentenced to die in the electric chair. From the outset, leaders of the African American community charged that the evidence against Watts was "suspicious" and that he had received an unfair trial because of a lack of minority representation on the jury. They were joined in their protests by Amnesty International and Human Rights Watch. But despite numerous legal appeals, Watts remained on death row.

The Watts case had galvanized some NABJ members, and, as the execution date approached, they were pressuring the board to take a public stance in an effort to win a last-minute stay and perhaps eventually a new trial. Mathias Washington had placed the matter on the agenda for the board meeting, which would be held just prior to the convention's opening session. A preview of the debate that was likely to ensue was reflected in the president's "working dinner" meeting with the board's executive committee: Asa Jackson, Clarence Post, and Tamara Landry.

"I'm not sure we should get mixed up in the Watts affair," said Jackson rather tentatively. "If we do, our stance could turn this organization into an advocacy group. If we're to maintain our credibility as journalists, we need to remain detached."

"I disagree," said Landry. "What's wrong with our getting involved as an organization? After all, other media organizations lobby and take public positions on behalf of their members. That doesn't mean that as individual reporters they can't be objective."

"But when journalistic organizations take positions," responded Post, "such as intervening in litigation involving First Amendment violations, they are usually related to journalistic issues. Watts might be a journalist—in fact, he's a former president of the NABJ—but his case isn't about journalism; it's a criminal case."

But Landry was insistent. "If we remain aloof, some members will view this as an abandonment of our association's commitment to equal justice. They might say we're out of touch with the plight of African Americans who are more likely to face the death penalty than white criminals. And many of our members have covered this issue. That makes it a journalistic issue."

"We may be African Americans, but in our professional duties, we must be journalists first," replied Jackson. "Otherwise we lose our credibility. Remember this: Although some of our members work for media targeted specifically to black audiences, many work for white-owned papers and stations that serve diverse audiences. If the NABJ becomes an advocate for a cause, there will always be a suspicion that our own reporting is biased. It will be a case of guilt by association. And we'll be accused of having a conflict of interest."

"That's a point to consider," said Post. "Besides, it may be that Watts didn't receive a fair trial, but I don't think we should risk our reputation and spend the association's capital on this one case. It's definitely a conflict of interest. If we get involved in the Watts case, our professional duties will then become hostage to our personal views on racial justice. Our best approach is to disassociate ourselves from this case. As journalists, we have an ethical obligation to remain detached."

"You act as though the so-called values of detachment and objectivity are moral imperatives for all journalists," responded Landry. "But who set these standards? White reporters and editors. We didn't have any input into the formulation of these standards. Besides, this case isn't just about the guilt or innocence of one man. It's about the disbursement of justice for all African Americans. This high-profile case has received national attention. The black community will watch to see how we handle this. If we don't take a firm stand in support of Watts's right to a new trial, then we might be accused of being disloyal to one of our own. There are times when our consciences must have priority over our professional duties."

Post was concerned about his colleague's apparent belief in race-based journalistic standards. "If we insist on a different set of ethical standards for African American journalists," he said, "and if we become advocates for a criminal just because he happens to be black, regardless of how unfairly *we* believe he was treated by the justice system, we will be accused of embracing a *double standard* for black journalists—the kind of thing we should be opposed to."

"On the other hand," said Washington, who had listened intently to the impassioned discussion among his colleagues, "keep in mind that many of our members chose journalism because they wanted to make an impact on society. They certainly didn't go into it for the money. They might feel drawn to the Watts case because it embodies the racist tendencies of the American justice system. Under these circumstances, it's difficult to sit on the sidelines."

But despite this bold assertion, Washington still felt the tug of competing loyalties as the board members continued to travel familiar terrain in their search for moral wisdom. The full executive board would meet later that afternoon to consider the issue. Their decision would then be conveyed to the full membership the following day. The NABJ president knew that Tamara Washington was right about one thing. This case wasn't just about the guilt or innocence of one man. *People v. Glendell Watts* would certainly disrupt the effort at consensus building that had distinguished the association's recent conventions and might even be a defining moment for the NABJ itself.

THE CASE STUDY

Media organizations often take public positions on issues affecting their membership. The SPJ, for example, has been at the forefront on First Amendment issues. But the controversy outlined here does not involve a journalistic issue. It raises the question of whether journalists should abandon their position of neutrality and detachment on matters that do not directly affect their profession.

In this scenario the NABJ executive committee is pondering the dilemma of conflicting loyalties: conscience versus professional duty or journalistic objectivity versus advocacy for social justice.

This case is full of ethical subplots. Of immediate concern to the NABJ board, of course, is whether the association should become an advocate on behalf of Glendell Watts. But beyond the official stance of the NABJ, there is the ethical question of whether individual African American journalists should become involved. Are they journalists first, or should their allegiance be to one of their own whom they feel has been the victim of racial injustice? Should the answer to this question depend on whether they are working for a news organization targeted to a general audience or a black-owned organization whose constituency is primarily the African American community? And is there any merit to the argument advanced by Tamara Landry that conventional news values, such as objectivity and detachment, are the product of the white journalistic establishment to which minority journalists do not necessarily owe allegiance?

Put yourself in the position of an African American journalist and a member of the NABJ (admittedly, this may be difficult if you are not an African American). And then, applying the SAD formula, explain how you will evaluate and resolve the ethical dilemma posed in this case.

▶ CASE 7-4
A Witness to Genocide[67]

Robert Ashmore's soul was on fire! Within just a few short months the ravages of war had consumed his spirit and had made him an unwilling witness to humankind's sinister instincts.

Ashmore was a reporter for the *Baltimore Mercury,* one of twenty-four papers, four of them overseas, owned by the Rupert Newspaper Group. Ashmore had received his degree in journalism from Northwestern's Medill School of Journalism in 1992 and, armed with his impressive academic credentials, had joined the *Mercury* first as a general assignment reporter and later as the paper's capitol correspondent. Under managing editor

Ellen Mabry's tutelage, Ashmore had prospered, winning several statewide awards for his insightful and vivid accounts of the political dynamics of the state's legislative machinery. Stories of national import or interest were syndicated to other papers in the Rupert chain, thus affording Ashmore the kind of national exposure that rarely accrues to a statehouse reporter. His journalistic enterprise had also captured the attention of the Rupert Group's management, which selected him for an assignment to the corporation's London bureau, from which he would be dispatched to cover European news.

Contrary to many of its journalistic competitors, the Rupert Group had fostered its reputation as an aggressive international news organization and had opened bureaus in London and Singapore, which served as clearinghouses for the various dispatches from wire services, stringers, and a few Rupert correspondents who serviced the company's voracious appetite for foreign news. NATO's decision to bomb Serbian installations and military units in support of the Kosovar Albanians had riveted the nation's attention on this part of the world that had been the genesis of the First World War and still threatened to embroil the global community in a wider conflict. NATO's sponsorship of this military engagement did not obscure the fact that the U.S. military had been cast in the leading role, a reality not lost on an increasingly concerned American public.

Thus, when the NATO buildup commenced, Rupert's London bureau chief lost no time in briefing Robert Ashmore on how to chronicle events in this region of ethnic confrontation. Ashmore's assignment was ostensibly to cover NATO's air strikes and ground operations, if they should materialize, but the irrepressible young reporter was determined to focus on the human facets of this cultural tragedy and the suffering of the innocent victims of Belgrade's alleged campaign of ethnic cleansing. However, like most American reporters assigned to an area of military conflict, Ashmore was dependent upon the military command structure for much of his logistical support as the international force unleashed its destructive energy on Serbian targets in both Kosovo and Belgrade and its immediate environs.

However, as the bombing campaign drew to a close with the capitulation of the Yugoslav president,

Slobodan Milosevic, and NATO troops attempted to pacify the Kosovar countryside, Ashmore joined his peers in sifting through the rubble. Armed with a notepad and a laptop computer, he began the painstaking task of interviewing witnesses, survivors, and community leaders in order to corroborate the relentless allegations of brutality and genocide. His days were spent listening to tragic accounts of the destruction of homes and villages and the persecution of innocent civilians. Ashmore listened sympathetically as nine Kosovar women individually relived the horrors of rape and torture at the hands of Serbian soldiers. On three occasions, he was led by Albanian militia to mass graves where scores of mutilated bodies were unearthed. Each time his sense of detachment and dispassion, which had served him well in the corridors of political power, abandoned him as he bore silent witness to the gruesome consequences of centuries of ethnic hatred. At the end of each day, he dutifully transcribed his handwritten notes to his laptop, thereby electronically memorializing the horrific testaments of the survivors and his own eyewitness accounts of the indisputable evidence of genocide, clinically referred to as "ethnic cleansing."

Ashmore was painfully aware that genocide was not the exclusive preserve of the Serbs in the long-standing Balkan conflicts, but his mission was to illuminate for his readers the circumstances that had precipitated the NATO intervention. His vivid and arousing dispatches from the "front lines" of Kosovo eventually earned him a Pulitzer nomination, but he did not emerge from the experience emotionally unscathed.

Within three months of his return to London, fiscal constraints in the London bureau necessitated the reassignment of Ashmore to his previous beat at the *Baltimore Mercury.* However, he was relieved to return to the "tranquility" of domestic politics. In the months following his Kosovo experience, Ashmore enthusiastically resurrected his legislative responsibilities and savored the additional recognition that his Pulitzer nomination had occasioned. He would never forget his baptism of fire in Kosovo, but Ashmore did not dwell on the more horrific images of his experience. However, his attempt to return to normalcy was abruptly interrupted with a call in late July from Jonathan Bryan-Smith.

Bryan-Smith was an attorney who was assigned to assist in the preparation of war crime trials at The Hague. The prosecutorial pace had accelerated with the delivery by Serb authorities of Slobodan Milosevic and other former Serbian officials into the custody of the war crime tribunal. Bryan-Smith invited Ashmore to testify as a witness before the tribunal. "According to your published accounts, you have information that would be extremely valuable to our staff," Bryan-Smith told Ashmore. "You have obviously talked to many Albanian nationals who were victimized by Serb forces and you saw the mutilated bodies uncovered in these mass graves. We need your testimony to corroborate the accounts of other witnesses. Quite frankly, some of our cases are weak—or at least the evidence may be too circumstantial for the judges—and testimony from journalists like yourself may be crucial to our winning convictions."

Ashmore told the attorney that he would consider the request, but even before the conclusion of the transoceanic conversation he was experiencing the uncomfortable claim of competing loyalties between his duty as a citizen of the global community and his professional mandate to remain impartial and objective.

Ashmore's first move was to seek the counsel of his senior colleague and mentor, managing editor Ellen Mabry. However, Mabry advised the reporter that, regardless of her own predispositions, approval for Ashmore to testify must come from Franklin Hughes, the *Mercury*'s executive editor. The next day Mabry and Ashmore found themselves engaged in a spirited dialogue in the well-apportioned office of Franklin Hughes.

Hughes was fascinated by the request from The Hague. It was certainly an unusual twist on reporters' traditional aversion to cooperating with criminal prosecutors. "I want to listen to your views," Hughes advised the reporter and his managing editor. "This is a tough call, and I want to make sure we do the right thing. Let's begin with you, Ellen. Do you think Robert should testify?"

"Absolutely not," declared Mabry categorically. If Mabry harbored any reservations about her ethical absolutism, she did not reveal them to Hughes or Ashmore. "Crimes against humanity should be punished," Mabry said. "But journalists must not

become intelligence agents for the prosecution. That's not our role."

"Do you agree with Ellen?" Hughes inquired of Ashmore without displaying any signs of agreement or disagreement with Mabry's posture.

"I would agree with Ellen in most circumstances," Ashmore responded, somewhat disappointed that his superior did not display more empathy with his moral dilemma. "But genocide is different. This is a horrific crime, the most brutal violation of human rights imaginable. Besides, bringing war criminals to trial or even collecting evidence is much more difficult than your average police investigation."

But Mabry was unyielding in her assessment of a journalist's responsibility. "I agree that genocide is the worst imaginable kind of crime. But how does this fact alone alter the duty of reporters to remain objective and to serve as neutral observers? In essence it's a conflict of interest for a reporter to gather information and interview witnesses and then use this intelligence to assist the prosecution."

"I must confess that I'm troubled by journalists who abandon their roles as neutral observers," acknowledged Ashmore. "But is there really a bright line here? Journalists are citizens, too, and there are perhaps times when this duty should take priority over their professional obligations. I've heard that the cases against the Serbian defendants may be threatened by the difficulties in establishing responsibility for the war crimes and by the unreliability of some of the witnesses. My testimony might be essential to the administration of justice in this case."

"Perhaps," responded Mabry in the first slight concession since the inauguration of the spirited dialogue. "But keep in mind the long-term consequences of cooperating with officials at The Hague. If it becomes commonplace to have journalists testify at war crime trials, this could jeopardize access of reporters to future military engagements and perhaps even their safety. Their integrity will be compromised if they acquire a reputation as intelligence agents."

Despite Mabry's apparently unyielding stance, she closed by acknowledging the moral challenge to her young associate's conscience. On this,

Hughes agreed and told Mabry and Ashmore that, while the *Mercury* might normally prohibit his voluntary cooperation as a witness in a criminal case, the exceptional nature of war crime prosecutions demanded more reflection. Hughes was not surprised at Mabry's stout opposition, but he was somewhat surprised at the reporter's willingness to *entertain* the idea of testifying. Of course, Ashmore could still refuse even if the executive editor gave his blessing to the reporter's appearance. "The call is mine," Hughes noted with an air of finality, "but I'll seek advice from others, including our attorneys, and tender my decision in a few days."

THE CASE STUDY

"Should journalists testify before war crimes tribunals about atrocities they've covered, or would that undermine their objectivity and cast them as intelligence agents rather than neutral observers?" That was the question posed in a recent issue of the *Columbia Journalism Review.*[68] As this narrative clearly suggests, the *Mercury*'s reporter, Robert Ashmore, is ethically conflicted. His conscience is plagued by the competing loyalties of his duty as a world citizen and his professional responsibilities as a journalist.

On the one hand, journalists are indeed citizens and they divorce themselves from this responsibility at their own peril. If their audiences believe them to be culturally aloof and governed by a set of norms that sets them apart from the expectations of citizenship, then they risk a loss of credibility.

On the other hand, the managing editor's concerns, as outlined in the discussion, should not be summarily dismissed. Is Ellen Mabry correct? Must journalists under all circumstances refuse cooperative overtures from prosecutors, even when the charge is genocide? Would it be an unacceptable violation of the values of objectivity and neutrality for Ashmore to testify before the war crimes tribunal at The Hague, or is this the kind of exceptional case that would justify a deviation from the ethical norm? If there is reason to believe that a conviction is doubtful without corroborating testimony of journalists, does that change the ethical equation?

For the purpose of resolving this dilemma, assume the role of executive editor Franklin Hughes. You have listened to the arguments from both your managing editor and reporter Robert Ashmore. Which you do find more persuasive? Applying the model for moral reasoning outlined in Chapter 3, decide whether you will approve Robert Ashmore's appearance before the war crimes tribunal at The Hague, assuming that the reporter wishes to appear.

CASE 7-5

A Television Station's Conflicting Messages

Conrad McGinnis inspected with pride Channel 5's most recent community service award as he placed it alongside the numerous other testaments to his station's commitment to the common good. McGinnis was Channel 5's president and general manager, and under his five-year stewardship the station had become an overall ratings leader in Phoenix City's four-station market. He was particularly pleased with the dominance of Channel 5's news operation under the leadership of news director Marsha Twain. Based upon the recommendations of the station's news consultant, Twain had constructed a news operation that skillfully blended serious journalism with a variety of lifestyle features, the most popular of which was *Healthwatch*, a biweekly health segment that relied upon both syndicated and locally produced material to accommodate the demands of an increasingly health-conscious public. Because of its appeal and popularity, according to marketing and ratings data, Channel 5 heavily promoted the health feature's edifying and reliable subject matter.

The popular *Healthwatch* feature had produced Channel 5's most recent award, which was presented to the station during a luncheon by Andrea Goldberg, the director of Phoenix City General Medical Center's Health Outreach program. This was the second time in three years that the community's largest hospital had recognized the station for its endeavors on behalf of a healthy lifestyle and physical fitness. McGinnis had accepted the award on behalf of his station, with appropriate accolades for his news director for *Healthwatch*'s enduring popularity.

With Phoenix City General's benediction firmly secured, Andrea Goldberg's impromptu visit to Channel 5's general manager just two weeks after the award presentation was unexpected and disconcerting. Following a brief exchange of pleasantries in which she again congratulated McGinnis on his station's health coverage, Goldberg got right to the point. Despite Channel 5's informative and timely *Healthwatch* segment, Goldberg told McGinnis, she believed the efforts were being compromised by the station's advertising on behalf of fast-food restaurants and a variety of junk foods, both through local and national spot advertising. She believed the station's credibility was at stake and that promoting unhealthy lifestyle choices through advertising while promoting good health in the station's newscasts constituted a conflict of interest. "You're serving two masters," she admonished McGinnis in concluding her lecture on institutional integrity. McGinnis told Goldberg that he would give serious consideration to her complaint but made no promises to tamper with what he realized was a fairly lucrative source of advertising revenue.

McGinnis was chastened by Andrea Goldberg's discordant comments and what she perceived as an ethical problem. Nevertheless, he was not prepared to concede the ethical high ground to his complainant without discussing the matter with Marsha Twain and Mark Miranda, Channel 5's director of sales and promotion. "I'm aware that we do derive significant revenues from fast-food restaurants and so-called junk food ads," Twain noted in response to McGinnis's summary of Andrea Goldberg's concerns. "However, Goldberg may have a point. *Healthwatch* is a popular feature with our audience, and we promote it as a guide to a more healthy lifestyle. It includes the latest research in medicine and nutrition and interviews with well-known experts in those fields. It does seem somewhat hypocritical to include this segment in our newscasts, with the avowed purpose to encourage healthier lifestyle choices by our viewers, and then to accept ads from companies whose products and food are unhealthy. Whether

the ads run in the news program or at some other time is really beside the point. The newscast is the only truly local production we do in the evening, and *Healthwatch* is inevitably linked in the public's consciousness with our station's image and reputation."

As expected, McGinnis's visit to Mark Miranda produced a contrary view. "I don't see this matter as a conflict of interest at all," stated Miranda emphatically, directly refuting Andrea Goldberg's accusation. "Goldberg is suggesting that we're attempting to embrace competing loyalties. But the commercial side is separate from the news operation. It's true that ads provide the revenue to sustain our news operation. In the case of *Healthwatch*, the news department's job is to provide accurate information to our viewers, who can then decide whether to heed the advice or utilize the material provided. In this respect, it's no different from political news. If we chose our advertisers on the basis of whether they might run afoul of what we report from time to time, this station would be out of business. Our viewers are sophisticated enough to understand that there's nothing wrong with promoting good health in our newscasts while running commercials for enterprises that some might feel could undermine this effort. If we remove these ads from the air, it will set a bad precedent."

"I'm not concerned about the sophistication of our viewers," replied McGinnis. "But that same sophistication might lead them to conclude that, from a corporate perspective, there is something incongruous about promoting good health through a regular segment in our newscasts while continuing to provide access to commercial products that are not particularly healthy. Nevertheless, I'm sensitive to the economic considerations that must be taken into account in deciding whether these competing loyalties really do constitute a conflict of interest."

THE CASE STUDY

Television stations, like most media in the United States, are commercially supported. Advertising provides the economic sustenance for both the entertainment and journalistic components of a station's operations. In most cases, there is no apparent conflict between the news accounts and the products advertised on the station. But in this scenario, the *Healthwatch* segment has apparently become identified in the collective public consciousness as a corporate commitment to good health. The station has won awards for this popular news feature. Andrea Goldberg, representing a local hospital's Health Outreach program, is convinced that the advertising of so-called junk food and fast-food restaurants undermines the station's efforts to promote good health and nutrition during its *Healthwatch* news segment. In fact, she considers this to be a conflict of interest, since the station appears to be serving two masters whose messages are contradictory.

Channel 5's news director, Marsha Twain, is aware of the financial consequences of dropping ads for fast-food restaurants and certain forms of food considered to be unhealthy but apparently accepts the ethical logic of Goldberg's complaint. The station's director of sales and promotion, Mark Miranda, not surprisingly, categorically rejects Goldberg's categorization of this matter as a conflict of interest. He does not believe that the station should serve as a moral gatekeeper in maintaining consistency between the commercial and journalistic enterprises. News departments sometimes report unpleasant news about advertisers, but within Miranda's framework the claims made by advertisers and the information provided by the news division occupy separate universes. Conrad McGinnis, the station's general manager, is concerned about corporate hypocrisy but is left to ponder whether Andrea Goldberg's concerns really constitute a conflict of interest. Is this a situation in which the public might indeed perceive an egregious conflict between the news and commercial enterprises in such a way that the station might suffer a blow to its integrity and a loss of public credibility?

For the purpose of addressing this question, assume the role of Channel 5's general manager and, utilizing the SAD formula for moral reasoning outlined in Chapter 3, decide how you will respond to the concerns in this case.

 CASE 7-6

Campus Journalists and the Tobacco Wars

The results of the student referendum were unmistakable. The antismoking crusaders had prevailed in their initiative to improve the quality of life at Southwestern University.

The idea of a smoke-free environment at Southwestern was first floated by the university's vice president for academic affairs, Dr. Patricia Jenkins, but the Student Government Association (SGA) had asked her to submit the proposal to a student vote rather than to implement it through administrative fiat. The SGA cited a recently completed survey revealing that 34.1 percent of the student body at Southwestern were smokers. And most of these opposed any further attempts to restrict what they believed was their right to smoke. Although this was certainly not a majority, the SGA president told Jenkins, it was significant enough to allow the smokers some input into the decision-making process. "They should at least have an opportunity to convert student opinion to their point of view," she noted in her appeal to the academic vice president.

As presented to the students on the referendum ballot, the new policy would ban the use of all tobacco products in all campus buildings. Students who wished to "light up" could do so outside, and for this purpose the university would provide ash cans at strategic locations around campus. The "tobacco war," as the university's campus newspaper, the *Watchdog*, dubbed the campaign, sometimes stretched the bounds of decorum and civility, but in the end the antismoking forces carried the day. Nevertheless, the results of the campuswide vote were somewhat surprising to faculty and students alike. Although slightly more than a third of the respondents in the SGA survey had identified themselves as smokers, 46 percent of the student voters had cast their ballots in opposition to the administration's proposal, the reflection perhaps of a tolerant generation who opposed any institutional incursions into their individual rights.

Tawana Deitch was proud of the *Watchdog*'s role in providing a forum for student opinion during the campaign leading up to the referendum. As editor of the campus newspaper, she had served as the primary gatekeeper in ensuring that the paper's op-ed page reflected a diversity of student and faculty opinion. This was no mean task considering that the debate on this issue seemed to have been hijacked by extremists on both sides of the issue. At times, Deitch labored to discover a voice of reason among the myriad letters and opinions submitted in support of or in opposition to the new smoking policy. The *Watchdog*, however, had not served as a mere conduit for the sentiments of others. Two years before the student vote on smoke-free campus buildings, the editors had joined the crusade against the besieged tobacco industry and had been unremitting in their efforts to remind their peers of the health risks associated with the use of cigarettes and other tobacco products. The paper's editorial involvement in the tobacco war had not been a painless decision. Although there was only one smoker among the editorial staff, some viewed the right to smoke as a civil liberty comparable to suffrage and free speech. They resisted the notion of passing judgment on their contemporaries or of the newspaper's editorially browbeating them into a nicotine-free existence.

Nevertheless, Deitch's elevation to the position of editor had brought with it a determination to place the *Watchdog* at the vanguard of the anti-smoking crusade on campus. Armed with the latest news on the effects of secondhand smoke, she had convinced the newspaper's staff that banning tobacco products from all university buildings, if not from the campus itself, was a reasonable accommodation between the tobacco users and those who demanded a smoke-free environment. These editorials complemented her own columns which consistently savaged the tobacco industry for targeting teenagers in their ads and for misleading the public about the narcotizing effects of nicotine. Her public posture had brought its own rewards in the form of an award from a local environmental organization and a complimentary letter from the state's attorney general, who was involved

in litigation against the tobacco industry to recoup the costs of Medicaid payments for smoking-related illnesses. But above all, Deitch was properly gratified by the results of the student referendum and her newspaper's role in the factious campaign.

However, her euphoria was short-lived. She and Samuel Lewis, the campus paper's advertising manager, were not kindred spirits. Whereas Deitch regarded the *Watchdog*'s public service role as a sacred trust, Lewis viewed the paper's news and op-ed pages as merchandising vehicles for national and local advertisers who wished to pitch their wares to the college crowd. Deitch attributed Lewis's lack of journalistic altruism to the fact that the paper's commercial gatekeeper was an advertising major and that, contrary to the curriculum model at many universities, advertising was taught in the School of Business, not Mass Communication. At Southwestern University, journalism and advertising were like two ships passing in the night, academically speaking.

Despite her devotion to the marketplace of ideas, Deitch was also pragmatic and gratefully acknowledged the role of advertising in supporting the *Watchdog*'s journalistic enterprise. She appreciated Lewis's determination to safeguard the paper's financial infrastructure, but their relationship had hardly been one of peaceful coexistence. On two occasions the editor had challenged Lewis's decision to accept ads for term paper services and off-campus bars that promoted happy hour. Both had been the subject of *Watchdog* editorials. She had lost on the first issue but prevailed on the happy hour promotions, possibly because of the untimely death of a university freshman resulting from binge drinking.

The tobacco industry's overture, in Deitch's view, was a well-calculated attempt to influence the most vulnerable and tolerant of its potential consumers. After more than a thirty-year self-imposed moratorium, the tobacco companies had again decided to mount an aggressive campaign to capture the soul of the college consumer. Given the significant number of smokers among Southwestern University's student population, the tobacco industry's interest in the *Watchdog* as a commercial vehicle came as no surprise. However, Deitch vowed to resist any attempt to dishonor her paper's moral chastity in the tobacco wars.

The meeting to discuss this apparent conflict between journalistic and economic values was convened by Dale Brooks, the director of student media. Although Lewis and his staff were responsible for advertising sales and scheduling, Brooks routinely reviewed all contracts for matters of taste and other violations of university policy. In this dispute between the editorial and commercial side of the *Watchdog,* he would be the moral agent. Deitch, Lewis, and Brooks were joined by Sarah Rabinowitz, the newspaper's adviser.

Brooks opened the meeting with a few pleasantries and then asked Lewis to brief the others on the proposed ad campaign. "In a nutshell, we've been approached by the Baldwin and Baldwin ad agency; they represent the R. W. Kaiser Tobacco Company," stated Lewis matter-of-factly. "They want to run a half-page ad twice a week—each one will cost $400. Most of the ads will alternate between their new smokeless tobacco product and their leading brand of cigarettes. For our paper, this is a big contract from a national sponsor. It'll bring in a lot of money."

"But how can we accept money from the tobacco industry when we have campaigned so aggressively against smoking and in favor of smoke-free campus facilities?" replied Deitch indignantly. "It would be hypocritical to accept money from tobacco companies while editorially disparaging the use of tobacco."

"I strongly disagree," responded Lewis without hesitation. "As you are constantly reminding me, the editorial and advertising functions of this paper are separate. Our readers understand this. They're clever enough to separate our editorial positions from the products we advertise. I don't see the ethical dilemma here. General Motors advertises on all of the major TV networks. But should their news departments refuse to cover a story critical of GM just because their journalistic and commercial messages don't agree? What's the difference?"

As newspaper adviser and university employee, Sarah Rabinowitz's perspective was usually less imperious than Deitch's, but at this point she came to her editor's defense. "The difference is that we have *editorially* trashed the tobacco industry," said

Rabinowitz. "Tobacco is a dangerous product. It's a health hazard. If we appear to be softening our position and accept these ads, we'll lose credibility with our readers."

"Which readers?" rebutted Lewis. "More than a third of our students, according to the SGA survey, smoke. That's a significant minority, and we also have a responsibility to them. Also, R. W. Kaiser currently runs ads in more than two hundred college papers. Tobacco is a legal enterprise. Any company should have the right to advertise a legal product. Students have a right to make up their own minds. If we refuse these ads, this is tantamount to economic censorship." Lewis's reference to economic censorship was obviously an attempt to challenge Deitch on her own turf.

But Deitch was not deterred. "This is not censorship," she replied with conviction. "The tobacco industry has no right of access to our readers. They can advertise elsewhere in more hospitable forums. It's a conflict of interest for us to discourage tobacco usage on our editorial pages and then accept money from a tobacco company."

"If the entire editorial philosophy of our paper related to this kind of issue—such as a magazine designed specifically to promote a more healthy and robust lifestyle among young professional women—I might agree," conceded Lewis. "But the tobacco campaign is just one among many for us. We're a general-purpose newspaper for the Southwestern campus. We're not going to be remembered by our devotion to this one issue."

"It's true that we editorialize on a lot of issues," admitted Deitch. "But our readers, who are here for only four years, will judge us by what we do today. Our editorial campaign on the evils of tobacco was done with the students' and the university's interests in mind. I'm not going to concede the point that the acceptance of tobacco advertising is now a conflict of interest."

"Keep in mind that advertising keeps this paper afloat," Lewis reminded Deitch. "We receive some funds from student fees, but most of our support comes from ads. If it weren't for our advertising, there would be no editorial page. And the fact is that our sales have been flat lately. These ads will provide a welcome infusion of funds. It's okay to reflect different messages in the editorial and commercial spaces. They serve different purposes. In my judgment, there's no conflict of interest."

Brooks felt emotionally drained by this rapid exchange among his two student antagonists and the paper's adviser. As student media practitioners, Tawana Deitch and Samuel Lewis were schooled in different intellectual traditions and were unlikely to have a meeting of the minds. Both had made persuasive arguments. As director of student media, Brooks would be the final arbiter of the *Watchdog*'s next installment in the tobacco wars.

THE CASE STUDY

Because the tobacco industry has historically targeted college newspapers, the facts described here could reflect the experience of many college newspapers across the country.[69] Traditionally, there has been a clear line of demarcation between the editorial and advertising functions of newspapers, although the lines have blurred gradually in recent years. And yet, editors have been quick to point out inconsistencies between their papers' editorial postures and the acceptance of certain kinds of ads. This has been of particular concern in certain kinds of specialized publications.

The internal conflict between student editor Tawana Deitch and advertising manager Samuel Lewis raises a fairly straightforward ethical question: Is it a conflict of interest for a publication to criticize an industry on the editorial pages and then accept advertising from that industry? For Deitch, the answer is simple. Any commercial accommodation with the tobacco interests is steeped in hypocrisy. The result is an indefensible two-tier ethical posture, which can't be defended. She is also concerned about consequences—that is, the loss of the paper's credibility. She also rejects as unimportant the claim of economic censorship that would result in the denial of information about a lawful product to a significant minority of the student body. Interestingly, Deitch does not appeal to her paper's possible role in promoting a continuing high level of smoking among Southwestern students if the ads are accepted. This could be a relevant consideration, regardless of the *Watchdog*'s previously stated editorial position on the issue.

Lewis doesn't share the editor's ethical qualms about running tobacco ads. He believes that the student readers have a right to information about any lawful product, regardless of how the editorial staff feels about that product. Denial of the tobacco industry's access to the *Watchdog*'s advertising space is economic censorship, in his view. College students are mature enough to make up their own minds. Lewis also notes the financially lucrative contract offered by the R. W. Kaiser Tobacco Company. In this respect, his thinking is decidedly teleological (consequentialist). In essence, Lewis has coupled his mercenary instincts with an appeal to reader autonomy.

The issue has been joined and is now in the capable hands of the director of student media, Dale Brooks. Assume his role and, based on the SAD formula, make a decision on this matter.

 CASE 7-7
Switching Sides in Public Relations

In her more desperate moments, Monique Andrews was reminded of the biblical account of David and Goliath. Goliath was MicroGro Enterprises, a large conglomerate that specialized in industrial development. David was Citizens to Save Endangered Wetlands (CSEW), a confederation of environmental activists and concerned citizens that opposed MicroGro's latest venture into urban renewal.

Andrews's graduation from college ten years before had brought immediate employment with Boutwell and Randolph, a large public relations firm in Pittsburgh, but little job satisfaction. Her clients derived primarily from the corporate sector, and the pace, workload, and tedium required in the care and feeding of her commercial benefactors had exhausted her reserves of professional enthusiasm. With her valuable experience and wisdom gained during her decade at Boutwell, Andrews had retreated to her hometown of North Hampton, a coastal community of 250,000 located adjacent to a pristine wetlands sanctuary. North Hampton had been economically stagnant even before Andrews departed for college, but she nevertheless defied conventional wisdom in returning to the place of her birth to earn her livelihood. Andrews established her own public relations firm, and with little competition, aggressive salesmanship, and a lot of luck she attracted enough clients, mostly small companies, to hire two junior associates, Lee Fong and Andrea Romero, both recent graduates of nearby Central State University. To keep overhead to a minimum, the firm was housed in one side of a rather modest duplex that Andrews had purchased. The Andrews and Associates client list soon expanded to include several nonprofit institutions, such as the North Hampton Council for the Arts, which appealed to Andrews's acute sense of civic responsibility. Unlike her commercial business clients, they did not significantly enrich her firm's coffers, but Andrews derived immense satisfaction from the belief that she was contributing to her community's cultural ambiance.

Andrews was also satisfied with the overture from the CSEW. MicroGro's proposal to convert much of the ecologically fragile wetlands area between North Hampton and the adjacent city of Covington to the north into a large shopping mall had galvanized local and state environmentalists and other activists into a determined opposition. Their financial resources were no match for MicroGro, but Andrews agreed to budgetary austerity in her firm's representation of CSEW. She had never been a committed environmentalist but believed that the issue was too important not to be fully contested in the public square.

The North Hampton community was divided on the construction of a shopping mall on the wetlands sanctuary. Because of the potential economic impact, the local Chamber of Commerce was firmly behind the project. They were supported in their view by some of the national chain stores, which saw the new mall as an opportunity for expansion, and business leaders who saw the proposed shopping complex as an economic shot in the arm for the community's stagnant economy. Most of the locally owned businesses, some of whom were Andrews's clients, opposed the MicroGro initiative as unwelcome competition; others objected because of its impact on local tourism, which depended in part on the uncultivated wilderness as its principal enticement.

At the outset, Andrews canvassed her clients to ascertain their views on the MicroGro project and to ensure that there was no conflict of interest in representing the CSEW. Having relieved herself of this concern, Andrews and her two young associates mounted an aggressive campaign to counter the prolific and costly crusade of MicroGro's prestigious PR representative, Hillsdale and Bowers. The corporation's most persuasive evidence came in the form of an environmental impact study, which was commissioned by the company, purporting to "prove" that MicroGro's project could be carried out with a minimum of disruption to the wetlands' ecosystem and that the remaining wilderness would still attract tourists to the North Hampton–Covington area. MicroGro also cited other projects in which it had successfully integrated malls into the community with a minimum of disruption to the surrounding environment. Though constrained by financial considerations, the CSEW countered with a study of its own that refuted MicroGro's claims that the shopping mall could live in harmony with its native surroundings. The system was so sensitive, according to the report, that any unnatural intrusion into the wetlands could be environmentally fatal.

However, the CSEW's modest war chest proved no match for MicroGro's seemingly unlimited financial resources, and after fifteen months the group was reduced to an occasional press conference and appearances on local talk shows. Andrews and Associates, sentimentally aligned with the environmentalists but unable to justify the pro bono representation that would be necessary if the firm continued its representation, withdrew as CSEW's public relations counsel.

Despite her indecisive finale, Monique Andrews had impressed her clients with her firm's creative energies and assertive strategy. She had also impressed her competitor, Hillsdale and Bowers. As Andrews was preparing to close the file on the CSEW project, Michael Hillsdale, the senior partner in the firm, approached Andrews about joining his team to help bring the MicroGro venture to fruition. "We've been moderately successful to this point," Hillsdale told Andrews, "but we need a local firm to help us with the details. We still need final approval from state and federal agencies, and we still have some work to do in convincing the community that our mall can coexist with the surrounding wetlands." Hillsdale said that Andrews and Associates, with its knowledge of the project and the local environmental concerns, would be an ideal ally in contributing to the economic progress of the North Hampton–Covington communities. He also pointed to a slight shift in public opinion that clearly reflected the community's increasing comfort level with the accommodation between MicroGro's proposed shopping complex and the surrounding wetlands.

"We've been asked to assist Hillsdale and Bowers in paving the way for the new shopping mall," Andrews told her two associates, Lee Fong and Andrea Romero, in recounting her conversation with Michael Hillsdale. Fong handled the creative end of the business, while Romero was the firm's account executive. "Although they've handled MicroGro's campaign for more than a year," she continued, "they now need local public relations counsel. The question is whether we should join them. After all, we're no longer involved with the CSEW. We fought a good fight, but we're no match for the competition."

"How will this look to our other clients?" asked Fong. "Many of them were opposed to the MicroGro project while we were working for the CSEW. Are they likely to jump ship if we join forces with Hillsdale?"

"We've checked this out," replied Andrews. "Two, perhaps three, say they will leave. But the others appear resigned to the shopping center. A couple have even said if the price is right they may consider leasing space in the mall."

"In that case, I don't see a problem," said Romero. "We may lose some revenue up front from the defection of two or three clients, but in the short term the Hillsdale contract will offset those loses. And in the long run, if we do a credible job, MicroGro might throw other business our way. The economic boost that this shopping center will provide should eventually expand North Hampton's industrial base, which should also benefit Andrews and Associates." As her firm's account executive, Romero seldom ignored the fiscal realities of the public relations enterprise.

But Fong had some reservations about Romero's assessment predicated strictly on economic values. "I'm concerned first of all about the public's perception, as well as the perception of our clients present and future, if we switch sides in this dispute," said Fong. "Perhaps some have voiced no objection, but at this point the business community and the citizens might question our commitment to the CSEW in the first place if we are so willing now to assist their antagonist. Second, because we worked for the environmentalists for more than a year we have some inside knowledge of their concerns and perhaps even the strategies they may employ if they continue the campaign on their own. Although we may not be representing clients with opposing interests *at the same time,* this arrangement with Hillsdale might still be viewed as a conflict of interest."

"I disagree," responded Romero. "The CSEW group is no longer our client. We fought a good fight and lost. And while we may have some environmental concerns of our own, the impact of this shopping mall project on the ecosystem is at best debatable. Our study and the one commissioned by MicroGro don't agree; but MicroGro's record in other communities appears pretty solid."

"At some point," declared Fong rather defensively, "we must decide where our loyalties lie. We accepted the CSEW as a client because we believed that the environmental interests needed to be heard—and because we were concerned about the mall's impact on the wetlands. Just because CSEW ran out of cash and we severed our relationship with the group doesn't mean that we should sell our services to the opposition just because they appear to have the upper hand."

"You speak of loyalties," replied Romero, "but we need to examine our priorities. Consider this: We no longer represent the environmentalists; they're likely to lose because MicroGro's proposal, despite some lingering doubts, appears to the business community to be ecologically sound, and even public opinion appears to be moving in MicroGro's direction."

"But public opinion is fickle," observed Fong. "I'm not surprised that it has shifted decidedly in MicroGro's direction. Hillsdale and Bowers has done a great job in the public arena, and for the past several weeks there has been little effective opposition, except an occasional interview with a CSEW member. The question is how much loyalty we have to what we believe is in the long-term best interest of the North Hampton community. Sometimes economic *progress* must give way to other concerns."

Monique Andrews listened attentively to the views of her two young associates. They had focused on the most relevant question, in Andrews's view. Where, indeed, should their loyalties lie? If this had been an issue involving the representation of clients with competing claims, there would be no question of a conflict of interest. But is it a conflict of interest, Andrews wondered, to switch sides in a dispute when you have severed your relationship with one of the parties to the dispute? As the senior member of the firm, Andrews would be the ultimate decision maker in deciding whether to join Hillsdale and Bowers in paving the way for the shopping mall. However, she promised that she would submit her recommendation to her two associates for one final venting before calling Michael Hillsdale.

THE CASE STUDY

The recently revised code of the PRSA requires members to "disclose promptly any existing or potential conflict of interest to affected clients or organizations" and to "avoid actions and circumstances that may appear to compromise good business judgment or create a conflict between personal and professional interests." The case at hand does not involve the concurrent representation of clients with competing interests. And, in fact, Monique Andrews has canvassed her clients to determine whether they have any serious objections to her firm's joining MicroGro's public relations team. Two or three questioned the move, but most indicated no serious reservations. However, this move was primarily a matter of courtesy and an attempt to evaluate the overall financial impact on the firm. And she has no personal interest (such as some hidden investment in the shopping mall project) that might conflict with her professional obligations.

Thus, the PRSA code doesn't provide any clear guidance in this particular case. The underlying questions still remain. Andrews and her colleagues developed an emotional bond with the environmentalists during their period of representation, but there is no evidence that they are so personally committed to the cause that they are willing to ignore other opportunities.

Both Romero and Fong address the question of competing loyalties, an important ingredient in any ethical decision involving public relations. As the moral agent, what duty do you owe to your conscience? To your firm? To your clients, past and present? To the community?

Because Andrews and Associates has severed its relationship with the environmentalists, Andrea Romero sees no conflict of interest in representing the other side in the dispute. Despite the loss of a couple of clients in the short term, she believes that the long-term financial benefits justify the move. In addition, it's at least debatable as to whether the initial concerns about the adverse ecological impact on the wetlands are justified. Indeed, public opinion appears to have shifted somewhat in MicroGro's favor, which, in Romero's judgment, is further evidence that the opposition to the mall is beginning to erode.

Despite the lack of any serious objections from most of the firm's clients (some of whom are no longer opposed to MicroGro's project), Romero's colleague, Lee Fong, is concerned about the firm's long-term reputation and the perception that a shift to the other side might be viewed as a conflict of interest. Or to put it another way, there is a danger, in Fong's view, that Andrews and Associates will be viewed by future clients as a "hired gun" rather than a reliable firm that is emotionally committed to the clients they serve.

Does Hillsdale's offer pose a potential conflict of interest? How would you evaluate the competing loyalties in this case? For the purpose of addressing these questions, assume the role of Monique Andrews and, using the model for moral reasoning outlined in Chapter 3, make a recommendation to your young associates concerning the offer to join the public relations team of Hillsdale and Bowers.

Notes

1. Martha T. Moore, "Bush Cousin Helped Fox Make Call," *USA Today*, November 14, 2000, p. 15A.
2. Bill Carter, "Counting the Vote: The Fox Executive," *New York Times*, November 14, 2000, p. A21.

3. This wording came from the code that was in effect prior to the 2000 update.

4. "The Bishops under Fire," *Newsweek,* April 23, 1990, p. 24. For a more thorough discussion of this case, see Dennis L. Wilcox, Phillip H. Ault, Warren K. Agee, and Glen T. Cameron, *Essentials of Public Relations* (New York: Longman, 2001), pp. 67–69.

5. Michele Orecklin, "Too Close for Comfort," *Time,* March 18, 2002, p. 65.

6. Jeffrey Olen, *Ethics in Journalism* (Upper Saddle River, NJ: Prentice-Hall, 1988), p. 25.

7. For example, see Elizabeth Lesly Stevens, "mouse.-ke.fear," *Brill's Content,* December 1998/January 1999, pp. 95–103.

8. Mitchell Stephens, *Broadcast News,* 2d ed. (New York: Holt, Rinehart & Winston, 1986), pp. 309–310.

9. F. Smith, *Groping for Ethics in Journalism,* 5th ed. (Ames: Iowa State University Press, 2003), p. 387.

10. Justin Ewers, "Is the New News Good News?," *U.S. News & World Report,* April 7, 2003, p. 48.

11. Jennifer LaFleur, "Embed Program Worked, Broader Coverage Lagged," *News Media and the Law,* Spring 2003, pp. 4–6.

12. For a more thorough discussion, see Smith, *Groping for Ethics in Journalism,* pp. 388–390.

13. Betsy Streisand, "True Confessions of a Tabloid Opportunist," *U.S. News & World Report,* March 2, 1998, pp. 24, 26.

14. Bruce Selcraig, "Buying News," *Columbia Journalism Review,* July/August 1994, p. 45.

15. Kelly Heyboer, "Paying for It," *American Journalism Review,* April 1999, pp. 28, 30.

16. See Gary Paul Gates, *Air Time* (New York: Harper & Row, 1978), pp. 353–354.

17. Steve McClellan, "Tabloids Pull Out the Checkbook, Proudly," *Broadcasting & Cable,* May 9, 1994, p. 42. The exact amount was not revealed, but most reports put the payment in the $500,000 range.

18. Heyboer, "Paying for It," p. 30.

19. H. Eugene Goodwin and Ron F. Smith, *Groping for Ethics in Journalism,* 3d ed. (Ames, IA: Iowa State University Press, 1994), p. 136, citing Ann Hodges, "Cult Interviews Worth Big Bucks to News Shows," *Houston Chronicle,* April 24, 1993, p. 6.

20. Quoted in Selcraig, "Buying News," p. 46.

21. "The Cost of Business," *U.S. News & World Report,* January 12, 2004, p. 13.

22. Bill Carter, "Critics Say ABC Opened Its Checkbook for a News Source," *New York Times,* May 31, 1999, p. C1.

23. All quotes taken from ibid.

24. Selcraig, "Buying News," pp. 45–46.

25. "Dubious Decisions; Details at Six . . . ," *Columbia Journalism Review,* July/August 2001, p. 14.

26. "Darts & Laurels," *Columbia Journalism Review,* May/June 1999, p. 22.

27. Sarah Jackson-Han, "Conflicting Interests," *Communicator,* November 1994, p. 24.

28. James Poniewozik, "Whose Flag Is Bigger?," *Time,* April 14, 2003, p. 71.

29. Ibid.

30. Thomas Bivens, *Mixed Media* (Mahwah, NJ: Lawrence Erlbaum, 2004), pp. 26–27. See also "Lawmakers Decry TV Station's Ban on Flag-Wearing Newscasters," AP online dispatch, September 28, 2001, at http://www.freedomforum.org/templates/document.asp?documentID=15017 (downloaded July 20, 2004).

31. Gina Barton, "Patriotism and the News: How 'American' Should the American Press Be?" *Quill,* December 2001, p. 18.

32. Ibid.

33. For example, see Maria Trombly, "Ethics and War," *Quill,* December 2001, pp. 14–17, for an examination of disagreements between critics who claim journalists go too far and those who believe they do not go far enough.

34. Gary Hill, "Search for Truth Is Journalism's Patriotic Role," *Quill,* November 2001, p. 35.

35. Michael Hoyt, "Journalists as Patriots," *Columbia Journalism Review,* November/December 2001, p. 5.

36. Susan Paterno, "The Intervention Dilemma," *American Journalism Review,* March 1998, pp. 37–38.

37. Ibid., p. 38.

38. Ibid.

39. Ibid., p. 66.

40. J. Max Robins, "NBC News Forces Gerald Rivera to Drop Mayoral Bid," *TV Guide,* October 14, 2000, p. 57.

41. Howard Kurtz, "Rather Spoke at Democratic Fundraiser," *Washington Post,* April 4, 2001, p. A1; Howard Kurtz, "Rather Apology Isn't Enough for Some Critics," *Washington Post,* April 5, 2001, p. C2.

42. Fred Brown, "Conflicts over Conflicts," *Quill,* September 2002, p. 52.

43. Associated Press dispatch, published in sacbee.com's *Recall Election Newsletter,* September 9, 2003, at wysiwyg://2/http://www.sacbeen.com/content . . . tics/recall/story/7382315p-8325882c.html (downloaded September 10, 2003).

44. Stephanie Saul, "Judgment Call," *Columbia Journalism Review,* July/August 1989, p. 50.

45. Quoted in "No Cheering in the Press Box," *Newsweek,* July 19, 1993, p. 59.

46. Valerie Alia, "A Conflict of Interest," in *Media Ethics* (Boston: Emerson College, 1997), p. 1.

47. Ibid., p. 12.

48. "Reading by 9," in *News Futures: Civic Innovations in Reporting* (The James K. Batten Symposium and Awards for Excellence in Civic Journalism, Sponsored by the Pew Center for Civic Journalism and the Medill School of Journalism, May 12, 1998), pp. 19–20.

49. Al Cross, "A Powerful Experiment," *Quill,* June 2002, p. 4.

50. E.g., see ibid., citing Philip Meyer, a journalism professor at the University of North Carolina.

51. Arthur Charity, *Doing Public Journalism* (New York: The Kettering Foundation, 1995), p. v.

52. Anthony J. Eksterowicz, "The History and Development of Public Journalism," in Anthony J. Eksterowicz and Robert N. Roberts (eds.), *Public Journalism and Political Knowledge* (Lanham, MD: Rowman & Littlefield, 2000), p. 3.

53. Bill Kovach and Tom Rosenstiel, *The Elements of Journalism* (New York: Crown, 2001), p. 101.

54. Charity, *Doing Public Journalism,* p. 15.

55. Rebecca Ross Albers, "Going Public," *Presstime,* September 1994, p. 28.

56. Cross.

57. Quoted in Liz Viall, "Crossing That Line," *Quill,* November/December 1991, p. 18.

58. Albers, "Going Public," p. 28.

59. Shepard, "The Gospel of Public Journalism," *American Journalism Review,* September 1994, p. 34.

60. Davis, "Buzz" Merritt, *Public Journalism and Public Life* (Hillsdale, NJ: Erlbaum), 1995, pp. 115–116.

61. Gloria Cooper, "Darts & Laurels," *Columbia Journalism Review,* March/April 2004, p. 6.

62. Ibid.

63. Seth Mnookin and Bret Begun, "Taking a Swing," *Newsweek,* October 20, 2003, p. 10.

64. "Darts & Laurels," *Columbia Journalism Review,* January/February 1996, p. 19.

65. "Darts & Laurels," *Columbia Journalism Review,* January/February 1999, p. 25.

66. This scenario is based on an actual case that was reported in 1995 in a national news magazine. However, the facts have been changed for the purposes of this hypothetical case study. See "Should Journalists Also Be Advocates?" *U.S. News & World Report,* July 31, 1995, pp. 27–28.

67. This case is based upon some questions raised in the following article: S. Austin Merrill, "Witnesses for the Prosecution," *Columbia Journalism Review,* September/October 1999, pp. 35–37.

68. Ibid., p. 35.

69. For example, in 1998, *The Chronicle of Higher Education* reported that the U.S. Tobacco Company alone was running ads in about 200 student newspapers. See Leo Reisberg, "A Tobacco Company Ends Voluntary Ban on Advertising in Student Newspapers," *Chronicle of Higher Education,* May 1, 1998, pp. A53–A54.

8

Economic Pressures and Social Responsibility

ECONOMIC INTERESTS VERSUS MORAL OBLIGATIONS

In his "Apology for Printers," the American sage Benjamin Franklin famously declared, in response to a customer who asked the young printer to publish a piece in his paper that Franklin found "scurrilous and defamatory": "I have formed a determination never to prostitute my press to the purposes of corruption and abuse of this kind for the sake of gaining a more comfortable subsistence."[1] But even the legendary Franklin's high-minded principles could not resist the more common marketing techniques to sell papers, such as sexual titillation, sensational crime stories, and gossip and scandal mongering.[2] Even in colonial America, it seems, Franklin was a man of modern sensibilities.

The profit motive and competition are the economic mainstays of Western democracies. No doubt, our capitalist system is responsible for most of our material wealth and commercial prosperity, and it has produced a highly diverse media system free from government control. But some have been critical of the excesses of our economic system. The critics view the unrestrained pursuit of profits as a parasitical practice that puts self-interest above any sense of social responsibility.[3] According to this view, whenever profit motives and altruistic motives

compete for the attention of corporate management, commercial interests always prevail.

Economic considerations are undoubtedly a powerful (and sometimes irresistible) motivator. And herein lies an ethical quandary. I noted in Chapter 1 that one who is motivated primarily by self-interest in situations calling for a moral judgment cannot, by definition, behave ethically. Does that mean, therefore, that moral agents who are driven by economic motives have rejected any allegiance to moral duty and social responsibility?

To answer this question, we should begin with a basic proposition: There is nothing *inherently* immoral in the profit motive or the accumulation of wealth. Many wealthy entrepreneurs and philanthropists have used their considerable economic resources to benefit social causes and charity. Likewise, certain businesses and corporations have revealed a sense of social obligation by plowing some of their profits back into the communities they serve. Self-interest *can* be the servant of the public's interest, because the pursuit of profits can work to the benefit of society at large. Ethical questions do arise, however, when commercial interests are allowed to dominate other social obligations. The issue, in any given situation, is how to *balance* economic pressures against individual or institutional duties to others.

This is a perennial problem, for example, for TV stations that might desire to position themselves as the "news leader" in their communities by programming more hours of news but must confront the realities of market competition. Entertainment programs frequently generate higher ratings, which means that local news is dispensable. KNBC-TV in Los Angeles, for example, decided to cancel its nearly twenty-year-old 4 P.M. newscast in September 2002 to make room for the newly syndicated *Dr. Phil.* This followed a decision by KCBS-TV to replace its news program in the same time slot with *Judge Judy.* Thus, of the "big three" news outlets in LA only KABC-TV, which had also lost viewers at 4 P.M., remained committed to local news during this time period.[4]

For the moral idealist, it is tempting to propose that commercial interests should always be subordinated to more noble causes. But suppose, for example, that a major advertiser for a small newspaper threatens to withdraw its support if the editor insists on publishing a story critical of that advertiser. One could argue that in the spirit of journalistic independence the editor should proceed with the story, undeterred by the threat of economic reprisal. But if the loss of advertising is likely to pose a severe financial hardship for the paper, it may then be unable to provide a quality service to the public in the rest of its news coverage. The *New York Times* may have the financial security to withstand such pressures, but small hometown newspapers often do not.

In a capitalist society economic pressures can come from many directions, but they generally originate from three sources: (1) financial supporters, such as investors, advertisers, clients, subscribers, and customers; (2) the competition; and (3) the public at large. The three are interdependent, of course, and economic concerns in one area can have an impact on another area. For example, competitive pressures often force companies to make countermoves in the interest of appeasing institutional financial supporters. Segments of the public sometimes chastise

advertisers or even boycott them to force them to pressure a network or publisher to withdraw objectionable material.

The media are in a unique position within the American economic system. Unlike most other businesses, they acquire most of their profits not directly from the consumer but indirectly through advertising. The media are also unique because of the constitutional protection accorded them as an institution. Their "product"—news, information, and even entertainment—has been given a legal sanctuary not available to the output of other industries. Thus, from the outset the media have always been viewed as servants of the public interest, a role that transcends purely commercial considerations. Nevertheless, since the turn of the twentieth century, the media have joined the ranks of big business, and economic pressures have competed aggressively for influence in management decision making. This uneasy alliance between the media's financial interests and the public's interests is reflected in three separate but related phenomena: (1) the trend toward concentration of ownership in the media, (2) the rise of the marketing concept, and (3) the influence of advertising on the media.

CONCENTRATION OF MEDIA OWNERSHIP

Since the beginning of the twentieth century, the media have marched relentlessly toward bigness and concentration of ownership.[5] The power of ideas must now compete with the power of the profit-and-loss statement. Nowhere is the evidence of concentration more noticeable than in the newspaper business. Since World War II, most U.S. papers have been gobbled up by groups or chains, a trend that has slowed recently but has nevertheless continued unabated. In 1930, for instance, 84 percent of the nation's daily newspapers were independent.[6] By the turn of the century, however, about 20 percent of the approximately 1,500 dailies were still independent and family-owned,[7] and during the six-year period between 1994 and 2000, 47 percent of all hometown papers changed hands, some of them three or four times.[8] Fewer than sixty cities are served by more than one daily newspaper,[9] and 99 percent of the daily newspapers are the only paper in their respective markets. Most daily papers are now the property of such groups as the Gannett Company, Newhouse Newspapers, Knight-Ridder Newspapers, the Times Mirror Company, and the Tribune Company, which became an even more formidable media conglomerate with its recent purchase of Times-Mirror, publisher of the the *Los Angeles Times*.[10] Thus, it is clear that the family-owned newspaper is moving steadily in the same direction as the family-owned farm.

Arguably, media concentration could result in a better product because of the pooling of economic resources. Indeed, chain ownership has allowed many newspapers that might otherwise have died to survive. Corporate ownership often results in an infusion of funds that can lead to an economic rejuvenation and even an improved editorial product. Furthermore, in most cases parent companies do not intrude into the editorial decisions of their news operations.

However, the obsession with cutting costs to maximize profits is systemic to large chains, and the ultimate loser is the reader and viewer. Ironically, newspaper comics (more commonly referred to as the "funny pages") have become "exhibit A" in the drive to cut costs. In July 2004 *Newsweek* magazine reported that cost-conscious newspapers in San Francisco, Dallas, and Atlanta had reduced the size of their funny pages to save on newsprint and paper. In addition, the major syndicates that distribute the comics are dealing increasingly not with local papers but with the chains that own them— chains that are publicly owned, obsess about costs and earnings, and are more beholden to stockholders than their readers. The magazine reported that one major chain, California-based Knight-Ridder, demanded a 20 percent reduction in the rates its papers paid for comics,

"while threatening the cancellation of more than $100,000 worth of business if the syndicates don't comply."[11]

One of the most disturbing trends lies in the monopoly of information by self-interested outside corporations that have no commitment to the journalistic imperative and spirit than in the group and chain ownership patterns themselves. Press accounts of media mergers are commonplace, documenting the relentless concentration of various facets of the media infrastructure. This lead from an Associated Press story in May 2004 is exemplary of this trend: "NBC clinched its big media prize Wednesday, completing a merger with the Universal television and entertainment businesses to create a major media conglomeration."[12]

The major TV news networks are the properties of nonjournalistic corporate enterprises (ABC, for example, is owned by Walt Disney and CBS by Viacom), but whether the fears of a loss of journalistic independence are overblown remains to be seen. However, some anecdotal evidence suggests that media watchdogs should not yet abandon their posts. In 1999, for example, ABC News President David Westin reportedly "killed" a story on Disney's lax hiring practices that led to the hiring of convicted pedophiles at its theme parks amidst suspicions that the story would have aired except for Disney's ownership of ABC.[13] Walt Disney company officials insisted they had nothing to do with the story's demise, but just days before Michael Eisner, Disney's chair, on National Public Radio had articulated his views on the network's coverage of Disney interests: "I would prefer ABC not to cover Disney. I think it's inappropriate.... ABC News knows that I would prefer them not to cover [Disney]."[14]

An equally troubling case, which precipitated a national debate within the journalistic community and inspired a movie (*The Insider*), arose as CBS stockholders were prepared to vote on a merger with the Westinghouse Electric Company. In 1995 CBS's *60 Minutes* had scheduled an interview with Jeffrey Wigands, a former high-ranking tobacco company executive who was prepared to offer devastating testimony against the Brown and Williamson Tobacco Corporation (B&W). CBS had apparently offered to indemnify their interviewee against legal fees and damages in any libel suit arising out of the broadcast.[15] B&W threatened to sue CBS for interfering with a contract between the tobacco company and Wigands that prohibited Wigands from commenting on the company's business. Under management pressure, CBS News decided to kill the interview amid speculation that the network's legal problems might dampen Westinghouse's enthusiasm as a corporate suitor and charges that CBS News president Eric Ober and general counsel Ellen Oran Kaden, who led the legal team in the merger negotiations, would profit handsomely from the cashing out of stock options in the takeover. Ober later derided these assertions as "absurd" and "a self-serving cheap shot."[16]

There are also a number of interlocking relationships between news divisions and book publishers. Hyperion Books and ABC News, for example, are corporate cousins. Time Warner Trade Publishing and CNN share a common corporate guardian, as do HarperCollins and the Fox News Channel. Since controversial books frequently generate news coverage, news divisions have a moral obligation to divulge any ties to publishers whose books they critique or report on. In the spring of 2004, for example, *60 Minutes* aired a story concerning Richard Clarke's allegations that the Bush administration had ignored the threat of terrorism prior to 9/11. Clarke was a former advisor to President George W. Bush and launched his allegations in a book titled *Against All Enemies: Inside America's War on Terrorism*, published by Simon & Schuster subsidiary Free Press. Simon & Schuster and CBS are both owned by Viacom, a fact that *60 Minutes* correspondent Lesley Stahl failed to mention. Stahl called it an oversight, but this did little to silence Clarke's critics.[17]

Whereas the number of daily newspapers has been inching downward in recent years, broadcast stations and cable systems have been proliferating. There are currently just under 1,500 daily newspapers, as compared with more than 12,000 broadcast stations[18] and an even greater number of cable systems. Until recently, the concentrations of broadcast ownership were not so pronounced, because of the limitation by the Federal Communications Commission (FCC) on single-market and nationwide station ownerships. Until 1984, for example, no licensee was permitted to own more than seven TV, seven AM, and seven FM stations. Beginning in the 1990s, the FCC has continuously liberalized its rules, resulting in an unprecedented amount of media concentration, but the commission's most recent initiative in 2003 prompted fierce resistance from a broad spectrum of consumers and pressure groups. However, as chronicled in the *American Journalism Review*, this unanticipated grassroots movement, which was publicly vociferous in its denunciation of the FCC's proposal to further loosen its rules limiting media concentration, received only modest coverage in many news outlets owned by the big conglomerates eager to cash in on the new opportunities for mergers and acquisitions.[19]

Perhaps the most ominous concentration of media power is found in the movie industry. Since the 1930s, no more than six or seven major studios have dominated the business, controlling at various times 80–90 percent of the films distributed in this country. Today, most of the business is in the hands of five theater chains; and Hollywood's six production studios, such as Time Warner (Warner Brother Movies), Viacom (Paramount), and Disney, are key constituents of vast media empires.[20] In some communities the studios have achieved a major monopoly of theatre ownership.

The verdict is still out on the trend toward media consolidation. In some cases the quality of content may suffer as corporate executives exhibit a "lowest common denominator" mentality to increase ratings and circulations and, therefore, the profit margin. On the other hand, some chains, such as Knight-Ridder, generally improve the papers they purchase. Mergers and consolidations do not inevitably result in a diminution of quality, but in the final analysis the result depends on whether the corporate managers are committed to the special position traditionally occupied by the media within the American cultural framework.

THE ALLIANCE OF MASS MEDIA AND MARKETING

As applied to the media, the marketing concept holds that all departments, including news, must contribute to the financial well-being of the organization. Thus, news executives are expected to package their news and information to attract a target audience and to exploit the economic potential of the marketplace.[21] In short, they must search for creative ways to infuse their news and editorial content with entertainment values. In fact, a recent survey of 130 editors and news directors showed that more than 75 percent of the respondents believed that entertaining readers and viewers comes before educating them. In another major survey by the Pew Research Center for the People and the Press and the *Columbia Journalism Review,* nearly eight out of ten of those surveyed attributed a decline in the coverage of important stories on their dullness, and a majority of respondents said the same of highly complex stories[22]—in other words, a lack of appeal to a mass audience.

The media are profit centers and as such can be expected to adopt marketing strategies similar to other economic institutions. But when commercial pressures jeopardize journalistic standards, then serious ethical questions must be addressed. As commercial values increasingly penetrate the journalistic terrain, influential industry voices, such as Barbara Cochran, president of the Radio Television News Directors Association, have warned of the ethical fallout from the tensions between business values and journalism values:

Stations are trying to maximize their profits, and the sales departments can come up with some ingenious schemes to generate revenues that may involve the news department. The best test for such plans is how it would look if it were exposed on the front page of the local newspaper. If it would be embarrassing, it's probably not a good idea. Stations that ignored that test have had to change their plans. The cost in credibility is huge compared to the dollars earned in revenue.[23]

The threat to journalistic standards posed by commercial pressures was the heart of a controversy in the summer of 1998, when CNN restructured its programming schedule in an effort to jump-start its static ratings.[24] On June 7 the debut of *NewsStand: CNN & Time,* a collaborative effort between CNN and *Time* magazine, featured a story accusing the U.S. military of secretly using nerve gas against defectors during the Vietnam War. Within a few days CNN staffers were beginning to question the accuracy of the story, the network's own military analyst resigned in protest over the piece, other news organizations such as *Newsweek* challenged the validity of the report, and the Pentagon ordered a full investigation into the charges.[25] CNN itself commissioned First Amendment attorney Floyd Abrams to conduct an in-house investigation of the story. In the end, CNN retracted the report, acknowledging "serious faults in the use of the sources who provided . . . the original reports."[26] In the wake of this fiasco, the two producers of the segment were fired but continued to stand steadfastly behind the truth of the report.[27] One CNN staffer summed it up with this query: "It begs the question, Did we cut corners to make a big splash with *NewsStand?*"[28]

If there is any lament among practicing journalists today, it is the discernible, and some say inevitable, erosion of the "wall" between the commercial and editorial sides of the media enterprise. For traditional reporters and editors who remember the "good old days," this separation, like the sacrament of communion, purified the newsroom and spiritually confirmed its journalistic sovereignty. But things have changed. Take, for example, this description of the transformation at the *Los Angeles Times* in the 1990s under the leadership of new CEO and publisher Mark Willes, who subsequently lost his job when the *Times* was sold to the Tribune Company in Chicago as part of a merger, characterized in the *Columbia Journalism Review:*

> Throughout the paper, editors are sitting down with delegates from circulation, marketing, research, and advertising to develop new sections and new offerings within sections, to establish targets and goals for revenue and readership, and to search for new ways to achieve overall increases in circulation, advertising, and profit. "There are teams everywhere," says an exasperated news employee. Each team is headed by a business-side executive—a "general manager" or, in the marketing lexicon now ascendant at the paper, a "product manager."[29]

If this account were merely anecdotal, it might be dismissed as one paper's radical experiment. Indeed, after several years of turbulence, the *Los Angeles Times* apparently rebounded under new leadership.[30] But a poll by *Presstime* magazine published in April 1998 found that at least 192 daily newspapers, 57 percent of the respondents, have marketing committees that include editorial members. Among the editors' responsibilities, according to the survey, is the development of ad-driven special sections and the targeting of demographic groups for coverage.[31]

While these once sacrosanct walls between editorial and advertising functions begin to crumble at conventional newspapers, online these walls have never been established. For example, at the end of many book reviews in the *New York Times* online edition, readers can purchase books just with a mouse click. For each purchase, the *Times* receives a small transaction fee. The practice prompted this complaint from Lehigh University journalism professor Jack Lule:

> I don't think the mighty *Times* is overly interested in the minuscule profits derived from the transaction fee. But it has crossed an ethical line on the Internet that perhaps it could not or would not cross in print.

With this example to follow, could we fault student journalists for thinking that student newspapers should run on-line reviews of restaurants and link the reviews to the restaurants' Web sites? Should students collect a fee from each restaurant every time a reader visits its site? Shouldn't the reviews be glowing, to assure profit? Why not have the restaurants pay for the glowing reviews, as well? Once the first ethical compromise is made, the next can quickly follow.[32]

Ethicist Deni Elliott, on the other hand, has challenged the very premises upon which this so-called wall between a medium's financial and journalistic interests resides. "The Wall was a lousy metaphor for the 20th century style of doing journalism," she writes, "and is completely unworkable for the corporate creation of news that journalists are doing today." She notes that the newsroom and business side are dependent on one another and that good journalism and good business are not mutually exclusive.[33]

This is sage (and practical) advice because to compete in the economic arena today, a business or corporation must master the principles of marketing. The media are no exception. The fundamental objective of any newspaper, magazine, broadcast station, movie studio, or cable system is profit. Without it the life span of any media institution will be a short one. In addition, an unprofitable operation is unlikely to attract the investment capital needed for expansion. On the other hand, a profit allows an organization to invest in the talent and hardware necessary for the production of a quality product. Nevertheless, when marketing values trump journalistic values, an inevitable disquiet grips the newsroom.

No news event in recent memory is more illustrative of the impact of marketing values on journalistic decision making than the coverage of the O. J. Simpson trial. In the weeks following Simpson's arrest for the double murders of his ex-wife Nicole Brown Simpson and her friend Ronald Goldman, the case received more intense coverage than any event since the Persian Gulf War. While critics subjected every aspect of this rather bizarre spectacle to the most exacting scrutiny, many of the concerns revolved around the conflict between the marketing aspects of the trial coverage and the media's role as socially responsible gatekeepers.

The news media devoted hundreds of hours and thousands of inches of copy to exploring every detail—some important, some trivial—of the case.[34] During live coverage of Simpson's preliminary hearing, ratings shot up dramatically, eclipsing even the popular soap operas. However, the public exhibited a degree of schizophrenia in its assessment of the Simpson coverage. At the same time that audiences were devouring every lurid and sensational detail of the case, surveys showed that a large percentage of Americans thought the media's performance was excessive or unfair.[35] Some critics complained about the influence of corporate values (that is, the "bottom line") and ratings on the journalistic decision-making process. Others complained that such entertainment masquerading as news trivializes real news. "There is a perversion of news values when a presidential visit to Eastern Europe and a presidential visit to a G7 summit cannot get . . . the same amount of time as a pretrial hearing of a former football player," noted Marvin Kalb, a longtime broadcast journalist and director of the Joan Shorenstein Center on the Press, Politics, and Public Policy at Harvard University.[36]

But others defended the media's performance, noting that the sheer drama and compelling public interest in the case were sufficient justifications for the extensive coverage. ABC's Ted Koppel, apparently rejecting the view that the marketing concept and journalism are incompatible, said that the fact that business decisions drive news decisions is a "virtue" because it gives the public a significant voice in shaping the news agenda. In short, the application of marketing principles to journalism has helped to "democratize" the profession.

For the ethical purist, the application of the marketing concept to electronic journalism has been a mixed blessing. As news operations have become profit centers, they have benefited from increased capital investment, expanded staffs, and higher salaries. On the other hand, consultants (sometimes referred to as "news doctors") have descended on newsrooms like the plague, dispensing their wisdom and advice to any client looking for impressive numbers. The result has been nothing short of a revolution in local TV journalism. Evidence of the influence of the marketing concept is present in almost all local news programs. Some have followed the lead of the tabloid programs in using graphic violence, human foibles, and tragedies and sensationalism in pursuit of higher ratings. Others have integrated civic-minded promotions (such as collecting coats for needy children and then airing news stories featuring the event) directly into their newscasts.

Some stations use consultants' advice and audience survey data to determine the audience appeal (i.e., marketability) of certain stories, which results in a form of populist journalism in which the audience is provided with what they want rather than what they need as citizens. A Magid survey in early 2003 exemplifies this form of market-driven approach to electronic journalism. According to the survey of 6,000-plus viewers, protestors came in last on a list of war-related topics viewers were interested in seeing in their local newscasts. A Magid consultant suggested that the amount of time a station devotes to coverage of protests and the placement of such stories in the newscast should be considered with viewer distaste for protest in mind.[37] However, *Broadcasting & Cable* magazine, the industry's trade publication, quickly took exception to the consultant's warning. "No news medium that takes itself seriously," editorialized the publication, "should allow focus groups or surveys to drive their coverage of any significant issue, especially war and peace. The fact that dissent may be marginalized for economic reasons, not political, would be cold comfort to those whose voices are not heard."[38]

There is also a disturbing inclination to use news programs as promotional vehicles for the entertainment divisions. When the NBC comedy *Seinfeld* completed its highly successful tenure, for example, both network and local news departments provided a journalistic benediction. Similarly, in the spring of 2004 *Dateline NBC* did at least two hours of stories on the NBC entertainment program, *The Apprentice*, surrounding its climactic episode. The news division defended its decision on the grounds the show was a cultural phenomenon and therefore newsworthy.[39] *Dateline* was also taken to task about the same time by media critic Kevin McDonough for devoting a two-hour episode to the finale of *Friends*, a popular entertainment program for several years.[40] A *TV Guide* survey of the morning shows on ABC, CBS, and NBC published in June 2004 revealed that all three networks devoted a significant amount of time to promoting their entertainment fare.[41]

Newspapers, as vividly illustrated in the opening scenario of this section, have not escaped the lure of the mass marketing concept. Confronted with stagnant or declining circulations and profits during the 1980s, many newspapers turned to marketing firms for assistance in helping them to reclaim their audience appeal. The result has been an increase in soft news and features and supplements, known as advertorials, actually paid for by advertisers but cloaked in the respectability of editorial content. The electronic variation of the advertorial concept is the *infomercial*, program-length commercials that have proliferated since the government's deregulation of commercial time limits. Infomercials are today a textbook example of marketing diversity, featuring everything from weight-loss regimens to self-improvement programs to labor-saving appliances. The financial stakes in the production of infomercials are tremendous, and competition for airtime is fierce. In 2002, for example, there were at least 400 infomercials vying for half-hour time slots.[42]

In addition, infomercial makers have concluded that dot-coms are uniquely suited to their form of advertising,[43] although this unpredictable venue may dissuade some companies from investing heavily for the foreseeable future.

Whether such program-length commercials should be provided with an unfettered entrée to the nation's airwaves and cable systems is a matter of public policy. But when infomercials blur the lines between advertising and entertainment and even editorial content, then serious ethical questions arise. Some journalists and even some advertisers are concerned that a trend in this direction is leading to a kind of "editorial pollution" that compromises the integrity of the media.[44] In fact, the industry's own trade organization, the National Infomercial Marketing Association, has expressed misgivings about infomercials that fail to distinguish between commercial objectives and entertainment.[45] Such was the case when the Federal Trade Commission (FTC) accused Synchronal Corporation, one of the largest producers of thirty-minute TV infomercials, of false advertising in connection with claims that certain products would dissolve cellulite and cure baldness. The infomercials were also disguised to look like ordinary TV programming, said the FTC, instead of paid advertisements.[46] In another case, a diet product company was cited for using a newscast scenario to promote the "discovery" of the company's weight-loss program, thus duping viewers into believing they were watching an actual program.[47]

The packaging of both news and entertainment to achieve some marketing objective is evidenced by the reference to such content as a "product." No longer is the news produced merely as a public service. It must be sold to the consumer and must contribute its share to the success of the marketing plan of the overall operation. Newspapers, for example, must position themselves journalistically to maximize the profit potential of their news product, which means devising a marketing scheme aimed at attracting a well-educated, affluent audience.

Marketing directors at many newspapers fear that large numbers of low-income readers would undermine the appeal of the demographics on which high advertising rates are based.[48]

Considering the competitive environment, the integration of the marketing concept into the various media enterprises is undoubtedly inevitable and does not necessarily imply some ethically misguided intent. And yet, the preceding discussion has a decidedly negative overtone, replete with examples of how the public interest has been subordinated to economic interests. Where, then, do the ethical problems reside in accommodating the marketing concept to the media's social responsibility mandate?

First, a "truth-in-advertising" problem arises when news operations dispense promotional content, celebrity profiles, and soft features under the guise of hard news. They are, of course, free to embrace all three within the scope of their newspapers, magazines, or broadcast day. But they should not attempt to dignify such material by including it in a "newscast" or packaging it in such a way that the average reader or viewer cannot distinguish it from editorial matter. Second, on a more philosophical level, when marketing strategies result in an unholy alliance between entertainment and journalistic values and undermine the media's imperative to service the democratic system through the discussion of serious and socially relevant issues, then significant ethical considerations are tendered. The most egregious form of this alliance, of course, is self-censorship, whereby certain stories are taboo simply because they might adversely affect the financial side of the media enterprise. Consider this example, recounted by former CBS producer Lowell Bergman, who stated that "[i]f you are the owner of an NFL team you have a virtual free pass, in terms of television news coverage," during a talk at New York University in 1999. "The network will not initiate a critical story about your business practices and history. No in-depth story will be commissioned." Bergman said he was told this by news executives at both ABC and CBS.[49]

Thus, it is within this rising tide of commercial expectations that ethical conflicts arise concerning the media practitioners' obligations to their institutions' own self-interests and their moral duties to the welfare of society. Is the marketing of news, for example, compatible with the journalistic imperatives of reporters, editors, and news directors? There is no law of nature that mandates the sacrifice of quality to the demands of the marketplace. Nevertheless, this is a thorny ethical issue that confronts media managers today, and in the long run its resolution will depend on the moral sensibilities of the policy makers who must ponder the true meaning of social responsibility within an industry that is increasingly infatuated with the marketing concept.

THE ROLE OF ADVERTISING

The Media's Lifeline: The Ethical Challenges of Commercial Sponsorship

It is perhaps belaboring the obvious to say that advertising is ubiquitous in the American media system. Advertising is the economic underpinning for both the information and entertainment functions of our mass of communication institutions and thus directly affects the quality of media content. Of course, advertising gives the mass media financial *independence* from government and other political interests, but it also creates a *dependence* on the commercial sector.

The economic pressures exerted by the influence of advertising are apparent in at least four areas. *First*, the quantity of commercial material determines the amount of space or time remaining for nonadvertising content— that is, news and entertainment. Newspaper editors are obliged to arrange their editorial content in the space remaining after the advertising department lays out its ads on the available pages. In television news, producers have to slot their stories around commercials, so that there is a limit on the amount of time devoted to each "package." And on the entertainment side of TV, programs are constructed to build to a dramatic climax, or peak, going into a commercial break.

Second, a ripple effect occurs when advertisers cut their budgets, as they do in periods of economic recession, or when they switch their buying from one medium to another. In other words, when the advertising industry sneezes, the media catch cold. Even the network giants were not immune to this phenomenon in the 1980s as the impact of cable television steadily eroded the audience levels of ABC, CBS, and NBC. The news divisions suffered severe budgetary cutbacks and layoffs during this economic upheaval, but other network divisions were affected as well. And in the past decade a significant loss of circulation at many of the nation's major newspapers has resulted in a reduction of ad revenues, less editorial content, and staff layoffs.[50]

A *third* way that commercial interests can affect the nonadvertising content is through direct pressure on media managers. Advertisers are understandably annoyed when they are the subject of unflattering news coverage and sometimes react by withdrawing their ads from the offending publication, station, or network or otherwise pressuring it into refraining from future negative publicity. Such was the case in San Jose, California, when automobile dealers complained because the *Mercury News* published an article titled "A Car Buyer's Guide to Sanity," in which the reporter counseled consumers, among other things, to rely on factory invoices rather than on what the dealer might say. San Jose automobile dealers were not amused and met with the paper's news executives, complaining that the article left the impression they couldn't be trusted.[51] Angry car dealers pulled at least $1 million dollars in advertising, although the FTC later held that the boycott was a violation of federal antitrust laws.[52]

According to Debra Potter, executive director of NewsLab, which works with TV stations on strategies to report complex stories, advertisers' influence is "seeping into television news."[53]

And testimonials for the increasing influence of advertisers on local news are not hard to find. For example, award-winning investigative journalist Tom Grant resigned from KXLY-TV in Spokane, Washington, because "when it comes time to deliver news, the lawyers and ad reps make the decisions." Grant cited eight specific issues he was forbidden to cover during his fifteen-year tenure in TV news, including stories about bad car dealers and bad restaurants, whose owners spent lavishly on local station advertising. One former news director says she knows of stations that "keep a printed list of people and issues they won't report on, for fear of alienating an advertiser."[54]

Finally, one of the most disturbing recent trends is the practice at some TV stations to disguise commercial content as news. Professor Dow C. Smith of the S.I. Newhouse School of Public Communications at Syracuse University has referred to this as a "hideous practice that violates basic journalism ethics." In a commentary for *Broadcasting & Cable,*[55] he cited an example in which a local TV station had "succumbed to the pressures of the bottom line by selling airtime, then packaging it like news," thus making it difficult "to tell which interviews are legitimate news and which are paid." In a story on an aqua-massage machine, for example, the reporter not only received a massage but also interviewed the store's owners. The story had little informational value. The station claimed the reporter did not do commercial interviews, but this may have not been obvious to the average viewer.

Even when advertisers are not directly implicated in the subject matter, they may withdraw their support if they believe their corporate values might be compromised through association with controversial content. In the spring of 2000, for example, Procter & Gamble decided to yank its sponsorship of the controversial Dr. Laura Schlessinger, who was known for her intemperate on-air remarks about gays and lesbians. This was followed by United Airlines' in-flight magazine's decision to stop accepting ads for Dr. Schlessinger's radio program.[56]

The threat of economic retaliation from a disaffected advertiser is a fact of life within a commercially driven media system. Nevertheless, even in today's highly competitive market, such repercussions are not a foregone conclusion, and some news executives have valiantly resisted advertiser pressure. Such was the case when San Francisco's KPIX-TV did an investigative series on fast-food chains in which they challenged advertising claims of new low-cholesterol, low-fat hamburgers. The station lost some ad revenues, but the station defended its report on the grounds that it was "in the best interest of the public."[57]

When commercials are actually blended with editorial content, some media ethicists believe that a sacred line has been crossed. Consider, for example, a report in the *Denver Post* in the fall of 2002 on World Cup skiing, accompanied by an AP photo. This legitimate account of a newsworthy event then morphed smoothly into what appeared to be further coverage of winter sports, complete with an integrated layout of photos, headlines, typeface, and text. In reality, the lower half of the page was an "advertisement" for a video game version of National Hockey League playoffs.[58]

Also exemplary of the commingling of commercial and editorial matter is *The View*, a daytime talk show produced by ABC's entertainment division, and cohosted by a former NBC correspondent, a former *60 Minutes* anchor, and ABC's Barbara Walters. In the fall of 2000 Campbell Soup Co. paid an undisclosed sum as "prominent sponsor" for eight episodes of the program. On one episode viewers saw coproducer Bill Geddie eating his Campbell's "soup of the day," while on another the show's cohosts competed to gather the most Campbell's Soup labels in a makeshift wind tunnel. Bob Steele, director of the ethics program at the Poynter Institute, a media think tank, was disapproving of this tie-in arrangement. "The problem," he declared, " is that 'The View' contracted with Campbell's Soup in a way that guaranteed Campbell's promotional time embedded within a program that is supposed to

serve the viewers' needs. Many viewers count on information-based programming, and when that programming is eroded by the sale of its content, the viewers are disserved."[59]

Of course, advertising's influence reaches far beyond the journalistic function of media enterprises. Whereas entertainment executives may complain about the economic influence of advertisers who aspire to exercise more control over program content, they are usually more reluctant than their journalistic brethren to defy such pressure. Entertainment does not possess the strong tradition of independence as the editorial function. In addition, society is more loathe to accord entertainment the same degree of constitutional respect as news and information. It is a courageous (or financially foolish, depending on your point of view) entertainment executive indeed who ignores threats of an advertiser boycott and airs a program on a sustaining basis. In any event, many advertisers are disinclined to sponsor entertainment programs that they feel are too controversial. For example, when a major sponsor of NBC's *Sisters* discovered that one episode of the program contained a scene featuring a group of women lolling in a sauna chatting about multiple orgasms, the advertiser threatened to cancel $500,000 worth of ads.[60] And several advertisers, following a threatened boycott by a major Catholic organization, abandoned their sponsorship of ABC's controversial program[61] *Nothing Sacred,* which portrayed a Catholic priest who questioned church doctrine. While the major entertainment networks do, in fact, occasionally test the boundaries of cultural acceptability in their content, the riskier ventures are still more common on cable TV where lower ratings expectations diminish the likelihood of advertiser pressures on producers and cable networks.

In the final analysis, the ethical pragmatist must search for an accommodation between the role of advertising as an expression of corporate self-interest and the institutional moral imperative of social responsibility. Of course, the two are so intertwined that it is sometimes difficult to examine them separately. Advertising is truly symbiotic with the other mass media functions, news and entertainment. Advertisers, of course, do not entirely share the vision of news managers and entertainment programmers that there should be a complete separation of church and state between the business side and the other mass media functions. Advertisers do *need* the media's vast and instantaneous distribution network to market their products and services. But in the process, they do not consider it unreasonable to exert some influence over the environment in which their valuable economic resources are being expended. And media managers are not entirely unsympathetic to this view. They understand that ad revenue provides the financial sustenance for their entertainment and editorial enterprises. In addition, they believe that advertising contributes to the economic health of society by providing valuable information. Media managers feel that sensitivity to ethical concerns in advertising is an important component of their image-building public relations or marketing effort.[62] On the other hand, they believe that undue advertiser pressure on program content—both news and entertainment—is just as inimical to "freedom of the press" as the power of government. The fragile and often ambiguous wall that insulates news and entertainment from undue commercial pressures is the inescapable collective responsibility of media managers, the ethical chaperons of the public interest.

The Challenges of Cyberspace

Cyberspace is a new frontier, an unregulated smorgasbord of information. Ads have become commonplace on many websites and search engines, although advertisers are still sailing uncharted waters in terms of the most effective strategies for utilizing the Internet. Clearly, the principles that have fueled commercial sponsorship of the mass media may be ineffective when applied to the new Web-based media. Thus, for advertisers the Web presents both challenges and opportunities.

The Internet is still really in its infancy, but ethical alarm bells have already been sounded over the "commercialization" of the Web. For example, accusations of deception and crass commercialism have been leveled against some search engines that allow website owners to pay for prominent placement on search engine pages. Thus, when a user types in selected key words looking for information, a particular company's web page always appears at the top of the list. "It's become possible, for the first time, to actually pay your way to the top of the listings at the major search engines," laments Danny Sullivan, editor of SearchEngineWatch.com, a website that tracks the industry. Commercial Alert, a consumer watchdog group founded by Ralph Nader, was indignant enough to file a complaint with the FTC against eight search engines, accusing them of violating deceptive-practices law by blurring the "murky line" between editorial judgment and advertising on the Internet. Industry representatives have responded that such commercial arrangements are essential to ensure the economic viability of Web search engines.[63] And as websites become increasingly expensive to maintain, the commercialization of cyberspace will continue unabated.

Consumer groups are also concerned that the glut of commercial voices on the Web increases the risk that hucksters will take advantage of unsuspecting Web surfers. Of course, hucksters have been a threat to unwary consumers for years in the classified ads and through direct marketing. "But on the Internet," noted a recent article in *U.S. News & World Report*, "with ads morphing from banners to pop-ups and now to searches, novices don't always know what's what."[64]

The problem may be high tech, but the solution is not. All listings on portals (i.e., sponsored content) should be clearly labeled as "paid," a practice that traditional media have followed for years. This is a classic case of old wine in new bottles. While the ethical challenges posed by the Web may be new (or at least creative), the values are of ancient vintage:

truth, honesty, respect for the dignity of the individual, and fairness.

PRODUCT PLACEMENTS

In 1982 Steven Spielberg charmed millions of moviegoers with his enchanting film *ET, The Extra Terrestrial.* He also charmed the manufacturer of Reese's Pieces, the chocolate-covered peanut-butter candy, which was used to coax ET out of hiding. In the weeks following release of the film the sales of Reese's Pieces soared 65 percent.[65] The modern era of "product placement" had arrived.[66] Because product placements embrace aspects of both the marketing concept and advertising, separate treatment is warranted here.

Product placement involves a business arrangement between a company and a movie producer whereby the company offers financial support, free products, or both in exchange for those products being featured prominently in the film. The practice is not new and has been described as a "lifesaver"[67] for producers with tight budgets. The year after the release of *ET,* for example, Twentieth Century-Fox announced it would feature brand-name products in its films in return for fees of $10,000 to $40,000 a movie.[68] Today, companies may pay several million dollars for the exposure. It is not unusual to find several products displayed at strategic locations throughout feature films. Tri-Star Pictures' *Short Circuit,* for example, included shots of Alaska Airlines, Apple computers, Bounty paper towels, and Ore-Ida frozen french fries.[69] Similarly, *Time* magazine played a prominent role in *Divine Secrets of the Ya-Ya Sisterhood* in which one of the leading characters gives an interview to a *Time* reporter, an interview that is mentioned repeatedly in the film.[70] Not coincidentally, the film was produced by Warner Brothers, another AOL Time Warner unit.

Product placements, however, are not the exclusive province of the big screen. Television movies and programming have been subsidized through product placements for many years.

For example, several of the characters on *Dallas* drove General Motors and Ford automobiles, supplied free of charge. *Roseanne* featured a shot of Quaker Oats Squares, and the secretaries on *L.A. Law* used IBM computers.[71] And more recently, Apple's introduction of the popular iMac computer was followed by appearances on more than twenty shows, including *Ally McBeal, Felicity, The X-Files,* and *The Drew Carey Show.*[72] And viewers could not have missed the couples on *House Rules* having an argument in the aisles of a Lowe's Home Improvement Warehouse or the promo clip for a GMC Envoy SUV on CBS's *Survivor: Pearl Islands.*[73]

The attraction of product placements for companies seeking to market their wares through integration with entertainment content is captured in this "pitch" from one product placement agency:

> Brand-name products are receiving "Rave Revues" in Hollywood. They can't sing, they can't dance, and they can't act, but they receive almost as much attention as their human counterparts. Imagine the impact of your customers seeing their favorite star using your products. Your company's name and visual footage become an integral part of film and television conveying subliminal messages and implied endorsements.[74]

Digital technology is likely to accelerate the proliferation of product insertions into entertainment programming. In March 1999 a Coca-Cola can and Wells Fargo billboard were quietly inserted into an episode of UPN's drama *Seven Days* to gauge viewer reaction.[75] Digital technology's potential for opening up new venues for sponsors is quite imposing, and, for critics of the increasing commercialization of the entertainment culture, also quite troubling.[76] For example, a virtual ad could be inserted into the original run of a program and then replaced with an ad for a different company in subsequent showings through syndication. This flexibility could significantly increase the revenue streams for producers of broadcast, cable, and Web-based programming.

Movie and television producers defend product placements on the grounds that they are a much-needed source of revenue for an industry with soaring production costs. Some studios even argue that the insertion of brand-name products adds a dimension of reality to their creations. "One way to reinforce the feeling of reality in a film is by using real products," explained one large studio executive. However, such rejoinders cannot ameliorate the concerns of media critics, who see ethical pitfalls in product placements.

First, the insertion of ads blurs the line between the entertainment and commercial elements, resulting in a potentially deceptive marketing practice in which audiences are subtly manipulated.[77] Commercial Alert, a Portland-based consumer activist group, has requested that the government investigate product placements and require that acknowledgments of the sponsor of embedded ads be included at the beginning of the program and that the word "advertisement" appear prominently on the screen. Naturally, advertisers resist such regulations because "[a]dvertisers are increasingly drawn to the subtle, seamless sell that separates them from commercial breaks that send viewers surfing away." In other words, an overabundance of candor would derail product placement's allure.[78]

Second, under some circumstances product placements can disrupt the film's narrative by focusing, albeit it briefly, on the products themselves. In addition—and perhaps most troubling of all—ad insertions can cause an undesirable shift in artistic control. For example, several years ago film critic Mark Crispin Miller lamented that producers often send scripts to product placement agents months before production begins to see how many products can be placed, which results in advertisers making the "basic decisions of filmmaking."[79] The danger, of course, is that companies may object to storylines or content that is not consistent with the aura surrounding the product being promoted.

Despite these concerns, the placement of commercial products in TV programming is likely to accelerate in view of the emerging TiVo technology, which allows viewers, among other things, to "zap" commercials more easily. With this much power in the hands of consumers, advertisers may increasingly be forced to rely upon product placements to gain the attention of their target audiences.

ECONOMIC PRESSURES: HYPOTHETICAL CASE STUDIES

The diversity of issues surrounding the discussion of economic pressures makes any generalizations risky at best. But the cases in this chapter are representative of the moral dilemmas confronted by media practitioners. In evaluating these cases, apply the SAD formula for moral reasoning outlined in Chapter 3.

◀ CASE STUDIES ▶

▶ **CASE 8-1**

Sports Reporting: Who Controls the Content?[80]

For ten years the Venice Motor Speedway, the latest entry in the amazingly popular auto racing circuit, had struggled for parity against such well-entrenched racing venues as Indianapolis, Daytona, and Atlanta. Venice, a progressive community located in New York's heartland, had recognized the economic potential of this highly competitive sport, which included enthusiasts from a wide variety of demographic groups. The public bonds used to finance the speedway were, in the view of Venice's political leadership, fully justified by the remunerative prospects of several highly publicized racing events each year. The Speedway's governing board was pleased with the unflinching loyalty of the racing fans from New York and surrounding states but still longed for a "crown jewel"—a prestigious event that would attract international media coverage and propel the Venice Motor Speedway into the big leagues of stock car racing. Such a media saturated event featuring the sport's superstars could make serious inroads into the dominance of the NASCAR events and the Indianapolis 500 and vindicate the community's financial investment in the speedway. Venice's "crown jewel" became known as Global Track One.

From the outset, Global Track One, the creation of a London-based company, Sports Enterprises, Ltd., was envisioned as an international event featuring racers from around the world, although American entries would certainly dominate the field in the inaugural competition. Sports Enterprises, Ltd. was an aggressive and experienced promoter of a wide variety of sporting events and used its considerable marketing skills to quickly cultivate interest and curiosity in this latest entry into the auto racing competition. Venice's enthusiastic citizens braced for the onslaught of media coverage and the ancillary economic benefits that the community anticipated from the Global Track One event.

Sports was a prominent feature of Venice's network affiliates' journalistic menu, a source of fierce competition for dominance in both the early evening and late night news slots. Nevertheless, Channel 7 had nudged aside its rivals and, in the days leading up to Global Track One's maiden voyage, legitimately promoted itself as Venice's *sports leader*. Despite the massive media coverage that was anticipated surrounding the event, the station's news director, Lisa Samuels, was confident that her station would find its niche in providing local viewers with a unique perspective on this latest entry in the sport of auto racing. However, she had underestimated Sports Enterprises's determination to dominate so thoroughly the lucrative financial remunerations of both the primary coverage and the multitude of spinoff news packages that would inevitably originate from both the international

carriers and the domestic networks and their local affiliates.

In their negotiations with the myriad of broadcast and cable outlets, Sports Enterprises executives set forth several conditions for access by local stations to Global Track One's inaugural race: They would have to agree to run short packages of no greater than two minutes in length produced by the race promoters themselves. Under the terms of the agreement, stations were prohibited from editing these news inserts. In addition, stations were allowed a seven-day "window" during which they could air their secondary video (driver interviews and profiles, features, etc.), but they were then required to turn over this video, as well as any unaired material, to Sports Enterprises and relinquish their rights to this material. Channel 7's competitors readily agreed to these stipulations, but Lisa Samuels demurred until she could explore the ethical dimensions of this dilemma with her station's Sports Director Mike Sanchez and Sports Reporter Nat Kaminsky.

"We don't have a lot of time to make a decision," Samuels declared as her two colleagues gathered around the small table in the news director's office. "The other stations in town have agreed to Sports Enterprises's conditions; if we don't do likewise, we'll be closed out of this event. But I'm concerned that we're relinquishing too much control of our content."

"There's no doubt that we're giving up some control," responded Sanchez. "But this is a trend that has been underway for years in the sports business. There are billions of dollars at stake, and all the major sports enterprises are attempting to maintain economic control of their products. After all, sports is primarily entertainment, and the sponsors and promoters view their events as products to be marketed. As the sports leader in the Venice market, we need access to this event. Are the stipulations really unreasonable?"

"I think they are," countered Kaminsky. "I agree that this is an important event for us. But the demands of big sports promoters are becoming unreasonable. Sports may be entertainment, but it also has journalistic value. We owe it to our viewers to provide uncorrupted, unvarnished information surrounding such events. We can't do this if we agree to air unedited packages provided by those who are sponsoring this event."

"This doesn't really bother me," replied Sanchez unsympathetically, "as long as we identify the source of this material. We can still do our own accounts, not only of the race itself but the personalities and side shows surrounding the race. Sports Enterprises isn't demanding censorship rights over our own material."

"But that isn't the issue," insisted Kaminsky, who had always considered himself a sports journalist and resisted the claim that his beat was nothing more than entertainment. "Those packages produced by Sports Enterprises will be nothing more than promotional pieces. They'll be using our news programs to hype Global Track One. This is more akin to advertising, not news. Even if we identify the source, we'll lose credibility with our viewers as an independent sports-minded station. In fact, if we succumb to this blatant form of self-promotion in our sports coverage, our viewers may begin to doubt the objectivity of our regular news coverage. We shouldn't abandon journalistic values just because Global Track One is a live sporting event."

"I disagree," argued Sanchez. "Fans understand that sports coverage is different from other forms of news. "They don't expect the same degree of detachment anyway. Those who can't personally attend this event expect their local stations to fill them in; that's why they watch the local news. Keep in mind that our competitors will be there. If we're kept at arm's length from the race and have to resort to secondhand accounts, we'll lose our viewers to the other stations in the market. Besides, your appeal to journalistic values rings a little hollow. Let's face it. Television news itself frequently indulges in self-promotion and is guided by marketing techniques to boost ratings."

But Nat Kaminsky was not persuaded by his colleague's appeal to competitive realities. "Keep in mind," Kaminsky noted, "that Sports Enterprises is not just insisting upon our accepting their unedited packages. They're also insisting upon the rights, after seven days, to all our video. This will severely limit our ability to do follow-ups and retrospectives. This is our material, and we should not have to relinquish it as a condition of access to the Global Track One race. If we agree to give up control of our material just to provide firsthand accounts of this event, as a sports journalist I consider this to be a serious ethical issue."

"But if we don't agree to Sports Enterprises's terms," insisted Sanchez, "then we'll have no first-hand coverage at all. All sports organizations, including those that sponsor major team sports, are tightening their financial control over their products. As long as their contracts don't preclude *any* original coverage, for competitive reasons I believe we must make some concessions."

News Director Lisa Samuels listened attentively to this frank exchange between her two subordinate colleagues. As a journalist, she was troubled by the loss of control over her station's content. Sports Enterprises, of course, was only one promoter, but she was disturbed that this might become a trend. Her managerial inclinations suggested that Channel 7 must do whatever was necessary to remain competitive. The station's viewers expected no less. If they were uncaring in whether the station had to sacrifice its editorial control to gain access, Samuels mused, then did Sports Enterprises's stipulations really present the station with a serious ethical dilemma? These were the questions that troubled Lisa Samuels as she pondered whether to accept the same conditions that had been agreed to by her local competitors.

THE CASE STUDY

In recent years, sports organizations have displayed a more aggressive attitude in controlling media access to their events. During the February 2000 running of the Daytona 500, for example, NASCAR added a provision to its media credential request forms that claimed ownership of everything that was printed, shot, or said at the event. This provision was quickly removed when members of the National Motorsports Press Association threatened either to boycott NASCAR races entirely or to cover events without seeking credentials. Similarly, in the spring of 2001 Major League Baseball attempted to require journalists to sign a contract to obtain credentials to cover games. The contract would have prevented newspapers from using their own photos in other media for promotional use.[81]

As one journalist, writing in a recent issue of *Quill Magazine,* noted: "Major sports organizations increasingly are seeking to use copyright law, contract law and the so-called tort of misappropriation to get their way with media outlets, and they are threatening to deny access to journalists who won't roll over."[82]

Sports organizations view their events as "products" to be marketed to a mass audience. Collectively, billions of dollars are stake. In their view, the entertainment value of sports trumps the journalistic dimensions of their public performances. News organizations with a lot of clout may forestall what they believe to be unreasonable demands limiting access, but in this case, the local network affiliates, with the exception of Channel 7, have acquiesced in Sports Enterprises's stipulations to media access. Reporter Nat Kaminsky views this as an ethical issue because it results in loss of editorial control, in effect, of the station's sports content. Given the stipulations insisted upon by Sports Enterprises, the quality of Channel 7's coverage will suffer. Station viewers will be the ultimate losers. Kaminsky believes that sporting events should be treated as journalistic endeavors, despite the fact that they are designed primarily as vehicles for mass entertainment.

Sports Director Mike Sanchez, on the other hand, has assumed a more tolerant posture toward the conditions set forth by Sports Enterprises. He sees acceptance of the stipulations as a necessary step to remain competitive. In this view, once Channel 7's competitors accepted the conditions on access, then marketplace realities trumped whatever ethical qualms station personnel might have had. While the audience might be disserved somewhat by the stipulations on media access, Sanchez argues that the audience would be more disappointed if the station is barred from the event and hence must resort to providing coverage from outside the track. Sporting events are not like traditional news events because they are staged by promoters and professional organizations with the intent of maximizing their profits through entertainment. And what's wrong with that? In Sanchez's view, utilitarianism trumps the deontological perspective in which news directors must ask whether they would like such restraints on sports

coverage to become universal fare within their industry.

News Director Lisa Samuels has listened attentively to the views of her sports director and reporter Nat Kaminsky and must now make a decision. For the purpose of evaluating this ethical dilemma, assume the role of Lisa Samuels and, applying the model of moral reasoning outlined in Chapter 3, describe what you would do and defend your judgment.

▶ **CASE 8-2**

Web-Based Ads and the Search Engine's Search for Financial Stability

Bill Crenshaw had never known life without computers. He had emerged from the womb at the inception of the technological revolution that would eventually bring a computer into virtually every middle-class home and alter the corporate landscape forever. He had received his first rather primitive computer at the age of 7, and as he stood on the threshold of adolescence he was referred to both affectionately and derisively as a computer nerd or geek. In high school his mastery of the technology had earned him a part-time job maintaining the hardware and installing the software that now adorned his academy's classrooms.

Crenshaw had enrolled in his state's flagship university, but after a couple of years his entrepreneurial spirit and impatience with the rather subtle and tedious plots of Shakespeare and the historical intricacies of the Peloponnesian War prevailed over the conventional wisdom of the necessity of a college education, and he departed quietly from the tranquility of campus life. Cyberspace was still an unconquered frontier, in his view, and he wanted to be a part of the pioneering spirit that would eventually harness the unlimited potential of the World Wide Web. At the age of 20 he joined a dot-com company that marketed electronic components online, but when the operation succumbed to the financial exigencies that were soon to become an epidemic within the dot-com industry,

Crenshaw departed for greener pastures. For two years he freelanced as a website designer, an occupation that was sufficiently lucrative to provide the seed money for his own company. With his own resources leveraged against an offer of venture capital, Crenshaw designed his own search engine named Lancelot to compete against such familiar appellations as Lycos, Netscape, Google, and AOL. Shortly after Lancelot's inauguration, it became a public company traded on the New York Stock Exchange, a move that produced a fresh source of revenue. Crenshaw then became president of Lancelot Enterprises.

Crenshaw's strategy for survival was to produce a faster and more coherently organized product than his competitors, although Crenshaw was not naïve about the financial risks inherent in such an undertaking in the untamed wilderness of cyberspace. He frequently referred to competition on the Web as *electronic Darwinism* because only the fittest survived. Crenshaw hoped to be one of the "fit."

At the outset, Crenshaw had assembled a small staff of technological whiz kids, a business manager to handle Lancelot's financial transactions, and a marketing director to devise a game plan for positioning the company as a legitimate contender in the cyberspace search engine competition. Within a few months Lancelot had achieved both visibility and respectability in the marketplace, a fact that did not go unnoticed by advertisers seeking direct access to millions of online Internet customers. Crenshaw had initially rejected the notion of accepting ads as a means of enhancing Lancelot's revenue stream for fear of alienating customers who were attracted by his search engine's incredible speed, operational proficiency, and uncluttered appearance. But as Lancelot's subscriber base grew, so did the pressure from advertisers.

Crenshaw was aware that revenues from subscribers and investors might not provide long-term salvation for his company, a fact that his business manager consistently brought to his attention. The time had come, in his view, to consider whether to accept ads as a fuel source for his search engine. However, he would make no decision without the counsel of his marketing director, Geneva Boscarino, and business manager, Sally Chen.

"It seems to me we have three options," Crenshaw asserted as he met with his two colleagues in his rather sparsely appointed office, a concession to the company's still uncertain financial future. "We could reject all ads, as we have done thus far. Or we could accept advertising but be selective in our clients. That would necessitate establishing standards. The third option is to accept all advertisers who are willing to pay for access to our search engine."

"I don't believe we can ignore the advertising industry any longer," replied Boscarino immediately. "As I've told you on several occasions, we need to enhance our revenue stream, and ads are increasingly commonplace on other search engines. And Web advertising guarantees the client access to consumers on a one-on-one basis. I'm not in favor of imposing barriers to advertiser access. Unless the copy or visuals are highly indecent or obscene, I don't believe we should pass judgment on the ad content. We can't be too choosy. At the moment there is a finite number of companies, some of them rather bizarre, willing to expend their resources on search engine ads."

"I have a different view," responded the business manager. "I've expressed my support for advertising as a revenue source, but I think we have to draw the line somewhere. Keep in mind that we have a captive audience. They probably will not be offended by the ads—after all, they can suppress them with just one click—as long as they are not obtrusive or annoying."

"What we consider obtrusive and annoying may be nothing more than target marketing in the minds of some advertisers," said Boscarino. "The major trend now is for website owners to pay for prominent positions on search engines. This allows consumers to click directly to those companies' websites. What's wrong with that?"

"It provides an unlevel playing field in the Web commercial marketplace," asserted Chen convincingly. "This is comparable to having a record company that pays a DJ to play its music on the air. For example, the other day I typed in 'study at home' on six different search engines and the name of the same virtual university popped up first. Of course, they paid for that kind of exposure. I don't mind accepting advertising, but we should insist that the messages stand on their own rather than link our users directly to the sponsors' websites. And we should not mix commercial and editorial content by guaranteeing to sponsors that certain key words will propel them to the top of the list on the Lancelot engine. We have a responsibility to those who use our engine as a device to search for knowledge and information."

"I don't think we're taking advantage of consumers," Boscarino countered with conviction. "They have a choice as to whether to click to those commercial sites listed on our engine. As for your concern with integrating commercial and editorial content by using certain key word groupings to guarantee a sponsor top billing, how is this different from current media practice? TV stations run promotions disguised as news. Companies pay to have their products promoted in movies and TV programs. Newspapers publish tabs and supplements that essentially integrate editorial matter with commercial matter. And the list goes on."

Chen paused for a moment and then decided to change the focus of the discussion slightly. "Putting aside the issue of accepting sponsored links on our search engine, I also believe we have a responsibility to serve as a gatekeeper for those purveyors of questionable products and services. The Internet is full of diploma mills, get rich quick schemes, and fraudulent business opportunities."

"This is impractical in my judgment," replied Boscarino. "While the traditional media often have policies about advertising acceptability based upon taste, they do not assume any obligation for validating their ads or the product claims. And quite frankly, many publications accept promotions for diploma mills, fortune tellers, and other bizarre enterprises. The Web is so fluid and unregulated that I don't think we should reject any sponsor just because it might involve some unorthodox product or service."

"But the Web is virtually unregulated," said Chen. "That places more responsibility in our hands. If we don't set some standards, then who will? There are a lot of scams on the Web, and for the average consumer they may be difficult to detect. In the short term, we might make money, but what have we gained if we drive away users in the long

run? There are already a lot of complaints about advertising on the Web. I think we have a duty to serve as a gatekeeper."

"We have to face the economic realities of our business," responded Boscarino. "In order to provide access to the vast array of information available on the Web we need this support. Our stockholders are watching closely to see how we manage the financial affairs of this company. Besides, consumers are autonomous individuals. They should be sophisticated enough to understand that the 'let the buyer beware' admonition is as true in cyberspace as it is on earth."

Crenshaw listened attentively, fully aware that his two colleagues were debating an issue that could determine the financial solvency of the Lancelot search engine. They agreed on the need for advertising, but parted company on the extent of corporate oversight that should be exercised by their Web-based enterprise. As he pondered their comments, Crenshaw was conflicted. Journalists had their ethical standards. Public relations professionals had theirs. There was no precedent for search engine entrepreneurs.

THE CASE STUDY

Bill Crenshaw's observation in the narrative's last sentence is an engaging one. Unlike other cases in this text, this one does not involve a traditional media professional or practitioner. Lancelot is a search engine company, operating as a new media entity in the unregulated cyberspace environment. In a sense, this is tantamount to humankind's return to nature, where there are both dangers and opportunities but few rules. Can traditional ethical values be transported to the Web?

Few portals screen their advertising clients. "Everyone would love to provide more and better information to users, but that has to be balanced against the economic realities this industry faces," notes Ted Meisel, president and CEO of GoTo.com, the pioneering pay-for-placement site. "It's a choice about providing this information or no information." Critics like Susan Grant, director of Internet Fraud Watch, a project of the National Consumers League, contend that this is a phony dilemma. "It's a disservice to consumers who come to your site to needlessly expose them to those kinds of frauds," she says.[83]

Advertising, of course, is ubiquitous. And in a marketplace economy commercial interests have a right to compete aggressively for the consumer's attention. One should not expect a great deal of self-restraint considering the relentless flow of advertising messages that assault our sensibilities each day. Finding a niche in the consumer's psychological recesses is increasingly difficult. Therefore, advertising gatekeepers must assume some responsibility for their role in the communication process. But what should be the nature of this responsibility? Consumers are autonomous individuals and presumably can ignore or reject the commercial messages presented to them.

But even that is becoming increasingly difficult when ads are integrated into the editorial content. In an earlier age, as one commentator has observed, the media exercised "rational restraint" in ensuring that one company held no competitive edge in the published ads. "Typographic splurges" to the detriment of others were not permitted.[84] In today's environment, of course, that kind of austere policy may be unrealistic, but its underlying theme—that some kind of rational limitations are ethically mandated—still resonates. Or does it? Should the new media managers simply shun any serious attempt at self-regulation until the public demands such Web-based paternalism, or should they become proactive as fiduciaries of the public interest?

These are intriguing questions and ones that some mass communication students will confront as they are attracted away from the traditional media to new opportunities in cyberspace. In this scenario, Lancelot's staff are balancing economic pressures against their responsibilities to consumers and the users of the search engine. Are the two necessarily incompatible? For the purpose of addressing the ethical dilemmas posed in this narrative, assume the position of company president Bill Crenshaw and, applying the formula for moral reasoning outlined in Chapter 3, make a decision on whether you will impose any kind of self-regulation on companies seeking access to your search engine. If you decide that some gatekeeping is necessary, you might include in your analysis a set of proposed guidelines.

 ### CASE 8-3

Impotency Drugs and the Promotion of Sexual Pleasure[85]

"The drug wars are heating up," mused Dale Alter, Director of Marketing Communication for DaxoRX, the third largest manufacturer of pharmaceuticals in the United States, as he contemplated the intense competition to respond to the nation's health needs through prescription drug advertising. Since 1997, when federal drug regulators relaxed restrictions on consumer drug advertising, DaxoRX had invested lavishly to capture a respectable market share for its treatments for high blood pressure, cholesterol, depression, and even hair loss. In the mid-1990s company executives, based upon recommendations from their medical consultants, approved research funding for an impotence drug designed to alleviate the effects of what doctors referred to as erectile dysfunction. However, the drug was not assigned priority status until DaxoRX's competitors introduced their impotence treatments under such brand names as Viagra, Levitra, and Cialis. The drug manufacturer's complacency was quickly replaced with a sense of urgency, and following the mandatory review by the Food and Drug Administration (FDA), Notox made its market debut as DaxoRX's contender for the treatment of erectile dysfunction.

As his company's top communications strategist, Alter was aware of the challenges of promoting a new product to consumers increasingly reliant upon the pharmaceutical industry as the panacea for a diversity of medical problems. Developing a strategy for Notox would be particularly vexing in light of its rather tardy unveiling and the fierce competition of the now established competitors. At the dawn of the twenty-first century, the subject of male impotence was no longer broached in hushed tones; in a sexually oriented society, male sexual prowess had assumed a position of prominence in the public square, with the fervent participation of the pharmaceutical industry. DaxoRX had to be competitive; over the long term billions of dollars were at stake.

As Notox approached its final stages of FDA approval, Alter summoned Heather Macelfresh and

Alvin Bernstein to a strategy conference for the advertising and promotion of Notox. Macelfresh was the corporate Director of Public Communication; Bernstein was DaxoRX's Director of Marketing. Macelfresh was responsible for the pharmaceutical firm's public relations and advertising initiatives and spent much of her time coordinating with DaxoRX's advertising agency, Barnes and Sheffield.

"We need to develop a marketing strategy for Notox," Alter declared without exchanging pleasantries as Macelfresh and Bernstein settled into their chairs in Alter's well-appointed executive office in DaxoRX's impressive headquarters building in Chicago. "Today I would like to discuss the advertising campaign."

"I've already been in touch with Laura Chase at Barnes and Sheffield," Macelfresh volunteered. "She's the new Creative Director. As you know, the marketing of new products is all about positioning. The agency will, of course, handle the campaign, but Chase is interested in what approach we would like to take in selling Notox."

"We can emphasize the fact that Notox's effects begin sooner and last longer than its competitors," offered Bernstein. "Also, the side effects are minimal."

"I have something different in mind," replied Macelfresh. "Our competitors have moved beyond their products' effectiveness in treating male impotence. Impotence is certainly not confined to older consumers—it's not uncommon among men in their 40s—but it does become more of a problem with age. But how many ads for impotence drugs really focus on their treatment for erectile dysfunction? The actors are fairly young, some appear to be no older than late 30s. The commercials are all about romance. The subtle message is that taking one of these impotence drugs will lead to greater sexual satisfaction, perhaps even some kind of sexual nirvana. Promoting merely the medicinal value of Notox won't get us a respectable market share; romance and the prospect of enhanced sexual performance will. We'll leave it up to our agency to decide how to do it better than our competitors."

"I realize we must be competitive," responded Bernstein. "The campaigns for the current drugs on the market have morphed from the restoration of sexual respectability for older Americans to recreational sex for men much younger. I have an ethical problem with this because Notox, like its competitors, is a prescription drug, a treatment for erectile dysfunction. It's designed to help those with physical difficulty in accomplishing sexual intercourse to overcome that difficulty. The goal is not merely to enhance the sexual satisfaction of its users, but a soft-sell approach featuring romance could give the wrong impression. Ads that highlight young actors in a romantic setting leave the impression that these drugs are virtual aphrodisiacs. This is nothing more than an appeal to male virility and ego. If we take this approach with Notox, where will it stop? Are there are other prescription drugs where the promotion of lifestyle becomes more important than the medical benefits of the drug?"

"We have a lot of money invested in Notox," countered Macelfresh. "We need to broaden our horizons to a younger demographic. Let's face it. Younger males are already pressuring their physicians to prescribe the latest and most effective impotence drug, even if they're not truly in need of it. And who is behind this? In many cases, their wives and girlfriends. Wives in particular are the guardians of the health care needs in many families. That's why some of our competitors' ads appeal as much to women as men. We need to do the same. And doctors are only too willing to oblige in prescribing these drugs. If our ads don't appeal to a broader population than just the older generation, we'll be at a competitive disadvantage."

"From an economic perspective, you make a persuasive case," acknowledged Bernstein. "But Notox is a prescription drug. It's designed for men who have a medically treatable sexual dysfunction. Most of these are older consumers, although admittedly the problem also affects some younger males. We should focus on the medical benefits of this drug. I'm aware of what our competitors are doing, but I don't think we should follow their lead."

"But there's nothing misleading about a soft sell," noted Macelfresh. "Notox's lab results support our product's sexual effectiveness, even for healthy males. Why not broaden its appeal? Even younger men are sensitive about their sexual prowess, and our competitors are taking advantage of this fact. Let's face it. Sex appeal has always been a mainstay of the ad industry. If the benefits of Notox appeal to the male's sexual vanity, why not encourage physicians to prescribe it?"

"Whether Notox enhances significantly the sexual performance of those males who don't suffer from true erectile dysfunction—and we can't be absolutely certain of that—is not the issue," replied Bernstein. "Notox is a drug, sold by prescription only. It's designed to treat a medical condition. If we use the soft sell you're proposing, it will be viewed as a weekend pill and an insurance policy for great recreational sex. We've used soft-sell campaigns for our heart and cholesterol medicines, but at least we've confined our claims to the medical benefits of those drugs. I think what you're proposing crosses the line."

"Over the next ten years $2 billion could be at stake," responded Macelfresh. "As long as our claims are not misleading and doctors are willing to prescribe our product for willing patients who feel they will benefit, I don't see that we've crossed any ethical line."

Bernstein refused to surrender to the economic pressures that animated his colleague's passionate defense of encouraging recreational sex through a soft-sell commercial appeal, but he made one last defense of his ethical propriety in the matter. "Doctors prescribe products such as Notox because of pressure from patients generated by emotional appeals contained in prescription drug advertising," he said. "Doctors themselves frequently don't have sufficient information on the drugs they prescribe, and requests from patients may lead them to prescribe certain brands. If our campaign were to stick with the medicinal benefits of Notox, I would feel better. Even if our claims aren't misleading, I don't believe it's proper for a pharmaceutical company to promote its drugs for any purpose other than to improve the physical or emotional health of the consuming public."

Alter had listened attentively as Macelfresh and Bernstein dueled rhetorically over how Notox should be commercially positioned in the already competitive field of impotence drugs. He was painfully aware of the huge financial stakes and the need to capture at least a respectable market share of the impotence drug market. But he was also concerned that the soft-sell campaign proposed by Macelfresh that could be construed as a pitch for recreational uses for Notox could tarnish the image of the pharmaceutical giant, DaxoRX, at a time when the industry was already under assault from a variety of consumer groups. Alter promised his two corporate subordinates he would take their competing views into account and render a decision within a few days on the directions to give Laura Chase at the Barnes and Sheffield Advertising Agency concerning his company's ad campaign for Notox.

THE CASE STUDY

In February 2004, *Newsweek* published an article on impotence drugs that projected the annual sales of the three leading impotence drugs at $6 billion by 2010. Driven by such advertising slogans as "When the moment is right, will you be ready?" (Cialis) and "When you're in the zone, it's all good" (Levitra), the industry had clearly evolved, as *Newsweek* described it, from "an old man's crutch" to a weekend pill fueled by ad industry–created "romantic images of tender moments."[86] Ad slogans such as these are what Alvin Bernstein has in mind when he complains that Heather Macelfresh is promoting sexual satisfaction rather than Notox's original goal of treating the physical causes of male erectile dysfunction.

Critics of prescription drug advertising are not hard to find. They complain that such ads encourage patients to put pressure on their physicians to prescribe certain brands without adequate product information. However, the ethical dilemma outlined in this scenario is more specific in its focus. Bernstein, the marketing director for DaxoRX, a large pharmaceutical company, is concerned that the proposed theme of the ad campaign for a newly approved impotence drug will forsake its health benefits in physically achieving sexual intercourse for a more hedonistic goal of pure sexual gratification and a higher level of sexual performance. Whatever the truth about the effectiveness of the drug in this respect, Heather Macelfresh believes that her company must be economically competitive with the other leading manufacturers of impotence drugs and that the only way to do this is to broaden the target audience and to market Notox to those who have successful sexual relationships but simply want to enhance the quality of those experiences. Bernstein objects to an ad campaign that departs significantly from the promotion of the health benefits of prescription drugs, their primary purpose, to one based strictly on ego and self-gratification. On the other hand, does such a campaign, featuring romance and intimating a noticeable improvement in the quality of sexual relationships, cross an ethical line when patients and their doctors are the ultimate decision makers on the need for the drug?

Research, testing, and production of prescription drugs are expensive, and pharmaceutical companies are under intense economic pressure to recoup these investments and to make a profit. Advertising is one mechanism to increase the demand for and sales of prescription drugs. In this scenario, Heather Macelfresh argues that DaxoRX must meet the competition head-on by advertising the enhanced sexual pleasure derived from its impotence drug rather than merely the drug's original purpose as a treatment for male sexual dysfunction. Alvin Bernstein sees this as an ethically slippery slope.

Dale Alter, Director of Marketing Communication for DaxoRX, is the moral agent in this case and must decide on the overall marketing strategy, including advertising, for his company's new product. DaxoRX's advertising agency will then develop a campaign based upon their client's desires. For the purpose of analyzing the ethical dimensions of this case, assume the role of Dale Alter and, utilizing the SAD model for moral reasoning outlined in Chapter 3, make a decision on this matter. In so doing, review carefully the views expressed by your corporate staff members, Heather Macelfresh and Alvin Bernstein.

▶ **CASE 8-4**

The Alumni Magazine: Journalism or Public Relations?[87]

This had not been an enjoyable year for university president Alexander Davidson. Some of his largest contributors to the Central State University (CSU) Foundation and the Alumni Association were

unhappy, and their collective indignation was likely to reverberate during the university's annual fund drive.

The cause of their disaffection was located in Chandler Hall, the home of the Office of University Relations and the *Central State Gazette,* the university's award-winning alumni magazine. In many respects, the *Gazette,* which was supported by a combination of university and alumni funding, was the prototypical alumni publication, with its methodical but informative accounts of campus life, faculty and student profiles, a survey of the activities of notable alumni, and obituaries. The magazine was distributed both to alumni and other patrons of the university. But despite its affiliation with Central State's public relations enterprise, the *Gazette's* editor and writers approached their mission with the mentality of journalists, producing several candid and uninhibited accounts of campus life that challenged some alumni's nostalgic recollections of their own college experiences. For example, one article documented the incidences of campus "date rape," including complaints that university officials were slow to respond to such charges. Another featured the winner of a "wet T-shirt" contest sponsored by a local fraternity during Homecoming weekend. The article was accompanied by a revealing photo of the smiling coed as she accepted her award. On another occasion, the *Gazette* revealed that the Central State Medical Center, which was located ten miles from the main campus, was under investigation for improperly disposing of medical wastes. This was followed in the next issue by an impressive article on the NCAA's investigation of the university's recruiting practices, a story that had appeared frequently in the commercial media but that some alumni viewed as an unpardonable sacrilege. All of the articles were balanced and provided ample opportunity for comments from university officials.

The *Gazette's* unflinching coverage had earned it the prestigious Robert Sibley Award, an annual competition sponsored by *Newsweek* magazine through the Council for Advancement and Support of Education to recognize excellence in alumni magazines. The day the award was announced Daniel Humphries expected a congratulatory phone call from the university's president. Instead, he received an urgent summons to meet with President Davidson. Humphries was Central State's director of university relations and frequently met with the president to apprise his superior of his department's public relations strategy on various issues. When Humphries arrived, Davidson was more agitated than usual.

"I'm catching a lot of heat from some influential alumni and the head of the CSU Foundation concerning our magazine's coverage," he began. "They're complaining that we're not projecting a positive image for the university. One alumnus was really incensed that we would publish a picture like the one of the wet T-shirt contest winner; he thinks things are out of control here." Davidson also said that the university's director of alumni relations, an office that provided a steady flow of material for the *Gazette,* had received similar comments.

"As you know," Davidson continued, "I've always been a supporter of the public relations efforts of your office. In general, as a taxpayer-supported institution, I feel we should be upfront with the public concerning the activities at Central State. But the alumni audience is different. With state support dwindling, we rely more and more on our alumni to support the CSU Foundation. And it's crucial that we stay on good terms with the alumni."

In recounting the conversation later, Humphries could not recall the litany of complaints cited by Davidson, but the president's message was clear: He was impressed with the *Gazette*'s journalistic enterprise in winning the Sibley Award, but he was concerned that the magazine's candor and what some alumni perceived as negative coverage of the CSU campus threatened the university's fundraising efforts. He asked Humphries to meet with his staff and develop a recommendation on what role the alumni magazine should play in the university's public relations arsenal. "Whatever your recommendation," Davidson promised, "I'll give it careful consideration."

As he returned to his office to confer with the two staffers who were most directly involved in university-sponsored publications—the *Gazette*'s editor and the editor of *Central State Perspectives,* the university's on-campus faculty and staff publication—he silently reviewed the historical role of the alumni magazine.

The *Gazette* had originally been established under the auspices of the Office of Alumni Relations as little more than an expanded newsletter, but fifteen years ago it had been moved to University Relations as part of CSU's consolidation of its public relations efforts. Its original charter had been rather modest: "To promote the accomplishments of Central State University alumni and to serve as a source of information for alumni concerning campus life and the University's activities, programs, policies, and achievements." Such a mandate was subject to interpretation, in Humphries's view, but for most of its history the *Gazette* had been fairly conventional and noncontroversial in its coverage.

But with the arrival three years ago of LeToya Michaels as editor, the magazine had taken on a more aggressive approach in covering campus events. She understood the *Gazette*'s role as a public relations organ but believed that the best public relations is to provide a candid assessment of the university's activities, both its sins and its virtues. With seven years' experience as a reporter on a small-town daily, Michaels rejected the notion of the *Gazette*'s role as nothing more than a cheerleader for the university. She had not dispensed with the sections celebrating the alumni's achievements and the more mundane aspects of campus life but believed that the magazine's investigative pieces added balance to an otherwise unimaginative publication. In Michaels's first year as editor, the *Gazette* had received accolades from the alumni faithful because of its innovative design and enterprising writing style. But in the past several issues she had apparently "pushed the envelope" on content, and the wolves were beginning to howl.

Upon his return to Chandler Hall, Humphries briefed Michaels and Manuel Montiel, the editor of *Central State Perspectives.* Montiel also served as a contributing editor of the *Gazette,* with primary responsibilities for the faculty and staff profiles and other personnel achievements. Montiel had joined the University Relations staff upon his graduation from Central State fifteen years ago with a master's degree in mass communication and a concentration in public relations. Humphries anticipated that his views would differ from those of the *Gazette*'s editor. He was not disappointed!

"I think we should stay the course," said Michaels confidently following her superior's summary of his meeting with President Davidson. "I appreciate the alumni's concerns, but our job is to give them an honest accounting of what's going on on campus, warts and all. The essence of good public relations is honesty."

"But you're forgetting what the purpose of an alumni magazine should be," responded Montiel. "Our job is to provide information to various publics. If the media asked us to comment on the NCAA investigation or the problems at the medical center, for example, then we should be as forthcoming as possible. But the *Gazette* targets the alumni and other patrons of the university. They're interested in the positive aspects of their alma mater—a relentless barrage of negative stories makes it sound as though things are out of control. And that could affect fund-raising."

"If that's the case," replied Michaels, "then the *Gazette* becomes an exercise in spin control. We should give our readers—the Central State graduates—a realistic view of campus life and events at the university. I'm not insensitive to the impact on fund-raising. But if we just report the positive side of campus life, then we lose credibility as a university publication."

"Credibility with whom?" Montiel asked defiantly. "The alumni—or at least some of the more influential ones—don't view the *Gazette* as a journalistic publication. They're not interested in investigative pieces. Credibility is related to expectations, and most alumni don't expect a university publication that thrives on the unattractive side of campus life. After all, alumni donate because they have a special affection for the university."

But Michaels was undeterred by what she perceived as her colleague's willingness to pander to the university's philanthropic interests. "Our coverage has been balanced," she remarked. "University spokespersons have been included in every article. This has provided them with an opportunity to tell the alumni what the university is doing. We might lose some donors in the short term, but over time the alumni will come to appreciate the *Gazette*'s candid assessment of university life. Writing honestly about our campus is not only good journalism—it's also good public relations."

The *Gazette* has received national recognition as the recipient of the Sibley Award, which has brought prestige to the university and the Office of University Relations. We shouldn't allow some disaffected donors to dictate the content of our magazine."

"But with the reduction in state appropriations, the university is depending more and more on the support of alumni. Just remember who signs our paychecks. The *Gazette* is not like a news magazine. It's a public relations tool—not a journalistic organ."

Humphries listened to the points and counterpoints offered by his two staff members. As the director of University Relations, he was the moral agent who would either respond to the alumni's complaints or convince the university president to support the magazine despite pressure from Central State's benefactors. If the second option were not chosen—or if President Davidson elected not to accept it—then LeToya Michaels might resign as the *Gazette*'s editor, and the magazine would retreat to safer but perhaps less prestigious terrain.

THE CASE STUDY

What should be the role of a state university alumni magazine? Should it be essentially a public relations organ, or can such a publication legitimately define itself as a campus news medium and embrace the journalistic virtues? Are these two philosophies incompatible?

This question has erupted on a number of campuses. Several alumni magazine editors have resigned rather than succumb to pressure from alumni and fund-raisers.[88] And yet, those who provide financial support to universities are major stakeholders who feel that, as the target audience for alumni magazines, they should be allowed to influence the editorial direction of these publications.

In this case, the editor of the *Gazette*, LeToya Michaels, apparently believes that good journalism and public relations are not mutually exclusive. This philosophy is captured in this observation in a recent issue of the *Chronicle of Higher Education*:

> Many editors acknowledge that they have a duty to pave the way for fund raisers by making connections with alumni. But they insist that they can best do so by having the editorial freedom to write honestly,

fairly, and openly about the institution, its students, and its alumni. The closer their magazines are to development, they argue, the harder it is to divorce themselves from the office's goals.[89]

On the other hand, Manuel Montiel argues for a much more restricted editorial philosophy for the university's alumni magazine. In his view, good public relations consists of putting the university in the best light, where possible, and targeting its messages to its various constituencies, which in this case are the CSU alumni and other donors. Economic reality appears to be a major motivation here, although Montiel also apparently feels that the *Gazette* has no mandate to cover issues or events that reflect unfavorably on the university and perhaps should avoid them altogether.

For the purpose of recommending an operating philosophy for the university's alumni magazine, assume the role of the director of university relations, Daniel Humphries, and render a judgment in this case.

▶ **CASE 8-5**

Product Placement in Prime Time

Abram Silverman may not have been a household name, but network programming executives spoke his name with an undisguised reverence. His 1992 network entry, *Silver Tongues,* a comedic rendition of a group of dysfunctional attorneys in an unorthodox law firm, had been an instant hit and remained in the top twenty for five years, a remarkable performance in an increasingly fickle industry. This was followed by several more entertainment triumphs on both the broadcast and cable networks, all of which contributed impressively to the TV industry's bottom line. Like his competitors, Silverman knew that a successful program would not only enhance his stature among his benefactors, the network brass, but would also boost the program's chances for syndication, which was the financial Holy Grail for Hollywood producers. The production of a first-run series was also accompanied by a great deal of nail biting and nervous anxiety as production costs continued to escalate and the networks' license fees failed to keep pace.

As Silverman prepared his latest entry for the networks' critical perusal—a show tentatively titled *On Deadline,* a realistic look at the techniques of two investigative reporters for a large daily newspaper—he maintained a fretful vigil over the program's costs and frequently had silent dialogues with himself on how to maintain the integrity of his comparatively modest budget. He envied his cast whose fictional characters provided a vicarious escape from the economic realities of the Hollywood set.

As Silverman's director was putting the finishing touches on the *On Deadline* pilot, the arrival of Arthur McNeil at the producer's Burbank office was not an unmixed blessing. McNeil was an agent acting on behalf of Unicor Computers, Inc., a small but aggressive competitor to the computer stalwarts in the field. Despite its size, Unicor had deep pockets and boasted a rather lavish advertising and marketing budget. TV, magazines, and the Internet had been its advertising strongholds, but McNeil's visionary prowess detected a rich opportunity in the convergence of the established technology of TV and the new digital revolution. McNeil was confident of the "star" quality of *On Deadline* and wanted a piece of the action. Or in the language of the industry, he was interested in product placement.

Silverman was familiar with product placements by which a manufacturer pays a producer to have its product featured prominently in a film. The practice was common in both theatre releases and TV, and Silverman's stringent budget compelled him to endure his visitor's financial proposal.

"Our offer is for two million dollars in the first season," McNeil said as he attempted to gauge Silverman's level of interest. "Since the newsroom set for *On Deadline* will be filled with computers, Unicor will supply the hardware. Our brand name will be affixed prominently to the front of the unit so that it is visible while the reporters are working at their desks. Ditto for the laptops they take on assignment. We would like an option to renegotiate the deal for the second season if the show is renewed. In addition—and here's the part I find attractive—if the show eventually goes into syndication, which I expect it will, we will offer additional financial incentives in exchange for replacing electronically the current computers with new models using digital technology. Thus, both the first-run shows and the syndicated versions can be used as marketing vehicles."

Silverman's inclination was to accept McNeil's offer, but he had had little direct experience with the practice known as product placement and thus deferred his decision for a few days. Silverman's ethical sensitivities had been tweaked by some comments from critics in the trade press, but he was unable to articulate clearly the true dimensions of the ethical concerns. The pragmatic producer was certainly not opposed to the commercial nature of network TV since advertising was ultimately the source of his daily bread. In addition, the economic pressures of producing a quality program within strict budget guidelines necessitated a consideration of supplemental sources of income. On the other hand, he was offended by *crass* commercialism in which marketing concerns eclipsed artistic or creative choices. Unicor's contract would undoubtedly require a certain number of exposures, which would have some modest impact on the aesthetic aspects of the production. In addition, commercials were clearly separated from entertainment content, and the messages and product claims could easily be ignored by consumers. But product plugs were woven into the very fabric of the program, and there was no escape for the viewer. And since viewers would be blissfully unaware of the paid insertion of Unicor computers into Hollywood's contrived newsroom set, Silverman worried about the subliminal effect on his audience.

But a counterpoint to his ethical qualms about product placements was his pragmatic assessment of the economic realities of the industry. Such commercial arrangements would enhance his revenue stream and thus ensure the continuation of quality entertainment fare. He also knew that to refuse McNeil's offer would be bucking a long-standing trend in Hollywood and one that was becoming more pronounced in the television industry. Besides, the use and visibility of brand-name products would replicate reality. Viewers are more sophisticated, Silverman reasoned, and expect to see brand names on the products and props that adorn the sets of their favorite shows.

Was this really a moral dilemma of some import or were product placements merely business

arrangements to which there no ethical obstacles? This was the point of departure for Abram Silverman's troubled reflection as he contemplated whether to accept Arthur McNeil's lucrative offer to subsidize the production of what he hoped would be another TV network success.

THE CASE STUDY

Hollywood is no less a servant to commercial interests than other mass media. For a number of years companies have paid handsomely to have their products inserted into theatre releases, and TV entertainment programming has recently jumped on the bandwagon. Economic concerns have led producers to form strategic alliances with manufacturers in order to subsidize production costs. Within TV programs marketers are looking for unconventional ways to influence consumers who are increasingly resistant to traditional commercials and who are likely to "zap" or fast forward the ads as they appear.[90]

Critics complain that there is no ethically acceptable manner of inserting ad images into a TV show because it blurs the line between the dramatic content and commercial interests. In a sense, then, the audience becomes a captive of both the producer's economic woes and the company's creative marketing ploys.

On the other hand, many producers and directors are philosophical about product placements and consider this to be a reasonable accommodation to stay within budgetary guidelines. They might also note that consumers are autonomous individuals who, despite the subtle commercial proselytizing by unseen sponsors, can still resist the influence of such product insertions and make their own purchasing decisions.

One question in considering this issue from an ethical perspective is whether members of the audience, if they were aware of this practice, would be offended by it. Or are commercial messages so ubiquitous that consumers are becoming more sophisticated in evaluating their underlying motivations and perhaps even resisting the influence of those that do not comport with their predispositions?

For the purpose of resolving the issues outlined in this scenario, assume the position of

Abram Silverman. What obligations do you owe your audience? Do they really care about product insertions into entertainment fare? Do you think that such intrusive marketing techniques are effective? Applying the SAD formula for moral reasoning described in Chapter 3, render a judgment on whether you will accept Arthur McNeil's offer to supply your fictional newsroom with his brand-name computers.

CASE 8-6
Slain Civil Rights Heroes as Commercial Props[91]

The African American Lifeline Institute was no longer a voice in the wilderness. The missionary spirit, determination, and unmistakable confidence of the institute's founders and their heirs had gradually earned it a position of prominence among the nation's most visible and influential institutional activists.

Three self-made African American entrepreneurs had established the institute twenty years ago as a nonprofit organization devoted to improving the quality of life for all black citizens but particularly those in the inner city. It had opened its doors with a modest budget but an ambitious agenda: restoration of the black family, job training, decent housing, and access to better health care and educational opportunities. The leadership had also targeted the persistent pathologies of life in urban America, such as drugs and prostitution, because of their corrosive effects on the psychological and emotional vitality of the nation's economically disinherited.

The institute's devoted staff was optimistic but pragmatic and measured their early successes in small increments. But their tenacity and moral fervor were indisputable and eventually attracted the attention of several philanthropists and foundations that had provided the long-term financial stability required for the institute's challenging program of sociological rejuvenation. Several federal grants and individual donations had also contributed to the organization's economic stability.

Much of the budget consisted of direct grants to specific community programs, but the institute's media-wise administrators had also committed a respectable sum for public relations and advertising. The public relations efforts were directed both at the African American middle class, with their increasing economic clout, and the public at large. Most of the advertising expenditures were allocated for radio because inner-city residents tended to be heavy radio listeners. TV also figured prominently in their entertainment fare, but the cost of TV time precluded the institute's involvement with this medium except in extraordinary circumstances.

This was one of those circumstances, in the judgment of Cassandra Davis, the institute's director of communications. Davis was the impresario of the institute's public relations and advertising enterprises and had commissioned the Bailey and Barnhart Advertising Agency to develop a campaign to counteract what she believed were the deleterious effects of the tobacco industry's marketing efforts within the African American community. Despite the industry's setbacks and strategic retreat in the face of both private lawsuits and legal initiatives from several state attorneys general, the tobacco interests still stood accused in the court of public opinion of promoting their products to the most vulnerable, such as children and the residents of black neighborhoods. Tobacco products could not be legally advertised on radio or TV, but billboards had proved to be an effective substitute within the African American community. Because blacks were heavy users of TV, Davis reasoned, the institute's expenditures on antitobacco commercials would be justified.

Bailey and Barnhart's campaign concept, which had to receive the institute's blessing before proceeding to production, was resourceful and enterprising. It also provoked an ethical debate within the institute's public relations hierarchy.

An account executive tendered his agency's storyboard in a PowerPoint presentation at the institute's Washington, DC, headquarters to communications director Cassandra Davis and her two subordinates, Washington Williams, the assistant director for community relations, and Eugene Simmons, the assistant director for advertising. The campaign's theme was not subtle. The ad featured pictures and film of three slain civil rights leaders—Dr. Martin Luther King Jr., Malcolm X, and James Chaney—that were dramatically intercut with pathetic shots of deceased smokers portrayed by African American actors. The spot effectively contrasted the courageous lives of the three luminaries with the wasted lives of smoking victims. The commercial concluded with a still-frame montage of the three figures, accompanied by this sobering question: "They died for a just cause. Will you?"

"The agency is planning to run this campaign on ESPN, BET, and stations with high viewership within the African American community," explained Davis. "They're also planning to run radio spots. They've sent us this storyboard for approval. The agency expects the TV ads to be particularly effective because African American teens, in particular, are heavy TV users."

"Most Americans have heeded the warnings about the health risks posed by cigarettes and other tobacco products," Davis continued. "But the industry targets African Americans with higher concentrations of advertising."

"That's a debatable point," responded Simmons. "The tobacco industry says they have no ethnic agenda. Nevertheless, the level of smoking among African Americans is unacceptably high. This is a powerful commercial; no one can ignore the message. I don't know whether it will be effective among black youth, but it should get their attention."

"I can't dispute the ad's effectiveness," replied Williams. "But I am concerned about the ethics of using the images and reputations of these famous civil rights leaders in a commercial context. I realize that we're attempting to counter the economic influence of the tobacco industry in the inner city; African Americans are still a major market for them. But somehow this kind of campaign seems to be degrading to the lives of these great men. What the agency is proposing, essentially, is to use these men as commercial props."

"I disagree," replied Simmons. "If they were alive today, Dr. King, Malcolm X, and James Chaney would be appalled that so little progress has been made in the lives of most African Americans. Alcohol and tobacco usage are real problems in the inner city. They would probably lend their names to our campaign."

"We don't know whether they would agree to the use of their names and pictures in commercials," responded Williams, "so we have to use our own judgment. These leaders died for a cause—a noble cause—and the integration of their images with those of pathetic-looking smokers who have a self-imposed death sentence appears to me to be an act of desperation. The commercialization of three men who should be put on a pedestal and held up as heroes to young blacks sends the wrong message—that their lives and images are available to the highest bidder."

"That's absurd," answered Simmons defiantly. "We're not selling a product. We're trying to save the lives of African Americans, especially teens, who are the most vulnerable. What could be a more noble cause than that?"

"The cause is noble," acknowledged Williams. "But do the ends justify the means? We can develop strategies that are just as effective. We don't need to resort to the appropriation of the reputations of these leaders in a commercial context. This campaign is degrading to their legacy."

"In this case I think the ends do justify the means," replied Simmons. "The tobacco billboards are slickly done. They're highly visual, prominently placed, and very effective. The advantage of using TV is that we have the field to ourselves; tobacco ads are banned. Of course, we could still run TV ads without these civil rights leaders. But quite frankly, I don't know of a more effective means of getting our message across. These men are role models and highly respected within the African American community. Their presence in this commercial should have a high impact."

"You're right. They are role models. And for that reason their historical legacy should be preserved. Linking them in this way to our antitobacco crusade in a commercial context is unseemly," concluded Williams.

Cassandra Davis listened attentively to her two staff members. Each was passionate in his beliefs, and each believed he was on solid ethical ground. The disagreement between Washington Williams and Eugene Simmons could presage a similar split among the African American leadership if this campaign should be launched as planned. The moral elites might object on the grounds that the ad violated the respect due to the three civil rights leaders. The social activists would counter that they would approve of invoking their names and reputations to improve the quality of life within the African American community. As an admirer of Dr. King, Malcolm X, and James Chaney and an opponent of the tobacco industry, Davis felt the tug of competing loyalties as she pondered her unenviable role as moral agent.

THE CASE STUDY

Should the images and reputations of these three slain civil rights leaders—martyrs in a noble cause to the African American community—be employed in a commercial context to counteract the influence of the tobacco industry?

Eugene Simmons's position is essentially utilitarian, predicated on the assumption that the only way to counter the tobacco industry's economic and marketing impact within the black community is to try to get the maximum effectiveness from the institute's modest expenditures within the TV medium. In this view, the heavy tobacco usage among African Americans, particularly those who live in the inner city where health care and lifestyle counseling are not as readily available, is a pathology that justifies invoking the reputations and images of the three slain civil rights leaders.

Washington Williams, no less concerned than Simmons about the impact of the tobacco industry within African American neighborhoods, is more reticent in "appropriating" the images of these men, who are identified with a noble cause, for commercial purposes. He questions whether soliciting their testimonials from beyond the grave will eventually diminish their stature within the African American community.

How far should the institute go in counteracting the tobacco industry's advertising and marketing strategies among African American consumers? Take the role of communications director Cassandra Davis, and make a decision on whether you will approve the antismoking TV campaign featuring the images of Dr. Martin Luther King Jr., Malcolm X, and James Chaney.

 CASE 8-7

The Junket as a Public Relations Tool

The political revolution in Eastern and Central Europe was like a breath of fresh air to Telepac, Inc. As an aggressive and successful player in the competitive telecommunications industry, Telepac's corporate management was increasingly seduced by the commercial opportunities in the emerging democracies of the former Soviet Empire as they struggled to master the intricacies and uncertainties of a capitalistic system.

Telepac had been a late entrant in the telecommunications field, but its cadre of ambitious and well-educated young managers, led by president Teri Hance, had quickly developed the company into an attractive Wall Street commodity. Its initial enterprise had been built around cellular phones loaded with novelty features designed to entice both consumers and corporate executives alike, but within a few years Telepac had added other products to its inventory of impressive advanced telecommunications technology. Telepac had indeed become an influential contender in the domestic information marketplace, and Hance began scanning the economic horizons for foreign investment opportunities. Hance and her management staff were determined to become actors on the global stage, hoping to establish a symbiotic relationship between their own financial self-interest and the proponents of economic reform in emerging democracies.

Hance had traveled to Eastern and Central Europe on both business and pleasure and was impressed by the marketing opportunities that awaited enterprising investors. However, she had also accommodated herself to the reality that any attempt to penetrate these foreign markets would be accompanied by sometimes long and protracted negotiations with government bureaucrats who were capitalistic neophytes. Telepac would have to establish a bond of trust between the company and its foreign suitors. And the public relations division, Hance knew, would play a prominent role in this process.

Earl Kohler, Telepac's vice president for communications and marketing, did not need to be prodded into action. At the first indication of Hance's interest in penetrating the markets of Eastern and Central Europe, Kohler had ordered his small staff to prepare a public relations strategy for maximizing the investment potential in these fledgling capitalistic nations. Sherri McLendon, Telepac's director of public relations, and Dale Knight, a product information specialist, soon developed a rather ambitious plan for providing their company with a public relations overture to these foreign markets.

"We're planning to kick off this campaign by bringing some business reporters and editors of the leading newspapers in Poland, Hungary, Slovakia, Bulgaria, and the Czech Republic to this country to tour our plants," said McLendon as she and Knight unveiled the plan to their superior. "We'll set up demonstrations so that they can see what our equipment can do—how it can revolutionize corporate and personal communications in their countries."

"The papers we've selected are among the most prestigious in their respective countries," added Knight. "They're read by government officials and corporate elites. If we get favorable news coverage, this should help pave the way for negotiations with their government representatives."

"It's an interesting idea, but I do have one ethical concern," responded Kohler. "I'm concerned that this will be perceived as nothing more than a junket designed to influence the decision makers in Eastern and Central Europe. Our competitors could have a field day with this. Remember that they're also trying to expand their markets in this part of the world. They could cry foul, and then our plan will backfire."

"But media tours are commonplace in the public relations field," replied McLendon. "Our job is to provide information to our public through the media, and that's all that we would be doing in this case. The journalists will still make their own decisions on what to report."

"That's true," replied Kohler. "But this will be an expensive trip, and we'll be picking up the tab. It may appear as though we're trying to buy influence."

"Let's face it," responded Knight rather candidly. "We spend a great deal of money trying to cultivate our corporate image. I don't see anything wrong with sponsoring a trip for a group of journalists, some of whom probably could not afford to come to this country anyway. Besides, it's mutually beneficial. If we do gain access to markets in these countries, we'll advertise in their papers. And for them, this could be an important event. The attraction of foreign capital and investment is important to their national economic development. This trip will have news value, and that should resolve the ethical dilemma."

"Perhaps. But does news value—or at least what we perceive as news value—really make a difference?" wondered Kohler aloud. "The fact is that we're still setting the agenda for this visit. The reporters and editors will go where we direct them and have access only to certain selective information about our company and our products. In a sense we're paying for access to the news columns of Eastern and Central Europe. How much of what we do here is news and how much is self-promotion?"

"That's not really our problem," replied McLendon. "The foreign journalists can make that decision. Our job is to provide information and to demonstrate what our products can do. A favorable corporate image will pay dividends later if we should gain access to their markets."

"Besides, self-promotion is part of our job as public relations practitioners," McLendon continued. "We're responsible for creating a positive corporate image for Telepac in the collective minds of government decision makers in Europe. And I see nothing wrong with inviting foreign journalists to tour our plants, even at our own expense. After all, someday we may be an important source of business news in their countries. This trip will help them to familiarize themselves with our operation and get to know us. And I agree with Dale—as a possible future investor in their economy, Telepac should have some news value to their readers."

As Telepac's vice president for communications and marketing, Earl Kohler had carefully nurtured his company's public relations activities, and his efforts had paid dividends in both the general circulation and the trade press. Media events were an important part of Telepac's public relations inventory, but the company had never sponsored an all-expense-paid trip for visiting journalists.

In Kohler's mind, his staff's proposal amounted to an ethically troublesome public relations initiative. On the other hand, considering the legitimate role of the public relations practitioner in the commercial marketplace, he found it difficult to articulate clearly the exact nature of the ethical dilemma. After all, such activities, sometimes referred to as junkets by the media, are commonplace in corporate America. Did the potential news value of such an event, for example, purge it of any moral suspicion? Because the proposed visit by the foreign journalists arguably had some news value, the answer to this difficult question, Kohler knew, would ultimately determine whether he would approve the public relations plan proposed by his two energetic and ambitious staff members.

THE CASE STUDY

When Dale Knight, Telepac's product information specialist, states that "[t]his trip will have news value, and that should resolve the ethical dilemma," he may have in mind the general principle that public relations practitioners should preserve the free flow of unprejudiced information and should not engage in any practice that has the effect of corrupting the integrity of the communications process. Would an orchestrated tour for media representatives violate this principle when they are given the opportunity for on-the-spot viewing of a newsworthy product, process, or event? Does the fact that the host company provides an all-expense-paid tour alter the equation? The authors of one leading text on public relations suggest that public relations initiatives that include such trips are acceptable as long as they have a legitimate news purpose.[92] For no purpose other than pleasure they would be unacceptable. Thus, Knight is apparently concerned that this all-expense-paid trip should have some journalistic value, thus adding credibility to the lines of communication between his company and the foreign business editors and reporters.

Is it ethical for a public relations practitioner to offer payments or other inducements to a member of the media in order to obtain preferential or guaranteed news or editorial coverage? If not, does a sponsored trip for foreign reporters and editors constitute a form of payment to obtain guaranteed news coverage?

Media tours and visits sponsored by corporations and government agencies are common tools within the public relations arsenal. Of course, participation in all-expense-paid junkets has increasingly been viewed as a conflict of interest within the journalistic establishment. Should there be any comparable ethical concern from the public relations perspective?

Certainly nothing is ethically amiss in cultivating media sources in the hopes of procuring favorable coverage. After all, as autonomous moral agents, reporters are free to render their own decisions on information sources and the kinds of information to include in their news stories.

On the other hand, a moral purist might argue that, although a symbiotic relationship does exist between the media and public relations practitioners, a corporate-sponsored junket is an undisguised attempt to influence the news value of an event and therefore undermines the integrity of the communication process. After all, unlike most pseudo-events to which the media are invited, reporters are offered a consideration (the cost of the trip) in return for their participation.

Assume the role of Earl Kohler, Telepac's vice president for communications and marketing, and decide whether you will approve the proposed all-expense-paid trip for the business editors from Eastern and Central Europe. In this case your decision-making process should be guided by the role of public relations in American society as an embodiment of persuasive communications, as well as whether you believe that an all-expense-paid tour for journalists runs the risk of corrupting the communications process in terms of the flow of accurate information to the consumer.

❡

Notes

1. Quoted in Walter Isaacson, *Benjamin Franklin: An American Life* (New York: Simon & Schuster, 2003), p. 67.
2. Ibid., 68–69.

3. Alan H. Goldman, *The Moral Foundations of Professional Ethics* (Totowa, NJ: Rowman & Littlefield, 1980), p. 234.

4. "Doctor Is In; News Is Out," *Broadcasting & Cable,* August 6, 2001, p. 26.

5. For a thorough examination of this problem, see Ben H. Bagdikian, *The Media Monopoly,* 6th ed. (Boston: Beacon Press, 2000), pp. 3–26; Robert G. Picard, Maxwell E. McCombs, James P. Wilson, and Stephen Lacy (eds.), *Press Concentration and Monopoly: New Perspectives on Newspaper Ownership and Operation* (Norwood, NJ: Ablex, 1988).

6. See John C. Busterna, "Daily Newspaper Chains and the Antitrust Laws," *Journalism Monographs* 110 (March 1989): 2.

7. James V. Risser, "Endangered Species," *American Journalism Review,* June 1998, p. 20.

8. Thomas Kunkel and Gene Roberts, "The Age of Corporate Newspapering: Leaving Readers Behind," *American Journalism Review,* May 2001, p. 38.

9. See *Editor & Publisher Yearbook,* Part 1, 1998, p. xxiii.

10. See Marci McDonald, "L.A. Is Their Kind of Town," *U.S. News & World Report,* March 27, 2000, p. 45.

11. Elise Soukup, "The Un-Funny Pages," *Newsweek,* July 19, 2004, p. 10.

12. Seth Sutel, "NBC Takes Place as Media Gain, Completes Merger with Universal," AP dispatch published in *The Advocate* (Baton Rouge, LA), May 13, 2004, p. D1.

13. See Elizabeth Lesley Stevens, "mouse.ke.fear," *Brill's Content,* December 1998/1999, pp. 95–103.

14. Quoted in Trudy Lieberman, "You Can't Report What You Don't Pursue," *Columbia Journalism Review,* May/June 2000, p. 45.

15. Richard P. Cunningham, "The Smoking Gun May Belong to CBS, Not Tobacco Firm," *Quill,* January/February 1996, pp. 18–19. See also Bill Carter, "'60 Minutes' Says It Held Story Due to Management Pressure," *New York Times,* November 13, 1995, p. C8.

16. See Lawrence K. Gross, "CBS, 60 Minutes, and the Unseen Interview," *Columbia Journalism Review,* January/February 1996, p. 45.

17. David Bauder, "Ties Become Issue for News Shows," AP dispatch published in *The Advocate* (Baton Rouge, LA), April 12, 2004, p. 4B.

18. "Broadcast Station Totals as of September 30, 2000" (online data from the Federal Communications Commission, November 29, 2000, accessed July 20, 2001), available from http://www.fcc.gov/mb

19. Charles Layton, "News Blackout," *American Journalism Review,* December 2003/January 2004, pp. 18–31. When the House of Representatives subsequently voted to block the new FCC rule allowing networks to own more stations, *NBC Nightly News* provided no coverage at all. "Dart," *Columbia Journalism Review,* September/October 2003, p. 6.

20. Bagdikian, *The Media Monopoly,* p. xxxv.

21. See Conrad C. Fink, *Media Ethics* (Boston: Allyn & Bacon, 1995), pp. 140–141.

22. See Andrew Kohut, "Self-Censorship: Counting the Ways," *Columbia Journalism Review,* May/June 2000, p. 42.

23. Quoted in Bob Steele, "A Crisis of Faith," *Communicator,* April 2004, p. 45.

24. For an interesting analysis of the mistakes that led up to this journalistic debacle, see Neil Hickey, "Ten Mistakes That Led to the Great CNN/Time Fiasco," *Columbia Journalism Review,* September/October 1998, pp. 26–32.

25. J. Max Robins, "CNN vs. the Army: A Premature Strike?" *TV Guide,* July 4, 1998, p. 37.

26. Deborah Zabarenko, "Retractions Suggest New Financial Pressure," Reuters dispatch, July 3, 1998, available from http://news.lycos.com/stories/business/19980703rtbusiness-media.asp, p. 1.

27. See J. Max Robins, "Air Still Far from Clear over 'Tailwind,'" *TV Guide,* July 18, 1998, pp. 39–40.

28. Robins, "CNN vs. the Army."

29. Charles Rappleye, "Cracking the Church-State Wall," *Columbia Journalism Review,* January/February 1998, p. 20.

30. See Susan Paterno, "Let the Good Times Roll," *American Journalism Review,* September 2001, pp. 20–26, 29–34.

31. Rebecca Ross Albers, "Breaching the Wall," *Presstime,* April 1998, pp. 31–36. See also Coyle, "Now, the Editor as Marketer," p. 37.

32. Jack Lule, "The Power and Pitfalls of Journalism in the Hypertext Era," *Chronicle of Higher Education,* August 7, 1998, p. B7.

33. Deni Elliott, "Getting Past 'The Wall,'" *Quill Magazine,* April 2000, p. 13.

34. See Jacqueline Sharkey, "Judgment Calls," *American Journalism Review,* September 1994, pp. 16–26. For a discussion of the controversial attempts at "marketing" O. J. Simpson following the trial, see John C. Coffee, Jr., "The Morals of Marketing Simpson," *New York Times,* October 8, 1995, p. F10.

35. Sharkey, "Judgment Calls," p. 20.

36. Ibid.

37. "Homefront: Coverage Protesters," *Broadcasting & Cable,* March 24, 2003, p. 56.

38. Ibid.

39. Bauder, "Ties Become Issues for News Shows."

40. Kevin McDonough, "Entertainment Honchos Corrupt 'Dateline' to Promote 'Friends,'" *The Advocate* (Baton Rouge, LA), May 5, 2004, p. 12A.

41. "TV Guide's Shill-O-Meter," *TV Guide,* June 20, 2004, p. 10.

42. "The Infomercial Index" (online index, July 18, 2001, accessed July 20, 2001), available from http://www.magickeys.com/infomercials/index.html

43. Patricia Winters Lauro, "The Media Business: Advertising; Will Dot-Com Advertisers Turn to the Infomercial to Bring Traffic to Their Web Sites?," *New York Times,* April 24, 2000, p. C18.

44. Paul Farhi, "Time Out from Our Commercial for a Word from Our Sponsor," *Washington Post National Weekly Edition,* March 2–8, 1992, p. 21.

45. "New Infomercials Test the Growing Industry's Ethics," *TV Guide,* September 4, 1993, p. 38.

46. "Infomercials Maker Agrees to Pay $3.5 Million to Settle FTC Charges," *The Advocate* (Baton Rouge, LA), June 5, 1993, p. 3C.

47. Farhi, "Time Out from Our Commercial," p. 21.

48. Ibid.; Fink, *Media Ethics,* pp. 154–155.

49. Lowell Bergman, "Network Television News: With Fear and Favor," *Columbia Journalism Review,* May/June 2000, p. 51.

50. Marci McDonald, "A Different Paper Chase," *U.S. News & World Report,* May 7, 2001, p. 35.

51. "Those Sensitive Auto Dealers Strike Again, and Another Newspaper Caves," *American Journalism Review,* September 1994, p. 14.

52. See Anthony Ramirez, "The F.C.C. Calls a Halt to Car Dealers' Protest against a Newspaper," *New York Times,* August 2, 1995, p. C3.

53. See Deborah Potter, "News for Sale," *American Journalism Review,* September 2001, p. 68

54. Ibid.

55. Dow C. Smith, "Disguising Ads as the Local News," *Broadcasting & Cable,* March 3, 2003, p. 40.

56. Susanne Ault, "P&G Abandons 'Dr. Laura' Talker," *Broadcasting & Cable,* May 22, 2000, p. 10.

57. "The Economics of Ethics: Doing the Right Thing," *Broadcasting,* October 1, 1990, p. 50.

58. "Dart," *Columbia Journalism Review,* May/June 2003, p. 8.

59. "Talk Show's Soup Tie-in Hard to Swallow for Some" (online AP dispatch and Nando.net, November 15, 2000, accessed November 16, 2000), available from http://www.nando.net/entertainment/st.../0,1087,300280007-300439366-302818323-0,00.html

60. "Sisterhood, Frankly Speaking," *Newsweek,* May 13, 1991, p. 65.

61. "In Brief," *Broadcasting & Cable,* October 6, 1997, p. 92.

62. Fink, *Media Ethics,* p. 165.

63. Margaret Mannix, "Search Me, Please," *U.S. News & World Report,* July 30, 2001, p. 37.

64. Ibid.

65. F. Miguel Valenti, *More Than a Movie: Ethics in Entertainment* (Boulder, CO: Westview Press, 2000), p. 145, citing W. Lackey, "Can Lois Lane Smoke Marlboros?: An Example of the Constitutionality of Regulating Product Placement in Movies," *University of Chicago Legal Forum* (Annual 1193), pp. 275–292.

66. Valenti, *More Than a Movie: Ethics in Entertainment,* p. 145.

67. See ibid., p. 144.

68. Steven L. Snyder, "Movies and Product Placement: Is Hollywood Turning Films into Commercial Speech?," *University of Illinois Law Review* (1992), p. 304.

69. Ibid., p. 309, note 69.

70. Howard Kurtz, "Multiple Tongues; Who Was Watergate's Deep Throat? John Dean Nominates Four Candidates," *Washington Post,* June 17, 2002, p. C1. (The reference to the *Time* interview in the film was buried in a commentary that dealt with a variety of topics.)

71. Snyder, "Movies and Product Placement," pp. 307–308.

72. See "iMac Attack" (online article *Entertainment Weekly,* December 14, 1998, accessed July 23, 2001), available from http://www.dearsally.org/felicity/articles/121498_apple_ew.html

73. Andrew Goldman, "Commercial Hide-and-Seek," *TV Guide,* November 29, 2003, p. 52.

74. Online promotion from Rave Revues (accessed August 16, 2001), available at http://www.ravereviews.com

75. Stuart Elliott, "A Video Process Allows the Insertion of Brand-Name Products in TV Shows Already on Film," *New York Times,* March 29, 1999, p. C11.

76. See Stuart Elliott, "Reruns May Become a Testing Ground for Digital Insertion of Sponsor's Products and Images," *New York Times,* May 23, 2001, p. C6.

77. Ibid.

78. J. Max Roberts, "See Spot Regulated," *TV Guide,* October 25, 2003, p. 34.

79. Snyder, "Movies and Product Placement," pp. 309–310.

80. Some of the information for this case study was taken from Abe Aamidor, "Sports: Have We Lost Control of Our Content?," *Quill,* May 2001, pp. 16–20.

81. Ibid., p. 17.

82. Ibid., p. 16.

83. Margaret Mannix, "Search Me, Please," *U.S. News & World Report,* July 30, 2001, p. 37.

84. See Randall E. Stross, "Pop Go the Weasels," *U.S. News & World Report,* August 13, 2001, p. 39.

85. Some of the information for this case is based upon Keith Naughton, "The Soft Sell," *Newsweek,* February 2, 2004, pp. 46–47.

86. Ibid.

87. This case is based on some events and concerns reported in the following source: Julie L. Nicklin, "Journalism or Public Relations?," *Chronicle of Higher Education,* January 26, 1996, pp. A23, A25.

88. See ibid., p. A23.

89. Ibid., p. A25.

90. For example, see Elliott, "Reruns May Become a Testing Ground for Digital Insertion of Sponsor's Products and Images."

91. The idea for this case is derived from an actual anti-smoking campaign that was funded by the Centers for Disease Control and Prevention's Office on Smoking and Health. Some of the facts are taken from the following source: Jim Cooper, "TV, Radio Ads Counter Tobacco Pitch to Blacks," *Broadcasting & Cable,* July 12, 1993, p. 68.

92. See Dennis L. Wilcox, Phillip H. Ault, and Warren K. Agee, *Public Relations: Strategies and Tactics,* 3d ed. (New York: HarperCollins, 1992), pp. 119–120.

CHAPTER

9

The Media
and Antisocial Behavior

THE INFLUENCE OF THE MEDIA ON BEHAVIOR

In February 2003 19-year-old Josh Cooke walked into his family's basement in Fairfax County, Virginia, and shot his father seven times and his mother twice with a shotgun. He then calmly called the police to report the killings. Cooke's attorney attributed his client's actions to his fascination with the hit movie *The Matrix*, a psycho-drama in which computers take over the world and crime is the natural order of things inside The Matrix. In the same week an Ohio woman who told police she lived inside The Matrix where "they commit a lot of crimes" was found not guilty by reason of insanity to charges of killing her husband.[1]

In December 1997, 14-year-old Michael Carneal entered a Kentucky high school with a pistol and five shotguns and started shooting, killing three classmates and wounding five others. His victims' parents sued several video-game, movie production, and Internet companies, alleging that exposure to the defendants' material made young people "insensitive to violence and more likely to commit violent acts."[2] The content "included violent, interactive computer games, pornographic websites, and a movie in which a student dreams of killing his teacher and classmates."[3]

Sarah Edmondson and her boyfriend, Benjamin Darras, were apparently fascinated with the violent crime spree depicted in the film *Natural Born Killers.* Several days later they went on a spree of their own, shooting a convenience-store employee in the neck, rendering her a quadriplegic. The victim's family and estate sued, among others, Time Warner and producer Oliver Stone, accusing them of producing a movie they "knew or should have known" would incite people such as Edmondson and Darras.[4]

Events such as these are often used to accuse the media of exerting a powerful influence on the antisocial behavior of readers and viewers. Such incidents provoke publicity and criticism, ranging from mild rebukes to lawsuits and even calls for government regulation. What is lost in these barrages is that the number of injuries, deaths, and other violent acts flowing from any given program, movie, or article is small indeed. Thus, the evidence would appear to suggest a cautionary approach in fashioning a moral framework within which to evaluate the impact of the media on antisocial behavior.

Much of our media content challenges societal norms. Without stories about crime, violence, drugs, and suicides, for example, both news and entertainment would be robbed of their dramatic vitality. It would be unreasonable and unrealistic to delete all controversial

282

content, even when the effects on the audience are unpredictable. The goal should be to devise strategies to promote the responsible treatment of antisocial behavior in the media and to avoid approaches that encourage moral degeneration.

The media occupy a pervasive presence in our lives, and it is at least reasonable to conclude that they affect our behavior in ways yet to be determined. One author, in commenting on the media's impact on criminal conduct, drew this logical conclusion:

> If so many commercial and political interests invest so much money in media advertising, it would seem absurd to believe that the media have no effect on our behavior, including, perhaps, our criminal behavior. Otherwise, billions of dollars are being wasted by advertisers. And if the media changed only the noncriminal aspects of our behavior, that would be only slightly less remarkable.[5]

Concern with the effects of the mass media is not new. When Goethe published *The Sorrows of Young Werther* in the eighteenth century, for example, authorities in several nations worried that readers would commit suicide in imitation of the book's tragic hero.[6] The preoccupation with possible imitation of dangerous behavior depicted in the media endures, but it would be unreasonable to expect the media to retreat entirely from controversy just because some readers or viewers are likely to imitate the behavior revealed through their content. From an ethical perspective the focus should be on the lessons (messages) communicated through the behavior of media practitioners themselves and the values and attitudes reflected in their material.

MEDIA LESSONS AND MORAL RESPONSIBILITY

Because of the media's high visibility and potential influence, they occupy a sensitive moral position within society. Both the conduct of media practitioners and the lessons incorporated into media content in the form of values, attitudes, and symbolic messages can raise ethical questions. The issues surrounding the media and antisocial behavior generally fall into two categories: (1) practitioners' commission of antisocial acts in connection with their professional obligations and (2) the media's influence on antisocial behavior.

Antisocial Acts and Professional Obligations

Media practitioners are watchdogs and gatekeepers, and for that reason they should usually avoid relying on antisocial conduct to fulfill their professional mandate. Like public officials, media practitioners should be expected to seek the ethical high ground in their conduct.

For example, although reporters would like to believe that they would never violate the law in pursuit of a story, many do. Some of the infractions are minor, such as exceeding the speed limit to get to the scene of a story. But what if a journalist, to demonstrate to the public a lack of military security, decides to gain access illegally to a Defense Department computer system? Or suppose that a reporter, gathering background information for a story on the proliferation of child pornography on the Web, downloads some representative material from the Internet, in violation of federal law that makes the mere possession of child pornography a felony. Does the public's interest in these stories outweigh the reporter's obligations to obey the law?

This was the question in the fall of 2003 when *60 Minutes* reporter Steve Kroft, a freelance contributor to the program, and a newspaper reporter were arrested for unlawful entry onto the grounds of a chemical plant in Pennsylvania while working on a story on lax security at such plants.[7] A similar issue concerning a journalist's professional obligations and respect for the law arose in May 2000 when Minneapolis TV reporter Tom Lyden was charged in criminal court for "lifting" a videotape of dogfighting from a car at the scene of a police investigation. Lyden defended his actions on the grounds that "he was an aggressive reporter whose responsibility was to the story he was doing on dogfighting." The Minnesota chapter of the Society of Professional Journalists (SPJ) condemned Lyden's act as "unethical and a violation of SPJ's code of ethics."[8]

The consequences were severe for investigative reporter Mike Gallagher who was fired by the *Cincinnati Enquirer* in 1998 for writing a series of "untrue" articles about Chiquita Brands International based on *illegally obtained* voice mail messages. The articles had questioned the business practices of Chiquita. The *Enquirer* issued a front-page apology and agreed to pay $10 million in damages to the fruit giant. "Information provided to the *Enquirer* makes it clear that not only was there never a person at Chiquita with authority to provide privileged, confidential and proprietary information," the black-bordered apology read, "but the facts now indicate that an *Enquirer* employee was involved in the theft of this information in violation of the law."[9]

Regardless of the circumstances, media practitioners are in a weak moral position when they commit serious breaches of the law. Although there are some rare exceptions, such antisocial behavior sends the wrong message to the audience. First, violating the law often places the reporter in the role of participant, rather than detached observer, because a story is, in a sense, created out of the reporter's behavior. If journalists are truly representatives of the public, they should not engage in conduct that they would not approve of in their constituents. Second, if the commission of criminal acts in search of a story became commonplace, respect for the rule of law within society would be undermined. And if the public interest became the sole justification for antisocial behavior, many groups within society might have a legitimate claim to exemptions from the standards of moral conduct.

The Media's Influence on Antisocial Behavior

Because of the media's pervasive influence in the affairs of society, they have often been accused of being accomplices to or influencing antisocial behavior. On other occasions, the news media have actually participated in the resolution of some criminal or other antisocial act, which usually brings praise from those who view the journalist as citizen first and criticism from tradition-bound reporters who complain that such participation compromises their independence and objectivity.

Of course, media practitioners are acutely aware of their critics' concerns and over the years have developed moral guidelines and policies. Under the unrelenting stress of deadline pressures and the spirit of competition, however, these guidelines are sometimes ignored, precipitating a fresh round of media criticism. The ethical issues involved in the media's role in influencing antisocial behavior touch on all three functions of the mass media: news, entertainment, and advertising.

News.   Crime, violence, and human tragedy are important parts of the reporter's stock-in-trade. It is not surprising, therefore, that the news media should be blamed for perpetuating the cycle of antisocial behavior that appears to have laid siege to U.S. society. Undoubtedly, some immature and impressionable members of the audience may learn lessons in antisocial behavior from news coverage and decide to imitate what they see or read. For example, in the wake of the pervasive media coverage of the Columbine High School massacre, an incredible number of copycat acts were reported across the nation. In Pennsylvania alone, police reported fifty-two bomb scares and other threats. In another case, three Canadian teens carried out a death pact following news coverage of rock star Kurt Cobain's suicide. Their death note lamented not having access to the same gun he used.[10]

As unfortunate as these incidents may be, however, no reasonable person would suggest that the media should retreat entirely from such coverage as a remedy for society's ills. Journalists should use common sense and good taste in balancing the news needs of the audience against the requirements of social responsibility. For example, a journalist might alert the public to the lax security surrounding some of the world's busiest airports but should avoid providing details on how that security might be breached. Likewise, in covering suicides reporters should avoid assigning celebrity status to a suicide, providing details of the incident, or romanticizing it. In addition, the media should educate the public on how to identify potential suicide victims, discuss solutions to suicide, and provide information on agencies uniquely qualified to treat those who are contemplating suicide.[11]

Some journalists and news executives have questioned television's handling of violent news. Several years ago in Seattle, for example, the American Federation of Television and Radio Artists (AFTRA), the union that represents reporters and anchors, attacked what it called "bodycount journalism." The AFTRA organized a public forum on TV news violence and even convinced two of the three local news directors to confront a hostile audience.[12] And in Los Angeles, news director Bill Lord of NBC-owned KNBC, upset over the broadcast of a surveillance tape showing the murder of a convenience-store clerk, ordered staffers not to show violent acts that have been captured on tape. In a staff memo, Lord said such a tape violates "any imaginable standard of good taste or good journalism."[13] Some stations went so far as to introduce "family-sensitive" newscasts by reducing or eliminating graphic depictions of murder and brutality on their early evening broadcasts. This was a risky move in a medium that demands visual intensity. Adherents claimed they were responding to an audience weary of "hyped" crime coverage and urban mayhem.

Skeptics, including some news consultants, viewed the move as nothing more than an attention grabber and marketing ploy. Such moves are cosmetic, they complain, because the network newscasts, which usually are juxtaposed next to the local news, and the stations' late news are not affected by such policies.[14]

One of the most risky forms of news coverage—and one that critics complain borders on "infotainment"—is the live transmission of police car chases or other crisis situations. Such events are unpredictable, and live coverage severely limits the opportunity for editorial reflection and judgment. In one such episode viewers in Los Angeles and elsewhere watched one man's bloody suicide on live television, as TV news helicopters from several local stations hovered over a busy freeway to get "close to the action."[15] In January 2000 a Phoenix audience witnessed the police fatally wound a suspect following a wild pursuit.[16] Former news director turned media critic Carl Gottlieb offers this sage advice: "Just because you can broadcast it live doesn't mean you have to. That's letting the technology determine the story. A car chase is a legitimate news event. The question is: Does it warrant live coverage? Tape is a wonderful alternative in that it gives you time to think about how the story should be presented."[17]

TV journalists, of course, cannot ignore violent crime as one of our most daunting cultural pathologies. But increasingly social scientists are arguing that the sheer overload of violence and disaster stories is giving the public a warped sense of reality. And many believe that this portrayal exacerbates racial tensions and distorts impressions about the urban crime problem.[18]

The ethical imperative for journalists is to cover the news responsibly so as not to encourage or incite further crime and violence. Perhaps no genre of story is more journalistically challenging and ethically vexing than the coverage of crisis situations, such as an armed standoff between law enforcement officials and a defiant group of militants, a hostage taking, or an act of terrorism. Under such stressful circumstances, ethical guidelines (if they exist at all) often fall prey to competitive pressures and the dynamics of newsroom crisis management.

A representative case in which the media emerged with mixed reviews was the standoff in Waco, Texas, between the Branch Davidians and government agents. During and following this event, the media received almost as much scrutiny as the confrontation itself.

The opening act in this journalistic morality play, which still resonates as a classic example of the media's potential influence in crisis situations, occurred when the *Waco Herald-Tribune* launched its remarkable seven-part series in late February 1993 about a secretive, little-known religious cult that called itself Branch Davidian. Citing their own investigation, officials of the Alcohol, Tobacco, and Firearms (ATF) agency met with the paper's staff and asked that they delay publication of the story. Following this meeting, several staff members discussed the request but decided to move ahead with publication. "We decided we had heard nothing that would mess up what the ATF was planning," said editor Bob Lott in defending the *Herald-Tribune*'s decision.[19]

From this rather modest request the ethical and legal turmoil surrounding local media mounted as events quickly unfolded. For example, a Dallas radio station broadcast a request for the Branch Davidians to fly a banner if they were listening. When sect members complied, federal authorities criticized the station for undermining their negotiating strategy, which included isolation. A station executive later said his station's message to cult members might have actually opened up negotiations. On another occasion, at the urging of federal authorities, KRLD-AM, an all-news station in Dallas, broadcast several messages from Koresh, after which the cult leader released pairs of children who had been living in the compound. Koresh then promised to surrender—a promise he later reneged on—if the station would broadcast another of his messages. Station manager

Charlie Seraphin told reporters that his station was not attempting to become part of the story but "was acting at the urging of federal officials."[20] In alluding to the conflict between the station's *particularistic* (objectivity, independence of judgment) and *universal* (humanitarianism, life-saving duties, cooperation with authorities) obligations, journalism professor Sara Stone of Baylor University defended the station's actions. "I think you deal as a human being first. You have the responsibility as any other citizen has. But I was amazed that they [the ATF] even asked to begin with."[21] Nevertheless, Professor Stone worried that such participatory behavior might establish some kind of worrisome precedent.

Despite such concerns, however, no ethical system, whether deontologically or teleologically based, would condone a principle whereby reporters, under the lofty standard of independence, must shun all pretense of humanitarian instincts. For example, at one point during the siege a TV reporter braved gunfire to make a radio request for ambulances and also used the station's news unit to remove three of the injured federal officers from the compound.[22]

The coverage of terrorist acts and hostage taking has also generated a great deal of controversy concerning the media's role in such events. No one would dispute the fact that such incidents are newsworthy. But there is also a real danger that the media, particularly television, can themselves become hostages to the political agenda of the terrorists. As noted in Chapter 4, during the coverage of the terrorist attacks on the United States in September 2001, the networks displayed an acute sensitivity to being used by interviewees, such as Osama bin Laden and a family member, as propaganda vehicles and forums for their political agendas. For the most part, they resisted preconditions for the interviews that would have compromised their journalistic independence. Although TV cameras do not *cause* terrorism, there is little doubt that the instantaneous and dramatic coverage afforded by TV has an appeal for those who are looking for a forum for some political cause.[23]

In searching for guidelines for the coverage of crisis situations, particularly where hostages are involved, any advice that might be rendered is more a matter of common sense and journalistic wisdom than divine providence. For example, reporters should avoid revealing, in words or pictures, information that might expose the positions or tactics of law enforcement officials. They should become involved in hostage negotiations only as a last resort and should avoid the temptation to make contact with a gunman or hostage taker. Journalists should also avoid going live from a crisis scene, unless there are compelling journalistic reasons for doing so. And they should notify authorities if a terrorist or hostage taker contacts the newsroom.[24]

Of course, cooperation with police and other government agents can sometimes pose ethical problems. Journalists cannot casually coexist with government authorities without jeopardizing their credibility and risking an ethical flogging. When the media "crawl into bed" with law enforcement officials, becoming in effect an arm of the law, they not only compromise their independence, but they also must contend with accusations that they have become government pawns. Perhaps the most egregious breach of journalistic independence is when a law enforcement agent impersonates a journalist in a crisis situation or criminal investigation. Journalists and commentators naturally worry that "such subterfuge can compromise journalists' credibility and even endanger them by calling their identity into question."[25]

Unfortunately, there is no bright-line ethical rule that can be invoked in such circumstances. While normally journalists do not relinquish their equipment (or their identities) to law enforcement agents, exceptions must be considered in life-or-death situations in which there appear to be no reasonable alternatives.[26] Such was apparently the case in Newark, New Jersey, when police seized a video camera from a photographer for the New Jersey Network following a request for an interview from a man suspected of killing his wife and mother-in-law and holding his 9-year-old son hostage. The camera was eventually returned, but the network did not protest the seizure. "The Newark Police Department seized the camera during emergency circumstances," said a network spokeswoman. "NJN understands that this measure was taken to address the crisis at hand."[27]

The daily newspaper at the University of Missouri set off a firestorm of criticism when it was accused of cooperating with police. While working at the paper, student-journalist Beth Darnell earned hundreds of dollars dancing topless or fully nude at parties. She claimed that she had entered a costume shop just a few blocks from the university campus expecting to apply for a clerk's job. When she left an hour later, she was on her way to her first topless dancing engagement. Darnell denied any desire to do nude dancing but acquiesced when the shop's owner, Tom Bradshaw, "made it sound like other girls were doing it." She said she was coerced into doing so by Bradshaw, who allegedly ran a prostitution ring out of the back of his shop. Angry at what she believed was the merchant's manipulation of her, Darnell decided to publish her first-person account of Bradshaw's business in the journalism school's daily newspaper, the *Columbia Missourian*. The story also alleged that other college students had been lured into the sex trade by Bradshaw.

A couple of days before the story went to press, however, the newspaper's faculty managing editor, George Kennedy, agreed to allow a male student reporter to wear a police "wire" (a recorder) to both corroborate Darnell's allegations and to assist the police in arresting Bradshaw. Kennedy's defense of the *Missourian*'s collaboration with the police was as follows: "[T]his was a problem we wanted to help solve—this was not a case where the newspaper would remain neutral. We decided to become an active participant in attempting to enable the police to do an act of public service." Critics challenged the paper's ethical judgment for publishing a first-person account of highly controversial activities by the person who committed them and for the participation of a reporter in the arrest of a suspect, which compromised the paper's credibility as an independent journalistic organ.[28]

Sometimes an organization's news-gathering activities actually produce evidence—evidence that might be relevant to the solution of a crime. Under such circumstances, unless there are clear-cut reasons for refusing official requests for such materials, the ethical arguments against cooperation become more problematic. Editors and news directors sometimes react defensively, for example, when they are asked to supply photographs or videotape footage that may contain evidence of criminal conduct, such as the actions of looters during a riot or demonstration. Some members of the journalistic establishment view such demands as a violation of their editorial prerogative and believe that cooperation with outside agencies could set a bad precedent. Although this argument may have some merit, refusal to cooperate under these circumstances should be based on a specific and defensible ethical principle, reflecting a critical analysis of the facts of the case. Reporters and editors should avoid knee-jerk reactions and the invocation of clichés, such as a general claim of "editorial privilege." One can appreciate reporters' fears of being viewed as arms of law enforcement and their desire to keep such outside agencies at a respectable distance. Nevertheless, their societal role does not *automatically* exempt them from the obligations imposed on the rest of us, and such exemptions must still be justified through the normal moral reasoning process. Their decisions must balance the need to maintain journalistic independence and to avoid the perception that they are the tools of the police against the universal obligation to comply with subpoenas (or more informal requests) for evidence of specific criminal conduct.

The decision whether to cooperate with law enforcement authorities must, of course, be made on a case-by-case basis. At times there is no apparent reason for refusing to do so. However, journalists must beware of entering into arrangements with the police and others that compromise their independence and damage their credibility. Such unholy alliances convert reporters into partners in the battle against antisocial behavior rather than mere observers of this unsavory landscape.

Entertainment.   In the spring of 2004 MTV News reported that pop singer Britney Spears was planning to include a scene in her *Everytime* video in which she appeared to succumb to suicide. Spears revised the content after the proposed concept leaked out, prompting numerous complaints from angry viewers.[29]

Does violence on TV and in the movies increase the aggressive behavior of children? Do programs about crime contribute to the growing crime rate in society? Is the drug culture glorified in prime-time television drama? Should Hollywood be blamed for the decline in family values?

These are just a few of the ethical questions confronting the entertainment industry. Through their reliance on all kinds of conflicts portrayed through stark characterization, clever dialogue, special effects, and dramatic situations, the entertainment media convey important lessons concerning both beneficial and antisocial behavior. They may, at times, merely reflect reality or, on other occasions, help to promote change, but there is no doubt that they occupy an important niche in the nation's moral development. Professor Deni Elliott, a frequent commentator on media ethics, has described some of the ethical concerns surrounding the entertainment media as follows:

> Mass media entertainment, in print or broadcast, does more than help people fill time between dinner and bed; entertainment pieces educate and socialize. We learn about moral heroes through feature profiles—people who risk their lives to help strangers. We learn how to deal with child molestation, drug use and other

crises through watching prime-time situation comedies. Yet when violence is shown, some of the learning may be not what the writers and producers intended. The basic concern about showing violent acts is that the dramatized event may lead people to commit the same acts. Does a TV movie that depicts gang rape encourage similar acts? Psychological experts disagree. Screenwriters and producers must consider the effect that such scenes could have on some members of the audience.[30]

For more than 60 years, the "effects" of media depictions of various forms of antisocial behavior have been placed under the experimental microscope of social scientists. But even if a definitive link can be established between media content and antisocial behavior, the Constitution would leave little room to maneuver in regulating this content. In the past thirty years several lawsuits have attempted to hold the media liable for disseminating material that allegedly led to imitative acts of violence.[31] But the courts have consistently held that the First Amendment protects such matters of artistic taste, unless the producer of the content "incites" the audience to unlawful behavior. With the legal protection of violent entertainment thus ensured, the *ethical* concerns surrounding the values being transmitted through the dramatic and sometimes controversial creations of the entertainment industry should assume a renewed sense of urgency.

Few producers of entertainment would intentionally set out to encourage or *incite* antisocial behavior. Such a goal could not be defended under any ethical norm. Nevertheless, regardless of whether the entertainment industry causes antisocial behavior, society, particularly vulnerable and impressionable youth, cannot escape the subtle behavioral and psychological cues inhabiting its seductive merchandise. For example, a serious subject such as drug abuse, even when dealt with in the sugar-coated format of situation comedy, must be realistic to capture the audience's attention. And yet every effort should be made not to glamorize drugs to

the point that the antidrug message (if there is one) is lost on the viewers. However, media practitioners are in an ethically delicate position, because they must function at that fragile crossroads between reality and entertainment, attempting to embrace simultaneously both the verities of an uncivil society and socially responsible messages that promote moral values to which that society itself may no longer be committed.

Unfortunately, Hollywood is no longer saying no to drugs in its dramatic and entertaining accounts of reality—at least not in any definitive way. For most of the 1980s drugs either vanished from popular entertainment or were depicted as villainous. But a decade later *Newsweek* reported that "drug use has gone prime time, and without the cautionary alarm bells or Devil's horns."[32] For example, in one episode of *Roseanne,* one of the top-rated sitcoms in the country, the principal characters discovered a cache of marijuana, lit up, and spent much of the show in stoned bliss. Pot humor was also featured on such satirical offerings as *Saturday Night Live* and *Comedy Central,* while MTV's top-rated Beavis and Butthead sniffed paint thinner.[33]

Such casual treatment of the drug culture has apparently continued unabated. In August 2001, for example, *TV Guide* lamented that Ecstasy appeared to be the "drug of choice" for TV scriptwriters. "In recent weeks," observed the magazine, "we've counted three programs in which the illicit drug has fallen into the hands of unsuspecting characters." In both HBO's *Six Feet Under* and Showtime's *Resurrection Blvd.,* the illicit drug fell into the hands of unsuspecting characters, but both shows, according to *TV Guide*'s account, presented the dosing as a "harmless lark."[34]

Of course, there are voices of moderation and responsibility within the entertainment industry. MTV, for example, which boasts a fairly sizable following among youthful viewers, has a policy against promoting drug use. This led the network to negotiate some changes with the artist Afroman's record label in the hot pop song "Because I Got High" before it was deemed suitable for airing in the video release. All visual references to smoking marijuana were removed.[35]

Some have accused the television industry itself of becoming a government accomplice in its war against drugs, an alliance that poses some disturbing ethical questions. A 1997 law requires the broadcast networks to match the amount of "antidrug" advertising bought by the federal government with an equal amount of "antidrug" public service announcements. But the White House Office of National Drug Control Policy allowed the networks to substitute programs with an "antidrug" message for public service announcements, a financial arrangement that was potentially quite lucrative for the industry.[36] In January 2000 Fox, ABC, CBS, NBC, and Warner Brothers admitted they had allowed the agency to review some one hundred scripts for such popular programs as *ER, Beverly Hills 90210,* and *Chicago Hope.*[37] While the networks insisted they made no changes because of government pressure, critics regarded the practice as government intrusion into free speech.[38] At the least it might be regarded as a subtle oversight of Hollywood's creative autonomy. Nevertheless, after a national brouhaha erupted, the White House agreed to stop previewing scripts of prime-time TV programs to confirm the presence of "antidrug" messages.[39]

The media are accused of promoting every conceivable form of antisocial behavior, from encouraging disrespect for authority to causing an increase in teenage suicide. However, violence continues to be public enemy number one for media critics, primarily because it is so pervasive and because the evidence is beginning to mount of a deleterious effect of the exposure of too much violence on young viewers. Nevertheless, violence remains a staple media fare. In 2003, for example, a study by the Parents Television Council revealed that TV violence was almost double that of four years earlier.[40]

Today the media are accused of moral high treason by religious conservatives and presidential candidates alike. In the 1960s the movie industry, in an effort to blunt some of this criticism, introduced a rating system as an early warning device for their patrons, but media critics consider this as an insufficient admission of moral responsibility in the value wars between Hollywood and "mainstream" America. The television industry remains under siege for its steady diet of graphic violence. Because of TV's pervasive intrusion into our home life and its pivotal role in our children's lives, this medium has born the brunt of public censure for its preoccupation with violence and its pernicious influence on society. Media watchdogs, government officials, and some industry executives themselves have been unerringly vocal in their denunciation of graphic and often gratuitous televised violence. Particularly in the wake of a rash of school shootings, the public reaction has ranged from proposals for restrictive government regulation to calls for tougher industry supervision.

Violence is the result of a complex interaction of individual and cultural variables, and industry representatives argue that it is unfair to blame the media for all of society's pathologies.[41] Nevertheless, Hollywood plays a pervasive role in the cultural life of the nation, and entertainment executives must assume at least their share of moral responsibility for society's quality of life. Thus, we ignore this warning from four major public health groups, including the influential American Medical Association, at our own peril. "[The effects of violent media] are measurable and long lasting," they declared in a joint statement in the summer of 2000. "Moreover, prolonged viewing of media violence can lead to emotional desensitization toward violence in real life."[42]

The record industry has also come under moral scrutiny because of its high-volume appeal and sales to teenagers. Lyrics that glorify the radically dysfunctional aspects of the human condition, say the industry's moral guardians, make a profound impression on the not-yet-mature worldviews of the young. As *Newsweek* noted in a recent article on teenage prostitution, a lyric such as "Bitch choose with me, I'll have you stripping in the streets" from the song "P.I.M.P" by superstar rapper 50 cent is hardly subtle in its glorification of pimping.[43]

Such musical genres as gangsta rap and heavy metal, though aesthetically offensive to true musical afficionados, are exceedingly popular among the young. Their lyrics are also often violent and sexually explicit. Time Warner, in particular, has been singled out because of the lyrics produced by some of the rappers under contract to the media conglomerate. The public condemnation of rapper Ice-T's cop-killing song was so great, for example, that Time Warner finally parted company with the artist. However, Time Warner chair Gerald Levin did not surrender easily to his critics, embracing the First Amendment as his moral savior. The fact is, however, that much of the gangsta rap music, which glorifies brutality and misogyny, is not the result of spontaneous expression but callous marketing. This reality is reflected in rapper Willie D.'s interview with *USA Today,* in which he expressed reservations about his shocking lyrics now that he has a month-old daughter. The lyrics to which he was referring included the rather startling claim that a woman deserved to get raped and murdered because she left her curtains open. "I have to put food on the table," he said. "For me, it's a business. I say it to get paid."[44] The music industry has responded to charges of such "cultural pollution" with a voluntary rating system in which some cassettes and compact discs containing violent or sexually explicit material are identified with warning labels.

A system of ethics need not demand that violence be eliminated entirely, an absurd prospect at best. But it is not unreasonable to expect producers of mass entertainment to bring to their craft a sense of responsibility toward the medium and the audience. A film director, for example, might treat a violent scenario differently for a family TV audience than for a theater audience. Likewise, violence in children's programs should be treated differently than that aimed at adults.

In constructing the guidelines for an "ethics of violent content," we might consider the following questions: (1) Is there an adequate warning by the producer, so that each individual or group in the chain of distribution (advertiser, network, station, movie theatre, consumer) can decide whether to reject the content? (2) Is the violence gratuitous, or is it essential to the plot and script? (3) Does the material depict violence as a desirable (or even inevitable) consequence or solution to a problem? (4) Is there just punishment for unwarranted acts of violence, or are such acts rewarded? (5) Are heroes and villains clearly delineated? (6) If there is no just punishment or if the heroes and villains are not clearly identified, is there some higher public purpose to be served by the use of violence in the plot or script?

An ethicist might ask: Who should assume moral responsibility for the menu of the entertainment industry? Although the producers of such materials may bear the ultimate responsibility, a reasonable argument could be made that all of the parties in the line of distribution must share in this moral duty: writers, producers, directors, networks, stations, newspapers, magazines, movie theatres, and the audience itself, including the parents of children. Nevertheless, producers of mass entertainment are in a particularly precarious position, because they must entertain and accommodate the needs of the creative community while at the same time being sensitive to the value-laden messages being communicated to a diverse audience. Controversial entertainment materials dealing with social issues are seldom neutral in the lessons they teach. They may be creatively balanced, but social or antisocial values are an inherent component of such dramatic fare.[45] Thus, media practitioners must be sensitive to their industry's role in influencing society's mores and should devise strategies to entertain their audiences while not abandoning them to moral anarchy.

Advertising.   The relationship between advertising and the problem of antisocial behavior is perhaps not as apparent as that in the news and entertainment functions of the mass media. One reason is that the unabashed purpose of advertising is to persuade, and few media practitioners wish to be accused of promoting illegal or violent conduct. Another reason is that a broad consensus has emerged among the media about the types of ads that are suitable for publishing or broadcasting. Most media institutions have codes that, in addition to rejecting advertising on the ground of taste, also refuse ads that violate laws or encourage unlawful conduct. Ads that promote illegal lotteries or offer mail-order weapons are two examples.

However, even mainstream advertising is beginning to "push the envelope" on propriety, leading one columnist to lament that "[t]here are no gatekeepers left at the networks."[46] Consider, for example, the Chevrolet TV commercial several years ago showing a frustrated woman in a Camaro passing a leering trucker. As she does so, she thrusts an out-of-focused arm into the air, a subtle imitation of an obscene gesture. Examples of other offensive commercials are one for a Maryland mall emphasizing the theme of defecation and another featuring oral sex described by *U.S. News* columnist John Leo as "an excruciatingly gross ad for a little-known hamburger chain."[47]

Among the mainstream media, the primary complaint in recent years has been directed against the glorification of violence, particularly in ads directed at children and adolescents. Consider this vivid description in *TV Guide* of a TV commercial promoting the video game *NFL Blitz*:

[The commercial] opens to the sight of Steeler QB Kordell Stewart picking off members of a marching band with passes that smash against the musicians' heads, knocking them cold. Next, we see the game's moving images. These feature players engaging in excessively brutal tackles or celebrating their feats in excessive acts of self-glorification. The narrator offers the ad's kicker:

"Deadly long-range passing. Linebackers without conscience. 'NFL Blitz'—it's a wretched assault on the sense of fair play. No refs, no rules, no mercy."[48]

TV Guide critic Phil Mushnick was merciless in his denunciation of what he described as a "twisted, kid-targeted portrayal of football." He accused the NFL of "greed and a distinct lack of conscience."[49]

Not surprisingly, Hollywood is an attractive target for critics who denounce movie studios for marketing their violent R-rated fare to teens. Although it is unknown how much of the movie industry's billion-dollar ad budgets are spent on promoting R-rated films, a critical assessment from the Federal Trade Commission (FTC) in 2000 caused the TV industry to review its movie ad policies. The FTC found that the industry routinely markets R-rated movies, music, and video games to children. In one case, for example, researchers asked children as young as 9 to help shape the sequel to the R-rated slasher film *I Know What You Did Last Summer*.[50] The report triggered a harsh rebuke of the film industry from political candidates and Congress alike,[51] prompting one network executive to describe such public excoriations as "political saber-rattling before the elections." Others were more charitable and characterized the FTC's findings as a forceful reminder of the industry's need to be more responsible.[52]

Media critics are not alone in their harsh assessments of violence-oriented ads. They are frequently joined by viewers who express their disapproval of ads that they believe exceed the bounds of ethical propriety. For example, in the fall of 2000 NBC, after a flood of viewer complaints, withdrew a Nike commercial that featured U.S. track star Suzy Favor Hamilton outrunning a chain saw–wielding madman. "We think people who understand Nike and who we are will get these ads," responded a spokesperson for the shoe company.[53]

Despite advertisers' traditional aversion to controversy, one should never underestimate the economic potency of the marketplace. In the past decade some advertisers have challenged the boundaries of propriety in their marketing strategies for young consumers, as reflected in this disturbing announcement in *Newsweek* magazine: "In an attempt to cash in on the multimillion dollar market for urban-inspired goods, experts say, a small but increasingly visible group of marketers is using tough-guy imagery to sell everything from malt liquor to music."[54] The magazine cited as an example a commercial for Snickers featuring a youngster emblazoning an inner-city wall with the candy bar's name—symbolic of a gang practice of "tagging" walls with graffiti. Similarly, an ad for Coty Wild Musk perfume titled "The Wild Ones" featured a model wearing what resembled a belt full of bullets around his waist.[55]

Ads such as these not only raise ethical concerns because of their questionable content but also because of the audiences to which they are directed. When such gang-related messages are targeted to urban youth, the advertising industry stands accused of introducing still another explosive element into an already hostile and violent environment. Moral agents, of course, are free to seek vindication for their behavior on whatever moral grounds they so choose, but they can never escape moral responsibility for the consequences of their actions.

THE MEDIA AND CIVILITY

If the teaching of ethics means anything, it means we must cultivate respect for others. This "value," which lies at the heart of Immanuel Kant's philosophy and is arguably the energizing force for all ethical behavior, commands us to treat persons as not just a means to an end but as ends unto themselves. In so doing, we should attempt to foster within ourselves the qualities of courtesy, compassion, and respect for the beliefs and opinions of others. In short, we should be civil. A civil society is more likely to be a virtuous society. But unfortunately, in recent years there does appear to be a decline in civility, as

evidenced by our growing intolerance and impatience in our relationships, a deterioration in the "quality" of rhetoric, an increase in uncivil behavior with which we express our opposition on public issues, and an overall cynicism toward and disrespect for society's norms.

In searching for answers to this malaise, we should avoid the temptation to blame the media entirely for this disturbing decline in civility. Nevertheless, because of the media's impact, it is certainly fair to inquire what role media practitioners have played in the depreciation of society's cultural life. With the proliferation of computer networks, enabling us as individuals to bypass traditional media gatekeepers and to communicate at will with other individuals, small target audiences, or large undifferentiated audiences, this is a vital and timely question. Uncivil speech within itself is harmless. But inflammatory and vitriolic rhetoric and the sanctification of violence may also beget antisocial attitudes and behavior. Among the lunatic fringe it may encourage violence. But even within society's mainstream such offensive speech and conduct can create a culture of incivility in which undisguised hostility is vented in front of millions of zealous onlookers and "trash thy neighbor" becomes a spectator sport. Any attempt to categorize the various kinds of uncivil behavior is risky since the lines among them are often blurred. However, for the purpose of a brief discussion we divide them into three categories: uncivil behavior, hate speech, and dirty tricks.

Uncivil Behavior

Several years ago, *The Jerry Springer Show*, plagued by low ratings, was in danger of cancellation. As they entered the May sweeps, a key ratings period that would determine the show's future, Springer and his new producer, Richard Dominick, made a momentous decision. The key to success was "relationship shows, Ku Klux Klan members and fights, lots of fights." "What we needed to do," said Dominick, in defending their controversial decision, "was get people as they were going through the channels [so that] at whatever second they hit our show, they would find it interesting."[56]

It worked! *The Jerry Springer Show* connected with an audience that apparently fancied (or at least were curious onlookers of) the dysfunctional and violent renditions of uncivil behavior. The program quickly challenged Oprah Winfrey for leadership of daytime talk TV. Within just one year Springer's ratings increased by an incredible 114 percent.[57] Even allegations that the show's acts of belligerency were staged did not deter the Springer faithful. As some television insiders observed, "Springer couldn't buy this much publicity heading into May sweeps if he tried."[58]

It is perhaps a solemn reminder of our culture's artistic permissiveness and complacency that the program escaped any significant critical scrutiny until it seriously challenged Oprah Winfrey for talk show dominance.[59] Finally, amid howls of protest from religious leaders, education groups, community activists, and media critics, *The Jerry Springer Show* agreed to a tactical retreat from its polemical content. In March 1998, for example, the Detroit Board of Education joined the city council in asking a local TV station to move the show from its 4 P.M. time slot to a time "when parents or guardians are more likely to be able to monitor their children's television viewing." The board's statement followed a Nielsen report confirming that *Springer* was watched by nearly 15 percent of twelve- to seventeen-year-olds and nearly 10 percent of six- to eleven-year-olds.[60] A group of community activists in Chicago, characterizing the *Springer* show as a "pornographic slugfest," went even further and secured an agreement from the producers to edit out the fistfights, chair throwing, and other violence.[61] Nevertheless, ten years after *The Jerry Springer Show*'s resurrection as the TV industry's personification of incivility, the program continued to command a loyal following.

From an ethical perspective, it is difficult to imagine a more perverse species of entertainment than a talk show that features a regular diet of fistfights, chair throwing, and other manifestations of uncontrolled rage. Such content cannot be reconciled with any moral framework. Antisocial behavior in the form of real-life violence and other acts of aggression packaged as entertainment is destructive of civil society because it validates incivility as a means of managing human relationships.

Hate Speech

Consider these two items from *Boston Globe* columnist Jeff Jacoby: In the summer of 2003 right-wing talk show host Michael Savage told a gay caller to "get AIDS and die, you pig." For this mean-spirited remark, he was fired by MSNBC. In 1995 liberal NPR commentator Nina Totenberg (proving that hate speech is not the exclusive province of the right) declared, with reference to Senator Jesse Helms: "I think he ought to be worried about what's going on in the Good Lord's mind, because if there is retributive justice, he'll get AIDS from a transfusion, or one of his grandchildren will."[62]

In the same year, right-wing talk show host G. Gordon Liddy said he had used handmade drawings of the President and Hillary Rodham Clinton for target practice and also claimed that shooting federal agents is legally justified.[63] He suggested that people, in defending their homes against agents, "shoot twice to the body, center of mass, and if that does not work, then shoot to the groin area."[64] Although critics condemned him for his intemperate and shocking remarks, not all agreed. For his "bravado," Liddy was honored with a "free speech" award by the National Association of Radio Talk Show Hosts.

The common thread in these three apparently unrelated incidents is the genre of hate speech—speech "attacking an individual or group on the basis of who they are."[65] We cannot just dismiss such mass-mediated rhetoric as the ravings of lunatics wandering in the cultural wilderness. They have struck a responsive chord among some segments of society and command a loyal following. For example, when a Michigan radio station suspended the program of James (Bo) Gritz, a retired lieutenant colonel in the Special Forces who had described the Oklahoma City bombing as a work of art, listener complaints convinced station management to restore the program to the airwaves.[66] And when radio station KCKC near Los Angeles canceled Liddy's syndicated talk show, callers threatened to blow up the station and murder the station manager.[67] One can hardly imagine a more uncivil response to an uncivil program.

The most common variety of hate speech, of course, is verbal or written attacks on various groups because of their racial, ethnic, or national origin. Beginning in the 1980s, for example, right-wing groups took a keen interest in public access cable channels as a platform for disseminating their racist rhetoric. On one occasion, a group calling itself the SS Action Group placed a recruitment message on Warner Cable's access channel in working-class Norwood, a suburb of Cincinnati. The message read, "Join the American Nazis and smash Red, Jew, and Black Power." Shortly thereafter, the same message was run on the cable system in Cincinnati under the joint sponsorship of the SS Action Group and the White American Skin Heads. They also aired a one-hour edition of a neo-Nazi program, *Race and Reason*. Local reaction was swift and emotional. The issue dominated the news for several days, as populist leaders denounced hate groups and called for censorship. One member of the cable board even resigned. Eventually reason prevailed in the form of an agreement by a coalition of groups, including the NAACP and the American Jewish Committee, to produce programs to counter the neo-Nazi message. The Norwood/Cincinnati experience was not unlike the conflicts involving neo-Nazis that arose in several other cities as geographically diverse as Atlanta, Georgia, and Sacramento, California.[68]

Several years ago the Ku Klux Klan was at the center of a controversy in Kansas City when it sought access to the local cable system. Although the city council attempted to thwart the Klan's initiative, apparently in violation of federal law,

the council, faced with a lawsuit it didn't think it could win, soon backed down. However, when KKK members showed up to produce a program, they became embroiled in a shouting match with some community members. Police arrested several on concealed weapons charges, and no Klansman returned after the incident.[69]

These cases, of course, concern a legally mandated right of access devoid of management censorship. Thus, media managers—in this case, cable system operators—are left to ponder this question: Should media practitioners simply defend their role in the dissemination of such hate speech on the grounds of legal obligation, or do they have an ethical duty to counter such speech with the presentation of opposing views? While public access channels have the potential for broadening the range of public discourse, some local officials have wavered in their support because of a fear that access channels might be dominated by such hate groups as the KKK.[70]

The Internet, of course, has made such intermediaries as cable TV unnecessary, and hate speech and other forms of uncivil behavior have certainly prospered in the unregulated culture of cyberspace. Because hate speech is inherently unreasonable and fanatical, it is not surprising that the apostles of hatred would view new technologies, such as those supporting the information superhighway, as a golden opportunity to expand their horizons. For example, a week after the terrorist bombing of a federal building in Oklahoma City in April 1995, Rabbi Marvin Hier, dean of the Simon Wiesenthal Center in Los Angeles, discovered this message on the Internet: "I want to make bombs and kill evil Zionist people in the government. Teach me. Give me text files."[71]

In searching for ethical strategies to combat the moral ravages of hate speech, we should remember that free speech is fundamental to a libertarian society. A civil society does not depend on governmental or societal controls on expression, no matter how offensive it may be. The proper antidote to hate speech is not suppression but even more speech. The key to a civil society lies as much with the audiences as the communicators. A talk show host whose stock-in-trade is shocking epithets and hate-filled messages is sustained through advertising generated by high ratings—in other words, audience appeal. The reality is that if we truly desire and deserve an ethical society, then the apostles of virtue and civility should emerge victorious in the marketplace of ideas in an open encounter with the cynical patrons of hate speech.

Dirty Tricks

In March 1995, the producers of the *Jenny Jones* TV talk show convinced 24-year-old Jonathan Schmitz to appear on an episode dealing with secret crushes. He came on assuming his admirer would be a woman but was instead confronted with a man he barely knew, Scott Amedure. Three days later, after receiving a note from Amedure, Schmitz allegedly drove to Amedure's home and killed him with two shotgun blasts to the chest. Schmitz later told police that the embarrassment from the show (which never aired) had "eaten away" at him.[72] Schmitz was convicted of murder in 1999.

Such occurrences may be uncommon, but they represent perhaps the fringe of a rather disturbing trend among TV talk shows. Such confrontational programming, which we might refer to as "dirty tricks," usually consists of "sandbagging" some unsuspecting guest. Consider, for example, one episode of *The Jerry Springer Show* in which a woman told her husband, John, that she was having an affair with another woman. "You bring me out to Chicago for me to find this out on TV?" John asked in a fury.[73] In the dirty tricks, confrontational mentality of the latest additions to the talk show genre, guests become pawns to be manipulated for the bizarre entertainment of studio and TV audiences and the financial enrichment of producers. Pop therapy becomes a spectator sport. Guests often wind up yelling at each other, and fistfights are not unheard of.

Dirty tricks, of course, are not confined to the visually engrossing TV talk shows. Take, for example, the Chicago disc jockey who suggested to listeners that a TV anchorwoman—and recent widow—was pregnant by a Chicago Bulls player. A judge refused to dismiss her defamation suit. In still another case with even more tragic consequences, a St. Louis radio station aired phone messages believed to be a TV weatherman talking about a love affair. Early the next morning, he died in a fiery plane crash believed to be a suicide.[74]

In searching for strategies to confront the cultural ravages of hate speech and mass-mediated dirty tricks, we must reject our natural inclination toward government censorship and instead approach the issue on an ethical plane. Even those who disdain civility have a "right" to search for a hospitable pulpit from which to dispense their messages. But media practitioners, except in cases in which the law mandates access, are under no moral duty to accommodate the purveyors of hate speech or dirty tricks. A station executive, for example, is certainly free to reject a talk show that traffics in confrontation and verbal violence. This is a difficult decision, because much of the fare currently on the air is popular with some audiences. Some media managers might argue that the public has a right to all viewpoints, even those that appear to be outrageous to media critics. Fair enough. But the fact remains that such decisions are driven more by market considerations than any altruistic desire to pay homage to the First Amendment or to serve the public interest. Besides, the issue here is not toleration of unpopular or even disgusting "views." The view, for example, that the Holocaust never happened—a position that is anathema to many in the Jewish community and elsewhere—can still be presented in a civil, rational fashion, even if it lacks any credible supporting evidence.

Thus, the issue revolves around the use of inflammatory language that is devoid of social value, dehumanizes its target, or *incites* violence or other forms of antisocial behavior. As in all areas of ethical concern, media practitioners are responsible for the content they disseminate, regardless of who actually produces it. And advertisers are ethically liable for providing the financial sustenance to the apostles of incivility. But the stark reality is that as long as audiences continue to patronize or at least indulge the purveyors of hate speech and programs that thrive on violent confrontation, the media will continue to contribute in their own way to the degeneration of cultural civility.

THE MEDIA AND ANTISOCIAL BEHAVIOR: HYPOTHETICAL CASE STUDIES

The cases in this chapter present moral dilemmas concerned with the depiction or encouragement of antisocial behavior by media practitioners. In analyzing these scenarios, keep in mind the three philosophical approaches to ethical decision making described in Chapter 3: duty-based ethics (deontology), consequence-based ethics (teleology), and Aristotle's golden mean.

A deontologist would examine the motives of the moral agent and would inquire whether the approach under consideration should become a universal rule for resolving such dilemmas. In evaluating gratuitous violence in TV programming, for example, a deontologist would reject this kind of content as being unworthy standard fare for the TV entertainment medium, even if there were no demonstrable harmful effects from such programming.

An alternative approach, of course, is to examine the consequences of the ethical decision. The moral agent considers the potential impact on all of the parties affected by the decision and then decides which course of action will produce the best consequences under the circumstances.

In situations involving the depictions of antisocial behavior, Aristotle's golden mean can provide a useful approach to moral decision making. The goal is to find a mean between the two extremes in an ethical dilemma. In applying the golden mean, the strategy should be neither to eliminate controversial material entirely (an extremely paternalistic approach) nor to approve of or encourage antisocial behavior just for the sake of titillating the audience. Rather, programs and published material containing depictions of antisocial behavior should include an appropriate dosage of positive lessons for the audience.

A case in point is a TV series that includes violence but discourages its use as a means of resolving human problems. In cases in which the scenes or dialogue are too graphic, warnings could be issued by the producers, thus allowing the audience to render its own judgment on whether to consume the material. Likewise, a TV news crew that covers demonstrations in unmarked cars and with unobtrusive equipment is displaying a sense of responsibility and a healthy respect for Aristotle's golden mean.

CASE STUDIES

▶ **CASE 9-1**

Animals as Mediated Entertainment: Property or Moral Beings?

Gary Bartello was one of Hollywood's most successful producers, and his latest film, *Triumph of the Species*, had premiered accompanied by the expected critical acclaim. With an evolutionary twist

on Charles Darwin's *Origin of the Species*, Bartello's production was based upon an intriguing premise: that at the end of nature's evolutionary cycle at some point in the distant future, the animal kingdom, particularly mammals, had surpassed their human counterparts in terms of intelligence and adaptation to the natural world and with revolutionary fervor had subdued the human species, thereby sentencing it to eternal captivity or cultural subordination. However, despite the featured roles of animals, *Triumph of the Species* was not intended for a family audience. The animal revolt that eventually resulted in the subjugation of their human overlords was graphically violent, and the film was awarded an R rating.

Bartello had employed animals in several of his previous films but never in such a starring role. He was acutely aware of the cinematic track record of movies whose storylines revolved around members of the animal kingdom or included significant sequences featuring them, such as *Cats and Dogs*, *Planet of the Apes*, *Jurassic Park*, *Rat Race*, and *A Knight's Tale*. He was confident that *Triumph of the Species* would take its rightful place among this genre.

Bartello's animal actors, which ranged from the traditional family pets, cats and dogs, to the larger mammals such as lions, elephants, and gorillas, were provided by Animal Entertainers, Inc., one of about two dozen animal rental companies that oblige Hollywood's insatiable demand for trained animal performers. Despite the fictional violence portrayed in the movie, Bartello took what he believed were appropriate measures to protect the animals during filming from harm or abuse, assigning Kara Miller, the communications manager for the production unit, to monitor the health and well-being of the animals. A representative of the American Humane Association's Film and Television Unit was also on hand to witness the treatment of the animals, a concession that would win *Triumph of the Species* the association's seal of approval, which could then be featured in the film's closing credits.[75]

Bartello was confident that during the production of his latest film he had behaved as a responsible steward of the animal performers. He was also satisfied that, despite the portrayals of violence of humans against animals, during which no animals were actually mistreated on the set, and the unexpected and dramatic retaliation and ultimate victory by the animal kingdom, *Triumph of the Species* was a tribute to our nonhuman kin and accorded them a degree of moral standing normally reserved for *homo sapiens*. To his staff, Bartello facetiously described the animal kingdom's intellectual maturation, the result of an evolutionary aberration, as an experiment in radical

egalitarianism. Sylvia Byers did not share Bartello's enthusiasm for his latest cinematic triumph.

Byers was president of the National Association for the Advancement of Animal Rights, one of the more radical and aggressive organizations devoted to animal rights and welfare. Bartello's movie studio was still tabulating the first week's box office receipts for *Triumph of the Species* when Byers demanded a meeting with the film's producer. Bartello was initially disinclined to grant an audience to someone reputedly as confrontational as Sylvia Byers but reluctantly agreed to a meeting with the animal rights activist. Since Kara Miller had supervised the production and the unit's treatment of the animal performers, Bartello invited her to join him in what was likely to be a spirited discourse with the irrepressible Byers.

The three met over coffee and pastries in Bartello's spacious but modestly adorned Hollywood office, and after a brief exchange of pleasantries Byers launched her opening salvo. "I have two problems with *Triumph of the Species*," she complained. "First, this film depicts an excessive amount of violence against animals. While in the end the animals prevail and understandably retaliate against their human masters, the subjugation and mistreatment of the animals is what prompts this revolt."

"But none of the animals are actually mistreated," Miller responded. "We took great pains on the set to insure their safety and welfare. The film is science fiction and in the end the animals win. Sure, the film depicts violence, but the animals themselves were well treated during the production."

"You miss my point," argued Byers. "My complaint has nothing to do with how the animals were actually treated. I'm well aware that Hollywood studios have safeguards in place to protect animal performers from abuse. But this film depicts, in a rather casual way, animals being subjected to violence and other forms of mistreatment. In the film humans are portrayed as justified in defending themselves against their attacks, even though their human oppressors goad them into striking back. And though the animals eventually prevail, they come across as vicious and vindictive. The overall effect is to sanction the use of violence against animals."

"But the animals in this film are actors," responded Bartello. "They are playing a role. And the fact is that in real life there is violence against animals just as there is violence against humans. As long as the animals themselves are treated humanely, I don't see this as an ethical problem."

"I'm well aware that violence is a part of our culture," replied Byers, "and that works of art must sometimes mirror this human condition. But as you know critics complain that so much of today's media violence is gratuitous and that acts of violence are frequently portrayed in a morally ambiguous fashion. That's one of my complaints with *Triumph of the Species*. Although the animals are victorious in the end, the violence against them appears to be justified while their campaign of retributive justice is unusually cruel to their human antagonists. This film is not even-handed, and it undermines the moral standing of animals."

Bartello and Miller remained silent for a moment while they reflected upon the implications of Byers's rhetorical volley. Byers took their silence as an invitation to continue the assault.

"My second complaint," she declared, "is even more fundamental. The members of my organization are uncomfortable with the very idea of training animals to perform for humans. It has always been our position that animals have rights and that keeping them in captivity for no other purpose than to train and employ them as entertainers is immoral."

Miller could not contain her incredulity at such a suggestion. "That would mean the elimination of animals from the movies and television. Audiences, particularly children and teens, love animals. As long as we don't abuse the animals, how is keeping and training animals for the purposes of entertainment a form of exploitation?"

"We're not opposed to *all* uses of animals," replied Byers. "We have no objection to using animals as background or for brief, nonperforming appearances. But giving them a starring role and requiring them to perform or to engage in unnatural behavior for the benefit of humans is a violation of their rights."

"I've always subscribed to the moral obligation of humans to refrain from the mistreatment of animals," stated Bartello. "But I can't accept the notion that they have rights comparable to those of humans. Having rights carries with it the ability to exercise those rights responsibly, and I don't see this as a trait of the animal kingdom. Animals are not comparable to autonomous humans. Training animals to perform for the entertainment of humans is not exploitation."

Before Byers could respond Miller decided to move the conversation in a slightly different direction. "As you can tell, we don't agree with what we believe is your extreme position on animal rights and the use of animals in films. But the day may not be too far away when many of the animals depicted in movies will be computer-generated. The process is still fairly expensive, but I believe the industry is moving in that direction. Wouldn't the use of virtual rather than real animals resolve some of your concerns?"

"Yes and no," Byers replied without hesitation. "My complaint about the use of animals for entertainment purposes would indeed be answered. But even the use of virtual animals, which look real to the audience, in films in which they are abused still sends the wrong message to society—that animals are less deserving of respect than humans. I compare this to the feminists' complaint that violent pornography is degrading to women as humans and perpetuates the view that women are nothing more than sex objects."

Miller shared Byers's view on violent pornography but silently questioned the analogy between the fictional depictions of animal violence in movies and the degradation women suffered at the hands of porn merchants. Similarly, Bartello was unresponsive to the feminist analogy but decided to terminate the meeting. Before making her exit, Sylvia Byers stated that she was planning to meet with the president of the Screen Actors Guild to express her concerns, as well as several other producers of recently released movies featuring animals. "*Triumph of the Species* is already in theatre release," she declared, "but as a prominent Hollywood producer with some influence I ask you to consider the concerns of my organization. Perhaps you can work within the industry to make changes."

Bartello made no promises except that he would reflect upon the ethical dimensions of the problems presented to him and Kara Miller during their relatively brief meeting.

THE CASE STUDY

In this scenario, the animal rights perspective is introduced within a media context, albeit in a rather restricted way. Animal rights activists have campaigned against a wide range of abuses, including utilizing laboratory animals for research, the killing of animals for their furs, and even the killing of some animals for food. Sylvia Byers's complaints are more modest: (1) depiction of violence against animals in films, even when the animal actors themselves are well treated, sanctifies violence against animals in real life and (2) holding animals in captivity and using them as performers for the amusement of humans is a form of exploitation. Most of us would never mistreat our family pets, but we are less concerned about violence against nondomesticated animals, even when the violence is initiated by humans.

Some argue that animals have moral rights because they are living creatures and have inherent value. Those who deny such rights to animals, in this view, are sometimes labeled specists, the animal equivalent of being a racist. Others respond, citing everything from scripture to moral philosophy, that animals cannot have rights because they are by nature subordinate to humans and cannot have rights without the capacity for exercising responsibility. The common ground is that a reasonable person would not inflict unnecessary harm on a helpless animal or participate in its torture. And where pets are concerned, most of us assume a duty of care when we become their owners.

In this case, the issues of media violence and exploitation are joined with some of those advanced by the animal rightists. Sylvia Byers is not concerned about the mistreatment of animals in films (there are safeguards in place to minimize the risks), but she does project her concerns about how the animals are used (as objects of violence) into society at large. She sees a cause and effect. Byers also considers the forced performance of animals as a form of exploitation.

Gary Bartello and Kara Miller, of course, have a different perspective. Depicting violence against animals, as offensive as it may be for some, is a realistic portrayal of a slice of life, similar to fictionalized human violence. Some animals, especially nondomesticated species, do suffer at the hands of humans. The issue of exploitation does not resonate with Bartello and Miller because history is on their side. Almost from the inception of visual communication, particularly movies and television, animals have played a prominent role and have entertained millions of people. Bartello and Miller view this as a truly radicalized expression of the animal rights perspective.

Hollywood producer Gary Bartello has promised Sylvia Byers, his animal rights antagonist, that he will reflect upon her concerns. That is, if he is to act in good faith, he must assume the position of moral agent and attempt to be fair in evaluating the ethical dimensions of this issue. For the purpose of evaluating the concerns of Sylvia Byers, step into the shoes of Gary Bartello and assume, just for the sake of discussion, that his latest release, *Triumph of the Species*, is typical of films that feature violence against animals. Taking into account the arguments of Sylvia Byers, as well as your own sentiments and those of Kara Miller as expressed in the case, decide whether, if given another opportunity, you would still produce films such as *Triumph of the Species*. Keep in mind that Sylvia Byers has advanced two concerns; you may reject both, concur with both, or concur with one and reject the other. As with the other cases in this text, you should frame your discussion within the context of the SAD model for moral reasoning outlined in Chapter 3.

▶ CASE 9-2

Online Ads for AIDS Drugs and the Promotion of Unsafe Sex

The Merrill-Schuster Company had been on the front lines in the battle against AIDS almost from the epidemic's inception. Merrill-Schuster was not among the top three drug companies in the nation, but it had developed and patented a number of drugs that had proven effective in heretofore fatal or debilitating diseases. Xecor, an HIV drug, was among those worthy entries into the prescription drug marketplace. Not only had it obtained the endorsement of many physicians, but Xecor's advertising campaign apparently had resonated with a significant segment of HIV carriers as well, according to surveys of both the medical profession and patients. The pharmaceutical company had launched newspaper ad campaigns in cities with sizable gay populations, but its most creative energies had been expended on websites targeted to the homosexual population or frequented by members of the gay and lesbian community.

Some HIV carriers and AIDS patients felt victimized by what they believed to be price gouging among some drug companies, but their protests against Merrill-Schuster were muted somewhat by Xecor's phenomenal results in the treatment of the disease. Lester Beck, founder of the San Francisco–based United Gay Front, was also impressed with Xecor's effectiveness. He was less impressed with Merrill-Schuster's Internet ad campaign for the drug.

While the ad copy itself did not, in Beck's judgment, overstate Xecor's effectiveness, all of the ads depicted healthy, handsome, and robust young men touting the drug's medicinal powers. "These ads," lamented Beck in a strongly worded letter to Merrill-Schuster's CEO, "may be encouraging unsafe sex. Their message is that those infected with HIV can just pop a pill, and they'll be healthy and strong. We respectfully request that Merrill-Schuster withdraw these ads." When his complaint went unacknowledged, the gay activist responded to this corporate snub with a massive letter-writing campaign from the United Gay Front membership and ads in several large newspapers. These initiatives in turn generated TV interviews, which propelled Merrill-Schuster onto the national news agenda, a dubious distinction in the mind of Gerald Brookhaven.

Brookhaven was Merrill-Schuster's executive vice president. Brookhaven should have reveled in his company's success and its undeniable contributions to the relief of human suffering, but he frequently felt pilloried by an unappreciative public. Accusations of "obscenely" high prescription drug prices and the refusal to commit company assets to so-called orphan drugs (those produced for less common diseases and thus less lucrative financially) were among the accusations with which Brookhaven had to contend as his company's number one troubleshooter. And now Merrill-Schuster's

commercial creativity was under siege for simply attempting to gain a competitive advantage in the prescription drug wars. Although the ads had been produced by an outside agency, company officials were the ultimate gatekeepers for the online promotion of their products. They had enthusiastically tendered their blessing to the agency's resourcefulness in targeting the gay population for the sale of their prescription HIV drug.

Beck was asking for nothing less than the withdrawal of an ad that, in Brookhaven's view, had been inordinately effective in increasing Xecor's sales. While the drug could not be purchased without a prescription, physicians were influenced not only by the ads but also by their patients' demands for the highly advertised drug. Although the executive vice president had the ultimate responsibility for deciding the fate of the Xecor online ads, as he usually did when confronted with such dilemmas, he sought the counsel of Sonia Getty, director of public relations, and Michael Chen, the company's director of advertising, marketing, and sales.

"I've explained the problem to you," Brookhaven began as he poured himself a cup of coffee in preparation for what he knew would be an animated discussion. "Beck wants us to withdraw these ads. Does he have a point? Are we encouraging unsafe sex?"

"He may have a point," replied Getty, always sensitive to the public relations implications of any form of protest, even the seemingly frivolous ones. "The sales of Xecor are certainly strong, and our surveys indicate that a high percentage of users received at least some of their product information from the website ads."

"But all that indicates is that the ads are effective," responded Chen. "The use of handsome, virile models is common in our industry. The technique is effective. The various drugs for impotence and hair restoration have all used such models."

"Your examples do not involve life-threatening situations," countered Getty. "Our ads could unwittingly encourage unsafe sex by minimizing the disease's debilitating effects. If consumers link the product claims with the stark images of handsome and healthy-looking HIV carriers, they may become sexually careless."

Getty paused as she turned to her computer with one of the website ads prominently displayed on her seventeen-inch monitor. "Beck may be right," she continued before Chen could issue a rejoinder. "Our research also indicates that Xecor users were influenced by the attractiveness and healthy appearances of the young male models. Human nature being what it is, they may consider Xecor an effective antidote for the consequences of unsafe sex. There is also evidence of a resurgence of the HIV virus in some communities, such as San Francisco."

"Our responsibility is to promote our product with the most effective message possible," replied Chen, after listening patiently to his colleague's remarks. "In fact, I consider it to be an ethical duty to our stockholders and to those who worked so diligently to bring Xecor to market. There are limits. But I don't believe we have crossed the line with these ads. In my opinion, consumers are rational individuals who can make up their own minds. Even if our research documents the effectiveness of the images in the ads, I can't believe that we are encouraging unsafe sex."

Getty was troubled by Chen's rather uncompromising retorts to her verbal thrusts, but she was equally disturbed by the public relations implications of her company's confrontation with the United Gay Front. They had attracted national news coverage, and the verbal thrashing that Merrill-Schuster had endured at the hands of Beck and his gay activist organization could erode Xecor's magnetism as a drug of choice among gay consumers and their physicians. Yes, Xecor was effective in the fight against the debilitating effects of the HIV virus and AIDS, but so were some of its competitors.

"Even if you are correct," observed Getty, "I think we should err on the side of caution. After all, we're not being asked to withdraw the drug from the market. But if there's any chance that our ads are encouraging antisocial behavior in the form of unsafe sex, they should be pulled and replaced with something less controversial."

"These images resonate with the very people we're trying to reach," replied Chen. "And I don't see any difference between the advice physicians give their patients when dispensing other drugs and the HIV drugs. When doctors prescribe cholesterol and heart medicine, for example, they also admonish the users to couple this medication with a healthy lifestyle. Why can't the same advice be dispensed

when prescribing Xecor? Doctors should warn patients to continue to practice safe sex, although no such warning should really be necessary."

Brookhaven listened attentively to the point–counterpoint of his junior staff members. He was stoic throughout and acknowledged their insightful exchange but did not reveal his own assessment of Beck's complaint. As Getty and Chen retreated from his office, he stared at the online ad once more as he contemplated his ethical duties to all of the stakeholders involved.

THE CASE STUDY

Prescription drug advertising is now ubiquitous in the mass media. The most innocent view of such advertising is that it opens a line of communication between patient and physician. Cynics complain that it puts pressure on physicians to accede to patient demands rather than to render prescriptions based strictly upon medical concerns and the physician's best judgment. However, this case is not about the ethics of prescription drug advertising as a class but rather particular visual images that critics believe may be promoting unsafe sex. The continuation of the ads themselves, therefore, might be viewed as a form of antisocial behavior because the consequence of unprotected sex is a resurgence of the HIV epidemic.

Nevertheless, it is not clear as to how much responsibility Merrill-Schuster should assume for this potential danger. The interests of a number of stakeholders must be taken into account. As Chen correctly noted, stockholders are interested in the corporate bottom line, and this drug has certainly contributed to the company's profits. And the research suggests that the Xecor online ads have been instrumental in the drug's commercial success.

Of course, the gay community is an important stakeholder. They have benefited from the drug, and many have been influenced by the online claims of the Xecor ads. If we accept the notion that advertising images to which consumers can relate are persuasive—and the advertising industry certainly subscribes to this idea—then we must assume that the pictures of handsome, robust, and healthy young men are effective marketing tools. But the next step is somewhat tricky. Even if some gay users assume that Xecor is so effective that they now have a license for unsafe sex, how much responsibility should Merrill-Schuster assume for this outcome? After all, there is a certain amount of hyperbole in all ads. The use of attractive, healthy-looking models is a mainstay of the industry for a wide range of products.

One could argue that within the marketplace of ideas there is certainly no dearth of information on the dangers of unsafe sex, and that as autonomous individuals HIV carriers and AIDS victims bear the ultimate responsibility for how to use the facts and images presented to them. Indeed, assuming that some users are practicing unsafe sex (and thus contributing to the spread of HIV), secure in the false knowledge that Xecor will provide a magic bullet to offset the consequences of this form of antisocial behavior, Merrill-Schuster certainly did not intend this as an outcome. Nevertheless, in an imperfect world the irrational (or perhaps emotional) impulses of humans sometimes dominate their more rational instincts. At least, that's what advertisers are counting on. Thus, can the advertising industry escape entirely its moral responsibility for the unintended consequences of its commercial messages?

For the purpose of evaluating the arguments outlined in this scenario and rendering a decision on whether to withdraw (or change) the Xecor ads, assume the role of executive vice president Gerald Brookhaven. And then, applying the model for moral reasoning described in Chapter 3, decide the fate of Merrill-Schuster's online ad campaign for its popular prescription HIV drug.

▶ **CASE 9-3**

Investigating Child Pornography: Limits of the First Amendment

When Mark Goldsmith's daughter, Laura, told him that there were rumors some of her high school classmates had been recruited to pose for sexually explicit photographs, her father took more than a passing interest. Goldsmith was the education beat reporter for the *Fort Houston Post* and maintained a wary eye on the myriad contentious issues within the Fort Houston Consolidated School District.

Goldsmith's byline was a regular feature on the paper's metro page as he documented such ongoing controversies as school bond elections, which often pitted the inner city against the suburbs; the role of sex education within the Fort Houston public schools; and the "no pass, no play" policy concerning student athletes. Laura's position as editor of her school's newspaper not only provided Goldsmith with some unique insights into the realities of academic life from the teen's perspective, but it also afforded common ground that exceeded the usual father–daughter relationship.

Laura's uncorroborated intelligence concerning her classmates was potentially explosive and particularly troubling to Goldsmith because of his knowledge, both personally and professionally, of Branson High's elite status within the educational hierarchy. From its inauguration in 1974 Branson High had been a paragon of academic excellence. Located in the conspicuously affluent suburb of Grammercy Hills, Branson also stood as a monument of middle-class flight from the inner city, an undefiled enclave apparently secure from the pathologies that threatened the urban educational institutions. Faculty and staff extolled the fact that students could arrive each morning without having to endure the indignities of metal detectors or searches. The correlation between decorum and discipline and academic performance, in their view, was undeniable. Branson High was a perennial leader in the results of the national achievement exams, and each year their graduates figured prominently among the freshmen classes at the Ivy League colleges. The school's heavy investment in technology, including Internet connections, and the faculty's commitment to the teaching of critical thinking and problem-solving skills justified Branson's reputation as a citadel of academic enlightenment.

Goldsmith could not allow the rumors of a child pornography ring operating within Branson High to go unexplored. With a continuing flow of information from his daughter and some corroboration provided by reliable sources within the school district office who were just beginning their own investigation, the rumors began to assume factual proportions, and the following picture began to emerge: The alleged perpetrator was David Britt, a local photographer who for the past five years had contracted with the Branson High yearbook staff to shoot their class pictures. According to Goldsmith's information, Britt would select the most attractive females from his photo sessions and then call them at home and entice them, for a lucrative sum, into posing nude and performing a variety of sex acts, all of which were captured on Britt's sophisticated digital camera. The photos were then uploaded to a website that specialized in child pornography, where for a fee pedophiles could satisfy their obsessive perversion.

Goldsmith asked the *Post*'s police reporter, Wanda Savage, for assistance in determining whether Britt had a police record. "Britt was arrested several years ago for possession of child pornography, but the charges were dismissed for lack of evidence," Savage told Goldsmith. "Apparently the search warrant was defective. This might explain why this information was never conveyed to school officials." Armed with this knowledge, Goldsmith confronted Britt with the allegations, which the photographer categorically denied. He threatened a libel suit if the *Post* published these accusations.

The reporter's next visit was to Branson High principal Michael Woolworth. Woolworth, an administrative rookie in his first year as Branson's principal, was justifiably proud of his predecessors' legacy. He had inherited an elite institution and was determined to continue the school's honorable tradition. Goldsmith's overtures were not what Woolworth had in mind for his maiden voyage. The principal told Goldsmith that he was aware of the rumors but doubted their validity. "I've asked my teachers to keep me informed if they hear anything suspicious," Woolworth said candidly. "If I find any evidence that these rumors are true, I'm duty-bound to notify the police." Goldsmith acknowledged the principal's duty but was undeterred in his determination to conduct his own investigation.

Goldsmith conceded the treacherous terrain of his investigation and the ethically slippery slope of his investigative techniques. At some point he might need the cooperation of some of the teen models themselves, but this would probably necessitate parental permission. However, the reporter's most immediate concern was to obtain tangible evidence that would link Britt to the pedophilia website. The

first step, in Goldsmith's view, was to document the presence of sexually explicit photos featuring Branson students. Goldsmith's briefing to Paul McKeithen, the *Post*'s managing editor, and city editor Rosalind Paulk resulted in a spirited debate. Goldsmith's proposal was controversial and would have to receive McKeithen's blessing.

"I have the Internet address that supposedly houses Britt's photos," said Goldsmith. "Britt doesn't run the site; he just contributes to it. The only way, in my judgment, to confirm these rumors is to download some of these pictures. Obviously, we won't publish the names or pictures of these underage models, but I need the photos to see if any Branson students are involved."

"But there's a problem," objected Paulk. "It's illegal under both federal and state law to even possess child pornography. You could go to jail for downloading these pictures."

"These photos are crucial to our investigation," replied Goldsmith. "We should be able to plead the First Amendment as a defense if any legal action ensues. When these laws were passed, surely the authors didn't have the press in mind. I'm not a pedophile; I'm just trying to do a story that should be of interest to our readers concerning child pornography in suburbia."

"But the statutes don't contain any exceptions for journalists," noted Paulk. "You're putting yourself at risk, as well as the reputation of the paper. Do you really need to access these Internet sites and download this material?"

"That's the only way to truly document this story," reiterated Goldsmith. "My sources have provided the leads, but I need to corroborate their information. I can match the photos from the website with the Branson High annuals and cross-check my evidence with the school's principal. This won't *prove* Britt's involvement, but in will be a major step in my investigation. Our readers deserve to know what is happening in one of the premier schools in the district."

"I agree that this is a serious problem," acknowledged Paulk. "But if this becomes a legal issue, can we defend our actions? The first question, of course, is whether we can convince the courts that under the circumstances journalists are entitled to a First Amendment privilege to violate the laws against possession of child pornography in pursuit of a story. But even if we are successful, there is the court of public opinion to contend with. Are we morally exempt from the obligations imposed on the rest of society?"

This was an intriguing question, but Goldsmith met the challenge head-on. "In this case I believe we are," he responded. "We're fiduciaries of the public. It's our job to keep them apprised of any corrupting influences within the community. Providing an early warning about this predator is a service to the community. The benefits clearly outweigh the harms in this case, even if we have to violate the law in the process."

The managing editor had listened to this exchange with interest and growing concern. On the one hand, the story needed to be told. This wasn't a report of an official investigation, in which the facts could simply be reported without viewing any of the material in question. Goldsmith's investigation was truly enterprising and matching the photos on the website with those in the Branson High yearbook was essential; it would at least authenticate the rumors that had preceded Goldsmith's painstaking investigation.

On the other hand, Goldsmith's news-gathering defense was constitutionally suspect. His proposal could put both the paper and the reporter legally at risk. And beyond the immediate legal concerns were the ethical dimensions of a journalist's violating the law to serve some higher public purpose. While he pondered this dilemma as his newspaper's moral agent, McKeithen was painfully aware of the indivisibility of the legal and ethical issues under these circumstances.

THE CASE STUDY

Are journalists ever justified in violating the law in pursuit of a story? If so, what threshold standards should be met to vindicate such a violation?

In most cases, the possession of child pornography is not essential to reporting knowledgeably about the subject. But in this scenario, journalist Mark Goldsmith believes that he must access a website frequented by pedophiles to validate the essential truth of the rumors concerning the recruitment of female students at Branson High. But

the law intervenes at this crucial juncture: It is illegal to even possess child pornography; journalists are not excluded from the law's reach.

In the only case on point, in 1998 a veteran journalist who worked as a producer for National Public Radio pleaded guilty to two counts of sending and receiving child pornography over the Internet to test the validity of the First Amendment as a defense. He said he was researching the explosion of child pornography on the Internet and the efforts of authorities to restrict it. Federal prosecutors responded that the reporter/producer was using the material for prurient interest, not journalistic research.[76]

In this case, there is no suggestion that Goldsmith is a pedophile. He is invoking the First Amendment as a legal defense, but he apparently also believes that it affords moral shelter for some lawbreaking in those rare circumstances when the information sought is essential to the public interest. The *Post*'s city editor, on the other hand, challenges both premises. A constitutional defense, in her view, will be ineffective as a legal defense and will also be of dubious value from an ethical perspective.

The paper's managing editor, Paul McKeithen, appreciates the validity of both arguments but is naturally concerned about the consequences for both his reporter and the *Post* if he approves Goldsmith's proposal to download this child pornography from the Web. McKeithen is the moral agent in this case. Therefore, for the purpose of weighing the pros and cons of Goldsmith's proposal, assume the role of Paul McKeithen and, applying the SAD formula for moral reasoning outlined in Chapter 3, render your judgment in this matter.

▶ CASE 9-4

Hiring the Criminal Element for Nation Building: Laytel's PR Problem

Thomas Steele had harbored misgivings about his nation's decision to invade Iraq in March of 2003, but his reservations had gradually receded as the process of nation building and the restoration of

Iraq's vital infrastructure had finally begun to bear fruit. Steele had graduated from college in the spring of 1990 with a major in public relations and a commission as a second lieutenant in the army, and within a few months he was dispatched to Kuwait to serve in a public affairs detachment in what became known as the Persian Gulf War. His responsibilities consisted primarily of arranging press pool coverage of his unit's combat operations and disseminating the military's version of events as they transpired. With the rapid cessation of hostilities, Steele was redeployed to Fort Hood, Texas, where he continued his work as a public affairs officer until the termination of his active duty obligation. His transition to civilian life was unproblematic as he joined a small public relations company in Houston, where he focused his energies on cultivating the public images and helping to execute the strategic marketing objectives of his firm's diverse clients.

However, after seven years of working long hours for a public relations company whose client list remained virtually static, Steele migrated to the headquarters of the Laytel Energy Corporation, where he served as the company's Director of Public Communication. Laytel was a large company that specialized in oil pipeline installation and maintenance and other vital aspects of a nation's energy infrastructure, and six months after coalition forces invaded Iraq and deposed Saddam Hussein the company had been awarded a government contract to repair Iraq's damaged oil distribution system and to resurrect the nation's power grid in those cities where military operations had taken their toll.

As a military veteran, Steele was pleased to be a participant in this nation-building process and initially devoted most of his energies to counteracting the seemingly endless barrage of negative press reports on the continuing instability and the consequences of the apparent lack of postwar planning. Suicide bombings and the almost daily accounts of American military casualties were the mainstay of journalistic coverage of postwar Iraq, but Steele labored diligently to neutralize this image in the court of public opinion. Laytel, of course, was only one of many players in the effort to rebuild Iraq, but Steele believed his company's

determination and accomplishments could serve as a vivid affirmation of the allegiance of America's economic community to restoring the energy infrastructure of Iraq's civil society. He was particularly pleased that Laytel had committed itself to hiring, insofar as possible, Iraqi citizens to help rebuild their own country. This initiative provided desperately needed jobs for the Iraqis, but it was also cheaper than importing more costly American workers. Steele's optimism was tempered somewhat by the realization that America's efforts at democratizing Iraq could fail, but he was still delighted to be a part of what he knew would require a Herculean effort at civic restoration in Iraq.

Many journalists continued to report the more dramatic and sensational accounts of America's presence in Iraq, but Steele had succeeded in sensitizing some to the less spectacular but significant process of rebuilding the country, specifically the reconstruction and protection of the country's energy resources. However, Steele's confidence in the nobility of his company's enterprise was shattered by a call from network correspondent Marsha Wiles. Wiles told Steele that she was working on a story, based upon information provided to her network's Baghdad bureau by a Laytel employee in Iraq, that part of the company's workforce in Iraq consisted of former members of Saddam Hussein's Baath Party and that some had been insurgents who were known to have killed American soldiers. Wiles wanted Steele to confirm or deny the accuracy of this account and inquired as to the thoroughness of the background checks conducted by Laytel before hiring Iraqi citizens. Steele told the correspondent he could not confirm the accuracy of the story but that he would investigate the matter further. A discreet inquiry to Laytel's Director of Human Resource Management (HRM), Richard Lancaster, brought an immediate denial of any irregularities in the company's employment profile in Iraq, a response that was confirmed by a similar query to the head of the Laytel field office in Baghdad. Steele was preparing a formal response to Marsha Wiles's overture when he received a disquieting call at home from Jacob Nannes, whom he recognized as an HRM staff member.

"I'm aware of your concern about some of our Iraqi employees," Nannes said. "The fact is that the story is true; some of our hires were supporters of Saddam Hussein, and there is evidence that some were insurgents who killed American soldiers, particularly right after the fall of Baghdad. Our project managers in Iraq felt they had no choice but to ignore their backgrounds. They needed skilled workers, and many of these were qualified. Besides, to our knowledge none of these Iraqis were leaders in the insurgency. Time was also not on our side; we were under pressure from the government to produce results quickly." Nannes paused briefly to allow Steele to digest what he had been told and then continued. "But I'm concerned that some of these may still be loyal to Saddam. They're being well paid, but I have concerns about their commitment to our mission. And it bothers me that we have hired workers whom we know or at least suspect may have been responsible for American deaths."

Confronted with denials from two company officials and a contrarian view provided by the HRM staff member, Steele asked Nannes how he knew that the project managers in Iraq had *knowingly* hired former insurgents to work on the Laytel energy ventures. Steele reasoned that such hiring practices might not have been deliberate but that, in the social disarray of postinvasion Iraq, perhaps it was impossible to perform thorough background checks. Nannes responded that his account could be verified through inspection of a confidential company file, the codes and password for which Nannes passed along to Laytel's Director of Public Communication. Steele promised Nannes that he would keep their conversation confidential.

When Steele returned to his office the following day, his voice mail contained a follow-up inquiry from Marsha Wiles concerning the story she was pursuing on the allegedly nefarious backgrounds of some of Laytel's Iraqi workers. The time was rapidly approaching, he knew, when he would have to provide some form of response to the persistent network reporter, but in the meantime he agonized over what was clearly a tedious ethical dilemma. The truth, apparently, was reflected in the company's confidential files, but if he accessed the files—files to which, according to company policy, he had no right—he might soon find himself in the unemployment line. Steele could, of course, remain the company loyalist,

refuse to examine the files, and then pass along the company's official denials to Marsha Wiles. The fact that a Laytel employee in Iraq and an HRM staff member at the company's Houston headquarters had accused project managers of knowingly hiring Iraqis with criminal backgrounds was disturbing. But at this juncture, company officials had no incentive to acknowledge the disreputable backgrounds of the former insurgents who were now working for Laytel in rebuilding their nation's energy infrastructure. Public condemnation might ensue that could quickly trigger political repercussions that in turn could result in the loss of a highly lucrative contract. In assessing the situation, Steele was not entirely unsympathetic to the rather daunting challenge of those project managers in Iraq who were under pressure to produce results. Perhaps the ends justified the means, but if the American public knew that taxpayers' money was being spent on workers who had resisted the coalition invasion and had in fact killed American soldiers, would they be indulgent or demand accountability?

Did the public have a right to know that Laytel Energy Corporation had engaged in employment practices that in this country might charitably be referred to as antisocial behavior (the hiring of Iraqis who were suspected of killing American soldiers) or more caustically as unpatriotic? If so, from a public relations ethical perspective, how should Thomas Steele respond to the dilemma described here?

THE CASE STUDY

Thomas Steele is Director of Public Communication for an energy company, Laytel, that is assisting in the effort to bring order out of chaos in occupied Iraq. When he hears the disquieting news that his firm may have cut moral corners in the hiring process, he is understandably distressed but is not entirely unsympathetic to the project managers' dilemma in finding qualified workers within such a short time span and under less than optimal hiring conditions. Of course, he has not truly confirmed the reports with documentary evidence—evidence that is apparently available in the company's confidential computer database to which

Steele does not have authorized access. If he uses the codes and password to inspect the file, he will learn the truth but in the process violate corporate policy and possibly lose his job.

Steele is clearly in an ethical box. So what are his options? His first option, of course, is to simply parrot the company line, and since he has not seen the confidential employment file, rationalize his actions on the grounds that he does not *know* the truth except for the version provided by company officials. However, if the network correspondent or any other reporter discovers the truth and is able to document it, Steele's credibility will be shattered and Laytel may have a PR disaster on its hands. A second option would be to convince Laytel managers to acknowledge publicly that they had hired some Iraqis with criminal backgrounds, accompanied by a vigorous defense of why they believed such a practice was necessary. However, this option might raise suspicions within the management hierarchy that Steele had accessed the confidential file.

Are these the only options, or are there other approaches that Steele might use in resolving this public relations dilemma? For the purpose of evaluating this case, assume the role of Thomas Steele, Laytel's Director of Public Communication, and, utilizing the moral reasoning model outlined in Chapter 3, decide how you would handle this situation.

▶ **CASE 9-5**

Sports Trash Talk and the End of Innocence[77]

Sports Gazette was the crown jewel in the American Cable Sports Network's impressive arsenal of talk shows. It ranked second only to ACSN's live telecasts of professional sporting events and had attracted a loyal following of sports enthusiasts and fanatics. Those who were attracted to trash talking and in-your-face superstars could reap a bountiful harvest from the show's daily diet of confrontational interviews, accompanied by video clips of bench-clearing brawls during the baseball season, the most aggressive and violent gridiron action

from the NFL, and under-the-net cheap shots from their NBA counterparts. Professional boxers could always be counted on for a quick flash of arrogance as they taunted their opponents, thereby continuing a rather dubious tradition among prizefighters. Some of the interviews were taped, frequently generating as much heat as light and a noticeable number of "bleeps" to mask the profanities that were now commonplace in athletes' public appearances.

Christopher Wiley, *Sports Gazette*'s new producer, had assumed his position with some reservations about the show's uncivil and controversial format, but he could not ignore the ratings data that documented its significant audience appeal. He also could not ignore the three bags of mail that had just been dumped on his desk by his efficient assistant.

Wiley recognized the letters as an orchestrated writing campaign, but the lack of spontaneity in the critical epistles did not invalidate the concerns that emerged from their authors. "I have practiced sports law for fifteen years," wrote an attorney, "and each year my caseload of Pee-Wee League, Little League and other recreational officials who have been assaulted gets heavier." One former Little League umpire wrote that he had quit after sixteen years of officiating because of abusive parents and threats of violence. Another said he had been spit on by parents and physically assaulted twice. "Even the kids are getting into the act," he wrote. "In the past several weeks I have ejected two young players for using abusive language, and recently we almost had a bench-clearing brawl—just like in the major leagues." The litany of complaints varied in their specifics, but the 300 letters had one thing in common: They indicted television for pandering to the incivility of professional athletes and providing a platform for them to disgorge themselves of whatever pent-up emotions were lurking just beneath the surface.

"I do not blame *Sports Gazette* or ACSN for all of the ills that have befallen youth sports," wrote one particularly articulate correspondent, "but this show is watched by many children and adolescents who aspire to become professional athletes. They take many of their cues from what they see on your program, and these interviewees are role models for their youthful followers. Their fathers are among *Sports Gazette*'s most loyal viewers, and they also are influenced by the show's intemperate demeanor. Therefore, you cannot simply ignore your own responsibility in the corruption of their sense of sportsmanship and fair play."

Wiley was suitably chastened by what he had read. He did not believe that *Sports Gazette* had been singled out for the ire of the discontented letter writers; they undoubtedly had tendered their complaints to his counterparts at ACSN's network rivals. In addition, TV's "blame" for such charges of corruption of the sportsmanship ethic had to be shared with parents whose violent and profane outbursts at youthful sporting events would undoubtedly be emulated by their offspring. But of course, the parents themselves were probably influenced by the uncivil in-your-face remarks that were the hallmark of the show's irrepressible interviewees. The network's own ratings data revealed the presence of many young people in the audience, and presumably many of them were participants in organized youth sports activities. Of course, the nightly violence on the entertainment networks made the combative nature of the show's guests appear to be the natural order of things.

As a rookie producer, Wiley was reluctant to move precipitously, despite his own misgivings. He would eventually confront *Sports Gazette*'s two anchors, who were influential in selecting the show's guests, and the "booker," who actually made arrangements for their appearances. However, he wanted to reflect upon this ethical dilemma and then confront the staff with at least a tentative decision.

Wiley was acutely aware of the talk show's phenomenal commercial success. He was reluctant to characterize *Sports Gazette* as journalism, since the anchors themselves made no pretense to objectivity. In fact, they frequently precipitated the uncivil responses through their impertinent questions. In Wiley's view, sports journalism was rapidly becoming an oxymoron on TV, but labels aside, the anchors did solicit insights and information that might otherwise go undiscovered during routine interviews. They were always prepared and probed the recesses of the professional athletes' psyches. Despite the show's aggressive interview

style, Wiley was not naive enough to believe that the interrogations suddenly transformed otherwise courteous and decorous athletes into coarse barbarians. Their superstar status had provided a liberal dose of cultural forgiveness, in their view, and their trash talk would find other venues, if not on one of cable TV's premier sports talk shows.

Sports Gazette had struck a responsive chord among the network's faithful. The nation's sports enthusiasts had turned professional athletes into cult figures, and they were now reaping what they had sown. Wiley wondered whether his network should shoulder any of the responsibility in this matter; his show was just giving the viewers what they wanted. Some would even argue that this issue is too complex for a single sports talk show to respond by confessing its sins, altering its format, and then expecting the same level of audience allure that it had enjoyed during its two-year tenure.

On the other hand, Wiley was troubled by the plaintive pleas of the letter writers who apparently viewed themselves as the conscience of a growing body of concerned citizens—concerned about the growing violence, profanity, and other forms of antisocial behavior surrounding organized youth sports and TV's role in creating this culture of incivility. While he was unwilling to shoulder all the blame, he was a part of a program genre that stood accused of corrupting the sportsmanship ethic. It was easy to blame the parents—they were the sources of the violence and most of the profanity at youth sporting events—but they were also influenced by the relentless trash talk and in-your-face remarks of some professional athletes. The problem had been clearly identified and documented by *Sports Gazette*'s critics. Christopher Wiley was the show's producer and gatekeeper. What ethical responsibility, he wondered, should he assume in playing a role in the restoration of youthful innocence on the athletic field?

THE CASE STUDY

Ratings, commercial appeal, and giving the people what they want versus TV's role in cultivating the social pathologies of incivility, antisocial behavior, and the corruption of the sportsmanship ethic—these are the competing interests that have emerged to challenge Christopher Wiley's moral imagination as he ponders the ethical issues raised in this narrative. Like other media gatekeepers and moral agents, he cannot just simply deny responsibility for his content. But the question is whether he should deny responsibility for corrupting the innocence of youthful athletes and predicate his defense on market considerations. He could argue that the *Sports Gazette* simply appeals to the darker side of human nature that was already present when his show made its debut. After all, trash talk and other forms of uncivil behavior existed long before the *Sports Gazette* made its maiden voyage two years ago.

On the other hand, each show that features this kind of content contributes in some small way to reinforcing the existing cultural values and to perpetuating the troublesome behavior patterns that afflict the youthful audience. Consider this lamentation from Phil Mushnick, writing in a recent issue of *TV Guide:*

> Think of your own relative reality. Where once you were horrified to read or hear about the softball umpire assaulted after the game or the pee-wee football coach beaten by a player's father, these reports have become so commonplace that they're moving farther toward the back of the newspaper and the final minutes of the news broadcast. For crying out loud, we're becoming desensitized to the desensitization.[78]

Christopher Wiley is not considering canceling his top-rated show. His dilemma is whether to alter the format to tone down the most aggressive rhetoric (which might admittedly result in some audience defections) or whether to retain the *Sports Gazette*'s current aggressive, confrontational style and reject the complaints that had precipitated this ethical dilemma in the first place. Therefore, for the purpose of addressing these concerns, assume the role of producer Christopher Wiley and, applying the SAD formula for moral reasoning described in Chapter 3, render your judgment on this matter.

▶ **CASE 9-6**
Alcohol Ads in the Campus Newspaper

Kendrick Haas was determined to mount an aggressive campaign against substance abuse on his campus, and alcohol was public enemy number one. As president of San Jacinto State University, Haas was accustomed to the casual and morally permissive atmosphere of college life in southern California. But he was chastened by a rather sobering report from his dean of students that alcohol consumption, particularly binge drinking, had shown a dramatic rise among San Jacinto students over the past three years. Although the drinking age in California is 21, college upperclassmen were not the only offenders. It was an open secret that many underage students frequented the local pubs using fake IDs.

Under Haas's tutelage, San Jacinto had evolved from a party school, where the class schedule was viewed as a smorgasbord of appetizing "gut" courses, to an institution with rigorous academic standards and a challenging teaching faculty with impressive academic credentials. But he was convinced that his university's commitment to the students' intellectual development should be accompanied by a corresponding devotion to their social and moral welfare. An unabated rise in alcohol abuse, he feared, would corrode the quality of life at San Jacinto and eventually lead to a noticeable decline in academic performance.

The President's Task Force on Substance Abuse, a twelve-person committee composed of both faculty and students, had devised a rather ambitious strategy to deal with the problem, including a three-hour drug awareness seminar during freshman orientation, the distribution of a wide variety of information pamphlets on the dangers of drug and alcohol abuse to student mailboxes, and an intensive training program for dormitory resident assistants on how to detect and manage problems of alcohol overindulgence among their young charges. Even the clergy of the various campus ministries were enlisted to add a spiritual dimension to the university's substance abuse agenda.

The *Daily Sentinel,* the university's student newspaper, editorially applauded the president's decisive action and provided impressive coverage of the task force's deliberations and recommendations. As the forum for student expression at San Jacinto State, the *Daily Sentinel* was a symbol of journalistic excellence. Its reporters and editorial staff had been recognized both regionally and nationally for their enterprise and were perennial finalists in the prestigious Hearst competition. But the *Daily Sentinel* was more than a platform for student expression at San Jacinto State. It was also a profit center, an economic oasis that stood in stark contrast to the university's academic units that existed rather fragilely on austere budgets and increasingly outmoded equipment and facilities.

But Kendrick Haas had not summoned his director of student media, Cassie Lake, to his office to discuss the paper's auspicious status as a campus cash cow. The president, who was not one to waste time on pleasantries, got right to the point. "As you know, we're already four months into our substance abuse campaign," he began. "And I appreciate the editorial support from the *Sentinel.* But I'm concerned about the ads from the off-campus bars that offer all kinds of inducements for students to overindulge. Most of our students read the *Sentinel,* and they're exposed to these ads. I would like for you to consider dropping them."

"I understand your concern," responded Lake. "But these bars are among our most lucrative and reliable advertisers."

"I understand that," replied the president. "But we're just asking our student paper to be a team player—to help us in our fight against alcohol abuse here at San Jacinto. The university attorney advises me that I might have the administrative authority to ban such ads outright. But I'm not inclined to do so. As you know I believe in a hands-off approach in dealing with the *Sentinel.* But let me make my position clear: The *Sentinel* is a part of the university community and has a duty to act responsibly. And running ads that glorify alcohol consumption among college students is not ethically responsible."

Lake was grateful that Haas had not played his trump card, the threat of outright censorship of the controversial ads. She was in no mood for a First Amendment confrontation with the president, but he apparently expected her to be his ethical conduit to the paper's business staff. As Lake assembled her staff to discuss the president's plea, she was plagued by her divided loyalties both as a university employee and as the head of a student-run journalistic enterprise. Her sounding board consisted of Harvey Miller, business manager; Lionel Brown, the student advertising manager; and Kenisha Washington, a bright, energetic, and very productive sales representative for the *Sentinel.*

"The president is pushing us to drop all of our alcohol advertising," said Lake. "That includes most of the bars and other student hangouts close to campus. As you know, he has made substance abuse prevention a priority in his program to improve the quality of student life at San Jacinto. And according to information provided to the Office of Student Affairs by the Health Center, alcohol appears to be the drug of choice at this university. Drinking—particularly binge drinking—is on the rise, and President Haas wants us to be a team player in his initiative."

"But I question his logic in this matter," responded Brown. "Ads can't encourage students to drink. They might be effective in helping our student readers decide *where* to go for their entertainment, but those who are already drinkers are going to do so anyway. An ad isn't going to convince a nondrinker to go to a bar."

"Perhaps," replied Lake, who had always been skeptical of claims that advertising was powerless to do more than persuade consumers to switch from one brand to another. "But the ads we run are pretty alluring. Most of these establishments also sell food, but the ads usually focus on what the advertisers believe will be the most appealing to college students—the alcohol. Many of them feature happy hour discounts, free snacks with the purchase of certain kinds of beer, tear-off coupons, and other incentives. The student patrons who take advantage of these inducements may already be drinkers, but by running these promotions we're encouraging overindulgence."

"But one of the purposes of advertising is to encourage consumers to behave in a certain way," responded Washington rather defensively. After all, she had negotiated lucrative contracts with several of the clients under scrutiny and was not about to surrender easily to what she perceived as President Haas's moral crusade. "Because it's legal for college students to drink," she continued, "these establishments have a right to advertise. And we're the medium most targeted to the student population. As long as the ads are in good taste, these merchants have a right to compete in the marketplace."

"You have a point, and I understand your concerns," responded Lake. "But I wonder if we aren't a little hypocritical. Our student editors have run columns pointing out the dangers of binge drinking and endorsing the president's program. If we run these ads, isn't the business side of our paper undermining our editorial position?"

"I don't see this as a real problem," countered Brown. "In the professional world editors insist on a clear separation between the editorial and commercial sides of the paper. Why should a college paper be any different? If we base our decisions on what our editorial staff has done, then we lose our independence."

"But a college paper *is* different," said Lake. "The *Daily Sentinel* is the only paper many of these students will read. We're a forum for student expression. And don't forget that student fees help to support the *Sentinel*. The president has asked for our help in combating a problem that contributes to antisocial behavior among some of our students. Isn't this a reasonable request? It boils down to a question of what our responsibility is to the students. After all, they're our audience."

"All of our readers are at least 18," responded Washington rather emphatically. "They are mature enough to make their own decisions. If we ban these alcohol ads to protect students from themselves, this strikes me as rather paternalistic. And this should not be the role of a student newspaper at a public university."

"I don't have any philosophical problem, as do Lionel and Kenisha, with complying with the president's request," said Miller, who had listened patiently to the debate. "But I am concerned about the financial impact on the paper. We could survive the elimination of the alcohol advertising, but it would seriously erode our profit base. And this would certainly affect our ability to upgrade the *Sentinel*'s

physical plant, including investments in new computer technology and software."

"Perhaps we can make the loss of revenue up somewhere else," said Lake, without any clear conviction that she was right. "We'll just have to be more aggressive. Besides, on any issue like this we don't want to be viewed as irresponsible. I wonder if we shouldn't give in on this and be a team player. After all, alcohol abuse is a serious problem at San Jacinto."

Kenisha Washington, who believed that commercial independence was as sacred as editorial independence, remained unconvinced: "If we thought that these ads really contributed to the problem of alcohol abuse and decided on our own to drop them, then I might feel differently. But if we cave in to administrative pressure, we'll lose credibility. It still comes down to a question of whether we want to be perceived as a student voice independent of administration control."

During this rather impassioned dialogue, Cassie Lake had exhibited a decidedly pro-administration posture. But she was unsure of whether she spoke from sincere conviction or more as a devil's advocate in attempting to stimulate the moral imagination of her staff. On the one hand, she was a university staff member who was expected to be a team player and to display a certain amount of diligence in implementing administrative policy decisions. On the other hand, she presided over a student-run enterprise that prided itself (both ethically and legally) in serving as an independent voice of student expression. President Haas had promised a hands-off approach, so at least her ethical capacities would be unfettered by legal concerns. Nevertheless, the mere fact that he had summoned her to his office constituted a form of pressure that had to be incorporated into the ethical decision-making process. However, if she appeared to accede too easily to Haas's request, she might jeopardize her own credibility with the *Sentinel*'s staff. Thus, like so many moral agents, she approached her ethical dilemma with divided loyalties.

THE CASE STUDY

Much of the ethical debate about alcohol advertising centers around assignment of responsibility. Opponents of such ads claim that youth-oriented messages that glamorize the social prominence of alcohol promote antisocial behavior, which violates advertisers' and the media's moral duty to society. Their defenders usually emphasize the autonomy of the individual to make rational choices from among the many competing voices in the marketplace.

According to the university's president, drinking is a serious health hazard at San Jacinto State University. His proactive stance to deal with the problem has embraced all facets of student life, and he sees no reason that the student newspaper should not contribute to the success of his campaign. Nevertheless, he has pledged an administrative hands-off approach and has instead appealed to the ethical sensibilities of the newspaper's staff.

The participants in the *Sentinel's* staff meeting have staked out various ethical positions. The student staffers, Lionel Brown and Kenisha Washington, emphasize the autonomy of college students to make their own decisions rationally and deliberately. In their view, the *Daily Sentinel* should not make moral judgments about the acceptability of ads, even though some ads may encourage antisocial behavior by some readers.

The paper's business manager, Harvey Miller, is less concerned with social and individual responsibility than with the economic impact on the *Sentinel.* Whereas the loss of this revenue might not be devastating, the *Sentinel's* future as a state-of-the-art student newspaper could be jeopardized.

Cassie Lake, the director of student media, appreciates the president's dilemma and believes the *Sentinel* has a responsibility to contribute to the quality of student life at San Jacinto State University. Nevertheless, she is sympathetic to the other points of view and does not want to accede uncritically to the president's request.

What is missing from this discussion is any consideration of a middle ground, an Aristotle's golden mean. The two extremes, of course, are a *laissez-faire* approach, in which moral responsibility is focused on the individual readers rather than on the paper, and a *paternalistic* approach, whereby the paper screens product ads that might encourage some form of antisocial behavior. Is there a reasonable middle ground in this case, or must the *Sentinel* predicate its policy on alcohol advertising on one of the ethical arguments advanced during the staff meeting?

To render an ethical judgment on whether the *Daily Sentinel* should continue to accept alcohol ads, assume the role of the director of student media. Using the SAD formula for moral reasoning discussed in Chapter 3, make a decision on this matter.

 ## CASE 9-7
Online Links to Terrorist Home Pages[79]

As the new media director and online editor of the *San Fernando Star,* Andrea Marcos was on the cutting edge of her paper's technological reformation. She had designed the *Star's* home page and was the gatekeeper of the newspaper's daily online edition, but Marcos had not allowed the technology to overwhelm her sense of journalistic propriety. Technology, in her view, should be the servant and not the master in the journalist's search for truth. The endless possibilities of cyberspace were intoxicating, but Marcos had achieved a respectable comfort level in negotiating the mysteries of the Internet and the World Wide Web.

Marcos applauded the state-of-the-art technology that offered instantaneous access to millions of bits of information with only the click of a mouse. But she was also disturbed by the glut of banal, uncouth, and even dangerous material that threatened to turn the Internet into an intellectual wasteland. From a historical perspective, online journalism was still in its infancy, but as its novelty slowly receded, reporters and editors had begun to view cyberspace with a sense of ethical wariness. On the one hand, the new technology allowed newspapers to compete more aggressively with their broadcast brethren in terms of the timely reporting of the day's events and to update stories as needed. For newspapers, it had revitalized the very meaning of news. On the other hand, the seduction of online editions intensified the probability of inaccuracies and the publication of uncorroborated and incomplete information. Marcos questioned whether cyberspace journalism could afford the luxury of ethical reflection.

One of the more promising innovations in the online repertoire, in Marcos's view, was the ability to provide the reader with links to other websites. For the intellectually curious, an online story could serve as a point of departure to an endless array of associated and unfiltered intelligence. However, Marcos did not believe that linking relieved an online editor of her ethical responsibilities as gatekeeper. If a newspaper, for example, were reluctant to include indecent, offensive, or inflammatory material within its regular edition, could it absolve itself of moral responsibility by linking to this information in its cyberspace edition?

During the four years that the *Star* had been online, for Marcos this question had been mostly academic. Where matters of taste were concerned, the newspaper's seasoned cadre of reporters had erred on the side of caution, thus avoiding the editor's moral scalpel. In a few cases Marcos had deleted links to commercial establishments to avoid the appearance of providing gratuitous publicity. But Toni Sanchez's story required more exacting scrutiny.

Sanchez, a seven-year veteran with the *Star,* was the newspaper's education beat reporter. She covered both the local educational establishment and the San Fernando State University campus at the edge of the metroplex. In recent months Sanchez had produced a series of articles describing the university's impressive record in new technologies research and the activities of the newly established Institute for the Study of Cyberspace Ethics, a research institute devoted to the ethical implications of the unregulated World Wide Web. In surveying the institute's daunting mission for story ideas, Sanchez had encountered Professor Benedictine Lasswell, who had received a government grant to study and map the activities of more than fifty terrorist and guerilla groups around the world, including Al Queda, most infamously associated with the 9/11 assault on the United States. Although some of his work was conducted under a cloak of confidentiality, Lasswell shared one interesting finding with the inquisitive journalist: Terrorists had emerged from the shadows and were now on the World Wide Web.

Marcos viewed Sanchez's story with a critical eye. It contained a fascinating account of how some terrorist groups have entered the mainstream and attempted to gain respectability through the Web. Marcos was impressed with the apparent sophistication of some of these groups, as evidenced by the creative design of their home pages. Once known only for their guns, bombs, and assaults on innocent civilians, the terrorists were attempting to soften their images and to use their home pages to counter what they claimed had been a campaign of disinformation about their causes and their political objectives. Cyberspace had provided a platform for terrorists and other rebel organizations to go directly to the people rather than depend on the mediating influences of the press or risk government censure. Guerilla and rebel groups such as the ELN in Colombia, the Zapatistas in Mexico, and the Hezbollah in Lebanon were now among the featured players on the Internet.

Although the contents varied, the terrorist websites were a virtual smorgasbord of propaganda, featuring everything from doctrinaire and intemperate political commentary to antigovernment invectives to the biographies of "martyrs." Many of the home pages described in Sanchez's well-researched article had links to other sites. The article also had links—to the terrorist home pages. Marcos did not consider the linkage a matter of great moment, but neither was she prepared to dismiss it casually. As the moral agent and the online editor who reported only to the executive editor, she would decide the fate of the home page links in Sanchez's article. In the exchange with her reporter, Marcos was still ambivalent but decided to play devil's advocate.

"I'm a little concerned about the links in your article," Marcos told Sanchez. "Although these home pages appear to be harmless—I accessed three of them earlier today—including them in the online edition of the *Star* may give these groups a legitimacy they don't deserve."

"I question your premise," responded Sanchez. "You're suggesting that by including links in this article that we have somehow helped to mainstream terrorism and these guerilla and rebel movements. But they're already in cyberspace. If someone wants to contact them, their addresses are readily available from other sources."

"But that's an ethical cop-out," replied Marcos. "We can justify just about anything by claiming that readers who want this information will find it anyway so why worry about it. Would you approve of the *Star*'s online edition linking to a site that provides instructions on how to manufacture a bomb from household products?"

Sanchez pondered her colleague's challenging inquiry but wasn't dissuaded from her opinion. "But this is different. We certainly don't want to link to a site that promotes violence. The home pages linked to my article may belong to terrorists, but they're not using the Web to launch an attack on the international computer network. I certainly don't condone their acts of violence, but they view themselves as politically oppressed minorities. The Web affords safe passage for their ideas past government censors. It provides an outlet for their frustrations and may even help to defuse their violent inclinations."

"But your argument misses the point," replied Marcos. "These home pages are still instruments of propaganda. Some of our curious readers will undoubtedly visit them. But we wouldn't include this kind of unfiltered information in the body of the story. Links should offer readers an opportunity to go beyond the coverage offered by our online edition, such as the full text of a Supreme Court opinion, but we should not abandon our editorial judgment just because we have the technical capacity to link our readers with the sources referred to in our articles. We're still gatekeepers. If we're doing a story about General Motors, would we link to their home page and provide them with free publicity?"

"Only if there is something there that we believe will supplement our own story in a meaningful way," said Sanchez. "When we link to an organization's home page, we aren't providing them with free publicity. Our readers are autonomous individuals. They can click to the sites if they wish, but the fact that we include them in the body of our texts doesn't imply our endorsement."

"Not directly," acknowledged Marcos. "But many of these groups are on the State Department's list of terrorist organizations. One strategy in the war against terrorism is to isolate them. In some respects their move onto the Web has circumvented that strategy. But the issue is whether

a newspaper should help to facilitate this facade of respectability—an attempt to legitimize their antisocial behavior through the unregulated forum of the Internet."

Sanchez persisted in countering her editor's objections. "I disagree that we're helping to enhance their credibility by linking to their home pages. Our readers can accept or reject what's there. The information there is harmless, and linking adds a dramatic dimension to the story."

"You may be right," admitted Marcos. "But keep in mind that home pages can change daily. Today they may be harmless; tomorrow they may contain a call for the violent overthrow of the regimes against whom they are revolting or a holy war against their enemies."

THE CASE STUDY

The pages of the World Wide Web are connected by a series of hyperlinks consisting of words, pictures, and phrases. A simple click of the mouse will instantaneously move you from one page to another. Linking the contents of an online publication to other sites allows journalists to share their documentary evidence and primary source materials with their readers. If done properly, over time linking may help to enhance journalistic credibility because it allows readers to review for themselves the points of interest referenced in the online article.

Does linking diminish an editor's moral responsibility as gatekeeper? As editor, would you be inclined to link to a site containing content that you would not include as part of the substance of the original article? If the case concerned child pornography, the decision would be more clear-cut. But the Web pages described in Toni Sanchez's article are essentially propaganda vehicles, an attempt by some terrorist organizations to soften their images and perhaps to gain sympathy within the global community.

Although she is keeping an open mind on the matter and is playing devil's advocate, online editor Andrea Marcos is concerned that by linking to these sites, her paper then becomes a political pawn for these organizations. Although the *Star*'s linkage to these web pages will not alone significantly enhance their influence, she believes that each news organization should assume its share of the responsibility for helping to spread the propaganda of these disaffected groups.

Marcos is also concerned about the transient nature of these terrorist home pages and the potential for quickly evolving from harmless propaganda vehicles to rhetorical devices for violent revolution. This reality of the cyberspace phenomenon is captured in this observation from Edward Mendelson in which he describes the use of the Web by a twentieth-century monk:

> The system of hyperlinks connecting the pages of the World Wide Web suggests a world where connections are everywhere but are mostly meaningless, transient, fragile and unstable. A would-be monk in the twentieth century who visits the Web page of the Monastery of Christ in the Desert will find the exhortation "Don't miss our Thanks Page." A few clicks, and he arrives at an image by a local artist, which will be replaced on screen automatically and randomly in a few seconds by another, and then another. You can create a link between your own Web page—the "homepage" that acts as a table of contents for all the pages linked to it—and someone else's homepage, but you have no assurance that the other person's page will display the same content from one day to the next.[80]

Sanchez obviously doesn't share her editor's apprehension and believes that linking to these web pages provides a more dramatic dimension to the story. Even if the content of the websites does shift, she still feels that the *Star*'s readers are sufficiently mature to evaluate this information for themselves.

Assume the role of online editor Andrea Marcos. Are you convinced by reporter Sanchez's plaintive plea, or are your reservations still sufficiently disturbing that you will delete the web page links from the article? In examining this issue and reaching a decision, you should apply the SAD formula, as described in Chapter 3.

Notes

1. Tom Jackson, "Escape 'The Matrix,' Go Directly to Jail; Some Defendants in Slaying Cases Make Reference to Hit Movie," *Washington Post*, May 17, 2003, p. A1.
2. *James v. Meow Media, Inc,* 300 F.3d 683 (6th Cir. 2002).
3. John D. Zelezny, *Communications Law: Liberties, Restraints, and the Modern Media* (Belmont, CA: Thomson/Wadsworth, 2004), p. 99.
4. Newsnotes, "Louisiana Judge Disposes of Case Against Filmmakers," *Media Law Reporter*, April 3, 2001. A Louisiana judge eventually dismissed the lawsuit.
5. James Q. Wilson and Richard J. Herrnstein, *Crime and Human Nature* (New York: Simon & Schuster, 1985), p. 337.
6. Ibid., citing D. P. Phillips, "The Influence of Suggestion on Suicide: Substantive and Theoretical Implications of the Werther Effect," *American Sociological Review* 39 (1974): 340–354.
7. "Reporter Convicted of Trespassing," *The Advocate* (Baton Rouge, LA), November 12, 2003, p. 2A.
8. "Reporter Charged in Minnesota," *Broadcasting & Cable*, May 22, 2000, p. 36.
9. Robert Weston, "Cincinnati Newspaper Pays $10 Mil to Chiquita," Reuters dispatch, June 29, 1998, available at http://news.lycos.com/stories/topnews/19980629rtnews-chiquita.asp, p. 1.
10. Paul Klite, "Media Can Be Antibiotic for Violence," *Quill*, April 2000, p. 32.
11. Elizabeth B. Ziesenis, "Suicide Coverage in Newspapers: An Ethical Consideration," *Journal of Mass Media Ethics* 6, no. 4 (1991): 241–242.
12. Bob Simmons, "Violence in the Air," *Columbia Journalism Review*, July/August 1994, p. 12.
13. Richard Cunningham, "No More," *Quill*, July/August 1995, p. 13.
14. For a discussion of how the station changed the focus of its newscast, see John Lansing, "The News Is the News, Right? Wrong! 'Family Sensitive' Shows Another Way," *Poynter Report*, Fall 1994, pp. 6–7.
15. Joe Schlosser, "Death along a Highway," *Broadcasting & Cable*, May 4, 1998, p. 12.
16. Dan Trigoboff, "Shooting Raises Coverage Issues," *Broadcasting & Cable*, January 31, 2000, p. 13.
17. Quoted in ibid.
18. "Local TV: Mayhem Central," *U.S. News & World Report*, March 4, 1996, pp. 63–64.
19. Quoted in Joe Holley, "The Waco Watch," *Columbia Journalism Review*, May/June 1993, p. 53.
20. Ibid., p. 52.
21. Quoted in ibid.
22. Ibid.
23. See Larry Grossman, "The Face of Terrorism," *Quill*, 74, 1986, p. 38.
24. For a more complete list and discussion of such guidelines, see Jay Black and Bob Steele, "Beyond Waco: Reflections and Guidelines," *Journal of Mass Media Ethics* 8, no. 4 (1993): 244–245.
25. Dan Trigoboff, "When a Reporter Is Really a Cop," *Broadcasting & Cable*, June 19, 2000, p. 4.

26. This is the view of the Poynter Institute's Bob Steele, who has written guidelines for crisis reporting distributed by the Radio Television News Directors Association (ibid, p. 5). These guidelines were reprinted on p. 18 of the April 26, 1999, issue of *Broadcasting & Cable.*

27. Quoted in Trigoboff, "When a Reporter Is Really a Cop."

28. Ed Bishop, "J-School Paper Criticized for Breach of Ethics, Cooperating with Police," *St. Louis Journalism Review,* December 1991–January 1992, pp. 1, 9.

29. Jennifer Vineyard, "Britney Spears Removes Suicide Plot from 'Everytime' Video," MTV.com, at http://www.mtv.com/news/articles/1485729/20040312/spears_britney.jhtml (downloaded March 18, 2004).

30. Deni Elliott, "Mass Media Ethics," in Alan Wells (ed.), *Mass Media and Society* (Boston: Heath, 1987), pp. 66–67.

31. For example, see *Olivia N. v. NBC; Zamora v. Columbia Broadcasting System et al.,* 480 F. Supp. 199 (S.D. Fla. 1979); *DeFilippo v. National Broadcasting Co. et al.,* 446 A.2d 1036 (R.I. 1982); *Herceg v. Hustler,* 13 Med. L. Rptr. 2345 (1987). The one notable exception in which a media defendant was held negligent is *Weirum v. RKO General, Inc.,* 539 P.2d 36 (1975). In this case a radio station was held liable for having broadcast a promotional contest that led to the death of a motorist.

32. John Leland, "Just Say Maybe," *Newsweek,* November 1, 1993, p. 52.

33. Ibid.

34. "Cheers and Jeers," *TV Guide,* August 18, 2001, p. 10.

35. David Bauder, "MTV Restricts Airing of Pop Song about Pot," AP dispatch published in *The Advocate* (Baton Rouge, LA), August 24, 2001, p. 10A.

36. See Betsy Streisand, "Network Noodling: Who Controls Content?" *U.S. News & World Report,* January 24, 2000, p. 26; Paige Albiniak, "TV's Drug Deal," *Broadcasting & Cable,* January 17, 2000, pp. 3, 148.

37. Streisand, "Network Noodling."

38. Ibid.

39. Betsy Streisand, "Cents, Censorship, and Videotape," *U.S. News & World Report,* January 31, 2000, p. 24.

40. David Bauder, "Study Says TV Violence Almost Double That of 4 Years Ago," AP dispatch published in *The Advocate* (Baton Rouge, LA), December 12, 2003, p. 24C.

41. For example, see comments by Proctor & Gamble spokeswoman Gretchen Briscoe in Paige Albiniak, "Media: Littleton's Latest Suspect," *Broadcasting & Cable,* May 3, 1999, p. 14, and comments from Motion Picture Association President Jack Valenti in Paige Albiniak, "Television under Fire Again," *Broadcasting & Cable,* May 10, 1999, p. 11.

42. Quoted in Paige Albiniak, "Violent Media, Violent Kids?" *Broadcasting & Cable,* July 31, 2000, p. 14.

43. Suzanne Smalley, "This Could Be Your Kid," *Newsweek,* August 18, 2003, p. 47.

44. Quoted in John Leo, "Stonewalling Is Not an Option," *U.S. News & World Report,* June 19, 1995, p. 19.

45. One study found an increase in the number of homicides after stories about prizefights, in which violence is rewarded, and a decrease in homicides after stories about murder trials and executions, in which violence is punished. See David P. Phillips and John E. Hensley, "When Violence Is Rewarded or Punished: The Impact of Mass Media Stories on Homicide," *Journal of Communication* 34 (Summer 1984): 101–116.

46. John Leo, "Foul Words, Foul Culture," *U.S. News & World Report,* April 22, 1996, p. 73, quoting Bob Garfield, a columnist for *Advertising Age.*

47. Ibid.

48. Phil Mushnick, "Unnecessary Roughness," *TV Guide,* October 24, 1998, p. 38.

49. Ibid.

50. Betsy Streisand, "Slasher Movies the Family Can Enjoy," *U.S. News & World Report,* October 9, 2000, p. 50.

51. Paige Albiniak, "Media Take a Pounding," *Broadcasting & Cable,* September 18, 2000, pp. 16, 18.

52. Steve McClellan, "The Scarlet R," *Broadcasting & Cable,* September 18, 2000, p. 15.

53. "Cheers and Jeers," *TV Guide,* October 7, 2000, p. 11.

54. "Do Gang Ads Deserve a Rap?" *Newsweek,* October 21, 1991, p. 55.

55. Ibid.

56. "Jerry Springer: Punching the Envelope," *Broadcasting & Cable,* December 15, 1997, p. 33.

57. Ibid.

58. Joe Schlosser, "'Jerry Springer': Scraps or Scripts?" *Broadcasting & Cable,* April 27, 1998, p. 10.

59. For example, see Clarence Page, "Springer's TV Show Debases Us All," syndicated column published in the *The Advocate* (Baton Rouge, LA), April 30, 1998, p. 11B; Kevin V. Johnson, "Show Battles Way to Top, Takes Care in Sweeps Fray," *USA Today,* pp. 1D–2D.

60. Dan Trigoboff, "Educators Don't Want to Keep 'Springer' after School," *Broadcasting & Cable,* March 30, 1998, p. 11.

61. Lindsey Tanner, "Show to Cut Violence after Boycott Threat," Associated Press dispatch published in *The Advocate* (Baton Rouge, LA), May 1, 1998, p. 4A.

62. Jeff Jacoby, "Hate Speech of the Left," *Boston Globe,* December 28, 2003, p. D11.

63. See Donna Petrozzello, "Talk Show Hosts Dispute Clinton's Criticism," *Broadcasting & Cable,* May 1, 1995, pp. 6–7.

64. David Stout, "Broadcast Suspensions Raise Free-Speech Issues," *New York Times,* April 30, 1995, p. 18.

65. For a more exhaustive definition and discussion of hate speech, see Richard Alan Nelson, *A Chronology*

and Glossary of Propaganda in the United States (West-port, CT: Greenwood, 1995).

66. Stout, "Broadcast Suspensions Raise Free-Speech Issues."

67. Richard Reeves, "We're Talking Ourselves to Death," *The Advocate* (Baton Rouge, LA), May 2, 1995, p. 6B.

68. Mark D. Harmon, "Hate Groups and Cable Public Access," *Journal of Mass Media Ethics* 6, no. 3 (1991): 149–150. For a brief discussion of the use of cable by extremist groups, see "Extremist Groups Spread Message via Cable Access," *Broadcasting & Cable,* May 1, 1995, p. 8.

69. Harmon, "Hate Groups and Cable Public Access," pp. 148–149.

70. E.g., Jessie Burchette, "County Officials Say No to Cable TV Idea," *Salisbury Post* online edition, Feburary 17, 2001, at http://www.salisburypost.com/2001feb/021701f.htm (downloaded January 3, 2004).

71. Hate, Murder and Mayhem on the Net," *U.S. News & World Report,* May 22, 1995, p. 62.

72. Janice Kaplan, "Are Talk Shows Out of Control?" *TV Guide,* April 1, 1996, p. 10.

73. Ibid, p. 12.

74. Sharon Cohen, "Radio Stunts, Reports Push Medium to Edge," *The Advocate* (Baton Rouge, LA), April 16, 1994, p. 13A.

75. Under a 1980 agreement with the Screen Actors Guild, producers are not required to invite the unit's field representatives on their sets, but if they do they are entitled to include the unit's seal of approval in their closing credits.

76. See "Radio Journalist Pleads Guilty to Child Porn Charges," online dispatch from the Associated Press and Nando.net, July 7, 1998 (accessed July 29, 1998), available at http://www.techserver.com/newsroom/ntn/info/070798/info4_20726_noframes.html; Raju Chebium, "Journalist Seeks First Amendment Protection in Child-Porn Case," online AP dispatch, April 28 1998 (accessed July 29, 1998), available from http://dispatches.azstarnet.com/joe/1998/0511jour.htm

77. Some of the ideas for this case were derived from Phil Mushnick, "On Sports: End of the Innocence," *TV Guide,* August 18, 2001, pp. 44–45.

78. Ibid., p. 45.

79. Some of the information in this case study was taken from the following source: Kevin Whitelaw, "Terrorists on the Web: Electronic 'Safe Haven,'" *U.S. News & World Report,* July 22, 1998, p. 46.

80. Edward Mendelson, "The Word and the Web," *New York Times Book Review,* June 2, 1996, p. 35.

10

Morally Offensive Content: Freedom and Responsibility

SOCIETY'S SURVEILLANCE OF OFFENSIVE MATERIAL

Near the close of the 2004 Super Bowl's halftime show, pop star Justin Timberlake popped off part of singer Janet Jackson's corset, exposing her right breast. Michael Powell, chair of the Federal Communications Commission (FCC), called the stunt "classless, crass and deplorable" and promised an immediate investigation.[1] Both CBS, which broadcast the game, and the show's producer, MTV, issued public apologies, but the forces of moral rectitude had been unleashed. In the weeks following the Janet Jackson affair broadcasters inserted tape delays on some live broadcasts and reviewed their entertainment fare for material that might further provoke the wrath of the FCC. This was followed by a congressional investigation, in which the theme was: *What happened to family TV?*[2]

When 10-year-old Anders Urmacher, a student at the Dalton School in New York City, received a mysterious e-mail file from a stranger on his computer, he downloaded it and then called his mother. When Linda Mann-Urmacher opened the mysterious file, the screen filled with ten small pictures depicting couples engaged in various acts of sodomy, heterosexual intercourse, and lesbian sex. A shocked Mann-Urmacher said, "I was not aware that this stuff

was on-line. Children should not be subjected to these images."[3]

In January 1997 freelance news photographer William W. Lewis was on hand to capture the carnage resulting from the ambush of two sheriff's deputies by a deranged man with an M-1 rifle in Riverside County, California. Among his photographs was a horizontal shot with the upper torso and head of a slain officer sprawled face up, with arms outstretched. Lewis sold his work to the *Press-Enterprise* in Riverside, which ran the photo of the dead officer on the front page. The decision prompted 800 calls of concern and outrage from readers, relatives of the dead men, and law enforcement officials accusing the newspaper of a lack of sensitivity.[4]

Among the featured films at the 2003 Cannes Film Festival was *Irreversible,* a revenge story that included a lengthy rape scene in a pedestrian underpass in which a pimp violated Monica Bellucci while repeatedly slamming her bloodied head against the concrete. Women viewers at the Festival were outraged and walked out of the film, which also included other grotesque renditions of violence, leading *Newsweek* magazine to ask: "When does the painfully unpleasant become the totally unwatchable?"[5]

Indecency at the Super Bowl, pornography in cyberspace, gruesome photographs in the local newspaper, violent cinematic depictions of rape and mayhem—just a few examples of controversial subjects that reflect people's sensitivity to what might be described as morally offensive content. Any material that offends the moral standards of certain segments of society could conceivably fall into this category, and thus the issues are often intertwined with those relating to the antisocial behavior dealt with in Chapter 9. Nevertheless, the continuing debate over the mass distribution of morally offensive material justifies a separate chapter devoted to an exploration of these concerns.

Society's watchdogs are never far from center stage when it comes to their moral surveillance of the nation's mass media. In some respects, the issue of offensive content is one of the most troublesome ethical dilemmas for media practitioners. The ethical dimensions of this problem are made more apparent by the fact that virtually all morally offensive content, except for the most blatant forms of obscenity, are protected by the First Amendment. Although most ethical transgressions prompt complaints only from media critics and perhaps those most affected, condemnations of morally offensive material can sometimes lead to mass protests and demonstrations. For example, some might object to pornography on the ground that it offends the community's standards of decency. Others object to shocking photographs published in the local paper. Religious conservatives protest the local showing of a movie they consider to be blasphemous. Some even object on moral grounds to ads for abortion clinics or beer and wine commercials. Morally offensive content is a broad and perhaps ill-defined subject.

Attempting to placate the moral sensibilities of all segments of society is, of course, impossible and even undesirable. Any such strategy would deprive our culture of its artistic vitality and render it aesthetically sterile. Nevertheless, media practitioners must be sensitive to these concerns and should blend their legal rights under the First Amendment with a healthy dose of social responsibility.

PORNOGRAPHY, INDECENCY, AND MORAL RESPONSIBILITY

Sex sells! Just consider these facts, as reported in the *New York Times:* The $4 billion Americans spend on video pornography is greater than the annual revenue accrued by any of the professional baseball, basketball, and football leagues. Americans pay more for pornography in a year than they do for movie tickets and all the performing arts combined. The Internet porn business may be one of the few to keep expanding in the midst of the dot-com collapse.[6]

With such a phenomenal marketplace presence, it is clear that fascination with pornography is not the exclusive preserve of the social misfits. It is ubiquitous and defies demographic profiling. And yet, pornography's alleged corrosive effects on society's moral infrastructure continue to occupy a prominent position on the nation's public agenda. Pornography's detractors predict a moral Armageddon if such fare is not vanquished from our cultural menu, while their opponents respond with charges of censorship.

The Supreme Court has ruled that obscenity is not constitutionally protected speech, but it has frequently struggled to define it. The justices may come to the Court with impressive legal credentials, but they are not literary critics. After all, one person's pornography may be another's art. A former justice, Potter Stewart, in a candid concession to pragmatism, once observed that he could not define obscenity but knew it when he saw it.[7]

One theme that underlies all of the Court's pronouncements on obscenity is that the justices are concerned with the idea that obscenity is harmful to society and may adversely affect a community's quality of life. In this respect, the Court's pronouncements on obscenity are more than just constitutional dogma. They also reflect a profound concern with a community's *ethical* standards.[8]

As the debate over obscenity continues, new emotional and political alliances have emerged. Some feminists aligned themselves with the forces for moral restraint by condemning pornography as an expression of the notion of male supremacy.[9] In the 1980s they won passage of some community ordinances that defined pornography as the depiction of the sexual subordination or inequality of women through physical abuse, but such legal successes were short-lived as the federal courts declared these ordinances to be unconstitutional.

During the Reagan administration, Attorney General Edwin Meese kept the debate over obscenity in the public consciousness by releasing the final report of the U.S. Attorney General's Commission on Pornography, commonly referred to as the Meese Report. Meese was the Reagan administration's point man in the "war on crime," and before the report was even released there were charges that the commission had already made up its mind about the detrimental effects of obscenity.[10] Although the panel was accused, even by some of its own members, of questionable interpretations of social scientific evidence and was unable to establish a definitive link between some kinds of pornography and sexual violence, some groups used the study to pressure stores to remove sexually explicit material.

The Constitution has been an enduring instrument for protection of *legal* rights, but it has not always proved to be a worthy moral compass, as evidenced by the continuing debates over abortion and the death penalty. Some states, for example, have enacted laws regulating the dissemination of recorded music containing indecent or obscene lyrics. There have been prosecutions of music-store owners for allegedly violating these laws. But despite the legal issues reflected in these cases, the moral debate will rage on in those communities that feel strongly that such music is offensive to societal mores.

Indeed, the inevitable failure of legal assaults on the dissemination of controversial content substantiates the significance of the ethical arena for confronting what some believe to be artistic pathologies. The campaign against pornography and other offensive material that degrades women is a case in point. Consider, for example,

the proactive stance of a group from the National Organization of Women, including Gloria Steinem, Betty Friedan, and Melba Moore, which picketed the New York City offices of Time Warner to protest the distribution of a music video titled *Smack My Bitch Up. Smack,* the video featuring the latest single from the British band Prodigy, was aired on MTV and contained lyrics that seemed to promote violence against women. The video also marked the first time in MTV's sixteen-year history that the music channel had allowed female frontal nudity. But the frequent sight of breasts was not the only thing that attracted the attention of the guardians of media morality. The clip, according to an account in *TV Guide,* forced "the viewer to binge vicariously from the point of view of a clubgoer who snorts drugs, belts liquor, gropes women's breasts, picks fights, vomits repeatedly and has consensual sex with a stripper." And the protagonist in this bizarre video spectacle was a woman. The Prodigy video was eventually pulled from the MTV rotation, but the music video channel denied that the protest had anything to do with its decision.[11]

In the past decade, hip-hop music, which has a broad appeal to a teen audience and has never been afraid to challenge the conventions of moral propriety, has been singled out for its advocacy of antisocial and morally offensive behavior. However, to restore some measure of respectability to their craft, some prominent rappers have renounced violence, "embracing philanthropy and donning pinstripe suits."[12] But as noted in the *New York Times,* some top acts have also crossed over to the "adult aisle":

[I]n deliberate defiance of this newfound respectability, some top acts have begun to pursue a less-than-wholesome sideline: commercial pornography. Pop music has always pushed sexual boundaries, of course, and rap has never shied away from gleefully smutty lyrics. But now, some stars are moving beyond raunchy rhetoric into actual pornographic matter, with graphic videos, explicit cable TV shows and hip-hop-themed girlie magazines.[13]

The practice of journalism resides at the core of First Amendment values, but reporters are often confronted with an ethical quandary when it comes to including material that might offend the moral sensibilities of the audience. Should a videotape of nudity, for example, be included in a TV news report if such visuals contribute to the public's understanding of the story? Should public figures be subjected to a different standard from ordinary citizens when deciding whether to include quotes containing colorful and indecent language? Should offensive language be deleted from a quote or cleaned up to avoid embarrassment to the interviewee and offense to the readers or viewers?

Of course, altering a quote raises an ethical question from the standpoint of truth and accuracy. Some publications employ what they believe to be a reasonable compromise by printing the first letter of the questionable word followed by a series of dashes. TV stations often "bleep" offensive language uttered by newsworthy subjects, which again raises questions of journalistic accuracy. Many local newspapers, because of their role as a community-based family medium, are still fairly conservative on the matter of offensive and indecent language. The size and nature of the market often determine how liberal media practitioners can be toward reproducing scatological language, but most are still reluctant to challenge the public's tolerance for such material.

When public figures are concerned, and that includes professional athletes, the question of whether to report profane language becomes a matter of ethical gamesmanship. Some editors take the position that if the questionable comments are essential to the story, they should be left in. Others are more comfortable with the use of euphemisms and indirect quotes in which the offensive remarks are sanitized. This is often a close call and may depend on the news figure's status and the context in which the remarks are made. It may also depend on the specific expressions used.

Sports figures are particularly troublesome, because their interviews are often peppered with colorful expletives. Sports editors usually sanitize these remarks before publication, although some use the bleep technique as a substitute for offensive language. Such editing can be justified, according to the rule stated earlier, because the rough language found in most interviews with sports figures is seldom essential to an understanding of the story. There are occasions, of course, when an athlete's reaction to a situation is so revealing that an exact quote is justified. This decision will still depend, of course, on the level of sophistication of the readers or viewers and the particular medium involved.

Unfortunately, the sports media environment reinforces the rather unorthodox and sometimes offensive behavior of athletes themselves. Sports television is increasingly filled with rude and crude behavior, including remarks by commentators that continue to expand the bounds of ethical propriety. "We've reached the point," observed *TV Guide*'s Phil Mushnick, "where we can't tune in on a Sunday afternoon without being hit with snickering, smug and wildly inappropriate stabs at humor, most of it aimed directly at the crotch."[14] He cited as examples of this "telecrudeness" an ESPN *Sportscenter* anchor's penchant for calling good hitters "master batters," a Fox Sports Net game show's heavy reliance on sexual wisecracks and categories attached to profane expressions, and comedian Jay Mohr's debut on the same network's *NFL This Morning*, during which he noted player injuries and said he had broken his wrist two years ago and had not "been able to masturbate since." Mushnick was uncompromising in his conclusion that "sports has joined the rest of television in targeting the lowest common denominator."[15] Fair enough! But it is also true that such coarse behavior could not thrive without the forbearance of an increasingly tolerant and permissive critical mass of viewers.

English contains many words that are offensive to society's linguistic norms, but some are considered more indecent than others. Certain references to specific sexual acts and other bodily functions are usually taboo in the mainstream media, but some taboos appear to be fading. The list of words considered to be offensive has narrowed considerably. In fact, the only common bond between Anita Hill and Lorena Bobbitt may be that they both have been instrumental in journalistically legitimizing some heretofore forbidden expressions. During the Clarence Thomas hearings before the Senate Judiciary Committee, Hill's graphic live testimony captivated a national TV audience with her repeated references to "large breasts," "penis," and the porn star "Long Dong Silver."[16] Perhaps because of the seemingly clinical descriptions of Hill's allegations of sexual harassment, the words that were once considered too raunchy for radio and TV barely caused a murmur. And in 1993 when the world was treated, through extensive media coverage, to the lurid details of how Lorena Bobbitt had taken a knife to her husband's penis, there were no significant demonstrations of moral outrage. And how did news executives decide that the Bobbitt case should make the headlines? "It was a story of public interest," said Richard Wald, ABC's senior vice president for editorial quality. "There is no such thing as a totally inappropriate news story. The problem is to figure out how you should tell it."[17]

Even when the use of scatological language is deemed essential to a story, news executives frequently issue warnings to the audience. In the O. J. Simpson case, for instance, when the 911 tapes made by Nicole Simpson a few years before her murder were released, ABC chose to air the obscenity-filled tapes unedited in its *Nightline* program. Prior to the program, which airs after the late news in most markets, the network warned viewers of what they were about to hear. ABC justified its decision on the grounds that the tapes "were the real thing and they indicated his anger and her fear."[18]

These shifting journalistic sands at the national level may have resulted in some liberalization of standards at the local level. For example, the president of Arkansas State University was accused by his two secretaries of masturbating in his office. During the public hearing on the

matter, the school official denied the charges and said it was impossible for him to have an erection because he was impotent. Radio station KBTM in Jonesboro, Arkansas, included both words in its news accounts without one critical phone call. "Does this mean," news director Wayne Hoffman wondered, "that 'masturbation' and 'erection' are okay to say on the air?"[19]

Of course, the use of indecent language in electronic media raises another host of moral problems because of the intrusion of radio and TV into the privacy of the home and the presence of children in the audience. Ever since the FCC first fined a Pennsylvania radio station for broadcasting an interview with the rock musician Jerry Garcia, of the Grateful Dead, that contained several indecent phrases, the commission has been concerned about the use of offensive language on the nation's airwaves. This concern was graphically reflected in the famous "seven dirty words" case, in which the FCC upheld a complaint against a New York radio station owned by the Pacifica Foundation. The complaint involved the broadcast of a satirical recording by the humorist George Carlin in which he repeated several words that one would never hear on the public's airwaves. In its order, the FCC described the language as "patently offensive as measured by contemporary standards for the broadcast medium."[20] The fact that children are in the audience at certain times of the day was also cited as justification for channeling indecent content into certain time periods. The commission's decision was upheld by the Supreme Court in 1978, thus putting licensees on notice that they were forbidden to broadcast indecent language for shock value.[21]

To allay the fears of broadcasters that a new era of governmental oversight was about to dawn, the FCC responded not with a twenty-four-hour ban on indecent content but with a requirement that broadcasters "channel" such programming into times of the day when children are unlikely to be in the audience. Despite this "safe harbor," explicit broadcast chatter has continued unabated in other time periods, and the commission has been busy policing the nation's airwaves.

Because of its pervasive intrusion into the privacy of the home, the TV entertainment industry has been a perennial battleground for the moral soul of the nation's viewers. The prevalence of foul language and sexually explicit content in prime time, motivated more by the search for ratings than any artistic pretense, is indisputable. According to a study by the Henry J. Kaiser Family Foundation, for example, 75 percent of prime-time series featured sex in 2000, up from 67 percent the year before.[22]

In fact, the pornography industry itself has recently received its share of prime-time exposure, as exemplified by Showtime's *Family Business,* a reality series about porn star Adam Glasser, or the Fox network's *Skin* that premiered in the fall of 2003 and featured a major character as a dad who just happened to be CEO of an adult-entertainment empire. *Skin* Executive Producer Jim Leonard defends the sudden popularity of the porn plotline because it "makes us question our values." "Why do we like [the porn king] more than the guy who's trying to bring him down?" asks Leonard. "There's a paradox." However, media watchdogs, such as Robert Peters, president of Morality in Media, not surprisingly disagree. "It's desensitizing people [to porn]," responds Peters. "Let's say we had a prostitute in every sitcom, in every drama. Over time, people would begin thinking, 'Prostitution? So what!'"[23]

As the TV networks increasingly push the envelope, eroding the bounds of propriety in the process, the critics are merciless in their denunciation of what they believe to be the TV industry's shameless shredding of the nation's moral fabric. For example, Bob Garfield, a columnist at *Advertising Age,* has observed, "There are no gatekeepers left at the networks. Aside from the F-word and saying that Advil is better than aspirin, you can get away with anything now."[24] And as the *New York Times* sadly observed (correctly) in its indignation at the morally depressed

state of prime-time television reflected in just one season's network lineup, the blame must be shared by several stakeholders: the TV industry, advertisers, and parents:

> Like a child acting outrageously naughty to see how far he can push his parents, mainstream television this season is flaunting the most vulgar and explicit sex, language and behavior that it has ever sent into American homes. And as sometimes happens with the spoiled child, the tactic works: attention is being paid.
>
> Ratings are high, few advertisers are rebelling against even the most provocative shows, and more and more parents seem to have given up resisting their children in squabbles over television. Often, in a nation of two-income families and single parents, children are left home to watch whatever they want.[25]

Of course, media critiques are frequently anecdotal and focus on the most provocative themes in certain shows. Nevertheless, such programs are often the most popular and may serve as a barometer of things to come. Network executives deny they are pushing the envelope of pop culture and note that stations and cable operators are the ultimate gatekeepers in reflecting their communities' artistic tastes. Regardless, the networks, caught between the realities of gradually eroding ratings on the one hand and an assault by morally conservative critics on the other, have been proactive in attempting to keep the wolves away from their door while searching for strategies to accommodate their own economic interests. However, at least in the short-term profits are likely to trump the moral restraint in the struggle for influence in the network executive suites. Network officials, in defending their controversial offerings, point to a more permissive society in which popular culture reflects reality and parents no longer appear to be as distressed about TV vulgarity as media critics.[26]

The latest and what could prove to be the bloodiest battle over pornography and indecency is in cyberspace. As the largest and most accessible online service, the Internet represents a virtually infinite marketplace of ideas, the purest form of democracy. It is also an endless menu of some of the most perverse sexually explicit material. Although much of this material can be found in adult bookstores, pornography is different on computer networks, as *Time* magazine noted in a recent cover article on "cyberporn":

> You can obtain it in the privacy of your home— without having to walk into a seedy bookstore or movie house. You can download only those things that turn you on, rather than buy an entire magazine or video. You can explore different aspects of your sexuality without exposing yourself to communicable diseases or public ridicule.[27]

Much of the early debate has reverberated around the easy access to cyberporn of children, many of whom are more computer literate than their parents but may not be emotionally prepared for what they see. It is under this banner that some concerned parents are supporting government regulation, a view that many congressional representatives are only too willing to indulge. Thus far, Americans appear to be divided on the issue. But if the past is truly a prologue, the Constitution will once again prove an unworthy taskmaster in the service of moral virtue, and society's combatants will again be forced (as in the case of abortion) to wage their ethical skirmishes in the marketplace of ideas. The Internet and other computer networks will, of course, increase the accessibility of pornography for children as well as for adults. But from an ethical perspective the solution, if there is one, does not differ appreciably from that recommended to combat the pernicious influences of sex and violence on television and cable: parental control and supervision.

OFFENSIVE SPEECH

In early 2001 conservative activist David Horowitz created an ad that he hoped would spark a debate on college campuses over whether the nation should pay reparations for slavery. Instead, the ad—entitled "Ten Reasons Why Reparations for Slavery Is a Bad Idea—and Racist Too"—ignited a free speech brouhaha and prompted apologies from several student newspapers for publishing the ad and refusals by others to do so. While a few did publish it without incident, students on many campuses abandoned any pretense of civility in what they considered to be a well-justified assault on bigotry and insensitivity. For example, at the University of California at Berkeley, fifty students stormed the offices of the *Daily Californian* and demanded an apology from the paper's editors for publishing the ad,[28] Brown University students absconded with the entire press run of the *Brown Daily* in apparent protest over the ad, while at the University of Wisconsin–Madison one hundred protestors stormed the student newspaper's office and demanded the resignation of the top editor.[29] This campus controversy was reminiscent of the one that erupted several years ago with the student press publication of Bradley Smith's ad, "THE HOLOCAUST CONTROVERSY: The Case for Open Debate," in which he denied the reality of the Holocaust.

Events such as these pit the values of free speech against those of tolerance and human dignity and respect. Increasingly, speech that is "offensive" to racial or religious groups has become forbidden fruit in the marketplace of ideas. In a survey by the First Amendment Center in 2000, approximately 67 percent of the respondents felt public speech offensive to racial groups should be restricted, while 53 percent felt speech offensive to religious groups should be prohibited. "Today, the First Amendment is very much in play," said Kenneth Paulson, executive director of the Freedom Forum's First Amendment Center in a candid assessment of the survey's results.[30] Clearly free speech is on the defensive in the court of public opinion.

The issue of offensive speech has created some interesting alliances. Calls for censorship have emanated from both conservatives and liberals.

Ironically, some of the most vociferous appeals for limits on speech rights have originated on college campuses, the traditional bastions of liberalism and freedom of expression and inquiry. Many institutions of higher learning have implemented "hate speech" codes, limiting expressions offensive to minorities and women, although some of these have not withstood constitutional challenges. And as just noted, the student press has found itself at the center of this firestorm for merely serving as a forum for expression of opinions, regardless of their majoritarian appeal.

As these events illustrate, censorship is not just a legal (constitutional) issue. It remains very much an ethical one because public opinion and concerted action can be just as effective as government regulation in silencing unpopular and offensive speech. Nevertheless, proponents of societal regulation argue that free speech is just one among the hierarchy of values and that our increasing cultural diversity requires a greater emphasis upon racial, ethnic, and religious tolerance. On the other hand, their detractors observe that our experience tells us that censorship has never been a successful antidote for offensive speech. This is not to suggest, they argue, that offended groups have no right to object strongly to what they consider to be insensitive and bigoted remarks, but they should do so in the public venues available for such discourse. For example, a few well-written responses to the "reparations" ad in student newspapers would have been far more effective than assaults on the newspapers themselves.

A MATTER OF TASTE: SHOCKING AND DISTURBING VISUALS

Offensive content does not always involve indecent or obscene material. Some photographs and TV news footage are so graphic as to shock the sensibilities of the average reader or viewer. Suppose, for example, that a state official who has just been convicted of a felony calls a news conference to announce his resignation. But instead of the expected resignation announcement, he pulls a gun and, with cameras rolling, places the barrel in his mouth and pulls the trigger. Would you air this graphic footage? That was the question confronting TV news directors in Pennsylvania in January 1987, when R. Budd Dwyer, the state treasurer, convened a news conference in his office the day before his scheduled sentencing on counts of mail fraud, racketeering, and perjury. Following a brief, rambling statement critical of the justice system, the press, and the outgoing governor, he shot himself. As he slumped to the floor with blood gushing from his nose and mouth, the cameras followed him.[31]

This tape was quickly fed by satellite to stations across the state. Most news directors chose not to show this public suicide, but a few made the contrary decision. The most common reason cited by those who decided not to show the moment of death was the graphic nature of the footage. They felt it would be in bad taste and shock the audience. Closely related to these concerns was the observation that showing the suicide itself was not necessary to the reporting of the story.[32] The three stations that chose to run the footage during the noon hour defended their decision on the values of newsworthiness and immediacy. They also argued that the footage they had shown was not particularly graphic.[33]

Viewers in Alexandria, Louisiana, apparently were not offended by the live TV coverage of a sheriff's deputy, distraught over his pending divorce, who placed the barrel of a pistol to his jaw and fired, splattering blood as his body slumped. Although some objected, 80 percent of those who called the station supported the decision to air the drama.[34]

"We did not televise a suicide," KALB-TV news director Jack Frost said. "The incident we televised was a situation that put the downtown area in danger, and our public needed to be aware of that." Roy Peter Clark, senior scholar at the Poynter Institute for Media Studies, refused to second-guess Frost and said there is value in seeing events as they unfold: "That's the ultimate sense of immediacy and, in a way, you get to vicariously experience a public event that may have some danger." However, Clark acknowledged that when stations go live they relinquish some measure of editorial control, thus running the risk that harmful consequences will occur.[35]

But Pat Monk, mental health therapist at an agency near the suicide scene, criticized the station for not turning the camera away at the crucial moment. "They must question whether unstable people will fulfill their threats," she said. "You can't base your coverage on the possibility they will not."[36]

Such forays beyond what some believe to be the limits of aesthetic and dramatic propriety usually subject journalists to charges ranging all the way from poor taste to voyeurism. In deciding whether to use potentially offensive and shocking pictures, media practitioners must weigh newsworthiness against other values. Unfortunately, many editors appear to be oblivious to the impact of photos. They view them as supplements to news stories, ignoring the fact that the impact of a story is often determined by the accompanying photograph.[37]

Television news directors may be more sensitive to visual effects because of the fact that pictures are an inherent part of any TV report. News video does not always explain the meaning of a story, but it can create powerful images. Given the inevitable psychological impact of such images, it is little wonder that graphic photos of human tragedies evoke such strong reactions from the audience and even the professional community. In the Dwyer case, for example, the popular press was uniformly critical of the airing of his suicide. At one station some advertisers even withdrew their support in protest of the coverage.[38]

Following the kidnapping and decapitation of *Wall Street Journal* reporter Daniel Pearl by Arab terrorists in Pakistan, CBS News was placed on the ethical hot seat by both the government and the victim's family. Correspondent

David Martin had received a videotape from a Saudi journalist, who had downloaded it from the Internet, depicting Pearl's torture and murder at the hands of his abductors. Both the State and Justice Departments, as well as Pearl's family, asked CBS not to air the tape, which was being used to recruit radical Arabs against the United States and Israel. Nevertheless, the network, after "much deliberation," chose to broadcast the tape minus the gruesome images of the victim's slaying and decapitation.[39]

Pearl's wife characterized CBS's decision as "heartless." "It is beyond our comprehension," she said, "that any mother, wife, father or sister should have to relive this horrific tragedy and watch their loved one being repeatedly terrorized." *CBS Evening News* Executive Producer Jim Murphy responded that his news division weighed the family's feelings heavily "against what we considered our mission: to inform the public." Tom Rosenstiel, director of the Project for Excellence in Journalism, agreed. "There's nothing morally or journalistically that dictates that tape is off limits," he asserted. "The job of a journalist is to provide information to the public in a way citizens can make up their own minds. What's hard for Americans to understand is how something so horrible could appeal to other people. CBS made the decision that we need to see some of this to try and understand that."[40]

The controversial decision in the summer of 2003 to air the gruesome images of former Iraqi president Saddam Hussein's slain sons was similarly defended on the grounds of newsworthiness and relevance. News executives called the images an "integral part of their coverage of the war in Iraq." Nevertheless, some refused to air the visuals because they were too gruesome. At the Poynter Institute think tank for journalism, broadcast professional Al Tompkins urged news executives to communicate with their audiences. "If you don't use them, you should explain why," he advised. "And those that do should 'limit the usage and justify why.'"[41]

In the spring of 2004, when four American contractors were killed in Fallujah, Iraq, some newspapers chose to publish a photograph of Iraqi youngsters on a bridge in front of the mutilated and charred bodies of two of the victims. The Raleigh *News & Observer,* for example, included one of the horrific photos in its news coverage and received about 120 complaint calls and e-mails. "The *News & Observer* seldom publishes such graphic photographs," declared an editorial to its readers, "but decided to do so in this case because the scene shows the brutal reality of the day's news. In making the choice to publish, *N&O* editors decided our report of the slayings would be incomplete without one of the many photographs from the front lines."[42]

Several weeks later, after *60 Minutes II* broke the story with graphic visuals of its own, most news organizations chose to publish or broadcast some version of the highly disturbing and politically embarrassing photos of American guards at the Abu Ghraib prison indulging in the ritualistic sexual humiliation of Iraqi captives (CBS agreed to delay the broadcast by two weeks at the request of General Richard Myers, chair of the Joint Chiefs of Staff, because of a concern for the safety of American hostages and the tension surrounding the city of Fallujah[43]). However, most news organizations declined to broadcast the video of the beheading of a civilian worker, Nicholas Berg, who was beheaded apparently in retaliation for abuse of those imprisoned Iraqis. In today's multimedia environment, of course, media gatekeeping, even by the most ardent moralist, is ineffective because of the ready availability of virtually anything on the Internet. Nevertheless, the permissive and unregulated environment of the Net does not absolve media managers of the moral obligation to serve their audiences in a responsible and ethical manner.

Photographs of the casualties of war are always disturbing and often gruesome. Who would not be repulsed by the picture, shot by a photographer on assignment for *Time,* of the dead Iraqi soldier just outside Kuwait City sitting in a jeep with his head charred down to his skull[44]—or by the graphic visual evidence of the genocide in Bosnia-Herzegovina, a shocking testament to the darker side of the human experience? Of course, the ethical consequences of such agonizing decisions often extend beyond expressions of moral indignation. Americans were horrified, for example, when TV news programs aired footage of jeering Somalis dragging the body of a dead U.S. soldier through the streets of Mogadishu. Newspapers ran similar photos. Following this coverage, thousands of Americans called Capitol Hill to demand that U.S. troops be withdrawn from this ill-fated operation. Members of Congress referred to the pictures in demanding that President Clinton withdraw the troops immediately. The pictures and the public reaction precipitated a national debate about the political and ethical implications of the pictures and the media's influence on foreign policy.[45]

Of course, examples such as the Dwyer case and the casualties of combat are subjected to more public and professional scrutiny than most photographic coverage. Despite the alleged newsworthiness of such visuals, media practitioners have a moral obligation to at least consider the sensibilities of family, friends, and relatives of the victims. Nevertheless, pictures of tragedies are a staple of photojournalism, and some editors feel that because they are so compelling and so memorable, such graphic representations must be used, even at the risk of distressing readers and family members. Many scenes of auto accidents, shootings, drownings, and suicides are prizewinners in annual news photography competitions.[46]

Media gatekeepers are confronted with another decision involving taste when news coverage includes nudity. Pictures of the human body often offend the moral sensibilities of the audience, prompting charges of sensationalism. Once again, editors and news directors must balance the news value of such pictures against other considerations. Assume, for example, that a TV news crew accompanies police officers on a raid of a topless bar. Should the evening news, presented during the dinner hour, graphically depict the arrest of naked dancers? Because TV is a visual medium, these shots are arguably at the heart of the news story. Nevertheless, many audiences are offended by such journalistic candor, and some stations sanitize this kind of material by electronically blocking out the bare breasts.

Many editors refuse to run nude photographs of even those involved in newsworthy events or matters of public interest. Despite the prevalence of sexually explicit material in our society, they apparently do not believe that the public will accept nudity in their hometown newspapers. When one considers that the audience is an important ingredient in the moral reasoning process, it is difficult to fault such caution.

News managers are essentially *teleological* in their approach to publishing or airing offensive language or visuals. For an ethical journalist, the reactions of their audiences and the consequences for the family and friends of those featured in the coverage should be a dominant concern in their decision making. In deciding whether to include morally offensive material in news coverage, we should keep one guideline clearly in mind: Such visuals should not be used just for shock value or to increase circulation or ratings. These pictures should be justified according to the same rules of good journalism as any other editorial matter. They should, first, be *newsworthy*. Once the news value of such photos has been ascertained, a determination should be made on whether they are *essential* to the story. Do the graphic visuals, for example, provide significant information or understanding that would otherwise be lacking in the story? These factors should then be weighed against other competing values, such as good taste and a respect for human decency.

THE LINGERING LEGACY OF BLASPHEMY

The "crime" of blasphemy is primarily a historical artifact, but despite the fading of blasphemy from the legal arena, the ethical dimensions of the debate remain problematical. The controversy surrounding *The Last Temptation of Christ* a few years ago demonstrates the continued vigilance of religious conservatives over what they consider to be blasphemy and irreverence in the mass media. In 1998, for example, a controversy erupted over Terrence McNally's still unfinished play, *Corpus Christi,* scheduled to open at the Manhattan Theatre Club in New York. Described by its author as a "spiritual journey," the script depicted Joshua as having a long-running affair with Judas and sexual relations with the other Apostles. In response, the Catholic League for Religious and Civil Rights promised unbridled warfare if the show opened as scheduled. After a phone threat of arson, administrators of the club canceled the production but reversed themselves when famous dramatists and writers complained that the club was being intimidated into self-censorship.[47]

Such examples of radical scriptural interpretation are rare today, but when they occur unbridled passions aroused among religious conservatives can be formidable. Indeed, blasphemy and other varieties of antireligious subject matter are considered by some to be among the most offensive forms of content because they challenge the fundamental principles of religious doctrine.

However, religion is such a delicate subject that even erring on the side of caution can precipitate an unexpected audience reaction. In May 2002, for example, ABC edited the word "Jesus" out of a broadcast of *The View.* On the show, Meredith Viera noted that the daily weigh-ins of her dieting cohost, Joy Behar, had ended. "Yes, and thank you, thank you, Jesus, is all I have to say," Behar replied. The live broadcast carried her exact words, but when ABC broadcast a taped version of the show on the West Coast, "Jesus" was edited out. The bleeped word drew the indignation of the Reverend Jerry Falwell, some conservative media watchdogs, and the women whose on-air conversation was edited. ABC, which apparently has few limitations on the use of expletives in prime time, said the use ran afoul of a clear-cut network policy against using the word "Jesus" as an exclamation. "Under the circumstances, we were concerned it would be offensive to our audience," noted ABC spokeswoman Julie Hoover.[48]

The controversy over morally offensive content, perhaps more than any other media ethics issue, touches on the kind of society we want to be. Our libertarian heritage propels us in the direction of freedom. But even in an open society there are limits, and much of the ethical debate has focused on them. The ferocity of this moral dialogue would challenge even the wisdom of Socrates in forging an accommodation of competing values in the intellectual marketplace.

On the one hand, a system of ethics based on moral prudishness would lead to such austere media content that it would probably be rejected by a majority of the audience. On the other hand, absolute freedom leads to moral chaos and destruction of cultural continuity. Practically speaking, neither extreme is workable. Thus, in a diverse society the strategy should be to reach some middle ground, an accommodation between the excesses of moral prudishness and moral chaos.

THE CASE FOR MORAL LIMITS

A search for an ethical meeting of the minds on the issue of morally offensive content must begin with an understanding of the arguments for and against societal controls. One way of approaching the matter of moral limits is to note the grounds that might be advanced to justify those limits. Four liberty-limiting principles are relevant to this inquiry: (1) the *harm* principle, (2) the *paternalism* principle, (3) the *moralism* principle, and (4) the *offense* principle. Although these grounds have most often been cited to justify the legal regulation of obscenity, they are equally applicable to the control of other forms of morally offensive content.[49]

The Harm Principle

Under the first concept, based in part on the ideas of John Stuart Mill in *On Liberty,* individual liberty may be reasonably restricted to prevent *harm to others.* For example, some allege that exposure to pornography is directly related to sex crimes such as rape. Even in a libertarian society few would disagree with the harm principle as a general notion. But there is little evidence that morally offensive content causes physical or psychological harm to others. Thus, the supporters of this principle have turned their attention to the detrimental impact on cultural values and the exploitation of certain segments of society. This view is reflected in an observation from Professor Franklyn S. Haiman in *Speech and Law in a Free Society:*

> If communication is so vital to the functioning of a free society as to warrant the extraordinary protection afforded to it by the First Amendment, it must have the power—we are often reminded—for harm as well as good. If speech can enlighten, it can also exploit. If literature can enrich our values, it can also debase them. If pictures can enhance our sensitivities, they can also dull them.[50]

The harm principle does attract an interesting cast of supporters, on both the right and the left of the political spectrum. In 1986, for example, a feminist, Andrea Dworkin, testified before the Meese Commission in favor of the regulation of pornography. Invoking images of women being brutalized and even killed for the profit of pornographers, Dworkin explained, "The issue is simple, not complex. Either you're on the side of women or on the side of pornographers."[51] Such a view shows that the cause of censorship is not the exclusive preserve of conservatives or liberals.

The Paternalism Principle

Under the second principle, morally offensive content should be controlled to prevent *harm to self.* In other words, exposure to obscene and other sexually explicit matter is harmful because it dehumanizes individuals and even corrupts their value system. In common parlance we need to be protected from ourselves. If nutritionists believe that we are what we eat, then proponents of paternalism believe that we are what we read (or view).

Some accuse the media of emphasizing freedom at the expense of responsibility. For example, depictions of a wide variety of sexual behavior are a media commonplace, but the potential consequences, such as pregnancy, venereal disease, and AIDS, are featured less prominently.

The paternalistic view is reflected in the Supreme Court's admonition that individual "free will," such as the desire to view or acquire obscene works, must sometimes yield to the state's interest in protecting "the weak, the uninformed, the unsuspecting, and the gullible from the exercise of their own volition."[52]

The Moralism Principle

According to the third view, society should control morally offensive content to prevent *immoral behavior* or *the violation of societal norms.* This principle raises the question of the kinds and degrees of regulation that should be tolerated in a pluralistic society. Some believe that ready access to pornographic material, for example, encourages promiscuous sexual behavior. But even if there is no demonstrable harm from exposure to content such as pornography and blasphemy, some support societal controls merely because this material offends community standards. This is an extreme position, because it could lead to social ostracism of even those who choose to consume controversial content within the privacy of their homes.

The Offense Principle

Some argue that society is justified in restricting individual liberty to prevent *offense to others.* In this context offensive behavior is understood as behavior that "causes shame, embarrassment, discomfort, etc., to be experienced by onlookers"

in public.[53] This principle is usually employed to justify the protection of nonconsenting adults from public displays of offensive material. Likewise, objections to the publication of gruesome or disturbing photographs are usually made on the basis of taste and the desire to avoid offending the moral sensibilities of the audience. When newspapers agree to accept only listings for adult theaters but no promotional ads, or when bookstores conceal adult magazines behind the counter for sales by request only, these decisions are grounded primarily on the offense principle.

THE CASE AGAINST MORAL LIMITS

The arguments against societal censorship are based primarily on the notion of individual autonomy and a rejection of the liberty-limiting principles just described.[54] Proponents of this view have little trouble, for example, dispensing with the harm principle as a viable foundation for regulation. There is no evidence, they say, that morally offensive material harms others (for example, by causing an increase in sex-related crimes), and they claim that the so-called societal harm is so speculative as to pose no immediate threat to the cultural order.

Likewise, libertarians find that paternalists are wrong when they argue that pornographic and blasphemous material harms the individual. But even if such harm did occur, according to those who oppose restrictions, paternalism is an unacceptable liberty-limiting principle.

The principle of moralism is also rejected, because the alleged consensus on what constitutes community standards does not exist. But even if it did, moralism would be unacceptable, because standards vary tremendously from community to community. Undoubtedly, the liberal cultural environment of New York City would be anathema in the Bible Belt. In addition, reliance on such fluid and often elusive criteria imposes the majority's will without respecting individual autonomy and minority interests.

Civil libertarians also argue that "offensiveness" is an ambiguous and virtually unproductive standard both legally and ethically. Some group might be offended by any controversial content, they argue, and in a democratic society offensive content actually serves as an invigorating influence in the diversity of the marketplace. Besides, it is a rare occasion when autonomous individuals become captive audiences for such fare, and critics of offensive content often base their views on an abstraction rather than any personal knowledge or insights into the nature of the material. How many Internet users or supporters of government regulation, for example, have actually seen any of the sexually explicit material supposedly polluting cyberspace?

The anticensorship position is rather persuasive from a legal standpoint, especially in view of the Constitution's expansive protection of speech and press rights. But it remains for the ethicist—and each of us should participate in this process—to search for that balance between individual autonomy and the need for moral standards.

THE SEARCH FOR STANDARDS

The notion of morally offensive content poses a problem for deontologists. These duty-based theorists would not desire such material to become common within society. The production and distribution of offensive material just for the sake of commercial exploitation cannot be justified, because (1) the purpose of artists in producing such content does not flow from any universal moral obligation and (2) exploitation does not show the proper respect for persons as ends unto themselves.

On the other hand, deontologists also acknowledge the right to free expression.[55] Under the duty-based approach to ethical decision making, the value of actions lies in motives rather than in consequences. Artistic freedom by itself does not justify such material, but works of art that in some way contribute to cultural

enrichment should be protected. Thus, the deontologist would examine the purpose and motive of the author in producing the allegedly morally offensive work, regardless of the ultimate consequences of the material. The problem with this approach is that it requires an exploration of the vast recesses of the author's mind, a perilous and uncertain journey. Sometimes the author's motives are evident, but at other times they are concealed.

Consequentialists (teleologists), as always, would look to the probable effects of the content. So far there does not appear to be any demonstrable physical or psychological harm resulting from the consumption of some forms of morally offensive material, such as obscenity. Nevertheless, a teleologist must still consider the more fundamental effects on societal values and attitudes. For example, does the viewing of sexually violent pornography result in the degradation and subordination of women in society's collective consciousness?

If there is no demonstrable harm to others or to society, perhaps censorship is unwarranted. Of course, teleologists rest more comfortably on this position than do deontologists, because they are not really concerned with the motives of the author but only the consequences. And some believe that even hard-core pornography, regardless of whether it is produced for the purposes of commercial exploitation, can have beneficial effects. For example, G. L. Simons, an Englishman who has written extensively on various aspects of human sexuality, believes that exposure to pornography can aid normal sexual development and that it can invigorate sexual relationships.[56] But even if one were to reject Simons's observations, a teleologist might conclude that the consequences of censorship are fraught with dangers in that some material possessing social value might be swept aside with that containing no demonstrable literary or cultural utility.

Aristotle's golden mean, on the other hand, seeks the middle ground between the excesses of moral prudishness and moral chaos. An ethicist, applying the golden mean, would examine the content, the medium of distribution, and the audience to which it is directed. The real centerpiece of the golden mean is "information and reasonable control." Distributors of potentially offensive content have a moral obligation to provide consumers with adequate information and warnings so that they can make rational choices about their reading or viewing. The film ratings system and the disclaimers included at the beginning of controversial network programs are two well-known examples.

The principle of reasonable control ensures the availability of material for consenting adults while protecting the sensibilities of nonconsenting adults and children. Zoning laws, bans on public promotions for offensive material, and the placement of adult magazines behind the counters at retail outlets would appear to be a reasonable middle ground between the excesses of prudishness and affronts to public morality.

The various media deserve different levels of control, depending on audience accessibility. Radio and TV, for example, are still predominantly family media and are almost ubiquitous. Newspapers, magazines, movies, and books, on the other hand, require consumers to make more active and conscious decisions.

Where children and unconsenting adults are concerned, greater controls would also be justified. This is the principle on which the FCC has built its programming standards regarding indecent content, as evidenced in the Pacifica case described earlier. But the technology that has made possible the information superhighway has also challenged traditional ethical approaches and has precipitated a public debate about its role as an instrument of cultural enrichment. Thus, the old strategies may no longer be feasible as distinctions among media rapidly disappear and all communication becomes increasingly electronic. The Internet is a classic example, as proponents of regulation argue that cyberspace should be governed according to the "broadcast" model, whereas free speech advocates favor a "print" model with little or no regulation.

MORALLY OFFENSIVE CONTENT: HYPOTHETICAL CASE STUDIES

The following cases afford the opportunity to apply the ethical guidelines described here to the media distribution of what some consider to be morally offensive content. The issues surrounding the production and dissemination of pornography and other varieties of material that offend the moral sensibilities of some segments of the audience are among the most emotional and contentious confronting media practitioners. It is a classic confrontation between the libertarians and the proponents of governmental paternalism. You may have personal feelings toward such material, but in resolving these ethical dilemmas, try to keep an open mind, and apply the principles of sound moral reasoning outlined in Chapter 3 to the facts of these cases.

CASE STUDIES

▶ **CASE 10-1**

The College Newspaper Columnist as Resident "Sexpert"

San Fernando State University was hardly a citadel of Puritanism, but Cecelia Shaw's weekly column for the university's student-run newspaper, *The* *Daily Post*, had morally polarized the usually docile student body. The 24-year-old Shaw held a master's degree in human sexuality and was a first-year doctoral student in clinical psychology, unusual and impressive credentials for a regular contributor to the paper's typically diverse op-ed page. The editor of *The Daily Post*, Marielle Sanchez, had approved Shaw's controversial column, *Sex Talk*, with some reservations but felt confident that Shaw's insights would contribute significantly to the sex education of the campus's more ignorant or naïve residents. The editor's misgivings were also assuaged by the knowledge that her paper was one of a small but growing number of college publications with writers who were willing to elevate the students' interest in human sexuality to a level of public discourse.

Sex Talk was a fascinating assortment of humorous anecdotes, coarse language, and uninhibited advice on the most intimate features of human sexuality. Shaw was not insensitive to the possibility of moral objections to her candid commentary and had inaugurated her column with such mundane topics as birth control and "the first time." Despite a breezy writing style punctuated by periodic flashes of humor and satire, the sex columnist attempted to preserve the serious tenor of her essays on human sexuality.

But by the fourth week she had moved decisively into heretofore forbidden territory, regaling her readers with reflections on such topics as masturbation, multiple orgasms, oral sex, and even anal sex. Her commentaries were not subtle but provided vivid descriptions of the various sexual techniques under review. Nevertheless, Shaw balanced her more sensitive topics with discussions of sexual health, reflecting at times a degree of clinical detachment, but this attempt at moderation went virtually unnoticed by those who were offended by the more unconventional sexual discussions. Predictably, Shaw's candid incursion into previously taboo sexual terrain precipitated an outpouring of both student approbation and moral censure. Her supporters—and that included a significant percentage of the student body—applauded her moral courage in sexually educating her young readers while her shocked critics accused her of encouraging unconventional sexual experimentation. Some indicted the paper and its editorial staff for publishing the column as a means of boosting readership and circulation. The paper's website became the most popular venue for this spirited exchange, but some employed the more traditional forum of letters to the editor. Many of the *Post*'s e-mail messages expressed approval of Cecilia Shaw's column, but others condemned her writings, often with personal attacks upon the "sexpert" herself. The

advertising staff reveled in the enlarged circulation that accompanied the debut of Shaw's popular but controversial column. "Sex is a great marketing tool," one enthusiastic staff member observed.

The campus brouhaha did not escape the attention of parents and donors, some of whom assailed the university administration for what they perceived to be a lack of moral leadership. In an interview with a local television reporter, university president Myron Beck had expressed misgivings about the column but promised to stay above the fray to avoid accusations of censorship. Nevertheless, as *Sex Talk* became increasingly graphic and the litany of complaints escalated, Beck privately urged the student newspaper's adviser, Ralph Larkin, to exert his influence with the editorial staff to either terminate the column or at least moderate its more offensive commentaries. As *The Daily Post*'s adviser, Larkin had assiduously avoided any appearance of paternalism and had confined himself to rendering advice on matters of style and story selection. Nevertheless, he was not unsympathetic to the president's concerns and the challenges of defending *Sex Talk* as a notable contribution to the campus newspaper's journalistic mission. He promised Beck that he would discuss the matter with the paper's editor.

"This is your decision, Marielle," Larkin assured his talented editor as he convened an impromptu staff meeting in his office on the first floor of the student union, which housed the rather modest editorial offices of *The Daily Post*. They were joined by managing editor Richard Lentz, a passionate defender of Cecelia Shaw's controversial column.

"As you know, *Sex Talk* has generated a lot of discussion on and off campus," Larkin began in his typically understated manner. "We've been inundated with mail, both supportive and critical, but the administration is also on the defensive with some outside the campus community. We need to at least discuss the future of this column as a regular feature in *The Daily Post*."

"We should rally behind Shaw and her column," Lentz replied without hesitation. "Her remarks may be too graphic for some, but *Sex Talk* provides some much-needed information to our student body. Many of them come from families where such topics as oral sex and masturbation are never discussed. They are taboo subjects. Besides, those who are offended don't have to read this column."

Larkin was ambivalent about the saliency of Shaw's column as an educational vehicle and continued his role of in-house critic. "Many of our readers, judging by our mail and letters to the editor, are offended," he correctly noted. "Is this really the role of a campus newspaper, to offer this kind of information and advice to students who are still in various stages of sexual maturation? What does this have to do with journalism?"

"*Sex Talk* may be uninhibited and offensive to some," replied Lentz, "but it still serves a valid journalistic purpose. Shaw provides information that is unavailable to our students from other sources, including their parents. And Shaw is qualified to comment on the subjects she writes about. She is performing a valuable public service to our student body."

But Larkin was unmoved by what he perceived to be an uncompromising posture. "I'm sure some students enjoy this uninhibited discussion of sex," remarked Larkin, "but keep in mind that student fees supplement our advertising revenues. Our students are stakeholders in this ethical decision. We should serve all students. And judging by our e-mail and letters to the editor, Shaw has a lot of critics. Should student fees support such content that is purely sensational and appeals to the prurient interest of some students and yet has such marginal value from a journalistic perspective?"

"Some of the material is coarse," admitted Lentz, "but it deals with an aspect of human sexuality seldom discussed in public. But what's more, the column is also laced with information on sexual health. The critics have chosen to focus on only the more risqué content."

"The risqué material overshadows the discussion on sexual health," responded Larkin. "In this respect, it trivializes human sexuality. Some of Shaw's critics even complain that she is attempting to legitimize an otherwise indecent column by sugar-coating it with material of a more mundane sexual nature. The fact remains that this column is offensive to many of our readers and does not concern a matter of public importance. Sexual practices are private matters. As a journalistic enterprise, *Sex*

Talk is suspect. I recommend that it either be dropped or that Shaw be required to refrain from including the more offensive material."

"I disagree with your characterization that Shaw's content trivializes human sexuality," declared Lentz, who was unwilling to concede the moral high ground to his older and more mature ethical adversary. "The fact that controversial topics are discussed within a sometimes humorous or light-hearted context does not trivialize the subject. This is simply an effective device to connect with the college audience. Shaw's purpose is not to titillate the readers but to provide much-needed information not readily available from other popular sources. What's wrong with that?"

"If students want to know about oral sex and other such topics," replied Larkin, "there are ample sources for them to go to on their own. Besides, many of the ideas discussed in *Sex Talk* are considered unconventional sexual practices by some of our readers. It's an affront to their moral sensibilities. What Shaw is doing is certainly not central to our journalistic mission as a forum for student information and expression. We could drop this column tomorrow without damaging our credibility with our readers."

Marielle Sanchez had listened attentively to this spirited exchange between her paper's managing editor and Ralph Larkin, the dedicated adviser of *The Daily Post*. She wasn't entirely sure as to whether Larkin was arguing from his own conviction or simply serving as a surrogate for the university's president. She agreed with Larkin that dropping the column based upon the editorial staff's independent determination that it provided little in the way of public service would not damage the paper's credibility, but terminating *Sex Talk* because of student or public pressure might.

Sanchez had remained silent because she wanted to internalize both points of view and digest the arguments advanced in favor of each. As student editor, she was about to assume the role of moral agent in confronting a contentious and delicate ethical dilemma. If she sided with Larkin and terminated the column or ordered that its content be diluted, Sanchez would be accused of surrendering to the forces of moral prudishness. On the other hand, if she remained steadfast in her support of Shaw's contentious column, she would stand accused of supporting moral anarchy and pandering to the lowest common denominator on the editorial pages of the student newspaper. As a student herself, Sanchez experienced some discomfort at Cecelia Shaw's unvarnished discussions of human sexuality, but in rendering her ethical judgment she felt an obligation to consider the interest of her paper and those of both the supporting and dissenting voices of the university community.

THE CASE STUDY

Yale columnist, others take sex out of the sack! This headline from the fall of 2002 trumpeted a growing trend among college publications to "detail the trials and tribulations of a favorite college pastime."[57] The authors of these unfiltered sex columns range from undergraduate students to those with graduate degrees who are more likely to take a clinical approach to their discussion of human sexuality.

In this case, the resident "sexpert" does in fact bring some graduate-level expertise to her commentary, but she obviously understands the market necessity of appealing to her youthful readers' natural curiosity and sexual impulses. She does not hesitate to invite her readers to partake of the heretofore forbidden fruit of public discourse on human sexuality. However, as Cecelia Shaw and the student newspaper's editor have discovered, the presumed permissiveness of the college generation does not necessarily extend to explorations of such sensitive topics as anal and oral sex. Even those who are sexually active might blush at such candor on the op-ed page of *The Daily Post*. Nevertheless, *Sex Talk* clearly has its share of supporters among the more sexually liberated readers as reflected in the paper's e-mail, website, and letters to the editor. The university's administration is obviously uncomfortable with the disapproving reaction of its off-campus critics but has left it to the good judgment of the student newspaper's staff to determine the future of the publication's controversial column.

The frank discussion of what some consider unorthodox (or offensive) sexual practices might be an affront to the moral sensibilities of some readers, but as the paper's editor, Marielle Sanchez must also consider countervailing values. Does *Sex Talk*, for example, provide a true public service to the campus community? In other words, does it have journalistic merit? Regardless of journalistic merit, can Sanchez ethically defend the column's survival based strictly on market appeal? Of course, if the editor insists on confining Shaw's commentaries to clinical discussions of human sexuality and deleting the more coarse and graphic content, this might result in an Aristotelian solution (i.e., the golden mean), but it would also put *Sex Talk*'s popularity at risk.

For the purpose of examining this moral dilemma, put yourself into the shoes of student editor Marielle Sanchez, and applying the SAD model of moral reasoning in Chapter 3, render your own decision in this case.

 ## CASE 10-2

A Condom Crusade Takes on the Vatican[58]

"Sexual abstinence has been a colossal failure, and it's irresponsible to continue to promote such a puritanical policy on birth control and safe sex," declared Hillary Parker, chair of Catholics For Individual Choice, a lay group. She leveled this broadside at Mary Lopex, senior account executive for Cardoza and Isaacson, one of Boston's newest but rapidly growing public relations firms.

Parker's organization had for several years been a dissident voice in the intramural controversy among Catholics over the Vatican's policy on birth control and the use of condoms. They had accommodated themselves to the realities of a more permissive society and embraced a utilitarian perspective on the role of condoms in preventing unwanted pregnancies and disease, including the AIDS virus. While abstinence had not resonated with contemporary American society as a moral norm, in Parker's view, Catholics For Individual Choice focused its energies on the practical consequences of unsafe sex, mainly unwanted pregnancies and the transmission of the AIDS virus.

In this view, condoms were an indispensable tool in combating these social pathologies. However, the Vatican, through the local diocese, had made its displeasure known concerning any Catholic lay group that advocated the use of condoms, even in third world countries where AIDS was known to be of epidemic proportions. The Catholic lay group's views were clearly offensive to both the Church's hierarchy and even many of the Catholic faithful.

Catholics For Individual Choice had been inaugurated as a fairly modest effort to challenge the Catholic Church's firm resistance to altering its policy on artificial means of birth control, including condoms, but had quickly expanded its agenda to include a concern for safe sex, with particular attention to the AIDS virus. With a rapidly growing membership, and hence a more secure financial base, Parker's organization sought professional public relations counsel to assist them in waging their campaign both domestically and in some foreign markets, particularly the third world. Parker was hoping that Cardoza and Isaason, with its growing reputation as an aggressive advocate for its diverse array of corporate clients, would become an ally of Catholics For Individual Choice in promoting its controversial agenda. Parker had contacted the PR firm and was directed to the senior account executive, Mary Lopez, as the initial gatekeeper in determining whether to forge a professional alliance between Cardoza and Isaacson and the Catholic lay group.

Lopez met briefly with Hillary Parker and told her she would forward the organization's request to the senior partner, Anthony Cardoza, for final disposition. However, Cardoza did not incline toward the autocratic, and he usually sought counsel from his diverse array of energetic and talented staff members. Lopez and the firm's junior partner, Lydia Isaacson, provided Cardoza with the requisite point-counterpoint in considering the merits of Parker's petition.

"I have my doubts about taking this account," declared Lopez, a devout Catholic, as the meeting commenced in Anthony Carodoza's lavishly decorated office. "Promoting condom usage over abstinence is morally offensive to many conservative Catholics. It is certainly offensive to the Catholic hierarchy. Regardless of whether the issue is birth control or AIDS prevention, they argue that abstinence is the best policy. It's a moral issue."

"This is a controversial question," acknowledged Isaacson. "But we should not base our decision on whether to accept this account on objections from the Catholic clergy and conservative Catholics. As far as birth control is concerned, abstinence has clearly not worked. And some Catholic clergy in AIDS-blighted countries have resisted the distribution of condoms. One cardinal has even asserted that condoms actually spread AIDS. Catholics For Individual Choice would like to correct this misinformation, and I don't see any reason why we should not take them on as a client."

"The cardinal's comment that condoms actually spread AIDS may be going a little too far," conceded Lopez, "but who are we to judge the accuracy of this claim. But more troubling is the possibility that we'll be accused of being complicit in sexual promiscuity by promoting condom usage. Many school systems, under pressure from conservatives touting family values, have added abstinence to their sex education instruction. They apparently haven't given up on abstinence as a method of birth control."

"Perhaps," responded Issacson, "but teenage pregnancies continue to be a problem, and AIDS is of epidemic proportions in many parts of the world. As a public relations firm—assuming we are willing to take this account—our mission is to help solve a problem, not worry about the moral overtones of this issue."

"But we have no ethical imperative to accept this account at all," replied Lopez. "This is a hot-button issue for faithful Catholics and most Catholic clergy. The promotion of condom use as opposed to abstinence is morally offensive to them. If we accept this account, we'll be accused of being an accessory to the promotion of immoral conduct."

"I believe this is an exaggeration," declared Issacson. "The fact is that many Catholics, particularly in this country, no longer subscribe to the Vatican's doctrine on birth control. Besides, I don't see this as a moral issue at all. The fact is that abstinence has been a failure, and the responsible and practical thing to do is to acknowledge this fact and encourage condom usage."

"I don't agree with you," said Lopez. "But even if I did, I don't believe that Cardoza and Isaacson should take on this client. Condom usage is a divisive issue. I don't believe that this firm should become embroiled in this controversy. We should stick to our more traditional, corporate clients, some of whom may not be enthusiastic with this firm if we become identified with a public controversy, particularly one involving the Catholic Church. I do believe that the matter of condom usage should be discussed. This is the role of the news media and talk shows. As a faithful Catholic, I don't even have any objection to the Vatican reconsidering its position. But I don't think our firm should help influence public opinion on this issue."

Anthony Cardoza sensed that the brief exchange between his junior partner and Mary Lopez was about to come to an end and thanked them for their remarks. There was wisdom in both views, he realized, and he promised them a decision within a couple of days. "Mary, please inform Ms. Parker that we'll give her request serious consideration," he said as the meeting adjourned.

THE CASE STUDY

The client list for the public relations firm of Cardoza and Isaacson consists primarily of corporate clients. Catholic dissident Hillary Parker has approached the firm because of its reputation and the belief that they will be aggressive in promoting the cause of her organization, Catholics For Individual Choice. The discussion within the firm's executive offices, as outlined here, centers around whether Cardoza and Isaacson should enter the moral thicket of the condom controversy.

From an ethical perspective, PR firms are generally free to choose their own clients. A client may be suitable or unsuitable for a variety of reasons. Thus, there is no moral imperative to accept Hillary Parker's organization as a client. The dialogue between Isaacson and Lopez centers around the ethical "wisdom" of representing a client whose moral views are antithetical to conservative Catholics and the Catholic hierarchy. In so doing, they might be accused of somehow being complicit in promoting sexual promiscuity, even if the use of condoms

might be an important weapon in the fight against AIDS in many countries.

Lydia Isaacson argues that abstinence hasn't worked and implicit in her remarks is the notion that her firm can play an influential role in combating the social problems of unwanted pregnancies and unsafe sex. Senior Account Executive Mary Lopez responds that this is a moral issue that's better left to marketplace forces other than her public relations firm. She is concerned that a certain segment of the Catholic population will be offended by Hillary Parker's challenge to the Vatican's policy and that somehow Cardoza and Isaacson will become publicly associated with this campaign and suffer as a result.

Senior partner Anthony Cardoza is the moral agent in this case and will make the decision on whether to accept Catholics For Individual Choice as a client. For the purpose of analyzing this case, assume the role of Anthony Cardoza and, applying the moral reasoning model outlined in Chapter 3, render your decision on this matter.

▶ CASE 10-3
Live! From Death Row!

Wilbert Lacey had languished on death row for ten years, but now his rendezvous with justice was apparently at hand. His last appeal having been exhausted, Lacey awaited the inevitable enforcement of the warden's third and final death warrant. After a six-month reign of terror in the usually tranquil community of Manderville, Lacey had been convicted for the brutal slayings of three families, all of whom had been ritually dismembered and some of their body parts stored in Lacey's refrigerator. Lacey's attorney had invoked the insanity defense, but the jury was in no mood for such legal ploys and lost no time in convicting him on all counts. He was subsequently sentenced to die in the electric chair, a device that in most states has been replaced by lethal injection as a means of carrying out the death penalty.

A decade after his incarceration, feelings were still running high in Manderville, whose citizens had grown impatient with the judiciary's indulgence of the convicted murderer's interminable appeals. Nevertheless, a small cadre of death penalty foes had assembled at Hapeville State Prison, just thirty miles from Manderville, to protest this "state-sponsored brutality" and "cruel and unusual punishment" prohibited by the Constitution.

But it was Robert Eaton's unexpected invitation, not the small gathering of vocal demonstrators, that attracted the attention of the state's journalistic establishment. Eaton, the warden at the Hapeville State Prison, was an avowed supporter of the death penalty. The warden had never cultivated a close relationship with the media, but in an abrupt change in both custom and policy he announced that the execution would "be available to live TV coverage to show that swift and certain punishment awaits convicted murderers." The only conditions, according to the warden's surprise announcement, would be that only one pool camera could be installed for the event and the faces of all witnesses would be electronically blurred. Thus, as Lacey, through his attorney, pronounced himself "at peace with the Lord" and prepared to suffer the consequences of his foul deeds, the state's TV news departments found themselves pondering the ethical dimensions of an issue that was not entirely of their own making: Should they take advantage of Eaton's offer to provide live coverage of Lacey's execution?

Channel 10, one of two network affiliates in Manderville, was among the first to render its own collective moral judgment and publicly proclaimed that it would disassociate itself from the televising of such a gruesome spectacle. Rondell Hayes was pleased that his counterpart at Channel 10 was apparently not plagued by moral ambiguities in this matter, and as news director of Channel 7 in Manderville, Hayes shared his competitor's discomfort at the prospect of carrying the state's first live telecast of an execution. However, the station's assignment editor, Martha Klein, and Sydney Fielding, the producer of the late night news who would also handle the execution telecast if it were approved by station management, disagreed in their ethical assessment of the situation.

"I don't think much of this idea," said Klein unequivocally in the hastily arranged meeting with Hayes and the spirited young news producer. "The televising of an execution is just too grotesque. Our audience may be overwhelmingly in favor of the death penalty, but I don't think they're ready for this."

"The execution isn't scheduled for prime time," replied Hayes. "It'll happen around midnight. And, of course, we'll issue the usual warnings."

"A lot of people will stay up and watch out of curiosity," said Klein. "I realize that's their choice. But should we cater to the public's fascination with the macabre? And besides, if we televise this event live at midnight we'll probably wind up airing tapes of the execution on the next day's newscasts. These things have a life of their own. Our competitor has already declined to televise this execution, and they have generated a lot of publicity about their decision. Whatever the public feels about the death penalty, they certainly won't fault Channel 10 for declining the warden's invitation."

"I don't think we should take our cues from our competitor," responded Fielding who, as a news producer, had applauded the TV media's success in introducing televised coverage into the state's court system. "As journalists, I think we have an obligation to televise this execution. The print media have for many years witnessed such executions. All we're seeking is parity, and the warden is apparently willing to give it to us, even if we didn't file a petition requesting this unprecedented access to an execution. After all, the camera provides a more accurate portrayal of the event than the vivid account presented narratively by our print brethren. The people of this state convicted Lacey; they now have a right to see the results. Considering the sentiment in this state for the death penalty, our viewers might even applaud our initiative."

But Klein was unmoved, partially because of her own opposition to the death penalty and partially because she did not believe that such ghoulish renditions of the state's handiwork belonged on public display. "There's also a matter of privacy here," she said. "Lacey has been convicted, and he's about to pay his price. We'll cover the execution, just like we would any other news story. But why is it essential, from a journalistic perspective, to televise Lacey's last gasp?"

"Lacey lost his right to privacy when he murdered his victims," said Fielding in a rejoinder to what he felt was a specious argument. "And this kind of televised execution might even serve as a deterrent to others."

"But that's an ideological argument, not a journalistic one," responded Hayes. "If we make our decision on that basis, then we're making a rather subtle editorial statement. The same would be true if we decided to televise Lacey's execution on the grounds that the horrific nature of such an event might convince the public that the death penalty is immoral or at least unconstitutional. Such reasons are good from an ideological perspective, but they don't serve the cause of journalism well."

"You have a point," conceded Fielding, who was sensitive to any insinuation that his reasoning was not journalistically sound. "But we have a history of public executions in this country. This wouldn't really be that new. We have a tradition in this country that government proceedings should be open to the media and the public. And until now the TV media have been closed out."

"It's true that many executions in the nineteenth century were public events," said Klein. "But TV is different. Bringing an execution live into the privacy of the home is going too far. I'm a journalist, too, and I'm sensitive to the public's right to know and our role in fulfilling that responsibility. But there are times when other values have to be considered. Televising an execution is gruesome without any clear-cut journalistic rationale."

"I think you're overreacting," responded Fielding. "Executions are not exactly unheard of on television. Take, for example, the execution of Romanian president Ceaucescu, the beheadings in Saudi Arabia, and executions in Iraq, Iran, and Vietnam. All of these were shown on the nightly news."

Klein was willing to acknowledge this appeal to precedent but not its moral standing. "I've seen some of the footage of these executions," she said. "Most of these were fairly rapid events and even edited for broadcast. In addition, these were public events; they took place in front of news cameras. At least in recent years, with the exception of a few witnesses, executions have been conducted outside of public view in this country. And although death comes relatively quickly when

the switch is pulled, the televising of this execution will last several minutes. It will just enhance the morbid nature of the event. Besides, the fact that there have been visual news accounts of other executions does not automatically justify providing live coverage of the Lacey execution."

As Hayes listened to both the ideological and ethical arguments advanced by his producer and assignment editor, he felt emotionally fatigued. Because of the controversial nature of this matter, any proposal to go live with Lacey's execution would have to be approved by the station's manager. But he would rely heavily on Hayes's recommendation.

On a personal level, Hayes felt emotionally repulsed by the idea of televising an execution. But he also had to concede the validity of the journalistic, if not ideological, arguments advanced by Fielding. In some respects, perhaps this was just another governmental proceeding to which the media deserved to have access. On the other hand, in his mind the very nature of an execution—actually killing a human being (albeit a very wretched one) in front of a live TV camera—relegated this kind of event to a special category. Were there sound journalistic reasons, he wondered, for televising Wilbert Lacey's last moments or was this tantamount to electronic brutality?

Channel 10 had already provided its response to this question. The fact that his competitor had declined the opportunity to beam Lacey's demise into his community's living rooms weighed heavily on Hayes's mind. "What an interesting twist," he thought as he began to ponder his ethical dilemma. "Normally I have to worry about taking a certain course of action because of what our competitor might *do*. In this case, I'm concerned about our own conduct because of what the other station is *not* planning to do."

THE CASE STUDY

"Should a TV station broadcast an execution?" To some, this might seem like a remote possibility, and until recently it appeared they might be right. But the approval by the U.S. attorney general of closed-circuit coverage of Timothy McVeigh's execution for the families of the victims brings us one step closer. This issue was examined several years ago in a *Newsweek* article following a request by a public TV station in San Francisco to televise the execution of Robert Alton Harris, convicted of the murders of two San Diego teenagers.[59] A federal judge eventually upheld California's ban on cameras at executions, and the station's petition was denied. However, this was not the first interest displayed by the TV industry in providing visual coverage of executions. In 1977, for example, a federal appellate court upheld Texas regulations prohibiting camera coverage of executions.[60] And more recently, Phil Donahue, in another "cutting-edge" initiative, sought permission to televise an execution in North Carolina. His request was denied, but the determined Donahue turned his attention to a scheduled execution in Ohio when a county judge actually urged the media to televise the execution of a convicted double murderer.[61]

The televising of executions is not among the most hotly debated issues in newsrooms. Nevertheless, as long as the death penalty itself remains controversial and the relentless competitive pressures that have driven the industry increasingly toward the sensational continue to exist, it is probably just a matter of time before the debate begins for real. One could argue that the televising of an execution cannot be justified because it demeans respect for life and is nothing more than an electronic catharsis for those who seek vengeance.

On the other hand, at a more detached and unemotional level a journalist might argue, as did Sydney Fielding, that the issue here is one of access to governmental proceedings and that the public has a right to witness the ultimate consequence of its system of justice. This argument tracks closely the one usually offered in support of TV camera access to criminal trials. In addition, proponents of access could claim that televised executions may help to shape public attitudes (either pro or con) in the ongoing public debate about the morality of the death penalty.

Taking the position of news director Rondell Hayes, decide whether you will accept the warden's invitation and televise Wilbert Lacey's execution.

▶ **CASE 10-4**

The Resurrection Conspiracy: Blasphemy or Artistic Freedom?

François Savoir had come of age as a producer of art films in the 1970s in his native country of France with two award-winning entries in the Cannes Film Festival. The first, a rather brazen and sexually explicit portrayal of a child prostitute, had won critical acclaim for its candid and realistic exploration of the coarse underside of French society; and the second, a biting satire of French culture prior to the Revolution, had won similar accolades. These awards eventually produced offers of financial backing for other projects, the culmination of which propelled Savoir into the forefront of avant-garde film producers.

Savoir's controversial themes and cinematic techniques were a constant source of irritation to the more conservative elements of French society, and two of his films had even earned him the enmity of the Catholic Church: *Mary of Nazareth*, a viciously satirical debunking of the "myth" of the virgin birth, and *The Choir Boy*, a story of a pedophilic priest's fall from grace. However, in published interviews, while acknowledging his secular humanism, Savoir insisted that his mission was not to destroy organized religion but to "purify" it, to release it from its mystical moorings. The church's censure notwithstanding, the unrepentant filmmaker continued to garner praise from some critics for his unorthodox and occasionally exploitative assault on traditional beliefs and values.

With his artistic bona fides thus established, Savoir had immigrated to the United States in 1987 and continued his work as an artistic radical with the production of several films that satirized, often with dark humor, America's cultural foibles and social pathologies. Mainstream film studios and distributors had shunned the unconventional producer, but Savoir had succeeded in getting at least limited distribution of his films through some small, independent production houses.

The Resurrection Conspiracy was Savoir's latest and potentially most explosive work. It was offered as an alternative to the biblical account of the Crucifixion and Resurrection, an event in which politics rather than divinity was the driving force. The film began with Jesus' ministry, subsequent trial and crucifixion, followed by the frantic determination of his disciples, for political reasons, to deify their fallen leader, and then dramatically portrayed the fate of the first Christians during the first century A.D. According to Savoir's narrative, Jesus was a charismatic leader who had attracted a following that the Roman authorities viewed as a threat to public order. Because of the possibility of political insurrection, Jesus was tried for sedition and sentenced to death on the cross. Pontius Pilate then ordered that Jesus be crucified between two thieves as a sign of their contempt for any challenge to the sovereignty of Rome from the Jewish community.

However, contrary to the biblical account, Savoir's Jesus did not rise from the dead three days later. Instead, Jesus' disciples, fearful of the Roman authorities but at the same time determined to continue the insurrection begun by their leader, conspired to propagate an account of a divine resurrection that would serve as the foundation for a movement that would eventually challenge Rome's authority over the Jewish people.

In Savoir's biblical revisionism, the woman identified in the Scriptures as Mary Magdalene was depicted as a pawn of the disciples to spread the "gospel" that Christ was resurrected, an account that was somewhat credible in light of the unexplained empty tomb three days following the crucifixion. The Apostles, who did not chronicle Jesus' life until many years after these events and could not corroborate their oral history, were depicted as unwitting accomplices to the conspiracy. The persecution and martyrdom of the early Christians, as creatively and graphically depicted in *The Resurrection Conspiracy,* were a solemn testament of the consequences of blind obedience to a false doctrine.

Savoir had produced the film using some of his own funds and additional financing provided by a small group of investors. This was a risky venture without a distribution contract in hand, but Savoir was as unconventional in the economic aspects of film production as in the creative facets.

He was confident that his latest masterpiece would find its niche on the nation's cinematic landscape. With his film in hand, Savoir had approached three major studios but his overtures had been rejected. With Hollywood under assault from the religious right and *The Last Temptation of Christ* still fresh in their memories, they were not interested in offending the sensibilities of the faithful, at least not in the flagrant manner reflected in Savoir's script.

In addition, although most movie deals are consummated away from the public glare, Savoir's quest for a distribution contract had not gone undetected by the media watchdogs. A passing reference in film critic Michael Shadwell's syndicated column was sufficient to galvanize a broad spectrum of Christians in opposition to what they believed was an assault on the bedrock principle of Christianity, the divinity of Jesus Christ. Some Christian leaders were unyielding in their public denunciation of Savoir's film as a "blasphemous rape of the Holy Scriptures."

Samuel Weintraub had also read Shadwell's column. Weintraub was an independent producer and film distributor who frequently contracted with the major studios to distribute their products to theaters and cable channels. Although the stockin-trade of his company, Redwood Productions, was mainstream cinema, Weintraub had occasionally handled the domestic distribution of several foreign films and had produced several of his own experimental films for limited release. Savoir's visit to Redwood Productions was not unexpected. Having been rejected by the major studios, the producer had now turned to the smaller but reputable enterprises to help him harvest the fruits of his labor in the marketplace. Savoir's project was intriguing to Weintraub, but he was cautious as he viewed Savoir's enterprising cinematic revision of the New Testament account of the Resurrection and its aftermath.

The script was well written, the roles were impressively cast, and Savoir's credentials as a creative genius were unassailable. Weintraub had no reservations about the project's artistic merit. But his moral radar was transmitting mixed signals. The distribution of Savoir's film was economically risky for Weintraub. If he signed a contract with the filmmaker and failed in his bid to book *The Resurrection Conspiracy* into mainstream movie houses in the major markets, he would suffer a financial loss. But while his economic concerns were not insignificant, his precarious role as a moral gatekeeper was his immediate consideration.

On the one hand, he was a strong supporter of free expression and believed no idea should be banned from the artistic marketplace because of its offensiveness, vulgarity, or unpopularity. Although devout Christians might consider any challenge to scriptural accuracy to be blasphemous, even the Bible should not be immune from probing inquiry. After all, Savoir had not promoted his film narrative as a historical truth; it was a political drama produced against the backdrop of the biblical account of the rise of Christianity. It was a work of fiction that for the less pious within the religious community might be viewed as harmless entertainment. Nevertheless, its conspiracy theory, even if presented as a work of fiction, directly challenged a fundamental tenet of the Christian faith.

On the other hand, though Weintraub appreciated Savoir's artistically executed plot, he wondered whether this film exceeded the bounds of cultural propriety. Weintraub's own beliefs were more secular than religious, but he questioned whether this public trashing of Christianity would serve any socially redeeming purpose. *The Resurrection Conspiracy* was virtually flawless from an aesthetic perspective, in Weintraub's view, but the community of devout Christians had already denounced the film's narrative as blasphemous. He did not question Savoir's right to his own atheistic worldview or the right of anyone to disagree with the scriptural rendition of historical events. But the French filmmaker had produced a work that was morally offensive to a significant number of movie patrons. They could, of course, boycott the film (as they assuredly would), but *The Resurrection Conspiracy* would, in the collective consciousness of its critics, exemplify the media's continuing assault on the moral fiber of American society. And Weintraub would be implicated in the chain of responsibility for the release of this controversial movie. As Savoir persisted in his pursuit of a distribution venue, Samuel Weintraub considered the consequences of entering into an alliance with the heretical filmmaker.

THE CASE STUDY

Religion is at the heart of some of the most emotional and divisive controversies in our culture. Blasphemy, of course, is morally offensive to many members of the Christian community, and media content that is at variance with scriptural accounts challenges the sincere beliefs of devout Christians. Libertarians would counter, however, that the strength of a free society lies in its willingness to tolerate and even encourage unpopular and offensive views. Of course, blasphemy has had a rather tortured history in American society, and for much of our early history laws against blasphemy were enforced. Nevertheless, once the legal underbrush is cleared away, the ethical question still remains as to whether some ideas are so repugnant to community values that they should be proscribed in the marketplace of ideas.

François Savoir's film *The Resurrection Conspiracy* does not purport to be a docudrama offering an alternative historical truth to that reported in the Scriptures. Instead, the director cleverly attempts to humanize the characters involved in the biblical accounts of Jesus' ministry, Crucifixion, and Resurrection and to ascribe to them political motives that are at variance with the traditional view of Christ's disciples. The film is a work of fiction—but fiction with a message that is offensive to many members of society.

Samuel Weintraub is a film distributor who must decide whether Savoir's film is worthy of his professional attention. Although he is not directly responsible for the content, he is in the chain of distribution and thus assumes the role of moral agent for the dissemination of this film. Therefore, he becomes a major player in whether Savoir's masterpiece is allowed to compete in the artistic marketplace.

Weintraub does not question the movie's aesthetic qualities but is disturbed by its brutal assault on the Christian canon as revealed in the biblical accounts. He wonders whether *The Resurrection Conspiracy* is just one more attempt by ethical relativists to marginalize the role of religion in

American society. On the other hand, censorship by private interests, just like government censorship, is inimical to liberal values, and Weintraub's strong belief in the freedom of artistic expression argues in favor of his facilitating the theatrical debut of *The Resurrection Conspiracy.*

Assume the role of film distributor Samuel Weintraub, and, using the model of moral reasoning outlined in Chapter 3, decide whether you will sign a distribution contract with Savoir.

▶ **CASE 10-5**

Cyberporn and Free Speech

Obscenity in outer space: The marketing of cyberporn. This snappy headline in the Southwestern University *Chronicle,* the university's student newspaper, highlighted a two-page article on the marketing of sexually explicit material through the Internet. It also presaged a public relations nightmare for university president William Calders.

The article, published under the byline of student reporter Scott Winters, had been the culmination of several weeks of painstaking research "surfing the Net" for any trace of online pornography, which he found in surprising abundance. Winters had availed himself of the university's connection to the World Wide Web that was available to students both in the library and in a special computer-equipped room in the student union. The *Chronicle*'s editorial offices were also hardwired for ready access to cyberspace. Winters had not targeted commercial bulletin boards that housed adult pictures and narratives, since those were available only upon payment of a fee. He was interested primarily in the availability of such adult-oriented fare online, including explicit "sample" materials (both pictures and narrative) that served as promotional and marketing tools for the commercial adult bulletin boards.

Not only was Winters surprised at the accessibility of such morally offensive content, but he was also able to identify the computers from which requests for pornographic materials originated because the Netscape browser tool provided by the university to facilitate student access to the Internet

also made a copy of each transaction. And much to the dismay of the university's administration, the young journalist had dutifully noted his classmates' keen interest in the material under investigation. Southwestern University students, it seemed, viewed the Internet as more than just an engaging medium for intellectual pursuits.

"I'm really catching some heat about this *Chronicle* article—or, more precisely, what the article represents," said President Calders as he convened a strategy session on what he called the "cyberporn flap." With him were Nathan Moses, vice president for academic affairs; Morris Feldman, director of university public relations; Joanne Michaels, the dean of students; and Jacob Samuelson, student government president. Calders usually consulted the president of student government on matters affecting student life at the university, because he liked to think of himself as "student-oriented" and also because he considered Samuelson a good source of intelligence about student opinion.

"I've had calls from several parents wondering why we're allowing students to have access to this kind of material," continued Calders. "And the chair of the board of regents isn't thrilled about it either. On the other side, the president of the local chapter of the American Civil Liberties Union heard we were considering blocking student access to this material and called to urge us to reconsider. I told him no decision had been made on the matter."

"It's been only a week since publication of this article, but my office has already handled numerous inquiries from the media, including the *Chronicle of Higher Education,*" volunteered Feldman.

"There's a lot of interest at every level," admitted the university president. "This is a complex issue—for us, it involves free speech, academic freedom, and our responsibility to the students and their parents. And because whatever we decide will also affect the image and credibility of the university, it's also a troublesome public relations problem. And that's your domain, Morris!"

"I think I speak for the faculty in opposing any limitation on access to any part of the World Wide Web," said Moses. "We invested heavily in this system to facilitate both faculty and student research. I'm aware that some of this usage may not be for legitimate research purposes. But I don't think we should spend our time policing how the students and faculty use this facility. This is a public university, and I don't think there should be censorship of any kind."

"I don't see this as censorship," responded Michaels. "Because we're facilitating the students' access to this material, why can't we control the conditions under which they have this access? I realize our students are adults. But our mission is to encourage earnest intellectual pursuits. Surfing the Net to gawk at pornography is not my idea of serious research. Besides, some of this material is probably illegal under current obscenity laws. Do we want to be in a position of providing access to material that may not even be legal to begin with?"

"But how can we recommend values to our students that promote freedom of inquiry and freedom of expression and then tell them that they are too immature to view this material?" asked Moses. "It's too paternalistic to try to distinguish between legitimate research interests and prurient interests."

"There are other values that are just as important as freedom of inquiry and expression," stated Michaels unequivocally. The dean of students was not bothered by the accusation of paternalism, because she viewed the moral behavior of many college students to be subject to the whims of unbridled youth. Their psychological maturity, she reasoned from her own experience, was not matched by their ethical development. "Just three years ago," she continued, "this university decided that the teaching of ethical values was important enough that now all students are required to take a course in moral philosophy. And two years ago the Faculty Senate approved an amendment to the Code of Student Conduct punishing hate speech directed at racial and ethnic minorities. Although a federal judge has just declared this provision to be unconstitutional, the point is that the faculty decided that the promotion of campus civility and tolerance was just as important as free speech. If we limit access to this so-called cyberporn, this will send a message that this kind of material has no socially redeeming value and doesn't contribute anything of significance to intellectual discourse. I don't see this as a free speech issue because it's not the students' speech that's at stake."

"Part of the free speech equation," responded Moses, "is the right to receive information. I realize that much of this material is trash. But I don't see how we can control access without interfering with legitimate research. Besides, even if we could, these students are mature enough to make their own decisions."

"But our situation isn't exactly comparable to making a rational choice to see a movie or purchase an adult magazine," said Calders. "It's true that students don't have to log on to this material. But it's certainly tempting. Should we be using public money to facilitate access to cyberporn?"

"How do the students feel about this?" Calders directed this question to Jacob Samuelson.

"There's some difference of opinion," responded Samuelson, who had patiently awaited his turn to join this engaging exchange. "But most seem to oppose any censorship by the administration. They feel they are mature enough to make their own decisions, especially because the university has set up this system partially for their benefit. However, there are a few who find pornography repugnant and would have no problem if the university blocked access to this material."

Calders then turned to the university's public relations director. "How do you assess the public fallout from all of this?"

"From a public relations perspective, there are two concerns: image and intellectual credibility," replied Feldman. "On the issue of credibility, quite frankly I don't think the public understands our intellectual debates about academic freedom. We'll catch some heat from our own faculty and probably from scholars across the country. And, of course, the civil libertarians will be heard from on the issue of free speech. But the public—and that includes the parents of our students—is fairly conservative. They aren't likely to understand why this university is providing access to pornography for our student body. We may suffer some short-term damage in terms of image. But it'll blow over. Most parents aren't likely to refuse to send their students here because of this flap, unless some other problem arises."

"What it boils down to," Feldman continued, "is what this university feels is more important: the right of students as autonomous individuals to choose their own materials, regardless of how morally offensive they might be to some, or the responsibility of the university to set standards and to promote virtuous behavior and attitudes. Of course, the two might not be mutually exclusive."

"This has been a productive dialogue," said Calders sincerely as he adjourned the meeting. "This is a serious matter. I want each of you to give this issue some thought and have your individual recommendations on my desk within a week. And then before a final decision is made, we'll reconvene to consider whether cyberporn will continue to be a prominent feature of Southwestern University's information superhighway."

THE CASE STUDY

Even as the ethics of the distribution of and access to sexually explicit and other morally offensive content through conventional media remains controversial, new technologies now pose more daunting challenges to society in confronting the ethical dimensions of their cultural influence. The traditional regulatory mechanisms constructed to control the flow of pornography seem inadequate in the face of unrestricted access to the Web by adults, adolescents, and children alike.

In this case, a public university is a facilitator in this process. University administrators, to remain technologically competitive, have provided their students and faculty with a system that is interactive with the Internet and other computer systems. Although the purpose of this access is research, there is little supervision of how the system is used. And now that the public is finally realizing the potential of this information technology, they are demanding accountability. And even the administration is divided. On the one hand, the dean of students rejects the notion that the university, having set up this system for students and faculty, must now abandon any control over the kinds of material that are examined or downloaded by its users. She sees this as another opportunity to teach values and virtuous behavior, to which the university has supposedly committed itself. She is also concerned about whether the university should provide unsupervised access to content that may not even be legal under current obscenity statutes.

On the other hand, the vice president for academic affairs sees this as a matter of academic freedom and free speech. Both positions, of course, raise the question of what role the university should play in facilitating access to content along the information superhighway that some consider to be at least morally offensive or perhaps even legally obscene under current law.

President Calders has requested each of those present at the meeting to submit a recommendation on whether to regulate access to the Internet. Much of the analysis, of course, will focus on the ethical dimensions of the issue. Taking the role of university public relations director Morris Feldman, formulate a recommendation to the president and defend your position.

▶ CASE 10-6

The Reparations Ad and the Limits of Free Speech

As the spring semester began, Teresa Guadelupe was enthusiastic about her new campus leadership role. The newly appointed editor of Austin State's student newspaper, the *Sentinel,* was determined to rescue her newspaper from its journalistic doldrums and to return it to a position of distinction in the campus lives of Austin State's multicultural student body. While the *Sentinel* was still respected as a forum for student expression, Guadelupe, a two-year veteran of the paper's staff, detected a certain amount of complacency and lack of imagination among her peers. She was also concerned that the *Sentinel*'s coverage did not adequately reflect the cultural diversity of the student body and that the paper was an ineffective watchdog when it came to scrutinizing the affairs of the university's administration.

Guadelupe was euphoric when, during her first staff meeting, she detected a refreshing level of passion that had been lacking during the last academic year. "We're the only newspaper that some of our students will read," Guadelupe observed correctly. "Our stories must be relevant to their interests. Our news coverage must be balanced and fair, but I don't care if we step on some toes on the op-ed page. They can throw stones at us for all I care, but I want the *Sentinel* to be at the forefront of campus debate."

Guadelupe didn't know it at the time, but David Horowitz was about to make her dream come true. Horowitz, an activist and self-proclaimed "provocateur," was editor in chief of FrontPageMagazine.com and president of the Center for the Study of Popular Culture. Horowitz would have languished in obscurity on most college campuses had it not been for his controversial ad titled "Ten Reasons Why Reparations for Slavery Is a Bad Idea—And Racist Too." In the ad, Horowitz did not mince words in outlining his thesis. While the commentary did contain some rational, intellectual arguments, it also included some statements that would inevitably inflame the passions of the African American community. For example, most Americans living today, according to Horowitz, were descendents of post–Civil War immigrants who had no responsibility for slavery. He claimed that advocating reparations reinforced African Americans' "crippling sense of victimhood." In one of his more provocative statements, Horowitz also declared that blacks owe white Americans a debt of gratitude for freeing them from slavery and that reparations had in fact already been paid in the form of welfare payments.[62]

As the *Sentinel*'s advertising manager, Theopolis Jones, stared in stark disbelief at Horowitz's incendiary claims, he was unaware that his counterparts at more than forty other universities were probably experiencing similar anxiety pains as the activist blanketed the country with his rhetorical hostility to the idea of reparations. Within seconds of digesting the ad, Jones presented it to newspaper adviser Stuart Ellis, a former journalist and strong proponent of student press autonomy. Ellis was imbued with a feeling of déjà vu as he recalled the brouhaha several years ago on some college campuses resulting from Bradley Smith's ad titled "THE HOLOCAUST CONTROVERSY: The Case for Open Debate," in which Smith had denied the reality of the Holocaust that resulted in the extermination of six million Jews under Hitler's Nazi regime. The ad had deeply offended many in the Jewish community, but the *Sentinel* was spared when Bradley apparently decided to bypass Austin State in his search for appropriate venues in which to

espouse his views. Nevertheless, Ellis briefed the staff on the controversy that surrounded this ad. "Some college papers published the ad while others declined," he said, "but it definitely polarized some campus groups."

"It's your call as to whether to run this ad," Ellis told Guadelupe as he met with the *Sentinel*'s staff, "but I think we should have a full discussion of this issue." The editor was joined by the paper's managing editor, Betsy Turnbull, and Theopolis Jones, who was unfailingly turf-conscious and insisted upon having a prominent role in any decision affecting his advertising department.

Jones lost no time in advancing his own view. "As an African American I'm offended by this ad," Jones declared. "This is nothing more than another form of hate speech that will be offensive to most of our black students. We should reject this ad."

"I could not disagree more," countered Turnbull. "Sure, this ad is strong medicine, and it will offend some. I'm not sure I agree with all of the arguments. I haven't had a chance to give it much thought. Nevertheless, Horowitz is entitled to free speech on this issue, and the campus community should hear his views, even if they are controversial and perhaps even inflammatory."

"I should point out that the idea of reparations for the descendents of American slaves has been around for years," interjected Ellis, attempting not to unduly influence this spirited discussion, "but some attorneys have taken the debate to a new level by threatening legal action."

Turnbull had been unaware of the historical pedigree of this debate, but Ellis's remarks reinforced her confidence in her position. "Horowitz's comments may be offensive to some," she said, "but if we don't publish this ad we'll be accused of free speech hypocrisy. I realize that Horowitz has no legal right of access to our paper, but we pride ourselves on being a forum for an exchange of views."

"These ideas are an abomination to African Americans," responded Jones. "Equating welfare with reparations and suggesting that blacks owe American whites a debt of gratitude is insulting and racist. We have achieved a good deal of racial harmony on this campus, but this could just open old wounds. What's the difference between the reparations ad and the Holocaust ad Stuart just described to us? Both are racist and offensive."

"If we had a policy against publishing any 'advertorial,' then we could reject this ad without being accused of viewpoint discrimination," replied Turnbull. "But we have published other issue-oriented ads. I don't think we should reject any ad just because of the nature of the content."

Turnbull paused for a moment to let her argument sink in, and then she continued. "And I see a big difference between Bradley Smith's Holocaust ad and the one submitted by Horowitz. Smith's ad was an attempt at historical revisionism. It was not based upon any credible evidence, and it certainly did not have the support of most Americans. The reparations ad, on the other hand, is essentially a statement of opinion, and like it or not, it probably reflects the feelings of a majority of Americans."

"What about minority rights?" countered Jones. "If Horowitz were just opposed to reparations, that's one thing. But he goes beyond that and suggests that slavery wasn't such a bad thing after all—that the slaves were better off here than they might have been in Africa and that such things as welfare erases any debts owed to the descendents of slaves. That's preposterous and it's offensive to African Americans."

"You have a point, Theo," conceded Turnbull. "But is that really for us to determine? We have promoted ourselves as an organ of news *and* opinion, a vehicle for the unrestricted exchange of ideas. Horowitz's ideas may be offensive, but he has a right to express them."

Jones detected a flaw in his colleague's logic and seized the moment. "Okay. Just for the sake of argument I'll concede his right to speak. There are other forums for him to express his racist views. The *Sentinel* is a paper for an exchange of *student* expression. I don't believe we have an obligation to accept all commentary that arrives in this office from outside sources. Keep in mind that the campus is a self-contained community, and its civility could be undermined if we publish this ad and the issue of reparations has a polarizing influence among our student body. The views contained in this ad reinforce the intolerance we have worked so hard to eradicate."

"I don't agree that the *Sentinel* is merely a forum for student expression," replied Turnbull. "Our students should be exposed to a wide variety of views, no matter how offensive, unpopular, or radical they may be."

"There's one other problem we haven't considered," responded Jones, attempting to change the focus of the debate slightly. "If we publish this ad, we might lose other advertisers. Advertisers hate controversy. And if they believe they may be asked to boycott the *Sentinel* by those opposed to this ad, they become skittish. Besides, if our papers are stolen from the newsracks in retaliation for our publishing this ad, some of our sponsors may ask for rebates. Just keep in mind the potential financial impact on our paper."

With that closing salvo, Stuart Ellis detected a stalemate in the debate between Betsy Turnbull and advertising manager Theopolis Jones. The paper's editor, Teresa Guadelupe, had intentionally remained on the sidelines during this dynamic exchange between her two colleagues. As the paper's adviser had noted at the outset, she would be the moral agent in rendering a judgment on whether to run David Horowitz's controversial ad. She needed time to reflect, to weigh the values of free speech against other countervailing values such as campus civility, tolerance, and fairness. In closing the meeting, Ellis offered to provide counsel but reaffirmed Guadelupe's role as the ultimate gatekeeper in resolving this thorny ethical dilemma.

THE CASE STUDY

When David Horowitz submitted his ad to more than forty college newspapers, a significant number refused to publish the ad. Some of those that did publish it were besieged by outraged students; editors were threatened, and newspapers were confiscated. This is a classic confrontation between the values of free speech and other interests that promote such values as tolerance, civility, and justice. Conservative critics complain that the campus furor surrounding the publication of such controversial views as those contained in the Horowitz ad is just another example of political correctness designed to erode the fundamental (moral) right to free speech. Their liberal respondents argue that free speech is just one value among many that must be balanced against other interests in an increasingly diverse and multicultural society.

The following is a typical defense of the Horowitz ad published on a website devoted to conservative commentary on matters of public interest:

> We accept certain limits on free speech in our society—the old example of yelling "fire" in a crowded theater has been joined by generally accepted cultural prohibitions on speech denigrating others for their religion, race, sex, or sexual orientation—but Horowitz's ad merely presents one side of a debate, and does so in an intelligent and rational manner. . . . Reasonable people can disagree about whether reparations are a good idea. It's not reasonable to assume that the conservative side of a debate is inherently wrong and should be stifled.[63]

However, others have maintained that the student editors who rejected the ad were correct in doing so. Anti Defamation League director Abraham Foxman, for example, has argued that the antireparations ad, like the Nazi Holocaust ad, was designed to foment racism and hate and was intended to make people angry. Supporters of reparations also complain that "blacks are still suffering the consequences of slavery and segregation that consigned them to the bottom of the economic ladder."[64] Commentaries such as these simply perpetuate the long-standing distrust between the races and racial animosities. Thus, some limitations are justified on offensive views in the interest of social stability and tolerance.

As Teresa Guadelupe reviews the Horowitz ad and considers its potential repercussions on Austin State's campus community, she must keep two facts in mind. First, unlike the Holocaust ad referred to in this case, opposition to reparations undoubtedly represents a majoritarian (though not necessarily racist) view within American society and probably on most college campuses. Second, the Horowitz ad, as noted in the narrative, is not merely an antireparations commentary; it also links reparations with welfare payments, claims that African Americans owe white society a debt of gratitude for freeing them from slavery, and declares

that reparations would only reinforce African Americans' "sense of victimhood." These are the statements, according to Horowitz's liberal critics, that depart from rational discourse on the issue and elevate passion over reason.

In this scenario, newspaper editor Teresa Guadelupe is considering her options at the same time that her editorial peers at other colleges and universities are doing likewise. She is not aware of the consequences that eventually befell many of those papers that did run the ad. Therefore, she must render her judgment with the interests of all of the stakeholders on her campus in mind. For the purpose of confronting this ethical dilemma, assume the role of Teresa Guadelupe and, applying the formula for moral reasoning outlined in Chapter 3, decide whether you will publish the David Horowitz ad.

▶ **CASE 10-7**

The Controversial Wedding Photo

Sandra Royce, managing editor of the *Columbia Times-Journal*, was transfixed by the visual documentation of what she knew would be the page one story for the next day's edition—the first gay marriage in her community's 150-year history. Beginning with the Massachusetts Supreme Judicial Court's decision several years earlier that prohibitions on same-sex marriages violated the state's constitution, demands for sexual parity had quickly spread across the nation, exacerbating further the moral dissonance between religious conservatives and the gay and lesbian population. However, Columbia's gay community had displayed little inclination to challenge the community's conservative moral norms and the state's law that prohibited same-sex marriages—that is, until Linda Maxwell and Marsha Boutwell decided to seek official recognition of their five-year partnership through the sanctity of marriage.

In view of the scores of same-sex marriages performed by public officials in such venues as San Francisco, the Maxwell-Boutwell union would have been unexceptional—except that the ceremony was performed on the high seas by the captain of a cruise liner during a voyage catering to gay and lesbian couples. Upon their return to port, the couple announced that they would seek their state's recognition of the marriage, an aspiration that was unrealistic and would undoubtedly precipitate a legal challenge. The unusual circumstances surrounding the wedding and the couple's challenge to marital orthodoxy quickly propelled them into the national spotlight and set them apart from the other gay and lesbian couples who had married under more traditional circumstances.

The *Times-Journal* was contemplating its local coverage of their two newsworthy citizens when a wire service transmitted the only visual documentation of the high seas nuptials—a vivid color photo purchased from the ship's cruise director featuring an embrace and a passionate kiss symbolizing their official union. As the only graphic representation of the Maxwell-Boutwell ceremony, photo editor Lee Mason quickly submitted the wire service photo as his contribution to the paper's local coverage of the couple's precedent-setting and bold initiative. However, city editor Bradley St. James, who would supervise the local news coverage of the event, was more reticent as he contemplated the moral firestorm that could erupt from the publication of such a pictorial in the pages of the *Columbia Times-Journal*. St. James quickly arranged a meeting with managing editor Sandra Royce, who would listen patiently to the arguments of her two subordinate editors and then assume the role of moral gatekeeper in passing judgment on the disposition of the contentious wedding picture.

"As you know, this is the only photo of the Maxwell-Boutwell wedding," declared Royce in initiating the dialogue with her two journalistic subordinates. "Their wedding on board a cruise liner is certainly unusual. And since they're a local couple, this is front-page news for us. But I'm concerned about publishing this photo. It might be offensive to some of our readers."

"We could run the story without the photo," responded Mason. "But I would object to that. The photo may offend some, but the very idea of gay marriage would be offensive to these readers. We are increasingly becoming a visual medium. For

several years we have run color photos to illustrate some of our stories. I believe the picture is relevant and should be published."

"I have reservations about publishing this photo," replied St. James. "Look at this picture. This is not just a kiss; it's a graphic picture of two women *passionately* kissing. The event itself is newsworthy and should be reported. But some of our readers will be offended by this photo. They may even feel that by running this photo we have given tacit approval to same-sex marriages."

"I disagree," countered Mason, without hesitation. "We wouldn't hesitate to run such a photo of a heterosexual couple kissing if it had news value. In fact, we've run wire photos before of newsworthy figures, such as entertainers, kissing following their nuptials. We can't base our decision on how offensive this picture might be to some. There might be some situations where I would feel differently—for example, a gruesome photo of American soldiers killed in battle—but this is a civil rights issue. In addition, the circumstances surrounding the event are unusual. It's newsworthy. I suspect that gay marriages will become increasingly commonplace."

"The story itself is newsworthy," conceded St. James. "After all, this is a local lesbian couple and certainly our first gay marriage, despite the fact that the ceremony took place on the high seas. But I don't see that the picture contributes much of value to the story. It offends but can't be justified by any countervailing journalistic principle."

"In today's journalistic environment, our readers expect pictures," responded Mason. "We live in a visual culture. Our readers expect pictures. If we had other, less graphic pictures of this wedding, perhaps we could avoid using this photo. But this is all we have. And it provides a good supplement to our story. Besides, if we choose not to publish this photo simply because it's offensive to some of our readers, isn't that a rather subtle editorial statement—that same-sex marriages are socially unacceptable?"

Royce wasn't quite convinced of the validity of Mason's closing statement, and she certainly did not underestimate the cultural sensitivity of her paper's readers—and perhaps even some local advertisers. Nevertheless, in the past decade there had been a noticeable decline in homophobia, if not widespread public acceptance of same-sex marriages, and she silently assessed both the news value of the photo and the risks of offending the loyal readers of the *Columbia Times-Journal*.

THE CASE STUDY

There is little doubt that the American public's threshold for tolerating offensive content is higher than it was just a few years ago. The proliferation of mediated sex and graphic violence and the media's relentless assault on our sense of moral proportion have perhaps numbed us to the coarser aspects of the human condition. Every day journalistic gatekeepers must decide whether to run photos that may be too invasive (such as pictures of grief), too shocking, or too gruesome. News value must be weighed against concerns about sensationalism and voyeurism.

However, in this scenario, the potential offensiveness of the photo emanates more from the symbolism surrounding lesbian relationships and same-sex marriages than from the content of the picture itself. The issue of homosexuality is still culturally divisive, despite evidence of a greater degree of social tolerance. As photo editor Lee Mason notes, the *Columbia Times-Journal* would not hesitate to run a similar photo of a heterosexual couple. Thus, the paper's editors are concerned about the depiction of a passionate kiss at the conclusion of the wedding ceremony between lesbian partners Linda Maxwell and Marsha Boutwell and the anticipated reaction from some readers. Can the paper justify the publication of this photo based upon traditional news values? Does it contribute something to the story that enhances its meaning for the paper's readers? If Sandra Royce decides to publish this photo with the story, should she include an explanation for the readers? If so, how should it be worded?

For the purpose of analyzing this ethical dilemma, assume the position of moral gatekeeper and managing editor Sandra Royce and, utilizing the SAD model for moral reasoning outlined in Chapter 3, render a judgment on whether your paper will publish the controversial photograph of

the kiss between lesbian partners Linda Maxwell and Marsha Boutwell.

Notes

1. "FCC to Investigate Super Bowl Breast-Baring," CNN.com, February 2, 2004 (downloaded on February 2, 2004), located at http://cnn.usnews.printthis. See also Bill Carter, "Bracing for Fallout from Super Indignation," *New York Times*, February 5, 2004, p. B1.
2. See Marc Peyser, "Family TV Goes Down the Tube," *Newsweek*, February 23, 2004, pp. 52–54.
3. Philip Elmer-Dewitt, "On a Screen Near You: Cyberporn," *Time*, July 3, 1995, p. 40.
4. Frederick R. Blevens, "When Journalistic Judgment Outrages Readers," *Chronicle of Higher Education*, May 16, 1997, p. B7.
5. David Ansen, "How Far Is Too Far?," *Newsweek*, March 3, 2003, p. 60.
6. Frank Rich, "Naked Capitalists," *New York Times*, May 20, 2001, Section 6, p. 51.
7. Stewart made this comment in his concurring opinion in *Jacobellis v. State of Ohio*, 378 U.S. 184, 197 (1964).
8. One author who takes this position is Harry M. Clor in *Obscenity and Public Morality: Censorship in a Liberal Society* (Chicago: University of Chicago Press, 1969).
9. For a discussion of the relationship between women's rights, pornography, and the First Amendment, see Dwight L. Teeter Jr. and Don R. Le Duc, *Law of Mass Communications*, 7th ed. (Westbury, NY: Foundation Press, 1992), pp. 360–361.
10. For a summary of this controversy, see Don R. Pember, *Mass Media Law*, 2000 ed. (Boston: McGraw-Hill), pp. 478–479.
11. "Smack Attack: Why MTV Pulled Clip," *TV Guide*, January 10, 1998, p. 62.
12. Martin Edlund, "Hip-Hop's Crossover to the Adult Aisle," *New York Times*, March 7, 2004, Section 2, p. 1.
13. Ibid.
14. Phil Mushnick, "Phil Mushnick's Sportsview," *TV Guide*, October 14, 2000, p. 64.
15. Ibid., p. 65.
16. See "Toppling the Last Taboos," *Newsweek*, October 28, 1991, p. 32.
17. Quoted in Wayne Hoffman, "No Longer Taboo," *Communicator*, October 1994, p. 85.
18. Ibid.
19. Ibid.
20. See *FCC v. Pacifica Foundation*, 3 Med. L. Rptr. 2553, 2554 (1978).
21. Ibid.

22. Suanne Ault, "Sex and the Survey," *Broadcasting & Cable,* February 12, 2001, p. 24.

23. Rochell D. Thomas, "TV Goes Soft on Porn," *TV Guide,* October 18, 2003, p. 16.

24. Quoted in John Leo, "Foul Words, Foul Culture," *U.S. News & World Report,* April 22, 1996, p. 73.

25. Lawrie Mifflin, "TV Stretches Limits of Taste, to Little Outcry," *New York Times,* April 6, 1998, p. A1.

26. Ibid., p. C8.

27. Elmer-Dewitt, "On a Screen Near You," p. 40.

28. "Would You Print This Ad?," *Chronicle of Higher Education,* March 16, 2001, p. A9.

29. "Brown Students Steal Univ. Paper," online Associated Press dispatch, March 17, 2001 (accessed March 20, 2001), available at wysiwyg://1/http://news.findlaw.com/ap_s...er/1110/3–17-2001/20010317161206400.html

30. "Americans: Don't Protect Offensive Speech," *Quill,* August 2000, p. 8.

31. See Patrick R. Parsons and William E. Smith, "R. Budd Dwyer: A Case Study in Newsroom Decision Making," *Journal of Mass Media Ethics* 3 (1988): 84–85.

32. Ibid.

33. Ibid., pp. 89–90.

34. Chevel Johnson, "Viewers Back Decision to Air Suicide Drama," *The Advocate* (Baton Rouge, LA), September 17, 1994, p. 4B.

35. Ibid.

36. Ibid.

37. William L. Rivers and Cleve Mathews, *Ethics for the Media* (Upper Saddle River, NJ: Prentice-Hall, 1988), pp. 137–138.

38. Ibid.

39. Dan Trigoboff, "CBS Takes Flak for Pearl Tape," *Broadcasting & Cable,* May 20, 2002, p. 15.

40. Ibid.

41. Allison Romano, "News Execs Defend Their Use of Gruesome Images," *Broadcasting & Cable,* July 28, 2003, p. 9.

42. E-mail from editorial staff member Andy Bechtel, April 1, 2004.

43. "CBS Delayed Abuse Report at the Request of Gen. Myers," *Washington Post,* May 4, 2004, p. A18.

44. See Linda Kulman, "Horror and Humanity," *U.S. News & World Report,* July 9/July 16, 2001, pp. 51–52.

45. Jacqueline Sharkey, "When Pictures Drive Foreign Policy," *American Journalism Review,* December 1993, pp. 14–19.

46. See John L. Hulteng, *The Messenger's Motives: Ethical Problems of the News Media,* 2d ed. (Upper Saddle River, NJ: Prentice-Hall, 1985), pp. 148–149.

47. John Leo, "Jesus and the Hustlers," *U.S. News & World Report,* June 15, 1998, p. 17.

48. David Bauder, "Beeping Out of Jesus' Name Puts ABC Network under Fire," AP dispatch published in *The Advocate* (Baton Rouge, LA), June 7, 2002, p. 19A.

49. These categories are based on those described by Joel Feinberg in *Social Philosophy* (Upper Saddle River, NJ: Prentice-Hall, 1973), Chapters 2–3. However, they are also dealt with in some detail in Thomas A. Mappes and Jane S. Zembaty, *Social Ethics: Morality and Social Policy,* 3d ed. (New York: McGraw-Hill, 1987), pp. 284–287; and Tom L. Beauchamp, *Philosophical Ethics: An Introduction to Moral Philosophy* (New York: McGraw-Hill, 1982), pp. 270–297.

50. Franklyn S. Haiman, *Speech and Law in a Free Society* (Chicago: University of Chicago Press, 1977), p. 164.

51. Described in Alan M. Dershowitz, *Taking Liberties: A Decade of Hard Cases, Bad Laws, and Bum Raps* (Chicago: Contemporary Books, 1988), pp. 179–180. The commission issued its report and conclusions in 1986. See U.S. Attorney General's Committee on Pornography, *Final Report,* 2 vols. (Washington, DC: U.S. Government Printing Office), pp. 19–86.

52. *Paris Adult Theatre II v. Slaton,* 413 U.S. 49, 64 (1973).

53. Mappes and Zembaty, *Social Ethics,* p. 285.

54. For a discussion of the pros and cons of these liberty-limiting principles, see ibid., pp. 285–287.

55. For a discussion of the moral arguments for and against censorship of pornography, see Thomas F. Wall, *Thinking Critically about Moral Problems* (Belmont, CA: Thomson/Wadsworth, 2003), pp. 369–410.

56. G. L. Simons, "Is Pornography Beneficial?," in Mappes and Zembaty, *Social Ethics,* pp. 301–306; Walter Berns, "Beyond the (Garbage) Pale or Democracy, Censorship and the Arts," in Harry M. Clor (ed.), *Censorship and Freedom of Expression: Essays on Obscenity and the Law* (Chicago: Rand McNally, 1971), p. 63.

57. Martha Irvine, "Yale Columnist, Others Take Sex Out of the Sack," AP dispatch published in *The Advocate* (Baton Rouge, LA), September 14, 2002, p. 4A.

58. Some of the information for this case was taken from Jason McLure, "Vatican Condom Crusade," *Newsweek,* December 15, 2003, p. 10.

59. "'Live, From San Quentin . . . ,'" *Newsweek,* April 1, 1991, p. 61.

60. *Garrett v. Estelle,* 556 F.2d 1974 (5th Cir. 1977), *cert. denied,* 438 U.S. 914 (1978).

61. "Judge Wants Execution Televised," *Broadcasting & Cable,* December 5, 1994, p. 89.

62. This summary is taken from "U.S. Campus Free Speech Undermined in Race Debate," *FindLaw Legal News,* online Reuters dispatch, April 11, 2001 (accessed April 12, 2001), available at http://news.findlaw.com/legalnews/s/22010411/rightsreparation.html

63. "A Liberal Dose of Free Speech Hypocrisy," online essay, March 18, 2001 (accessed August 17, 2001), available from http://usconservatives.about.com/library/weekly/aa031801a.htm

64. "U.S. Campus Free Speech Undermined in Race Debate," p. 2.

Media Content and Juveniles: Special Ethical Concerns

JUVENILES AND CULTURAL PATERNALISM

Does kindergarten need cops? Kiddie films sport smoking and drinking! FTC calls for new law to protect kids online! Headlines such as these serve to remind us of the community's concern with our most vulnerable citizens. The passage from childhood to adulthood is a perilous one, and in the first decade of the twenty-first century society's duty to safeguard this passage remains undiminished. Undoubtedly, juveniles occupy a special niche in our culture. Because the juvenile audience is unique, media messages directed at that audience warrant our undivided attention in a separate chapter. We live in an uncivil world in which children are perhaps at risk as never before. With such formidable odds, it might be tempting to abandon the struggle for moral direction and certitude in the lives of our children.

But morally untutored children develop into morally ambivalent adults, a reality that justifies bracketing the juvenile audience for special consideration and continuing the campaign for moral edification among the nation's youth. Obviously, the media should not be blamed for the myriad of emotional, behavioral, and moral problems that afflict children and adolescents. But to the extent that they are influential in shaping the youthful audience's worldview—and they are—the media must also shoulder their share of the responsibility.

Historically, Americans have committed themselves to the protection of youthful innocence and to the rehabilitation of those who have lost or been deprived of that innocence. Cultural paternalism is greatest when applied to children and adolescents, and this moral obligation has even been codified in the legal system. The juvenile justice system, prohibitions against child pornography, child labor laws, and laws establishing the legal age for buying alcoholic beverages and exchanging marriage vows without parental consent reflect this interest in protecting society's youth.

This web of legal paternalism would appear to defy the principles of freedom and autonomy that have been alluded to several times in this book as necessary for making rational decisions about ethics. But children are not autonomous and depend on others for their moral guidance and sustenance. Conventional wisdom holds that the value systems of juveniles are still immature and, therefore, need protection

353

and nurturing. In recent years the U.S. Supreme Court has acknowledged this lack of intellectual and emotional maturity by restricting free speech rights in secondary school.[1]

This immaturity rationale for insulating society's youth from undesirable influences was addressed directly by the thinkers of the European Enlightenment, the architects of the libertarian tradition. Although these philosophers advocated individual freedom—a prerequisite for autonomous moral reasoning—they did not believe that such rights should be extended to those below the age of majority. John Locke, for example, noted children's limited capacity to rationally exercise the privileges of freedom and argued for special protection:

> To turn him [the child] loose to an unrestrained liberty, before he has reason to guide him, is not allowing him the privilege of his nature to be free, but to thrust him out amongst brutes, and abandon him to a state as wretched and as much beneath that of a man as theirs.[2]

John Stuart Mill also addressed the subject in his classic work, "On Liberty." In promoting the notion of individual liberties, Mill observed that "this doctrine is meant to apply only to those human beings in the maturity of their faculties. We are not speaking of children, or of young persons below the age which the law may fix as that of manhood or womanhood."[3]

Such observations provide credible support for the need to treat juveniles as special. It must be acknowledged, however, that this vision of children as innocent and weak has changed dramatically as the "psychological space" between childhood and adulthood has shrunk in our complex and fast-paced society. The disintegration of traditional family structures and the diminishing tranquility of the nurturing environment have accelerated the maturation process.

This altered view of the juvenile segment of society is reflected in cracks in the legal protections for children and adolescents. For example, states have traditionally shielded youthful offenders from the glare of publicity by closing juvenile courts and records to the public, asserting a "compelling state interest" in the rehabilitation of juvenile delinquents. The embarrassment caused by the publication of the names of youthful offenders, it was felt, would hamper the states' efforts to restore some sense of moral direction in their younger citizens.

But our society has begun to reassess its view that juvenile offenders should be accorded a safe haven from the glare of publicity. The rash of school shootings in the past several years by alienated teenagers, for example, confounded the nation and publicly confronted the myth of childhood innocence. An increasing number of states have opened their juvenile courts and records for public inspection,[4] and the U.S. Supreme Court has struck down state laws that prohibit the publication of juvenile offenders' names lawfully obtained.[5] The trend toward trying the more violent youths as adults, even to the extent of imposing the death penalty in some cases, is further evidence of the erosion of special legal sanctuary for juveniles.

Of course, this changing reality is of more than passing sociological interest. As the lines among childhood, adolescence, and adulthood become less distinct, ethical questions remain. Because the mass media are important agents of socialization,[6] some consideration must be given to what role the media should play in the lives of a youthful audience that is admittedly more knowledgeable and less innocent than its predecessors.[7] Should media content aimed at children merely reflect reality, or should it attempt to inculcate the young audience with positive values? What responsibility do media practitioners have when they develop programs targeted to adults but accessible to children? How graphic should mass media material be in confronting the juvenile audience with discussions of sensitive and controversial subjects? What moral obligations do media practitioners have in dealing with children and adolescents as consumers?

These are difficult questions, and the challenge, given the current permissive environment, is to construct strategies that will avoid the intellectual and emotional prudishness of a bygone era while maintaining a sense of moral obligation toward children and adolescents as impressionable audiences in the media marketplace. It should be remembered that the juvenile audience is not monolithic. Media content prepared for younger children should be considered differently from that prepared for adolescents. Thus, age and maturity are important considerations in evaluating media content aimed at the younger generation.

INFLUENCES ON THE JUVENILE AUDIENCE

The concern with the protection of the youthful audience from the harmful effects of artistic subversion is of ancient vintage. Plato, in his *Dialogues,* for example, advocated the censorship of "bad fiction" to insulate children from its undesirable influences:

> And shall we just carelessly allow children to hear any casual tales which may be devised by casual persons, and receive into their minds ideas for the most part the very opposite of those which we should wish them to have when they are grown up?
>
> We cannot.
>
> Then the first thing will be to establish a censorship of the writers of fiction, and let the censors receive any tale of fiction which is good, and reject the bad.[8]

Plato's counsel would be welcomed by those who continue to be concerned about the artistic and literary tastes of American youths.

Movies

Of course, this concern with the special nature of the juvenile audience extends far beyond what young people read. The film and sound-recording industries are essentially youth-oriented enterprises. Teenagers are a significant part of the movie audience, and Hollywood has not been oblivious to this fact of economic life. Although producers have been far from puritanical in their approaches to films designed for teenagers, the movie ratings have at least served as a warning to parents and adolescents.

The ratings system grew out of the ashes of the movie code, which by the late 1960s was considered by Hollywood to be a virtual failure. The code had incorporated strict standards for depictions of, among other things, violence, sexually explicit material, crime, and racism. But film producers ignored these lofty standards, thus rendering the code a moral failure.

In 1968 the Motion Picture Association of America (MPAA) formalized the current ratings system. Films were originally accorded a G, PG, R, or X rating.[9] The system has since been revised with the addition of a PG-13 rating and the replacement of the "X" with an NC-17 rating. The ratings may be evidence of Hollywood's sensitivity to its moral obligations to all audiences, but the industry has been publicly indicted for violating the spirit of its own ratings system. In September 2000 the Federal Trade Commission (FTC) released the results of a study that found that nearly 80 percent of R-rated movies are marketed to juveniles under 17. This report so antagonized one state attorney general that he threatened to sue the entertainment industry.[10] Nevertheless, even when the films are properly rated and marketed, the effectiveness of the system depends, in the final analysis, on the good-faith efforts of both theatre managements in enforcing the code and parents in maintaining an interest in the cinematic tastes of their children. While some theatre chains have made a good-faith effort to enforce the code, compliance is not industry-wide. For example, in the spring of 2004 *Newsweek* reported that GKC Theatres, a Midwestern chain, had instituted a system whereby parents could sign a consent form for their children to view R-rated movies, thereby negating the requirement for adult accompaniment for such films. However, Jack Valenti, president of the Motion Picture Association of America, was unsympathetic to GKC's permissive initiative. "I think it's ruptured the intent of the rating system," he observed critically.[11]

Distressingly, technology may overtake the usefulness of the ratings system. The same technology that facilitated music swapping by Internet users can be used by children to locate hard-core pornography, including obscene movies.[12] Of course, the ratings cannot "flag" all content that might be unsuitable for juveniles. Consider this rather sobering lead paragraph, for example, from an article in *U.S. News & World Report*:

> A glamorous schemer trails thick streams of smoke, cigarette holder in hand. Pals chug a keg's worth of beer. Scenes from an R-rated movie, perhaps? No, just memorable bits of two children's classics: *101 Dalmatians* and *All Dogs Go to Heaven*.[13]

Historically, alcohol and tobacco have figured rather prominently in some genres directed at the child audience. One study found that of fifty G-rated animated features released between 1937 and 1997, 68 percent depicted at least one incident of smoking or drinking. Good characters were just as culpable as villains. The results are not particularly surprising for the earlier releases, but with the public's concern over rising tobacco use among teens, one would expect a more restrained approach from Hollywood's cultural gatekeepers. However, smoking was included in all seven animated features released in 1996–1997, at the conclusion of this 60-year survey, "from pipe-puffing Esmeralda in Walt Disney's *The Hunchback of Notre Dame* to sailors with cigarettes in 20th Century Fox's *Anastasia*."[14]

We cannot casually dismiss the imitative effect of such on-screen behavior on the young audience. For example, according to a study released in June 2003 teens who watched the most movies with smoking were almost three times more likely to start smoking than those who watched the fewest number of movies with smoking.[15] Similarly, a study published in 2004

in the journal *Pediatrics* revealed that students 10–14 years old whose parents let them see R-rated movies, where smoking is more likely to be displayed, were almost five times as likely to have tried smoking during the two-year study period as those who never saw the movies.[16]

Nevertheless, in fairness we should be cautious about ascribing all of the blame to movie producers and studio executives for the pathologies of the youthful experience. Studies still indicate that parents, peers, and siblings are principal forces in influencing the drinking and smoking habits of teens and that other scenes (a vicious dog, for example) are more likely to leave a lasting impression than those depicting smoking and drinking.[17] But the fact remains that children and adolescents inhabit a vicarious universe dominated by irresistible market pressures, and there is an ever-present danger of perverse or at least undesirable influences on the morally immature value systems of the nation's youth. For example, a study published in June 2003 in the health journal *Lancet* reported that children who watch films featuring actors smoking are three times as likely as their comrades to light up.[18]

Recordings.   Teenagers and even preteenagers are the largest segment of the record-consuming audience. Although some parents whose musical tastes are more reserved might find rock music aesthetically offensive, the lyrics often reflect the frustrations and uncertainties of adolescence and strike a responsive chord in impressionable teenagers. Music is a powerful communication medium for adolescents, who often associate the music with such emotions as excitement, happiness, and love.[19] But when lyrics and album covers contain obscenities, indecencies, and glorifications of certain forms of immoral conduct, such as drug abuse, ethical considerations arise in connection with the distribution of such material to a youthful audience. Concerned citizens have complained about the sexually explicit lyrics and record covers often associated with "raunchy rock" and rap albums, and the Federal Communications Commission (FCC) continues to impose sanctions against stations that air "shock jock" programs, featuring bawdy commentary, as well as stations that consistently play records containing indecent language.[20] The commission's policy on indecency is aimed particularly at the airing of offensive program material at times of the day when children are likely to be in the audience.[21]

This paternalistic attitude reflects a sensitivity to the special interests of the juvenile audience. From an ethical perspective, indecency and obscenity are not essential to the communication of socially relevant messages to adolescents, even within the lyrics of rock music. But the challenge for media practitioners, in an era of liberated youth, is to develop artistic models that avoid the extremes of moral Puritanism and moral anarchy.

Television

In October 2003 the Henry J. Kaiser Family Foundation announced that an astonishing 43 percent of the children 2 years old and under in the 1,065 families surveyed watched TV on a typical day and that 26 percent had a TV in their room. The median amount of time spent watching television was two hours a day.[22] Television clearly enters the lives of children even before their cognitive skills acquire the capacity for rational discernment and discrimination, leading media critics to fret about the potential for artistic mischief in the lives of society's most vulnerable.

Television has been at the forefront of the debate over freedom versus responsibility in programming content to which children and adolescents are likely to be exposed. And perhaps for good reason. In a print culture, before the advent of television, adult characters in children's books were traditionally depicted as positive and even stereotypical role models. In this idealized world parents really did know best, politicians were usually honest, and teachers were respected and omnipotent. In addition,

parents were worthy gatekeepers who channeled their children's reading habits and maintained a constant vigil over their literary consumption. But television is omnipresent, and both newscasts and TV dramas now confront the juvenile audience with political corruption, dysfunctional families, and ambiguous role models that challenge the moral affiliation between parents and their children. Such portrayals have a leveling effect and tend to narrow the gulf between childhood and adulthood.

There was a time when childhood consisted of a parade of fictional heroes, youthful icons whose virtuous qualities and messages were unambiguous. Such heroes were influential in reinforcing positive values and helping to build self-esteem. The comic books that children read and the TV shows that were derived from those comics, such as *The Adventures of Superman*, reflected that belief in heroes. But then the social upheavals and the counterculture movement of the 1960s and 1970s severely undermined our faith in heroes.[23] And children's programs reflected this new sad reality as a new generation of action-packed adventure cartoons, in which the "good guys" were virtually indistinguishable from the "bad guys," confronted the nation's youngest viewers in a cultural environment already adrift in a sea of ethical relativism.

However, the industry has not been entirely unresponsive to the moral concerns of its critics. In the mid-1990s, for example, DIC Entertainment, producers of a number of popular children's shows, announced a twelve-point plan to guide writers and directors who work for the company. The standards included development of story lines to enhance self-esteem and foster cooperative behavior and an admonition against portraying antisocial behavior as glamorous or acceptable.[24]

The TV program decision makers have also been criticized for the rather subtle and not-so-subtle messages that their prime-time offerings send to the adolescent audience, particularly those who lack parental guidance and whose moral anchors are adrift. In Chapter 9, we discussed the potential impact of excessive televised violence on its young audience. But the concerns go beyond graphic depictions of such antisocial behavior. For example, TV critic Faye Zuckerman took NBC to task for airing "A Family Torn Apart," a fact-based film in which a teenager, apparently chafing under his parents' strict disciplinary code, decides to kill them. "Here the weak script so narrowly defines its characters," complained Zuckerman, "it irresponsibly delivers the message that it's acceptable for a teenager to kill both of his parents because they refuse to let him date."[25]

Does this mean that Hollywood producers and TV programmers should maintain a healthy distance from any reality-based story lines? In a diverse society, where artistic expression is a virtue, that would be unrealistic and undesirable. But Zuckerman's complaint is not so much that such a program was aired but that it portrayed the attacker as the victim and thus preyed on parents' "worst fears about their kids."[26]

The influence of TV in the lives of children and adolescents poses an ethical dilemma for producers of entertainment programming. They must have the artistic freedom to develop quality shows that reflect the realities of contemporary society for a mass audience, a segment of which is children and adolescents. But there is now little doubt that juveniles learn values, social roles, and behaviors from watching TV. For example, TV portrayals of minorities, sex roles, and family relationships can have a profound effect on children's attitudes about society.[27] Similarly, dozens and perhaps hundreds of studies have convincingly linked aggressive behavior in children to exposure to violence on TV and in movies, video games, and other media. "The size of the effect is almost as strong as the relationship between smoking and cancer," notes psychologist Jerome Singer, codirector of the Yale University Family Television Research and Consultation Center.[28]

Thus, in light of this electronic influence on the socialization process, producers and programmers should at least pause to consider the nature and extent of their moral responsibility to develop positive role models for children and adolescents. They must be sensitive to the moral needs of young viewers who might be less innocent than their predecessors but are nevertheless still vulnerable and impressionable. This obligation is particularly important in an era of declining parental supervision and influence.

Of course, this responsibility does not absolve adults of their parental mandate to guide children's viewing habits.[29] To assist in this endeavor, the television networks have instituted a ratings system of their own.[30] Nevertheless, many parents are imperfect gatekeepers, either because they are not present to witness their children's program selections or have not learned how to "just say no." Under these circumstances, the pressure would inevitably be on the producers and distributors of TV programming to step into the moral vacuum left by this parental abdication.

Advertising

Advertising to children is at an all-time high, "creating cravings that are hard to ignore but impossible to satisfy."[31] The annual expenditure for advertising directed at children, according to experts, is about $12 billion,[32] and these efforts appear to have paid dividends. Children under 12 spend a staggering $28 billion a year and teens spend $100 billion, according to market expert James U. McNeal.[33] Children also influence another $300 spent by their parents.[34] Twenty-five years ago, according to Eric Schlosser, author of *Fast Food Nation*, only a few American companies, such as McDonald's and Walt Disney, directed their marketing at children. Today, children are targeted by an incredible diversity of companies, ranging from phone, oil, and automobile companies to clothing stores and restaurant chains. "Hoping that nostalgic childhood memories of a brand will lead to a lifetime of purchases," remarks Schlosser, "companies now plan 'cradle-to-grave' advertising strategies."[35]

Clearly, kids wield a lot of power in the marketplace; they are a force to be reckoned with on Madison Avenue. However, media critics are concerned about the influence of advertising on children. Much of their attention has focused on the commercialization of TV programs produced for children.[36] And broadcasters themselves have not been unmindful of their special responsibilities in this area. For more than half a century, the National Association of Broadcasters (NAB) worked with the TV networks to limit the amount of commercialization in programs designed for children. But in 1982 the Justice Department filed an antitrust suit against the NAB, charging that its commercial codes were a restraint of trade. Shortly thereafter, the NAB agreed to abandon all efforts to negotiate further limitations on broadcast advertising.[37]

Beginning in the early 1970s, Action for Children's Television (ACT), a citizens' group, began pressuring the FCC and Congress to regulate the commercialization of children's programming. Until recently the FCC did provide guidelines, limiting the number of commercial minutes per hour of programs designed for children. But in 1986 it eliminated those guidelines,[38] and the industry's reaction was swift: Many stations increased the number of commercial minutes in children's programming, and the networks began airing what were really program-length commercials, cartoon shows built around popular toys such as G.I. Joe and Smurfs.[39] The ACT mounted a legal challenge to this deregulation and won a technical victory when a federal court ruled that the FCC had failed to justify adequately its policy change.[40] But in 1991 Congress passed legislation reinstituting commercial limits on children's programming—10.5 minutes per hour

on weekends and 12 minutes on weekdays—and also ordering broadcasters to serve the special educational needs of children.

These efforts at legal regulation aside, the ethical questions remain for the television and advertising industries. Those who view juveniles as a special audience argue that children and adolescents are vulnerable and should not be exploited by TV advertising.[41] Their concerns may well be justified, because research findings suggest that children do not always understand that the primary purpose of advertising is to sell and that very young children have difficulty distinguishing between advertising and program content.[42]

"Mothers and fathers are locked in an intense and increasingly unfair competition with advertisers and marketers," notes Enola Aird of the Institute of American Value's Motherhood Project. "Advertisers have overstepped their bounds and it's time to put them back in their place."[43] Elizabeth Lascoutx, director of the Advertising Review Unit of the Better Business Bureau, takes a more temperate and cautious view of the deleterious influences of advertising. "If you take as a premise that marketing to kids is evil, I have to part company," she says. "I don't understand how it protects a child to shield them from advertising until they reach a certain age."[44]

Because of consciousness-raising efforts by the nation's health experts, the most recent battleground in the ad wars has been the "junk-food" industry. There is now little doubt that obesity threatens the well-being of the nation's youth, and TV ads have been indicted for their contribution to this health crisis, prompting *Broadcasting & Cable* magazine, the industry's leading trade publication, to ask: "How much longer can TV gorge itself on children's advertising?"[45] More than 90 percent of the products advertised on children's television are high in fat, sugar, or salt, according to a recent news account. And a nutritional analysis of afternoon and Saturday TV ads aimed at children found that 50 percent were for foods in the "fats, oils, and sweets" categories. Indeed, in the decade from 1992 to 2002 food marketing aimed at children increased from $6.9 billion to $15 billion.[46] Even the most diligent parents must compete with the barrage of junk-food ads that assault their childrens' sensibilities.

However, advertisers have not confined their marketing techniques to messages directed at children as consumers. There is now evidence that advertisers are enlisting kids to influence the purchasing habits of their parents for such "adult" products as automobiles and computers. "[C]ompanies that have never given the slightest thought to an audience they once scorned as ankle biters," mused an article in *U.S. News & World Report*, "are retailoring their messages for the kindergarten crowd and their adult 'co-viewers,' be they parents or nannies."[47] John Geraci, vice president of youth research at Harris Interactive, readily agrees: "The real story of kids' market power is not their spending. It's their influence on the household."[48] This explains why advertisers such as Gateway, the Ford Windstar, and Embassy Suites Hotels recently found Nickelodeon to be an attractive venue for their commercials.[49]

Of course, the influence of advertising extends beyond the electronic media. The marketing of tobacco products to young people, in particular, has been of concern to media critics, as well as government officials. The opening salvo in this battle was fired in 1988 when a campaign for Camel cigarettes debuted featuring a cartoon character known as Old Joe Camel. From the outset, he maintained a pervasive presence on billboards, phone booths, and magazine pages.[50] Suspecting that the campaign was really aimed at children—a charge that R. J. Reynolds, the manufacturer of Camels, denied—three teams of researchers attempted to find out. Although there was no evidence that Joe Camel affected the overall teenage smoking rate, the findings suggested a phenomenal increase in Camel's share of the youth market. In addition, Old Joe also had an impact on much younger

children. For example, fully 91 percent of the 6-year-olds surveyed could match Old Joe with a Camel cigarette.[51] An aggressive assault by state attorneys general compelled the tobacco industry in 1998 to stop advertising on billboards and avoid the "Joe Camel" type of ads that apparently appealed primarily to young people.[52] Some states have also mounted an antismoking commercial campaign of their own, apparently with impressive results.[53]

The most controversial campaign of the past decade was not about smoking but sex. In 1995, Calvin Klein introduced a campaign that promoted jeanswear by picturing young men and women in suggestive sexual poses with their underwear showing. The ads were in keeping with Calvin Klein's reputation except that they ran in *YM* magazine, whose readers are as young as 12 years old. Because one model was a child, Klein was accused of publishing "kiddie porn," an accusation that also prompted an FBI investigation. Several groups urged a boycott of the Calvin Klein products. Although Klein defended his sexually provocative campaign as strategically sound, the designer soon pulled the plug on the ads.[54]

Younger segments of the public are more impressionable than adults and more likely to be deceived by production values that increase the attractiveness of products in the minds of the viewers.[55] Thus, commercials aimed at children, especially younger children, take advantage of those who are the least powerful among consumer groups and the least capable of making rational and independent decisions in the marketplace.[56]

In addition, children are actually secondary consumers, because they have no real buying power of their own. Nevertheless, the available research suggests that heavy TV viewers do, in fact, approach their parents with requests for toys, games, and other products that they have seen featured in commercials.[57] Some critics believe that "this places an unfair burden on parents, who are required to spend significant portions of their parental energies vetoing purchases of new toys, breakfast cereals, candy products and soft drinks."[58] However, this mass marketing to the child audience is not confined to the TV industry. The highly acclaimed film *Jurassic Park,* for example, featured a scene in which the child characters pass through a Jurassic Park gift shop where the shelves are lined with "JP" shirts, caps, toys and other souvenirs—an inside-the-movie ad for the many Jurassic Park products that were being marketed around the country. This tactic evoked this complaint from Alan Entin, past president of the family psychology division of the American Psychological Association: "They're doing an awful lot to sell that movie and all its spin-offs. And it's misleading. I think it's taking advantage of kids and a market and parents who feel they are coerced into buying these things for kids and taking them to the movie."[59]

Some people, however, do not approach the role of commercialization in children's lives with such a caustic eye. Children are consumers, too, they argue, and there is nothing inherently evil or immoral in attempting to influence their product choices.

In a society in which advertising is ubiquitous and mass marketers attempt to cultivate consumer behavior at an early age, developing strategies to reconcile the views outlined here could be a formidable task. But we might consider as a point of departure the following guidelines for TV ads targeted to the child audience:

- Commercials directed at children should avoid "high-pressure" tactics to compel the young consumer to purchase the product.

- Children's commercials should not make exaggerated claims or mislead their audiences about the characteristics or benefits of the product advertised.

- In commercials directed at children, premiums or other promotional inducements should be depicted as clearly secondary to the original product being advertised.

- Children's commercials should never use violence, verbal abuse, or other forms of antisocial behavior as a selling technique, nor should such behavior be depicted as socially beneficial or acceptable.

- Children's commercials should avoid the use of weasel words, such as *only* and *as low as,* to promote price or exclusivity claims.

- In programs targeted to children, program content should be clearly separated from commercial content, and the major characters in the programs should not also be used to promote products to the juvenile audience.

In conclusion, the media do play a significant role in children's lives and can be influential in the formation and adoption of attitudes and values. Some media content is a reflection of the youthful subculture, but it also has something to say about the moral tone of that subculture. Thus, there is an ethical imperative for society to examine the media messages aimed at its youthful members.

THE JUVENILE AUDIENCE: HYPOTHETICAL CASE STUDIES

The cases in this chapter reflect a diversity of situations in which media content is directed at youthful audiences, both children and adolescents. In reading and evaluating these scenarios and providing your own solutions to the ethical dilemmas, keep in mind the special nature of the audience involved. You may wish to review the three philosophical guidelines for ethical decision making described in Chapter 3. Then, as you have done in the preceding chapters, examine each situation from the perspective of the duty-based moral agent (deontologist), the consequentialist (teleologist), and Aristotle's golden mean. Base your judgment on one of these philosophical foundations, and defend your decision.

CASE STUDIES

▶ **CASE 11-1**

Madison Avenue's Youngest Consumers[60]

As an executive with Hobart and Tyson, one of Madison Avenue's largest advertising agencies, Sherri Jackson had watched with concern as the ad industry challenged the limits of moral propriety and cultural civility. Jackson believed passionately in advertising's influential role in a free market economy and had few qualms about the personal integrity of her agency's staff and the other executives who contributed to Hobart and Tyson's success. However, as consumer complaints mounted against the industry and the FTC began scrutinizing advertisers and corporate marketers more rigorously, she became increasingly apprehensive that the ad industry was navigating without a moral compass.

After eight years with Hobart and Tyson, Jackson departed for a less hectic lifestyle, but she did not consider herself a disaffected critic who now felt it her calling to transform her former benefactor. Nevertheless, she believed her industry would benefit from an ombudsman who could objectively evaluate some of the industry's more controversial practices and respond to consumer complaints. With a rather modest infusion of funds from several small foundations and some private donations, Jackson established the Center for Responsible Advertising. The industry itself responded with undisguised hostility, but utilizing her professional contacts, Jackson convinced some skeptics that the Center would serve as an impartial forum for citizen complaints against advertisers rather than as a citizen watchdog organization. The more enlightened agencies even acknowledged the public benefit of such an organization and agreed to tender some financial support.

Jackson had launched her enterprise with only one assistant, but as the Center began to evaluate complaints against the advertising industry and to issue reports that were applauded by both industry critics and insiders as fair and balanced, the

number of financial benefactors grew. Within three years, the Center had expanded its roster to nine, most of whom were engaged in researching and writing the Center's reports. Jackson's minions were both proactive and reactive. Some of their projects were self-initiated studies of various industry practices, but the Center's essential mission was to serve as an ombudsman. Complaints against specific advertisers, particularly those implicating ethical concerns, were investigated, and if they appeared to have some merit, the advertiser in question was invited to submit a written response to the complaint. Jackson would then appoint two of her staff members to argue the opposing views in front of her, after which she would write a draft report rejecting or sustaining the complaint. On other occasions, the Center received complaints indicting the advertising practices of an entire corporate sector, such as the fast-food industry, and Jackson would then ask one or more representatives from that sector to respond in writing. However, no report was finalized until it had received a majority vote of her staff. While there was some resistance on Madison Avenue to cooperating with this self-appointed ombudsman, the fact that the Center published all of its findings persuaded some reluctant advertisers of the wisdom of submitting their own rebuttals to consumer complaints.

As the Center looked forward to its fourth year of operation, Jackson's staff began the arduous task of sifting through and evaluating the myriad of complaints against the fast-food industry and food products heavily marketed to children. The grievances focused not just on the unhealthy aspects of the marketed food products but also on the advertising techniques designed to persuade children to convince their parents to purchase the products. Such devices as tie-ins with cartoon characters, the use of professional athletes and entertainers to promote such products, and collection of product labels that could be traded in for a gift or prize were representative of such complaints.

Jackson was not unsympathetic to such criticisms because, as the mother of two, she had trouble competing with the barrage of junk-food advertising on television. Nevertheless, as an ombudsman she was obliged to exercise a degree of restraint and professional detachment and was determined to subject this genre of advertising to the same rigorous standards of fairness and balance that had become the hallmark of the Center's probing inquiries. To obtain a fair sampling of industry views, Jackson solicited responses from several cereal, candy, and fast-food companies that marketed their wares to children. She then appointed John Brownell, who had joined the Center two years ago with a newly minted marketing degree, to argue on behalf of the consumer complainants and Amber Foster, the most experienced staff researcher, to represent the industry views as delineated in their rather thoughtful and thorough submissions.

"Let's be clear about the seriousness of this issue," declared Brownell, as he prepared to set out the indictment against the fast-food industry and what some derisively referred to as the junk-food industry. "The amount of money spent on marketing food to children has more than doubled within the past decade. Children have become a major target audience for such advertisers. Some product ads include toys, websites, movie, and television tie-ins to persuade kids to eat the featured foods, much of it unhealthy. Food marketing is so pervasive—it has even penetrated school programs—that it's virtually impossible to escape its influence. Food advertising is especially effective because of the pivotal role that the media, particularly television and the Web, play in the lives of children."

"Madison Avenue might object to the label *junk food*," responded Foster, "but the fact is that we are a fast-food and junk-food culture. Our lifestyle has changed, and the food industry is simply responding to a need. Parents are the ones who purchase most of this food for their kids, and it's their responsibility to monitor their eating habits. I don't see this as an ethical issue within the industry. There is nothing deceptive in most of these ads. No one is led to believe these products are healthy. They simply appeal to the tastes of young people. The companies comply with the food labeling requirements, and parents can determine for themselves whether certain products are unhealthy for their kids."

"Deception is not the issue," Brownell quickly replied. "But food marketers are taking advantage of children's immaturity. Young children in particular don't understand that the purpose of advertising is to manipulate them into buying a product; their cognitive development is not sufficiently advanced to appreciate sophisticated persuasion techniques. In this respect, marketing to children is a serious ethical issue. Parental responsibility has an appealing ring to it, but it's difficult for parents to resist the *nag factor*. In fact, a recent study showed that one in every three visits to a fast-food outlet was attributable to children's begging—that is, the *nag factor*."

The *nag factor* obviously did not impress Foster. "But you appear to be opposed to any persuasive communication aimed at children or to which children might be exposed. Within your framework, children should be insulated from political messages because, heaven forbid, they should become political activists at such a young age. We are a consumer society, and I see nothing wrong with socializing our youngest members into the consumer culture. At the risk of redundancy, it's parents' responsibility to help their children become discriminating consumers."

"But the marketing of food products to children is different from, say, promoting toys and games," said Brownell. "This is a health issue. Most of the foods being marketed to kids are unhealthy. Just watch the news. Obesity is public enemy number one in children's health, according to recent studies. The overall well-being of the nation's youth has declined in the past several decades. And the food industry and its aggressive advertising campaigns targeted to children must share part of the responsibility."

"The issue of children's health is more complicated than just subsisting on certain kinds of food," replied Foster. "There are other factors, such as lack of exercise. The food industry can't be blamed for lack of parental oversight and communal concern. Parents can control their childrens' eating habits, and if they stopped purchasing what they believed to be unhealthy food products, then the industry itself would change. Let's face it. Parents enjoy fast-food restaurants as much as their children. Food manufacturers and the fast-food industry are just responding to market demand. Children want certain kinds of food, and the marketplace is just accommodating these desires. Children are consumers, too, and have the right to express their preferences. If parents have no objection, then why should a moral imperative be forced upon food marketers to help improve the health of the nation's youth?"

Jackson, as usual, had been listening attentively but, with Amber Foster's last rejoinder, decided that she had been sufficiently informed to write a draft report for her staff's consideration. She realized that, with the barrage of negative publicity, the food marketers and fast-food industry were on the defensive and that public opinion had begun to turn against them. On the one hand, she believed that those who advertised and marketed unhealthy food to children should be held accountable. On the other hand, Madison Avenue responded primarily to market demands and trends, and the fact was that children had been socialized into a consumer culture. Should those who targeted kids with their advertising now be held responsible for fulfilling a demand from the nation's youngest consumers? Was there something unethical about the use of advertising techniques designed to appeal specifically to children (such as the allure of professional athletes or entertainers)? For that matter, why should the responsibility be placed entirely on the shoulders of parents?

THE CASE STUDY

For several decades, consumer groups, such as Action for Children's Television (ACT), worked to limit advertising aimed at children. But the recent realization, supported by research, that the physical fitness of our nation's youth is at risk has brought this concern into stark focus. Obesity, in particular, has been identified as the major threat to children's health. And the fast-food industry and food manufacturers that market their wares to children have been singled out as the primary culprits in this crisis. In such an environment, a defense of food marketers becomes increasingly problematical.

Nevertheless, there is another side to this issue. As noted by Richard Campbell and his coauthors writing in *Media & Culture*: "Children and teenagers,

living in a culture dominated by TV ads, are often viewed as 'consumer trainees.'"[61] We have created the consumer culture and therefore should not be surprised that television (and now the Internet) has helped to socialize children into this culture. Much of the success of the food industry and fast-food outlets is predicated upon their appeal to children. To the extent that food marketers have promoted an unhealthy lifestyle, parents are willing participants. Thus, should the indictment of the practice of targeting children as consumers be resolved on ethical grounds, or is this nothing more than a legitimate marketing strategy to which some overzealous citizens groups object?

For the purpose of considering these questions and the criticisms of the food industry outlined here, assume the role of advertising ombudsman Sherri Jackson. And then, utilizing the SAD formula for moral reasoning outlined in Chapter 3, make a decision on what ethical posture you will recommend to your staff for inclusion in the Center's written response to the complaints against the fast-food industry and those companies that market food products to children.

▶ CASE 11-2
The Suspended Football Players

St. Jude's gridiron trouncing of their cross-town rivals, the Harding High Wildcats, was not entirely unexpected in the wake of the startling announcement shortly before the highly publicized game. Three days before this final contest of the regular season to determine which of the local undefeated teams would move on to the state playoffs, Harding High coach John MacAlister revealed that five starting players, including the starting quarterback, had been suspended for disciplinary reasons and would not dress out for the Friday night classic. He provided few details and skillfully deflected inquiries from the press concerning the nature of the offenses that had led to the suspensions. Just a week before kickoff, local sports prognosticators had declared the game a "tossup" but, in light of Coach MacAlister's terse declaration, quickly gave the winning edge to

St. Jude. St. Jude's 35-7 victory over Harding High vindicated that reassessment.

Harding was one of five high schools that serviced the educational needs of Victoria Falls' adolescents, but the school's athletic prowess rivaled its academic reputation. The football program in particular was a perennial contender for state honors and during the fall season dominated the sports coverage of both the *Victoria Falls Chronicle* and the sports segments of all three local TV stations. The Wildcats' sudden fall from gridiron grace and their unexpected thrashing at the hands of their cross-town rivals was readily attributable, in the minds of the community's sports journalists, to the last-minute suspensions of five first-string players. While rumors circulated as to the reason for the suspensions, Stephen Doucet's ongoing investigation of the matter quickly morphed from rumor into fact. Doucet was Channel 5's sports director, who also took the lead in his station's coverage of Victoria Falls's high school athletic events. While Coach MacAlister had refused to divulge the reasons for the suspensions of five players just three days before the Wildcats' most important game of the season, the team's trainer, who was also a science teacher at the school, confided to Doucet that the players had been suspended for drunkenness. According to the trainer, the five student athletes had left the Harding High premises early one afternoon and went to a downtown bar where, using fake IDs, they were served several alcoholic beverages. The five had returned to school intoxicated just in time for the afternoon team practice but Coach MacAlister had immediately suspended them from the team. He also notified police, who were investigating the bar's owner for serving alcohol to the underage clientele. Doucet then contacted an acquaintance of his in the Victoria Falls police department, who corroborated the trainer's account and the investigation of the downtown bar.

By the night of the matchup between St. Jude and Harding High, Doucet was confident of the reliability of his information, but he also recognized the ethical dimensions of reporting the rather disturbing results of his investigation, particularly considering the age of the offenders. But as it became clear that the suspensions were perhaps instrumental in dooming the Wildcats' chances for a shot at the state championship, Doucet's journalistic instincts competed annoyingly with his normally compassionate nature. However, he knew that the decision of whether to report the reasons for the suspensions and to identify the delinquent players would not be his alone. News director Latrelle Perkins, representing the station's management perspective, would be the moral gatekeeper. Janie Parham, the producer of Channel 5's early evening newscast, joined the conference between Perkins and Doucet.

"As you know," Perkins noted in commencing the hastily called ethics summit on the Monday morning following the Friday night classic, "Channel 5 has a policy against reporting the names of juvenile offenders unless they are charged as an adult or, in rare cases, when they are accused of a heinous crime. But these players are not charged with a crime; they've just been suspended for disciplinary reasons. The station policy doesn't cover this situation."

"Normally I would be opposed to reporting the names of students suspended for drinking," replied Doucet. "That usually isn't newsworthy. But this is different. I've agonized over the matter, but let's face it. These are not just students; they're also athletes whose names are frequently on the sports pages. They used fake IDs to buy booze. And their suspensions cost their team dearly."

"They may be athletes and from time to time their names do appear in our news coverage," Parham acknowledged. "But they're also juveniles who made a mistake. This could scar them for life. They've suffered enough by being deprived of the opportunity of playing in the most important game of the season. In fact, three of them are seniors and won't have an opportunity to compete again at this level."

"If these were second-string players whose absence would be unlikely to affect the outcome of the game, I might agree," argued Doucet. "But the suspension of five starters, including the quarterback, is a serious matter. It was bound to have a detrimental effect on team morale and was undoubtedly instrumental in the Wildcats' lopsided defeat. These suspensions are directly related to the outcome of the game against St. Jude and are therefore newsworthy."

"You're assuming that the absence of these players from the team caused Harding High's embarrassing defeat," responded Parham. "You don't know this for a fact. Perhaps the team just had a bad night."

"That's highly unlikely," declared Doucet. "We're journalists, and it's our job to probe for explanations as to why the Wildcats were outmatched Friday night. I've already reported on the technical reasons—the second-string quarter, David Egbert, had difficulty with reading his receivers, and the defense couldn't penetrate their offensive line. The blocking wasn't that sharp either. But the fact remains that these five starters were team leaders, and their absence undoubtedly hurt the team. They just didn't play inspired football. And I think we have an obligation to tell our viewers why."

"But we can do that without naming the players," replied Parham. "The fans surely must be aware that the suspensions—which were publicly announced by Coach MacAlister—were instrumental to the outcome of the game."

"According to your logic," responded Doucet as he became more entrenched in his position, "we could refuse to publish the name of anyone involved in an embarrassing situation. It seems to me that once the coach announced that five players had been suspended from the team, then the reason for those suspensions became journalistically relevant. And once we identify the reason—drunkenness—we may as well identify the players, since everyone in town who attended the game is aware of who was on the sideline and who wasn't."

"Undoubtedly, some in the community are aware of which players were suspended," declared Parham. "But they probably don't know the reason. Besides, providing media coverage of this episode and publicly identifying the players could create a stigma that will follow the players after they graduate. Publicity can have enduring consequences."

"Media coverage can be embarrassing," admitted Doucet. "But perhaps that's what's needed here. This could teach these players a lesson they'll never forget. Even juveniles need to realize there are consequences to their actions. And as I noted before, these are not just ordinary adolescents. They are starting players on one of the state's most competitive football teams. If this information leaks out and our viewers learn that we knew about the suspensions but refused to report them, then we could lose credibility."

"I don't accept your 'they need to be taught a lesson' rationale," replied Parham. "I believe the suspensions are a sufficient lesson. Besides, this argument has little to do with journalistic relevance. These players are students first and athletes second and need to be viewed in that light. And as far as losing credibility, I'm more concerned about the reaction of the viewers to our reporting the names of the players. I don't think we'll be applauded for doing so."

"I think I understand fully the competing arguments in this case," interrupted Perkins. "If we go with your story, Stephen, it will run in our 6 P.M. newscast tonight. I'll think it over and decide whether we should report what you've uncovered, including the names of the suspended players." Channel 5's news director had no reason to believe that his station's competitors were aware of the specific reason for the suspensions or, if they were, that they were about to divulge this information to their viewers. Regardless, in this case Latrelle Perkins was determined to not allow competitive factors to distort his moral compass concerning the reporting of the names of the suspended football players.

THE CASE STUDY

News coverage of adolescents and children who commit various infractions has always been particularly vexing. In recognition of the public interest in an alarming increase in juvenile crime, some states now allow media access to their juvenile justice system. There is some skepticism that shielding juvenile offenders from the glare of publicity really serves the cause of rehabilitation. Nevertheless, society's protective attitude toward its youngest citizens continues.

This case, of course, does not involve criminal behavior but a fairly common problem among today's teens—consumption of alcoholic beverages. However, the juveniles in question are not just ordinary members of the student body at Harding High. They are starters on the school's championship-caliber football team, and their indiscretions and subsequent suspensions may have cost their team an opportunity to compete for the state championship. In a rather modest way, they are media celebrities, since their names have frequently appeared in connection with the local media's coverage of the Harding High football games.

And yet, these players are still adolescents who clearly made a mistake. The coach, apparently believing he had to provide some explanation in advance as to why several starters would not dress out for the big game, simply stated they had been suspended. He declined to elaborate, a clear indication that he intended to protect these players to the extent possible. TV sports director/reporter Stephen Doucet believes that the reasons for the suspensions and hence the names are journalistically relevant because of the suspensions' impact on the outcome of the game. But producer Janie Parham is probably correct in her assessment that the station's viewers will not applaud the reporting of the players' names in connection with the infractions that led to the suspensions.

For the sake of analyzing this ethical dilemma, assume the position of Channel 5 news director Latrelle Perkins and, utilizing the SAD model for moral reasoning outlined in Chapter 3, render a judgment on this ethical dilemma. In analyzing the facts of this case, you should take into account (1) the ages of the offenders, (2) their unique role as football players with some celebrity status within the Harding High community, (3) the journalistic relevance of the information, and (4) the potential harm of the release of the student athletes' names and the specific nature of their indiscretion balanced against the news value of this information.

▶ CASE 11-3

Nottoway Landing's Cult Following among Young Female Viewers

Michael Belo was in a foul mood! Along with the other three network chieftains, he had just returned from the nation's capital, where he had endured two days of hostile interrogation from a congressional committee demanding to know why

the television industry persisted in its efforts to corrupt the morals of the nation's youth. "The American people are fed up with the networks' using the public's airwaves to feed them a daily dose of sex and violence, especially when children and teenagers are likely to be in the audience," Robert Russell, committee chair and conservative Republican, declared during one of his frequent lapses into rhetorical hyperbole. Russell urged the network executives to return to the family viewing hour concept the industry had embraced more than two decades ago. He adjourned the two-day hearing with a threat of government regulation if the networks did not assume more moral responsibility in devising their prime-time menu.

Despite the ritualistic nature of such committee hearings—his predecessors had endured such indignities regularly since the TV quiz show scandals in the late fifties—Belo was chastened by this assault on his company's lack of moral propriety. Nevertheless, he was impressed by Congressman Russell's profound knowledge of the four major broadcast networks' prime-time schedules and the ratings data that were the lifeblood of the industry's program decision making. The chair had adroitly deconstructed every program that, in his judgment, featured excessive sex and violence and demanded a defense of that program's cultural merit. However, Belo had arrived at the hearing armed with his own program research and notes on the network entertainment division's decision to include each offering in its prime-time schedule. He had performed reasonably well, in his view, in responding to the congressman's offensive, but he had been blindsided by one research report cited by his antagonist concerning *Nottoway Landing.*

Nottoway Landing, a prime-time soap opera that aired at 9 P.M. Eastern time, had been singled out for particularly harsh criticism. Set in a New England seacoast community, *Nottoway Landing* focused on the rather untidy lives of the town's affluent occupants and attempted to embrace contemporary culture in all of its manifestations. Sexual promiscuity, substance abuse, teen suicide, high school shootings, interracial dating, homosexual relationships, date rape, and abortion had all provided grist for the writers' mill as the show quickly moved into the top ten, where it remained for most of the season.

Nottoway Landing's target audience was females 18 to 34, but the latest rating book also revealed a significant number of male viewers who had been attracted to what Chairman Russell referred to as the program's "hedonistic themes." His ire was directed not so much at individual topics, such as abortion or school violence, but at the recurring depictions of steamy and seemingly casual sex and the relentless depictions of alcohol as the "drug of choice" for the show's male characters. "I realize that this program is designed for adult viewers," Chairman Russell asserted to the witnesses and the television audience that would hear his sound bites on the evening news broadcasts, "but this study shows that young girls ages 10 to 16 are attracted to the male 'hunks' on *Nottoway Landing*. And their heartthrobs are depicted week after week having unprotected and casual sex, *without any apparent consequences,* and some of the action takes place in bars or luxurious homes where alcohol is usually consumed during the dialogue. In some episodes, these male sex symbols, along with their beautiful girlfriends, consume several drinks and then drive away intoxicated in their flashy sports cars. This is the kind of behavior that is corrupting our young people because shows such as *Nottoway Landing* air in the middle of prime time. You can defend this show as an adult drama if you wish, but many of the viewers are young people who are heavily influenced by what they see on TV."

Chairman Russell's study had caught Belo off guard because it had been commissioned by the committee in preparation for these hearings. While it contained a comprehensive and "scientific" analysis of the entire prime-time schedule of all four networks, the congressman had selected *Nottoway Landing* as the most egregious example with which to assault the unsuspecting network president.

Like his industry rivals, Belo had made no specific commitments to his congressional critics except to review his prime-time schedule to see if adjustments were warranted in response to the ongoing national debate about TV's role in the lives of the nation's youth. Nevertheless, he did take this obligation seriously as a means of keeping the legislative wolves and consumer watchdogs away from his door.

Belo had been back in New York for less than an hour when he quickly disgorged himself of his frustrations at the public thrashing he had endured at the hands of the congressional committee, excerpts of which had been aired on the nightly news, including his own network. "This hasn't been a pleasant experience, but we need to do a good-faith review of our prime-time schedule," Belo told Solomon Rubenstein, the network's vice president for entertainment, who had been summoned to his superior's office within minutes of the president's return to his fortieth floor office suite. "But I want to focus first on *Nottoway Landing,* with which Chairman Russell seemed to be so occupied." They were soon joined by Cassandra Fertita, the associate vice president for prime-time programming.

"As you know, *Nottoway Landing* is one of our hits," noted Rubenstein correctly. "It's an adult drama—some would describe it as a soap opera—and it does feature adult themes. This program is hardly a novelty in prime-time TV. Why has this show been singled out?"

"I'm aware that its target audience is females ages 18 to 34," replied Belo. "And sex and alcohol are a part of our culture. Let's face it, we live in a rather permissive society. But Russell's concerns are based upon the young girls we've picked up along the way in our demographic mix. I was aware from our ratings data that some young viewers are tuning in, but the chairman's study provided more qualitative information on why females as young as 10 are being turned on by the show's male stars."

"But isn't this a danger with any program?," countered Fertita. "We design our schedule to appeal to certain demographics, which may change as the evening wears on. If our target audience tunes in in sufficient numbers, then we have a hit as far as our advertisers are concerned. Are we responsible if underage girls are attracted to the male leads in *Nottoway Landing*?"

"In a sense, you have a point," replied Belo. "But scheduling plays a role in who tunes in. *Nottoway Landing* is situated between our first and third hours of prime-time programming on Tuesday nights. The first hour is sitcoms; the 10 P.M. time slot is occupied by our highly rated medical show, *The Residents.* Would it make sense to move *Nottoway Landing* to the 10 o'clock position on another night?"

"Forgive the cliché, but if it ain't broke don't fix it," declared Fertita emphatically. "*Nottoway Landing* is getting the numbers and the demographics in its current position. Keep in mind also that it serves as a strong lead-in for *The Residents.* If we move *Nottoway,* then both shows might suffer. Besides, how will a time shift address Chairman Russell's concern? It's naïve to think that young girls will be in bed by 10, oblivious to the rather liberal lifestyle of their male heroes."

"But what you refer to as 'liberal' conservatives might consider to be promiscuous," responded Belo. "Thus far we have mentioned only time shifting as a possibility, but this doesn't deal with the primary moral accusation against the program, namely that young, impressionable females—some as young as 10—are bonding vicariously with the beautiful people of this fictional community known as Nottoway Landing and are learning that casual sex and alcohol consumption are admirable traits. It's hard to explain to either Congress or the viewing public why we don't share some ethical responsibility for such consequences."

It was difficult for Rubenstein to provide a direct counterpoint to Belo's argument because, despite his twenty-year tenure in the broadcasting industry, he still harbored certain puritanical tendencies, which he conveniently bracketed when making decisions on which shows to include in his network's prime-time schedule. "You may have a point," Rubenstein finally conceded. "But if we make major revisions in *Nottoway Landing,* we may as well cancel it. It's a realistic look at life in an upscale, contemporary community. Sex and alcohol are a part of this kind of lifestyle. Don't the parents have the primary responsibility for monitoring their children's viewing habits?"

"I agree with parental responsibility," replied Belo, "but let's face it. Most kids have TVs in their rooms. And quite frankly, some of these young girls are undoubtedly watching the show with their parents, who are also addicted to it."

"I won't deny the charismatic nature of the cast and their attraction to young teens," acknowledged Fertita. "This is the same phenomenon we see with rock stars. And many of the male characters are indeed 'hunks' who always seem to land in bed with beautiful women. And alcohol is always a part of this mix. There are few homely people in this show except for villains and an assortment of cultural misfits. Since we approved this program for our prime-time schedule, we are indeed responsible for it. But are we to *blame* for the deleterious effects of *Nottoway Landing* on a segment of the audience for whom this show is not intended? We're entertainers, not psychologists."

"I don't think that Chairman Russell is concerned *just* with the inclusion of sex and drinking as part of the plot," asserted Belo. "During the hearings he also charged—correctly, in my judgment—that we never show consequences of such a permissive lifestyle, such as unwanted pregnancies and fatalities resulting from drunk driving, not to mention the emotional toll from casual relationships."

With that closing observation, Belo adjourned the meeting. As he reflected on his subordinates' remarks, he knew that *Nottoway Landing* was really a surrogate for what TV's critics considered to be a vast cultural wasteland. Should the highly rated program become a sacrificial lamb to the congressional committee's artistic paternalism, or would this be seen by his industry peers and libertarians as a surrender to government pressure? Could changes be made in the show to placate his congressional critics without destroying its commercial success? And at a higher level, could he deny any ethical responsibility for *Nottoway Landing*'s influence on young girls when the program was not targeted to this demographic segment of the TV audience?

Network president Michael Belo pondered these questions as he adjourned the meeting with his two subordinates. He confirmed to Solomon Rubenstein that normally this decision would be left to the Entertainment Division but that he would assume the responsibility for making the ethical call in the case of *Nottoway Landing.* Nevertheless, he promised to make no decision or to communicate further with his congressional critics without full consultation with Rubenstein and Fertita.

THE CASE STUDY

Sex and alcohol abuse are common within the teen subculture. In addition, studies show that heavy TV viewing is correlated with such pathologies as sexual intercourse at an early age and an increase in the level of aggression. TV undeniably plays an influential role in the lives of the nation's youth, even with the Internet (which poses problems of its own) competing for their attention.

The issues posed in this narrative are enduring and have plagued cultural gatekeepers since virtually the inauguration of mass media entertainment. Government threats and attempts at intimidation are commonplace, and all parties know that congressional options are limited because of First Amendment concerns. But this also serves to shift the emphasis to the ethical arena, where consumer watchdogs maintain a constant vigilance.

As representatives of a government-licensed industry and fiduciaries of the public interest, broadcast executives cannot simply ignore the persistent inquiries of their congressional critics. There may be no reasonable way to satisfy all stakeholders in this ongoing moral disputation. Industry executives cannot be expected to respond to every study that reflects TV's pernicious influence on certain segments of the audience. But neither can they simply deny all responsibility for the social influences of their programming fare. The libertarianism impulse does have its limits.

The major concerns have been set forth in the case narrative. For the purpose of addressing this complicated issue, assume the role of network president Michael Belo and, utilizing the SAD formula for moral reasoning described in Chapter 3, make a decision on the fate of *Nottoway Landing*. In your analysis, be sure to identify the options available to you and clearly delineate the pros and cons of each.

▶ CASE 11-4

Teen Therapy on the Airwaves

Dr. Georgina Sellers (or "Dr. George," as she was affectionately called) had struck a responsive chord among the nation's youth. Dr. George's ethical wisdom and sage counsel dispensed daily through her two-hour radio broadcast had attracted an unexpected cross section of teens, including those from morally stable environments and those who were culturally disaffected and morally adrift. Like most talk show hosts she was not universally applauded by her listeners, but she had captured their attention with her "Character First" campaign and uncompromising and often strident insistence upon her unyielding code of moral discipline. Her fans lauded her message and the missionary spirit with which it was delivered. Despite a caustic style that tolerated no whining or feeble attempts at rationalization from her young callers, Dr. George's quick wit and ability to understand and address adolescents forged an unquestionable bond with her fans. Her less charitable critics derided her profound sense of self-righteousness and the uncertain consequences of what they referred to as "pop therapy."

However, Dr. George was not a therapist without credentials. She had earned a PhD in psychology from the University of Pittsburgh, married an attorney from Chicago, and moved to the Windy City to begin what would eventually develop into a lucrative practice in child psychology. Her growing reputation as a therapist was augmented with an impressive record of scholarship, including three books and countless journal articles and academic treatises presented to her peers at professional conferences. However, after fifteen years of counseling children with behavioral and emotional problems and attending to the desperate testaments of adolescents in the privacy of her office, she had decided to expand her practice into the electronic marketplace. Dr. George's overtures to the station manager of Chicago's most highly rated station among the city's teens was greeted with some skepticism, but the irrepressible psychologist had persisted until the manager agreed to a two-hour phone-in segment in the late afternoons during which Dr. George would respond to questions from her inquisitive adolescent callers.

Within six months, Dr. George's talk show had become the most popular in the Chicago market, a track record that caught the attention of both *Newsweek* and *Time*. It also attracted the attention of McKnight Communications, which purchased the syndication rights to the show and placed it on

299 radio stations, including those in the top thirty markets.

Dr. George's "tough love" approach to her electronic counseling sessions confounded her critics, most of whom embraced the conventional wisdom that teens were impervious to advice from those over 30. Predictably, her callers had confronted her with a wide range of adolescent problems, including teen sexuality, fractured relationships, abortion, obesity, loss of self-esteem, and even incest. She also welcomed calls from teenagers who were apparently morally mature and frequently offered their own advice in response to a previous caller's desperate plea.

In dispensing her wisdom, Dr. George was patient but firm. She gave no quarter to those callers who wished to debate the prudence of her guidance and took advantage of her electronic bully pulpit to scold those who stubbornly resisted her counsel. But regardless of the issue, her advice was animated by two fundamental and related precepts: moral health and the cultivation of character. The popular therapist was convinced that a morally healthy teen could survive the traumatic passage from childhood to adulthood, and she was eager to contribute to that safe passage. Her on-air dialogues were often peppered with references to honesty, integrity, respect, commitment, and self-discipline.

As Dr. George began her second year on the air, discordant notes threatened the show's character. A 16-year-old girl, apparently following what she believed was advice tendered by Dr. George during a live-on-air exchange, ended a tumultuous relationship with her boyfriend and three weeks later committed suicide. The girl's parents then sued Dr. Georgina Sellers and McKnight Communications for negligence. In a less drastic response, the father of a 15-year-old boy complained in a letter to the *New York Times* that his son had talked candidly on the *Dr. George Show* about his parents' pending divorce and the events leading up to the estrangement, including the father's adulterous relationship. This prompted a public round of soul-searching in the press and from opponents of the pop therapy genre of radio programming. Nevertheless, Dr. George's image with her fans was untarnished, and the American Psychological Association even presented her with their prestigious media award for her efforts on behalf of troubled teens, a coveted affirmation from her peers. Letters from teens who had benefited from her sagacity far surpassed those who were disappointed with her counsel. And her continuing high ratings further validated her influence among the nation's youth, a marketplace triumph that prompted McKnight to search for new outlets for its most popular syndicated offering.

"McKnight Communications wants us to be their three hundredth station on the *Dr. George* lineup," declared Marion Faye, as he opened his meeting with program director Leslie Pine and the station's program manager, Maria Guadelupe. Faye was the general manager of KABE-FM in San Marino, a culturally diverse metroplex of 750,000 in the desert Southwest. The visit from McKnight's sales rep was not unexpected, but the recent controversy surrounding the *Dr. George Show* had transformed what under normal circumstances would have been a routine programming and financial decision into an ethical dilemma. Faye would be his station's moral agent and gatekeeper in deciding the fate of the *Dr. George Show* in the San Marino market, but he was not reticent in soliciting input from his two subordinates.

"As you know, the show is one of the most popular phone-in talk shows, particularly among teens—our demographic group. But the *Dr. George Show* is not without controversy," Faye continued, as he awaited comments from his program director and promotion manager.

"I vote in favor of adding this show to our lineup," said Pine without hesitation. "It's the number one talk show in a majority of markets that carry it. It could be a big moneymaker for us. Besides, Dr. George is a refreshing counterpoint to so much of the morally ambiguous fare aimed at teens today."

"I have some reservations," replied Guadelupe. "Her 'tough love' approach to dealing with adolescent problems is appealing at first glance. There's no doubt that a lot of teenagers are morally adrift and need some direction. But no one knows for sure how these callers are using this advice. I'm skeptical of this kind of program in which therapists dispense advice to listeners they've never met, particularly in the case of teenagers."

Pine, however, was unconcerned by what one unflattering article had described as "Dr. George's ten easy steps to moral health." "I don't have a problem with the show," she stated. "A lot of teens have nowhere to turn. If they get comfort from Dr. George, whether they take her advice or not, I don't see any real harm. It would be great if all teenagers could talk to their parents, a friend, or a minister. But some don't have confidence in these resources. Dr. George has connected with a lot of teenagers, and she has a large following."

"But the teen years are delicate ones," noted Guadelupe. "I have two daughters of my own. I know what's best for them, even though they don't always appreciate my advice. I applaud Dr. George's 'Character First' agenda, but I question her 'one size fits all' approach to dispensing advice. She may appear to be talking one-on-one to her callers, but in fact other listeners with similar problems may well act on her advice."

"But Dr. George is accessible to thousands of teens and in the process she's entertaining," replied Pine. "And her message and no-nonsense approach to moral behavior are what kids need to hear. They'll pay attention to a media celebrity like Dr. George, whereas they often turn a deaf ear to those closest to them. Who can really object to her 'Character First' crusade? It certainly beats the lessons conveyed through TV and much of the pop music that teens listen to today."

"I have no objection to Dr. George's message or her intent," stated Guadelupe uncategorically. "But I do think that this kind of instant therapy dispensed to anonymous callers, regardless of its apparent merit, undermines the moral authority and influence of those who are in the best position to assist those adolescents with emotional or other personal problems."

The dialogue between the program director and promotion manager had been brief, but Faye was confident that their comments reflected the most important countervailing arguments that might be advanced concerning his decision on whether to provide Dr. George with an entrée to the San Marino market. On the one hand, he could not fault her motivations in attempting to restore some measure of moral health to the nation's youth. She had apparently met with some measure of success.

And in a more practical vein, the program was a huge economic success, the fruits of which would enrich the station's own financial coffers.

On the other hand, the recent events documenting the darker side of radio pop therapy, as anecdotal as they were, challenged Faye's sense of social responsibility. With such a vast and anonymous audience, there was really no way to measure the benefits and harms of the psychologist's daily disbursements of moral guidance. Although Dr. George's professional credentials were unassailable, her program still smacked of pop psychology, and he was concerned that a radio personality might exert an inordinate amount of influence on his adolescent listeners and thus undermine the moral authority of those who know them best. But the fact that stations in 299 other markets had welcomed Dr. George apparently without any moral qualms did not make his decision any easier.

THE CASE STUDY

In recent years radio psychology and therapy have evolved into a popular genre. Of course, advice columns have been a mainstay of the print media for many years, as evidenced in such popular features as "Ann Landers" and "Dear Abby." But their radio counterparts—the content of which is sometimes derisively referred to as "pop therapy"—are usually more highly focused in their audiences and the nature of the problems that are addressed.

The dilemma confronting station manager Marion Faye does not revolve around whether he believes the *Dr. George Show* has some socially redeeming value or whether he views this program as nothing more than entertainment masquerading as serious therapy. His concern is more fundamental: Dr. George's audience consists primarily of teenagers who apparently feel more comfortable confiding in this media celebrity (albeit with impressive academic and professional credentials) than in a family member or a close friend. He wonders whether, in the long run, the harm done by advice rendered to anonymous juvenile callers will outweigh the benefits.

However, he must also admire her uncompromising adherence to a strict moral code and what appears to be reasonable counsel tendered to her youthful fans. And teens, like anyone else, are free to accept or reject her advice. In the end, they are responsible (or are they?) for their own decisions.

Despite the potential financial rewards (not an unimportant consideration), Faye is obviously bothered by the *Dr. George Show*. Has he unnecessarily converted a purely economic and programming decision into an ethical one?

For the purpose of making a decision on whether the *Dr. George Show* will make its debut in the San Marino market on KABE-FM, assume the role of station manager Marion Faye. Then, applying the SAD formula for moral reasoning outlined in Chapter 3, render a judgment in this matter and defend it.

▶ CASE 11-5
Advertising in the Public Schools

Braxton Hutto surveyed the fallout from Saturday's school bond election with a profound sense of pessimism. As the superintendent of the Parkersville School District, Hutto had led a TV and newspaper advertising campaign to convince taxpayers to rescue the financially destitute system from economic ruination. But the voters had once again rejected the educational establishment's plea, apparently unconvinced that increased funding would appreciably improve the academic quality of their community's schools. The vote had been close—51 percent to 49 percent—but "close counts only in horseshoes," Hutto remarked rather dejectedly to one of his assistants.

Hutto grappled with his melancholy for a few days and then decided to take matters into his own hands. The Parkersville School District had once been among the state's most exemplary, and there was no reason, in his judgment, why it could not once again aspire to academic excellence. If he could find "outside" sources of funding for books, supplies, lab equipment, and state-of-the-art computers, the superintendent reasoned, then perhaps he could unencumber some money in the budget to provide small pay increases for both faculty and staff.

Hutto's natural instincts inclined him toward the rather lucrative benevolence of the corporate world, which had provided an abundance of educational materials to his district during his tenure. Of course, there was a trade-off in that each company's corporate logo was featured prominently on each packet, and suspicion concerning the educational value of materials provided by institutions with a vested interest always existed. Nevertheless, teachers had found them to be a welcome addition to their other pedagogical tools.

The superintendent wondered whether the time had come to become more fully engaged with corporate sponsorship of the educational enterprise. His proposal, which would have to be approved by the school board, would not be revolutionary, since other school districts around the country had already given corporate sponsors an entrée into their schools. This included Channel One television, which contained commercials and was beamed directly into the nation's classrooms. Specifically, Hutto's plan called for the selling of advertising space along school hallways, which would become a virtual arcade of target marketing. The money raised by such a commercial venture, Hutto reasoned, could pay for a lot of computers, software, and supplies.

Hutto viewed his plan as an economic necessity. He also recognized it as a potential public relations problem, a perception confirmed by Robert Lane, the school district's affable publicity director. Lane suggested that they move cautiously, first introducing the concept on a one-year trial basis at Parkersville High and then soliciting as many views as possible on the proposal. "We should begin," Lane said, "by meeting with the head of the teachers' union, the president of the PTA, Parkersville High principal Leslie Holiday, and perhaps even a teacher and the president of the school's student council. In this way, all of the constituencies will be represented." Lane also suggested that they meet together because group dynamics, in his judgment, often produced more reasonable results.

Hutto convened the meeting in his office after school hours. He was joined by Leslie Holiday, Parkersville High principal; Sandra Land-Johnson, president of the district's PTA; Marsha Braxton, union president and a social studies teacher at the high school; and Lisa Stanley, student council president. Robert Lane was also in attendance to assess the public relations implications of the proposal and to consider the advice that he would recommend to his superior on whether the plan should be implemented.

"I assume you have all read my proposal," Hutto said as he began his pitch in support of corporate sponsorship of his educational enterprise. "Simply put, we would like to sell ads to companies such as McDonald's, Pepsi, and others that appeal to the youth market. We don't plan to saturate our school buildings, of course. The ads would be strategically placed along the hallway and in our cafeteria. The revenue from this venture can help support a lot of our needs that taxpayers apparently are unwilling to pay for."

"I support the proposal," responded Braxton. "The teachers haven't had a raise in several years, and we have little money for supplies. And in this information age our students need computers. If the taxpayers are unwilling to approve a bond issue to help pay for these necessities, then we have to take matters into our own hands."

"I'm the principal of Parkersville High," said Holiday, "and I'm certainly sympathetic with our financial plight. But this seems rather drastic to me. We could open ourselves to charges of selling out to corporate interests. In addition, if we can so easily raise money through this means, that will take the state legislature and the local taxpayers off the hook. Politically, a better approach might be to let things get so bad that our citizens have no choice but to support the schools."

"I'm not concerned with the politics of this matter," responded Land-Johnson indignantly. "We should put the kids first. The fact is that if we allow advertising in our schools, these sponsors will have a captive audience. We'll be assisting them in taking advantage of these students. The purpose of school should be to teach—not to promote products."

"But isn't that rather elitist?" replied Hutto, unable to resist the temptation to defend his proposal at this point. "After all, these kids have grown up on advertising. It's ubiquitous in their world—on TV, in shopping malls, and even on the scoreboard in the municipal stadium where we play our games.

What's the difference here? These students are mature enough to make their own buying decisions."

"The difference," stated Land-Johnson, "is that in this case we would become in a sense partners in commercializing our public schools. Advertisers would have a captive audience. And we would be helping them to take advantage of these students. Having these ads—many of which are cleverly done and are very entertaining—in our hallways and cafeteria would distract from the seriousness of our schools' educational mission."

"I agree with Sandra," said Holiday. "Schools are supposed to be institutions that students trust. If these ads go up in the public schools, they will assume a certain amount of credibility. Our community role and responsibility to these students distinguish us from advertising in other contexts. And we don't have the personnel or the time to sift out the good ads from the bad."

"I realize it's a trade-off," responded Braxton. "I'm not crazy about the idea of having ads in our hallways and lunchroom. But the bottom line is we need the money. The materials provided by corporate sponsors so far have been helpful. In a market-driven world, I just don't agree that we're somehow taking advantage of impressionable youths. They're more worldly and materialistic than many of their parents."

The superintendent then turned to Lisa Stanley, who had been uncharacteristically quiet, for the student perspective. "I'm not concerned about the ads," she replied, without hesitation. "After the 'newness' wears off, most of the kids at Parkersville High will probably pay little attention to them. Besides, we're mature enough to make our own judgments about products. Our whole world is saturated with ads. If these advertisements produce money for the district, the students certainly won't complain."

"I am concerned about the public's perception," said Lane, who had been listening to the discussion and taking notes. "Our critics might accuse us of selling out to commercial interests, thus diluting the quality of the educational environment. And if our relationship with corporate sponsors continues for an extended period, we might even be publicly indicted for propagandizing rather than educating our students. On the other hand, in our advertising and media-saturated world, even the public may not care. This just may not be a big issue for them. In any event, from a public relations perspective, we might use this plan to convince taxpayers how desperate our financial condition is. Perhaps, then, they'll come to our rescue."

As Superintendent Hutto brought the meeting to a close, Lane began to ponder the ethical dimensions of the proposal. Although Hutto was certainly favorably disposed toward some kind of marketing alliance with corporate America, he would lean heavily on his publicity director's recommendation, especially because the proposal had to have school board approval and eventually public endorsement. On the one hand, Lane agreed with the superintendent that the support from advertising revenues could be the economic salvation of the district's educational support system. And besides, in a commercially saturated youth culture, what harm could result from placing a few ads in the school's passageways?

On the other hand, it did seem rather unseemly to introduce commercial values into an institution that was committed to academic concerns, particularly to a captive audience for which the school assumed responsibility for its educational maturation. He had visions of an ad adorning the Parkersville High cafeteria that read, "This lunch break is brought to you today by. . . ."

THE CASE STUDY

Because of economic concerns, many school districts across the country have provided access to corporate sponsors to promote their products directly to students within their educational environment. However, such a practice is not without controversy, as noted in this observation from a recent article in *U.S. News & World Report:*

> Once relatively free from reminders of the outside commercial world, schools today are fast becoming billboards for corporate messages. . . . Whatever their port of entry into the schools, advertisements and product endorsements are creating a stir across the country. While supporters argue they are harmless, critics blast school-based commercial plugs as not only distasteful but manipulative. . . .[62]

In this case, the superintendent feels his options are limited considering the district's bleak financial picture. Teacher union president Sandra Land-Johnson agrees and sees the corporate sponsorship as a means of at least improving the district's educational support system. And student council president Lisa Stanley doesn't anticipate any objection from the students given the commercial environment in which they have matured.

On the other hand, the school's principal is reluctant to have his institution become a marketing vehicle despite the financial benefits that might accrue. But he also cites political motives—that is, accepting outside funding sources might send the wrong signal to the legislature and taxpayers. The PTA president, who supposedly speaks for the parents' concerns, is unconditionally opposed to the proposal because of its potential impact on the students.

Thus, all of these concerns might be addressed in response to this question: Does the placement of ads in the public schools to enhance the quality of the educational enterprise raise ethical concerns, or it is really more of an amoral business decision based upon economic reality?

You are the school's publicity director, Robert Lane, and must now make a recommendation to the district superintendent on whether to go forward with his proposal to the school board. Keep in mind the public relations aspect of this dilemma and, if you should recommend approval, what strategies you might use to sell the idea to the public, assuming, of course, that you anticipate some resistance.

▶ ## CASE 11-6
Video Games and the Promotion of Incivility[63]

Pro Football Combat was not subtle in its invitation to video game enthusiasts to experience the vicarious thrills of professional football's organized mayhem. Its packaging included some of the most aggressive and brutal scenes from the NFL's gridiron action and an assertive rhetorical appeal to the nation's youngest fans. "You be the coach. Call your own plays. Experience the thrill of victory and smash mouth football at its best. No rules, no officials, no penalties!," proclaimed the game's compelling and imaginative box top.

Pro Football Combat was an intense litany of action-packed and aggressive football plays, accompanied by reaction shots of player celebrations, unsportsmanlike conduct manifested in taunting of opposing players, and inebriated fans, some of whom were naked to the waist or sported colored hair and a bizarre array of unconventional attire. These were designed to enhance the reality of the professional football environment. However, the game was not without its socially redeeming qualities. It required participants to develop strategies and to make decisions on how to neutralize the effectiveness of the other team's game plan. Trinitone was hopeful that these benefits would silence the game's most savage critics. Although Trinitone Enterprise's latest entry into the competitive video game marketplace was not licensed by the NFL, the company was confident that its target audience of ages 10 to 16 would readily embrace *Pro Football Combat*'s fast-paced action.

Trinitone had been a pioneer in producing games and toys for children and adolescents and had marketed its wares to generations of youthful consumers and their parents. Its innovative management teams had always adapted to commercial realities, and the company had been one of the first entrants into the video game marketplace. From its inception, Trinitone had cultivated its reputation as a company committed to the fortification of childhood fantasies and the preservation of youthful innocence. However, competitive pressures had forced Trinitone into a strategic reassessment of corporate philosophy, and beginning in the early 1990s, the company's products had appealed progressively to a youthful generation nurtured on a culture of moral permissiveness.

With the Christmas season—a lucrative period for manufacturers of toys and video games—just a few months away, Robin Montgomery was not unduly surprised at the visit from Matthew Crankshaw, the director of marketing and promotion for Trinitone Enterprises. With its diverse inventory, Trinitone relied on more than one agency to handle its lucrative advertising expenditures. Prior to Crankshaw's arrival, the rumor mill had identified Byron and

Oleson, a small but successful agency in Chicago, as Trinitone's beneficiary of the *Pro Football Combat* campaign that would commence two months before the Christmas shopping season. As Byron and Oleson's media director, Montgomery would represent her agency in deciding whether to respond favorably to Trinitone's overtures.

"Trinitone Enterprises wants to shift part of their account to our agency," noted Montgomery, as she convened the meeting with two agency colleagues who would offer their counsel on whether to accept the Trinitone account: Elva Bourg, the senior account executive, and Delbert Burgess, the creative director. "They're particularly interested in having us handle the ads for their video game business. The Christmas season is only four months away, and they have a lot of money to spend. They believe that their first sports video game—*Pro Football Combat*—will be a winner, and that's where they want to put their ad dollars."

"I've read the specs on the game you provided in preparation for this meeting," said Burgess without hesitation. "This is a pretty violent video. It's full of bone-crushing tackles, complete with sound effects, and plays that should be flagged for unnecessary roughness. But of course there are no officials here, and the game is programmed to highlight the most brutal aspects of professional football."

"You apparently have an objection to marketing this game to young consumers," replied Bourg. "But professional football is violent, and it comes into our homes every weekend during the fall. Kids are in the audience. It's a part of our culture, and Trinitone Enterprises is doing nothing more than satisfying a consumer demand to become more interactive with the finer points of gridiron strategy. Besides, this game isn't just about violence and fan behavior. It teaches skills that kids can use later in life."

"But these consumers are children and young teens," responded Burgess. "I agree that they can learn a lot about strategy and decision making from this video game. It's one of the most sophisticated sports videos on the market. It does require the users to think, and in that respect *Pro Football Combat* might even be educational. But these benefits are overshadowed by the game's violent and uncivil aspects. If we accept this account, then we'll be a party to the glorification of athletic violence and poor sportsmanship."

But Bourg was unpersuaded by Burgess's seemingly puritanical posture. "If consumers or critics have a problem with this game, they should address their concerns to Trinitone. Our job is to produce ads to help our clients sell their products. Sure, there are limits, but Trinitone is a reputable company that simply wants to compete on a level playing field. Their competitors are marketing games that some would consider unsuitable for young people. But these games are popular, and they're selling. If parents don't want their children to interact with these kinds of video games, then it's their responsibility to serve as moral gatekeepers. Besides, if we don't accept this account, then one of our competitors will. One way or the other, *Pro Football Combat* will launch an all-out blitz between now and Christmas to ensnare their young target audience."

"I agree that parents must shoulder a heavy share of the responsibility in this matter," acknowledged Burgess. "But saturation campaigns such as the one Trinitone has in mind for the Christmas season must naturally tie in with the product's theme, as reflected on the packaging. To be effective, our ads will have to have high-energy production values that focus on the game's more violent and unattractive aspects. This will make it difficult for parents to resist their childrens' entreaties to place a copy of *Pro Football Combat* under their Christmas tree. Therefore, I don't agree that we can just absolve ourselves of any moral duty to move cautiously in advertising violent video games to a youthful audience. I'm aware that if we don't accept this account, then one of our competitors will. There's a lot of money involved. But should we adjust our own moral compass based on what our competitors are likely to do?"

"Your position is unnecessarily paternalistic," responded Bourg. "Media violence is pervasive, even in some cartoons directed at children. Children are consumers. They have the right to make their own decisions. Many of them watch football on TV, and they're aware of the sport's violent aspects. They're also aware of the other unattractive aspects of the game: player celebrations in the end

zone, taunting, and uncivilized fan behavior. This game doesn't sanctify any of this. It attempts to portray realistically the nature of professional football and to allow young fans to interact in a way that provides an entertaining vicarious experience."

But Burgess was undeterred by his colleague's assault on his paternalistic instincts. "Children may be consumers," he replied, "but they're not autonomous. Television is very influential in their lives, and if we produce ads that highlight this game's primary selling points, then our actions will in fact sanctify the less attractive aspects of professional football. And when it comes to advertising products for children and adolescents, I do feel that our industry must be more selective in its clients—or at least in the kinds of advertising produced for them."

Robin Montgomery, Byron and Oleson's media director, listened impassively as Bourg and Burgess debated the merits of Trinitone's controversial video game. She was not surprised at their failure to reach common ground because they had previously engaged in such spirited exchanges concerning the moral implications of various advertising campaigns and messages. Bourg was an unreconstructed libertarian who rejected moral squeamishness in her industry's selection of clients, even when the ads were directed at children. She held parents fully accountable for their offsprings' viewing habits. Burgess's view did not differ significantly from his colleague's "autonomous consumer" rationale for ads directed at adults, but he believed that Byron and Oleson must assume some moral responsibility in filtering the relentless barrage of commercial messages directed at children.

Like it or not, ad agencies that target children are a part of the moral universe. As the moral agent in this case, Montgomery has to decide what role her agency will play within this universe.

THE CASE STUDY

Report finds "pervasive and aggressive marketing" of films and video games, trumpeted a headline in the *New York Times.* The headline was in reference to an FTC study reporting, among other things, that 70 percent of the 118 electronic games with a mature rating for violence selected by the commission targeted children under 17.[64] Media violence is an enduring concern of both consumer and government watchdogs, particularly violent content directed at children or to which juveniles have easy access. The complexities of this issue are exacerbated by such dichotomies as *gratuitous* versus *plot-essential violence, verbal* versus *physical violence, graphic* versus *sanitized violence,* and *morally judgmental* versus *amoral depictions and consequences.*

Video games are of particular concern because of the young consumer's one-on-one interactive participation in the games' high-energy entertainment. In this narrative, it is tempting to view *Pro Football Combat* as just another violent video game with little socially redeeming value. However, the game does challenge its users to plan strategy and to reason, two outcomes of educational value. In addition, one could argue, as account executive Elva Bourg did, that this video game does little more than package the natural environment of professional football—the same environment that is visually depicted to millions of viewers on national TV. In this view, an ad campaign that accurately depicts the dominant features of the video game—violent plays, disrespect for one's opponents, and unsavory fan behavior—can be justified. In such cases, the full weight of responsibility falls upon parents; ad agencies are simply amoral agents of clients who have a right to promote their wares to youthful consumers.

The contrarian view, of course, is that all producers of media content—and that includes ad agencies—must be somewhat paternalistic in their appeals to those whose value systems are still in their formative stages. Thus, society has a collective responsibility for the moral development of the nation's youth. Parents must indeed exercise moral oversight, but all who compete for some role in the lives of children must share this burden. That is the view of Delbert Burgess, who acknowledges the educational value of *Pro Football Combat* but is concerned that the video game's more sensational features will devour its feeble attempts at respectability.

For the purpose of providing your own perspective on this issue, assume the role of media director Robin Montgomery. You have listened to the competing ethical visions of your two colleagues,

and now it's time to make a decision on whether you will respond favorably to the overtures from Trinitrone Enterprises. In rendering your decision, apply the SAD formula for moral reasoning outlined in Chapter 3.

▼

Notes

1. See *Hazelwood School District v. Kuhlmeier,* 14 Med. L. Rptr. 2081 (1988); *Bethel School District No. 403 v. Frazer,* 106 S. Ct. 3159 (1986).
2. John Locke, "Second Treatise on Civil Government," in J. Charles King and James A. McGilvray (eds.), *Political and Social Philosophy* (New York: McGraw-Hill, 1973), p. 117.
3. John Stuart Mill, "On Liberty," in ibid., p. 186.
4. For a discussion of this issue, see Louis A. Day, "Media Access to Juvenile Courts," *Journalism Quarterly* (Winter 1984): 751–756, 770.
5. See *Smith v. Daily Mail Publishing Co.,* 99 S. Ct. 2667 (1979).
6. Charles R. Wright, *Mass Communication: A Sociological Perspective,* 3d ed. (New York: Random House, 1986), pp. 185–201; Karl Erick Rosengren and Sven Windahl, *Media Matter: TV Use in Childhood and Adolescence* (Norwood, NJ: Ablex, 1989), pp. 159–241.
7. For an examination of some of the early research on the effects of mass media on children, see Ellen Wartella and Byron Reeves, "Historical Trends in Research on Children and the Media: 1900–1960," *Journal of Communication* 35 (Spring 1985): 118–133.
8. Plato, *The Republic, The Dialogues of Plato,* 2 vols., ed. and trans. B. Jowett (New York: Oxford University Press, 1892), vol. 2, p. 323; quoted in Joseph E. Bryson and Elizabeth W. Detty, *The Legal Aspects of Censorship of Public School Library and Instructional Materials* (Charlottesville, VA: Michie, 1982), pp. 14–15.
9. Most producers of pornographic films do not submit their works to the ratings board but instead just self-supply an X rating and go to market.
10. David Shuster, "South Carolina AG Threatens Suit Against Entertainment Industry," online Fox news dispatch, September 15, 2000, accessed September 19, 2000, available at http://www.foxnews.com:80/elections/091500/sc_shuster.sml
11. Ramin Setoodeh, "13 Going on 17?," *Newsweek,* May 24, 2004, p. 12.
12. "Congressmen Warn About Online Porn," online Associated Press dispatch, July 27, 2001, accessed July 27, 2001), available at http://news.findlaw.com/ap/ht/1700/7–27-2001/20010727144549000.html
13. Mary Lord, "Cruella Lights Up," *U.S. News & World Report,* March 29, 1999, p. 66.

14. Ibid.

15. Marc Kaufman, "Study: Teens Who See Smoking in Movies More Likely to Light Up," *Washington Post,* June 10, 2003, p. A7.

16. John O'Neil, "See a Movie, Then Light Up?," *New York Times,* July 6, 2004, Section F, p. 6.

17. Lord, "Cruella Lights Up."

18. "Seeing Spots," *U.S. News & World Report,* June 23, 2003, p. 10.

19. Alan Wells and Ernest A. Hakanen, "The Emotional Use of Popular Music by Adolescents," *Journalism Quarterly* 68 (Fall 1991): 445–454.

20. "FCC Crackdown Sparks Debate," *Morning Advocate* (Baton Rouge, LA), September 15, 1989, p. 14C.

21. 56 F.C.C.2d 94, 98 (1975).

22. Claudia Wallis, "Does Kindergarten Need Cops?," *Time,* December 15, 2003, p. 53.

23. James Kaplan, "Superheroes or Zeros?" *TV Guide,* October 29, 1994, p. 33.

24. "Cartoons with a Conscience Are in the Works," *The Advocate* (Baton Rouge, LA), December 15, 1993, p. 8A.

25. Faye Zuckerman, "NBC Movie Sends Wrong Message to Troubled Teens," *The Advocate* (Baton Rouge, LA), November 20, 1993, p. 11C.

26. Ibid.

27. See F. Earle Barcus, *Images of Life on Children's Television* (New York: Praeger, 1983).

28. Wallis.

29. For an examination of this problem, see Aimee Dorr, Peter Kovaric, and Catherine Doubleday, "Parent-Child Coviewing of Television," *Journal of Broadcasting and Electronic Media* 33 (Winter 1989): 35–51.

30. One study that compared programming between 1990 and 1997, when the ratings system was introduced, found that offensive language actually decreased in 1997 to pre-1990 levels. See Barbara K. Kaye and Barry S. Sapolsy, "Offensive Language in Prime Time Television: Before and After Content Ratings," *Journal of Broadcasting & Electronic Media* (Spring 2001): 303–319.

31. Nancy Gibbs, "Who's in Charge Here?," *Time,* August 6, 2001, p. 44.

32. David Crary, "Critics: Ads 'Exploitation' of Children," *The Advocate* (Baton Rouge, LA), September 11, 2001, p. 7A.

33. Rebecca A. Clay, "Advertising to Children: Is It Ethical?," *Monitor on Psychology* (online edition), Vol. 31, No. 8, September 2000, at http://www.apa.org.monitor/sept/00/advertising.html (downloaded on January 12, 2004).

34. David Crary, "Critics: Ads 'Exploitation' of Children," AP dispatch published in *The Advocate* (Baton Rouge, LA), September 11, 2001, p. 7A.

35. Eric Schlosser, *Fast Food Nation* (New York: Houghton Mifflin, 2002), pp. 42–43.

36. For a recent study of the role of children's advertising in electronic media, see Dale Kunkel and Walter Gantz, "Children's Television Advertising in the Multichannel Environment," *Journal of Communication* 42 (Summer 1992): 134–152.

37. See *United States v. National Association of Broadcasters,* 536 F. Supp. 149 (D.D.C. 1982).

38. "Programming Commercialization Policies," 60 R.R.2d 526 (1986).

39. See Don R. Pember, *Mass Media Law,* 2000 ed. (Boston: McGraw-Hill), pp. 597–599.

40. *Action for Children's Television v. FCC,* 821 F.2d 741 (D.C. Cir. 1987).

41. An examination of the prevalence of commercials aimed at children is provided by John Condry, Patricia Bence, and Cynthia Scheibe in "Nonprogram Content of Children's Television," *Journal of Broadcasting and Electronic Media* 32 (Summer 1988): 255–270.

42. See Laurene Krasny Meringoff and Gerald S. Lesser, "Children's Ability to Distinguish Television Commercials from Program Material," in Richard P. Adler et al. (eds.), *The Effects of Television Advertising on Children* (Lexington, MA: Heath, 1980), pp. 32–35.

43. Crary, "Critics."

44. Ibid.

45. Bill McConnell, "One Fat Target," *Broadcasting & Cable,* March 8, 2004, p. 1.

46. Amanda Spake, "Hey, Kids! We've Got Sugar and Toys," *U.S. News & World Report,* November 17, 2003, p. 62.

47. Marci McDonald, "Call It 'Kid-Fluence,'" *U.S. News & World Report,* July 30, 2001, p. 32.

48. Quoted in ibid.

49. Ibid.

50. "I'd Toddle a Mile for a Camel," *Newsweek,* December 23, 1991, p. 70.

51. Ibid. The cigarette industry has recently responded to criticism that they are targeting the young. In 1995, for example, Philip Morris announced a comprehensive program to discourage juvenile smoking. See Glenn Collins, "Philip Morris Seeks to Curb Cigarette Sales to the Young," *New York Times,* June 28, 1995, p. A11.

52. See Marc Kaufman, "Tobacco Firms Probed Over Ads" (online *Washington Post* dispatch, May 18, 2000, accessed May 19, 2000), available at http://www.washingtonpost.com/wp-dyn/nation/A21755–2000 May 17.html

53. See Marianne Lavelle, "Teen Tobacco Wars," *U.S. News & World Report,* February 7, 2000, pp. 14–16.

54. John Burnett and Sandra Moriarity, *Introduction to Marketing Communication: An Integrated Approach* (Upper Saddle River, NJ: Prentice-Hall, 1998), p. 220.

55. Evidence also indicates that younger viewers do not distinguish between the real and unreal on television. See Peter Nikken and Allerd L. Peeters, "Children's

Perceptions of Television Reality," *Journal of Broadcasting and Electronic Media* 32 (Fall 1988): 441–452.

56. For example, one study that examined children's understanding of network commercial techniques found that they did not understand the concept of a "balanced breakfast." See Edward L. Palmer and Cynthia N. McDowell, "Children's Understanding of Nutritional Information Presented in Breakfast Cereal Commercials," *Journal of Broadcasting* 25 (Summer 1981): 295–301.

57. Ibid.

58. *Children's Television Report and Policy Statement,* 31 R.R.2d 1228 (separate statement of Commissioner Glen O. Robinson, at 1255), *affirmed,* 564 F.2d 458 (D.C. Cir. 1977).

59. "'Jurassic Park' Hype Masks Disturbing Question," *The Advocate* (Baton Rouge, LA), June 21, 1993, p. 3E.

60. Some of the information in this case is derived from Amanda Spake, "Hey, Kids! We've Got Sugar and Toys," *U.S. News & World Report,* November 17, 2003, p. 62.

61. Richard Campbell, Christopher R. Martin, and Bettina Fabos, *Media & Culture: An Introduction to Mass Communication* (Boston: Bedford/St. Martin's, 2004), p. 402.

62. Betsy Wagner, "Our Class Is Brought to You Today by . . . ," *U.S. News & World Report,* April 24, 1995, p. 63.

63. The idea for this case was derived from Phil Mushnick, "End of the Innocence," *TV Guide,* August 18, 2001, pp. 44–45.

64. See "Violence in Media Is Aimed at Young, F.T.C. Study Says," *New York Times,* September 12, 2000, pp. 1A, A20; and "Excerpts from the Report on Violence," ibid., p. A20.

CHAPTER

12

Media Practitioners and Social Justice

SOCIAL JUSTICE AS A DOMINANT MORAL VALUE

When the Society of Professional Journalists (SPJ) issued its guidelines to assist journalists in avoiding racial, ethnic, and religious profiling in the wake of the 9/11 attacks, the SPJ office in Indianapolis received about twenty angry e-mails in one weekend. These unenthusiastic rejoinders to what the SPJ undoubtedly viewed as a helpful reminder of journalistic responsibility, while admittedly modest in number, were unexpected. Typical of the responses were these vehement remarks: "*Islam needs a reformation . . . not an ass-kissing.*" "*Head for the Middle East and stay there.*" "*Members of these suddenly protected groups want to slaughter Americans and wipe out our culture.*"[1]

A sample of twenty, of course, should not be taken as representative of thousands of journalists, but such comments are nevertheless disappointing from media professionals who should serve as catalysts in the evolution toward greater tolerance and social justice within a democratic society. But despite overwhelming evidence that the American public is poorly informed about and even prejudiced toward other cultures and traditions (including the Islamic religion), studies of news continue to reveal a glaring omission of coverage of certain groups.

In fact, complains Sally Lehrman, chair of SPJ's Diversity Committee, journalists "repeatedly make the error of portraying America as primarily white and middle class."[2]

Historically, the media have been accused of institutional indifference to the cause of social justice as evidenced by their lack of representation of a broad spectrum of constituent groups, the absence of coverage of the economically and socially disenfranchised, and the often unfair media depictions of certain minorities. The explanations have ranged from outright prejudice in some cases to marketplace realities that cater to majoritarian tastes and interests. However, as noted in the text that follows and in Chapter 13 on stereotypes, there have been some noticeable advances in the media's sensitivity to an increasingly culturally diverse environment.

Is social justice a dominant moral value? Communitarians, who trace their lineage to Aristotle's concept of the *polis* (community), believe that it is. Justice is thus inescapably an ethical imperative of the democratic enterprise, despite the fact that there will always be some disparity between the ideal and the reality. Communitarian thinking, as Philip Patterson and Lee Wilkins so aptly note in their engaging media ethics case book, "allows ethical discussion to include values such as altruism and benevolence on an equal footing with more

381

traditional questions such as truth telling and loyalty."[3]

We should not discount the complexities inherent in the concept of justice that may obscure its claim to cultural dominance—after all, millions of words have been expended on its exposition—but if we begin with the rather simplistic notion of "justice as fairness," then the idea of social justice as a dominant moral value becomes more credible. And since the media play such a pivotal role within contemporary democratic culture, media professionals cannot avoid the penetrating and sometimes tantalizing questions concerning their role in the promotion of social justice. Nevertheless, communitarians are not alone in the public square, and their critics do not always share their view of the dominance of social justice as a moral value. And the precise role (if any) that the media should play in the promotion of social justice is not without controversy.

In the final analysis, the approach that one takes to this issue depends on how one perceives the functions of the media in a complex society. Should the media be true participants in the social arena, or should they be viewed merely as transmitters of information? Should media practitioners see themselves as merely reflectors of the social landscape, or should they consider themselves as catalysts for change? The role of the media as instruments of social justice will depend on how we, both as individuals and collectively as a society, answer these questions and how we respond to the communitarians' claim that social justice is fundamental to a well-ordered civil society.

THE PRINCIPLE OF FORMAL JUSTICE

There are many ways of viewing the idea of justice, but common to all of them is this fundamental principle: *like cases should be treated alike;* there should be no double standards.[4] This notion, which has traditionally been attributed

to Aristotle, is sometimes referred to as the *principle of formal justice* because it is a minimal requirement for any system of justice but advances no criteria for deciding the question of when two parties should be considered equal.[5] The formal principle of justice provides a point of departure for debates about social justice but must be supplemented with other principles to serve as a blueprint for meaningful moral reasoning about the matter.

For example, many people believe that race, gender, or sexual preference should not be used as bases for hiring, but there is nothing in Aristotle's view to preclude using them. In fact, race has been used as a legitimate employment criterion to compensate for past injustices. Thus, theories other than Aristotle's formal principle must be brought to bear to justify the consideration of race as a just hiring practice. It remains for the individual or institution dispensing justice to establish the criteria for equitable consideration. But once the standards are in place, the formal principle of justice requires that all parties be treated alike in the application of those standards. This idea is reflected in the salary scales of media practitioners, who deserve the same pay as those colleagues with similar experiences and job profiles.

MEDIA PRACTITIONERS AND SOCIAL JUSTICE: TWO VIEWS

Most of us would not quibble with a system of justice that seeks equality of treatment for all members of society. It is certainly a noble goal. But how this goal is to be achieved has posed some interesting political, legal, and philosophical questions and has precipitated some sharp cultural divisions. At one extreme are those who believe that justice can best be achieved by relying on individual freedom and marketplace forces to provide for equality of opportunity. This view is represented by the traditional libertarian theory that media practitioners should be independent and autonomous, without any moral obligation to society. At the other extreme are those who doubt that justice can ever be achieved through a blind faith in the self-interests of individuals and profit-centered corporations and that some form of social responsibility, enforced through public pressure or governmental action, is often necessary to ensure equality of opportunity. Proponents of this view believe that the media have a moral duty to promote equality and justice. These opposing philosophies have influenced the media's institutional role in achieving social justice and are reflected in such practices as employment, responsiveness to the cultural needs of minorities, and the coverage of controversial issues.

The Libertarian Concept of Justice

The libertarian conception of justice is closely aligned with the traditional view of the media's role in U.S. society.[6] The libertarian philosophy grew out of the writings of such notables as John Milton, John Locke, and John Stuart Mill and is characterized by the marketplace of ideas as the primary determinant of social and political truths.[7] Under this theory justice consists of the maximizing of individual freedom from government coercion. Freedom of the press is codified in the First Amendment, and media practitioners have historically favored an independent press, responsible to no one except their own consciences. This philosophy was reflected in a comment attributed to William Peter Hamilton of the *Wall Street Journal:* "A newspaper is a private enterprise owing nothing whatever to the public, which grants it a franchise. It is therefore affected with no public interest. It is emphatically the property of the owner, who is selling a manufactured product at his own risk."[8]

Media practitioners may report on social injustices but do not necessarily feel any responsibility to crusade on their behalf. Libertarians reject mandated rights of access for political and social groups and prefer to leave it to the competitive forces of the marketplace to determine the extent of media exposure for various causes. Thus, libertarians advocate the right to espouse a cause in the belief that competing views will provide a "self-righting" effect if everyone has the same opportunity to speak. Critics of this philosophy point out that not all members of society have the same opportunity. Political, social, and economic considerations often serve as barriers to the marketplace of ideas.

Libertarianism is clearly concerned with self-interest. But proponents of this theory, such as the economist Milton Friedman, argue that individuals' and institutions' pursuit of their own interests will ultimately benefit society. Involvement in righting social wrongs, according to this view, compromises the media's role as an objective observer and threatens journalistic and artistic freedom.

Even when media coverage itself threatens the cause of justice, libertarians prefer to seek alternatives to governmental coercion. A case in point is the extensive and sometimes sensational publicity surrounding the trial of a defendant accused of committing a particularly heinous crime. Such news coverage, especially when it involves the release of incriminating evidence before a jury can be selected, threatens the defendant's right to the fair administration of justice. Libertarians stress the alternatives to "gagging" the press, such as a change of venue, postponing the trial, and uncovering bias through the jury selection process. The objective is to protect both the right to a free press and the right of the defendant to a fair trial, which can sometimes precipitate an awkward balancing act.

One could argue that this issue of free press versus fair trial is more a legal matter than a question of social justice. But because the issue raises questions of media responsibility, the ethical concerns underlying the dangers of "trial by media" are worthy of consideration. The media are the representatives of the public in maintaining vigilance over the criminal justice system. Thus, to the extent that their coverage is prejudicial and irresponsible, they have violated their public trust and perhaps undermined society's commitment to the principle that a person is innocent until proved guilty. It is not overstating the matter to point out that the media's interest in a defendant's right to a fair trial is as great as that of the society they serve.

The Egalitarian Concept and Social Responsibility

Whereas libertarianism emphasizes individual self-sufficiency, egalitarianism focuses on ensuring equality for all members of society. Egalitarians are more willing to sacrifice individual liberty in the name of justice than are libertarians. Thus, these philosophers would argue that media practitioners should relinquish some editorial discretion to ensure that various segments of society have access to the nation's organs of mass communication.

In its most extreme form egalitarianism appears to be implausible as a foundation for a system of justice, because it demands equality regardless of what people deserve. But most egalitarian theories are highly qualified. Some take the form of *distributive justice,* in which such things as property, rights, and opportunities are allocated to members of society in equal shares according to merit. A system of equal pay for equal work is such an example. Others emphasize a theory of *compensatory justice,* which holds that whenever an injustice occurs that results in harm, some form of moral compensation is required. Affirmative action programs, for example, are designed to afford this kind of equal opportunity in employment and to remedy past injustices. Likewise, the increasing visibility of minorities in prime-time programming might be viewed as an attempt to compensate for the historical absence of minorities from TV except in the most stereotypical of roles.

Those who oppose affirmative action programs reject the very notion of compensatory justice on the grounds that it is unfair to attempt to remedy past wrongs by holding the present generation accountable. Individuals, they argue, should be rewarded strictly on the basis of merit. But even a meritocracy poses some rather intriguing questions. Assume, for example, that a managing editor hires an African American reporter over a more "journalistically" qualified white reporter to cover inner-city racial problems. Clearly race was instrumental in this hiring decision. But it's also true that the editor considered race to be a "merit" in providing qualitative coverage of the African American community.

The egalitarian approach to justice clearly offers an alternative to libertarianism's endorsement of unfettered individual choice. Although there are many variations of this theory, one of the most influential contemporary versions is that proposed by John Rawls in *A Theory of Justice.*[9] For Rawls, justice is "the first virtue of social institutions."[10] As noted in Chapter 3, Rawls introduced the concept of the "veil of ignorance" behind which all participants in a moral situation would serve as "ideal observers." These moral agents would behave as rational thinkers, free from the knowledge of special talents, socioeconomic status, political influence, or other prejudicial factors concerning the other parties to the arrangement.[11] Media practitioners, therefore, would make their ethical decisions without regard for whether the other participants in the situation were women, members of racial minorities, corporate vice presidents, bag ladies, or politicians. The goal is to protect the weakest or most vulnerable parties in the relationship from injustice.

One application of Rawls's theory is in the coverage of news events. Journalists should report on the activities of an individual based on the person's inherent newsworthiness, rather than merely on the person's social status. Thus, behind the veil of ignorance, reporters and their subjects would establish a working relationship in which not all politicians would be depicted as dishonest, cultural labels and stereotypes would be discarded in news and advertising, the media would base their coverage on a group's legitimate claim to representation rather than merely marketing considerations, and journalists would approach their assignments with a respect for people rather than with undisguised cynicism. Under this approach, a more harmonious relationship would develop between reporters and society.

The Mainstream:
A Philosophical Blend

The ethical concerns of the contemporary media are too complex to fit neatly into a two-theory configuration of social justice. Most media institutions do not conform nicely to either the libertarian or the egalitarian view but fall somewhere between these two extremes. Thus, it is more accurate to speak of an organization's tendencies to be more or less concerned about its commitment to social justice.

A newspaper, for example, might make a concerted effort to attract African American employees while at the same time exhibiting little interest in improving its coverage of black urban problems. On the other hand, another paper might view the hiring of African American reporters as an opportunity to appeal to minority audiences through better news coverage. Some news organizations might distribute their content to minority audiences only if it were profitable to do so. Others might view this profitability as an obligation to use their resources to produce material targeted to the culturally deprived. Under this hybrid philosophy, the media's role in the cause of social justice usually revolves around four concerns: information access, media coverage and representations of minorities and the disadvantaged, diversity in the workplace, and the media's impact on criminal justice.

Information Access. Is access to information a fundamental "need" like food, shelter, and medical care? Skeptics might argue that this is just another absurd rights-based claim of those who cannot afford to travel the information superhighway. Neither media practitioners nor the government has a moral obligation, they argue, to ensure that the disenfranchised are full beneficiaries of today's information-rich culture. Or, to put it another way: On what moral basis is society obligated to ensure that all citizens have access to an abundance of information regardless of economic status or geographic location? This view, of course, represents the orthodoxy that information is just another economic resource and that the marketplace should be the ultimate determinant of access to this resource. Social reform–minded egalitarians counter that society, and the media, as wealthy and powerful members of that society, should subsidize those who cannot afford access (such as offering reduced-rate cable TV or Internet access to the inner-city poor). As a model for such humanitarianism, proponents of this view might cite public utility companies that often subsidize (sometimes through contributions from their customers) the poor.

This issue embraces pivotal political, economic, and social policy questions. Perhaps the point of departure should be to pose the question of whether information is indeed a fundamental need. From a purely physical survival perspective, one can hardly envision information as an economic soul mate of food and shelter. After all, most of us survive the exigencies of life in various stages of ignorance, and although knowledge (part of which is based on "information") may be essential to rational decision making and effective political and economic participation in the democratic process, access to information is more akin to a luxury than a "need." Information is just another commodity to be merchandised (as evidenced by the resurgence of checkbook journalism), just another manifestation of an affluent society. In pursuing this argument, one might also point out that even the disadvantaged have access to a minimum level of information through our system of compulsory education. In addition, radio and TV are prominent fixtures even among the urban poor; thus, there is no ethical imperative for society to subsidize their access to the vast array of services that are available on a 500-channel-capacity cable TV system or the information-rich Internet.

In a society founded on the principles of individual achievement and initiative as the measures of "deservedness," these arguments are undoubtedly appealing from an ethical perspective. On the other hand, one could contend that in an information-rich society, there is a moral obligation to share the benefits of that wealth, based not so much on what one deserves (after all, who are *we* to judge?) but on the common good of society. If "knowledge is power," then access to a diversity of information empowers the disenfranchised and makes them full partners in the democratic experiment. Rather than being marginalized, they become key players. Even if the media or society must subsidize their access to the full range of information services, this is a small price to pay to improve the psychological (if not always the economic) state of the poor. According to this view, a "need" should not be defined as something that is essential to survival but any commodity that contributes to one's humanity and makes one a productive member of society. This philosophy is captured in this ethical appeal from media ethicists Clifford Christians, Mark Fackler, Kim Rotzoll, and Kathy McKee:

> People as persons share generic endowments that define them as human. Thus, we are entitled—without regard for individual success—to those things in life that permit our existence to continue in a humane fashion. Whenever a society allocates the necessities of life, the distribution ought to be impartial. Free competition among goods and services has been the historically influential rationale for media practice, but in the case of a total national structure performing a vital function, the need-based criterion appears to be the more fitting ethical standard.[12]

Media Coverage and Representations. In August 2002 the *New York Times* announced that it would commence publishing reports of same-sex commitment ceremonies. Gay rights advocates, though not describing this as "true equality," nevertheless heralded the decision as a step in the right direction. Opponents of gay marriages, however, accused the *Times* of legitimizing gay unions that many Americans oppose. "Newspapers are in a position to affirm or reject values," opined Richard Cizik of the National Association of Evangelicals. "It's a value statement running counter to Christian tradition and values."[13]

Regardless of whether one agrees with Cizik's conservative beliefs, he is right about one thing. In their prominent role as cultural gatekeepers, the media can and do influence social values. Their initiatives on behalf of what they perceive to be social justice and individual fairness often run afoul of popular sentiments and are unlikely to win them moral accolades from many of their constituents, as evidenced in the case of Ronald Edward Gay. Gay, a lonely drifter and self-described "Christian soldier," entered a gay bar in Roanoke, Virginia, in September 2000, surveyed the crowd, and then when two men started kissing in front of him, pulled a pistol and opened fire, killing one man and wounding six others. He was quickly arrested and subsequently pled guilty to first-degree murder and malicious shooting.

The shooting lifted the veil of obscurity surrounding the rather sizable gay and lesbian community that had thrived amidst the tolerance and opportunity of this small Virginia city. The *Roanoke Times,* which coincidentally had initiated a reporting project on Roanoke's gay population several months prior to the shootings, pursued their story with a renewed sense of purpose. The paper's staff considered it to be one of the finest pieces of journalism ever produced by the *Times.* Angry readers accused the *Times* of being "godless" and of promoting homosexuality and the gay lifestyle, trying to "shove the gay agenda" down the throats of the community, and glamorizing and sensationalizing "a sick and dangerous practice."[14]

The *Times* had anticipated that its candid assessment of gay life in Roanoke would be controversial, but they were unprepared for the virulent reactions from their readers. "The newspaper had highlighted a subject many readers thought taboo—a biblical sin, even—and we had dared to open a once-shuttered window wide on a part of the community that many readers wish could remain hidden," remarked editor Michael Riley, writing in the *American Journalism Review*.[15]

The *Roanoke Times* should be heralded for its courageous enterprise. But as this case illustrates, the cost of promoting social justice can indeed be high when honest and accurate depictions of minority groups run afoul of cultural taboos and prejudices. Even when the news media attempt to serve as the public's conscience and the voice of tolerance and social progress, they may be accused of desecrating the community's conventions and offending its way of life. Nevertheless, in a democratic society social justice is a virtue, and the media have a duty to attempt to represent faithfully society's various elements. And there is ample evidence that over time the media can play an influential role in the promotion of social justice.

However, progress has been slow. As noted in Part I of this text, in its review of the media landscape in the 1940s, the Hutchins Commission chided the press for its inattention to the demands of minorities and challenged it to present a "representative picture of the constituent groups of society."[16] Critics contend that the commission's challenge still has not been met and that the problems of minorities and the disadvantaged are still underrepresented in the media except to the extent that sporadic news events (such as an urban riot) dictate otherwise. They have indicted the media for ignoring those segments of society that do not reflect substantially in their readership or ratings profiles.

Some research supports the critics' complaints. "Journalists repeatedly make the error of portraying America as primarily white and middle class," complains Sally Lehrman, chair of the Society of Professional Journalists' Diversity Committee. Certain groups are virtually ignored.

Journalists, according to Lehrman, have a "simple duty" to cover all segments of society fairly and accurately, and "to make informed distinctions."[17] And in some cases, the coverage remains stereotypical. Consider, for example, a project at the Poynter Institute in which researchers found that almost half the people of color featured in the newspapers they surveyed were sports figures or entertainers, leading the authors of the study to observe that such stereotypical depictions reduces them to "curiosities or sources of amusement."[18]

Despite this rather dismal assessment, some significant achievements have been made. Television, for example, was instrumental in converting the civil rights marches of the 1960s into a national mandate for social justice. In recent years media practitioners have been more active in combating racial and sexual stereotypes and more attention has been paid to social ills such as poverty and homelessness.

Perhaps the greatest journalistic sin in the coverage of minorities has been one of omission—the marginalization of minorities as news sources. Cultural diversity has not been matched by diversity in "sourcing." One recent content analysis of local newscasts found that "rarely were Latinos, Asian Americans, or Native Americans interviewed as news sources," whereas "African Americans were used as news sources more than other racial and ethnic groups when 2 or more people were involved."[19] Mainstream journalists have reached a "comfort zone" with their sources and tend to rely on them repeatedly because they are convenient, are known to the reporters, or have a proven track record of providing good quotes. Reporters should make a good-faith effort to include a reasonable diversity of sources in their journalistic agenda but should not necessarily confine their consultations to minority issues. For example, despite some progress in this area, a paucity of minorities is still represented among "experts" in fields such as law, medicine, and economics who are frequently interviewed on TV news programs.

Unfortunately, the frustrations at the lack of progress in covering underrepresented groups sometimes lead to radical solutions that tend to politicize editorial policy. Such was the case when Mark Willes, publisher of the *Los Angeles Times,* told the *Wall Street Journal* that he intended to establish specific goals (quotas) for the number of women and minorities quoted in his newspaper.[20] Willes's proposal drew a quick response from *U.S. News & World Report's* John Leo, who castigated the idea for favoring group representation over merit in news coverage. "On some stories, this heavy emphasis on ethnicity and/or gender makes sense," Leo wrote. "But on most stories it doesn't. Such emphasis misleads readers and creates the impression that almost every report should be looked at through the prisms of race and gender."[21]

Nevertheless, in the past decade the matter of diversity has reinvigorated media critics who accuse the media of a continuing moral indifference to the needs of society's constituent groups. For example, even though Hispanics comprise the nation's largest racial or ethnic minority, a survey of 16,000 news reports in 2000 revealed that the TV networks and CNN featured Hispanics in only about .5 percent of stories on their evening news broadcasts.[22] Race has become such a pervasive concern within our society that the news media sometimes frame stories within a racial context while ignoring the basic journalistic requirement of relevance. In today's multicultural environment, however, such ethical lapses are less likely to go unacknowledged. Following the 2000 summer Olympics, for example, syndicated columnist Michelle Malkin took the media to task for referring to 19-year-old swimmer Anthony Ervin as African American when in fact he is multiracial. According to Malkin, reporters ignored his achievements while consistently asking him "how it feels to be the first black American to make a U.S. Olympic swim team." "Only the U.S. media, with their zeal for race-based affirmative action and constant ethnic

categorizing," she wrote, "would subject one of our nation's athletic heroes to such relentless harassment over his skin color."[23]

The entertainment industry has also been taken to the public woodshed for the lack of a fair representation of minority groups. "Not only are we underrepresented on television, but when they do show us, it's frequently in a negative, stereotypic fashion," complains Gary Kimble, head of the Association on American Indian Affairs.[24] A recent study in the *Journal of Broadcasting & Electronic Media* found that the portrayals of African Americans in prime time were more negative than their Caucasian or Latino counterparts. According to the study, they were "judged as the laziest and the least respected" and "their dress was the most provocative and most disheveled."[25]

One explanation for the absence of African American characters in starring roles on TV has been lack of interest on the part of white audiences, still the most influential audience demographic. However, there have been some incremental improvements. In the 1990s, for example, the number of minority characters in commercials increased dramatically as Madison Avenue discovered the buying power of middle-class minorities. And in February 2002 *Time* magazine, citing such sitcoms as ABC's *My Wife and the Kids* and Fox's *The Bernie Mac Show,* both featuring well-known black comics and appealing to white audiences, announced: "After years of video apartheid, African-American oriented sitcoms are starting to reach white viewers."

But this sudden flurry of artistic enterprise featuring minority characters and directed at minority audiences should not obscure the marketing reality. Economic considerations and ownership patterns have traditionally deterred the media from becoming full partners in the cause of social justice. Ratings and circulation are the driving forces of media institutions, and content, including advertising messages, has traditionally been directed at white middle-class audiences.[26] But there is cause for optimism.

For several years program producers and advertising executives have been responding to an increase in consumer spending among minorities, particularly African Americans. In fact, it was only after the TV industry discovered the black middle class that African American characters (with a few notable exceptions) made significant inroads into TV's lucrative prime-time schedule and achieved a representative niche.

Likewise, the recent sensitivity to the Hispanic and Latino audiences is a reflection of the fact that the annual buying power of these groups is formidable, and advertisers are "hot" for this lucrative market, according to a recent report in *U.S. News & World Report*.[27] Nevertheless, Hispanics and Latinos continue to be underrepresented in comparison to their census figures. According to the 2000 census, Hispanic Americans account for 12.5 percent of the population—a nearly 58 percent jump since 1990—but the number of Hispanic television characters stood at only 2 percent in the 2001 season.[28]

The explanation for this dearth of Hispanic presence is not hard to find. Hispanics are barely represented in TV's executive suites, and network series remain dominated by white male writers "inclined to write about what they know—themselves." Network executives profess to be committed to greater program diversity. Fox's H. Mitsy Wilson, for example, cites the network's outreach to minority groups and declares: "Our goal is to place Hispanic writers on all shows." Similarly, CBS senior vice president/diversity Josie Thomas says: "We're working on it. There are opportunities for guest stars; recurring roles are still open. This isn't the end of the story."[29]

One reason for the minimal representation of Latinos may be their own attraction to TV shows favored by Anglos. One senior advertising executive has observed that "[a] lot of Latinos live white lifestyles," which might explain why there is a dearth of TV programs targeted to Latinos.[30]

Diversity in the Workplace.   It is unlikely that media coverage and representations of minorities will improve without a corresponding improvement in the employment picture for minorities within the media establishment. Minority employment has not kept pace with the minority population in the United States. A 2004 RTNDA/Ball State University survey, for example, reported that 21.8 percent of the TV workforce was minorities, compared with about 32.8 percent of the population at large, while almost 11.8 percent of the radio workforce was minorities. Unfortunately, the percentage of minorities in radio and television has not changed appreciably for a decade.[31]

In those stations with rather dismal minority staff profiles, news directors often say they can't find qualified minority candidates for jobs in their newsrooms, especially in small- or medium-sized markets. Some admit they're likely to give minorities more of a break to attract them as candidates, a practice that again sparks debates about the dimensions of social justice.

Minority recruitment within the newspaper industry has also been disappointing. The 2000 census figures profiled a nation whose non-white population stood at 30 percent, but in newsrooms the percentage was 11.64 percent, down from 11.85 percent in 1999. African Americans remained the largest minority group (5.23 percent), followed by Hispanics with 3.66 percent.[32] In 1978 the American Society of Newspaper Editors (ASNE) set a target of 17 percent for minority employment by the year 2000,[33] but in light of the disappointing progress in newsroom diversity, it subsequently lowered its expectations.

One explanation for this reassessment is "diversity fatigue" in which hiring targets are viewed as social goals rather than as essential elements of good journalism and good business. On the other hand, some ASNE members have argued that newsroom diversity is crucial to the cultivation of new readers, can strengthen credibility, and can "help produce a nuanced news report that readers will trust."[34] And in all fairness, most of the major news organizations have launched aggressive initiatives to recruit minorities.

There are a number of reasons that nonwhites have traditionally shunned careers in the newspaper field, some of which may be difficult for media managers to overcome: a lack of role models, relatively low pay, feelings of isolation, inadequate language skills, and poor advising in high school, to name a few. In addition, large metropolitan newspapers usually have policies of hiring mostly experienced reporters who have cut their journalistic teeth on smaller papers. To compound this problem, nonwhite reporters are reluctant to seek out beginning newspaper jobs on smaller papers in rural areas.[35] Thus, the traditional hiring practices within the newspaper business become self-defeating where minorities are concerned.

But Vanessa Williams, an assistant city editor at the *Washington Post* and former president of the National Association of Black Journalists (NABJ), blames this trend on entrenched racial biases, as well. "Managers still too often hesitate, express doubts and demand proof," she says, "that black journalists can handle assignments that they wouldn't think twice about handing to white journalists."[36] Herbert Lowe, a *Newsday* reporter and an officer of the NABJ, agrees: "We can stop this trend," Lowe told the Associated Press, "but it will take some real effort by newsroom leaders to show that they honestly value black journalists and the diversity that everyone says they want and the latest census numbers demand."[37]

However, even when a newsroom improves its diversity profile, there is a problem with retaining minorities. This is puzzling to many news executives, and the reasons are not common to all minority groups. For example, African Americans might see little opportunity for advancement,[38] whereas there is evidence that Latino journalists are leaving the English-language media for the rapidly growing array of Spanish-language news outlets.[39]

The advertising industry also now has an interest in gays and lesbians and has directed some of its communications strategies at this increasingly vocal, visible, and economically influential group. In 1995 this trend led the prestigious public relations firm, Hill & Knowlton, to form a unit for marketing communications efforts that address gay men and lesbians.[40]

The public relations profession has made a good-faith effort to recruit women and minorities and has met with some success. Today, about two-thirds of PR professionals are women, and minorities have made significant inroads into the profession. For example, according to the Public Relations Society of America, the corporate, nonprofit, and government sectors of the industry each contain about 20 percent of African American PR professionals.[41]

The available data indicate that women have fared better than racial minorities in some segments of the media industry. For example, recent studies have revealed that women now comprise about a third of the workforce in radio and TV news.[42] In addition, about 20 percent of the news director positions are held by women.[43] These figures are still far below the percentage of women in the population at large, but they do reflect some progress in promoting women into decision-making roles within the broadcast industry. Indeed, in 1998 *Broadcasting & Cable* magazine reported that, although women are still excluded from many of the top jobs in television, many women are poised to move up to high-profile positions within the industry. This optimistic assessment is attributed in part to the fact that more women are pursuing MBA degrees, which provide them with the financial credentials essential to success in the highly competitive electronic media.[44]

On the print side, more women are in top journalism jobs in markets of all sizes, and with the number currently in the pipeline, the industry should see a continuing increase in women occupying management-level positions.[45] There is some evidence that the influence of women editors has a positive influence on the news agenda. A recent study of stories from 30 newspapers' websites, for example, found that papers with a high percentage of female editors appeared not to differentiate between male and female reporters when assigning beats, as is apparently the case at male-dominated newsrooms. Additionally, papers with predominately male editors contained more negative news.[46] Another study indicated that the presence of females in the byline is a significant predictor of females appearing within the news story.[47]

The most recent claimant for social justice in the nation's newsrooms is the National Lesbian and Gay Journalists Association, which had its genesis in 1990. Just three years after its formation, the group held its first job fair in New York—an event underwritten by a $40,000 grant from the *New York Times* and attended by such prestigious media institutions as the *Washington Post,* the Associated Press, and ABC News.[48]

Despite the noble intentions of those who embrace the egalitarian philosophy, including programs that advocate compensatory justice for those who have been denied employment opportunities, for some white males "diversity" has become a code word for reverse discrimination. The perception is fueled both by rumor and by the aggressive manner in which media organizations are recruiting minorities: the hiring of consulting firms, conducting of sensitivity seminars, participating in minority job fairs, and announcing special hiring policies.[49] The aftermath of such policies can result in a less than harmonious working environment. For example, a diversity study by the Associated Press Managing Editors revealed that many minority journalists don't think whites have to work as hard, whereas their white counterparts held a similar view about minorities.[50]

In searching for strategies to confront the ethical dimensions of this issue, some troubling and complex questions must be raised. In so doing, perhaps we should begin with the common ground: In the cause of social justice,

it is wrong to deny a person employment simply on the basis of color, gender, sexual preference, or any other characteristic. But beyond the issue of employment per se, we must ask ourselves exactly how diversity can best serve society's interests. There is an unstated assumption that diversity in the workplace will improve the qualitative diversity of the content. But does diversity, for example, automatically improve the *quality* of the news product?[51] Or more specifically, are middle-class African American reporters more attuned to the problems of the inner city than their white counterparts, or are urban problems as much a matter of economic class as race? Are gay and lesbian journalists more understanding of and compassionate in their treatment of the gay community than heterosexual reporters? Can only a disabled reporter empathize with the physically challenged in their daily struggles for respectability? Must journalists be over 55 to write about the problems of the aged? And the list goes on.

There is, of course, a certain impertinence in such questions, and they should not deter media managers from attempting to develop an employment profile that more closely mirrors the society of which they are a part. But they must also be careful that whatever policies they implement do not lead to an unhealthy balkanization in the workplace environment that is in the long run inimical to the cause of social justice.

The Media's Impact on Criminal Justice.   In April 2004 the $12 million corruption trial against Tyco executives abruptly ended in a mistrial when the judge learned of a report of a juror receiving a phone call and a letter that were viewed as putting pressure on her. Both the *Wall Street Journal* and *New York Times* had published her name and the Associated Press had published her photograph, prompting Columnist Thomas Sowell to accuse the media of irresponsibility, "which not only is costing taxpayers millions of dollars but can corrupt the whole system of justice."[52]

Criminal trials, particularly high-profile cases, are news, and the press has a responsibility to witness these proceedings and to provide a reasonable account of the justice system at work. However, the media are powerful institutions that are instrumental in the formation of public opinion. When this reality is blended with the other interests at stake—the defendant, prosecutor, and the jurors, for example—ethical concerns arise when media coverage threatens the quality of justice guaranteed by the U.S. Constitution. The Sixth Amendment guarantees a criminal defendant the right to a fair trial, that is, the right to a public trial before an impartial jury of peers. The First Amendment guarantees the media freedom from government censorship or sanction. That these two bold declarations of individual and institutional liberties should sometimes clash is perhaps ironic, since they are both predicated on a healthy distrust of government. The criminal justice system revolves around juries that are unprejudiced before trial as to guilt or innocence. Although they may indeed hear prejudicial information during the trial, safeguards regulate the introduction and evaluation of evidence and witness testimony. No such precautions prevent the media from disseminating such information to the public before or during the trial.

Thus, those who consider the right to a fair trial the most fundamental among our constitutional guarantees criticize the media, particularly in high-profile cases, for their irresponsible dissemination of inflammatory and incriminating evidence and even "extrajudicial" statements (for instance, comments by opposing attorneys outside the courtroom) resulting in a trial before the court of public opinion rather than a court of law. Free press advocates, on the other hand, respond that only through media access to the judicial process and the right to serve as surrogates for their constituents can the citizenry be confident that justice is indeed being dispensed.

The *Dallas Morning News,* for example, created a brouhaha in February 1997 when it posted on its website a story reporting an alleged confession by Timothy McVeigh, a defendant on trial for bombing the federal building in Oklahoma City. This marked the first time that a major newspaper had broken a story online ahead of both the competition and its own printed edition. McVeigh's attorney attacked both the authenticity of the confession and the newspaper's conduct.[53] Ralph Langer, executive vice president and editor of the *News,* responded that the confession was both authentic and legally obtained. And in response to criticism that the paper's editors were indifferent to the ethical ramifications of their decision, Langer declared: "At least a few critics have suggested that the *News* gave no thought whatsoever to the effect on the trial. We had concern about the trial but, ultimately, came to believe that the information in that part of the material was of national importance and that we were obligated to publish it."[54]

The American judicial system, despite its shortcomings and occasional failures, is considered to be a paradigm of justice, a reflection of our culture's fundamental commitment to fairness and equality of treatment. Strictly speaking, the Supreme Court's vigilance in balancing the rights of a criminal defendant against the media's right to cover judicial proceedings, particularly when couched in constitutional terms, is a matter of law. But in reality the criminal justice system reflects our more general concern for social justice, with its emphasis on fairness, procedural safeguards, and rewards and punishments based on what people deserve. And when the media act irresponsibly and a defendant is denied the right to a fair trial because of pervasive and sensational publicity, then serious ethical questions are implicated.

Of course, sometimes the media have performed admirably in fulfilling their ethical imperative in pointing out the imperfections in the judicial system, such as the disparate sentencing patterns of whites and African Americans convicted of similar crimes. At other times, however, the herd mentality consumes the media and trial coverage takes on a circuslike atmosphere. Such cases usually reflect the conflict between news as a commodity to be marketed and the notion that the news media, because of their First Amendment protections, also have a social responsibility. And the presence of cameras in the courtroom, providing live coverage, has introduced a high degree of irresistible drama into this conflict.

The best example of recent vintage is the O. J. Simpson trial. From the outset, there was a great deal of skepticism that Simpson could get a fair trial because of the exhaustive and sometimes sensational coverage. Although the concerns underlying "trial by media" are at the heart of all high-profile cases, the Simpson case was unique in at least three respects: the amount of coverage, dismissal of a grand jury because of potentially prejudicial publicity, and the unprecedented access of media to information.[55] And much of the press coverage was centered in the exact location where an impartial jury was supposed to be impaneled, Los Angeles County. But it was the quality of information, not the amount of coverage, that threatened the justice system.

First, many of the items reported were either false or unsubstantiated. Second, even some of the matters that were reported accurately were so compromised by the level of media coverage that they similarly compromised the search for truth in the criminal process. For example, one witness reported seeing the defendant near the crime scene. Unfortunately, after it was learned that reporters had paid the witness for her "exclusive story," the prosecutor decided not to use the witness's testimony before a grand jury or during a preliminary hearing because she had been hopelessly compromised as a credible witness.[56]

In any high-profile trial, we might expect that the contending parties—both prosecution and defense—would appeal to the conscience of public opinion. And there is nothing unethical in doing so. Public opinion, after all, has an invigorating influence on the democratic

process. Thomas Jefferson understood this vital principle more than 200 years ago when he courted public opinion in search of support for the Declaration of Independence. Whereas the media have sometimes served as public advocates or conduits for those who have sought a hearing before the court of public opinion,[57] attorneys have never hesitated to serve as their own publicists in the interests of their clients.[58] For example, several weeks after Timothy McVeigh was charged with bombing a federal building in Oklahoma City, McVeigh's court-appointed attorney released a videotape, which received national TV coverage, showing a decidedly more relaxed and "friendly" McVeigh than had been portrayed in media coverage.

But the recent proliferation of high-profile trials and particularly the ubiquitous coverage of TV have led some attorneys to solicit professional assistance in creating favorable images for their clients. This alliance between the public relations and legal professions has become increasingly collaborative, as evidenced by the frequent reference in the literature to "litigation public relations." The list reads like a virtual "Who's Who" of criminal defendants. The perceived "need" for litigation public relations is captured in this observation from Professors Susanne Roschwalb and Richard Stack writing in *Communications and the Law*:

> A big error many lawyers make, according to public relations executives, is in failing to recognize that while silence should be accorded a presumption of innocence in the court, it is likely to be taken as a sign of guilt in the pressroom. The innocent, when accused, are expected by the public to proclaim their innocence promptly and emphatically. Absent such proclamation, any courtroom claim of innocence may be more skeptically perceived.[59]

The introduction of the public relations function into the criminal justice system (it has also assumed a more prominent role in civil litigation) does raise some serious ethical concerns for everyone involved: attorneys, public relations professionals, and the media themselves.

The reasons for using communications strategies vary among attorneys and even from case to case, but proponents of "litigation public relations" cite at least two reasons in its defense. First, although prosecutors portray themselves as "above public relations," they have an effective media network. Prosecutors have an early advantage in the court of public opinion because the government initiates and controls the criminal investigation, evaluates the evidence first, and often conducts news conferences to announce indictments. Under such a scenario, the first message the public receives about the accused is a negative one. Defense attorneys are then pressured to remind the public that their clients are innocent until proven guilty.[60] Second, advocates often target the public to sway potential jurors. A well-orchestrated public relations campaign on behalf of a client is sometimes effective in at least softening the harsh image generated by the prosecution. And such publicity does not threaten the criminal justice system because jurors are carefully screened and then admonished to render a verdict based solely on the evidence and testimony introduced during the trial.

Critics counter that it's absurd to believe that jurors can completely separate the publicity generated in the (sometimes circuslike) court of public opinion from the carefully scrutinized evidence and testimony adduced in a court of law. Despite the best intentions of the attorneys and the judge, it is impossible to ferret out all bias. In addition, opponents argue that, depending on the communications strategy devised, the use of public relations professionals can leave the impression that the defense team is attempting to massage the facts. Under such circumstances, public relations practitioners can quickly become coconspirators in frustrating the search for truth.

Clearly, the entertainment value intrinsic to the legal difficulties of public figures is often irresistible even to the mainstream news media, but equally disturbing are the plethora of programs that disregard the presumption of innocence and render their own guilty verdict in the court of public opinion. Consider, for example, Court TV, which has frequently provided substantive coverage and commentary on a wide variety of judicial proceedings. But when pop star Michael Jackson was arrested for child molestation, Cable TV's Diane Dimond quickly rendered her verdict: "Michael Jackson bought his way out of a very serious criminal situation [in 1993], and I think he surrounds himself with people who enable him to be near children when he shouldn't be." She later asserted "we might be watching the demise of a superstar." In a similar vain, Nancy Grace, a former Atlanta prosecutor and the host of the network's *Closing Arguments*, admitted that she thought Richard Ricci, the suspect in the Elizabeth Smart kidnapping case who died of a brain hemorrhage while in police custody, was the "perfect suspect." This comment ignored one inconvenient fact: Ricci didn't do it.[61]

But putting aside such personality-driven renditions where ratings trump fairness, the demands of the justice system are subjected to their most compelling challenges in high-profile cases where the public interest is greatest and the news coverage is pervasive. In a democratic system, the media are charged with both a mandate and a responsibility. Reporters should understand that their ethical imperative to provide meaningful and comprehensive intelligence on the performance of the judicial system is not incompatible with a simultaneous commitment to the cause of justice. Each time that a criminal defendant is accorded a fair trial, uninfluenced by prejudicial publicity, society itself is the beneficiary. On the other hand, the media should be mindful that unfair or slanted coverage (which may include publicity generated by either prosecutors or defense attorneys or their public relations consultants) has the potential for compromising the integrity of the process of criminal justice. Thus, the potential consequences both to the cause of justice and the credibility of the media are too serious to ignore.

SOCIAL JUSTICE AND ETHICAL DECISION MAKING

Justice is a central moral principle of society.[62] At the most formal and abstract level, as noted, it relates to giving individuals what they deserve. But what is each due? And how are competing interests to be balanced when justice for one might result in injustice for another?

These are complex questions, particularly for institutions that serve such a pivotal and pervasive role as the mass media. Libertarians tend to focus on individual media practitioners and the liberty to make decisions free from outside coercion. Egalitarians emphasize social responsibility and the duty to ensure justice for all segments of society, even at the expense of infringing on the liberty of media practitioners. Although these two concepts appear to be at the opposite ends of the philosophical spectrum, each has something to offer in constructing an ethical framework for social justice. The self-interest orientation of the libertarian concept must be rejected as contrary to sound moral reasoning. But the emphasis on individual autonomy places the focus where it should be: on the individual moral agent. As noted in Chapter 2, media practitioners are singularly accountable for the institutional decisions of their corporations. When a newspaper, for example, decides not to publish special inserts directed at minorities because of a perceived lack of advertiser interest, this decision is made by individuals acting on behalf of the institution. These executives are morally responsible for this decision.

Nevertheless, we often speak of "institutional responsibility" when referring to the various cultural roles of the mass media. Thus, from the egalitarian camp we can draw the notion of social responsibility in constructing an approach to ethical decision making for social justice. Because the media draw their sustenance from the communities of which they are a part, society has a right to expect media institutions to at least be sensitive to the cause of social justice. The question, of course, is how far this responsibility should extend and how this commitment to justice should be balanced against other obligations. The media, for example, have obligations to their subscribers, advertisers, and audiences (and perhaps stockholders), and these must be weighed carefully before honoring the demands of special segments of society.

In considering a dilemma involving issues of social justice, a duty-based theorist (deontologist) would examine the motives of the moral agent. Under this approach media practitioners act out of a sense of duty regardless of the consequences.

Duty-based theorists view justice as fairness, without consideration of whether the results of the ethical decision will benefit the greatest number of people. For example, a TV executive who programs to minority audiences out of a sense of duty rather than because the decision is commercially viable is following this approach to moral reasoning.

On the other hand, those who consider consequences to be important (teleologists) examine the potential effects of a decision on the cause of social justice. The positive consequences are weighed against the possible harm to the various parties in arriving at a just solution for the problem. In those cases in which the goal is to achieve positive ends for particular groups within society, some believe that individual liberties, such as freedom of expression, may be restricted in the name of social justice. This principle has been invoked by some feminists, who support censorship of pornography on the ground that it exploits and dehumanizes women.

Aristotle's golden mean can also be a welcome companion in confronting complicated situations in which the ethical extremes are unacceptable. Suppose, for example, that a TV news crew is sent to cover a prison riot. Such civil disturbances always pose a danger that news organizations will become a part of the story and will be used as pawns by those who seek publicity. The vices at either extreme involve providing no coverage, on the one hand, and covering every detail and angle regardless of the consequences, on the other. The challenge is to provide responsible reporting of the disturbance without offering a platform for the rioters to solicit public support.

Of course, not all moral dilemmas involving social justice can be accommodated through the golden mean. Sometimes fairness resides at one extreme or the other, and then the moral agent must approach the situation from the perspective of either the consequentialist or the deontologist.

To Aristotle justice was a virtue consisting, among other things, of equality of treatment based on merit. The problem, of course, is to determine whether the criteria for merit are just, which can challenge even the most rational media practitioner. For example, in deciding which spokespersons are to be accorded publicity during the news coverage of minority issues, should editors rely on those who appear to represent the largest constituency, the most articulate community leaders, or those who are the most vocal in pressing their cause? This is a practical journalistic problem because spokespersons, even within the same segments of society, do not always have the same agenda and may not even represent a significant following. As Paul Sagan, news director of WCBS-TV in New York, has observed, "But in doing a story about the minority community, I think a lot of us don't know who speaks for them. We

tend to listen to whoever talks the loudest, or who holds news conferences."[63]

The golden mean also allows for compensatory justice to rectify past injustices.[64] For example, affirmative action programs and demands by minority groups for fair treatment from media producers are viewed as compensation for past injustices and an attempt to equalize social relationships. A true mean is one that attempts to rectify past wrongs—that is, restore a sense of balance and proportion—to more accurately reflect the reality of the cultural diversity of society's constituent groups.

THE MEDIA AND SOCIAL JUSTICE: HYPOTHETICAL CASES

In this section you will confront a variety of issues. Some involve traditional questions of social justice, such as racial discrimination in the media. One case concerns a more recent issue of social justice, environmental justice. Another involves the issue of justice within the judicial system. The diversity of these cases demonstrates that the concept of justice exists at every level of our cultural experience. In reasoning through these cases, you should consider which ethical guideline described in Chapter 3 and the previous section best serves the cause of justice.

◀ C A S E   S T U D I E S ▶

▶ **CASE 12-1**

The Jewish Reporter: Religion and the Workplace

Bernard Weiss had been raised an orthodox Jew, and he was committed both intellectually and spiritually to the heritage that was bequeathed to his ancestors through the Hebrew patriarch Abraham.

For Weiss, his bar mitzvah at the age of 13 was more than just a formal rite of passage; it was the beginning of a spiritual journey. During his formative years, his family had lived in an upper-middle-class neighborhood of Moss Pointe, a community of 750,000 along the New England coast. Weiss's emotional and physical maturation was accompanied by an acute awareness of the creeping secularism that had infected the sanctity of the Hebrew religion exacerbated by the reality that one out of every two Jews in the United States marries outside the faith. However, Weiss's parents had successfully inoculated their son against such challenges to the purity of their religious identity and at one point even expressed an interest in their son becoming a rabbi.

But it was Lancaster High, not Bernard's parents, that exerted the greatest influence on his vocational ambitions. Lancaster High was Moss Pointe's most prestigious academy of secondary education. Its students were perennial competitors in the national merit scholar competition and were featured prominently in the freshman classes at such elite institutions of higher learning as Harvard, Yale, Princeton, and Dartmouth. Intellectually, Weiss felt a close kinship with his classmates, most of whom had set their sights on careers in medicine, law, engineering, or business, but Weiss's vocational aspirations diverged sharply from those of his peers. His sophomore English teacher detected in the young student a natural curiosity and a facility for written communication that required cultivation beyond the confines of the traditional classroom setting. She commended his talents to the school newspaper's advisor, who promptly enlisted Weiss as a reporter for Lancaster's journalistic organ.

Weiss's interest in reporting and writing news for the school paper quickly evolved into an extracurricular passion, and he set his sights on journalism as a career. Upon graduation, Weiss departed for Princeton University, his first choice among the Ivy League schools, where he majored in English and honed his journalistic skills as a staff member for The Daily Princetonian, the university's newspaper. To enhance his marketability as an entry-level reporter, Weiss then enrolled in Columbia University's journalism graduate program, which would provide him with the academic and professional bona fides to succeed in a highly competitive job market.

Weiss's ambition was to report and write for the nation's most prestigious newspaper, the New York Times, but he resigned himself to the wisdom of cultivating his skills in much more modest surroundings. After considering several job offers, Weiss selected the Lake Charles Gazette as his training ground. Lake Charles was a sizable

community of just over a million inhabitants located along the Atlantic seaboard about 200 miles from New York City. Unlike Moss Pointe, Lake Charles was not a Jewish enclave, but the Jewish community was sufficiently large to support a small synagogue, which would allow Bernard Weiss to practice his religious orthodoxy.

Weiss launched his journalistic career as a general assignment reporter, but after four months Martha Hitchcock, the paper's online editor, noticed his technological skills and arranged for Weiss's transfer to her division. Weiss quickly gained the reputation as an enterprising reporter and resourceful writer, which resulted in more challenging and interesting assignments. His job satisfaction and rapport with the Gazette's editors were undeniable—until the arrival of Yom Kippur, the Jewish high holy day, in October of his first year of employment. Weiss was assigned to cover the mayor's press conference during which time the mayor was expected to refute allegations of corruption in office. When the young Jewish reporter informed Hitchcock that he was an observant Jew and needed time off to observe the high holy day of Yom Kippur, Hitchcock reacted with surprise and told Weiss that the managing editor would need to clear such an unexpected absence without a commensurate reduction in pay. "Our company policy makes no provision for religious holidays," she told Weiss.

Hitchcock informed the Gazette's managing editor, Randolph Oschner, of Weiss's request and requested a meeting to discuss the matter. She also invited city editor Darrell Kimble, who had originally hired Weiss, to the meeting in Oschner's office.

"Bernard says he can't cover the mayor's press conference because of the Jewish high holiday known as Yom Kippur," Hitchcock told Oschner and Kimble as they reviewed Weiss's written request for dispensation. "We've never had such a request, and I told him I would have to clear it with you, Randolph. Needless to say, if you approve Bernard's request, this would be an absence with pay; otherwise, the approval would carry a price tag that would be financially punitive."

"As you know, Marvin Kaplan is Jewish," remarked Kimble. "He's covered the metro beat for three years and has never asked for time off for religious holidays. Why is Bernard so insistent?"

"Unlike Kaplan, Bernard is a true practicing Jew," replied Hitchcock. "He's orthodox. In many organizations, including the public schools, Jews are entitled to time off for religious observances. It's a tradition."

"Other institutions can do as they please," responded Kimble, somewhat unsympathetically. "We have no such policy, and I don't know of many newsrooms that do. When they enter the profession, journalists must understand they are journalists 24 hours a day. We can't make special accommodations just because one of our employees is Jewish."

"But according to a policy published 10 years ago, our newspaper is committed to diversity," declared Hitchcock. "And we have made significant strides in attracting women and minorities to our newsroom. If we are serious about diversity, we must be prepared to accommodate the special needs of our employees."

"But Weiss's situation is different," insisted Kimble. "When the *Gazette* committed itself to diversity, this was simply a matter of justice. We believed the paper should reflect the makeup of the community and that more diversity would enhance our news product. And I believe it has. But none of our employees hired under this policy—women and minorities, for example—have asked for special considerations in their employment situation. But Weiss is asking us to give him time off—with pay, naturally—to observe a religious holiday."

"If we're serious about diversity, we must include religion," countered Hitchcock. "And that may necessitate recognizing some religious observances. We should be able to adjust our work schedules to accommodate such holidays."

"But if we allow Bernard time off to observe Yom Kippur," objected Kimble, "then we'll be obligated to recognize other religious holidays. What if we hire a Muslim, for example? That person would have a right to insist upon similar treatment. I don't see this as a problem with most of our employees, but as the newsroom becomes more diverse, we could be confronted with demands for religious observances from other religious minorities."

"You're anticipating a problem that isn't likely to materialize," replied Hitchcock. "I don't know how many of our staff consider themselves devoutly religious, but the fact is that few religions require such strict observance of special holidays. Bernard is an observant, orthodox Jew. He takes his religion seriously. If we aren't willing to accommodate his need to celebrate Yom Kippur, he may leave."

Kimble was sobered by the prospect of losing Weiss, who was liked and respected by the entire staff. "Weiss is a good, young reporter," he said. "And I don't want to lose him. I'm just afraid that if we allow him time off with pay because of a Jewish holiday—and keep in mind that Yom Kippur is not the only such holiday—other reporters might consider this to be unfair."

"I'm not so sure," responded Hitchcock, in a last-ditch effort to deflect the city editor's objections. "Jewish holidays are a special case and have traditionally been recognized by schools and other institutions. There's no injustice to others in providing this benefit to one of our Jewish employees."

Managing editor Randolph Oschner listened passively throughout this exchange, realizing that he would be the moral agent in this matter. He wondered whether his paper's commitment to diversity required a nod to the religious dictates of his employees and, if not, whether he could acquiesce to Weiss's request without appearing to be unfair to other employees.

THE CASE STUDY

Does diversity require that employers take into account the religious preferences of their employees when to do so affects their job responsibilities? This question is implicated in the facts of this case. What is clear is that this is not a mainstream diversity case that focuses upon recruitment by gender, racial or ethnic status, or sexual orientation on the grounds that a diverse newsroom enhances the quality of the news product. There is nothing in the facts of this case to suggest that Bernard Weiss was hired because he is Jewish. In fact, his orthodoxy was not even an issue and did not become a job-related concern until he declined an assignment in order to be absent during a Jewish holy day.

So what exactly is meant by diversity? How far does a commitment to diversity extend? Should religious practices that occasionally impact upon one's professional responsibilities be accorded deference in the workplace in the name of diversity? Is there any injustice to other reporters and editors (who may have to pick up the slack for an absentee staff member) to provide time off with pay to a Jewish reporter who wishes to observe a religious holiday?

These are intriguing questions and raise some interesting ethical dilemmas for news managers. For the purpose of responding to these questions and Bernard Weiss's request for an approved absence to observe the Yom Kippur holiday, assume the position of managing editor Randolph Oschner. And then, utilizing the SAD model for moral reasoning outlined in Chapter 3, render a decision in this matter.

▶ **CASE 12-2**
Jury Deliberations as Reality TV[65]

For thousands of devoted fans, The Law cable channel was another captivating contribution to the genre of reality court TV. To Chief Operating Officer Faye Nance, it was an effective device for unraveling the intricate mysteries of the judicial process for viewers who were content to participate vicariously in one of democracy's most solemn and momentous pursuits. Criminal trials, accompanied by expert commentary, formed the core of The Law's diverse programming menu, but Nance surrounded such proceedings with engaging discussions with law professors, attorneys, judges, and ordinary citizens, as well as movies and syndicated television series that featured a variety of legal themes. Since most states now allow at least some televised coverage of criminal trials, the possibilities for engaging courtroom drama were endless.

Nance had matriculated at the University of Florida's College of Communication with a major in public relations, compiling an undergraduate record that qualified her for admission to Yale Law School. She embarked upon her legal education with some ambivalence because of what she perceived as a disturbing dualism in the law: the majesty of the law on the one hand and failures of the criminal justice system on the other. To help remedy this imbalance, Nance had flirted with the

notion of practicing public interest law to serve those who had effectively been disinherited by the legal process. But as she approached graduation and the obligation to pay off her student loans, her idealistic fervor yielded to financial realities, and she eagerly sought out the recruiters from the various law firms who journeyed to the Yale campus each year in a quest for fresh talent.

Nance's interview schedule was rigorous and included some of the most prestigious law firms in New York, Boston, and Chicago, but she was particularly attracted to the presentation by the representative from Holbrook and Haskins. Holbrook and Haskins was a small but thriving law firm in Los Angeles representing several prominent corporate clients in the entertainment field in protecting their legal interests against a variety of legal transgressions. During the interview, the firm's recruiter told the young law student that her public relations training and her exemplary academic record at Yale both commended her for an associate's position with Holbrook and Haskins. Hollywood's allure was irresistible, and three months after graduation she was living in close proximity to the world's largest entertainment center and was soon mixing and mingling with some of Hollywood's corporate elite.

Nance immersed herself in the highly competitive thicket of entertainment law, a legal specialty she found both challenging and fascinating. Her learning curve was a steep one, and she quickly acquired an intimate knowledge of both the corporate and creative aspects of the entertainment business. In the process, Nance attracted her share of influential clients. But after ten years of accommodating the corporate demands of her law firm's clients and experiencing what she recognized as the early stages of professional burnout, Nance departed Holbrook and Haskins and, with venture capital raised with the support of several influential contacts, launched The Law cable channel. The Law would join its primary competitor, Court TV, as an educational vehicle for those viewers who were untutored in the intricacies of the criminal justice system. Nance maintained her ties with Holbrook and Haskins as a legal consultant, but most of her energies were devoted to the successful inauguration of her fledgling cable enterprise.

She assumed the title of Chief Operating Officer but kept a watchful eye on the creative aspects of the business. She surrounded herself with a small but talented staff, including Barnett Dowden, a successful television producer, who was anointed with the rather impressive title of Executive Producer and Program Coordinator.

With aggressive marketing and an appealing program lineup, The Law slowly found its niche, and the audience levels began to rise. As the channel began its third year of operation, Nance was intrigued by a remark in a *Time* magazine article attributed to Jeffrey Abramson, author of *We, the Jury: The Jury System and the Ideal of Democracy*: "The jury remains the last great black box of American democracy. It's the government institution we know the least about."[66] Perhaps, Nance mused, it was time to remove the veil of secrecy surrounding jury deliberations. If so, then she was determined that The Law should play a pivotal role in this innovative method of civic education. Nance was aware that her initiative would not be entirely unprecedented; courts in Arizona and Wisconsin had been the settings for documentaries that included jury deliberations. The Ohio Supreme Court had given its blessing to the filming of jury deliberations, which had resulted in a six-part series on ABC in the summer of 2004. But these were the rare exceptions, and Nance believed that nothing less than full coverage of such proceedings, on a continuing basis, would produce the maximum educational benefit for her channel's viewers. *Inside the Jury Room*, as the program was tentatively titled, would begin with the California courts, a venue that produced its share of interesting and frequently sensational criminal trials. Success here, in Nance's view, would probably encourage experimentation in other state court systems, since California frequently sets the judicial tempo for other jurisdictions.

However, Nance did not underestimate the formidable obstacles to penetrating the sanctity of the jury room. She knew that the California state bar association and the state supreme court would have to provide their benediction to such an experiment, an experiment that even if approved would be scrutinized very closely. Nance was aware that such a proposal would raise ethical concerns,

and she was determined to vet those concerns before proceeding with her ambitious project to televise jury deliberations. To avoid undue public pressure on nonsequestered jurors during the trial, her proposal called for taping the deliberations and then televising them in their entirety immediately following the verdict.

"You know the purpose of this meeting," Nance declared, as she prepared to entertain the opinions of her colleague and two legal advisers. To deliberate the ethical dimensions of her jury project, Nance had summoned Barnett Dowden, the channel's Executive Producer and Program Coordinator, Sampson Sharp, an appellate court judge, and Berkeley University law professor Lydia Dawkins. "The idea of televising jury deliberations for public dissemination may not be entirely innovative—it's been done a couple of times before on a rather modest basis—but the broadcasts of entire jury deliberations, even on a tape-delayed basis, may indeed be unprecedented. Even if we think it's a good idea, we must get approval from the state bar association and the state supreme court. But we need to have a frank ethical discourse on the matter before The Law submits a formal proposal to the proper authorities."

"You know my feelings, Faye," Dowden asserted in what would be the opening salvo of an intellectually engaging exchange. "It's time we demystify the jury process. Many of our viewers have never served on a jury, and deliberations are always conducted behind closed doors. The jury is a powerful institution—it can convict defendants of crimes and recommend the death penalty—and yet it's one of the least understood of our democratic institutions."

"As a judge I have a different view," Sharp countered with an air of determination. "In this case, justice is more important than the public's right to know. They learn the verdict when it's announced in open court, but it's not imperative that curious citizens witness the dynamics of the decision-making process. Jurors often say things and behave in certain ways in the jury room that might be misinterpreted."

"But that's also an argument for openness," replied Lydia Dawkins, whose reputation as a radical thinker within the academic community was well known. "If there's any misconduct within the jury room, the tape will provide a public record of that behavior. In this sense, the knowledge that they're being taped for television may discourage such conduct."

Judge Sharp acknowledged the validity of Dawkins's comment with a nod and a grunt but was unwilling to contemplate what he considered to be an unwarranted violation of the sanctity of the jury room. "The presence of cameras might make some jurors behave more responsibly," he conceded, "but in all likelihood they will be distracted by these cameras, even if they are concealed from view. They may be reluctant to talk freely. The knowledge that they will be featured on national TV might prevent some from expressing their honest opinions. Others might go along with the majority to avoid being perceived as obstructionists. And of course, there are some who might use this as an opportunity to seek celebrity status."

"Perhaps," conceded Dowden, "but in the long run I think that televised jury deliberations will cultivate a keener sense of social responsibility among jurors. Besides, during the jury selection process the judge could dismiss any juror who might be nervous with cameras in the jury room."

"That's not a solution," replied Sharp. "There are so many people who are excused now from jury duty that I sometimes wonder if defendants really are tried by a jury of their peers as required by our Constitution. If jurors are excused because they object to having their comments televised, impaneling a jury will become even more difficult and time-consuming. This will be just one more stake in the heart of the criminal justice system."

"But witnesses and jurors both appear every year in televised trials across the country," objected Dawkins, "and most seem to be oblivious to the coverage. I doubt that many jurors would ask to be excused just because of the presence of cameras in the jury room."

"But this analogy doesn't work," countered the judge. "In a trial, jurors don't participate; they sit passively, and even if some are a little nervous about the cameras—and that's a big "if" in today's media-saturated environment—they aren't concerned about taking a stand or being made to look foolish. A jury room is a place for deliberation, and some jurors may be reticent in expressing their views if they know their comments may be televised to a large audience."

"But that argument cuts both ways," replied Dowden, detecting what he believed was a weakness in Judge Sharp's retort. "Jurors might act more responsibly if they knew the public was watching. I'm not suggesting that most jurors are irresponsible, but some do speak without a great deal of thought or reflection. In fact, the public might be shocked if they could eavesdrop on some jury deliberations. They would have serious doubts about the justice system. Having TV cameras document jury proceedings might discourage such gratuitous remarks and in the process restore the American public's confidence in the criminal justice system. Of course, there's a danger that witnessing such deliberations might further erode the public's confidence in the system. But that's a risk we must be prepared to take in a democracy."

But Judge Sharp was unconvinced and in closing offered one final observation: "The closed jury system has worked well in this country for over 200 years. It's an enduring pillar of our justice system. Why change it now? I can't think of a compelling moral argument for doing so."

Judge Sharp's closing argument, in Nance's view, was not particularly persuasive, but resistance to change was deeply ingrained in the criminal justice system. And after listening to the conflicting arguments, she had to admit to a certain degree of ambivalence. Any change in the jury deliberation system was not to be taken lightly, and she wanted to ensure that her proposal would contribute to the cause of democracy while not distorting the wheels of justice.

THE CASE STUDY

The criminal justice system is one manifestation of our commitment to social justice in a more cosmic sense. It is enshrined in our Constitution and is considered fundamental to a well-ordered society. Technological innovations that threaten our justice system's commitment to due process of law are usually greeted with skepticism or even outright hostility by the guardians of our legal conventions until their civic value and potential consequences can be thoroughly assessed. Televised criminal proceedings, which initially posed some troubling questions for the legal establishment, are now commonplace in most states.

However, Faye Nance's desire to televise jury deliberations is even more controversial than the admission of TV cameras to criminal trials. When the PBS program *Frontline* asked a Texas judge to permit cameras in the jury room and the judge agreed, the district attorney was outraged (an appellate court subsequently reversed this decision). As noted in this case, there have been a few other examples of attempts to penetrate the sanctity of jury deliberations. Criminal proceedings have been historically open to the public in this country; jury deliberations have not. Thus, the ethical concerns that permeate her proposal are more acute than in the case of televised criminal trials.

There are persuasive arguments on both sides of the ethical equation, as forcefully articulated by the participants in the ethical dialogue just described. On the one hand, proponents argue that televised jury deliberations would open up and document the process, provide the public with an opportunity to make their own decisions about fairness and the effectiveness of the criminal justice system, and function as a tool for public education about the justice system. Critics respond that televised deliberations might adversely influence the jury selection process (that is, those who object to cameras in the jury room would refuse to serve), increase the likelihood of a hung jury, and influence the willingness of some jurors to participate candidly in the proceedings. In addition, some jurors might fear retaliation, while others might seek celebrity status.

In one case where ABC News was allowed to film jury deliberations in a death penalty case, *Newsweek* conducted interviews with trial participants to garner their reactions. Six jurors, defense lawyers, prosecutors, and the judge said the filming had not affected their behavior or the case's outcome. Most said they had ignored the tiny, remote-controlled cameras. However, some of the jurors said that others had acted differently, knowing they would be on TV (for example, they accused one of "showboating").[67] Such comments are revealing but inconclusive for the long-term implications for televised jury deliberations.

As an attorney herself, Faye Nance is not unsympathetic to the concerns of the opponents of televised jury deliberations, but she believes that *Inside the Jury Room* might make a valuable addition to her legal showcase. As the moral agent in this case, she appreciates the wisdom of proceeding cautiously. For the purpose of analyzing the ethical dimensions of televised jury deliberations, assume the role of COO Faye Nance. And then, applying the SAD model for moral reasoning outlined in Chapter 3, make a decision on whether you will submit a proposal to the proper legal authorities in California to open criminal court jury deliberations to your television cameras.

▶ **CASE 12-3**

Diversity in the Public Relations Workplace: Race and Social Justice

The call for diversity that had permeated this year's annual convention of the Public Relations Society of America (PRSA) in Boston had touched Jefferson Metcalf Jr.'s soul. As president and CEO of Metcalf and Rutherford, one of the Southeastern region's largest public relations firms, Metcalf was painfully aware of the lack of racial and ethnic diversity within this profession. While women had made significant inroads, though the glass ceiling still barred promotion to top managerial positions at some firms, many public relations executives had been tardy in responding to the nation's call for social justice in employment of minorities. Metcalf counted himself among those who had for too long remained insensitive to the need for his firm to diversify, but he returned from the PRSA convention with a renewed sense of purpose.

However, unlike some of his public relations colleagues, Metcalf also viewed his commitment to diversity through the prism of compensatory justice. Metcalf and Rutherford had been founded by Metcalf's father, Jefferson Metcalf Sr., and Thomas Rutherford in 1949, and the firm had flourished in the post–World War II economic boom. As industrial and manufacturing enterprises began shifting their operations to the South because of cheap labor, Metcalf and Rutherford readily assisted these companies in forging civic links with their host communities. Like most companies in the deep South, the public relations firm remained a white male bastion, until Metcalf Sr.'s retirement in 1978. By this time the women's movement was well underway and significant strides had been made on the civil rights front. Jefferson Metcalf Jr.'s ascension to the corporate throne signaled a more progressive and proactive approach in the hiring practices at Metcalf and Rutherford. His initiatives in recruiting women had been fruitful, undoubtedly because the gender mix in most university public relations programs had begun to shift decidedly in the direction of females. In the early nineties Metcalf had made a sincere effort to attract African Americans into his firm, but few had applied. He had succeeded in hiring one African American in 1995, but after just a year his newest employee had left the firm for a more lucrative position in Chicago.

Despite his personal commitment to compensatory justice—that is, Metcalf believed that his firm had an obligation to "compensate" for past injustices in hiring—he could not ignore what he believed was a practical consideration in recruiting and hiring minorities, particularly African Americans. Most of his clients were companies governed by white males, many of whom had come of age in a culture in which racial prejudices, though more circumspect than in the old segregated South, were still a barrier to social justice. Metcalf did not believe that most of them were overtly racist, but he sensed some discomfort in dealing with an African American public relations practitioner across this rather subtle racial divide. However, at the dawn of the twenty-first century, Metcalf was confident that his renewed commitment to racial diversity would resonate with both his peers and his clients, and he lost no time in converting his convention-inspired ardor into a concrete plan.

Within six months of his return from Boston, Metcalf had formulated his diversity plan and distributed it to his firm's staff. His first move was to mount an aggressive advertising and recruiting campaign for a new entry-level position at Metcalf and Rutherford. He had considered setting aside the position for a minority but was concerned that might precipitate legal problems. Metcalf was determined not to compromise his enduring policy of hiring based on merit but was confident that his applicant pool would produce a critical mass of qualified African Americans. He was disappointed when only four of the applicants out of forty-seven were identified as minorities, two of which were African Americans. With the assistance of the firm's human resources management director, Metcalf narrowed the pool to two finalists—several were discounted because they appeared to be overly qualified for the position—and then convened a meeting of the firm's junior partner, Brad Rutherford (Thomas Rutherford's son), and the senior account executive, Staci Ponder-Longworth.

"We have two finalists for our entry-level account executive position," stated Metcalf as he spread the two dossiers on the table in front of his two colleagues. "One is African American. I had hoped for a larger applicant pool of minorities, but the minority public relations enrollment in the region's colleges and universities is not that great. They have a diversity problem of their own. Nevertheless, we have to begin somewhere."

Metcalf paused for a moment as Rutherford and Ponder-Longworth perused the two resumes. "As you can tell," he continued, "Tyrone Foster just received his degree from G.W. Carver University, a historically black institution. His major was public relations; he graduated with a 3.2 GPA and was active in his department's chapter of PRSSA. He also has an internship to his credit. His letter of application was well written, and the interview went well. Teresa Lucky received her master's degree two years ago from the University of Missouri, one of the top programs in the country. Since her graduation, she has been employed by a small firm in Missouri. During the interview she said that despite the fact that ours is an entry-level position, she is ready for a move to a larger market and our financial package is superior to her current employer's. I don't believe her two years of experience makes her overly qualified for this job."

"We had more than forty applicants for this position," noted Rutherford. "I can't believe that there were not others with some experience. And is Lucky the only one with a degree from one of the leading programs in our field?"

"There were others with experience," acknowledged Metcalf candidly. "Some had worked several years in public relations, but we discounted them because they appeared to be overly qualified. Their salary requirements exceeded what we're willing to pay. Others had rather modest experience. And yes, there were others with degrees from top-ranked public relations programs. Lucky is probably the best of the lot. But as you know, I've committed this firm to a policy of diversity, and I believe that Foster is a viable candidate for this entry-level position at Metcalf and Rutherford."

"But is Foster really comparable to Lucky? He does have some internship experience, and he apparently was a pretty good student. But his degree is not from one of the top programs. Teresa Lucky has a master's degree from a prestigious university and two years of solid experience."

"Quite frankly, I think you're being a little too formalistic about this," responded Ponder-Longworth. "When it comes to the apparent disparity in education, is there really a significant difference? Foster has a bachelor's degree; Lucky has a master's. But in the real world of practical experience that makes little difference. Lucky has worked in the profession for two years. That may give her some advantage, but quite frankly if we hire Foster, within a few months of employment that advantage could evaporate. I'm also not impressed by the argument that Lucky received her degree from a prestigious institution, whereas Foster went to a lesser-known historically black university. Missouri is a terrific school, but we have no reason to doubt the quality of the public relations program at G.W. Carver. Many African Americans choose to attend historically black colleges because they feel that there are still vestiges of racism at some state universities, especially those with low minority enrollments."

"Even if what you say is true," replied Rutherford, "the odds favor Lucky because of her educational background and successful work experience. We know she can do the job. She is better qualified, and if we hire Foster we'll be guilty of reverse discrimination because race will govern our decision."

"I object to your description of this situation as reverse discrimination," asserted Ponder-Longworth.

"I'll concede that on a purely quantitative basis Lucky wins. But if we're serious about diversity we should give Foster a chance. We've always hired on merit here, but keep in mind that Foster is surely not unqualified for this job. And in cases where there is not a tremendous gap in qualifications I believe that race can be taken into account to ensure diversity. In this case, I believe that considering race is actually a *merit* toward diversity. A certain amount of compensatory justice is required to make our diversity goals work, and I don't believe we're prostituting our standards by giving the edge to Tyrone Foster in this case."

"Let's assume you're correct and that we hire Foster," replied Rutherford. "A couple of our clients are African American. Do we assign him to those accounts, or do we press the envelope and run the risk that he may not be accepted by some of our white clientele? That could incur financial risks."

"If we allow that to become a barrier to our hiring minorities," responded Ponder-Longworth, "then we may as well ditch our diversity policy. As senior account executive, it's my responsibility to pave the way for minority acceptance by our clients. Attitudes have changed, and I don't see this as a tremendous problem. But if we hire Foster and he does a competent job for our clients, the racial divide will cease to be a problem. If he doesn't work out, he won't be here next year anyway."

"There's probably not much more to say on this subject," noted Rutherford as he anticipated an abrupt end to this rather animated exchange. "I'm in favor of social justice—of providing equal employment opportunities without regard to race—but when race is taken into account in employment decisions, even for the purposes of diversity, in my opinion the very foundations of justice are undermined."

Jefferson Metcalf, Jr., listened patiently to this intellectual (and yet somewhat emotional) disagreement between his two colleagues. He thanked them for their advice and informed them he would render his decision within two days, the deadline by which he had told Tyrone Foster and Teresa Lucky he would inform them of whether they had been accepted as a member of the public relations team at Metcalf and Rutherford.

THE CASE STUDY

Diversity in the workplace is not an issue that is confined to the communications and media-related industries. Nevertheless, because of the pivotal role that media practitioners and public relations professionals play in the marketplace of ideas and the free flow of information in a democratic system, some representation of the cultural diversity that is reflected in society at large is essential. Although there have been some pockets of success, the employment figures for the communications industry overall have not been encouraging. At this juncture, there is less debate about whether diversity is a desirable objective than with the matter of how best to achieve diversity.

Diversity is clearly a component of a much broader concern of social justice. But both ethicists and media practitioners might, in good faith, disagree about what social justice requires under the circumstances. A minimalist position is that justice requires egalitarianism based upon merit. In other words, there should be no discrimination in hiring based upon race, gender, sexual orientation, or other personal characteristics, but the best-qualified applicant should receive the job. Supporters of this view argue that any policy that accords minorities preferential treatment is actually antithetical to the principles of justice.

Their opponents respond that there is some compensatory justice due those who have been denied employment opportunities. Compensatory justice does not require hiring those who are clearly unqualified, they argue, but a more imaginative approach to recruiting and hiring and perhaps even some risk taking is essential if diversity in the workplace is to become a reality.

In analyzing this narrative, a good point of departure is the firm's stated policy of diversity in the employment of minorities. Thus, race becomes a factor in any employment decision, but the assumption is that all finalists—in this case there are two under consideration—meet at least the threshold requirements for the position.

The junior partner, Brad Rutherford, believes that the white woman's credentials—including a master's degree from one of the top programs in the country and two years of professional experience—give her a decided edge for this entry-level position. Staci Ponder-Longworth, the senior account executive, counters that for an entry-level slot this distinction is insufficient to make Teresa Lucky the front-runner. In her view, sometimes race must be a factor in order to provide opportunities for those who might otherwise be denied employment. A formalistic approach, as she describes Rutherford's stance, can be inconsistent with a proactive diversity policy. While Foster doesn't have the proven track record of his competitor, sometimes employers must make concessions in the interest of diversity.

If one accepts Ponder-Longworth's perspective, the focus in comparing the two applicants shifts away from their academic and professional credentials to one of institutional goals—in this case, an increase in minority employment, which might precipitate applications from other minorities. But if Metcalf hires Foster he is still left with the question of fairness to Lucky. Is that what Rutherford meant when he said that hiring a minority who is less qualified than a white applicant would actually undermine the foundations of social justice?

In this narrative, there is a brief discussion of whether an African American would be acceptable to the firm's clients. This is always a risk, and in assessing the situation Metcalf must consider the potential financial impact on the firm. But he should also develop strategies for confronting any recalcitrant client who refuses to deal with an African American representative. In the meantime, he must weigh the arguments from his two colleagues and decide whether to extend an offer to Teresa Lucky or her African American competitor, Tyrone Foster.

For the purpose of making your hiring decision, assume the position of Jefferson Metcalf, Jr., and, using the SAD model for moral reasoning described in Chapter 3, decide whether you will invite Tyrone Foster to join your public relations firm or whether you will accept the argument that Teresa Lucky should be hired because of her superior credentials.

> ## CASE 12-4
> ## The African American Publisher and Divided Loyalties

Washington Roundtree's credentials as a longtime crusader for civil rights were unimpeachable. As a young college student in the early 1960s, he had marched with Dr. Martin Luther King, Jr., in Alabama and had participated in the black voter registration drives in Mississippi. He had challenged the segregated lunch counters in Montgomery and had been arrested in Birmingham for taking part in a peaceful demonstration to protest segregation in the city's public transportation system. For this act of civil disobedience, Roundtree had spent three nights in jail. He had emerged from these experiences convinced that African Americans were on the precipice of a new era of social justice in which these descendants of slaves would finally share in the economic opportunities and social parity that had symbolized the white middle class. On a philosophical level, his emotional spark had been stoked by the doctrine of nonviolence embraced by Dr. King. From a political and legal perspective, his optimism was sustained by the passage of landmark civil rights legislation during the Johnson administration and the continuing vigilance of the federal courts in their determination to eradicate constitutionally the vestiges of segregation.

Upon his graduation from Morehouse University, a historically black college in Atlanta, Roundtree found employment in a black-owned print shop in Jackson Falls, a racially diverse city of half a million in the heart of the Deep South. But despite the demands of earning a livelihood and attending to the needs of his family, Roundtree continued his commitment to the ongoing struggle for racial equality through his participation in the NAACP and support for African American legislative candidates. His print shop responsibilities were not intellectually challenging, and the young civil rights activist applied for and was hired as a reporter for the *Jackson Falls Gazette*, whose progressive-minded publisher was eager to have minority representation in his newsroom. At a time when most newspapers in the South were neglecting their black audiences owing to, in part, their lack of commercial appeal to advertisers, the *Gazette*'s publisher was determined that the problems of the African American community would have a forum in the pages of his newspaper. And Washington Roundtree would be his representative in the economically impoverished and socially volatile black enclaves of Jackson Falls.

For ten years Roundtree chronicled both the struggles and the triumphs of the black residents of Jackson Falls, but despite his publisher's alleged commitment to racial equality, the activist-turned-journalist was disappointed in the rather modest amount of space accorded his stories by the *Gazette*'s editorial staff. "You're doing a great job, and we feel the black community is fairly represented in our paper. But we also have to sell papers, and our advertisers aren't interested in targeting audiences with no purchasing power," became an increasingly frequent rejoinder when Roundtree challenged his editors' decision to cut or eliminate one of his stories.

With this journalistic seasoning and a low-interest loan, Roundtree founded the *Freedom Fighter,* a paper that would service exclusively Jackson Falls' African American citizens while continuing his campaign for social justice and cultivating the growing black middle class. From his perch as publisher and editor of the *Freedom Fighter,* Roundtree was an unapologetic advocate for compensatory justice. He editorially promoted affirmative action initiatives, government antipoverty programs, and busing as a means of achieving school desegregation. And as the corridors of political power became increasingly accessible to African Americans, Roundtree enthusiastically endorsed black candidates for local office, the state house, and Congress. He was particularly pleased when, in 1986, the legislature, under pressure from members of the influential black caucus, had redrawn his Tenth Congressional District to ensure a majority black voter representation. Black legislators referred to this as social justice; their opponents called it racial gerrymandering. Nevertheless, the move had ensured the election of an African American representative, as conservative white politicians abandoned the Tenth District race as a lost cause, politically speaking.

But in 1994 an increasingly conservative Supreme Court had ruled that the Tenth District had been unconstitutionally redrawn specifically for the purpose of ensuring black congressional representation, and within a few months the legislature complied with the Court's edict as it revisited the Tenth District's geographic configuration. Thus, Roundtree's residence once again became an attractive plum for the white political establishment.

Elections normally did not pose a moral dilemma for the *Freedom Fighter*'s publisher-editor. In the past he had simply endorsed and actively supported African American candidates in their races against white opponents, reasoning that a commitment to racial justice could easily compensate for political inexperience. In the past two contests in the Tenth District, in which no white candidates ran, he had supported the incumbents because of their proven track record. But the upcoming congressional race—the first since the legislature's most recent redesign—challenged Roundtree's racial loyalty.

Thomas Whatley, the white candidate in the race, had survived the Democratic primary by virtue of a formidable coalition of white, progressive, pro-choice female voters and black middle-class voters. Whatley depicted himself as a political moderate, but his liberal record on civil rights, government assistance for the disadvantaged, and a woman's right to choose an abortion were undeniable. The Democratic entry was also politically experienced, having served two terms on the city council and two terms as a state senator. Whatley's black Republican opponent, on the other hand, was a political neophyte, but it was not his political inexperience that concerned Roundtree. Brewster Fields was the product of a black middle-class environment, undoubtedly a significant factor in what Washington perceived to be an opportunistic endorsement of Republican conservatism. Fields had not publicly repudiated affirmative action—a move that would be political suicide in a district in which African American voters were still influential—but in interviews with the media he consistently preached the gospel of individual initiative and self-help, not "paternalistic indulgences," as the keys to economic prosperity. Fields professed his support for civil rights but did not apparently share

Roundtree's commitment to compensatory justice in a society that appeared to be less racially tolerant today than at any time since the struggles for racial equality in the 1960s.

As the election neared, Roundtree was confronted with the nagging uneasiness of his competing loyalties as he considered his editorial posture on the congressional race. If he broke with tradition and supported the white candidate, his constituency might accuse him of abandoning them in their continuing efforts to maintain black political representation. Fields might be conservative, but he *was* an African American and could probably be educated as to the viability of affirmative action. Fields was also politically inexperienced, but Roundtree had never considered that to be a litmus test for public office, especially when blacks were trying to gain access to the corridors of political power. In addition, Fields's election would ensure that the Tenth Congressional District's seat would remain in the hands of an African American. This would at least preserve the visible trappings of social justice if not ensure its ideological progression.

On the other hand, Whatley's liberal credentials appealed to Roundtree's sense of social justice. His civil rights record was undeniable, and this made him, in Roundtree's judgment, the better qualified of the two candidates. If he publicly supported the Democratic candidate, he could explain his reasons in his editorial endorsement, and his black readers might forgive his political transgression. He could, of course, refuse to endorse either candidate as being unworthy of his blessing, but this position carried the same risk as not supporting Brewster Fields.

As a respected publisher and editor of a newspaper devoted to the cause of racial justice, Roundtree wondered, where should his allegiances lie in this election: race or affirmative action? During his more activist days in the service of Dr. King, the now middle-aged journalist had never dreamed that his dual commitments to his race and the greater cause of social justice might be politically incompatible. Which candidate, he wondered, would better serve the cause of racial justice, and what role should the *Freedom Fighter* play in bringing about that candidate's election?

THE CASE STUDY

During his professional career as a publisher and editor, Washington Roundtree has, without exception, supported African American candidates for public office on the grounds that racial progress can best be achieved through those who truly understand the black experience. Thus, in Roundtree's view the notion of race and his own vision of social justice for African Americans are inevitably linked. But Brewster Fields, a conservative Republican black candidate, doesn't share Roundtree's vision. In fact, Fields's white opponent appears to be more firmly committed to Roundtree's views on civil rights than Fields himself. And this has posed a dilemma for the publisher-editor of the *Freedom Fighter*. He must choose between his loyalty to race and his loyalty to a particular vision of racial justice (that is, compensatory justice), which in this case is more closely aligned with that of a white candidate.

For the purpose of analyzing this ethical dilemma, apply the SAD formula for moral reasoning, and decide which course of action available to Washington Roundtree would better serve his own view of social justice.

▶ CASE 12-5

International Public Relations, Morality, and Social Justice

Since the Nixon administration's overtures three decades ago to the leaders of the People's Republic of China that eventually led to a normalization of relations between our two countries, the U.S.–Sino alliance had remained politically fragile. American foreign policy had adopted a controversial strategy of pressuring the Chinese to end its human rights abuses, while at the same time pursuing the more pragmatic path of cultivating an economically viable trade policy with Beijing. On the one hand, the White House continuously expressed its moral indignation at China's use of forced labor to produce goods for export, an inhumane practice that had been documented by a naturalized citizen and scholar who had returned

to the People's Republic and secretly videotaped the abuses inside that country's exploitative prison system. On the other hand, administration pragmatists, as well as their supporters in Congress, argued that it was in our national interest to negotiate with the Chinese to open their markets to American goods and that congressional confirmation of most-favored-nation status, which the Chinese currently enjoyed but which was now in jeopardy, was essential to that foreign policy objective.

However, even as the Chinese appeared to covet most-favored-nation treatment, which would also ensure greater access to American markets, they stubbornly refused to acknowledge American charges of human rights violations and expressed their resentment, both publicly and privately, at such insulting indictments. In addition, periods of diplomatic tranquility were always interrupted by some disquieting episode that resulted in a regression in Sino–U.S. relations. There had been the controversial visit to the United States, for example, of Taiwanese professor Wang Wai, who had been invited to give a series of lectures at Harvard University. Wang, a frequent critic of the communist regime on mainland China, was not reticent during his three-day visit to Cambridge in once again condemning the Beijing government for its dismal human rights record. This action prompted a swift protest from the Chinese ambassador in Washington, followed by a suspension of the most recent negotiations between the U.S. trade representatives and their Chinese counterparts. And then, there was the downing of an American reconnaissance flight off the coast of China, which resulted in the internment of the aircraft and crew for a period of time.

But despite these highly publicized diplomatic repercussions, the Chinese government persisted in its efforts to procure congressional reaffirmation of its most-favored-nation status. However, recent evidence that China was selling medium-range missiles to Pakistan, as well as the continuing allegations of human rights abuses, had put the issue in doubt, particularly in a politically conservative Congress where any communist regime was viewed with suspicion. And the enduring balance of trade deficit with the People's Republic did little to soothe Congress's bipartisan pique at what they perceived to be the moral callousness of the Chinese leadership.

To Dong Teng-hui, the Chinese trade representative assigned to the embassy in Washington, the message both from his diplomatic contacts and in America's news media was unmistakable: His country's most-favored-nation status was in jeopardy. And it was within this environment of political uncertainty that Dong sought counsel from Knopp & Bryce, a Washington, DC, public relations firm with branches in five countries. The firm's client list included both domestic and multinational corporations, but Knopp & Bryce had also been a successful advocate within the halls of Congress for foreign governments and the private sector.

Anne Barker-Lane was Knopp & Bryce's director of international relations and served as the gatekeeper in selecting those clients who were worthy of her firm's attention. But despite the autonomy that she enjoyed within her company's hierarchy, Barker-Lane often sought the advice of her coworkers. Thus, Dong's overtures and the issue of whether human rights violations should be an obstacle to representing the Chinese government soon became a point of contention among Barker-Lane, Bryan Hardy, the firm's congressional liaison, and Jacob Wiley, the international account manager.

"The Chinese have approached us about representing them before Congress on the most-favored-nation issue," began Anne Barker-Lane, as she briefed her two colleagues on Dong's visit. "Despite the recent flap over the downing of our spy plane, trade is still economically vital to them. American markets are important, if not absolutely essential, to the leaders in Beijing."

"This will be tough," remarked Hardy. "The mood on Capitol Hill isn't very good. In the Senate, some of the older and more conservative members still resent our recognition of China. Taiwan has friends in Congress. Some are just looking for an excuse to withdraw most-favored-nation status from the Chinese."

"It may be a tough sell," responded Wiley. "But that's our job: to represent our clients as faithfully and skillfully as we can, even when the odds aren't good. And as you know, we have represented many clients on Capitol Hill, including foreign governments. But this one is different. The Chinese government is still seen by many as a repressive regime. The pictures of the Tiananmen Square massacre are still vivid in America's consciousness more than a decade later. In fact, recent polls indicate a majority of Americans favor holding the Chinese accountable for their alleged human rights violations. They insist upon applying our own standards of social justice to the Chinese."

"It's true that they would be an unpopular client in some quarters," conceded Hardy. "But should we select our international clients based on our own country's sense of morality? If the Chinese were clearly an outlaw regime, committing such atrocities as genocide, then I would have no problem with rejecting such a client out of hand. But even our own government continues to deal with the People's Republic. And as long as we still have diplomatic relations with this nation, don't they have a right to be heard in America's court of public opinion, as well as have representation in the halls of Congress?"

"I'm not so sure," replied Wiley, who had on several occasions expressed the opinion that any economic affiliation with a nation where human rights abuses could be documented amounted to an abdication of moral virtue in foreign policy. "We are an American public relations firm. As such, our values should count for something. As long as these human rights abuses continue, we should refuse to represent the Chinese. What do we stand to gain by taking on the regime in Beijing as a client? This could be an unpopular decision that might reflect unfavorably on this agency, and if we succeed in protecting their most-favored-nation status on Capitol Hill, this will not affect Beijing's attitude toward human rights and social justice."

"It's true that we could take some heat if we sign China as a client," conceded Hardy. "But I don't see this as an issue of moral virtue. The administration and its supporters in Congress apparently feel that the most effective means of combating the human rights abuses is to reach out to the Chinese and provide them with most-favored-nation status. In the long run, this relationship may give us more influence over China's domestic behavior. The integration of the People's Republic into the international community has to be gradual. And our own efforts on behalf of the Chinese could be significant. And you never know. A more open relationship with the Chinese might indeed improve their record on human rights."

"But this is speculation," responded Wiley. "In my judgment, the Chinese should earn the right to be represented in America's court of public opinion. Unless there's some movement on the human rights issue, I don't think we should represent them. And let's face it. The historical record on improving the human rights records of foreign regimes through more open communication is not particularly good."

"The standard has already been set by the administration and several before it," said Hardy. "Despite the Beijing regime's sensitivity and resentment, the White House continues to press them on the human rights issue, but the president and his congressional supporters feel it's in our national interest to cultivate a meaningful trading relationship with the Chinese. This may not be the most desirable approach, but politically it may be the most sensitive."

"I appreciate the political delicacy of this matter from a foreign policy perspective," replied Wiley. "But our position is different. I don't think we can do a good job for a client that we don't really believe in, particularly when they have such a dismal record on human rights. When Knopp & Bryce does business overseas or represents foreign clients in this country, we shouldn't abandon our own moral beliefs and standards. American corporations and the public relations firms that represent them are unofficial ambassadors. It may be true that if we refuse to represent the Chinese, they'll go to some other firm. But that's not our problem. We have to make a decision that we'll be comfortable with."

As Barker-Lane began to ponder the solicitation from the Chinese trade representative, she appreciated the competing philosophies just advanced by her two colleagues. Jacob Wiley favored moral virtue over political reality, even on the international stage, and believed that American values, as imperfect as they might be, should dominate our relations with foreign governments. And that was particularly true, in Wiley's view, of American firms in their international activities. On the other

hand, Bryan Hardy was a pragmatist who believed that all clients, even those who might be morally suspect, deserved some representation in the corridors of American political power. Anne Barker-Lane was painfully aware that her decision could have political consequences, not only for her firm but for American foreign policy as well.

THE CASE STUDY

At one level this case involves a familiar question in the practice of public relations: Should a public relations firm be a "hired gun" for all who seek representation, or should it assume representation only for those who causes it can, in good faith, support? But from a much broader, international perspective, this case also raises the issue of whether, in dealing with foreign enterprises (either private or governmental), American public relations firms should apply their own culture's moral values or whether they should provide representation for any foreign patron regardless of that client's moral worth. Should such firms represent client states whose sense of social justice (the most egregious violation of which concerns human rights) is more primitive, in our view, than our own? Should our own commitment to free speech and access to America's court of public opinion be extended to those nations whose cultural and political values differ from our own?

According to a survey several years ago, more than 150 American public relations firms work in this country for nations as diverse as Egypt, Japan, Hungary, and El Salvador. These client countries pursue both political objectives and commercial interests.[68] One could argue that, in a democratic system that prides itself on an unfettered marketplace of ideas, all speakers (including unpopular governments) have a right to be represented in the court of public opinion. In this view, public relations practitioners should assume a politically pragmatic posture in which the primary consideration is the "fit" between the client and the capabilities of the firm. Thus, the application of American moral standards, including our own ideas about human rights and social justice, becomes secondary to the decision-making process.

A counterpoint to this view is that, while foreign governments have the right to attempt to influence American foreign policy, public relations firms also have a right to select their clients based on their own self-interests (or the interests of others) and that the moral behavior of the client can and should be an important consideration.

For the purpose of rendering a judgment on whether Knopp & Bryce should assist the Chinese government in salvaging its most-favored-nation status, assume the role of Anne Barker-Lane. Using the formula for moral reasoning outlined in Chapter 3, make a decision on this matter.

▶ **CASE 12-6**

Environmental Justice and Media Access

The Reverend Jeremy Washington's soul was on fire. The NirvTech Corporation's proposal to build a chemical plant near Montrose in LaFitte Parish just two miles from his church had galvanized his moral energies to do battle in the public square against this corporate enterprise. NirvTech, a Malaysian-based multinational corporation specializing in the production of chemicals and pesticides, had promoted its proposal to the state's political leadership as an "economic shot in the arm" for the state and the economic salvation of LaFitte Parish. Washington minced no words in describing NirvTech's initiative as "environmental racism."

NirvTech was an aggressive player in the international arena, and the state's governor had enthusiastically applauded the company's decision to open its first U.S. plant in his political domain. Early in his first term, Governor Peter McBlade had become a suitor of international partners as a means of rescuing his state from the economic doldrums that had persisted for more than ten years. He had traveled abroad twice in pursuit of corporate white knights that would provide employment for his constituency and additional enrichment for the state's corporate tax base. The proposed site's proximity to the nation's inland waterway, an abundance of cheap labor, and generous tax incentives

from the state were instrumental in luring NirvTech to this backwater community on the banks of the Mississippi.

NirvTech's original proposal had targeted Baker's Bluff, a racially mixed middle-class city a hundred miles north of Montrose, for the company's American debut, but opposition from local citizens, communicated to the governor through the community's influential legislative representative, led to a "strategic reassessment" by corporate management. LaFitte Parish was then selected as the construction site for the NirvTech plant.

Washington was no novice in the fight for racial justice. As an idealistic college student, he had marched with Dr. Martin Luther King, Jr., and had later worked for the Southern Christian Leadership Conference. But following a rather lengthy apprenticeship under some of the nation's most influential civil rights leaders, Washington had returned to his roots in the Mississippi Delta to minister to the spiritual needs of his economically disenfranchised brethren. After more than twenty years as the pastor of the Mount Zion Baptist Church, his faith that the meek would someday inherit the earth remained undiminished, and he was determined to expedite, if possible, the fulfillment of this biblical prophecy. His public opposition to NirvTech's bid for corporate citizenship was just another skirmish to protect his community from the ravages of industrial pollution. Although not all of the African American citizens in LaFitte Parish were members of his church, Washington had become the de facto leader of the black opposition to NirvTech's proposal to locate in their community. A small minority had resisted his guidance because of the employment prospects that would accompany NirvTech's arrival, but Washington had convinced most African American citizens to place principle above self-interest, a tough sell among an economically depressed population.

Washington may have been a man of spiritual simplicity in the pulpit, but his temporal wisdom was usually the energizing force for his unobstructed moral vision. He readily conceded the practical limits of the occasional sound bite on the evening news and his access to the media to counter NirvTech's influence and public relations strategies. He needed reinforcements and was willing to make a pact with the devil if his long-term objectives could be accomplished. The "devil" in this case turned out to be Abercrombie and Associates, a small public relations firm in the state capital with a branch office in Baker's Bluff.

Abercrombie was known as an aggressive public relations firm with a steady clientele of local and regional clients. Calvin Abercrombie, the senior partner, had frequently accepted clients with unpopular views and in the process had often dueled with the state's power brokers and vested corporate interests. The firm's successful representation of such clients led Washington to Abercrombie's doorstep. Washington got right to the point. He briefly described his campaign against NirvTech's proposal to locate its plant in LaFitte Parish, the outlines of which Abercrombie had already gleaned from the news media. "We need your help in keeping out this industrial polluter," said Washington. "This is nothing but environmental racism. NirvTech may bring jobs to LaFitte Parish, but most of them won't go to our people. We'll still be unemployed. We need an advocate who can help us gain access to the media to tell our story." Washington then told Abercrombie that he had no funding for the campaign but wondered whether the firm would be willing to take him on as a pro bono client—without charge and for the good of society.

During Washington's brief presentation, Abercrombie had listened attentively and promised to tender the minister's request to his staff. Although Abercrombie had prided himself on the firm's willingness to represent controversial clients, his pride had always been amply rewarded by lucrative financial incentives. Reverend Washington had brought no such inducements to the table.

As senior partner, Abercrombie would be the moral agent in this case, but he valued the youthful insights and wisdom of his two young associates, Rebecca Nunez and Cassandra Brown. Both Nunez and Brown were junior partners in the firm, and both had brought to the enterprise that rare blend of creative talent and business acumen. In addition, Brown was the firm's first African American employee and had provided some invaluable insights into the views and concerns of the state's black population. However, despite their cordial working relationship, Nunez and Brown were not philosophical soul mates, and Abercrombie expected a spirited debate. He was not disappointed!

"I have a problem with representing Reverend Washington just on the merits of this issue," declared Nunez as she settled in for what undoubtedly would be an animated dialogue. "It may well be that NirvTech chose LaFitte Parish because it's a poor community, but we don't know that for a fact. Besides, the governor may have a point. This plant will benefit the state and the local economy. I understand Reverend Washington's frustration. This plant may indeed be a polluter. But let's face it. This area is already polluted. And NirvTech will bring jobs to the area and will provide a boost to the economic fortunes of the area."

"As an African American who grew up not far from Montrose, I happen to think Reverend Washington is right about environmental racism," said Brown. "But we're not going to settle that issue here. As a public relations firm, we don't have to believe passionately in their cause to represent them. The fact is they have no one to speak for them, to help them frame their message. They're powerless in the court of public opinion."

"But Reverend Washington is asking for charity," said Nunez unsympathetically. "I understand his concerns, but we're not a nonprofit organization. We can't take on clients who can't afford to pay. And we have no moral obligation to do so."

"I strongly disagree," replied Brown not unexpectedly. "Powerful corporations and other special interests employ public relations firms and lobbyists to influence the political system. And they have access to the media to do so. People such as Reverend Washington's congregation are effectively disenfranchised. They have no means of exercising political influence. I realize that we can't accept a lot of nonpaying clients, but we have a social responsibility to do some pro bono work to help those who have nowhere to turn."

"I understand your concern, Cassandra," responded Nunez, "but there's a practical matter of where you draw the line. If we accept this group without compensation, then where will it end?

Besides, the media are covering this issue. That should provide sufficient publicity for Reverend Washington's point of view."

"I acknowledge that there has been some media coverage, but quite frankly I'm not sure that it's been balanced. Both the governor's office and NirvTech have flooded the media with press conferences, interviews, and press releases. How can Reverend Washington expect to counter such a media deluge? He doesn't have the money or the clout with the media. His parishioners can't compete in the marketplace of ideas."

But Nunez was unconvinced. "But that's the way the system works. I'm sorry that these citizens can't afford the services of high-priced public relations counsel, but it's not our responsibility to make up the difference. It's the job of the media to afford Reverend Washington his day in the court of public opinion. If they fail in that ethical mandate, that's too bad. But it should not be the responsibility of Abercrombie and Associates to ensure media access for the disenfranchised."

"But one of the functions of public relations," insisted Brown, "is to frame the issues according to our clients' wishes to minimize the filtering process that inevitably occurs with media coverage. The fact is that the media's coverage, with a couple of notable exceptions, has been one-sided. Reverend Washington needs our expertise to help level the playing field."

Nunez wasn't sure whether her African American colleague really believed the media coverage was unbalanced or whether she thought the state's press should be more proactive in campaigning against NirvTech's proposed corporate citizenship. Brown was certainly convinced that NirvTech—and the state's political leadership, for that matter—was insensitive to the citizens' opposition because they were black and they were poor. Nevertheless, as the senior partner leaned forward to bring an end to this spirited debate, Nunez made her closing argument.

"Keep in mind that this is a controversial issue," Nunez said. "If we expect to keep our client base— some of whom are quite influential—and attract new clients, we don't want to be seen as a radical firm. Our position could be seen as antiprogressive. The environmental position doesn't sell well

among the power brokers in this state, especially those who view corporate investment as an economic necessity."

"We may suffer as a result of this," conceded Brown. "But we should represent Reverend Washington's cause because it's the right thing to do."

Calvin Abercrombie wasn't so sure. He had always embraced social responsibility as an abstract principle, but he was now being called on to commit his firm's resources to a cause without any prospect of financial compensation. And he wasn't even confident of the locus of social responsibility in this case. On the one hand, he found Brown's concerns about environmental racism convincing. And there was no doubt that Washington's parishioners were no match for the deep pockets of the opposition. On the other hand, environmental pollution was a way of life in LaFitte Parish. Besides, NirvTech would still be required to meet the federal and state standards for pollution controls, the enforcement of which was admittedly sometimes inadequate.

As Abercrombie pondered the ethical dimensions of his predicament, he asked himself whether the public relations profession owed some kind of moral duty to the culturally disinherited to provide them with a degree of political empowerment.

THE CASE STUDY

The mass media are instrumental in public opinion formation, but the economically disenfranchised have little or no access to the media to state their case. Even when this group is the subject of news accounts, journalists frame the issues through their own refracted lenses. Powerful special interests, on the other hand, can afford expensive public relations counsel to communicate their views to government officials and to the public through the media. In this way, they control the public square.

Egalitarians complain that, in a democratic society, the poor and other culturally disinherited groups are also members of the moral community and deserve to be heard. In this view, the right to be heard is a moral "right," and the media and those who provide information to the media have a responsibility to ensure access for the voices of the disaffected. Libertarians counter that the media have no such responsibility and that news organizations should be free to provide coverage and to frame these issues as they see fit unencumbered by claims of access from those who are unhappy with that coverage.

Public relations professionals, of course, are in the business of seeking access for their clients to the corridors of public opinion, but this access is costly. Those without the financial resources are at a decided disadvantage. Thus, the following question might be posed: What moral obligation should the public relations profession assume for contributing to the cause of social justice through pro bono work?

In this case, an African American minister representing an impoverished constituency is fighting a proposal to build a chemical plant in his community. Although the plant will create jobs and help to resurrect the local economy, most of the jobs will not go to those most in need of employment. He views this as an act of environmental racism because NirvTech selected LaFitte Parish, a predominantly poor African American region, after residents of a more affluent community used their political clout to reject the company's overtures. He has asked the public relations firm of Abercrombie and Associates for assistance in communicating his message to the public and the politicians in the state capital.

The firm's staff disagrees on whether they should take on Washington as a pro bono client. Cassandra Brown, an African American, argues that public relations practitioners have a moral responsibility to help narrow the gap between the "haves" and the "have nots" in terms of their relative political influence. Her colleague, Rebecca Nunez, who is less certain about the justice of Washington's cause to begin with, is not enthusiastic about the firm's committing itself to such an egalitarian posture.

Assume the role of Calvin Abercrombie and, using the SAD formula outlined in Chapter 3, decide whether you will honor the Reverend Washington's plea to assist his parishioners in their resistance to NirvTech's proposal.

Notes

1. Sally Lehrman, "Getting Past a 'White, Middle-Class' America," *Quill,* March 2002, p. 30.
2. Ibid.
3. Philip Patterson and Lee Wilkins, *Media Ethics: Issues & Cases,* 4th ed. (Boston: McGraw-Hill, 2002), p. 13.
4. See Tom L. Beauchamp, *Philosophical Ethics: An Introduction to Moral Philosophy* (New York: McGraw-Hill, 1982), p. 223.
5. Aristotle considers the subject in Book V of the *Nicomachean Ethics.*
6. For a discussion of the relationship of libertarianism to institutional press freedom, see John C. Merrill, *The Dialectic in Journalism: Toward a Responsible Use of Press Freedom* (Baton Rouge: Louisiana State University Press, 1989), pp. 113–114.
7. Fred S. Siebert, Theodore Peterson, and Wilbur Schramm, *Four Theories of the Press* (Urbana: University of Illinois Press, 1956), pp. 39–71.
8. Quoted in ibid., p. 73.
9. John A. Rawls, *A Theory of Justice,* rev. ed. (Cambridge, MA: The Belknap Press of Harvard University Press, 1999).
10. Ibid., p. 3.
11. For a discussion of the relationship of Rawls's theory, as well as those of other influential philosophers, to the notion of "responsibility," see Merrill, *The Dialectic in Journalism,* pp. 37–54.
12. Clifford G. Christians, Mark Fackler, Kim B. Rotzoll, and Kathy Brittain McKee, *Media Ethics: Cases and Moral Reasoning,* 6th ed. (White Plains, NY: Addison Wesley Longman, 2001), pp. 98–99.
13. Holly J. Morris and Vicky Hallett, "Public Displays of Affection," *U.S. News & World Report,* September 9, 2002, p. 42.
14. See Michael Riley, "Backlash," *American Journalism Review* (June 2001): 56–59.
15. Ibid., p. 57.
16. Commission on the Freedom of the Press, *A Free and Responsible Press* (Chicago: University of Chicago Press, 1947), pp. 26–27.
17. Lehrman, "Getting Past a 'White, Middle-Class' America."
18. Ibid.
19. See Paula M. Poindexter, Laura Smith, and Don Heider, "Race and Ethnicity in Local Television News: Framing, Story Assignments, and Source Selections," *Journal of Broadcasting & Electronic Media* 47, no. 4 (December 2003).
20. See John Leo, "Quoting by Quota," *U.S. News & World Report,* June 29, 1998, p. 21.
21. Ibid.
22. Lehrman, "Getting Past a 'White, Middle-Class' America."

23. Michelle Malkin, "Racial Politics Permeates Media Olympics Coverage," *The Advocate* (Baton Rouge, LA), September 29, 2000, p. 13B.

24. Neil Hickey, "Many Groups Underrepresented on TV, Study Declares," *TV Guide,* July 3, 1993, p. 33.

25. Dana E. Mastro and Bradley S. Greenberg, "The Portrayal of Racial Minorities on Prime Time Television," *Journal of Broadcasting & Electronic Media* (Fall 2000): 690–703.

26. For an insightful commentary on news coverage of groups outside the mainstream, see Clifford Christians, "Reporting and the Oppressed," in Deni Elliott (ed.), *Responsible Journalism* (Beverly Hills, CA: Sage, 1986), pp. 109–130.

27. See Marci McDonald, "Madison Avenue's New Latin Beat," *U.S. News & World Report,* June 4, 2001, p. 42.

28. James Poniewozik, "What's Wrong with This Picture?," *Time,* May 28, 2001, p. 80.

29. Ibid., p. 81.

30. Mastro and Greenberg, "The Portrayal of Racial Minorities on Prime Time Television," p. 699.

31. See Bob Papper, "Recovering Lost Ground," *Communicator* (July/August 2004): 24–28.

32. Kelly Heyboer, "Losing Ground," *American Journalism Review* (June 2001): 39.

33. Donald L. Guimary, "Non-Whites in Newsrooms of California Dailies," *Journalism Quarterly* 65 (Winter 1988): 1009. For an examination of the organization's plans to improve minority recruitment and hiring, see "Minorities in the Newsroom," *ASNE Bulletin,* February 1985, pp. 3–35, and May–June 1987, pp. 16–23.

34. Felicity Barringer, "Editors Debate Realism vs. Retreat in Newsroom Diversity," *New York Times,* April 6, 1998, pp. C1, C8.

35. Ibid.

36. "NABJ Suggests Changes to Increase Diversity," *Quill,* June 2001, p. 71.

37. Quoted in ibid.

38. For a discussion of this trend, see Kelly Heyboer, "Losing Ground," *American Journalism Review* (June 2001): 39–43.

39. Laura Castañeda, "Bilingual Defections," *American Journalism Review* (June 2001): 44–49.

40. Stuart Elliott, "Hill & Knowlton Forms a Unit to Direct Public Relations Efforts toward Gay Men and Lesbians," *New York Times,* June 23, 1995, p. C5.

41. PRSA Press Release (New York), August 22, 2003, p. 1.

42. See Bob Papper and Michael Gerhard, "About Face?" *Communicator* (August 1998): 26–32.

43. "Women and Minorities in Radio and TV News." *Communicator* (July 1999): 28.

44. See Elizabeth A. Rathbun, "Woman's Work Still Excludes Top Jobs," *Broadcasting & Cable,* August 3, 1998, pp. 22–28.

45. Christi Harlan, "Role Models in Transition," *Quill,* July/August 1995, pp. 39–40.

46. Stephanie Craft and Wayne Wanta, "Women in the Newsroom: Influences of Female Editors and Reporters on the News Agenda," *Journalism & Mass Communication Quarterly* 81, no. 1 (Spring 2004): 124–138.

47. Cory L. Armstrong, "The Influence of Reporter Gender on Source Selection in Newspaper Stories," *Journalism & Mass Communication Quarterly* 81, no. 1 (Spring 2004): 139–154.

48. "Newsrooms Recruit Gay Journalists," *Quill,* November/December 1993, p. 8; Cal Thomas, "Group Urges Media to Hire Homosexuals," *The Advocate* (Baton Rouge, LA), September 22, 1993, p. 4B.

49. See Alicia C. Shepard, "High Anxiety," *American Journalism Review* (November 1993): 19–24.

50. Gilbert Bailon, "Gulf between Minority, White Journalists Wide" (ASNE home page), accessed June 6, 1998, available at http://www.asne.org/kiosk/editor/october/bailon.htm

51. For some thoughts on whether reporting by minority journalists on their own ethnic groups results in better coverage, see Gigi Anders, "The Crucible," *American Journalism Review* (May 1999): 22–31.

52. Thomas Sowell, "Changes Needed to Fix Jury System," *The Advocate* (Baton Rouge, LA), April 14, 2004, p. 6B.

53. "The McVeigh Dilemma," *Quill,* April 1997, p. 17.

54. Ralph Langer, "Our Story, Process Correct," *Quill,* April 1997, p. 19.

55. Kathy R. Fitzpatrick, "Life after Simpson: Regulating Media Freedom in Judicial Matters," *Media Law Notes* 22 (Spring 1995): 4.

56. "O. J. Simpson Coverage: Reflecting on the Media in Society," *Poynter Report,* Fall 1994, p. 3.

57. Susanne A. Roschwalb and Richard A. Stack, "Litigation Public Relations," *Communications and the Law* 14 (December 1992): 6.

58. For a good discussion of how O. J. Simpson's lead attorney manipulated the media, for example, see Robert L. Shapiro, "Secrets of a Celebrity Lawyer," *Columbia Journalism Review* (September/October 1994): 25–29.

59. Roschwalb and Stack, "Litigation Public Relations," p. 3.

60. Ibid., p. 13.

61. See Andrew Goldman, "And the Verdict Is . . . Guilty," *TV Guide,* January 17, 2004, pp. 51–54.

62. For a discussion of the relationship of justice to various disciplines, see Ronald L. Cohen (ed.), *Justice: Views from the Social Sciences* (New York: Plenum, 1986).

63. Joann Lee, "New York City NDs Reflect on Their Coverage of the Tawana Brawley Story," *Communicator* (August 1989): 29.

64. Aristotle's conception of compensatory justice is sometimes described as "rectifying justice." See Norman E. Bowie, *Making Ethical Decisions* (New York: McGraw-Hill, 1985), p. 268.

65. Some of the ideas for this case are discussed in Nadya Labl, "Cameras? Jury's Still Out," *Time*, December 9, 2002, p. 66. In November 2002 a judge in Texas ruled that PBS's *Frontline* could film jury deliberations in a capital murder case, but that decision was reversed by the Texas Court of Criminal Appeals.

66. Ibid.

67. Debra Rosenberg, "Cameras Report, the Jury Decide," *Newsweek*, August 9, 2004, p. 8.

68. Dennis L. Wilcox, Phillip H. Ault, Warren K. Agee, and Glenn T. Cameron, *Essentials of Public Relations* (New York: Addison-Wesley Education Publishers, 2001), p. 294.

13

Stereotypes
in Media Communications

STEREOTYPES
AND VALUE FORMATION

In 1996, an ad for T. J. Maxx featured an ultra-feminine man throwing a hissy fit and playing the notes F-A-G on the piano, a classic representation of the enduring stereotype of the gay male. Six years later a 7UP ad using prison-rape jokes was pulled after a flurry of complaints. About the same time, Subaru, acutely aware of its lesbian following, felt sufficiently comfortable to hire Martina Navratilova, shunned by marketers in the 1980s because she was openly gay, as its pitchwoman.[1] These three anecdotal examples plucked from the vast array of commercial messages that confront American consumers each day are a testament to the ambivalence with which Madison Avenue employs stereotyping as a marketing strategy. But underlying this ambivalence is a painful reality: Stereotyping is a part of the human condition, a mental shortcut that most of us use to bring order to our individual worldviews. Because we seek and find common ground in stereotyping, it is not surprising that this technique should easily germinate within mass entertainment and information content.

However, we should not allow the inevitability of stereotyping to deter us from confronting and rejecting the socially destructive and unjust consequences of this habit. Journalism Professor Tom Brislin, writing in the *Honolulu Advertiser,* has eloquently articulated the undesirable consequences of stereotyping and society's duty to resist the propagation of stereotypes: "While informing and entertaining, media are powerfully transmitting social values. . . . Media stereotypes perpetuate real-world discrimination, harassment and, all too often, violence against groups and gender portrayed as outsiders. . . ."[2]

Some segments of the audience have heeded Brislin's advice and have not remained on the sidelines in the campaign against offensive stereotypes. Consider, for example, the brouhaha that erupted when NBC bid farewell to its highly acclaimed comedy *Seinfeld* in 1998. In the next to the final episode, while returning from a Mets baseball game, the featured characters, Jerry, Elaine, George, and Kramer, get stuck in a traffic jam created by the Puerto Rican Day parade. At one point Kramer tosses a sparkler, accidentally igniting a Puerto Rican flag. Angry parade-goers chase Kramer while a mob begins shaking Jerry's empty car and throws it down a stairwell. Kramer later remarks that "it's like this every day in Puerto Rico."[3]

The reaction to this controversial display of ethnic humor was swift. Manuel Mirabal, the president of the National Puerto Rican Coalition, called it an "unconscionable insult" to the

Puerto Rican community. Fernando Ferrer, president of the New York City borough of the Bronx, accused the *Seinfeld* episode of crossing the line between humor and bigotry. Ferrer said it was a slur to depict men rioting and vandalizing a car and to imply that this is an everyday occurrence in Puerto Rico. NBC took issue with the show's critics. "We do not feel that the show lends itself to damaging ethnic stereotypes," the network said in a statement, "because the audience for 'Seinfeld' knows the humor is derived from watching the core group of characters get themselves into difficult situations."[4]

Was *Seinfeld*'s use of ethnic humor distasteful stereotyping or just another typical amusing predicament that confronted the program's bizarre cast of characters? Regardless of one's perspective on this controversy, the *Seinfeld* incident is a solemn reminder that, despite an increasing sensitivity within the Hollywood community and on Madison Avenue, stereotyping is still one of the most contentious issues confronting the contemporary media establishment.

A *stereotype* is a "fixed mental image of a group that is frequently applied to all its members."[5] In a world full of complexities and ambiguities, we are constantly seeking ways of confronting and simplifying the confusion of everyday reality. Most of our knowledge of the universe is experienced vicariously, and we tend to compartmentalize this secondhand information and to fit it into our preconceived notions about other groups of people. When this happens, we are participating in the process of stereotyping. Stereotypes are frequently used as a defense mechanism to conceal our inadequacies or to justify our fragile feelings of superiority. For example, negative stereotypes of African Americans originally served to justify the Anglo enslavement of Africans and have since become deeply ingrained in Anglo-American culture.[6]

The concepts discussed in this chapter are related closely to some of those in Chapter 12. Stereotyping can lead to social injustices for those who are its unfortunate victims, and

when this happens, serious ethical questions arise. Stereotypes sometimes extend beyond the matter of social justice, however, and thus they deserve to be examined in a separate chapter.

There is a tendency to associate stereotypes with such visible issues as sexism and racial and ethnic prejudice. These are undoubtedly related to the most controversial of our stereotypes, but unfair labeling extends to all areas of social interaction. Overweight people, for example, are often pictured as slovenly and lazy. The faddish "dumb blond" jokes are used to stereotype a significant portion of the female population as intellectually suspect. The homeless are all lumped together as bums and social misfits who have chosen their unconventional lifestyle and economic circumstances. The mentally ill are frequently depicted as violent and dangerous, whereas most are at greater risk of harming themselves than others.[7] Certain nationalities are depicted as romantic and fun-loving, and others are pictured as cold and authoritarian.

Stereotyping is a human trait of ancient vintage, but the modern concept of stereotyping was introduced into our social consciousness by the distinguished author and columnist Walter Lippmann. Writing in his often-quoted *Public Opinion* in 1922, Lippmann made the following observation about the necessity (or perhaps inevitability) of relying on stereotypes to manage our environment and social relationships:

> For the attempt to see all things freshly and in detail, rather than as types and generalities, is exhausting, and among busy affairs practically out of the question. . . . Modern life is hurried and multifarious, above all physical distance separates men who are often in vital contact with each other, such as employer and employee, official and voter. There is neither time nor opportunity for intimate acquaintance. Instead, we notice a trait which marks a well known type, and fill in the rest of the picture by means of the stereotypes we carry about in our heads.[8]

In other words, stereotypes are an economical way of viewing the world. Because individuals cannot personally experience most of the events in which they have an interest, they rely on the testimony of others to enrich their impoverished knowledge of the environment. The mass media, of course, are an important window for this vicarious experience and function as our eyes and ears for that part of the universe we cannot directly observe.[9] They are cultural catalysts and inevitably influence our worldview. Thus, because of their undeniable cultural influence, media practitioners have a moral responsibility to understand the differences between stereotypes and reality and to maintain a steady vigilance against stereotypical portrayals that perpetuate real-world discrimination.

Lippmann noted, quite correctly, that a "pattern of stereotypes is not neutral." Because stereotyping involves our personal perceptions of reality, it is "highly charged with the feelings that are attached to them." Thus, as he instructs us, stereotypes are a vital defense mechanism behind which "we can continue to feel ourselves safe in the position we occupy."[10] This view suggests that stereotyping, as a natural process, has a role to play in maintaining sanity and that to arbitrarily reject it as unsavory or unworthy of our respect would be a mistake.

Nevertheless, in our egalitarian society, stereotypes are often unfair. Their use leaves little room for perceiving individual differences within a group.[11] Thus, to the extent that we judge others according to some misguided stereotype, we have undermined their right to self-determination, a basic value within our society.[12]

However, what makes stereotyping such a formidable cultural foe is that stereotypes are frequently based upon reality. Or to state it bluntly, some stereotypes are not entirely false. A case in point is a report from the Rand Corporation, which supplies research to the Pentagon, describing army wives as a "sorority" whose members are "typically considered to be young, immature, lower-class spouses who are in financial difficulty and who have difficulty controlling their reproductive tendencies." Echo Gaines, a website designer and a soldier's fiancée, accused the think tank of perpetuating a stereotype and launched an Internet counteroffensive against the report's findings. The book's author, Margaret Harrell, replied that the stereotype was "rooted in reality." "The book does reflect the stereotype," she said, "but it's one that's out there in the military community."[13]

Be that as it may, it is when we make inaccurate and unfair judgments about individuals based upon these mental images that ethical questions arise to confront our prejudices. For example, the media have traditionally depicted male homosexuals as flamboyant and effeminate, traits that do represent a segment of the gay population but are not necessarily representative of the group as a whole. Because such images often erect psychological barriers between the gay community and society at large, the question is whether they should be avoided entirely, even if they are an accurate portrayal of a segment of the offended group.

The media have been the focal point for much of the criticism of the perpetuation of stereotypes. In recent years they have become increasingly sensitive to these accusations, and some offensive stereotypes have been eliminated. Ironically, some critics have occasionally chastised media practitioners who presented nonstereotypical portrayals. A case in point was the criticism of the controversial Spike Lee film *Do the Right Thing*. Some movie reviewers observed that the film's ghetto neighborhood was not populated by addicts and drug pushers and thus was not a true depiction. This criticism ignored the fact that millions of African Americans live in neighborhoods that are not populated by drug pushers and street gangs.[14]

Nevertheless, media professionals must still struggle with the moral dilemma of responding to the concerns of those who object to unflattering or unrealistic portrayals while protecting the legitimate and acceptable roles that some stereotypes play in the presentation of media content. In other words, some stereotyping in the production of media content may be inevitable, but strategies should be deployed to confront those stereotypes that are particularly offensive and unfair to certain segments of society.

THE ROLE OF STEREOTYPES IN MEDIA CONTENT

Media content of all kinds—news, entertainment, advertising—abounds with stereotypes. If stereotypes are indispensable for an individual's comprehension of the environment, as Lippmann suggested in 1922, and because the media are the primary means by which we vicariously sample the world around us, stereotyping is probably inevitable as media practitioners attempt to construct their mediated reality for dissemination to a mass audience. But the media are powerful institutions. Their selection of symbols and images can sanctify some lifestyles and disparage others. Scholars disagree as to the degree of harm caused by media stereotypes, but the assignment of moral responsibility does not need to await the resolution of this debate. Like all moral agents, media professionals are responsible for the consequences of their decisions, as ethicist Deni Elliott pointedly reminds us:

> Media institutions fulfill social functions. News media tell citizens what they need to know for effective self-governance; persuasive media sell their clients' messages to an audience; and entertainment media sell their clients' brand of pleasure. All media institutions, of course, have the economic function "to attract and hold a large audience for advertisers," but that is irrelevant to a discussion in the moral realm. That is, economic realities don't provide justification for causing people to suffer harms. Neither does doing one's job necessarily provide justification for causing harms.[15]

The primary harm that accrues from stereotyping is that it leads to discrimination and prejudice. Ethical issues arise when the employment of media stereotypes becomes so pronounced as to dull the audience's critical faculties in making value judgments concerning individual members of society. In a pluralistic culture such as ours, media practitioners have an obligation to consider the fundamental fairness of a system that has traditionally projected stereotypical images of certain segments of society.

Stereotyping, however, does not concern just matters of cultural discrimination or prejudice. The prevalence of stereotypical symbols and messages in media content implicates the persistent question of what the media's role in society should be. Should the media serve as social engineers, attempting to construct a more egalitarian culture, or should they simply reflect society's values, thereby reinforcing cultural norms, some of which inevitably entail a stereotypical rendition of reality? These two views are briefly described in this assessment of stereotyping in advertising:

> Critics claim that many advertisers stereotype large segments of our population, particularly women, minorities, and the elderly. The issue of stereotyping is connected to the debate about whether advertising shapes society's values or simply mirrors them. . . . If you believe that advertising has the ability to shape our values and our view of the world, you will believe it essential that advertisers become aware of how they portray different groups. Conversely, if you believe that advertising mirrors society, you will think that advertisers have a responsibility to ensure that what is portrayed is accurate and representative. Advertisers struggle with this issue every time they use people in an ad.[16]

Such disputes have occupied the academic community and media critics for generations, prompting some fascinating Socratic dialogues within university classrooms. But for the practitioner, the ethical dimensions of the media's role in perpetuating or dispelling stereotypes involves a continuous struggle to balance the commercial allure and mass appeal of some stereotypes against the values of accuracy, fairness, and respect for the individual members of society. Media stereotypes of minorities, women, the elderly, and the disabled have been among the most visible and most criticized.

The examples presented in the following text are not intended to exhaust the discussion of stereotypes but are merely representative of this domain of ethical concern.

Racial and Ethnic Minorities

Nowhere have stereotypes been more prevalent than in the entertainment industry, and despite some progress in confronting unfair or offensive stereotypes, the fictional depictions of minority groups still occasion disapproval from cultural guardians. For example, author Maria Laurino is one of those guardians and, as an Italian American, is eminently qualified to object to the media's stereotypical depictions of this ethnic group. In commenting on the success of HBO's prime-time hit *The Sopranos,* Laurino remarked that "even a mention of 'The Sopranos' in some Italian American circles provokes a sigh of despair at the persistence of the Mafia stereotype. With all of the show's sensitivity to class tension and its perceptive radar for equally dangerous, equally false positive stereotypes," she wondered, "could 'The Sopranos' have maintained both its masterly look at Italian American culture and its extraordinary success without the plot device of the Mafia?"[17] Similarly, in critiquing an episode of the CBS series *That's Life,* which told the story of an Italian American bartender who "shocks" her family by breaking off her engagement and enrolling at a local New Jersey college, Laurino offered this assessment: "The insulting notion that it's a miracle for an Italian American woman like me to attend college makes the show's premise particularly dated, but it's in keeping with decades of television assumptions and stereotypes."[18]

The recognition of harmful stereotypes as an ethical problem in media content has been measured and deliberate. Generations of Americans, for example, were treated to conventional images of African Americans as comical, fun-loving, and dim-witted caricatures. By the late 1970s, however, some changes were evident, and fifteen years later prime-time TV had more programs than ever dominated by African American characters. Surveys also showed that African American households were watching TV in record numbers,[19] a discovery that did not go unnoticed on Madison Avenue. African American characters are no longer invisible to the prime-time TV audience, as evidenced by such recent programs as *Dave's World, Homicide,* and *NYPD Blue* in which African American actors have had leading roles.[20] And as reported in Chapter 12, African American characters have become increasingly prominent on network sitcoms. Nevertheless, even as late as the 1990s, a decade that some labeled as "progressive" in its eradication of many of the post–World War II media stereotypes, African Americans were still most frequently depicted as prostitutes, pimps, killers, and drug dealers. And in a spring 2004 review of the movie *Soul Train*—"a raunchy spoof of the disaster movie lampoon *Airplane!*"—film critic Carrie Rickey laments the producer's use of stereotypes, including one in which a token white is shamed by a black man's sexual prowess.[21]

Another group that has long suffered from media stereotypes are American Indians (sometimes referred to as Native Americans). Portrayals of the "savage Indian" did not begin in the movie studios of Hollywood. In the nineteenth century, long before the emergence of film, news reporting about American Indians was distorted in such a way that it encouraged or at least condoned brutal treatment of them. Mass-produced books reinforced the popular image of American Indians as subhuman renegades. With the rise of the giant film studios, Hollywood succeeded in erasing the cultural and ethnic distinctions among the more than 400 distinct American Indian tribes and nations by developing one-dimensional figures who mercilessly slaughtered innocent women and children.[22]

However, such stereotypes die hard and are not merely a historical relic of Hollywood's fantasy. Native Americans have taken their concerns into the American mainstream by challenging the use of Indian names, logos, and symbols by such professional sports teams as the Atlanta Braves, the Washington Redskins, and the Cleveland Indians. For example, during the 1995 World Series between the Atlanta Braves and the Cleveland Indians, the American Indian Movement (AIM) protested the teams' use of mascots and symbols, accusing them of encouraging racism and stereotyping.[23] And in May 1998, a Native American coalition argued to a U.S. trademark board that the Washington Redskins should lose federal protection for their "Redskins" trademark because the logo violates part of the Trademark Act forbidding protection for "scandalous" or "immoral" terms.[24]

The news media, which we depend on for an accurate representation of our national fabric, are not blameless in the perpetuation of stereotypes. For example, African Americans are often depicted as poverty-stricken and un-educated (and some are), but this ignores the reality of a large and influential black middle class. Black suspects are still more likely to be shown in handcuffs being taken into custody, while their Anglo counterparts are frequently photographed with their attorneys.[25] These images may accurately portray a segment of the black community, but the news media have usually ignored the sizable African American middle class. How many African American attorneys, for example, are interviewed on TV concerning their opinions of Supreme Court decisions (unless, of course, the ruling involves civil rights)?

Sports coverage is particularly susceptible to the perpetuation of stereotypes. According to Richard Lapchick, chair of the DeVos Sport Business Management Program at the University of Central Florida, this situation is the result of a glaring disparity between the race of a majority of athletes and the sports fans:

> The conviction that athletes are poor role models and bad leaders for children is fueled by media images, which are themselves fueled by racial stereotypes. Some white people who used to express openly their racial stereotypes about

intelligence, work ethic, drugs, violence, and gender violence now express them about athletes, consistently and regularly in the press, and when Americans think about athletes they generally think about black athletes. . . . The fan base in the United States is mostly white. They read about our athletes through a media filter primarily created by white male journalists and writers.[26]

In 2002, laments Lapchick, there were only two African American sports editors and nineteen African American columnists on major American newspapers. Ninety percent of our daily newspapers did not have a single African American sportswriter on their staffs.[27]

Insensitivity to racial stereotypes in the news media may well reflect the fact that minority representation in media management positions is still relatively low. But part of the problem is inherent in the nature of the news business. Social problems are newsworthy, and coverage of these problems inevitably focuses on those who are most likely to represent preconceived images, such as inner-city blacks who are school dropouts and gang members, and Hispanics and Latinos who are illegal aliens.[28] Under such circumstances, the values of fairness and accuracy often fall prey to the perniciousness of stereotypical thinking. A study of ABC, CBS, NBC, and CNN broadcasts released in late 2003, for example, showed that two-thirds of the stories about Latinos were devoted to illegal immigration, terrorism, and crime.[29]

Representative of such stereotypical coverage is an *NBC* report on the condition of a set of conjoined twins born in Mexico and surgically separated in the United States. In reporting the story, correspondent David Gregory, apparently assuming the illegal status of the parents, informed viewers that they had "snuck across the U.S. border" from Tijuana to get medical help. However, Gregory's version was contradicted by the coverage of the *San Diego Union-Tribune* and others that correctly reported that the family was fully supported by the San Diego Children's Hospital, which had donated its medical services and had also provided the ambulance that transported them across the Mexico-California border.[30]

The Arab-as-terrorist stereotype may have been responsible for the initial descriptions of the suspects in the 1995 bombing of the federal building in Oklahoma City. As emergency crews responded to the worst terrorist attack on American soil in history, the FBI issued an alert for a pickup truck containing three male passengers, two of them described as "Middle Eastern with dark hair and beards." In fact, two Anglo-American males, Timothy McVeigh and Terry Nichols, were arrested for the crime and ultimately convicted.[31] And the fact that all of the 9/11 hijackers were Arabs, mostly from Saudi Arabia, has done little to dispel the pernicious stereotype of the Arab-as-terrorist, with sometimes regrettable consequences for the public's perception of the Arab American community. Ironically, while the West has embraced the stereotypical view of the Arab world as a breeding ground for terrorists and a distressing habitat of oppressed peoples, Hollywood has perpetuated a more romantic stereotype of the Middle East as a region of Arabian nights. On the other hand, many Arabs view Westerners, particularly Americans, as morally decadent, excessively materialistic, and narcissistic. There is clearly a cultural divide based upon mutually destructive stereotypes and an overall ignorance of the other's history and values. However, there is a glimmer of hope. In the aftermath of the 9/11 tragedy, there have been some modest efforts to open the lines of communication between the two worlds and to dispel the stereotypes upon which this mutual distrust has been based.

The advertising industry must also plead guilty to stereotyping racial and ethnic minorities. Because advertisers are in the business of creating images and selling a product within a brief message, stereotyping is inevitable. And before the 1960s and 1970s, the economic reality that campaigns were produced primarily for a white audience led advertisers to appeal to the perceived attitudes and prejudices of the majority. Ads featuring stereotypical racial and ethnic characters, such as Chiquita Banana and Aunt Jemima, were commonplace until groups representing the various minority groups began protesting vigorously, thus forcing a retreat by agencies and companies.[32]

Nevertheless, stereotypes persist in the ad business, generating the predictable condemnations from critics even as they resonate with some segments of the target audience. Such was the case with a series of ads posted throughout the San Francisco area with the noble intent of preventing rape. In one such ad a picture of an African American male with a badly bruised nose and eye is accompanied by a written command below his face, "Don't take rape lying down." Other ads in the series featured a Latino and a white man. Cori Couture, director of an Oakland women's group backing the ad, defended the campaign as an effective means of showing potential rape victims that "men's bodies are not invulnerable to women." But critics of the ads, concerned both about the symbolic stereotypes lurking in the ads as well as their effectiveness, responded that such ads send the wrong messages about men of color and "place the onus of stopping rape on victims."[33]

Hispanic and Latino stereotypes have persisted within the advertising industry, precipitating a cacophony of complaints even as the characters have resonated with some segments of the audience. A case in point is the Taco Bell commercial introduced several years ago featuring a charming Chihuahua named "Dinky" strolling down a street ostensibly in search of female companionship but in reality looking for a treat from Taco Bell.[34] The Spanish-speaking Dinky quickly attracted a loyal following with his famous line, "Yo quiero Taco Bell" ("I want Taco Bell"). But while Dinky was adored by many fans, others found the dog offensive. The former mayor of Clearwater, Florida, Gabriel Cazares, for example, described the Chihuahua as a "demeaning stereotype that has no place in American mass-market advertising." Some members of the Cuban American community also condemned Dinky's use of a red-badge beret like the one worn by Ernesto "Che" Guevara, the communist revolutionary who helped Fidel Castro take power in Cuba.[35] However, Jose Limon, an English and anthropology professor at the University of Texas at Austin, saw Dinky as more of a cultural contradiction. While Dinky's "very small form and relationship to Mexico . . . encourages the American public to literally and stereotypically look down on Mexicans," acknowledged Limon, "Dinky [also] represents an increasing 'Mexicanization' of American society."[36] However, despite cries of stereotyping from some quarters, the commercial won critical acclaim from the American Marketing Association, and in a 1998 survey of Hispanic teens the Taco Bell spots ranked high among their favorite commercials.[37]

Female Stereotypes

The depiction of women has traditionally been one of the media's most pervasive stereotypes. In the 1950s most women were homemakers, and ads often portrayed them as being preoccupied with better ways to do the laundry and discovering new ways to please their husbands. Television programs featured the perfect wife, who maintained a spotless home for the family patriarch and the children and displayed none of the signs of stress that one associates with contemporary living. Such early TV fare as *Father Knows Best, Leave It to Beaver,* and *The Adventures of Ozzie and Harriet,* some of which are still in syndication, were fantasy insights into the model American family.

Other programs, such as *I Love Lucy,* featured silly and trouble-prone wives, a stereotype that continues to attract and amuse the mass audience. Nevertheless, neither image of women in the 1950s was an accurate portrayal of reality, although one might struggle to find real fault with these programs in light of the hours of clean entertainment they have provided TV viewers. In the 1970s and 1980s, the TV roles of women began to change as such

popular shows as *M*A*S*H, The Mary Tyler Moore Show, One Day at a Time, Murphy Brown,* and *The Golden Girls* began to feature female characters who were assertive and self-sufficient. Later, we find popular TV personalities like Roseanne as an independent wife and also a working-class hero.

At the dawn of the twenty-first century, network television has drawn mixed reviews in its depiction of women from the National Organization for Women (NOW). According to NOW's third annual feminist report on prime-time television, NBC's *The West Wing* and *Law & Order,* CBS's *Judging Amy,* and UPN's *Girlfriends* portray women as "smart, resourceful and in charge," while such network entries as NBC's *Fear Factor,* ABC's *The Bachelor* and *The Drew Carey Show,* and UPN's *WWE Smackdown!* show women as objects to be "ogled, used and demeaned."[38] Of course, NOW's assessment may not be shared by a preponderance of women viewers, which undoubtedly accounts for a sizable female presence among the audiences for TV programs that do thrive on female stereotypes.

The advertising industry has also thrived on female stereotypes. This is not surprising because throughout most of the twentieth century, women were the primary audience for much of the advertising, whereas men produced most of the ads.[39] In the early history of television, product ads often featured woman as submissive housewives and naïve or emotional, "needing the experienced voice of a rational male narrator to guide them around their own homes."[40] By the 1980s, the dependent housewife had virtually disappeared from TV commercials, but she was supplanted by the "supermom" who calmly and skillfully balances the demands of family and career. Both images are unrealistic, of course, and they exemplify the difficulties of constructing media content that is devoid of stereotyping.

In the 1990s traditional gender roles returned with a vengeance. Consider, for example, the Brut ad featuring a gorgeous young woman in a lacy black dress, her car stuck by the side of the road. A sexy young man arrives, slowly removes his T-shirt, uses it to remove her overheated radiator cap, and then ignores her "come hither" look as he saunters away. An appreciative female voice, her words appearing on the screen as they are spoken, says, "Brut. Men Are Back."[41] And then there was the Pepsi commercial in which Cindy Crawford, wearing a skimpy red sequinned dress and dangling earrings, enters a Pepsi deprivation tank as she announces, "I'll do anything for science!" After being deprived of Pepsi for a month, Crawford emerges from the tank as Rodney Dangerfield. This led one commentator to wonder whether Pepsi's intended message was "Drink Pepsi, get respect" or "Drink Pepsi, look sexy."[42]

In the twenty-first century, advertising strategies must maintain a delicate balancing act. Advertisers today must attempt to portray women realistically, in diverse roles, without alienating any significant segment of the female population. High-tech industries are a classic example of this conundrum. Technology companies realize that they must look beyond their traditional male base with the boom in the home computer market and with women controlling household budgets. Some TV commercials, for example, aimed squarely at stay-at-home moms have focused on how easy the systems are to use and on children's software—considered by marketers to be a surefire avenue to women's pocketbooks. But some women complain that such commercials ignore the female managers who have mastered the most complex spreadsheets and engineering software.[43]

Undoubtedly, the women's movement, with its harsh assessment of the advertising industry, has succeeded in diversifying the social roles of female characters. Nevertheless, images of women as preoccupied with beauty, sex appeal, and youth still abound in commercial messages directed at the mass audience. Although these images of women, like many other stereotypes, are probably an accurate reflection of some segments of the female population, they reinforce the notion of a culture anchored in superficial

values. Of course, if this cultural portrayal is realistic, a related ethical question arises: What is the media's moral responsibility in promoting such transparent values? This discussion brings us back to the perennial question of whether the media should merely reflect societal norms or whether they have an affirmative obligation to promote positive images.

Sexual Orientation and Stereotypical Depictions

To be young and gay is no longer a prime-time taboo, trumpeted a recent headline in *TV Guide.*[44] This announcement might seem unremarkable to a TV generation that came of age in the 1990s, but it belies a tradition in which the entertainment industry virtually ignored homosexuality except through the prism of stereotypical depictions. Until recently, homosexual relationships were a taboo subject for Hollywood's cultural guardians, and gay characters were generally depicted as amusing (or perhaps pathetic) and flamboyant caricatures or as victims of violence or villains.

The gay liberation movement that began in the late 1960s was undoubtedly responsible for the gradual erosion of industry reluctance to confront the realities of the homosexual lifestyle. In addition, increasing news coverage of the gay community and its campaign for social parity in the form of legal recognition of gay unions and marriages has also produced a greater climate of tolerance.

As early as the 1970s homosexual themes were cautiously introduced on TV. In 1971, for example, the controversial sitcom *All in the Family* aired an episode that tendered what is arguably TV's first sympathetic portrayal of a gay man. The following year ABC ran *That Certain Summer,* a made-for-TV movie, in which two gay men were shown touching on the shoulder.[45] In 1977 Billy Crystal introduced Jodie Dallas as an openly gay character on the hit TV show *Soap.*[46] Nevertheless, a conservative backlash against the gay liberation movement and what was viewed as the moral permissiveness of the 1960s and 1970s ensured a continuation of artistic prudence within the entertainment industry.

The 1990s were a watershed in the culture wars surrounding the controversy over sexual orientation in the mass media. *Roseanne, Northern Exposure, Ellen,* and *Melrose Place* were among the first to introduce, in a serious fashion, continuing gay or lesbian characters on network television. All of these series were successful, of course, and thus had market power. However, in early 1994 ABC at first refused to air an episode of *Roseanne* because it involved a kiss between Roseanne and a lesbian character played by Mariel Hemingway. It would be "bad for the kids" to see a woman kissing a woman, in the network's view, and would result in a heavy loss of advertising. The predictable storm of publicity and debate led some skeptics to suspect that the controversy was contrived to boost the ratings for the episode, which was scheduled to air at the beginning of the spring sweeps month. Nevertheless, ABC finally agreed to air the program, which attracted a large audience and only about one hundred calls to the network, most of them positive.[47]

Today, gay characters on television, for the most part, are no longer an anomaly and are neither one-dimensional nor objects of ridicule. For example, *NYPD Blue*'s openly gay and extremely efficient police administrative aide, John Irvin, debuted in the 1990s and eventually evolved into a well-respected and prominent member of the police precinct staff. And in July 2003, Bravo unveiled *Queer Eye for the Straight Guy,* a reality show that some reviewers described as "subversive" because it depicted a form of cultural bonding between gay and straight men that defied conventional wisdom. Both TV executives and advertisers were impressed with the program's ratings.[48]

The inclusion of the homosexual lifestyle in entertainment fare still offends moral conservatives, particularly with the recent initiatives in some states to recognize same-sex marriages, and thus will continue to be a debating point for the foreseeable future, but there is little doubt that today's gay and lesbian characters are more likely to be fully dimensional. Serious inroads have been made into unfair stereotypes. Stereotypes persist, of course, but if recurring visibility begets realism, then significant progress has been made in the past decade, a fact supported by recent research on gay characters and culture. Research by a communications professor at the University of Minnesota, for example, found that seeing likable gay characters on shows like *Will & Grace* had similar effects to knowing gays in real life. In one study, the levels of antigay prejudice dropped by 12 percent after students with few or no gay acquaintances were shown ten episodes of HBO's *Six Feet Under.*[49]

Historically, gays and lesbians have also been virtually absent from the nation's news agenda. The lack of coverage has resulted in a missed opportunity for the news media to confront erroneous stereotypes. The AIDS epidemic finally ended the journalistic invisibility of gay people. High-profile AIDS victims, such as Rock Hudson and Liberace, made the disease front-page news, but as communications Professor Larry Gross has noted, this has been a mixed blessing:

> At present AIDS stories appear in print and broadcast news—often with little or no new or important content—and the public image of gay men has been inescapably linked with the specter of plague. Media coverage of AIDS is very likely to reinforce hostility to gays among those so predisposed—there is abundant evidence of growing anti-gay violence in many parts of the country—and to further the sense of distance from a strange and deviant "subculture."[50]

The intense and at times acrimonious debate over whether states should legalize same-sex marriages has ensured that gays and lesbians will continue to be featured prominently on the nation's news agenda.

Moral considerations no doubt fuel a community's perception of the homosexual lifestyle as "deviant" behavior, but stereotypes—the way that individuals "frame" their view of the world—are also instrumental in shaping public opinion. A journalist's responsibility is to provide context and understanding so that a citizen's opinion can be an informed one. Indeed, the news media have increasingly expanded their horizons with their coverage of the gay rights movement and legislative initiatives to combat discrimination based upon sexual orientation. From an ethical perspective, the values in play here are truth, accuracy, and justice, and the perpetuation of inaccurate stereotypes undermines the news media's mandate to provide a comprehensive and truthful account of one of society's most vocal minorities.

Older People

In a 1993 Frito-Lay campaign, an elderly woman walks in front of a runaway steamroller at a construction site as she munches a bag of Doritos Tortillo Thins. Comedian Chevy Chase, seeing the impending disaster, jumps on a swinging wrecking ball to rescue the bag of chips. The woman is plowed into wet cement. However, in a follow-up Doritos ad several months later, the woman was allowed to get the better of Chase. Some seniors saw that as a tacit admission by the company that the previous ad was offensive to elderly viewers,[51] and the "contrite manufacturer delivered cases of free chips to a food bank."[52]

More than a decade has passed since this ill-conceived attempt at commercial humor, but the perceptible negative response from some seniors may have been a harbinger of things to come unless Wall Street adjusts its creative radar to the needs of more mature audiences. Baby boomers are now coming of age and represent a significant percentage of the country's discretionary income and financial assets. And contrary to one conventional stereotype, older

Americans increasingly have good health and are generally satisfied with their position in life.[53]

In our youth-oriented culture, the elderly have been among the most psychologically abused segments of society. Negative stereotypes about older people appear to be ingrained in U.S. society.[54] And because the media generally reflect our value system, it is little wonder that the elderly have been the victims of stereotyped characterizations. They have often been depicted as infirm, forgetful, childlike, and stubborn. Although these images might be applicable to some segments of the elderly population, they are clearly unfair to many others. Many elderly people concur. In a survey by the Ogilvy and Mather advertising agency, 40 percent of the over-65 respondents agreed that Madison Avenue usually presented older people as unattractive and incompetent.[55]

Like many other stereotypes, distorted images of the elderly in the media are now undergoing some slow renovation. Pressure groups, such as the Gray Panthers, have raised the collective consciousness of society to the plight of the elderly. More positive images are beginning to emerge in the media, as evidenced by the increasing depiction of the elderly in TV commercials as alert, energetic, and perfectly capable of sustaining romantic feelings—reflected, for example, in the Bud Light campaign featuring an elderly couple in an unusually lively romantic exchange in a living room.

There may be a certain degree of inevitability in the negative stereotyping of the elderly in commercials because the copywriters themselves are usually young. However, this generation gap can hardly serve as an excuse given the wealth of demographic research now available on older consumers. The real problem, however, lies not in advertising prepared for senior citizens but in that designed for younger audiences in which the elderly are used as foils. Under such circumstances, agencies must make every effort to sensitize their creative staffs to erroneous portrayals of the elderly as a strategy to eliminating unwarranted stereotypes.[56]

People with Disabilities

People with physical and mental disabilities have been among the most misunderstood and forgotten groups. To the extent that they have been allowed at all into the public's consciousness, the media have frequently portrayed the disabled as victims (such as in fund-raising telethons), heroes (derisively referred to by the disabled as "supercrips" because they take away from the real disability issues), evil and warped (as symbolized by a limp, a hook for a hand, or a hunchback), unable to adjust (such as programs that depict the disabled as bitter and full of self-pity), a burden on family and friends, and one who shouldn't have survived (as depicted in the 1980s TV dramas *An Act of Love* and *Whose Life Is It, Anyway?* in which physically disabled characters beg to be assisted in suicide because their life is not worth living).[57]

Critics complain that although some conventional stereotypes might accurately represent some segments of the disabled population, collectively they paint a rather distorted picture that is at odds with the way disabled people see themselves. Indeed, in 1981 one writer lamented that those with disabilities were seldom shown living their lives in interaction with those who do not have disabilities:

> The absence of positive portrayals that belie stereotypes and depict comfortable interaction between handicapped and non-handicapped people suggests that prime time television is not exerting a significant influence in shaping positive societal attitudes toward individuals who are handicapped, nor is it facilitating comfortable relationships by providing models of interaction.[58]

However, just a few years later there were visible signs of improvement among network TV fare. NBC's highly acclaimed *LA Law* featured a mentally disabled office worker in the law firm. In the fall of 1989 ABC premiered *Life*

Goes On, a family program starring Chris Burke, an actor with Down's syndrome who played a teenager with the same condition. In the 1990s, the physically impaired assumed a more prominent role in commercials. Some TV ads, for example, featuring the hearing impaired were done in total silence with the main characters "signing," while the narrative was superimposed on the screen.

These examples notwithstanding, disabled people still have not assumed a prominent role within the nation's mainstream media fare. The persistent media stereotyping of those with disabilities has spawned an alternative disabled press, with such descriptive titles as *Mainstream* and *New Mobility.* Although their coverage is diverse, the goal of such publications is to counter the negative images of pity and hero worship with images of people leading independent, active lives.[59]

People with Mental Illness

Perhaps no group is less understood by the general public or socially marginalized to a greater degree than people with mental illnesses. And since research indicates that the media play a pivotal role in the formation of public perceptions concerning the mentally ill, they cannot escape their share of moral responsibility for perpetuating unfair or distorted images of those who suffer from mental illness. Among the news media, for example, mental illness is most commonly framed in the context of crime, danger, and community fear.[60] However, as Pattrick Smellie, a news editor and Harkness Fellow at the Bazelon Center for Mental Health Law in Washington, DC, has lamented: Such values help "to perpetuate deep-rooted and largely unjustified public attitudes which make the lives of the vast majority of peaceable, de-institutionalized mentally ill people more difficult than they already are."[61]

While some crime might be attributed to mental illness, "the relentless framing of mental illness in the context of violence, and criminality, is amplifying, sustaining, and legitimizing a largely false picture of mental ill-health."[62] The fact is that most mentally ill people are not violent and dangerous, but many do find themselves unemployed, at the bottom of the socioeconomic ladder, and frequently estranged from family and friends. The mentally ill are among the most vulnerable of society's disadvantaged to discrimination, and since public perceptions of this group are framed by the media, there are clear ethical implications to the media's perpetuation of unfair stereotypes and their failure to provide a more balanced depiction of mentally ill people.

As the representative groups described in the preceding paragraphs illustrate, stereotyping of all kinds has traditionally been pervasive in media content. In some respects it is a tool for communicating with the mass audience. But used in the improper context, stereotypes can also lead to human degradation and prejudice. Thus, the moral responsibility for media professionals is to search for strategies that will discourage such pejorative stereotypes while not abandoning the commitment to artistic freedom and cultural diversity.

STRATEGIES FOR CONFRONTING MEDIA STEREOTYPING

The production of media content that is intended to perpetuate patterns of discrimination and prejudice cannot be justified under any of the ethical theories examined in Chapter 3. Duty-based theorists (deontologists), such as those applying Kant's categorical imperative, would argue that racism and prejudice should never become universally recognized standards of conduct. Stereotypes promoting such practices undermine the fundamental idea of respect for persons, which plays such a crucial role in ethical decision making.

Deontologists would examine the motives of the moral agent without regard to the specific consequences of the decision. For example, the television producer Norman Lear had high hopes for his classic series *All in the Family* when it premiered in the early 1970s. The lead character, Archie Bunker, was clearly and blatantly a bigot, a composite of all the dominant prejudices of U.S. culture. Lear used stereotypes as a means of confronting society's racist attitudes, a video version of "reality therapy" that was designed to satirize bigotry and prejudice. Unfortunately, there was some disagreement about whether all viewers recognized the program as a satire or whether this family comedy served to reinforce and sanitize prejudice.[63]

Teleologists (consequentialists), of course, are interested in the potential consequences of their decisions. The teleologist is not necessarily concerned with the motives of the media practitioner, which may not flow from moral purity. Because degrading stereotypes are unfair and offensive to certain segments of society, they must be rejected as harmful to the self-image of those groups. But beyond the specific harm to the targeted group, such stereotypes breed prejudice and discrimination within society at large. Nevertheless, there may be times when potentially damaging stereotypes serve a useful purpose by forcing society to confront the reality of its prejudices. Under such circumstances, the teleologist must weigh the positive and negative consequences before abandoning the use of controversial images altogether. For example, a documentary's use of stereotypes in exploring the issue of genetic racial differences would undoubtedly be controversial. But such a program might be justified as beneficial for society on the ground that it is better to confront the issue and examine the evidence publicly than to allow such stereotypical myths to fester beneath the surface of societal discourse.

The golden mean is particularly useful when stereotyped characters are representative of some individuals within a group (such as the flamboyant gay or the traditional housewife) but are seen as prejudicial to the group as a whole. Under such circumstances, media practitioners should treat these characters with sensitivity while not holding them up as typical of the entire group.

In addition, the golden mean calls for diversity in media presentations. Media practitioners, in other words, should strive for overall balance in attempting to portray the range of lifestyles within a particular group, not just those that are the most prejudicial to the group.

Nevertheless, we must recognize that a society cannot retreat entirely from its cultural heritage and that many classic works of art and literature contain stereotyped characters. Mark Twain's *Huckleberry Finn*, for example, has been attacked in some quarters as racist, and there have even been calls to ban it. Such drastic actions would be an affront to a democratic society. Under such circumstances the contemporary artistic marketplace should be the proper

mechanism for remedying whatever prejudicial lessons might be reflected in American cultural history.

STEREOTYPES AND THE MEDIA: HYPOTHETICAL CASE STUDIES

The cases in this chapter cover a wide range of ethical concerns involving stereotypes, though they are by no means exhaustive. As you work your way through these cases, keep in mind that perpetuation of offensive stereotypes can result in a diminution of social justice. Thus, some of these cases have a close kinship with those of the preceding chapter.

◄ C A S E   S T U D I E S ►

▶ CASE 13-1

Dirty Laundry and the Editorial Cartoon[64]

At the dawn of the twenty-first century, China was on the precipice of joining the family of nations as a progressive and politically congenial partner. Its newfound respectability had earned it a position as host of the 2008 Olympics, its liberal economic policies had moved it toward greater parity as an international trading nation, and China-watchers thought they detected a greater degree of political freedom, despite the continuing suppression of antigovernment news in the state-owned press. In recognition of the "new China" and to encourage further liberalization by the traditionally conservative Communist Party leadership, Congress extended most-favored-nation status to the Chinese, further assuring them greater access to U.S. markets. China's claim on Taiwan remained problematical, but the continuing American support for the Taiwanese and the enduring promise of military retaliation for any act of aggression served as a

deterrent to any menacing Chinese maneuvers against the island state.

However, the U.S. State Department's experts on U.S.-Chinese relations were apprehensive as a new premier assumed the reins of power in the Chinese hierarchy. Little was known about the new Chinese leader, Zhou Tang, but the available intelligence indicated that he was a hardliner who believed the pace of economic reform had proceeded too rapidly. His political views and those of some of his closest advisers were quite doctrinaire. A Soviet-style collapse of the communist system was unlikely under his regime, according to the State Department's most knowledgeable experts. Nevertheless, because of the continuing presence of some reform-minded officials in the Chinese hierarchy, the U.S. administration remained cautiously optimistic that China would not reverse its path toward liberalization. However, two disquieting events had a sobering effect on the prospects for continuing improvement in U.S.-Chinese relations.

The first occurred on the anniversary of the 1989 bloody suppression of pro-democracy demonstrators in Tiananmen Square in Beijing by the

Chinese military. In commemoration of this event, thousands of residents of Hong Kong took to the streets to protest the Chinese government's continuing opposition to meaningful political reforms. The demonstrators in Hong Kong felt relatively secure in their public display since the Chinese government had assured the former British colony that it would not seriously interfere with its liberal economic and political policies once the colony reverted to Chinese control. However, as the rally grew in size and the protestors became more vociferous in their denunciation of the regime in Beijing, the Chinese military responded with a vengeance, killing or injuring several of the protestors and arresting seven of the "ringleaders" who had organized the demonstration, including two Chinese Americans with business interests in Hong Kong. The U.S. president, as well as the congressional leadership, quickly denounced the crackdown, calling it an unprovoked attack on peaceful demonstrators exercising their right to free speech. The State Department announced that it was unsure of the whereabouts of those arrested but believed they had been imprisoned at an undisclosed location in China. During a press conference, the Secretary of State declared that the incarceration of the organizers of the peaceful demonstration in Hong Kong as political prisoners was a violation of human rights and "not helpful" in the move toward normalization of relations between the two nations.

The second event was more chilling in its potential consequences. During the presidential election campaign in Taiwan, the Chinese once again publicly declared their claim on the island of Taiwan and began naval exercises just a few miles outside Taiwan's territorial waters. The United States promptly cautioned the Chinese against any aggressive moves against Taiwanese sovereignty.

Throughout the thaw in U.S.-Chinese relations, one American administration after another had castigated the Chinese for their human rights violations, and in light of the recent events, the United States again resurrected its concern over Beijing's dismal human rights record, a move the State Department hoped would remind the community of nations of the fragility of China's claim to international respectability. However, the government in Beijing responded with a diplomatic broadside of its own, accusing the United States of hypocrisy on the issue of human rights, citing the prisoner abuse scandal in Iraq and the indeterminate incarceration of hundreds of prisoners at Guantanamo Bay in Cuba.

The U.S.-led invasion of Iraq in the spring of 2003 and the dispatching from power of Iraqi dictator Saddam Hussein had occupied the attention of many of the nation's editorial pundits for more than a year, but domestic issues again attracted their attention as the United States and its coalition partners cautiously and deliberately returned sovereignty to the Iraqi people. The provocations by the newly anointed Chinese leadership produced a new round of foreign policy commentary on the op-ed pages of the nation's newspapers. Most supported the administration's firm response to the troubling Chinese behavior, although a few noted this nation's vulnerability on the human rights issue as a result of the treatment of Iraqi prisoners during the U.S.-led invasion. There was virtual unanimity on the U.S. response to the Chinese saber-rattling over Taiwan, but a few opined that the time had come for the United States to distance itself from this ongoing dispute between China and this island nation.

The editorial staff at the *Los Marino Courier* were among those who responded swiftly and unambiguously to the Chinese provocations. The *Courier* served a community of 500,000 in Southern California and directed most of its editorial energies to state and local matters and national politics, but it did not hesitate to comment forcefully on international issues when the editorial staff deemed them of sufficient interest to their local readership. *This was one of those issues.* The day following the second event—the naval maneuvers just outside Taiwan's territorial waters—managing editor Lewis Irvin, reflecting the collective wisdom of his editorial colleagues, produced an uncompromising editorial in which he pondered whether China's program of liberalization had gone into full remission under the new Chinese leadership or whether the forces of liberalization already in motion were too irresistible in the long run to succumb to Zhou's more cautious style of leadership. This opening salvo was quickly followed by a submission from the paper's political cartoonist,

Hugo Etheridge, known for both his biting satire and subtle irony. Etheridge's handiwork had frequently precipitated e-mails, letters, and phone calls from annoyed readers. The managing editor routinely scrutinized Etheridge's cartoons but had never suppressed one because of its controversial content. But his representation of the Chinese issue gave Irvin ethical indigestion.

Irvin was not concerned about Etheridge's political viewpoint, although it was likely to be unpopular with some of the *Courier's* more conservative readers, but his framing of the issue was disturbing. The cartoon portrayed a caricature of a smiling Zhou Tang with glasses, a broad smile, and protruding teeth in front of a Chinese laundry. He was handing a laundry bag labeled "Dirty Laundry" to Uncle Sam with a label jutting out from the top with the words "Human Rights" written on it, a clear reference to the prisoner abuse scandals during the American occupation of Iraq and the incarceration of noncombatants at Guantanamo Bay. Beneath the cartoon was a caption that read: "Ah so, you solly Amellican, you too have dirty laundry." Etheridge's intent was to portray the hypocrisy of grounding the U.S.'s criticism of the Chinese in human rights violations in light of its own recent record.

"Hugo, we're not concerned about the editorial view of your cartoon," declared Lydia Rosenberg, the paper's executive editor, as she reviewed Etheridge's editorial cartoon with Lewis Irvin. "Some of our readers will undoubtedly be upset at your resurrecting the embarrassing prisoner abuse situation, but that's not our concern. Lewis has raised some questions about the way you have depicted the Chinese. I'll have the final say in whether we publish your cartoon, but I would like to hear both sides of the issue."

"My concern," began Irvin, "is with the way you've portrayed the Chinese leader. Using a laundry as a backdrop is relying upon an old stereotype of Asians. And the caricature of Zhou with glasses, a smile, and protruding teeth and the caption using stilted dialect reinforce this stereotype."

"I confess to the use of stereotypes," replied Etheridge without hesitation. "But in this case it's justified. This cartoon is intended to make two political statements. It's intended, first, to highlight what the Chinese see as our hypocrisy on the

human rights issue. But my cartoon doesn't let the Chinese off the hook either. The other message is that China has over the past decade attempted to portray itself as the new China. That's one of the reasons they were awarded the 2008 Olympics. But their recent behavior conjures up memories of the old China. The use of these outmoded stereotypes is an effective way of contrasting the old with the new."

"I'm not sure the average reader will understand the subtlety of your political message," said Luther Trance, the editorial-page editor who regularly participated in all discussions concerning the content of the paper's op-ed section. "They may not understand why you're using such Asian stereotypes. Nevertheless, this is an editorial cartoon, and you have a right to be outrageous in expressing your views. Some editorials contain intemperate language, but we run them as long as they contribute to the public debate on an issue. This cartoon, with its obvious stereotypes, is sure to generate controversy, particularly among our Asian American readers. But as long as the underlying political message is sound, I don't think we should refuse to run such cartoons."

"I don't have a problem with your political view," responded Irvin. "But this may get buried in the controversy over the use of offensive stereotypes. This cartoon makes a political statement at the expense of Asians. It's an unfair caricature that simply reinforces traditional stereotypes about Asians."

"But I'm using stereotypes for the purpose of exaggeration," countered Etheridge. "Political cartoons frequently rely upon exaggeration because they must connect with the audience immediately. Except for a short caption, we don't have the written word to develop for the reader, step by step, the major ideas. Our readers will quickly identify with familiar stereotypes. In this case, stereotypes are a legitimate communication device to connect to readers."

"I agree with Hugo," declared Trance. "Stereotypical caricatures are easily identifiable. Photos and cartoons must utilize symbols, even stereotypical symbols, to attract attention. And in this case, I believe Hugo's explanation that his intent is to point out recent events as reminiscent of the old

China justifies his use of stereotypes to communicate that message."

"In my opinion, any deliberate use of unfair stereotypes by the news media is unwarranted," remarked Irvin. "Unfair or inaccurate stereotypes, regardless of the purpose, serve to reinforce prejudices. The news media should be in the business of dispelling such stereotypes."

Lydia Rosenberg had listened attentively to the brief exchange among her three subordinates. The concerns were clearly not related to the cartoon's political message per se—she had always given Hugo Etheridge a great deal of latitude in this respect—but the *Courier's* managing editor was concerned about the framing of the message with stereotypes. Rosenberg knew that the publication of this editorial cartoon would generate protests from the Asian American community, but she was also sensitive to Etheridge's argument that he had used stereotypes as a means of calling attention to the recent events as symptomatic of the old China. As executive editor, Rosenberg was the moral agent, and with the publication deadline rapidly approaching, she pondered the ethical concerns surrounding Hugo Etheridge's political cartoon.

THE CASE STUDY

Stereotyping has a negative connotation in today's tolerant society, but most commentators agree that the use of stereotypes can be a slippery slope. Some clearly are offensive and perpetuate an injustice to groups or individuals unfairly represented by those stereotypes. But others may be justified under some circumstances, and this implicates the requirement for *justification*.

> Justification is the process by which a morally questionable act becomes a more or less morally permissible act. It becomes more or less morally permissible based on whether the questionable act is strongly or weakly justified. Although there are moral limits on how one does one's job, role-related responsibilities, fulfilling one's social function, can sometimes themselves justify morally questionable acts.[65]

Thus, the moral acceptability of cartoonist Hugo Etheridge's use of stereotypes depends upon the strength of his justification. While the

overt message of his political cartoon revolves around human rights—a controversial issue that's not at the heart of this ethical case—Etheridge argues that his use of stereotypes is a device to question whether the Chinese have really changed their stripes, despite the apparent initiatives toward liberalization in recent years. His antagonist, managing editor Lewis Irvin, isn't convinced of the moral strength of Etheridge's justification. The implication is that his message will be ineffective, while the use of stereotypes will just reinforce existing prejudices against Asian cultures.

The purpose of an editorial cartoon is to express an opinion. How much latitude should be afforded such artists in depicting certain groups? Are stereotypes justified if they are used to make a larger political point? Is the justification offered by Hugo Etheridge convincing? Or should the danger of reinforcing existing prejudices trump all justifications for stereotypical portrayals? These are some of the questions in play in this scenario.

For the purpose of considering these competing claims, assume the position of executive editor Lydia Rosenberg and, using the SAD model for moral reasoning described in Chapter 3, make a decision on whether you will publish this political editorial.

▶ CASE 13-2

Framing the Gay and Lesbian Issue for the Public Square

There were still ten weeks remaining before the referendum, but the battle lines had been drawn. In early November an "antigay" constitutional amendment would be placed before the state's voters that would effectively prohibit the legislature or local communities from recognizing gays and lesbians as a protected class. Two cities had already enacted such ordinances, extending a menu of rights and privileges to gays and lesbians, and this was sufficient to arouse the religious right's acute sense of moral indignation in support of the proposed amendment. In their view, a constitutional amendment was the only permanent remedy for such assaults on traditional family values by local communities with gay populations, and within a matter of weeks they had procured the required number of signatures to place the matter before the state's electorate. They arrived on the battlefield with deep pockets, as some churches collected special offerings to finance a saturation TV campaign. The Gay and Lesbian Coalition responded with an aggressive TV ad campaign of their own. Their local constituency could not match their antagonists' financial war chests, but various gay and lesbian organizations from outside the state had provided the subsidy necessary to combat the aggressive electronic proselytizing of the antigay forces. In its campaign, the religious right cited the AIDS virus as evidence of God's verdict on the immorality of homosexuality and blamed homosexuals for undermining traditional family values. The Gay and Lesbian Coalition responded with accusations of bigotry and homophobia and invited their opponents to read the federal Constitution's guarantee of equal protection under law.

The Counsel for Social Justice (CSJ) watched this emotional point–counterpoint with growing concern as the marketplace of ideas succumbed to the incivility of two groups who did not appear interested in rational discourse. The CSJ was a nonprofit organization whose mission it was to serve as a government watchdog and specifically to fight for justice and equality of treatment for all citizens. CSJ's lobbyists were always visible in the legislative corridors when bills or constitutional amendments were being debated that they believed were detrimental to the public interest or the state's minorities. However, the council did not believe that victory resided in falsehoods or half-truths and had committed itself from the outset to truthful communication within the public square. To this end, the CSJ also served as a "truth squad" in countering the distorted presentations of special interests.

From the outset, Michael Chatworth, CSJ's director of media relations, had begun planning strategy for what he knew would be his organization's influential role in the public disputation surrounding the proposed constitutional amendment. While the two opposing camps exchanged insults through the medium of thirty-second TV spots, Chatworth did not believe that true political discourse could be conducted in such a truncated

form. His strategy was twofold: to arrange a series of public debates on the issue and to produce a thirty-minute documentary that would air statewide just a few days before the referendum. TV time of this magnitude was expensive, but Chatworth refused to place a price tag on the truth. The goal of the CSJ, as it had so often been in the past, was to protect a culturally disinherited minority group from the naked power of majoritarianism. The proposed constitutional amendment would, in the council's view, institutionalize the intolerance and prejudices of many of the state's more conservative citizens.

With the approval of CSJ's management board, Chatworth had commissioned the project to a local documentarian, Kenneth Mills, who had produced campaign videos for the state's politicians and had even won an award for a documentary that was aired on PBS. Since time was short, Mills worked overtime on his project and then submitted the initial cut to Chatworth for his review and recommended changes. Chatworth was interested in a balanced documentary, not one that would be perceived as propaganda. In keeping with the council's philosophy, Mills had produced an initial cut that provided an unvarnished look at the gay community. There were shots of a recent gay pride parade that featured those who embraced the unconventional lifestyle, such as cross-dressers, bare-breasted lesbians, and men adorned in leather, whips, and chains. But the documentary was balanced with shots of the more "mainstream" gay lifestyle. The interviews that were inserted among the other visuals within the documentary also featured those who embraced both the conventional and unconventional gay and lesbian lifestyles. However, the theme of the project was to "humanize" the gay community and to convince the state's electorate that homosexuals did not pose a threat to their code of moral deportment.

Chatworth felt unworthy to evaluate the subtle nuances of this video. Framing, he knew, was inevitable in such dramatic portrayals, but he wanted to minimize the risk of distortion. In short, he wanted to avoid accusations of stereotyping that frequently accompanied any discussion of minority groups. Chatworth would be the decision maker in this case. He would be the ultimate gatekeeper on the moral worth of Mills's skillfully produced documentary, but this was a complex and sensitive issue. The views of Cecelia Maybury, CSJ's legislative liaison, and Tony Alvarez, special projects coordinator, would be instrumental in his judgment.

"I have mixed emotions about this documentary," stated Maybury. "I realize that within this gay and lesbian community there are many different lifestyles. The depiction of gays dressed in a bizarre fashion and bare-breasted lesbians is not entirely inaccurate, but they represent only a small group of the homosexual population. In the parade scenes, they're not on the screen for a long period of time, but I'm concerned that that's the image that will stick in the viewer's memory. The interviewees from this segment of the gay community reinforce this image. If we expect to win this referendum, perhaps we should just focus on the more mainstream elements."

"But that would be only a half-truth," replied Alvarez. "We have always committed ourselves to winning through truth in the marketplace. The public has been conditioned to believe that most gays and lesbians embrace the more unconventional lifestyle. The news media are partially responsible for this because in their coverage of gay pride parades they frequently focus on this element of the marchers."

"That's precisely my concern," responded Maybury. "The public perception is distorted because of the nature of the news coverage. We need to counteract this. I realize the documentary is, in a sense, balanced—it does include the more mainstream elements—but these bizarre depictions are likely to be more memorable in the public's collective consciousness. These visuals and interviews just reinforce the prevailing stereotypes of gays and lesbians."

"I question your characterization of the unconventional gay lifestyle as a mere stereotype," declared Alvarez. "This view is an accurate portrayal of one segment of the gay and lesbian community. If we eliminate this segment of the documentary, perhaps it will be more palatable at least to those voters who are still undecided on this issue. But if we don't include them, will this be just to those who choose to behave in an unconventional manner? Framing is everything, but what kind of message will this send to those who are omitted from this documentary? It might help us pick up a few votes, but in doing so we could be contributing to another injustice. If we don't provide balance in this documentary, it might be viewed as just another piece of propaganda."

"Sometimes we must sacrifice our short-term concerns for long-term gains," replied Maybury. "Our goal is to win at the ballot box, to convince the voters that this amendment is morally wrong. In the end, the entire gay and lesbian community will benefit if this measure is defeated. I realize that those with unconventional lifestyles are a part of the gay community. But this segment represents the stereotype associated in many people's minds with the entire gay population, and they find this offensive."

"We have always committed ourselves to truth in the marketplace," repeated Alvarez. "There's nothing in this documentary that's untrue, but it's an incomplete truth. If we include all segments of the gay community perhaps we can help dispel the stereotype that whips, chains, cross-dressing, and bare-breasted lesbians are typical of this minority group. Through proper framing we should be able to send the message that gays and lesbians are as diverse as the population in general. Thus, even if voters object to unconventionality, do they really want to deny human rights to an entire group just because of the unorthodox lifestyle of a few?"

"This sounds very noble," responded Maybury, continuing with her theme of political pragmatism. "But the reality is that the state's electorate—at least a majority of them—do their own framing when it comes to issues relating to homosexuality. In the court of public opinion, the unconventional gay lifestyle is mainstream, and we would be well advised not to include this kind of portrayal in this documentary. The choice is ours. Do we want to stand on principle and diminish our chances of winning, or do we take the politically wise course of action and optimize our potential for victory at the ballot box?"

With that challenging question, Michael Chatworth decided that the opposing views had been suitably ventilated and adjourned the meeting. He was clearly conflicted after hearing the opposing views of his two colleagues, but under such severe time constraints he told Alvarez and Maybury that he would inform Kenneth Hill within twenty-four hours whether to re-edit the documentary or proceed with his current rendition.

THE CASE STUDY

References to justice and stereotypes permeate this case. It would reside as comfortably in Chapter 12 on social justice as here in the chapter on stereotypes. However, the two are inescapably linked because at the level of group rights stereotyping influences how we respond to demands for social justice.

In this narrative, Michael Chatworth understands that most voters probably view the gay lifestyle through the prism of a very narrow stereotype—one that is not inaccurate but clearly does not embrace the entire truth. The council has always entered the public square based upon the principle that truth is the most formidable weapon, while understanding that truth does not always prevail. But the measure before the voters is fundamental to the CJS's mission—justice for all citizens. While the religious right might view all homosexuals as immoral, many voters might be more tolerant if they could get beyond the visual image of gays and lesbians as cross-dressers, dressed in whips and chains, or parading bare-breasted in public view. Passage of this constitutional amendment would be a serious blow to the cause of liberty for a significant segment of the state's citizenry. Should the documentary marginalize a visible, though small, segment of the gay and lesbian population for the purpose of achieving a just end for all?

Tony Alvarez is concerned that the documentary will become a work of propaganda if it doesn't contain some balance among the various segments of the gay and lesbian population. Considering the council's role, there is no ethical imperative for fairness and balance, unlike the news media. But in this narrative, the CSJ's own historical commitment to truth does implicate the need for balance. And yet, as Cecelia Maybury has cautioned, political realities might dictate otherwise if the chances for victory are to be optimized.

Of course, there's no guarantee of victory, but in a close election, a well-produced documentary

that skillfully presents the gay community as morally worthy citizens, which might necessitate deleting the fringe elements, could influence the outcome. The fact is that unconventionality, regardless of its source, is unacceptable to some conservative voters.

Decision time is at hand. For the purposes of analyzing the issues posed in this scenario and analyzing the competing arguments, assume the role of Michael Chatworth, the council's director of media relations, and, utilizing the SAD formula for moral reasoning described in Chapter 3, render a judgment on this matter.

▶ CASE 13-3

Gender Wars and Sexual Stereotyping

Lydia Caldwell was a veteran of the gender wars. She had matriculated at Briarfield College, a prestigious women's school in Connecticut, and had embraced the controversial ideology of the feminist movement with undisguised zeal. Upon graduating with honors from Briarfield, Caldwell accepted a position as copywriter for a large ad agency in New York, where her youthful idealism was quickly challenged by the commercial socialization process of her newly adopted corporate culture. She had struggled for recognition and advancement in a male-dominated world—a world that she was convinced, at least initially, was responsible for the perpetuation of commercial sexual stereotypes. However, as she moved from agency to agency in search of new challenges and career advancement, Caldwell's perspective had gradually evolved from one of idealism to marketplace reality. As a market-sensitive commodity, advertising, she believed, reflected rather accurately the state of gender relations in society at large. And from her present vantage point as creative director for the Patterson and Rheinhold agency in Chicago, things had changed for the better. Caldwell had applauded her industry's growing cultural sensitivity in the 1980s as career professionals, capable of skillfully balancing both career and family, replaced the harried housewife as the typical commercial caricature, a market-driven monument to the incredible success of the women's movement. However, as it became apparent that such "supermom" commercials might place even more pressure on women to fulfill society's heightened expectations, traditional male-female roles began to make a somewhat tentative comeback within the advertising industry.

Even in her most activist days, Caldwell had never equated feminism with being "antimale" and believed strongly that her industry could play a crucial role in bringing the gender wars to an end. Advertising, she believed, could be an important catalyst in the cause of social equality. Therefore, she was particularly interested in her creative team's campaign concept for the agency's newest client, Lancelot Malt Liquor.

The proposed commercial featured an athletic-looking male (or a "hunk," to use the vernacular) holding a can of Lancelot Malt Liquor in a lounge, while two very attractive and "leering" women looked on from across the room. As the camera focuses on various aspects of the male's physique, his two female admirers engage in a subtle dialogue concerning his athletic prowess. The spot ends with the hunk looking toward the women and holding up the Lancelot Malt Liquor can in a toast, as a female narrator's voice says rather enticingly, "Lancelot Malt Liquor . . . the choice of champions . . . and their fans."

"These are the storyboards and the script for the Lancelot account," said Caldwell as she displayed her unit's handiwork to Nancy Tibbs and Todd Austin. Tibbs was the agency's media director, and Austin was senior account manager. Caldwell often solicited input from Tibbs and Austin because of their units' roles in commercial placement and marketing among various media outlets.

"There's a quality of egalitarianism about this spot," continued Caldwell, as she pointed to the storyboards displayed in front of her two colleagues. "At last women have the right to express their sexual desires in commercials, just as men always have had the right to admire beautiful women."

"I'm not so sure," responded Tibbs. "Aren't we replacing one stereotype with another? It's not just a question of male dominance or female

independence. In the past, too many female characters were depicted as sex objects. And men were portrayed as being interested in only one thing—sex appeal. Now we have a role-reversal. Doesn't this ad promote false values?"

"I don't think so," insisted Austin. "The message in this spot is that now women can be just as candid in their sexual attraction to men. The fact is that this commercial will be successful. Sex sells! And the reason it sells is that it appeals to traditional sex roles. Women *do* place physical attractiveness of men high on their list of values—and in this sense I don't see sex appeal as a false or superficial value."

"I disagree," responded Tibbs. "In this spot the male is a sex object. His sex appeal is all that matters. The message is that, if you're a hunk, the world is at your feet, sexually speaking. This is nothing more than stereotyping. Whereas women use to be leered at in commercials, now men are accorded the same treatment."

"I'm a feminist, but that doesn't mean that we have to ignore traditional gender roles in our commercials," said Caldwell. "The fact is that women are just as interested in men's sexuality as men are in female sex appeal. However, I must concede, Nancy, that perhaps a spot such as this is one-dimensional. Perhaps it does promote superficial values, even as it reflects reality to a certain degree."

"I don't see equality as the issue," responded Tibbs with an air of moral superiority. "Crudeness is crudeness, regardless of who is doing the leering. We have criticized men for being interested in only one thing. This commercial just reverses the roles. And you consider that liberating?"

"I don't see anything distasteful about this spot," responded Austin. "It just reflects the reality of gender relationships in today's society. It's okay for women to be as aggressive as men—to admire openly the male's sexuality. Advertising is market-driven. And the market reflects contemporary cultural norms. All we're doing is exhibiting in commercial form the current state of gender relationships."

Caldwell had approached this discussion with her two management-level colleagues confident that the proposed Lancelot Malt Liquor commercial would serve their client well. And she still believed that it reflected the contemporary reality of gender relationships. But as she pondered the arguments advanced by Nancy Tibbs and Todd Austin, she also wondered whether the agency's media director had a point. Did the Lancelot Malt Liquor spot replace one stereotype with another and in the process depict women as one-dimensional? Perhaps it was inevitable that in a thirty-second commercial the dimensions of complex human relationships had to be accommodated to the production requirements of the TV medium, as well as the realities of the marketplace.

THE CASE STUDY

Critics accuse the advertising industry of stereotyping large segments of society, that is, ascribing certain characteristics to the undifferentiated group (for example, women) without sufficient sensitivity to individuality. In a sense, this issue comes back to an age-old question of whether advertising helps to shape society's values or just reflects them. Proponents of the "value shaping" view argue that advertisers should be particularly sensitive of how they portray different groups and that they should strive to eliminate or at least minimize stereotyping.

On the other hand, those who ascribe to the "reflective" view argue that because ads mirror society, sponsors have a responsibility to ensure that their ads accurately depict the constituent groups within society. Commercials are perhaps the most market-driven of TV content, they note, even more so than entertainment programming. As such, they reflect our cultural values and our worldview. And stereotypes are undeniably one paradigm that helps to shape our worldview. There are times, of course, when stereotypes are clearly unfair to individual members of a group and help to perpetuate harmful prejudices.

In this case, the debate appears to center around whether advertisers and advertising agencies have a responsibility to erase sexual stereotypes entirely as a means of pacifying the so-called war between the genders. On the one hand, such stereotypes based on little more than sex appeal are viewed as the promotion of superficial values for both males and females. In this view, the advertising industry should attempt to eliminate

stereotypes to the extent that men and women are depicted as dependent on one another from the perspective of sex appeal.

On the other hand, traditionalists argue that some stereotypes are permissible because they reflect reality. And the *reality* in this case appears to be that the modern woman now feels comfortable with expressing openly her admiration for a male's sexuality. And in this view, such portrayals are not inaccurate or unfair. In the past, of course, men were often depicted as interested in only a woman's sexuality, and commercials often portrayed women in this fashion. Does a role-reversal replace one stereotype with another, and if so, is this unfair or could it reinforce some harmful prejudice? Or, to put it another way, does the proposed commercial for Lancelot Malt Liquor raise important ethical questions concerning sexual stereotypes?

For the purpose of discussing these issues, assume the role of Lydia Caldwell and, applying the SAD formula discussed in Chapter 3, render a judgment on this matter.

▶ **CASE 13-4**
The Disabled Athlete in Television Fiction

The cultural divide could not have been greater between Terrence Sandburg and Joseph Hall. Sandburg was an Emmy Award–winning Hollywood producer whose social agenda featured frequent congregations with the entertainment industry's rich and famous. Hall was a Vietnam veteran in a wheelchair who subsisted on the meager wages earned as a clerk at a VA hospital in Los Angeles. Their worldviews were decidedly bipolar, but circumstances had conspired to bring them together in an unpretentious restaurant just a couple of blocks from the hospital where Hall was employed.

Sandburg was anxious to embark on his latest project for network television, a made-for-TV movie, tentatively entitled *Legacy of Despair*, which revolved around a professional football player with physical disabilities. Although commercial considerations were never far from center stage in the highly competitive television marketplace, Sandburg approached this enterprise with an undisguised sense of altruism, a desire to portray realistically the daily struggles of what some now refer to as the "physically challenged." With the script in hand, his next step was to hire a consultant who could offer counsel on the integrity of his story line. His industry sources had produced the names of several promising prospects, but all were somehow connected to the Hollywood establishment, an intervening variable that might color the consultant's perspective on the underlying message of the film. When a colleague suggested that he contact the local VA hospital, Sandburg did not hesitate. After interviews with both patients and three disabled employees, the producer hired Joseph Hall as his mentor to help guide his project to fruition. Sandburg had supplied Hall with a copy of the script and had suggested a subsequent rendezvous at a place of Hall's choosing not far from the hospital to discuss the literary merits of the work before going into production.

Legacy of Despair was the story of a professional football player, Tyrone Benchley, who had been a number one draft choice by an NFL franchise on the West Coast after winning all-American honors at Florida State. In his rookie year—the highlights of which would be revealed through a series of flashbacks in the film—he had won the starting role as wide receiver, an impressive feat within itself, and had produced statistics that won him accolades from both the coaching staff and the sports writers who covered the team. Benchley's sophomore year in the NFL had begun less dramatically. Because of a contract dispute, he had reported to training camp late and by the fourth game against his team's division archrival was just beginning to round into shape for what he hoped would be a successful second half. But for Benchley, there would be no second half.

In the third quarter of the game, with his team down 13–10, Benchley ran a crossing pattern twenty yards downfield. As he gripped the incoming, high-speed pass from quarterback Mark Sabine, a fleet-footed muscular safety converged on the wide receiver and hit him full force in the upper torso. With anxious teammates and opponents looking on, Benchley was taken from the field on a stretcher. The initial reports from the hospital, conveyed both

to team members and the television audience, were that the young player had suffered some form of paralysis, the extent of which was as yet undetermined. Forty-eight hours later, with no signs of improvement, doctors told Benchley and his bride of three months, Teresa, that he had suffered a spinal cord injury and might never walk again. Tyrone Benchley's dreams of a professional football career had ended with a rather innocuous-sounding play called "Blue Light 34 Right Cross Go."

In the initial stages of his rehabilitation, all at the expense of his former team, Benchley's "winning attitude," which had been instilled in him from his first organized gridiron participation in high school, sustained him in his efforts to discredit his doctor's prognostication of his chances for recovery. But after several months of excruciating pain and no significant progress in rehabilitating his useless extremities, Benchley became increasingly despondent and hostile to those who were his primary means of moral support. His father, a high school football coach, continued to offer unsolicited advice such as "Never give up" and "I understand your pain, but you have a wonderful and supportive family and you need to get on with your life." Although silently bereaved by his son's desperate struggle, Tyrone's father displayed an uncanny understanding of the problem, but his moral sustenance consisted primarily of invoking motivational metaphors in attempting to energize his disabled son to respond optimistically to life in a wheelchair.

Teresa, determined to be a pillar of strength in the face of this unexpected tragedy, became increasingly tolerant of her husband's disturbing but understandable frame of mind. She displayed amazing insights into his mental anguish and engaged in a pattern of enabling behavior as her own anecdote to Tyrone's despondency. A recurring theme, as Benchley continued to wallow in self-pity, was his belief that his football injury had robbed him of his manhood and that he could not offer his wife any degree of meaningful sexual satisfaction, which, in Benchley's view, is part of the marriage contract. Although the doctors never specifically ruled out a return of his sexual function, Tyrone was unforgiving in his own assessment of the situation. "You need someone who can be the husband that you so richly deserve," he told Teresa in one particularly poignant scene. However, Teresa ignored her husband's bid for pathos and searched for strategies to resurrect his sense of self-worth.

But even the long-suffering Teresa eventually tired of her husband's cynicism and issued him an ultimatum: Tyrone must either turn things around mentally, or she will leave him. As Tyrone began to deal with the reality of Teresa's unexpected mandate, a former teammate, Jason George, intervened. George recommended Benchley to a friend, a local college football coach who offered Benchley a job as a recruiter and assistant offensive coordinator. Tyrone reluctantly accepted the position, which involved both travel and participation in the development of the weekly game plan. Though still using a wheelchair, he quickly gained the respect of the other coaches and players, an emotional tribute that begins the healing process for his tortured soul and an accommodation to his physical impairment.

After Sandburg and Hall had placed their orders with the waitress, they lost no time in discussing the merits of the proposed script for the network debut of *Legacy of Despair*. "I'm curious as to why you selected a professional athlete as the star rather than some ordinary citizen who is a paraplegic," said Hall. "After all, pro athletes have access to the best medical care. They're not typical of the ordinary disabled person."

"That's true," replied Sandburg. "But *Legacy of Despair* is based on a true story. I've taken some liberties with the facts, but I thought this kind of story would attract a larger audience. Besides, the athlete as hero is a symbol that everyone can identify with. But this film lays bare the reality of life after football for injured players. The public perception is that they all rely on their disciplined training as athletes to conquer life's seemingly insurmountable obstacles. But the fact is that they frequently suffer the same bouts of depression as ordinary people."

"I suppose that I don't have any real objection to focusing this story around a professional football player," responded Hall with some lingering doubt. "But it does perpetuate the stereotype of disabled people as bitter and resentful of those close to them who offer support."

"In some respects, this image may be stereotypical," acknowledged Sandburg. "But it also reflects the reality of a segment of the paraplegic population. Besides, in another respect this film serves to dispel a stereotype—that of the injured athlete as the consummate winner, able to overcome life's most formidable obstacles. And through identification with the average paraplegic, Benchley can serve as a role model, a source of inspiration."

Hall considered a rebuttal to the producer's confident rejoinder but decided to continue with his critique of the film script. "There are other problems," he noted. "This film falls into the trap of focusing on the victim's preoccupation with his sexual prowess after the accident—as though an individual's manhood begins and ends with the sex drive. One of the most degrading stereotypes, in my judgment, is this obsession with the impact of paralysis on a male's sex life."

"I don't see anything stereotypical about this aspect of the film," Sandburg quickly replied. "For a young married couple—particularly where the husband is a well-conditioned athlete—the male's virility is certainly important to their relationship."

"I'm not suggesting that sex is unimportant to a paraplegic," said Hall somewhat defensively. "But to insinuate, as this film does, that a paraplegic's life revolves around this issue is misleading. There are so many other necessities of life that disabled people must cope with that to focus on the sexual aspect of Benchley's relationship with his wife perpetuates, in my judgment, still another stereotype."

Hall paused to take another bite of food and to allow Sandburg to reflect on his comments. "One final observation," he continued. "This film is like most of those featuring a disabled person who feels sorry for himself and is bitter because of life's injustice. There is the inevitable confrontation between the paraplegic and a family member, in this case Benchley's wife, who challenged her husband to come to grips with his affliction or else face dire consequences."

"But TV is a dramatic medium and thrives on conflict," Sandburg responded. "I realize that TV also frequently oversimplifies reality, and because audiences often view the world through the prisms of stereotypes, there is a danger of perpetuating unfair images of some cultural groups. But I think confrontations such as the one between Tyrone and Teresa are not unrealistic, nor do they unfairly portray the life of an embittered disabled person."

"You may have a point," replied Hall in a cautious concession to the producer's rebuttal. "But just be sure that this scene flows naturally from the characters and plot and is not contrived just to add drama to the script."

"Your comments are helpful, and I'm taking notes," Sandburg told Hall as a means of reassuring his consultant that his advice would be seriously considered though perhaps not entirely decisive in the script's revision. Sandburg was also not unmindful that he was paying Hall for his counsel and could not afford to simply disregard his consultant's concerns.

On the other hand, he wasn't quite convinced of the saliency of all of Hall's criticisms. The world as depicted through the entertainment media was a distortion of reality, in Sandburg's view. And although some might consider his portrayal of the fictionalized paraplegic to be somewhat stereotypical, he was convinced that his film, despite the fact that the lead character was a professional athlete, still mirrored the real-life experiences of some disabled people. Nevertheless, as one who had never experienced a physical disability, he could claim no empathy with Tyrone Benchley. He depended on his consultant, Joseph Hall, to provide the vital link to the world of the disabled. But as the producer of *Legacy of Despair* and the moral agent in this case, Sandburg would be the final authority on how to interpret Benchley's cynical view of life after football to the network's TV viewers.

THE CASE STUDY

From a historical perspective, much of our criticism concerning offensive and unfair media portrayals of certain segments of society has been directed at racial, ethnic, and gender stereotypes and increasingly stereotypes involving sexual preferences.

However, until recently, disabled people were not on our moral radar screen. Nevertheless, stereotypes of the physically disabled are among the most enduring in our society. In popular entertainment, disabled people have been depicted at various times as victims, evil and wicked, bitter and unable to adjust, or a burden to family, friends, and society. At the other extreme and perhaps as a form of compensatory justice, some disabled characters have been portrayed as heroes, derisively referred to as "supercrips"—always triumphing over great odds.[66]

As noted earlier in this chapter, stereotypes are not *necessarily* false representations. They sometimes reflect a slice of reality, albeit perhaps an oversimplified one. In this scenario, there does not appear to be a bright-line distinction between unfair stereotyping and a realistic portrayal of one individual's battle with the personal demons that threaten to destroy his ability to perform as a productive member of society. Film producer Terrence Sandburg believes that, although the situation dramatically depicted in *Legacy of Despair* may not mirror the experience of all physically disabled people, it does fairly reflect the experiences of some. Joseph Hall's concern appears to be with the script's preoccupation with Benchley's sexual dysfunction, the confrontational scene in which Benchley's wife sets her pitiable husband straight, and the depiction of the disabled as bitter and incapable of confronting the reality of their predicament.

Based on Joseph Hall's comments, does this script strike you as unfairly stereotypical in its portrayal of the disabled football player? Are some media stereotypes acceptable if they accurately depict one segment of the targeted group? Or is the use of a stereotype that realistically portrays the characteristics of only some members of the group unfair to the group as a whole?

For the purpose of addressing these issues, assume the role of film producer Terrence Sandburg and, applying the SAD formula for moral reasoning outlined in Chapter 3, decide whether you will take your consultant's advice and approach the story from a different perspective or move ahead and go into production with the present script.

If you decide that the current script is unacceptable, based on the description of *Legacy of Despair* presented here, what changes might you recommend?

▶ CASE 13-5

The American Indians' Battle with the Major Leagues

As the newly installed commissioner of Major League Baseball, Peter Backus had assumed command of a professional sport under siege but was determined to return baseball to its rightful position as America's favorite pastime. He was confronted, first, with rescuing the major leagues from the ravages of a devastating players' strike the preceding season that left in its wake disaffected fans from coast to coast and what might be charitably described as an uncivil relationship between the players and team management. The dramatic decline in attendance and television revenues even threatened the financial security of the franchises in the smaller markets, but Backus, with his business and Wall Street background, was confident that he could at least secure the economic stability of his athletic domain. Indeed, within a couple of years of Backus's inauguration, Major League Baseball appeared to be on the road to economic recovery. He was confident that the American League's most recently approved expansion teams in Jacksonville and Oklahoma City would enter the competitive arena in an environment of relative tranquility, as well as demonstrable fan support. The owners of the Jacksonville franchise had selected "Sharks" as their nickname, while Oklahoma City had tentatively settled on "Warriors," reflecting the state's rich Native American heritage. The owner of the Oklahoma City franchise had also selected the team's logo—a fierce-looking, scowling image of an Indian warrior with a decidedly red cast.

As Backus settled into his position as baseball commissioner, he was troubled by the recurring complaints of racism against some team owners. His egalitarian and nonjudgmental instincts were offended by such charges, but he was also astonished that such prejudice existed in light of the fact that both African American and Latino players had featured so prominently in the sport for many years. Not one to let such problems fester, Backus had dispatched the director of team relations as his ambassador to consult with team owners on the matter.

But racism comes in many guises, as the commissioner soon discovered in a meeting with a delegation from the American Indian Movement (AIM) only three months after taking office. Backus was aware that AIM had protested against the use of Indian mascots during the 1995 World Series between the Atlanta Braves and Cleveland Indians and that three years later a Native American coalition had legally challenged the federal trademark protection for the Washington football team's "Redskins." Nevertheless, AIM's visit was unexpected because the power centers of Major League Baseball were the leagues and team owners. And in the past, AIM had lodged its complaints about the use of Indian names, logos, and mascots directly with team owners. Apparently, the organization, which admittedly did not reflect the views of all American Indians, had decided that an assault on the commissioner's office would generate greater national publicity.

In just the past three weeks, as the major league teams prepared for the season's opener, AIM activists had held two well-attended press conferences in which they denounced professional sports franchises for their "institutionalized racism in the form of stereotypical use of American Indian names and logos." AIM had also called on the commissioner to use his influence to eliminate such stereotypes from the game. Backus had noticed, much to his chagrin, that AIM had taken out full-page ads in several newspapers complaining about the use of Indian names and logos in professional sports.

Backus said little but listened attentively as John Hawks, the leader of the AIM delegation, made his appeal to Major League Baseball's social conscience: "We're here to protest the use of American Indian names, mascots, and logos in some major league franchises. We're conveying similar concerns to the National Football League. Such symbols are degrading; they perpetuate offensive stereotypes. They are nothing more than caricatures. You have a reputation as a person of fairness, committed to social justice. AIM is asking that you develop a plan to eliminate such vestiges of racism from Major League Baseball. We know it isn't practical to change all the team names—such as the Cleveland Indians and Atlanta Braves—immediately; we just want a pledge that you'll work toward it."

"But there is something you can do," Hawks continued, "about the proposed name for the new Oklahoma City franchise. Their name and logo—the Warriors, depicting a scowling, savage-looking brave—is offensive to us, and we're demanding that this name be rejected. They don't start play until a year from now, so there's still time to change the name. As you know, we have already set up pickets at the construction site of the new stadium in Oklahoma City. And on opening day we plan to picket all stadiums with teams that have Indian names. This is how strongly we feel about this issue."

The thought of approaching Ted Turner with the suggestion that he consider changing the name of his Atlanta Braves was not one that brought a smile to the commissioner's face. The Oklahoma City franchise was perhaps more within reach but still problematic. Nevertheless, Backus, responding both diplomatically and truthfully, told the Indian delegation that he appreciated their concerns but that they should, as in the past, be directed at team owners and perhaps the executive committee of Major League Baseball.

Because AIM had already moved aggressively in appealing to the court of public opinion through its public protests, press conferences, and newspaper ads, the organization's next strategic move on the eve of a new season was to again confront the owners concerning their use of offensive stereotypes. Their first target was the league's newly enfranchised but still inoperative team in Oklahoma City. AIM's leadership did not plan to relinquish their pressure on the teams in Atlanta and Cleveland, but they were not naïve about their chances of exerting any immediate influence on the ownership and management of those well-established and traditional franchises. Oklahoma City, however, was a different matter. There was still time, they reasoned, to block the proposed

name and logo for a team with no tradition and no established fan loyalty.

Margaret Roundtree, the daughter of a recently deceased wealthy Oklahoma businessman, was the owner of the Oklahoma City team. She listened patiently as the same AIM delegation that had pleaded their case to Commissioner Backus again stated their objections to the unfair appropriation of Indian names by professional sports franchises. "If our voices go unheard," John Hawks promised, "we will continue our public campaign against Major League Baseball, including picketing of offending teams and encouragement of fan boycotts."

As a community-minded owner who was culturally sensitive to the Sooner state's most visible minority, Roundtree was not entirely unsympathetic to AIM's concerns. Nevertheless, she promised only to discuss the issue with her staff. AIM obviously viewed its plea as a humanitarian issue; Roundtree saw it as both a public relations and marketing problem.

Roundtree lost little time in convening her brain trust to discuss AIM's vociferous complaints about her team's name and logo. She was joined by team president and general manager Michael Davenport, director of publicity Jonathan Salters, and the Warriors' marketing director, Frank Antoine. Roundtree had asked Antoine to participate in the discussion because of the financial and marketing aspects of team names and logos.

"The commissioner and some team owners are concerned about this protest from the American Indian Movement," noted Roundtree as she opened the meeting with her enthusiastic young staff. "They're threatening to throw up pickets at every stadium that hosts one of our teams with an Indian name or mascot—Cleveland, Atlanta, and Oklahoma City—if we go through with our plans to call ourselves the Warriors. In fact, they're already picketing the construction site for our stadium."

"What exactly is their complaint?" asked Antoine. "Even if we should concede to them, the fans will be unhappy. The polls we conducted before settling on this name reflect public support for the Warriors. And we've already tied up capital in marketing and the initial negotiations on licensing agreements. If we back down now, it'll cost us, both financially and in terms of public credibility."

"They say the use of Indian mascots and the commercialization of Indian names result in demeaning stereotypes," responded Roundtree. "They say this is nothing more than institutional racism."

"I can see their point," replied Salters who was under no illusions about the unpopularity of his view, especially within the multibillion-dollar entertainment enterprise known as baseball. However, the team's owner had hired Salters precisely because he was known as somewhat unorthodox, both enterprising and unafraid of risky initiatives. He carried a reputation as a person with a social conscience and humanitarian instincts. "The symbols associated with these mascots and team logos," he continued, "such as the fierce, scowling face of an Indian warrior, as proposed for Oklahoma City, for example, do tend to perpetuate negative images. And this in turn affects society's attitudes toward the American Indian. I think AIM realizes that Indian names for established franchises aren't likely to disappear overnight. But they apparently are convinced they have a realistic chance of blocking expansion teams from following the same path as their predecessors."

"But I would think they would be proud of having their names associated with so many public institutions," said Davenport. "I view team names and mascots as a celebration of the American Indian."

"This is not a peripheral issue for them," replied Salters. "They're serious about eliminating the use of stereotypes in team names. And they've had some success. I know of one newspaper—the Portland *Oregonian,* I believe—that has actually banned from its sports pages such names as Indians, Braves, and Redskins."[67]

"That's carrying political correctness too far," responded Davenport. "It shouldn't be the media's job to censor such names, even if they are offensive to some. But we're the *source* of such names and thus have the power to do something about them—assuming, of course, that there really is a problem here. I wonder if AIM isn't being sensationalistic about this issue."

"In their meeting with the commissioner, I think AIM was quite clear on this point," said Salters, as he became increasingly comfortable with playing devil's advocate. "This is an important issue for them. AIM's position is that the use of these symbols, particularly in connection with professional sports, perpetuates the stereotype of Indians as savage warriors. They argue that they should be able to set their own agenda, to define themselves on their own terms."

"I sympathize with them," said Antoine, "but many of these team names have been around for years. There's a tradition built up around these franchises, such as the Cleveland Indians and the Atlanta Braves, not to mention a lot of money invested in their logos. I suppose that we could reconsider the proposed nickname for the Oklahoma City team, but then every group with an objection to a team name would surface. The fact is the fans are on our side; most consider this issue as sensational. If we even consider removing the Indian logos and nicknames, we'll have more to worry about than AIM."

"There's another consideration," said Davenport. "AIM has generated a lot of publicity, but it doesn't speak for all Native Americans. For some, the use of Indian names by professional sports franchises may not be that important. In fact, some have even profited off this phenomenon. You may recall several years ago when the tomahawk chop became popular in Atlanta, and AIM protested. And then it was discovered that the Cherokees were actually making some of the tomahawks and marketing them to the Braves."

"The issue is *not* whether all tribes agree with AIM's objectives," responded Salters. "The fact is that Native Americans have complained for a number of years of unfair stereotyping. The only question is whether these names and logos are fair representations. AIM's position, if I understand it correctly, is that Indians—not non-Indians—should determine how they're depicted. Other minority groups—African Americans and Hispanics, for example—have made inroads into removing offensive stereotypical symbols from products. Shouldn't Native Americans be accorded the same consideration?"

"Let's face it, Jonathan," replied Antoine, who was becoming increasingly irritated at what he perceived to be the irrational idealism of the team's publicity director. "Caricatures such as Aunt Jemima had no constituency. Who would really complain if it disappeared altogether? Team names are a part of American culture; they're as much a part of some cities' history as politics. There's a lot of fan support out there, and they're the ones we have to appeal to—both through our marketing and the stories in the media. I think AIM is being sensational; team names, in my judgment, don't denigrate American Indians. If we cave in to them, even in the case of Oklahoma City, the fans will really be unhappy—*and most of them aren't Indians.*"

"Thanks for your sensitivity," responded Salters with undisguised sarcasm. "You appear to be more interested in the impact on marketing and the fans' reactions rather than in the justice involved. I'll admit that the fans must be taken into account. But if we develop a plan to change team names over the long term—after all, we're not talking about a large number of franchises—that'll give us breathing space to help to educate the fans. I agree it's unrealistic to consider changing all of our team logos immediately, but it's not too late here in Oklahoma City. Perhaps AIM will accept this as a good-faith effort to work toward the elimination of stereotypes. Some other name will work just as well for this franchise. All I'm suggesting is that we should at least be sensitive to AIM's complaint."

Roundtree had learned from experience that there would never be a meeting of the minds between the idealistic Jonathan Salters and the market-driven Frank Antoine. But as the team owner, the decision would ultimately reside with her. Roundtree was aware that she was the proprietor of a potentially hot media property whose marketing capabilities could be lucrative for both the team's corporate structure and the community that it served. Her decision would be closely scrutinized by the media, the fans, the general public, the baseball industry, and Native Americans themselves, some of whom lived in the shadows of the American League's newest franchise. In such an environment, the question of social injustice as perpetuated by unfair stereotyping was inevitably challenged by marketplace realities and public apathy toward the cause of Native Americans.

Roundtree knew that sports writers were almost uniformly unsympathetic to AIM's concerns. And their complaints about unfair stereotyping were just as unconvincing to baseball fans and team owners alike. With so little support, Roundtree reasoned, perhaps she should dismiss their pleas as nothing more than an attempt by a handful of activists to use the high-profile institution of Major League Baseball as a vehicle for furthering their own political agenda. On the other hand, Roundtree's sense of fairness and sensitivity to the plight of Native Americans compelled her to consider their complaints with the same degree of respect as those of other minorities who had persevered in the face of so much initial public apathy to their charges of racism.

THE CASE STUDY

This case is not so much about the unfair portrayal of American Indians by the media as it is about the use of stereotypical symbols (namely, team names and logos) in promotion and marketing that in turn are conveyed through various media channels and other avenues of dissemination. And in recent years, some members of the Native American community have expressed their displeasure at what they perceive as "institutional racism" in the use of such symbols. In this case, the path of least resistance would be to recommend that AIM's protest be rejected as unworthy of consideration—a position that might appear to be insensitive but would certainly draw no protest from the fans. There is a danger that AIM might become more aggressive in the arena of public opinion, but it is unlikely that it would garner much support from non-Indians, especially because Native Americans do not appear to speak with one voice in this matter.

On the other hand, Major League Baseball is an American institution and perhaps some team owner should take the lead in eradicating offensive stereotypes from the sport. Clearly, the matter of changing established team names is a long-term proposition, but the Oklahoma City franchise has not yet received final approval for its name. Nevertheless, developing public relations strategies to convince fanatical fans of the social worth of this cause could prove to be a daunting task.

Margaret Roundtree, who is the moral agent, is not a media practitioner in the strict sense of the word, but she holds a franchise for a potentially hot media property, both through national licensing arrangements and the sales of local TV rights. And much of her staff's efforts are devoted to public relations, publicity, and marketing. The team's name and logo will be featured prominently in both the journalistic and the more entertainment-oriented aspects of this multimillion-dollar enterprise. Thus, for the purpose of analyzing this case, assume the position of team owner Margaret Roundtree and, utilizing the SAD formula described in Chapter 3, evaluate the concerns of the leadership of the American Indian Movement and decide how you will respond.

Notes

1. Steve Friess, "Sensitivity Training," *Newsweek*, December 2, 2002, p. 9.
2. Tom Brislin, "Media Stereotypes & Code Words: Let's Call Media to Task for Promoting Stereotypes," *Honolulu Advertiser*, February 23, 1997, p. 2, article online, accessed July 21, 1998, available at http://www2.hawaii.edu/~tbrislin/stereo.html
3. "Hispanic Leaders Protest 'Seinfeld' Flag-Burning Show," Associated Press dispatch published in *The Advocate* (Baton Rouge, LA), May 9, 1998, p. 5A.
4. Ibid.
5. Charles Zastrow and Karen Kirst-Ashman, *Understanding Human Behavior and the Social Environment* (Chicago: Nelson-Hall, 1987), p. 556.
6. Carolyn Martindale, "Newspaper Stereotypes of African Americans," in Paul Martin Lester (ed.), *Images That Injure: Pictorial Stereotypes in the Media* (Westport, CT: Praeger, 1996), p. 21.
7. See Patrick Smellie, "Feeding Stereotypes," *Quill*, March/April 1999, pp. 25–27.
8. Walter Lippmann, *Public Opinion* (New York: Macmillan, 1922), pp. 88–89.
9. See Bruce E. Johansen, "Race, Ethnicity, and the Media," in Alan Wells (ed.), *Mass Media and Society* (Lexington, MA: Heath, 1987), p. 441.
10. Lippmann, *Public Opinion*, pp. 88–89.
11. Peter B. Orlik, *Electronic Media Criticism: Applied Perspectives* (Boston: Focal, 1994), p. 23.
12. Zastrow and Kirst-Ashman, *Understanding Human Behavior*, p. 516.
13. Mark Thompson, "Fighting Words," *Time*, July 16, 2001, p. 36.
14. Patricia Raybon, "A Case of 'Severe Bias,'" *Newsweek*, October 2, 1989, p. 11.
15. Deni Elliott, "Ethical and Moral Responsibilities of the Media," in Lester, *Images That Injure*, p. 6 (note for quotation within the text is omitted).
16. William Wells, John Burnett, and Sandra Moriarty, *Advertising Principles and Practice*, 4th ed. (Upper Saddle River, NJ: Prentice-Hall, 1998), p. 49.
17. Maria Laurino, "From the Fonz to 'The Sopranos,' Not Much Evolution," *New York Times*, December 24, 2000, Section 2, p. 31.
18. Ibid.
19. See Joshua Hammer, "Must Blacks Be Buffoons?" *Newsweek*, October 2, 1989, pp. 70–71.
20. For a discussion of the changing tide in prime-time TV, see Leonard Pitts Jr., "The Changing Faces of Race on TV," *TV Guide*, July 6, 1996, pp. 16, 18.
21. Carrie Rickey, "Stereotypes Threaten to Ground *Soul Plane*," Knight Ridder Newspapers wire dispatch published in *The Advocate* (Baton Rouge, LA), June 4, 2004, Fun Section, p. 20.
22. For a discussion of contemporary stereotyping of Native Americans, see Richard Hill, "The Non-Vanishing American Indian," *Quill*, May 1992, pp. 35–37; Cynthia-Lou Coleman, "Native Americans Must Set Their Own Media Agenda," *Quill*, October 1992, p. 8.
23. "Native Americans Protest Braves-Indian World Series" (online article of The News and Observer Publishing Co. and the Reuter Information Service, 1995, accessed July 21, 1998), available at http://www.tennisserver.com/newsroom/sport...mlb/mlb/feat/archive/102095/mlb43814.html
24. Shaheena Ahmad, "Redskins Logo under Fire," *U.S. News & World Report*, May 4, 1998, p. 58.
25. Martindale, "Newspaper Stereotypes of African Americans," p. 24.
26. Richard Lapchick, "Sports and Public Behavior," in Judith Rodin and Stephen P. Steinberg (eds.), *Public Discourse in America* (Philadelphia: University of Pennsylvania Press, 2003), p. 74.
27. Ibid.
28. For a viewpoint on the continuing biased and stereotypical portrayal of blacks in news coverage, see Raybon, "A Case of 'Severe Bias,'" p. 11.
29. "Study Shows Skewed Coverage of Hispanics," *Quill*, March 2004, p. 25.
30. "Darts & Laurels," *Columbia Journalism Review*, May/June 1996, p. 23.
31. Nancy Beth Jackson, "Arab Americans: Middle East Conflicts Hit Home," in Lester, *Images That Injure*, p. 63.
32. Johansen, "Race, Ethnicity, and the Media," p. 444.
33. Elizabeth Bell, "Rape Ads Criticized by Men of Color," *San Francisco Chronicle*, June 25, 2001, p. A13.
34. For a discussion of this case, see Clifford G. Christians, Mark Fackler, Kim B. Rotzoll, and Kathy Brittain McKee, *Media Ethics: Cases and Moral Reasoning*, 6th ed. (White Plains, NY: Addison Wesley Longman, 2001), pp. 171–173.
35. Gene Kotlarchuk, "Chihuahua under Fire," *Lawrence Online*, vol. 119, no. 4, October 23, 1998, online opinion article accessed August 15, 2001, available at http://www.lawrenceville.org/special/thelawrence/9810_23_98/15.html

36. Michael Lafleur, "Taco Bell Advertisement Reflects Poorly on Mexican-Americans, Speaker Says," *Arizona Daily Wildcat,* October 20, 1998, online article accessed August 15, 2001, available at http://www.wildcat.arizona.edu/papers/92/41/09_1_m.html

37. Christians, *Media Ethics: Cases and Moral Reasoning,* p. 171, citing "Teens Pick Their Favorite TV Spots," *Advertising Age,* August 24, 1998, p. S10.

38. Paige Albiniak, "Real Women Aren't on TV," *Broadcasting & Cable,* November 4, 2002, p. 16.

39. Richard Campbell, *Media and Culture: An Introduction to Mass Communication* (New York: St. Martin's, 1998), p. 326.

40. Richard Campbell, Christopher R. Martin, and Bettina Fabos, *Media & Culture: An Introduction to Mass Communication* (Boston: Bedford/St. Martin's, 2004), p. 398.

41. "Old-Fashioned Gender Roles Are Back—In a Commercial," *TV Guide,* November 6, 1993, p. 39.

42. Bonnie Drewniany, "Super Bowl Commercials: The Best a Man Can Get (or Is It?)," in Lester, *Images That Injure,* p. 89.

43. Wells, *Advertising Principles and Practice,* p. 51, citing Kyle Pople, "High-Tech Marketers Try to Attract Women without Causing Offense," *Wall Street Journal,* March 17, 1994, p. B1.

44. See Frank DeCaro, "To Be Young and Gay Is No Longer a Prime-Time Taboo," *TV Guide,* May 1, 1999, pp. 45–46.

45. Larry Gross, "Don't Ask, Don't Tell: Lesbian and Gay People in the Media," in Lester, *Images That Injure,* p. 153.

46. DeCaro, "To Be Young and Gay," p. 45.

47. Gross, "Don't Ask, Don't Tell," p. 153.

48. John Weir, "Queer Guy with a Slob's Eye," *New York Times,* August 10, 2003, Section 9, p. 1.

49. Debra Rosenberg, "The 'Will & Grace' Effect," *Newsweek,* May 24, 2004, p. 39.

50. Ibid., p. 155.

51. "Senior Citizen Gets Last Laugh in New TV Ad," *The Advocate* (Baton Rouge, LA), February 5, 1994, p. 3A.

52. Ted Curtis Smythe, "Growing Old in Commercials: A Joke Not Shared," in Lester, *Images That Injure,* p. 113, citing Mary Nemeth, "Amazing Greys," *Maclean's* (January 10, 1994).

53. Smythe, "Growing Old in Commercials," p. 115.

54. Zastrow and Kirst-Ashman, *Understanding Human Behavior,* p. 431.

55. Ibid.

56. See Smythe, "Growing Old in Commercials," p. 116.

57. Jack A. Nelson, "The Invisible Cultural Group: Images of Disability," in Lester, *Images That Injure,* pp. 120–122.

58. Jack A. Nelson, "The Invisible Cultural Group: Images of Disability," in Lester, *Images That Injure,* p. 123, citing J. Donaldson, "The Visibility and Image of Handicapped People on Television," *Exceptional Children* 47, no. 6 (March 1981): 413–416.

59. Douglas Lathrop, "Challenging Perceptions," *Quill,* July/August 1995, pp. 36–38.

60. See Pattrick Smellie, "Feeding Stereotypes," *Quill,* March/April 1999, p. 27.

61. Ibid.

62. Ibid.

63. See Christopher Lasch, "Critical View: Archie Bunker and the Liberal Mind," *Channels of Communication* 1 (October–November 1981): 34–35, 63.

64. The ideas for this case were derived from a similar case involving Pulitzer Prize–winning cartoonist Patrick Oliphant and some of the responses to his cartoon.

65. Deni Elliott, "Ethical and Moral Responsibilities of the Media," in Lester, *Images That Injure,* p. 7.

66. For an insightful discussion of the various images of the disabled, see Jack A. Nelson, "The Invisible Cultural Group: Images of Disability," in Lester, *Images That Injure,* pp. 119–125.

67. This issue is discussed in Robert Jensen, "Banning 'Redskins' from the Sports Page: The Ethics and Politics of Native American Nicknames," *Journal of Mass Media Ethics* 9, no. 1 (1994): 16–25.

A COUPLE OF LESSONS
FROM THIS TEXT

Becoming a moral adult is hard work. Moral virtue is not just the by-product of memorizing a set of rules or abstract principles. Ethical fitness requires dedication, reflection, and perseverance. It also requires a body of *moral knowledge,* a commitment to a *set of core values,* and a facility in *moral reasoning.* We shall never reach our destination of ethical perfection—self-doubts will always be a part of moral maturation—but the journey itself can be profoundly gratifying.

At the end of the day, we should be willing to allow others to judge us by the content of our character. In other words, *character matters!* This is the energizing principle of this text. Enthusiastic teachers' engaging prose can inspire our moral imagination, but in the final analysis the cultivation of character is the responsibility of each of us.

For students of mass communication, the serious examination of ethical principles and their application to real-life situations through hypothetical case studies can contribute to their ethical fitness in preparation for the professional workplace. This book has forged a rather broad path through the moral landscape. There is certainly no dearth of ethical dilemmas confronting

the media, but the text material and the cases at the end of each chapter have explored what, in my judgment, are the most important of these. However, as noted at the outset, the purpose of this book is not to furnish an encyclopedia of media issues but, rather, to provide training in moral reasoning in the context of some of the most important ethical problems confronting media practitioners.

The ethical standards of media practitioners do not stand apart from the rest of society. Those in the media must resolve their ethical quandaries through the same process of moral reasoning as the rest of us. That, at least, is one lesson of this book. And because they occupy such a pivotal and prominent position in society's communication channels, journalists, advertising and public relations professionals, and producers of mass entertainment should be among the leading moral opinion leaders of our diverse society.

Another lesson of this book is that, at least insofar as universal moral principles are concerned, the conduct of media practitioners should be judged by the same standards as those applied to the rest of us. There is a universality associated with ethical principles that provides consistency across the entire spectrum of cultural inhabitants, regardless of one's professional or personal station in life. Of course, as noted throughout this book, several approaches can be brought to bear on any ethical dilemma. But the fundamental values underlying such decisions do not vary with the occupation of the moral agent.

THE STATE OF MEDIA ETHICS: MIXED SIGNALS

The public takes a jaundiced view of the nation's news media. That rather terse assessment was the result of a survey conducted in 2004 by the First Amendment Center and the *American Journalism Review* in which 60 percent of the respondents said they believed that the fabrication of stories is a widespread problem and just 30 percent believed news organizations tried to report without bias.[1] However, despite the public's continuing cynicism toward the ethical demeanor of the news media, we should not allow episodes such as the Jayson Blair affair, in which a young reporter for the *New York Times* put at risk the credibility of the nation's newspaper of record, to blind us to the fact that every day thousands of journalists and other media practitioners perform their craft with a sense of professional responsibility and moral virtue. Such highly publicized cases inevitably do a disservice to those who perform nobly without public applause or recognition.

Having said that, there is still a detectable concern among some media professionals about the moral health of their enterprises. In the formative years of the twenty-first century, the moral direction of our media institutions and the practitioners who work in them is unclear. This lack of clarity is exacerbated by the fact that there does not appear to be any enthusiasm for a culture of moral excellence in general. Our tolerance for unethical behavior and our attempts to rationalize it are greater than they should be. Nevertheless, the fact that we are willing to engage in public discourse on the subject

of ethics and to demand greater accountability are grounds for optimism.

Because of the gradual erosion of public confidence in the media, as evidenced by polls, there appears to be a heightened sensitivity within the industry to ethical issues. This concern is reflected in the fact that the media have begun to turn the spotlight on themselves and to debate the moral dilemmas that confront the creators of mass-produced content. In addition, media practitioners are participating in ethics seminars and workshops in ever-increasing numbers. And media organizations are paying more than lip service to moral issues at their professional conferences. For example, ethics programs and workshops are now a prominent feature at the annual conventions of the various professional associations of media practitioners.

It is still too soon to tell what impact this internal reexamination of moral values will have. But trends such as these signify a growing recognition that some of the techniques of investigative journalism raise ethical issues and that reporters cannot operate on a moral plane separate from society at large.

The development of written statements of principles has also been a step forward in at least codifying the moral precepts of the various media enterprises. As noted in this text, all areas of media communications—journalism, advertising, public relations, and the entertainment industry—are represented by codes. Many media organizations now have their own codes, and "company policy" is often cited in support of why a particular course of action was followed. Although these codes may not offer solutions in ticklish ethical situations, they do reflect a philosophy about the moral values to which homage should be paid.

The development of codified ethical standards can imbue the cause of self-regulation with a certain amount of credibility and dignity, but these are still rather modest steps. In the final analysis, the moral environment of media institutions will depend on the determination of individual practitioners to aspire to lofty standards of ethical conduct. But the issue is not whether the occasional deviation from ethical norms can be justified according to some more important principle but whether particular forms of behavior, such as the use of deception or invasions of privacy in news gathering or the use of gratuitous violence in entertainment fare, should become the industry standard. Unfortunately, too many decisions are still made on an ad hoc basis—a form of situation ethics, if you will—rather than from any set of well-constructed ethical principles.

Although there has been some recent ethical consciousness-raising within the community of media practitioners, consistent and systematic self-criticism is still rare. For example, a relatively small number of daily newspapers have ombudsmen to evaluate readers' complaints. In fact, the number of ombudsmen has actually decreased in recent years, as some newspapers have chosen to eliminate such internal watchdogs. The demise of the National News Council several years ago also left a void of organized media soul-searching at the national level.

Despite some public grumbling over the ethical conduct of the media, there is surprisingly little consistent external criticism. A number of citizen media watchdog groups exist and serve a useful purpose in expanding the diversity of media criticism in the intellectual marketplace. Some journals, including the *Columbia Journalism Review* and *American Journalism Review,* offer incisive and illuminating media criticism. The debut a couple of decades ago of the *Journal of Mass Media Ethics* reflects the concern of the scholarly community with the academic exploration and critical analysis of ethical standards within the media professions. Nevertheless, as worthy as these contributions are, they are still modest and are unlikely to result in any systematic and broad-based program of external media criticism.

THE NEWEST FRONTIER: THE ETHICAL CHALLENGES OF CYBERSPACE

Even in the midst of a spirited debate involving the more traditional ethical issues, we are confronted with new concerns engendered by the explosion of the information age and the new technologies that service the information superhighway. The proliferation of computer data banks, the digitalization of information storage and retrieval, and the staggering potential, both for good and evil, of cyberspace have already challenged the moral imaginations of ethicists and media practitioners alike. What should be remembered, however, is that the fundamental values that have served us well in moral reasoning about the more conventional ethical issues— truth, honesty, respect for persons, fairness, and so forth—are timeless and should serve us well in confronting the challenges of the information age.

There is a certain amount of ethical hysteria concerning the unregulated Internet. Needless to say, the lack of regulation requires a higher degree of ethical decorum by media practitioners, but ethicists are concerned that the rogues and cyberspace pirates will marginalize those voices who are clamoring for moral restraint in cyberspace. However, history suggests that, after a period of chaos, regulation of some kind will be imposed on the Web, probably at the insistence of those who wish to maximize the commercial advantages of the new technologies. Virtually every technology that has revolutionized the communications process—from the invention of the printing press to the age of geographical exploration to telegraph and radio—has created a certain amount of chaos followed eventually by government and self-regulation.[2] Interestingly, those who are most likely to profit from a new technology are also the ones who have traditionally sought government intervention. At this juncture, it is unclear as to how the regulation of cyberspace might be effected, but it is the natural order of things for the subversive tendencies of new technologies to submit eventually to some form of regulatory design. The ethical deportment of those who travel the Internet, of course, will partly determine the severity of such regulatory initiatives.

TOWARD GREATER ETHICAL AWARENESS: WHAT CAN BE DONE?

Beyond study in the classroom, several things can be done to improve the ethical environment of media institutions. First, media managers should take the lead in identifying the moral standards of their organizations and in codifying those principles. These codes should then be published and explained to employees. Unfortunately, the national codes are too abstract and general to serve as a foundation for a pragmatic ethical blueprint. But the detailed standards of some newspapers and the commercial TV networks, for example, can be valuable in at least serving as guideposts for journalists and other media practitioners as they confront moral dilemmas.

Some organizations have declined to commit to writing what they believe to be appropriate ethical behavior. They apparently believe that in our litigious society such codified principles will be used against them in lawsuits accusing them of negligent conduct. But the existence of such codes can also be cited as evidence of a socially responsible institution that is unwilling to condone unethical practices.

It is insufficient, however, to confine publicity about these ethical codes to the institutions and employees themselves. The public should be informed of the existence of organizational codes of conduct and the standards of behavior expected of media professionals. For example, newspapers could periodically publish the codes for their readers, an acknowledgment of public accountability.

Another means of improving the moral climate of media institutions is for media managers to conduct regular sessions on ethical standards and conduct. Other problems are discussed at staff meetings at all levels; ethical issues should be included, especially at the moment when they arise. Media managers should not be afraid to invite critics and moral philosophers to offer their own analyses and counsel on ethical dilemmas that confront staff members. Consultants have been helpful in improving the commercial posture of media organizations. In a similar fashion, ethicists have something to contribute to the moral tone of such institutions. And why not occasionally invite representatives of the reading or viewing audience to participate in these internal ethics discussions? This avenue of external criticism would not only provide a different perspective on the issues under discussion but would also increase public awareness of the media's sensitivity to ethical concerns. Above all, every employee should be involved in this process. Employee involvement usually results in a more congenial work environment, and "Come let us reason together" should be the hallmark of corporate ethical decision making.

In addition, media practitioners could benefit from attendance at workshops on ethics and moral behavior. Professional organizations, such as the Society of Professional Journalists and the Public Relations Society of America, often sponsor such seminars. Some colleges and universities and media-supported institutes, such as the Poynter Institute for Media Studies in St. Petersburg, Florida, have also been instrumental in providing continuing education in ethics and moral reasoning.

Finally, media practitioners should continue the periodic public examination of ethical issues now in evidence. As noted in the preface, various news organizations have discovered ethical malaise to be a social ill worthy of their attention. One can only hope that this is not a transitory infatuation that receives intense scrutiny while the topic is "hot," only to fade from the media's consciousness. Of course, as part of their coverage of the ethics issue, the media should engage in their own rigorous self-examination. This process would both sensitize media professionals to the moral dilemmas confronting their own enterprises and enhance their credibility with the public.

One means of approaching this matter of self-criticism is for media organizations to reverse the trend against the use of ombudsmen and to hire such internal critics to review public and internal complaints of ethical misconduct. For the larger institutions, the ombudsman might be a full-time staff member. Others might choose to employ ethics "experts," such as university professors, in a consulting capacity to handle such complaints. The results of these internal reviews should then be published as a means of reassuring the public that the media are serious about their own policies of self-regulation.

One could argue that media institutions merely reflect the moral relativity of their culture and that any significant change in the ethical standards of the media must await a similar metamorphosis in society at large. But one could argue just as convincingly that media practitioners should be leaders in this moral revival, willingly serving as role models for their audiences.

We have no reason to believe that the more traditional ethical issues that have confronted the media for many years will be any less troublesome in the future. What we can hope for, however, is a move away from situation ethics and toward a system based on more reasoned judgments based in turn on a positive set of moral principles.

These recommendations are fairly modest, but they can serve as a starting point for confronting the crisis in public confidence that has beset some of our media institutions. With the subject of media ethics now at center stage, media practitioners should become more aware in the future of the fallacies of situation ethics and should be more prone to engage in a dialectic on their industry's moral standards. The optimistic view is that they will do so willingly. The more pessimistic view is that they will have no choice because the public will demand greater accountability.

The media are important transmitters of our moral heritage. In this information age, they also sit at the vortex of the democratic process and our pluralistic social structure. Thus, media practitioners have a special responsibility to the culture of which they are a part and should consider it a professional mandate to improve the ethical climates of their own institutions. Because this book will be read primarily by future media practitioners, perhaps the lessons learned here in the pursuit of sound moral reasoning will someday pay dividends in the fulfillment of this professional mandate.

Notes

1. See Paul McMasters, "Low Marks," *American Journalism Review* (August/September 2004): 70–73.
2. For a thoughtful discussion of this matter, see Debora L. Spar, *Ruling the Waves: Cycles of Discovery, Chaos, and Wealth from the Compass to the Internet* (New York: Harcourt, 2001).

Society of Professional Journalists: Code of Ethics*

PREAMBLE

Members of the Society of Professional Journalists believe that public enlightenment is the forerunner of justice and the foundation of democracy. The duty of the journalist is to further those ends by seeking truth and providing a fair and comprehensive account of events and issues. Conscientious journalists from all media and specialties strive to serve the public with thoroughness and honesty. Professional integrity is the cornerstone of a journalist's credibility. Members of the society share a dedication to ethical behavior and adopt this code to declare the society's principles and standards of practice.

SEEK TRUTH AND REPORT IT

Journalists should be honest, fair, and courageous in gathering, reporting, and interpreting information.
Journalists should:

- Test the accuracy of information from all sources and exercise care to avoid inadvertent error. Deliberate distortion is never permissible.

- Diligently seek out subjects of news stories to give them the opportunity to respond to allegations of wrongdoing.

---

*The SPJ Code was revised in 1996. Reprinted by permission of the Society of Professional Journalists.

- Identify sources whenever possible. The public is entitled to as much information as possible on sources' reliability.

- Always question sources' motives before promising anonymity. Clarify conditions attached to any promise made in exchange for information. Keep promises.

- Make certain that headlines, news teases and promotional material, photos, video, audio, graphics, sound bites, and quotations do not misrepresent. They should not oversimplify or highlight incidents out of context.

- Never distort the content of news photos or videos. Image enhancement for technical clarity is always permissible. Label montages and photo illustrations.

- Avoid misleading re-enactments or staged news events. If re-enactment is necessary to tell a story, label it.

- Avoid undercover or other surreptitious methods of gathering information except when traditional open methods will not yield information vital to the public. Use of such methods should be explained as part of the story.

- Never plagiarize.

- Tell the story of the diversity and magnitude of the human experience boldly, even when it is unpopular to do so.

- Examine their own cultural values and avoid imposing those values on others.

- Avoid stereotyping by race, gender, age, religion, ethnicity, geography, sexual orientation, disability, physical appearance, or social status.

- Support the open exchange of views, even views they find repugnant.

- Give voice to the voiceless; official and unofficial sources of information can be equally valid.

- Distinguish between advocacy and news reporting. Analysis and commentary should be labeled and not misrepresent fact or context.

- Distinguish news from advertising and shun hybrids that blur the lines between the two.

- Recognize a special obligation to ensure that the public's business is conducted in the open and that government records are open to inspection.

MINIMIZE HARM

Ethical journalists treat sources, subjects, and colleagues as human beings deserving of respect.

Journalists should:

- Show compassion for those who may be affected adversely by news coverage. Use special sensitivity when dealing with children and inexperienced sources or subjects.

- Be sensitive when seeking or using interviews or photographs of those affected by tragedy or grief.

- Recognize that gathering and reporting information may cause harm or discomfort. Pursuit of the news is not a license for arrogance.

- Recognize that private people have a greater right to control information about themselves than do public officials and others who seek power, influence, or attention. Only an overriding public need can justify intrusion into anyone's privacy.

- Show good taste. Avoid pandering to lurid curiosity.

- Be cautious about identifying juvenile suspects or victims of sex crimes.

- Be judicious about naming criminal suspects before the formal filing of charges.

- Balance a criminal suspect's fair trial rights with the public's right to be informed.

ACT INDEPENDENTLY

Journalists should be free of obligation to any interest other than the public's right to know.

Journalists should:

- Avoid conflicts of interest, real or imagined.

- Remain free of associations and activities that may compromise integrity or damage credibility.

- Refuse gifts, favors, fees, free travel, and special treatment, and shun secondary employment, political involvement, public office, and service in community organizations if they compromise journalistic integrity.

- Disclose unavoidable conflicts.

- Be vigilant and courageous about holding those with power accountable.

- Deny favored treatment to advertisers and special interests and resist their pressure to influence news coverage.

- Be wary of sources offering information for favors or money; avoid bidding for news.

BE ACCOUNTABLE

Journalists are accountable to their readers, listeners, viewers, and each other.

Journalists should:

- Clarify and explain news coverage and invite dialogue with the public over journalistic conduct.

- Encourage the public to voice grievances against the news media.

- Admit mistakes and correct them promptly.

- Expose unethical practices of journalists and the news media.

- Abide by the same high standards to which they hold others.

American Advertising Federation: Advertising Principles of American Business*

1. Truth—Advertising shall reveal the truth, and shall reveal significant facts, the omission of which would mislead the public.

2. Substantiation—Advertising claims shall be substantiated by evidence in possession of the advertiser and the advertising agency prior to making such claims.

3. Comparisons—Advertising shall refrain from making false, misleading, or unsubstantiated statements or claims about a competitor or its products or services.

4. Bait Advertising—Advertising shall not offer products or services for sale unless such offer constitutes a bona fide effort to sell the advertised products or services and is not a device to switch consumers to other goods or services, usually higher priced.

5. Guarantees and Warranties—Advertising of guarantees and warranties shall be explicit, with sufficient information to apprise consumers of their principal terms and limitations or, when space or time restrictions preclude such disclosures, the advertisement shall clearly reveal where the full text of the guarantee or warranty can be examined before purchase.

6. Price Claims—Advertising shall avoid price claims which are false or misleading, or savings claims which do not offer provable savings.

7. Testimonials—Advertising containing testimonials shall be limited to those of competent witnesses who are reflecting a real and honest opinion or experience.

8. Taste and Decency—Advertising shall be free of statements, illustrations, or implications which are offensive to good taste or public decency.

*Reprinted by permission of the American Advertising Federation.

3

Public Relations Society of America: Code of Ethics*

The PRSA Assembly adopted this Code of Ethics in 2000. It replaces the Code of Professional Standards (previously referred to as the Code of Ethics) that was last revised in 1988.

PREAMBLE

Public Relations Society of America Member Code of Ethics 2000

- Professional Values
- Principles of Conduct
- Commitment and Compliance

This Code applies to PRSA members. The Code is designed to be a useful guide for PRSA members as they carry out their ethical responsibilities. This document is designed to anticipate and accommodate, by precedent, ethical challenges that may arise. The scenarios outlined in the Code provisions are actual examples of misconduct. More will be added as experience with the Code occurs.

The Public Relations Society of America (PRSA) is committed to ethical practices. The level of public trust PRSA members seek, as we serve the public good, means we have taken on a special obligation to operate ethically.

The value of member reputation depends upon the ethical conduct of everyone affiliated with the Public Relations Society of America. Each of us sets an example for each other—as well as other professionals—by our pursuit of excellence with powerful standards of performance, professionalism, and ethical conduct.

Emphasis on enforcement of the Code has been eliminated. But the PRSA Board of Directors retains the right to bar from membership or expel from the Society any individual who has been or is sanctioned by a government agency or convicted in a court of law of an action that is in violation of this Code.

Ethical practice is the most important obligation of a PRSA member. We view the Member Code of Ethics as a model for other professions, organizations, and professionals.

PRSA MEMBER STATEMENT OF PROFESSIONAL VALUES

This statement presents the core values of PRSA members and, more broadly, of the public relations profession. These values provide the foundation for the Member Code of Ethics and set the industry standard for the professional practice of public relations. These values are the fundamental beliefs that guide our behaviors and decision-making process. We believe our

---

*Reprinted by permission of the Public Relations Society of America.

professional values are vital to the integrity of the profession as a whole.

Advocacy

- We serve the public interest by acting as responsible advocates for those we represent.
- We provide a voice in the marketplace of ideas, facts, and viewpoints to aid informed public debate.

Honesty

- We adhere to the highest standards of accuracy and truth in advancing the interests of those we represent and in communicating with the public.

Expertise

- We acquire and responsibly use specialized knowledge and experience.
- We advance the profession through continued professional development, research, and education.
- We build mutual understanding, credibility, and relationships among a wide array of institutions and audiences.

Independence

- We provide objective counsel to those we represent.
- We are accountable for our actions.

Loyalty

- We are faithful to those we represent, while honoring our obligation to serve the public interest.

Fairness

- We deal fairly with clients, employers, competitors, peers, vendors, the media, and the general public.
- We respect all opinions and support the right of free expression.

PRSA CODE PROVISIONS

Free Flow of Information

Core Principle
Protecting and advancing the free flow of accurate and truthful information is essential to serving the public interest and contributing to informed decision making in a democratic society.

Intent
- To maintain the integrity of relationships with the media, government officials, and the public.
- To aid informed decision-making.

Guidelines
A member shall:
- Preserve the integrity of the process of communication.
- Be honest and accurate in all communications.
- Act promptly to correct erroneous communications for which the practitioner is responsible.
- Preserve the free flow of unprejudiced information when giving or receiving gifts by ensuring that gifts are nominal, legal, and infrequent.

Examples of improper conduct under this provision:

- A member representing a ski manufacturer gives a pair of expensive racing skis to a sports magazine columnist to influence the columnist to write favorable articles about the product.
- A member entertains a government official beyond legal limits and/or in violation of government reporting requirements.

Competition

Core Principle
Promoting healthy and fair competition among professionals preserves an ethical climate while fostering a robust business environment.

Intent
- To promote respect and fair competition among public relations professionals.

- To serve the public interest by providing the widest choice of practitioner options.

Guidelines
A member shall:

- Follow ethical hiring practices designed to respect free and open competition without deliberately undermining a competitor.
- Preserve intellectual property rights in the marketplace.

Examples of improper conduct under this provision:

- A member employed by a "client organization" shares helpful information with a counseling firm that is competing with others for the organization's business.
- A member spreads malicious and unfounded rumors about a competitor in order to alienate the competitor's clients and employees in a ploy to recruit people and business.

Disclosure of Information

Core Principle
Open communication fosters informed decision making in a democratic society.

Intent
- To build trust with the public by revealing all information needed for responsible decision making.

Guidelines
A member shall:

- Be honest and accurate in all communications.
- Act promptly to correct erroneous communications for which the member is responsible.
- Investigate the truthfulness and accuracy of information released on behalf of those represented.

- Reveal the sponsors for causes and interests represented.
- Disclose financial interest (such as stock ownership) in a client's organization.
- Avoid deceptive practices.

Examples of improper conduct under this provision:

- Front groups: A member implements "grass roots" campaigns or letter-writing campaigns to legislators on behalf of undisclosed interest groups.
- Lying by omission: A practitioner for a corporation knowingly fails to release financial information, giving a misleading impression of the corporation's performance.
- A member discovers inaccurate information disseminated via a Web site or media kit and does not correct the information.
- A member deceives the public by employing people to pose as volunteers to speak at public hearings and participate in "grass roots" campaigns.

Safeguarding Confidences

Core Principle
Client trust requires appropriate protection of confidential and private information.

Intent
- To protect the privacy rights of clients, organizations, and individuals by safeguarding confidential information.

Guidelines
A member shall:

- Safeguard the confidences and privacy rights of present, former, and prospective clients and employees.
- Protect privileged, confidential, or insider information gained from a client or organization.

- Immediately advise an appropriate authority if a member discovers that confidential information is being divulged by an employee of a client company or organization.

Examples of improper conduct under this provision:

- A member changes jobs, takes confidential information, and uses that information in the new position to the detriment of the former employer.
- A member intentionally leaks proprietary information to the detriment of some other party.

Conflicts of Interest

Core Principle
Avoiding real, potential, or perceived conflicts of interest builds the trust of clients, employers, and the public.

Intent
- To earn trust and mutual respect with clients or employers.
- To build trust with the public by avoiding or ending situations that put one's personal or professional interests in conflict with society's interests.

Guidelines
A member shall:

- Act in the best interests of the client or employer, even subordinating the member's personal interests.
- Avoid actions and circumstances that may appear to compromise good business judgment or create a conflict between personal and professional interests.
- Disclose promptly any existing or potential conflict of interest to affected clients or organizations.

- Encourage clients and customers to determine if a conflict exists after notifying all affected parties.

Examples of improper conduct under this provision:

- The member fails to disclose that he or she has a strong financial interest in a client's chief competitor.
- The member represents a "competitor company" or a "conflicting interest" without informing a prospective client.

Enhancing the Profession

Core Principle
Public relations professionals work constantly to strengthen the public's trust in the profession.

Intent
- To build respect and credibility with the public for the profession of public relations.
- To improve, adapt, and expand professional practices.

Guidelines
A member shall:

- Acknowledge that there is an obligation to protect and enhance the profession.
- Keep informed and educated about practices in the profession to ensure ethical conduct.
- Actively pursue personal professional development.
- Decline representation of clients or organizations that urge or require actions contrary to this Code.
- Accurately define what public relations activities can accomplish.
- Counsel subordinates in proper ethical decision making.
- Require that subordinates adhere to the ethical requirements of the Code.

- Report ethical violations, whether committed by PRSA members or not, to the appropriate authority.

Examples of improper conduct under this provision:

- A PRSA member declares publicly that a product the client sells is safe, without disclosing evidence to the contrary.
- A member initially assigns some questionable client work to a non-member practitioner

to avoid the ethical obligation of PRSA membership.

RESOURCES

Rules and Guidelines
The following PRSA documents, available online at www.prsa.org, provide detailed rules and guidelines to help guide your professional behavior.

- PRSA Bylaws
- PRSA Administrative Rules
- Member Code of Ethics

SELECTED BIBLIOGRAPHY

BOOKS

The following books, some which are cited in this text, are recommended for further reading:

Adams, Julian. *Freedom and Ethics in the Press.* New York: Rosen, 1983.

Bagdikian, Ben H. *The Media Monopoly,* 6th ed. Boston: Beacon, 2000.

Baker, Lee W. *The Credibility Factor: Putting Ethics to Work in Public Relations.* Homewood, IL: Business One Irwin, 1993.

Bayles, Michael. *Professional Ethics,* 2d ed. Belmont, CA: Wadsworth, 1989.

Beauchamp, Tom L. *Philosophical Ethics: An Introduction to Moral Philosophy,* 2d ed. New York: McGraw-Hill, 1991.

Benedict, Helen. *Virgin or Vamp: How the Press Covers Sex Crimes.* New York: Oxford University Press, 1992.

Black, Jay, Ralph Barney, and Robert Steele. *SPJ Ethics Handbook,* 3d ed. Greencastle, IN: SPJ National Headquarters, 1998.

Bok, Sissela. *Lying: Moral Choice in Public and Private Life.* New York: Vintage Books, 1999.

Bowie, Norman E. *Making Ethical Decisions.* New York: McGraw-Hill, 1985.

Brody, Baruch. *Ethics and Its Methods of Analysis.* New York: Harcourt Brace Jovanovich, 1983.

Broom, Donald M. *The Evolution of Morality and Religion.* Cambridge, England: Cambridge University Press, 2003.

Bugeja, Michael J. *Living Ethics: Developing Values in Mass Communication.* Boston: Allyn and Bacon, 1996.

Callahan, Joan C., ed. *Ethical Issues in Professional Life.* New York: Oxford University Press, 1988.

Christians, Clifford G. *Communication Ethics and Universal Values.* Thousand Oaks, CA: Sage, 1997.

Christians, Clifford G., John P. Ferré, and P. Mark Fackler. *Good News: Social Ethics and the Press.* New York: Oxford University Press, 1993.

Christians, Clifford G., Kim B. Rotzoll, Mark Fowler, Kathy Brittain McKee, Robert H. Woods, Jr. *Media Ethics: Cases and Moral Reasoning,* 7th ed. New York: Addison Wesley Longman, 2005.

Cohen, Elliot D. *Philosophical Issues in Journalism.* New York: Oxford University Press, 1992.

Cohen, Elliot D., and Deni Elliot, eds. *Journalism Ethics: A Reference Handbook.* Santa Barbara, CA: ABC-Clio, 1997.

Cooper, Thomas W., Clifford G. Christians, Frances Forde Plude, and Robert A. White, eds. *Communication Ethics and Global Change.* White Plains, NY: Longman, 1989.

Elliott, Deni, ed. *Responsible Journalism.* Beverly Hills, CA: Sage, 1986.

Ettema, James S., and Theodore L. Glaser. *Custodians of Conscience: Investigative Journalism and Public Virtue*. New York: Columbia University Press, 1998.

Fink, Conrad C. *Media Ethics*. Needham Heights, MA: Allyn and Bacon, 1995.

Frith, Katherine Toland, ed. *Undressing the Ad: Reading Culture in Advertising*. New York: Lang, 1997.

Gert, Bernard. *Morality: A New Justification of the Moral Rules*. New York: Oxford University Press, 1988.

Goldman, Alan H. *The Moral Foundations of Professional Ethics*. Totowa, NJ: Rowman & Littlefield, 1980.

Goldstein, Tom. *The News at Any Cost: How Journalists Compromise Their Ethics to Shape the News*. New York: Simon & Schuster, 1985.

Gordon, A. David, John M. Kitross, and Carol Reuss. *Controversies in Media Ethics*, 2d ed. White Plains, NY: Longman, 1999.

Greenberg, Karen Joy, ed. *Conversations on Communication Ethics*. Norwood, NJ: Ablex, 1991.

Gross, Larry, John Stuart Katz, and Jay Ruby, eds. *Image Ethics: The Moral Rights of Subjects in Photographs, Film and Television*. New York: Oxford University Press, 1988.

Jaska, James A., and Michael S. Pritchard. *Communication Ethics: Methods of Analysis*, 2d ed. Belmont, CA: Wadsworth, 1994.

Johannesen, Richard L. *Ethics in Human Communication*, 3d ed. Prospect Heights, IL: Waveland, 1990.

Kidder, Rushworth M. *How Good People Make Tough Choices*. New York: Morrow, 1995.

Kidder, Rushworth M. *Shared Values for a Troubled World*. San Francisco: Jossey-Bass, 1994.

Kieran, Matthew. *Media Ethics: A Philosophical Approach*. Westport, CT: Praeger, 1997.

Klaidman, Stephen, and Tom L. Beauchamp. *The Virtuous Journalist*. New York: Oxford University Press, 1987.

Knowlton, Steven R. *Moral Reasoning for Journalists: Cases and Commentary*. Westport, CT: Praeger, 1997.

Knowlton, Steven R., and Patrick R. Parsons. *The Journalist's Moral Compass: Basic Principles*. Westport, CT: Praeger, 1994.

Lambeth, Edmund B. *Committed Journalism: An Ethic for the Profession*. Bloomington: Indiana University Press, 1986.

Lesley, Larry Z. *Mass Communication Ethics: Decision Making in Postmodern Culture*, 2d ed. Boston: Houghton Mifflin, 2004.

Lester, Paul Martin, ed. *Images That Injure: Pictorial Stereotypes in the Media*. Westport, CT: Praeger, 1996.

Limburg, Val E. *Electronic Media Ethics*. Boston: Focal, 1994.

Maienschein, Jane, and Michael Ruse, eds. *Biology and the Foundation of Ethics*. Cambridge, England: Cambridge University Press, 1999.

Merrill, John C. *Legacy of Wisdom: Great Thinkers and Journalism*. Ames: Iowa State University Press, 1994.

Merrill, John C. *The Dialectic in Journalism: Toward a Responsible Use of Press Freedom*. Baton Rouge: Louisiana State University Press, 1989.

Merrill, John C., and Jack S. Odell. *Philosophy and Journalism*. White Plains, NY: Longman, 1983.

Merrill, John C., Peter J. Gade, and Frederick R. Blevens. *Twilight of Press Freedom: The Rise of People's Journalism*. Mahway, NJ: Lawrence Erlbaum, 2001.

Merritt, Davis "Buzz." *Public Journalism and Public Life*. Hillsdale, NJ: Erlbaum, 1995.

Meyer, Philip. *Ethical Journalism: A Guide for Students, Practitioners, and Consumers*. White Plains, NY: Longman, 1987.

Oakley, Justin, and Dean Cocking. *Virtue Ethics and Professional Roles*. Cambridge, England: Cambridge University Press, 2001.

Olen, Jeffrey. *Ethics in Journalism*. Upper Saddle River, NJ: Prentice-Hall, 1988.

Patterson, Philip, and Lee Wilkins. *Media Ethics: Issues and Cases*, 4th ed. Boston: McGraw-Hill, 2002.

Phelan, John M. *Disenchantment: Meaning and Morality in the Media*. New York: Hastings House, 1980.

Philips, Michael J. *Ethics and Manipulation in Advertising: Answering a Flawed Indictment*. Westport, CT: Quorum, 1997.

Piper, Thomas R., Mary C. Gentile, and Sharon Daloz Parks. *Can Ethics Be Taught?* Boston: Harvard Business School, 1993.

Pojman, Louis. *Ethics: Discovering Right and Wrong*, 4th ed. Belmont, CA: Wadsworth/Thomson Learning, 2002.

Rivers, William L., and Cleve Mathews. *Ethics for the Media.* Upper Saddle River, NJ: Prentice-Hall, 1988.

Rosenthal, David M., and Fadlou Shehaili, eds. *Applied Ethics and Ethical Theory.* Salt Lake City: University of Utah Press, 1988.

Russell, Nick. *Morals and the Media: Ethics in Canadian Journalism.* Vancouver: UBC Press, 1994.

Seib, Philip. *Campaigns and Conscience: The Ethics of Political Journalism.* Westport, CT: Praeger, 1994.

Seib, Philip, and Kathy Fitzpatrick. *Journalism Ethics.* Fort Worth, TX: Harcourt Brace, 1997.

Seib, Philip, and Kathy Fitzpatrick. *Public Relations Ethics.* Fort Worth, TX: Harcourt Brace, 1995.

Smith, Ron F. *Groping for Ethics in Journalism,* 5th ed. Ames: Iowa State Press, 2003.

Solomon, Robert C., and Clancy W. Martin. *Morality and the Good Life: An Introduction through Classical Sources,* 4th ed. Boston: McGraw-Hill, 2004.

Thayer, Lee, ed. *Ethics, Morality and the Media.* New York: Hastings House, 1980.

Tivnan, Edward. *The Moral Imagination: Confronting the Ethical Issues of Our Day.* New York: Simon & Schuster, 1995.

Williams, Bernard. *Ethics and the Limits of Philosophy.* Cambridge, MA: Harvard University Press, 1985.

Wilson, James Q. *The Moral Sense.* New York: Free Press, 1993.

JOURNALS AND PERIODICALS WITH FEATURES ON MEDIA ETHICS

American Journalism Review, 8701 Adelphi Road, Adelphi, MD 20783-1716

Columbia Journalism Review, 700 Journalism Building, Columbia University, New York, NY 10027

The Journal of Ethics, Kluwer Academic Publishers, 101 Philip Dr., Norwell, MA 02061

Journal of Mass Media Ethics, Lawrence Erlbaum Associates, 10 Industrial Ave., Mahwah, NJ 07430-2262

Media Ethics, c/o Department of Visual and Media Arts, Emerson College, 100 Beacon St., Boston, MA 02116

Quill, Society of Professional Journalists, 16 S. Jackson St., Greencastle, IN 46135-0077

RTNDA Communicator, Radio-Television News Directors Association, 1000 Connecticut Ave. N.W., Suite 615, Washington, DC 20036

SELECTED WEBSITES FOR ETHICS MATERIALS

Associated Press Managing Editors (http://apme.com/index.shtml)

The Association for Practical and Professional Ethics (http://php.indiana.edu/~appe/)

Dartmouth College Ethics Institute (http://www.dartmouth.edu/~ethics/about.html)

Fairness and Accuracy in Reporting Media (http://www.fair.org/)

Institute for Business and Professional Ethics (http://commerce.depaul.edu/ethics)

Josephson Institute of Ethics (http://www.josephsoninstitute.org/)

Minnesota News Council (http://www.mtn.org/~newscncl)

The Poynter Institute for Media Studies (http://www.poynter.org/)

Society of Professional Journalists (http://www.spj.org)

INDEX